Slave Portraiture in the Atlantic World

Slave Portraiture in the Atlantic World is the first book to focus on the individualized portrayal of enslaved people from the time of Europe's full engagement with plantation slavery in the late sixteenth century to its official abolition in Brazil in 1888. While this period saw the emergence of portraiture as a major field of representation in Western art, "slave" and "portraiture" as categories appear to be mutually exclusive. On the one hand, the logic of chattel slavery sought to render the slave's body as an instrument for production, as the site of a non-subject. Portraiture, on the contrary, privileged the face as the primary visual matrix for the representation of a distinct individuality. The essays in this volume address this apparent paradox of "slave portraits" from a variety of interdisciplinary perspectives. They probe the historical conditions that made the creation of such rare and enigmatic objects possible and explore their implications for a more complex understanding of power relations under slavery.

Agnes Lugo-Ortiz is Associate Professor of Latin American and Caribbean Literatures and Cultures at the University of Chicago. She is the author of *Identidades imaginadas: Biografía y nacionalidad en el horizonte de la guerra* and co-editor of *Herencia: The Anthology of Hispanic Literature of the United States*; *En otra voz: Antología de la literatura hispana de los Estados Unidos*; and *Recovering the U.S. Hispanic Literary Heritage, Volume V.*

Angela Rosenthal (d. 2010) was Associate Professor of Art History at Dartmouth College. She was the author of *Angelika Kauffmann: Bildnismalerei im 18. Jahrhundert* and *Angelica Kauffman: Art and Sensibility,* which won the 2007 Historians of British Art Book Award in the pre-1800 category. She also was co-editor of *The Other Hogarth: Aesthetics of Difference.*

Floras profili
Flora

Slave Portraiture in the Atlantic World

EDITED BY

Agnes Lugo-Ortiz
The University of Chicago

Angela Rosenthal
Dartmouth College

CAMBRIDGE
UNIVERSITY PRESS

One Liberty Plaza, 20th Floor, New York, NY 10006, USA

Cambridge University Press is part of the University of Cambridge.

It furthers the University's mission by disseminating knowledge in the pursuit of education, learning, and research at the highest international levels of excellence.

www.cambridge.org
Information on this title: www.cambridge.org/9781107004399

First published 2013
Paperback edition first published 2016
3rd printing 2022

Printed in Great Britain by Ashford Colour Press Ltd.

A catalog record for this publication is available from the British Library.

Library of Congress Cataloging in Publication data
Slave portraiture in the Atlantic world / [edited by] Agnes Lugo-Ortiz, Angela Rosenthal.
p. cm.
Includes bibliographical references and index.
ISBN 978-1-107-00439-9 (hardback)
1. Slavery in art. 2. Portraits. 3. Slavery – Atlantic Ocean Region – History.
I. Lugo-Ortiz, Agnes I. II. Rosenthal, Angela.
N8243.S576S54 2012
704.9'49306362–dc23 2011036251

ISBN 978-1-107-00439-9 Hardback
ISBN 978-1-107-53375-2 Paperback

CONTENTS

PLATES AND FIGURES

Plates

Color plates follow page 116

Figures

CONTRIBUTORS

David Bindman. Emeritus Professor of the History of Art at University College London. He has written extensively on British art and most recently on art and race. He is the author of *Ape to Apollo: Aesthetics and the Idea of Race in the 18th Century* (Cornell, 2002) and is currently editing, with Henry Louis Gates, Jr., *The Image of the Black in Western Art* in ten volumes, the first eight of which have been published, with the final two, on the twentieth century, to appear in 2014.

Rebecca P. Brienen. Associate Professor of Art History and director of the Art History program at the University of Miami. She is the author of *Visions of Savage Paradise: Albert Eckhout, Court Art in Colonial Dutch Brazil* (Amsterdam, 2006) and was a Kluge Fellow at the Library of Congress in 2010–2011.

Toby Maria Chieffo-Reidway. Independent Cultural Historian, B.A., Georgetown University; M.A. and Ph.D., The College of William and Mary. She is a recipient of a NEH research grant and was a Smithsonian Institution predoctoral Fellow, National Museum of American History and National Portrait Gallery.

Tom Cummins. Dumbarton Oaks Professor of the History of Pre-Columbian and Colonial Art and chairman of the Department of the History of Art and Architecture, Harvard University. He is the author of *Toasts with the Inca: Andean Abstraction and Colonial Images on Quero Vessels* (Michigan, 2002) and *Beyond the Lettered City: Indigenous Literacies in the Andes* (with Joanne Rappaport; Duke, 2012), which received the 2013 Latin American Studies Association's Bryce Wood Book Award.

Carmen Fracchia. Lecturer in Early Modern Spanish Visual Studies and former director of the Centre for Iberian and Latin American Visual Studies, Birkbeck University of London; Visiting Professor, Department of Social Anthropology, University of Granada, Spain, and a member of international collaborative networks, sponsored by the Spanish government, on the Anthropology of Slavery, Memory of Slavery, and Slavery and Abolitionism.

Agnes Lugo-Ortiz. Associate Professor of Latin American literatures and Caribbean cultural history at the University of Chicago. She is the author of *Identidades imaginadas: Biografía y nacionalidad en el horizonte de la guerra (Cuba, 1860–1898)* (Puerto Rico, 1999) and co-editor of several collections on Latino/a literature including *Herencia: The Anthology of Hispanic Literature of the United States* (Oxford, 2002). She is currently working on a book on the visual cultures of slavery in colonial Cuba (1727–1886).

Susan Scott Parrish. Associate Professor in the Department of English Language and Literature at the University of Michigan. She is the author of *American Curiosity: Cultures of Natural History in the Colonial British Atlantic World* (North Carolina, 2006), which was awarded the Ralph Waldo Emerson Prize and the Jamestown Prize.

Marcia Pointon. Professor Emerita in History of Art at the University of Manchester and Honorable Research Fellow at the Courtauld Institute of Art. Her books include *Hanging the Head: Portraiture and Social Formation in Eighteenth-Century England* (Yale, 1993) and *Brilliant Effects: A Cultural History of Gem Stones and Jewellery* (Yale, 2009). *Portrayal and the Search for Identity* was published by Reaktion Books in 2013.

Geoff Quilley. Senior Lecturer in Art History at the University of Sussex. His research focuses on British art and empire in the long eighteenth century; his most recent book, *Empire to Nation: Art, History and the Visualization of Maritime Britain, 1768–1829*, was published by Yale University Press in 2011. He has just completed a two-year Leverhulme Fellowship toward research for a new book on British art and the East India Company.

Angela Rosenthal. Educated in Germany and the United Kingdom, she was Associate Professor of Art History and chair of the Department of Art History at Dartmouth College. Her work focused on British and continental European art within a global perspective. She authored *Angelika Kauffmann: Bildnismalerei im 18. Jahrhundert* (Reimer, 1996) and *Angelica Kauffman: Art and Sensibility* (Yale, 2006), which won the 2007 Historians of British Art Book Award in the pre-1800 category, and she co-edited the volume *The Other Hogarth: Aesthetics of Difference* (Princeton, 2001).

Viktoria Schmidt-Linsenhoff. Professor Emerita of Art History at the University of Trier, Germany. She was co-author and co-editor of *Das Subjekt und die Anderen: Interkulturalität und Geschlechterdifferenz* (Berlin, 2001) and of *The Family of Man 1955–2001: Humanism and Postmodernism: A Reappraisal of the Photo Exhibition* (Marburg, 2004). Two recent publications include her two-volume *Ästhetik der Differenz: Postkoloniale Perspektiven vom 16. bis 21. Jahrhundert* (Marburg, 2010) and "On and beyond the Colour Line: Afterimages of Old and New Slavery in Contemporary Art since 1990" in Birgit Haehnel and Melanie Ulz (eds.), *Slavery in Art and Literature: Approaches to Memory, Trauma, and Visuality* (Berlin, 2010).

Eric Slauter. Associate Professor of American cultural, intellectual, and literary history and director of the Karla Scherer Center for the Study of American Culture at the University of Chicago. He is the author of *The State as a Work of Art: The Cultural Origins of the Constitution* (Chicago, 2008).

James Smalls. Professor of Art History and Theory at the University of Maryland, Baltimore County. His research focuses on the intersections of race, gender, and queer sexuality in the visual culture of the nineteenth century and that of the black diaspora. He is the author of *Homosexuality in Art* (Parkstone, 2003) and *The Homoerotic Photography of Carl Van Vechten* (Temple, 2006).

Helen Weston. Professor Emerita of Art History at the University of London. Her work has focused on political and post-colonial questions concerning the art of the French Revolution, with some emphasis on portraiture. She co-edited, with William Vaughan, *David's The Death of Marat* (Cambridge, 2000).

Daryle Williams. Associate Professor of History at the University of Maryland. He is the author of *Culture Wars in Brazil: The First Vargas Regime, 1930–1945* (Duke, 2001), winner of the American Historical Association's John Edwin Fagg prize. He served as associate director of the David C. Driskell Center for the Study of the African Diaspora from 2002 to 2004 and is currently writing a book on the Free Africans of Brazil.

ACKNOWLEDGMENTS

This book travels back and forth across the Atlantic, through a dilated span of almost four centuries, in search of traces left by those often lost to the history of art or to philosophical accounts on the "modern subject." Such a project could not have been possible without the anchoring support, faith, and sustenance of countless people during the many years that the two of us devoted to its preparation. We would first like to thank the institutions and units that provided material help to secure permission to use the many images discussed in the following essays or that provided a structural foundation for our work: at Dartmouth College, the Office of the Dean of the Arts and Humanities and former dean Kate Conley, the Leslie Center for the Humanities and its former directors Jonathan Crewe and Adrian Randolph, the Hood Museum of Art and its former interim director Katherine Hart, and the Department of Art History; at the University of Chicago, the Center for Latin American Studies and its director Mauricio Tenorio and former acting director Alan Kolata, and the Center for the Study of Race, Politics, and Culture and its former director Ramón Gutiérrez. This kind of support is always about more than funding or hosting. It is an expression of belief in the importance of a project and of confidence in its stewardship, and for this we are deeply grateful. The staff at all of these units was extremely generous in good and, especially, in difficult times. We would like to make particular mention of Jan Smarsik, Steve Dyer, Kathleen O'Malley, Isabel Weatherdon, and Betsy Alexander at Dartmouth, and Josh Beck and Clare Buttry at Chicago. Their unwavering disposition to lend a helping hand with good humor and a sense of commitment made all the difference and was fundamental to keeping the project on track at crucial moments. We would also like to acknowledge the Paul Mellon Centre, the Yale Center for British Art, the Clark Art Institute, and the W. E. B. DuBois Institute at Harvard University for their collegial sharing of information and intellectual support, as well as those individuals and institutions, mentioned throughout this volume, who have granted us permission to reproduce some of the works that appear here.

The anonymous readers for Cambridge University Press provided thoughtful suggestions and productive critiques of the manuscript version of this book. To them, to our editor Beatrice Rehl, to our assistant editors Anastasia Graf and Amanda Smith, and to the members of the Cambridge production team, especially James Dunn, Holly Johnson, and David Anderson, we offer our thanks for their care of and trust in this work.

Friends and colleagues from all quarters of our lives have followed throughout the years, to varying degrees, our obsession with and passion for the questions raised in this volume. Many listened with interest to our reflections about the project and offered, often inadvertently, useful insights. Others were simply there to provide love and support, which is in itself no small feat. There are too many to list here, and we have no doubt that our faulty memory, not a lack of gratitude, leads us to some involuntary omissions. Yet, mindful of this risk, we nonetheless wish to thank the following: First, Marianne Hirsch and Mario Santana for their generous and encouraging readings of an earlier version of our introduction to this book (its limitations are, of course, our sole responsibility); at Dartmouth, Mary Desjardins, Mark Williams, Amy Lawrence, Kathleen Corrigan, Irene Kacandes, Silvia Spitta, Gerd Gemünden, Jonathan Crewe, Melissa Zeiger, Ada Cohen, Joy Kenseth, Mary Coffey, Annelise Orleck, Alexis Jetter, Michelle Meyers (d. 2012), Josie Harper, Francine A'Ness, Doug Moody, Paula Sprague, Miguel Valladares, Israel Reyes, and Katherine Hart; in New York, Diana Taylor, Leo Spitzer, Eric Manheimer, Lori Novak, Jill Lane, and Lauren Jacobi; in New Haven, Jacqueline Goldsby and George Chauncey; in Cuba, Raida Mara Suárez Portal, Orelvis Rodríguez Morales, Margarita Suárez, Zoila Lapique, Luisa Campuzano, Ambrosio Fornet, and Carlos Venegas; in Madrid, Maricruz de Carlo; in México, Zaide Silvia Gutiérrez and Richard McDowell; in or from Puerto Rico, Ivette Hernández, Luis Avilés, Malena Rodríguez-Castro, Rubén Ríos-Avila, Mara Negrón (d. 2012), Licia Fiol-Matta, Aldo Lauria, Arcadio Díaz-Quiñones, Maruja García-Padilla, Angel Quintero Rivera, Juan Gelpí, Carlos Pabón, Edna Román, Mari Quiñones, and Carmen Luisa González; in Chicago, Miriam Hansen (d. 2011), Stephan Palmié, Daín Borges, Loren Kruger, Darby English, Elisa Martí-López, Bernadette Fort, Miguel Amat, and Nathalie Bouzaglo; in London, John Brewer and Marcia Pointon; in Frankfurt, Viktoria Schmidt-Linsenhoff (d. 2013); and in Washington, Yuriko Jackall. Special thanks go to Toula Polygalaktos for her help during the final push. We would also like to evoke here the beloved memory of Suzanne and Half Zantop, whose lives were shared with ours, and whom we senselessly lost in January 2001. They would have been eager to support us in this endeavor, and we know that something good must be missing from the content of this book because of their absence.

INTRODUCTION

ENVISIONING SLAVE PORTRAITURE

Angela Rosenthal and Agnes Lugo-Ortiz

A Tale of Erasure

In 1987 the African British artist Maud Sulter encountered in the Touchstones Rochdale Art Gallery a painting by John Michael Wright (ca. 1617–94) that, were it not for the astonishing history that underwrites it, she might have overlooked as a mere curiosity. The portrait in question, probably dating to the 1660s, represents a woman of the wealthy Butterworth family of nearby Belfield Hall (Fig. I.1). Before the painting had been cleaned in the 1960s, the figure had oddly gestured toward a column at her side, as if pointing out its presence to the viewer. Technical analysis had revealed the reason for this rather bizarre gesture, for beneath the column x-ray imaging exposed ghostly traces of a figure, a black male slave, who appears in a servile position pouring water onto his mistress's hand, and whose presence overpainting had eliminated. Maud Sulter concluded "and then, obviously, when slavery had been abolished and was no longer quite as fashionable, the portrait had been doctored, so as to paint out that history, that black presence in Britain."[1]

The inclusion of servants and pages of African descent in portraits of white European sitters had indeed, as Sulter remarked, become "fashionable" throughout Europe in the age of slavery and colonial expansion.[2] The word "slave" evolved from the Latin word for Slavs – *sclavus* – pointing to the great numbers of Slavic slaves in Western Europe in the Middle Ages and Renaissance. From the beginning of the fifteenth century and increasingly through the sixteenth and later, it was mostly people from the west coast of Africa who were captured and shipped to the Americas and Europe to be enslaved. Sold to European courts as luxury items, enslaved Africans (adults and children, female but especially male) entered portraiture as a stereotypical motif in European painting, most

I.1. John Michael Wright, *Portrait of Miss Butterworth of Belfield Hall*, Rochdale, 1660s. Oil on canvas. Courtesy of Touchstones Rochdale, The Esplanade, Rochdale, U.K.

obviously, but not only, as signs of status.[3] It was, however, with the expansion of the transatlantic slave trade and of the colonial plantation system that the demand for and availability of black slaves across Europe and the Americas exploded. Between the mid-fifteenth and mid-nineteenth centuries an estimated twenty-one million people were taken from their local villages in Africa with the intention of transforming them first into captives, then into commodities, and finally into slaves, to labor in the sugar, cotton, coffee, and tobacco fields of Brazil, the Caribbean, and North America – sites far from what are traditionally thought to be art centers.[4] Nevertheless, in Europe a black page remained for the longest time a desired asset and expensive rarity, and the inclusion of such servile figures in portraiture often became conventionalized into a type, as the Butterworth portrait itself testifies. This practice also imprinted the visual cultures of both the colonial and early republican Americas, where regional elites in the process of symbolizing their local power based upon slavery adopted its hierarchical structures (see Figs. 1.1 and 7.5). Thus, for instance, even during the transitional period from the colonial to the republican order, some important portraits of the patrician framer of the new North American republic, George Washington, still included black slaves dressed in the elegant garb of pages gazing in admiration at their heroic master, as in John Trumbull's *George Washington* (Fig. I.2). In this image – which was painted in London and not commissioned by Washington himself, but still forms part of the early heroic iconography of the Republic – the American patriot/painter Trumbull also equips the slave with the orientalizing outfit that is often found in European portraiture (see Fig. 2.6). It is this sort of typing, in tandem with the broader social and visual dynamics of the Atlantic slave trade, that helped to forge the still indelible link between black existence and enslavement, the disquieting equation between dark skin and subjection that has borne upon the way in which art and cultural histories have faced up to the challenge of interpreting both enslaved subjects and black individuals in representation.[5]

I.2. John Trumbull, *George Washington*, 1780. Oil on canvas. © The Metropolitan Museum of Art/Art Resource, New York.

Maud Sulter's powerful narrative of historical and visual occlusion, as well as revelatory cleaning, points to the central problem addressed by this book: the paradoxical presence and erasure of the enslaved subject in portraiture, a genre founded in Western modernity on the power to evoke and revoke subjectivity by producing the visual fiction of an individualized and autonomous self. The cleaning of the Butterworth painting, and the reemergence of the black figure from behind the column, does not simply bring to life a lost identity. Actually, *stricto sensu*, it does not do this at all. If anything, even at the moment of its initial inscription, the subjected black figure was already, symbolically, under erasure, his presence predicated on a relation that effected his symbolic absenting in the face of the dominant and nonchalantly subjugating white presence. Central to the Butterworth painting is the way in which the enslaved presence in representation often becomes a constitutive component of white identity. Thus, in Wright's painting the uniformed slave who rushes forward to pour water over the playfully outstretched hand of his mistress appears to be, in some ways, a part of the white woman. In a Hegelian twist, however, her presence in the pre-restoration portrait makes as little sense as his presence without her. Still, as Sulter suggests, the painting-out of the enslaved figure's likeness, even if done with the best of intentions (for instance, to "liberate" the figure from his position of subordination by "excising" him from the canvas), leads to a further marginalization and blindness, one that eliminates the visual trace of subjection against which the white sitter's identity as a free subject was intended to emerge. Yet, it is through these very acts of erasure that his enslaved presence claims existence.

We begin, then, with three erasures: (1) the ideological erasure in which the subordinated presence of the enslaved figure is the condition of possibility for the visual fantasy of masterly subjectivity granted to the white sitter, (2) the historical, painterly erasure that obliterated the traces of slavery, and (3) the erasure of the role of portraiture as a technology deployed, in this case, for the illusory freezing of permanent subjection. It is almost as if the black subject in the Butterworth painting were first crossed out – set "under erasure" (*sous rature*) – and then literally erased. Building on Martin Heidegger, who in his reflections on existence had crossed out the word "Being" ("Sein") and let the word along with its erasure stand, Jacques Derrida developed his central deconstructivist concept of *sous rature*. Derrida's insistence on the necessity of retaining a term under erasure means that even though its use may be problematic we must maintain it until it can be effectively reformulated or replaced. Similarly, the figure under erasure in the Butterworth painting demands critical attention and conceptual reconfiguration.

Painting may require a different vocabulary than the textualist crossings-out of both Heidegger and Derrida, and, perhaps, openness to different accounts of what presence might mean in the *visual* realm. Neither Heidegger's existential reflections on Being and Not-Being "in-the-world" nor Derrida's critique of Western metaphysics and of its notion of presence in language captures the ontology of paint.[6] This is not to claim social or physical presence as origin in the figures represented but rather to acknowledge the recalcitrant physicality of paintings, where the presence of Beings cannot be crossed out or erased in textual fashion. Within a figurative aesthetic, the enslaved figure, although not there, is there. The materiality of his image, despite occlusion through paint, insists and produces its own reality. One might consider his presence a haunting, a translucent invisible visibility.

Not only does the ghostly enslaved subject exist within and without portraiture, but the very focus of this collection on slave portraiture must exist as well in a liminal space of undecidability and paradox. If portraiture as a genre, in its most conventional pre–avant-garde fashion, has been understood as demanding that the viewer grant a subject-reality to the image made visible on the canvas, what then are the particularities of the dynamics of visualization and subjectification that underwrite the portrayal of enslaved beings whose conditions of existence and visibility have been historically under erasure? The essays in this collection place the terms "slave" and "portraiture" into useful friction and bring to the fore the specific historical and discursive circumstances that made such a conceptual and material encounter possible at key moments during the long history of transatlantic slavery.

Portraiture and the Scopic Dynamics of Plantation Slavery

The period running from the sixteenth to late nineteenth century marks a significant shift in the history of slavery – a history understood here not linearly, but as a series of variations and dissonances around the theme of "the human as property" and of its many ideological justifications. This period saw a progressively exponential expansion of the trade in human flesh to satisfy the demands of the colonial plantation economy, which became, in contrast to early Spanish colonial settlements, the dominant feature of the pan-European colonial venture in major areas of the Americas. The geographical displacements spawned by the intersection of the slave trade, the plantation system, and the modern colonial enterprise produced a new territoriality that Joseph Roach, in dialogue with Paul Gilroy's notion of the "Black Atlantic," has called the "circum-Atlantic world." This concept of "the circum-Atlantic," whose theoretical underpinnings inform our understanding of "the Atlantic world" in the title of this book, "insists on the centrality of the diasporic and genocidal histories of Africa and the Americas, North and South, in the creation of the culture of modernity."[7] Or, as Stephen Shapiro has put it, it entails a recognition of a matrix formed by Europe, Africa, the Caribbean, and the broader indigenous Americas in its constitution.[8] This is not to suggest that such a matrix yielded homogeneous patterns of plantation enslavement, which, of course, it did not, but to acknowledge the kernel of shared violence that constitutes modern territorialities and their histories. This violence also entailed, as we will see, a visual dimension.

Scholars have paid attention to the specifics and permutations in the structures of colonial and republican slavery in the Americas from a range of perspectives. These include the analysis of divergent patterns of plantation ownership (e.g., predominantly absentee/corporatist in the British Caribbean versus ownership by local white elites in the Spanish, Portuguese, and North American colonies); the definition and position of the slave within different legal traditions (the provisions, for example, within Spanish legislation that allowed for slaves to acquire their freedom through mutually agreed contracts with their masters – a right known as *derecho de coartación,* and which was totally absent from English slave law); the structures of sociability within various plantation regimes and the forms of slave familial organization these enabled (the Portuguese patriarchal *casa-grande* versus the conjunctural emergence of the Cuban jail-like *barracón,* for instance); to the various degrees of regulation and/or suppression of African religious practices that took place within different colonial contexts and that yielded heterogeneous forms of cultural syncretism (the development of *candomblé* in Brazil or *santería* in Cuba by contrast to the emergence of black Christian churches in the U.S. South).[9] Yet, despite this diversity of topics and approaches, we wish to focus on a concern common to them all: the production of the slave as a "hypervisible" entity – to borrow Saidiya Hartman's fruitful term – as a being whose existence had to be permanently subject (at least theoretically within the logic of chattel slavery) to the surveilling gaze of the master and/or its surrogate figure, the overseer.[10]

In juridical terms, and regardless of their variations, slave codes across the Americas made hypervisibility a disciplinary imperative. Enslaved persons had to be unyieldingly available to the scopic lust of a domineering gaze. Conversely, it was through hypervisibility that the masterly gaze constituted itself as such and attempted to render the slave subjectless (i.e., a mere instrument for economic production, a surface without depth). This is not to say, of course, that in the daily practices of slave life such an imperative was not constantly undermined through multiple modes of resistance – the most radical of these possibly being the act of the runaway slave, who quite literally escaped, erased him- or herself, from the masterly field of vision.[11] Nevertheless, slave codes were unequivocal in their will for visual control. Practically without exception, from the infamous 1661 "Barbados Act" onward, the slave was expected by law to be permanently visible to the eye of the master. Thus, for example, the 1842 Hispano-Cuban Slave Code in no uncertain terms stated:

> Slaves of one estate shall not be able to visit those of another without the express consent of the masters or overseers of both. When they have to go

> to another estate or leave their own, they shall take a written pass from the owner or overseer with the description of the slave, the date of the day, month, and year, the declaration of his destination, and the time he must return.[12]

Not incidentally, permission to leave the premises of the plantation involved not just a written document stating that such a license was indeed granted to a particular slave (within restricted spatial and temporal limits) but also an ekphrastic act of verbal portraiture – "the description of the slave" – by which his or her visual particularities (e.g., a scar on the shoulder, a tribal mark on the face) were to be recorded so as to make the document nontransferable, the slave visible to other overseers/masters, and the coercive will enforceable. The main concern of this volume is to underscore, through a series of case studies, the relationships between the placement of the slave's hypervisible body within the violent foundational dynamics of the trans-Atlantic, from 1599 to the date of the official abolition of the regime in its last hemispheric stronghold (Brazil, 1888), and the specifics of the representational practice of portraiture – most specifically, painted, printed, and sculpted portraits.[13]

In the context of imperial and colonial slavery, portraiture occupied an ambivalent position. The period marked by an expanding trade in human bodies coincided with the emergence of portraiture as a major field of representation in Western art. Yet, the two categories "slave" and "portraiture" appear to be mutually exclusive or, as David Bindman puts it, oxymoronic.[14] The logic of chattel slavery strived to produce the body of the slave in a very restricted manner: as a purely instrumentalized being, as a body dwelling in the eternal present of labor, reproduction, and punishment. The body of the slave appears as the site of a nonsubject, of an entity without memory or history – the slave as pure bodiliness and immanence. Portraiture, on the other hand, insists on the face as a primary site of an imagined subjectivity, often at the expense of the rest of the body. Its metaphysical aura of transcendence has been conventionally understood as a privileged tool for the visualization of "being," and for the production of the subject as visuality. Gilles Deleuze and Félix Guattari might have called it a machine for "facialization." It is their contention that in Western culture the face has acquired a privileged signifying status over the rest of the body. The face is produced, they say, when the head ceases to be coded by the body "so that the body, head included, has been decoded and has to be *overcoded* by something we shall call the Face." That act of overcoding the body by the face is what they call "facialization."[15]

However, in the logic of chattel slavery, it is the face that seems to be overcoded by the subjected body, and "facelessness" the means by which the slave is theoretically rendered a nonsubject.[16] This is perhaps the most profound significance of the passages in Juan Francisco Manzano's autobiography (1837), where the Cuban slave poet insistently narrates his experiences of torture as a constant assault against his "face" ("daily receiving blows on the face, that often made the blood spout from both my nostrils"), while covering with a "veil of silence," as he puts it, the violence wielded against the rest of his body. The body, in Manzano's autobiography, is insinuated yet concealed from the voyeuristic gaze of his well-intentioned (although perversely fascinated) abolitionist reader, and the drama of his dehumanizing subjection staged as a visualization of the broken face. This dialectic of bodily occlusion and facial display is central to the figuration of personal dignity and to the undoing of the slave subject position subtly at work in the text.[17]

Thus, what is at stake in producing the *likeness* of a slave's face, however illusory this production might be? What are its challenges?

Portraits and Types, Once Again

Few potential constraints hover with such force over the study of slaves of African descent in portraiture as our modern history of racism, which has denied singularity and individuality *as subjects* to non-Europeans and especially to those who have been enslaved.[18] This denial has taken place, though, through a rather paradoxical logic. Construed as "others" within racialized Western/modern notions of personhood (which, in its pre-Freudian Enlightened version, are structured by concepts of autonomy, sovereignty of rational consciousness, self-possession, and freedom), the existence of these "others" has been conceived of as a radical singularity, as a difference that subtracts them from the condition and destiny of "Man" as the universal subject of world history.

An exemplary, and rather foundational instance of this view is found in Hegel's *Lectures on the Philosophy of World History*. For Hegel, in sub-Saharan Africa: "history is in fact out of the question. Life there consists of a succession of contingent happenings and surprises. No aim or state exists whose development could be followed; and *there is no subjectivity*, but merely a series of subjects who destroy one another." In the *Lectures*, Africa is a site where the "principle of cultural backwardness" predominates, a place of historical impossibility where movement and progression is understood to be detained – in both senses of being "trapped" and "stopped."[19] Therefore, the singular and hyper-contingent difference of this "otherness" ("a succession of contingent happenings and surprises") grants Africans the status of a nonuniversal "generality" lacking in *subjectivity* (i.e., agency, *telos*). Or inversely, the African "other" is not universal because of its collective singularity vis-à-vis a no less phantasmatic "Europe." Racial types and stereotypes are a performative expression of this logic. If slave portraiture could be thought of as "oxymoronic" (to use again David Bindman's provocative term) it is also because it represents a moment of impossibility within the modern paradox set forth by Hegel. The

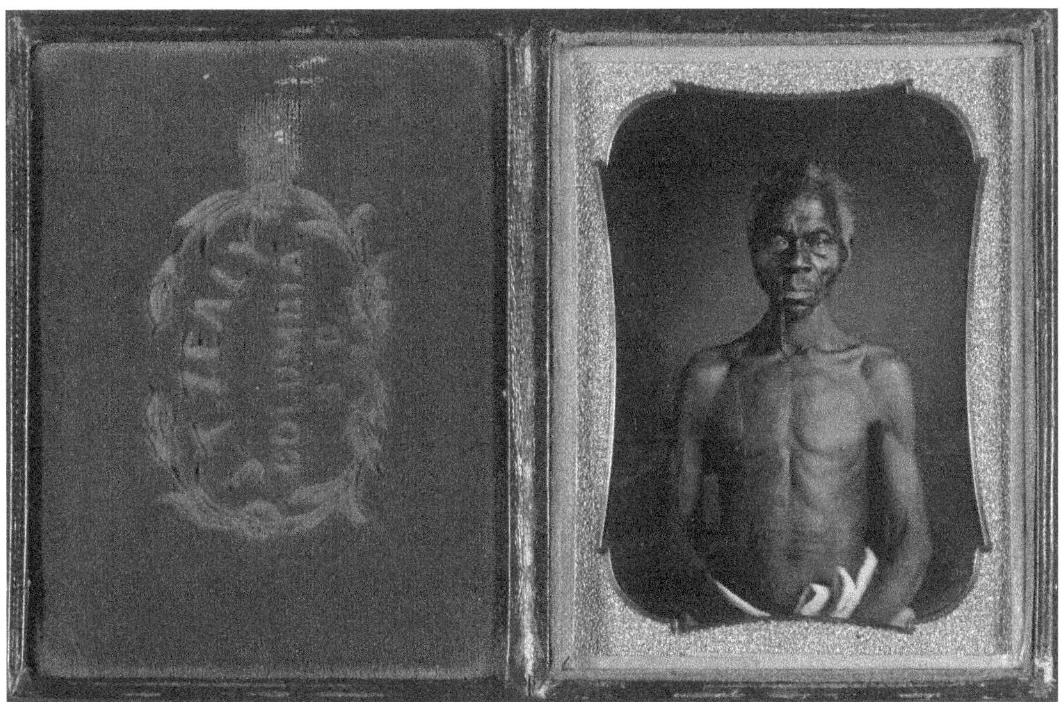

I.3. J. T. Zealy, *Renty, Congo, Plantation of B. F. Taylor, Esqu.* Columbia, S.C., March 1850 (frontal). Daguerreotype. Peabody Museum of Archaeology and Ethnology, Harvard University, 35-5-10/53037, Cambridge, Mass.

type casts its shadow over the singular, and the singular is forced to carry on under the shadow of the type.

Brian Wallis has provided a useful, although debatable, differentiation between "type" and "portrait" in his study of the colonialist and, at points, overtly pornographic daguerreotypes of slaves made by J. T. Zealy for the Harvard scientist Louis Agassiz in 1850.[20] By focusing on images such as that of *Renty, Congo, Plantation of B. F. Taylor, Esqu.* (Fig. I.3), Wallis problematizes historian Alan Trachtenberg's iconographic linking of Zealy's slave daguerreotypes to Roman portrait busts – an affiliation that leads him to underline the complicated status of subjecthood and presence at work in Zealy's images and to claim that, against Agassiz's intentions of zoological classification, they end up visualizing the performance of a self-aware denied personhood.[21]

While building on Trachtenberg, Wallis takes distance both from his iconographic and humanistic accents, insisting that Zealy's daguerreotypes are fully invested in a project of scientific racism and have very little to do with traditions of Western portraiture, much less with that of Roman busts. Far from portraits, they are "types." The type, unlike the portrait, he argues, "discourages style and composition, seeking to present the information as plainly and straightforwardly as possible. Thus, the images are frequently organized around a clear central axis with a minimum of external information that could distract from the principal focus ... objectivity is the goal." In the type, as he sees it, the subject is already "positioned, known, owned, represented, spoken for, or constructed as silent; in short, it is ignored.... Fundamentally nonreciprocal, [the type] masks its subjective distortions in the guise of logic and organization. Its formations are deformations."[22]

Wallis's contentions exemplify the challenges posed to our understanding of slave portraiture by the pressures that discursive regimes of racialization exercise over the rhetoric of singularity at work in the genre. However, although we agree with the sentiment of his criticism, and with his formal characterization of "the type," it seems to us that there are two issues that cannot be bypassed in examining the presuppositions at work in this analysis. The first of these concerns the sharp distinction Wallis makes between portraits and types, which tends to underestimate the extent to which "types" too, just like portraits, follow conventions and employ a style, even though this style might be one of "stylelessness." In other words, types are constituted by a rhetoric of authenticity and objectivity, just like portraits can be understood to employ, in the words of Marcia Pointon, a rhetoric of portrait-likeness. Ironically, many of the Roman "portrait busts" to which we ascribe individuality and character, are, as Sheldon Nodelman has demonstrated, not based on individuals at all, but on portrait types.[23] Thus, the distance between portrait and type may not be as unbridgeable as Wallis suggests, and questions pertaining to the rhetoric of subjectivity not as irrelevant to the typological. Likewise, the occlusion of singularity may not be so estranged a fact from acts of portraiture.

The second issue concerns, precisely, the status of discourses of "subjecthood" within the type. Depending on the circumstances, "types" can also subvert their "muted" condition if, for instance, the information contained in or excited by the image exceeds its frame of discursive intentions. This is certainly the case with Zealy's daguerreotypes. Anthropological as they no doubt are, they also allow for a different kind of gaze – one potentially moved by oppositional ethical concerns and values and, thus, able to register (in the material *thereness* of the image) the inescapable presence of subjects in pain. The perception of such a presence troubles the subjects' purported status as "specimens" and has the potential to overwhelm a viewer with the intensity of their suffering, with the agonic trace of a subjective singularity. More than inciting in the viewer the realization of "the universal humanity we share with them" (as Trachtenberg would have it),[24] that encounter does open up a fissure that upsets the viewing prescriptions of the "type." Once dislocated from their discursive framework, once they travel, as they belatedly did, "elsewhere," beyond Agassiz's meaning-making archives, the "type," despite itself, sets free (so to speak) the potentialities of "the portrait" that the images also contain – for as much as they are indeed constituted by the gaze of scientific racism, we may say, somehow with and against Barthes, that as daguerreotypes they are first, and unavoidably, the mark of an irreducible presence, a subjected contingency.[25]

The works of Zealy/Agassiz and the fruitful interpretive dissonances between Wallis and Trachtenberg point to some of the complexities in the study of slave portraiture undertaken by various essays in this book. The entanglement and/or frictions between the conventions of portraiture and typology are brought to the fore not only by ethnographic portraits (studied in this volume by Brienen, Parrish, and Smalls). It is an issue that hovers more generally, as we suggest above, over the representation of black subjects and thus requires pointed analytical attention. Two of the major problematics at work in the Wallis-Trachtenberg exchange – the iconographic traditions that are engaged (or disengaged) in the production of images of black subjects vis-à-vis the discursive regimes within which slave portraits appear, as well as the question of their historicity versus the phenomenological dynamics that may produce (or not) unsuspected ethical responses – are revisited by essays in this volume (Schmidt-Linsenhoff, Weston, Chieffo-Reidway, and Williams). Equally important is the problematic of the archive, so central to the Zealy/Agassiz images and to the project of this book. The archive is understood here in a Foucaultian sense: the sum of texts that a culture gives itself as testimony of its past and its identity and the institutions that preserve them, but also the law of what can be uttered, the rules of cultural decidability.[26] Buried as they were for over a century in the Harvard Library, until new political dispositions of the gaze, other paradigms of knowledge, and a reconsideration of the limits of the visual arts endowed them with significance, the Zealy/Agassiz images force us to interrogate the sites of production and preservation of slave portraiture, the violence of their origins and their unintended paradoxes. These sites were not restricted to the dusty and arcane repositories of a library, but range from the courtesan palaces and bourgeois interiors for which some of them were originally made, to churches and artists' studios – such as those of the Comtesse Benoist, who established a relationship of intimacy with the slave likenesses she painted, refusing to let it go during the artist's lifetime, only to have it enter, upon the artist's death, the collections of a royal museum (i.e., the Louvre) – to frontispieces of books that were deployed as visual evidence for the authenticity and truth value of authorial claims (e.g., Equiano and Wheatley), and abolitionist lithographs geared to influence public opinion against slavery. This book, which in itself attempts to be an archival endeavor, participates in and seeks to advance an interrogation of the circuits and rules that enabled the production of slave portraiture and of the possibilities for their historical afterlife.

A Critical Field on Slavery, Race, and Visuality

In the 1980s and 1990s art historical and literary projects of recuperation sought, in the footsteps of feminism, to recover absent or absented subjects. In literary studies much work has addressed slave narratives, autobiographies, and poetry. Some of these studies have paid significant attention to the processes of subjectification that take place, for example, through mimesis, parody, and complex language games (*signifyin'(g) practices*, as Henry Louis Gates has called them),[27] as well as through other textual strategies that destabilize the norms of "enslaved existence" with regard to the law and dominant forms of cultural authority.[28] For their part, art historians, especially those studying periods like early modernity, have focused on iconographical matters, leading to publications such as the first edition of the monumental *The Image of the Black in Western Art*.[29] Those few studies that address the portrayal of slaves more precisely often foreground biographical information on subjects such as Ignatius Sancho, Olaudah Equiano, Angelo Soliman, and Quobna Ottobah Cugoano, or look at the symbolic function of the inclusion of page boys of African descent in Western portraiture without raising the question of the visual rhetorics of slave subjectivity.[30] In the Luso-Hispanic world these kinds of studies are relatively scarce. This is particularly puzzling insofar as Brazil was the last country in the Western Hemisphere to abolish slavery officially (in 1888) preceded by the then Spanish colony of Cuba (in 1886).[31]

However, under the pressure of theoretical critiques such as those found in Henry Louis Gates's *"Race," Writing, and Difference*, and as part of the general development of the field of critical race theory, art historians increasingly have sought to study the representation of black figures not only as an iconographic subfield or as an enterprise of recuperation, but rather as part of broader discursive constructions of race. The essays in Gates's pioneering 1985 collection took up the task of unearthing race as "an invisible quantity, a persistent yet implicit presence" of literary and cultural production, and as a "dangerous trope" that demands the deconstruction "of the ideas of difference" that sustain it and the explication of the regimens of power/knowledge within which these ideas emerge and operate.[32]

Among these critical shifts in the study of race, "whiteness studies" in particular has overtly proposed that the invisible norm of whiteness structures and defines the notion of black as "other."[33] For instance, in *Playing in the Dark: Whiteness and the Literary Imagination* (1992), a brilliant meditation on the construction and rhetorical functions of the "Africanist" presence and persona in the founding writers of the young United States, Toni Morrison has argued that "Africanism, deployed as rawness and savagery ... provided the staging ground and arena for the elaboration of the quintessential American [*sic*] identity."[34] It was against such a presence, conceived as a "blank darkness," that concerns with autonomy and authority, newness and difference, and absolute power and freedom were elaborated.[35] In a culture that was built economically and socially upon slavery (as the most visibly central historical problematic of U.S. social relations), every cultural element was connected, directly or indirectly, to this foundation:

> The slave population, it could be and was assumed, offered itself up as surrogate selves for meditation on problems of human freedom, its lure and its elusiveness. This black population was available for mediations on terror – the terror of European outcasts, their fear of failure, powerlessness, Nature without limits, natal loneliness, internal aggression, evil, sin, greed. In other words, the slave population was understood to have offered itself up for reflections on human freedom in terms other than the abstractions of human potential and the rights of man.[36]

Within this analytical paradigm the question of the "identity" of the black (or indeed white) subject is no longer central, having been displaced by a critical concern for the racial constructions that emerged from the scientific and pseudo-scientific discourses on human difference in early modernity and their heterogeneous rhetorical articulations. Or as Morrison herself puts it, this project entails an "effort to avert the critical gaze ... from the described and imagined to the describers and imaginers; from the serving to the served."[37] The goal of criticism here is no longer to rehabilitate the injured subjectivity of the "other" along the Euro-American prototype but the recognition of the ruthlessness of these invisible norms and the analysis of their underlying mechanisms.[38]

Today, these two modes of analysis coexist, with iconographic studies revealing new and interesting information about the black presence in art and visual representation (more generally speaking), on the one hand, and deconstructive/critical race studies offering reflections on the discursive elaboration of racialized roles, on the other. Within the past decade scholars as theoretically diverse and wide reaching as David Bindman, Albert Boime, Magali M. Carrera, Beth Fowkes Tobin, Simon Gikandi, Darcy Grimaldo Grigsby, Michael Harris, Ilona Katzew, K. Dian Kriz, Maurine McInnis, Nicholas Mirzoeff, Catherine Molineaux, Felicity Nussbaum, Elizabeth L. O'Leary, Geoff Quilley, Joseph Roach, Alan Trachtenberg, Brian Wallis, Kathleen Wilson, and Marcus Wood, among others, have made major critical interventions exploring the diverse and contradictory visual culture of colonialism and slavery in Europe and the Americas.[39] Moreover, most recently, the bicentennial commemoration of the abolition of the British slave trade in 2007 incited a significant number of groundbreaking exhibitions and new publications that have brought to the fore a closer examination of the relationships between the visual arts and slavery.[40] The focus has frequently fallen on landscape art, genre scenes, natural history, and pro- and antislavery propaganda in print and popular culture and the performance of everyday life. With notable exceptions, slave portraiture has remained a practically uncharted territory.[41]

Over all of these approaches necessarily hover the unassimilable concept and reality of "slavery," which cannot and should not be equated with black subjects in representation. Yet these issues – the representation of black subjects and the representation of race more generally – demand that we grapple with slavery. We have found the work of contemporary artists to offer insights into how to address these visual and theoretical impasses. Artists who choose to work precisely at the difficult limit of racial representation suggest ways to conceptualize the analysis of the enslaved body in portraiture.

On Figuring Slave Portraiture

One of the reasons that American artist Kara Walker's powerful, disturbing, and beautiful works appear to speak so directly to so many contemporary viewers is that they seem to keep the terms "race" and "slavery" in play, without having relations concretize into dysfunctional chains. Her silhouetted narratives, suggesting shadows but also early-modern portraiture, posit the inescapable dialectic linking whiteness, blackness, and slavery. Rather than having one term explain the other, they coalesce onto one plane, the silhouette. Outlines define forms in which bodies meld and stereotypes merge into provocative pseudo-narratives. Here, on the positive/negative surface of the silhouette/shadow, we find a *historical* projection, a way to figure the inheritance of slavery in understanding figurations of race. Here are the shadows that haunt the collective memories and that provide a path to a productive history of the slave portrait.

In contrast to her crowded panoramic narratives of twisting and twirling bodies, Kara Walker's *Untitled* (1995) (Fig. I.4), tackles the conventions of portraiture head on. At first glance *Untitled* confronts us with a somewhat stiff and rather traditional rendition of a full-length male protagonist, one leg jutting forward with the other firmly planted on the ground, as if he were caught in the moment of slowly exiting the frame to the left. His whiteness emerges effortlessly from his black silhouetted outline through the chiseled aquiline and thus "noble" profile. The signs of his elevated class status are accessorized by what could be a wig or, simply, loosely coiffed hair. His long-tailed coat further intensifies the sense of entitlement that infuses his demeanor, upright and self-assured. Little prepares us for the blubbering and grotesque caricature profile of a "primitive" African woman, whose short "frizzy" hair, neck extensions, and raffia skirt along with her naked tipping breast encapsulate everything he is not. As Darby English points out, in a political sense she is "black, female and unfree." In contrasting their otherness, the figures evoke the intertwined history of white men and black women under slavery, "the black monkey on the back" of every white man, the "Sugar Daddies," including relationships such as the one between Thomas Jefferson and Sally Hemings.[42] If post-abolitionist discourse on subjectivity can tell us something, then, it is the insight that black and white subject positions have shaped and articulated each other.[43]

I.4. Kara Walker, *Untitled*, 1995. Cut paper on paper. Collection of Anne and Joel Ehrenkranz. Photo: Adrian Piper Research Archive, Berlin.

This book aims to provide an analytical analogue to Walker's practice, in that we wish to acknowledge and study the paradoxical presenting and absenting of enslaved individuals in visual representation; like a silhouette, the figure of the present/absent slave offers a vexed outline and a shadowy being, flickering between positive and negative space. We also wish to engage, productively, with the problematic entwining of the term "slave" with the representation of black individuals. Here again Walker's silhouettes are suggestive, with the blackness of her figures operating, sometimes, to represent black skin mimetically, while simultaneously denying such reference, positing the cut-out as a universal means of capturing figural narrative. The acceptance and denial of skin offers a pragmatic approach to the history of enslavement: It acknowledges the problem of blackness, while undermining the often automatic equation between blackness and slavery.

Perhaps some practical examples of the challenges posed by the modern historical and visual entanglement of race with enslavement, three, to be precise, will help explain what we mean.

One. There is nothing in Diego Velázquez's powerful portrait of Juan de Pareja of 1650 (Fig. I.5; Plate 1) that suggests the sitter is a slave. Pareja emerges from the warm dark background as a strikingly corporeal presence. Velázquez confronts us with a self-assured and confident subject that dominates the picture plane. He gazes out toward the viewer with calm and steady eyes; one eyebrow is raised, offering a note of sociable query. Understanding the act of portrayal as intersubjective, the painting stages a powerful dialogue between Velázquez and Pareja, between master and servant/slave/apprentice, while contesting the structures of ownership, power, and reciprocal responsibilities entailed by these positions. Indeed, the celebrated Spanish painter Velázquez was doubly master to Juan de Pareja: He was both his owner and his teacher.[44] Pareja became an artist in his own

I.5. Diego Velázquez, *Juan de Pareja*, 1650. Oil on canvas. Metropolitan Museum of Art, New York. Purchase, Fletcher and Rogers Funds, and Bequest of Miss Adelaide Milton de Groot (1876–1967), by exchange, supplemented by gifts from friends of the Museum, 1971. Photo: Malcolm Varon. © Metropolitan Museum of Art/Art Resource, New York.

right, and the emphasis on the sitter's questioning and responsive eyes highlights issues concerning vision and visuality. It is also telling that we see the fingers of his right hand spread apart and grasping the thick fabric of his robe. The hand, which served his master, would become the hand that created art.

This painting presents a paradox. Portraiture of the Spanish Baroque was, as Victor Stoichita has pointed out, reserved by definition for "important individuals" and thus excluded slaves as the subject of representation. If Pareja were portrayed, he would no longer be enslaved. Put differently, the sitter entered a mode of representation that abolished the premises of slavery. Arguably, the act of painting the portrait figuratively frees Pareja from the shackles of enslavement and transposes him into the realm of the *liberal arts.*[45] The goal of Velázquez's painting was not, however, to create an abolitionist icon. As Carmen Fracchia argues in her essay in this volume, other artistic issues were at stake. The painting sets forth this book's central paradox: How can there be a visual representation that is at once a portrait and a depiction of a slave, given historical definitions of the genre (since Pliny the Elder)?[46] Does not the act of sitting for one's portrait cross out or undermine the notion of enslavement? Rather than imagining there is a logical resolution to this tension, we embrace it, believing that in analysis the two terms render one another more complex, interesting, and productive.

Two. More than 250 years after Velázquez painted his portrait, the British artist John Philip Simpson exhibited a painting entitled *The Captive Slave* at London's Royal Academy (Fig. I.6). Dated 1827, the large canvas shows a young, life-size man of African descent seated on a bare stone ledge. The shallow

I.6. John Philip Simpson, *The Captive Slave*, 1827. Oil on canvas. The Art Institute of Chicago. Restricted gift of Mary Winton Green, Dan and Sara Green Cohan, Howard and Lisa Green and Jonathan and Brenda Green, in memory of David Green, 2008.188.

brown-gray background resembles that of Velázquez's painting, but in Simpson's composition it fails to serve as a backdrop against which his sitter's subjectivity emerges. Instead, it is a limit, a marker of his captivity, for the man's wrists are shackled and we see to the right, on the stone bench, the links of an enormous chain. If the shackles and chain signify his captivity, it is his dark complexion, read within the context of the Atlantic slave trade, which underwrites his identification as a slave in the work's title. Wearing a loose, red robe, which evokes an unspecified foreignness, the man raises his moist eyes – whether toward the light, toward his jailer, or toward divinity, we do not know.

This captive slave is a figure of hegemonic cultural imagination, one inflected by white masterly desires. Unlike the rebellious slaves reported on the plantations, Simpson's slave is nonthreatening, plaintive, and awaiting the goodwill of others for his liberation. It is a presence devoid of agency. The wide-open collar of his deep orange-red cloak reveals a smooth unblemished chest that suggests both sensuality and vulnerability, especially in light of the punishments captive slaves had to endure.[47] In contrast to Velázquez's ennobling subject this painting speaks directly of enslavement. At the time Simpson exhibited his painting the abolitionist movement in Britain was at a renewed height. Simpson's work of a submissive shackled black man articulates a strong antislavery position, one that gains its currency through comparison with portrait conventions. Like a Christian saint the man as an icon of enslavement appeals to the viewer for pity, but the captive's individualized features foster a sense that this is a particular person, and that this painting is a portrait.[48] The image rests on a line, or perhaps better in a zone, between genre painting or history painting and portraiture. Yet it is precisely the subject's submissive impassivity that resists the traditional (modern and liberal) categorization as a *portrait* – or to say it in Hegelian terms, of fitting the visual register of a *self-for-itself*. Like the Christian motto over the seal of the abolitionist society (Fig. I.7), Simpson's shackled black man appeals to the viewer for mercy: *Am I Not a Man and a Brother?* Seen in these terms, the man would surely be read as a dependent, perversely relational, subject, one tied to the compassionate gaze and shackled precisely for its benefit. As these two examples – the Simpson and the Velázquez – show, the category, or the oxymoronic anti-category, of slave portraiture puts pressure on the definition of both slave and portraiture. In challenging conceptual boundaries it demands historical specificity as well as careful reading, not necessarily of the biography of artist or figure represented (although the

I.7. William Hackwood for Josiah Wedgwood, *Am I Not a Man and a Brother?*, 1787. Black and yellow jasper medallion. Image by courtesy of the Wedgwood Museum, Barlaston, Staffordshire, U.K.

biographical may, too, factor into analysis), but, above all, the visual means employed in these works.

How can the "liberatory" or disciplinarian protocols of portraiture – its power to *capture* a likeness while conveying the sense of freeing and producing the subject – be reconciled with the position of the enslaved?[49] If Simpson's painting is a portrait, it is most likely a role-portrait of the free-born American Ira Aldridge (1807–67), the first great black Shakespearean actor in Great Britain, who at the time the painting was executed was establishing his career in London.[50] Were this figure Aldridge – and comparing the features of the figure in *The Captive Slave* to the documented pictures of the actor, we see no compelling reason to think this is not the case – the picture begins to dissolve the boundary mentioned above, between history/genre painting and the portrait. Actors' portraits, especially those that represent the sitters in a role, are clearly hybrids. They show the actor *as* a character. In this instance, however, even if the man represented Aldridge, one cannot call this an "actor's portrait," per se. At the Royal Academy in London it was simply shown with the title *The Captive Slave*.[51] Thus, if we do see Aldridge, it is in part despite, not because of, the painting's genre. Moreover, given the historical moment of the painting's public display, and even though Aldridge was a freeborn man, it would have been his dark skin color that would have signified enslavement.

What is, then, the "likeness" of a slave? What does it mean to *capture* a slave in portraiture? Does the genre actually allow for an enslaved subject to figuratively escape its bondage, as Juan de Pareja's portrait seems to suggest? Or, on the contrary, could it be possible that within the very dynamics of portraiture it is the notion and the practice of "the likeness of a slave" that works as a subtle means for the reassertion of subjection? Simpson's portrait (like José Correia de Lima's portrait of the heroic free Cape Verdean sailor Simão discussed by Daryle Williams in this volume) deploys conventionalized visual markers of enslavement as performative signifiers. If anything, such works exemplify the ideological and aesthetic problematics in which "slave" and the representation of dark-skinned people have been historically entangled. If the liberal arts have the potential – albeit metaphorical – power to free a subject in the realm of its own fiction, these examples demonstrate the complex manner in which the art of portraiture should indeed have a central role in discussions about slavery.

Three. The recording of the physical likeness of slaves in eighteenth- and nineteenth-century slaveholding cultures across the Americas was, for the slave, mostly associated with captivity, recaptivity, punishment, and bondage. When slave owners were interested in representing the individuality of a slave and his or her appearance, it was more often than not in order to capture a fugitive. Like twentieth-century police photographs of "wanted" people, verbal mini-portraits published as newspaper advertisements for runaway slaves had no other goal than criminal identification.[52] To this purpose, runaway ads paid

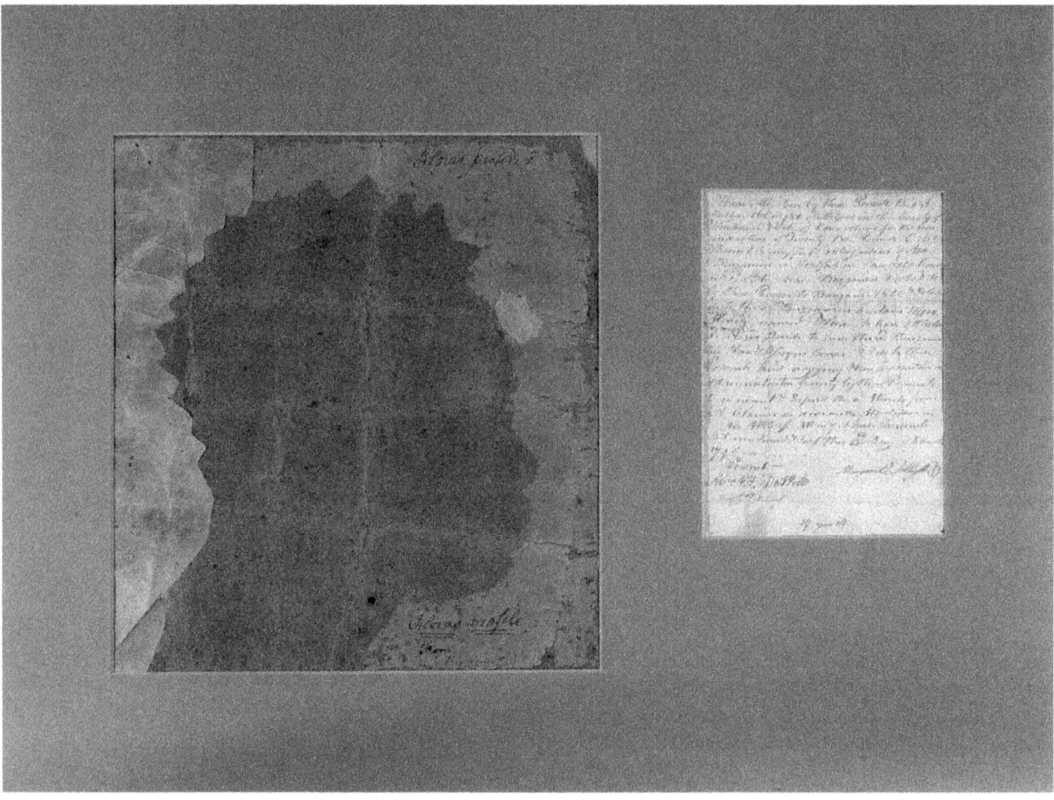

I.8. Anonymous, *Flora's Profile*, 1796. Silhouette, cut paper and brown ink with bill of sale, unsigned. Stratford Historical Society, Stratford, Conn.

particular attention to physical appearance and special characteristics, often including specific accounts of tribal markers, the bodily traces of past punishments and torture, and hairstyles.[53] These traits are ambivalent markers in visual representation.

For example, hair and its varied styling played an important role in the communal life of early-modern North American slaves and, therefore, in the verbal "wanted posters" for runaways.[54] The diversity of hairstyling might on the one hand be aligned with the great variety of artful treatments – braids and plaits, decorated with shells or beads, or hair cut to different lengths, partially shaven or wrapped up – that travelers encountered in their contact with western African populations. There are, as Shane White and Graham White propose, other possible sources and readings. These include contestation of "aesthetic standards of the dominant culture." Thus, the hairstyles of slaves in the Americas might be seen as a form of cultural resistance.[55] Although hair was cropped or shaved off as a form of punishment, White and White describe as a "slippage" in an otherwise "tight system of slaveholder control," that "by and large, slaveholders in the British mainland colonies seem to have allowed African Americans to style their hair as they pleased."[56] Thus hair can be seen as a significant medium for cultural expression, contestation, and social commentary.[57] This bears upon visual representation.

A remarkable wash drawing of 1796 inscribed "Flora's profile" (Fig. I.8) shows the silhouette of a young woman of African descent. The drawing on cut paper facilitated Flora's sale: the silhouette, with the angle of the long firm neck projecting the head forward, is accompanied by a bill of sale (Fig. I.9), which relates

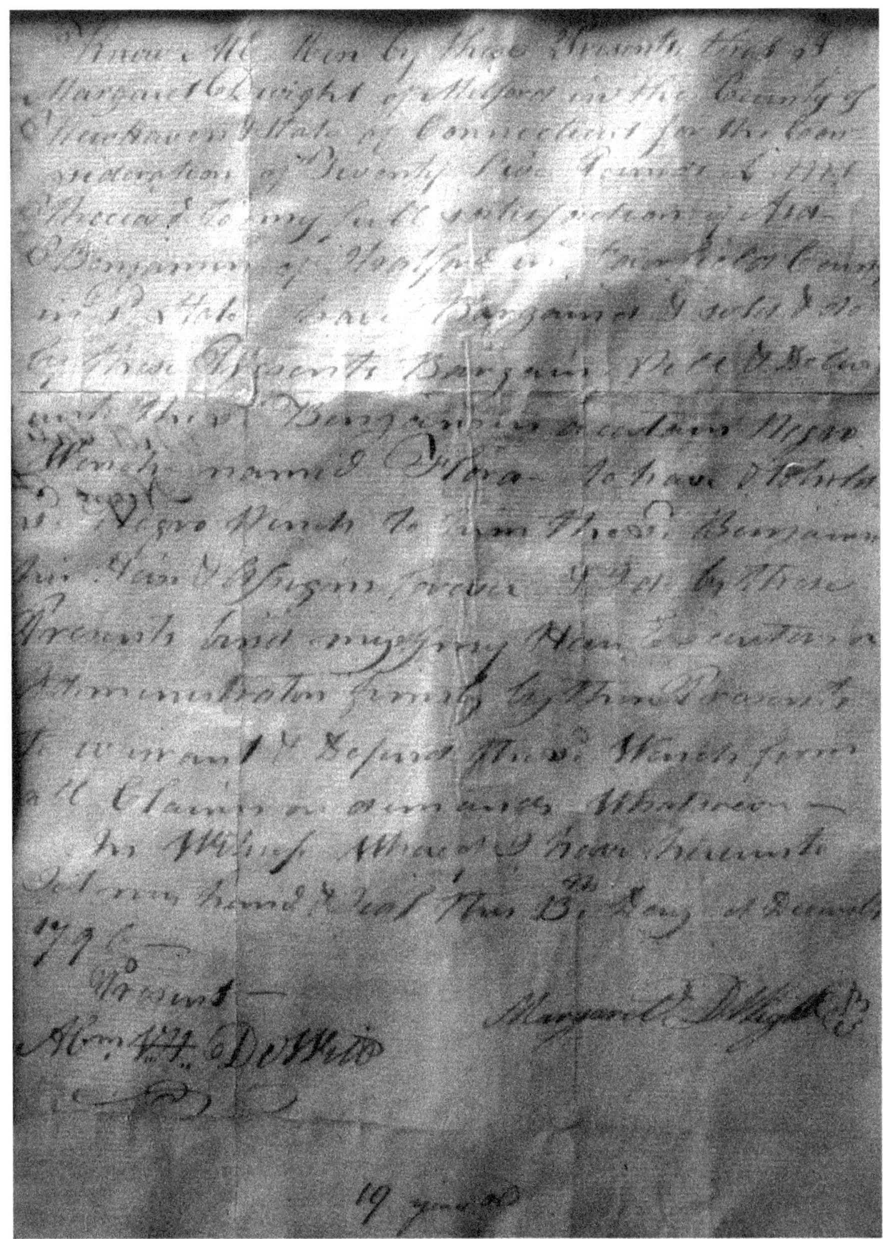

I.9. Detail of Figure I.8 (bill of sale). Anonymous, *Flora's Profile*, 1796.

that a nineteen-year-old slave of the name Flora was sold by Margaret Dwight of Milford in the County of New Haven and State of Connecticut, to Asa Benjamin of Stratford in Fairfield County, Connecticut, for the sum of twenty-five pounds sterling.[58] Not "Flora" herself, but her captured likeness was presented to facilitate the sale. Drawn from life, and thus recording indexically her physical form, inspecting the "portrait" replaced the actual inspection of the enslaved subject practiced at slave markets.

The silhouette, often considered to be a particularly powerful record of likeness, was in the late eighteenth and early nineteenth centuries a preeminent token of memory. Frequently mechanically reduced, silhouettes were exchanged between family, friends, and lovers for the purposes of recording features and calling into being a recollecting gaze. But the silhouette could also serve, more scientifically, to record appearance and type. The rounded features of Flora's youthful face, with its blunt nose, protruding lips, little chin and perpendicular but softly curved forehead, offer the kind of physiognomical "information" that by the end of the eighteenth century was often "read" as providing cues about the inner character and being of the individual. Such legibility was championed by the Swiss pastor and moralist Johann Caspar Lavater, especially in his immensely popular and widely disseminated *Essay in Physiognomy* (1789–92, first published in the 1770s in German).[59] For Lavater, the silhouette profile – which recorded the size, angle, and shape of the brow, the nose, and the chin – constituted the most salient view for the interpretation of character. He contended that the profile could be measured against an ideal human scale, with African traits at its lower reaches opposed to Greco-Roman ideals of whiteness.

Flora's Profile, while inescapably invested with connotations of the memorial and the physiognomic, replaces the recollecting and scientific gaze with a commodifying one. The silhouette and its portraying protocols grant specificity to the subject whose personhood was shopped. Yet, historically, that stolen specificity emerges as a positive marker of Flora's identity. Gwendolyn DuBois Shaw has drawn attention to "the visual and the verbal amalgamation of 'Flora' and 'flower,' of woman and object" for "in its organic regularity" Flora's hair "becomes like the petals of a flower.... Her image, like a pressed blossom, is sandwiched into the two dimensions of the paper. And like flowers, one could purchase slaves."[60]

Given the function of *this* silhouette as facilitating the trading of its sitter, "Flora" would have experienced the actual making of the image – taken by candlelight – as a potentially terrifying experience, as a flattening out and commodification of the self, rather than enabling or ennobling. Can and should this silhouette thus be called a "portrait" or a "slave portrait"? This volume is not concerned with trying to argue firmly one way or the other, but rather seeks to trouble our assumptions about the role and function of portraiture and to probe the limits and possibilities of the genre in relationship to questions of subjectivity, stereotyping, and enslavement.

MAPPING THE BOOK

Slave Portraiture in the Atlantic World is the first book to focus on the portrayal of enslaved subjects from the period marking the West's full engagement with slavery to its abolition. It is not a history of slave subjects and their visual representation. Rather, it explores portraiture and enslavement in order to throw both into question. The point here is not to survey a "genre" or to provide a comprehensive account of a type; indeed, to propose such an agenda would be counterproductive. As our comments and examples in this Introduction have shown, the very instability of the words "slave" and "portraiture" when brought together precludes such closure. Instead, we accept the instability, along with the voids, absences, and erasures; we look for those "oppositional gazes" and "oppositional attitudes" around which one might construct an account of presence, while acknowledging the fiction of pictorial and sculptural representations.[61] We turn to biography, without imagining closure in the biographical; we study portraits, understanding them as material historical traces, without reducing them to mechanical reflections of states of affairs.

The essays that make up this volume are set within a four-part conceptual framework, an organization that strives to deepen the theoretical and methodological dialogues that emerge in and between the contributions. They are also arranged in roughly chronological order, so as to convey a sense of the historical dimensions of the colonial and imperial cultures that have shaped the works under consideration.

Part I, *Visibility and Invisibility*, showcases three historical, theoretical, and methodological studies that take a broad approach to the questions at hand. In the first of these essays, "Slavery and the Possibilities of Portraiture," Marcia Pointon draws on her deep knowledge of Western art and reflects upon the ways in which the often-overlooked subject of the slave in representation not only troubles notions of a stable European self but also unsettles the fundamental conventions of the genre of portraiture as a whole. The essay moves from ancient art and art theory to early-modern paintings and photography, as well as contemporary concerns of conceptual diasporic art. Pointon's provocative reading of the power relations intrinsic to the portrait encounter as a colonizing practice of rendering a subject's object-ness opens a dialogue with other scholars in the volume who respectively concur, contest, and expand upon such theorizations.

David Bindman's essay, "Subjectivity and Slavery in Portraiture: From Courtly to Commercial Societies," offers a historical overview of slave representation (in particular that of the black page) in European art and of its transit from courtly to commercial societies. This shift is relevant to the broader cultural dynamics that characterized the period under consideration and that reemerges as an important context in subsequent essays. Bindman's contribution draws attention to the need for historical specificity by foregrounding both the continuities and changing cultural and aesthetic attitudes toward slavery and its visual depictions.

Eric Slauter's contribution, "Looking for Scipio Moorhead: An 'African Painter' in Revolutionary North America," emblematizes for the volume the methodological challenges presented by the historical search for enslaved subjects who have been rendered invisible by the slaveholding archive. Slauter sets out to look for this enslaved "African painter" working in pre-Revolutionary North America and about whom very little is known besides the rather remarkable fact that he is the subject of an entire poem written by the slave poet Phillis Wheatley. By looking critically for the things that Moorhead must have seen, by "looking with him" as it were, and by carefully poring over the fragments and traces left behind, Slauter produces a remarkable visual field from which the subject of the enslaved emerges from the inscriptions and gaps in the master's archive. The essay, like many others in this volume, thus puts pressure on the question of *invisibility* in relation to enslaved subjects in representation and considers multiple and shifting positions of reception and interpretation.

The second part of the volume, *Slave Portraiture, Colonialism, and Modern Imperial Culture*, foregrounds questions of representation posed by slave portraiture in relation to the dynamics of imperial expansion and colonialism that historically underwrote the emergence of chattel slavery economies. Four case studies offer paradigms keyed to the period examined in this book.

Tom Cummins's essay, "Three Gentlemen from Esmeraldas: A Portrait Fit for a King," focuses on the oldest known signed portrait in South America, Andrés Sánchez Galque's *Portrait of Don Francisco Arobe and his sons Don Pedro and Don Domingo*, which was painted in Quito in 1599. It was produced in the context of a struggle launched by a mulatto community in the emerald-rich region of Esmeraldas (in today's Ecuador) to counter attempts by the Crown and local authorities to enslave them, following the logic that their ancestors were runaway slaves and they were thus not legally entitled to freedom. Cummins analyzes the portrait in view of this contest and within the broader colonial politics and economics of the times. He also explores the new ("New World") questions of legal and racial subjectivity that were incipiently at work in these events and the new representational languages through which identity was visually articulated in the portrait. The painting thus emerges from within the history of slavery as the first powerful visual articulation of mulatto identity in the art of the Americas.

Carmen Fracchia's "Metamorphoses of the Self in Early Modern Spain: Slave Portraiture and the Case of Juan de Pareja" explores one of the most famous European slave portraits, Diego Velázquez's *Juan de Pareja*. Fracchia traces Pareja's remarkable personal transformation from slave and model into a free man and ambitious painter in the context of courtly culture in imperial Spain.

Offering new archival material and subtle visual analyses, the essay places these dynamics in dialogue with the theme of "metamorphosis" codified in Pareja's large-scale history painting of a religious event, *The Calling of Saint Matthew*. This painting includes a self-portrait of the formerly enslaved Afro-Hispanic painter of Muslim ancestry. Fracchia argues that through this juxtaposition Pareja aligns the spiritual awakening of Matthew, in the biblical story, with the artist's personal transformation from slave to free man, from model to artist.

The essay by Geoff Quilley, "Of Sailors and Slaves: Portraiture, Property, and the Trials of Circum-Atlantic Subjectivities, ca. 1750–1830," marks a shift from the dynamics of courtly and colonial cultures to commercial and imperial ones. Quilley argues that the representation of sailors in British art (ca. 1750–1830) reveals some of the tensions within the apparently oxymoronic category of slave portraiture. He treats directly the relations between subjectivity and property, the self and the thing within art, drawing parallels between the sailor and the slave with respect to their lack of a proper territory, or firm roots, their perceived "brutishness" and "otherness," and labor at sea. While avoiding simple conflation of sailor and slave, Quilley makes the strong case that the dialectics of freedom and slavery at work in the image of the sailor touch upon questions of racial and national belonging and of self-possession and subjectivity fundamental to an understanding of the historicity of eighteenth-century slave portraiture, by paying special attention to the frontispieces of Olaudah Equiano's book *The Interesting Narrative of the Life of Olaudah Equiano, or Gustavus Vassa, the African, Written by Himself* (first published 1789).

In her essay, "Between Violence and Redemption: Slave Portraiture in Early Plantation Cuba," Agnes Lugo-Ortiz explores the circumstances surrounding the creation of the first portrait of a slave in Cuban history and the attempts to consolidate symbolically the power of colonial elites through such image making. This extraordinary portrait of a mature and confident black male slave appears prominently among the members of the family he served in Nicolás de la Escalera's *Family of the Count of Casa Bayona* of the mid-1770s. Significantly, this monumental painting is the culminating scene in a cycle of religious images in Santa María del Rosario, a church built upon the ruins of the Bayona family's sugar mill outside Havana, which was destroyed in a slave rebellion in 1727. In a reading rich in methodological implications for the analysis of the social conditions and bodily dynamics that made possible the entrance of slaves into the dignified and dignifying realm of oil-painted portraiture during the colonial era, Lugo-Ortiz weaves archival information, visual evidence, oral history, and local myths into a dense fabric that allows an image of the slave to emerge as a healer of his master's body. At the same time the essay examines the portrait's politically charged role within the redemptive rhetoric of the painting cycle, one that sublimates the violent memory of past slave resistance while reasserting the sense of being of the Creole planter class.

Central to the modern imperial enterprise was the development of new conceptions of taxonomies and categorizations of the human that emerged from the encounters with different cultures as a consequence of travel and exploration. The fascination with natural history and the mapping of the world led in the Age of Enlightenment to the increasing professionalization of fields such as anthropology, medicine, ethnography, and biology. The essays making up Part III, *Subjects to Scientific and Ethnographic Knowledge*, address these shifting paradigms of knowledge as they relate to visual representation and conceptions of colonial subjectivity.

Rebecca Brienen, in her essay "Albert Eckhout's *African Woman and Child* (1641): Ethnographic Portraiture, Slavery, and the New World Subject," discusses a remarkable series of eight full-length portraits of individual adult members of different ethnic groups painted by Dutch artist Albert Eckhout in the first half of the seventeenth century in his country's colonial holdings in Brazil. Monumental in scale, these paintings combine natural history's interests in local costume and customs as well as scientific racial categorizations that were later popularized in Mexican casta paintings, with Western portrait conventions that stress frontality. Brienen approaches the question of subjectivity most closely when looking at a small oil sketch of an enslaved African woman in Dutch Brazil that most likely served as a source for the oil painting of an *African Woman and Child*. Displaying what Brienen calls "ethnic voyeurism" in its attention on the woman's exposed breasts and vulnerable facial expression, she observes traces of the model's "oppositional attitude" that marks her as a subject, albeit one subjugated and colonized.

In her contribution, "Embodying African Knowledge in Colonial Surinam: Two William Blake Engravings in Stedman's 1796 *Narrative*," Susan Scott Parrish describes European natural sciences in the context of British Guyana, but she inverts the equation by examining the presence of the slave not as an object of ethnographic knowledge but (like the Cuban slave discussed by Lugo-Ortiz) as a producer of local knowledge. Her essay focuses on an engraved portrait of an exceptional healer known as Kwasi who served as a scout for the Scottish regiments engaged by the Dutch to suppress the famous maroon insurgency of Surinam in the 1770s, and that was memorably recorded by John Gabriel Stedman in his *Narrative of a five years' expedition against the Revolted Negroes of Surinam* (1796). Kwasi's services to colonial power – that is, placing at its service his knowledge of the local geography as well as the medicinal and dietetic properties of local flora and fauna – not only, Parrish argues, upsets many of the presuppositions of European standards of scientific knowledge at the time, but also helped to create the conditions to render him representable in portraiture.

James Smalls's essay, "Exquisite Empty Shells: Sculpted Slave Portraits and the French Ethnographic Turn," looks at sculpted slave portraits in early- to mid-nineteenth-century France and discusses their relationship to ethnographic discourses. In particular, he analyzes Charles Henri Joseph Cordier's sculptural busts of highly aestheticized *types raciaux* in the context of the debates for the abolition of slavery in France (1848), of the Napoleonic colonial expansion into Africa, and of the elusive dynamics between the artist and the real-life African sitter. While Brienen, in search of subjectivity, moved from the generalized ethnographic portrait toward an oil sketch seemingly of a particular subject, Smalls proceeds conceptually in the opposite direction. In Smalls's narrative we witness the gradual loss of subjectivity that art manages to suggest, describing this process as a hollowing out of the subject to a mere decorative/ethnographic "shell" of colored stone.

The collection's concluding part, *Facing Abolition*, brings together four essays devoted to portraits that were produced at a volatile historical moment, namely, during the period marking the abolition of slavery in different geographic and cultural contexts. During this time new forms of subjectification and subjection emerged, entailing new and elusively complex redeployments of "facialization" in portraiture. In her essay "Who Is the Subject? Marie-Guilhelmine Benoist's *Portrait d'une Négresse*," Viktoria Schmidt-Linsenhoff argues that sociohistorical interpretations of this painting (originally exhibited at the Paris Salon of 1800) have been insufficient in accounting for the work's cultural and political significance. Instead, by carefully unpacking the iconographic field within which the painting was produced, she underscores the ways in which this image of a woman from Guadeloupe simultaneously works within and upsets visual discourses dominant at the time by which notions of French national belonging were established. In so doing, Schmidt-Linsenhoff argues, the painting opened a contested space for the incorporation of black female bodies into the body/imago of the nation.

Toussaint Louverture, the quintessential black revolutionary hero of the French abolitionist movement and former Haitian slave, is the subject of Helen Weston's essay. In "The Many Faces of Toussaint Louverture" Weston tackles the large body of visual as well as textual portrayals of the slave leader in dialogue with significant biographical moments in his life. As Weston demonstrates, the multiplicity of these images play out between the opposing poles of heroicization, on the one hand, and denigration and deformation, on the other, and are indicative of the ideologically loaded field of "faces" for which he was simultaneously celebrated and feared. Because of the kind of conventions deployed in many of these images (iconographically akin to established representations of slaves), Weston suggests that many of Toussaint's invented portraits (as no likeness of him was ever recorded during his lifetime) were produced at the borders of visual reenslavement.

Toby Chieffo-Reidway's essay, "*Cinqué*: A Heroic Portrait for the Abolitionist Cause," offers a novel interpretation of Nathaniel Jocelyn's renowned portrait of Sengbeh Pieh, who was also known as Cinqué, the leader of the 1839 *Amistad* rebellion. Chieffo-Reidway traces the history of the painting (its commission and the political climate within which it was produced), offers new archival material, and highlights the complex iconographic traditions mobilized by Jocelyn in the composition of the image to subtly convey his abolitionist message and produce an image framed by notions of human dignity.

The book closes with an essay by Daryle Williams, "The Intrepid Mariner Simão: Visual Histories of Blackness in the Luso-Atlantic at the End of the Slave Trade," that explores the ambiguous portrayal of the Cape Verdean sailor Simão in the context of the debates concerning the abolition of slavery at the end of the slave trade in nineteenth-century Brazil. Simão was a freeborn man who, during his lifetime, was celebrated as the hero of the *Pernambucana*, a Brazilian steamer run aground in a storm off the coast of southern Brazil in October 1853, and whose portrait was painted in 1854–55 by one of the most important Brazilian academic painters of the time, José Correia de Lima. However, and despite all evidence to the contrary, Simão's identity as a freeman has been consistently called into question at different moments in Brazilian history. This inclination to read the black freeman as a slave – which Williams partly relates to aesthetic traditions, activated in the painting, that fixed black bodies as laborers, slaves, and runaways – serves as a salutary reminder about how the "visual histories of blackness" are shadowed by the concept of slavery.

As we write the final words of this introduction, we are reminded that slavery, a system of labor that has actually existed throughout most of human history, is not a fact of the past and that the new globalized economy has activated old as well as unprecedented forms of human bondage. This slavery is no longer exclusively tied to the visible markers of African chattel slavery or to the scenarios of plantation economies, and because of this its invisibility is all the more perverse. Our rather unreflective associations (in Europe and the Americas especially) between blackness and slavery – that is, our centuries-old legacy of visual representations of the transatlantic slave trade – have been symbolically key to the occlusion of contemporary slavery, blocking its incorporation into our social imagination: debt bondage in India, contract subjection in southeast Asia, Thailand, and Brazil, the selling of children for domestic service (*restavecs*) in western Africa and parts of the Caribbean, ritual enslavement in Ghana, and the widespread sex trafficking of women and children all around the world, including the United States and Europe (a robust business that, according to Kevin Bales, entailed in 2005 an underestimated total of 200,000 human beings, with approximate revenues of $10.5 billion).[62] Slavery and its dynamics of facelessness are matters of the present. Nicholas Kristof, with relentless passion, constantly thrusts these facts before us in his weekly columns for *The New York*

Times and in the documentaries one finds among his links in the digital version of the newspaper.[63] There we again encounter the lived tragedy of the face within the scene of subjection, perhaps with no less visual lust "to display" and "to document" than that often shown by well-intentioned abolitionists of the eighteenth and nineteenth centuries. Or rather, to say it with Levinas, we find ourselves confronted with the "epiphany of the face," by which he means that nonviolent encounter with the infinitude of the other and her suffering, whose transcendence and exteriority calls upon our sense of ethical responsibility and instantiates our freedom.[64]

One of those faces belongs to Long Prass, a young Cambodian woman kidnapped and forced into prostitution when she was thirteen years old, and who is the focus of *The New York Times* documentary *The Face of Slavery*.[65] Virginity being highly prized in Cambodia, especially by men suffering from AIDS (who, in a paroxysm of misogyny, believe that having sex with a virgin may cure them of the disease), is key to Long Prass's story. Her virginity was sold four times, which meant that the opening of her vagina was repeatedly stitched and restitched in order to extract extra profits from her childish body. At one point she became pregnant and asked her madam for some days of rest. Angry at the request, the mistress stabbed her in the right eye, rendering her (according to Kristof, who is the narrator of the short film) a "valueless monster." The documentary dwells, just as Manzano's *Autobiography* does, on close-ups of her face. On her left side, "she is a pretty girl," on the right, she carries "the mark of slavery." The drama of her psychological, moral, and bodily injury, despite the smiling happy ending of the film (which, in a candid twist of U.S.-American optimism, announces a better future, thanks in part to education and plastic surgery), is nonetheless printed on her face as a visual metonym of her biography and of her mutilated selfhood. It is her portrait, a portrait where the slave appears as a being upon which violence has left the brutal visual traces of an aesthetic and spiritual split. This book has been written under the shadow of these realities, and our reflection upon the past aims not just to illuminate a key moment in the history of transatlantic slavery, but also to provide a lens to understand a broader field marked by suffering and, most often, despair, even within its moments of exception – its concealments and revelations in portraiture.

NOTES

1 Mark Haworth-Booth (interviewer), "Maud Sulter," *History of Photography* 16, no. 3 (Fall 1992), 263–6.

2 For further examples see the contributions by Marcia Pointon (Figs. 1.1 and 1.2), David Bindman (Figs. 2.1–2.3, 2.6), Geoff Quilley (Fig. 6.3, Plate 5), and Agnes Lugo-Ortiz (Figs. 7.3–7.5) in this volume.

3 In Italian courtly circles black servants were already popular toward the end of the fifteenth century. Reportedly Isabella d'Este, Marchesa de Mantua and leading

figure of the Italian Renaissance, was keen to acquire a black girl in 1491. Katja Wolf, "'Und ihre siegreichen reize steigert im Kontrast ein Mohr': Weiße Damen und schwarze Pagen in der Bildnismalerei," in *Weiße Blicke: Geschlechtermythen des Kolonialismus*, ed. Viktoria Schmidt-Linsenhoff, Karl Hölz, and Herbert Uerlings (Marburg: Jonas, 2004), 19–36, here 19.

4 Most recent statistics calculate that a total of about 21 million Africans were captured with the goal of being shipped to the Americas between 1450 and 1900. Of these, about 2 million (10 percent) died in the transatlantic crossing, and another 7 million died in transit from the interior of Africa to the trading posts on the western coast of the continent. In sum, historians estimate that about 10.2 and 11.3 million arrived in the Americas during this period. Most of these were destined for the plantations of the Caribbean (about 60 percent) and Brazil (35 percent). The North American colonies received just 5 percent of the estimated total. See Hugh Thomas, *The Slave Trade* (New York: Simon and Shuster, 1997), 804; Robert Edgar Conrad, "Trans-Atlantic Trade," in Seymour Drescher and Stanley Engerman, eds., *A Historical Guide to World Slavery* (New York: Oxford University Press, 1998), 371–82; Paul Lovejoy, *Transformations of Slavery* (Cambridge: Cambridge University Press, 2000); Basil Davidson, *The African Slave Trade* (Boston: Little Brown, 1980); and Alan Thomas, *Third World Atlas* (Bristol, Penn.: Taylor and Francis, 1994). For a powerful account of the process by which captive Africans were first turned into commodities and finally into slaves, see Stephanie E. Smallwood, *Saltwater Slavery: A Middle Passage from Africa to American Diaspora* (Cambridge, Mass.: Harvard University Press, 2007).

5 It was only in the age of Atlantic slavery that black skin became inextricably linked with enslavement/slavery. Before that time, slavery was, if not color-blind, at least hardly connected exclusively with sub-Saharan Africans. "White" slavery associated with the eastern sex-trade continued, but given the enormity of the traffic in black bodies in early modernity, it was black skin that came to be naturalized as the color of enslavement in the Western imagination. In Orientalist paintings these bodies were mostly associated with sexuality, not labor, as the paintings of the French Jean-Léon Gérôme make abundantly evident.

6 Martin Heidegger, *Being and Time* (New York: Harper and Row, 1962); Jacques Derrida, *Of Grammatology* (Baltimore: John Hopkins University Press, 1967).

7 Joseph Roach, *Cities of the Dead: Circum-Atlantic Performance* (New York: Columbia University Press, 1996), 4; Paul Gilroy, *The Black Atlantic: Modernity and Double Consciousness* (Cambridge, Mass.: Harvard University Press, 1993).

8 Stephen Shapiro, "Method and Misperception: The Paradigm Problem of the Early American Novel," in *The Culture and Commerce of the Early American Novel: Reading the Atlantic World System* (University Park: Pennsylvania State University, 2008), 24.

9 The bibliography pertinent to these questions is voluminous. Some key works include Laird W. Bergad, *The Comparative Histories of Slavery in Brazil, Cuba, and the United States* (Cambridge: Cambridge University Press, 2007); Robin Blackburn, *The Making of New World Slavery: From the Baroque to the Modern, 1492–1800* (London: Verso, 1997); David Brion Davis, *Inhuman Bondage: The Rise and Fall of Slavery in the New World* (New York: Oxford University Press, 2006); Laura Foner and Eugene D. Genovese, eds., *Slavery in the New World: A Reader in Comparative History* (Englewood Cliffs, N.J.: Prentice-Hall, 1969); Herbert Klein, *Slavery in the Americas: A Comparative Study of Virginia and Cuba* (Chicago: University of Chicago Press, 1967) and *African Slavery in Latin America and the Caribbean* (New York: Oxford University Press, 1986); Paul E. Lovejoy, ed., *Identity in the Shadow of*

Slavery (London: Continuum, 2000); Gilberto Freyre, *Casa-grande e senzala* [1933], ed. Guillermo Giucci, Enrique Rodríguez Larreta, and Edson Nery da Fonseca (Madrid: Coleção Archivos, 2002); José C. Curto and Paul E. Lovejoy, eds., *Enslaving Connections: Changing Cultures of Africa and Brazil during the Era of Slavery* (Amherst, Mass.: Humanity Books, 2004); Manuel Moreno Fraginals, *El ingenio: el complejo económico social cubano del azúcar*, 3 vols. (Havana: Comisión Nacional Cubana de la UNESCO, 1964) and *La historia como arma y otros estudios sobre esclavos, ingenios y plantaciones* (Barcelona: Editorial Crítica, 1983); Juan Pérez de la Riva, *El barracón: esclavitud y capitalismo en Cuba* (Barcelona: Editorial Crítica, 1978); Eugene D. Genovese, *The World the Slaveholders Made: Two Essays in Interpretation* (New York: Vintage Books, 1969) and *Roll, Jordan, Roll: The World the Slaves Made* (New York: Vintage Books, 1974); John W. Blassingame, *The Slave Community: Plantation Life in the Antebellum South* (New York: Oxford University Press, 1972); Laurent Dubois, *A Colony of Citizens: Revolution and Slave Emancipation in the French Caribbean, 1787–1804* (Chapel Hill: University of North Carolina Press, 2004); Luis Díaz Soler, *Historia de la esclavitud negra en Puerto Rico, 1493–1890* (Madrid: Revista de Occidente, 1953); Andres Ramos Mattei, ed., *Azúcar y esclavitud* (Río Piedras: Universidad de Puerto Rico, Recinto de Río Piedras, Biblioteca General José M. Lázaro, Departamento de Selección y Canje, 1982); Luis A. Figueroa, *Sugar, Slavery, and Freedom in Nineteenth-Century Puerto Rico* (Chapel Hill: University of North Carolina Press, 2005); Thomas Holt, *The Problem of Freedom: Race, Labor, and Politics in Jamaica and Britain, 1832–1938* (Baltimore: Johns Hopkins University Press, 1992).

10 Saidiya V. Hartman, *Scenes of Subjection. Terror, Slavery, and Self-Making in Nineteenth-Century America* (New York: Oxford University Press, 1997), 36. An insightful and philosophically pertinent meditation on invisibility (either via an excess or a lack of discourse) is offered by the Puerto Rican writer Eduardo Lalo in his beautiful essay *Los países invisibles* (San Juan: Tal Cual, 2008).

11 In Miguel Barnet's testimonial account of the former runaway Cuban slave Esteban Montejo, this removal from the field of masterly vision appears as a disengagement from human sociability altogether. Montejo, in his errancy through the mountains, severs all bonds of human contact and language. Distrust of other human beings guides his actions. Animistically, his most intense engagement is with nature: with plants and trees, with the language of the birds – a radical disappearing act from human visuality. See Miguel Barnet's *Biografía de un cimarrón* (Mexico City: Editorial Siglo XXI, 1966). This work has undergone several changes in title, most recently published as *Cimarrón, historia de un esclavo* (Madrid: Siruela, 1998). For a discussion of runaway slaves in the field of masterly vision see Agnes Lugo-Ortiz, "Poder, resistencia y dominación en las Américas esclavistas: Apostillas a Michel Foucault (paradojas y aporías)" in *Revista de Estudios Sociales* 43, Universidad de los Andes, Bogotá, Colombia (August 2012), 74–93. On maroon communities more generally see Richard Price, ed., *Maroon Societies: Rebel Slave Communities in the Americas* (New York: Anchor Press, 1973).

12 "Los esclavos de una finca no podrán visitar a los de otra sin el consentimiento expreso de los amos ó mayordomos de ambas; y cuando tengan que ir á finca agena ó salir de la suya, llevarán licencia escrita de su propio dueño ó mayordomo con las señas del esclavo, fecha del día, mes y año, expresion del punto á que se dirigen y término porque se les ha concedido." Article no. 19 of the "Reglamento de esclavos. Código Negro Hispano-Cubano." Spanish version, with original grammar, in Fernando Ortiz, *Los negros esclavos* (Havana: Editorial de Ciencias Sociales, 1987), 442–49, article 19, 444–45. English translation by Robert Paquette, "The Slave Code

of 1842," in *Sugar Is Made with Blood: The Conspiracy of La Escalera and the Conflict between Empires over Slavery in Cuba* (Middletown, Conn.: Wesleyan University Press, 1988), 267–72; article 19, 269.

13 Photographic portraits fall outside the purview of this volume.

14 See Bindman's essay in this volume.

15 Gilles Deleuze and Felix Guattari, "Year Zero: Faciality," in *A Thousand Plateaus: Capitalism and Schizophrenia*, trans. Brian Massumi (Minneapolis: University of Minnesota Press, 1987), 188.

16 See Agnes Lugo-Ortiz's essay in this volume for a further reflection on the face, the head, and the body within the visual logic of plantation slavery.

17 *Autobiografía, cartas y versos de Juan Francisco Manzano. Con estudio preliminar de José Luciano Franco* (La Habana: Cuadernos de Historia Habanera, Municipio de La Habana, 1937; reprint, Nendeln/Lichtenstein: Kraus Reprints, 1970). For the English version, see Juan Francisco Manzano, *The Life and Poems of a Cuban Slave*, ed. Edward J. Mullen (Hamden, Conn.: Anchor Books, 1981). This is the only extant slave narrative from the centuries-long period of Spanish colonial rule in the Americas.

18 For a productive distinction between "racist" and "racialist" discourses see Anthony Apphia, "Racisms," in *Anatomy of Racism*, ed. Gary David Goldberg (Minneapolis: University of Minnesota Press, 1990).

19 Georg Wilhelm Friedrich Hegel, *Lectures on the Philosophy of World History. Introduction: Reason in History* [1837], trans. H. B. Nisbet, introduction by Duncan Forbes (Cambridge: Cambridge University Press, 1975), 176 and 172; italics in quotation are our emphasis. On Hegel's complex and transformed philosophical stands on slavery and the Haitian Revolution see Susan Buck-Morss's *Hegel, Haiti, and Universal History* (Pittsburgh: University of Pittsburgh Press, 2009). Relevant for these issues also is Michel-Rolph Trouillot's "An Unthinkable History," in his *Silencing the Past: Power and the Production of History* (Boston: Beacon Press, 1995), 70–107. For a critical take on the notions of universalism, world history and the exclusions that constitute them see Ranajit Guha, *History and the Limit of World-History* (New York: Columbia University Press, 2002). On slavery, race, and the Enlightenment see David Brion Davis, *The Problem of Slavery in the Age of Revolution, 1770–1823* (New York: Oxford University Press, 1999); and for a useful introductory selection of texts on these issues see Emmanuel Chukwudi Eze, ed., *Race and the Enlightenment: A Reader* (Malden, Mass.: Blackwell, 1997).

20 Brian Wallis, "Black Bodies, White Science: Louis Agassiz's Slave Daguerreotypes," *American Art* 9, no. 2 (summer 1995), 38–61.

21 Taking as a point of departure Sheldon Nodelman's theorization of ancient Roman portraiture, Trachtenberg argues that Zealy's daguerreotypes project by their very "composure and formality . . . an acute awareness of the spectator." Such an awareness, which Nodelman recognized in the Roman artifacts and Trachtenberg transposed to the Zealy's images, "opens a wedge [according to Nodelman] between mask and self, persona and person – between self-representation and self-awareness." This wedge is understood to be the site that establishes the subject as a subject, not just as the object of a gaze, implicating in turn the subject position and ethical consciousness of the viewer. Trachtenberg, *Reading American Photographs* (New York: Hill and Wang, 1989), 52–60. Quotation from Nodelman is on page 54.

22 Wallis, "Black Bodies, White Science," 54.

23 Sheldon Nodelman, "How to Read a Roman Portrait," *Art in America*, 63 (1975), 26–33.

24 Trachtenberg, *Reading American Photographs*, 60. Reading against their taxonomical intentions, Trachtenberg seems to propose that Zealy's images themselves (because of their iconographic composition, reminiscent of Roman busts) could universally incite reactions of identification and empathy without considering the different ethical make-ups that inform particular acts of looking.

25 "In the Photograph the event is never transcended for the sake of something else: the Photograph always leads the corpus I need back to the body I see; it is the absolute Particular, the Sovereign Contingency, matte and somehow stupid, the *This* (this photograph and not Photography), in short, what Lacan calls the *Touché*, the Occasion, the Encounter, the Real, in its indefatigable expression." As has been pointed out by many critics, Barthes (who, among other things, was not able to consider the tricks of Photoshop and other technologies and underestimated the cultural mediations of sight and the instrumentalization of photography; see Marcia Pointon's critique of Barthes with regard to slave portraiture in this volume) is over-enthusiastic about the sovereign condition of the contingent in the photograph. We would rather speak about the subjected condition of the contingency and keep both terms (subjection and contingency) in a tense interplay. See Roland Barthes, *Camera Lucida* (New York: Farrar, Straus and Giroux, 1981), 4.

26 Michel Foucault, *L'Archéologie du savoir* (Paris: Gallimard, 1969). On slave portrait archives see Agnes Lugo-Ortiz, "Tras la visualidad del rostro esclavo: Exploraciones para un archivo," *e-misférica* 9.1–9.2 (2012); hemisphericinstitute.org/hemi/es/e-misferica-91/lugoortiz.

27 Henry Louis Gates, *The Signifying Monkey: A Theory of African-American Literary Criticism* (New York: Oxford University Press, 1988), especially ch. 2.

28 See, for example, Vincent Carretta, *Equiano the African: Biography of a Self-Made Man* (Athens: University of Georgia Press, 2005), and with Philip Gould, ed., *Genius in Bondage: Literature of the Early Black Atlantic* (Lexington: University Press of Kentucky, 2001); Henry Louis Gates, *The Trials of Phillis Wheatley: America's First Black Poet and Her Encounters with the Founding Fathers* (New York: Basic Civitas, 2003), and with Charles T. Davis, eds., *The Slave's Narrative* (New York: Oxford University Press, 1985). On the Cuban slave Juan Francisco Manzano see Sylvia Molloy, "From Serf to Self: The Autobiography of Juan Francisco Manzano," in her *At Face Value: Autobiographical Writing in Spanish America* (Cambridge: Cambridge University Press, 1991), 36–54; Julio Ramos, "*La ley es otra*: Constitución del sujeto jurídico. María Antonia Mandinga en el archivo de la ley," in Beatriz González Stephan, ed., *Esplendores y miserias del siglo XIX: cultura y sociedad en América Latina* (Caracas: Monte Ávila Editores, 1995), 193–220; Antonio Vera-León, "Juan Francisco Manzano: el estilo *bárbaro* de la nación," *Hispamérica: Revista de Literatura* 22, no. 60 (1991), 3–22; Sonia Labrador, "La intelectualidad negra en Cuba en el siglo XIX: El caso de Manzano," *Revista Iberoamericana* 174 (1994), 13–25; and Marilyn Miller, "Rebeldía narrativa, resistencia poética y expresión 'libre' en Juan Francisco Manzano," *Revista Iberoamericana* 211 (2005), 417–36.

29 Ladislas Burger, general ed., *The Image of the Black in Western Art*, 5 vols. (Cambridge, Mass.: Harvard University Press, 1979–89). This project has been brought to a renewed level of completion by Henry Louis Gates, Jr., and David Bindman in their monumental ten edited volumes of *The Image of the Black in Western Art*. The first eight of these have already appeared by May 2012 and the final two, on the twentieth century, will be published in 2014.

30 See the very informative small publication in conjunction with an exhibition at the National Portrait Gallery on the life and representation of Ignatius Sancho (his

portrait is discussed in this volume by David Bindman); Reyahn King, Sukhdev Sandhu, James Walvin, and Jane Girdham, *Ignatius Sancho*, exhibition catalog (London: National Portrait Gallery, 1997). Pertinent to this subject also are David Dabedeen, *Hogarth's Blacks: Images of Blacks in Eighteenth-Century English Art* (Athens: University of Georgia Press, 1987); Beth Fowkes Tobin, *Picturing Imperial Power: Colonial Subjects in Eighteenth-Century British Painting* (Durham: Duke University Press, 1999); Kim Hall, *Things of Darkness: Economies of Race and Gender in Early Modern England* (Ithaca: Cornell University Press, 1995); Gwendolyn DuBois Shaw, *Portraits of a People: Picturing African Americans in the Nineteenth Century* (Andover, Mass.: Addison Gallery of American Art, Phillips Academy, and University of Washington Press, 2006); Richard J. Powell, *Cutting a Figure: Fashioning Black Portraiture* (Chicago: University of Chicago Press, 2008).

31 Most Latin American work on art, race, and slavery has been done by Brazilian scholars. See Boris Kossoy and Maria Luiza Tucci Carneiro, *O olhar europeu: o negro na iconografia brasileira do século XIX* (São Paulo: Edusp, 1994); Carlos Eugênio Marcondes de Moura, *A travessia da Calunga Grande: três séculos de imagens sobre o negro no Brasil, 1637–1899* (São Paulo: Imprensa Oficial SP, Edusp, 2000); Ministério da Cultura, Fundação Cultural Palmares, Associação dos Amigos da Pinacoteca do Estado de São Paulo, EXPOMUS, *Para nunca esquecer: negras memórias/memórias de negros* (Rio de Janeiro: Museu Histórico Nacional, Ministério da Cultura, 2002); *Brasileiro, brasileiros*, exhibition catalog, Emanoel Araújo, curator (São Paulo: Prefeitura da Cidade de São Paulo: Museu Afrobrasil, 2005); Raul Giovanni da Motta Lody, *O negro no museu brasileiro: construindo identidades* (Rio de Janeiro: Bertrand Brasil, 2005). Relevant for the Francophone context are Jean Metellus and Marcel Dorigny, under the direction of Philippe Monsel, *De l'esclavage aux abolition: XVIIe–XXe siècle* (Paris: Éditions Cercle d'Art, 1998); Thierry Lefrançois, *L'esclavage dans les collections du Musée du Nouveau Monde* (La Rochelle: Editions du Musées d'Art et d'Histoire, 1998); Maurice Lengellé-Tardy, *Art et histoire de la France créole: du racisme à l'abolition de l'esclavage* (Mayenne: Imprimerie de la Manutention, 2004). An important overview of Latin American portraits is found in the exhibition catalog *Retratos: 2000 Years of Latin American Portraiture* (New Haven: Yale University Press, 2004).

32 Henry Louis Gates, Jr., *"Race," Writing, and Difference* (Chicago: The University of Chicago Press, 1985), 2, 5, and 6.

33 Maurice Berger, *White Lies: Race and the Myths of Whiteness* (New York: Farrar, Straus and Giroux, 1999); Ruth Frankenberg, ed., *Displacing Whiteness: Essays in Social and Cultural Criticism* (Durham: Duke University Press, 1997). Mike Hill, ed., *Whiteness: A Critical Reader* (New York: New York University Press, 1997); bell hooks, "Representations of Whiteness," in *Black Looks: Race and Representation* (Boston: South End Press, 1992), 195–278; Eric Lott, "White like Me: Racial Cross-Dressing and the Construction of American Whiteness," in *Cultures of United States Imperialism*, ed. Amy Kaplan and Donald Pease (Durham: Duke University Press, 1993); Gail Ching-Liang Low, *White Skins/Black Masks: Representation and Colonialism* (London: Routledge, 1996); Peggy McIntosh, "On the Invisibility of Privilege," *Wellesley College Center for Research on Women Working Paper Series* 189 *Peacework*, 1991; Charmane A. Nelson, "White Marble, Black Bodies and the Fear of the Invisible Negro: Signifying Blackness in Mid-Nineteenth-century Neoclassical Sculpture," *RACAR* 27, nos. 1/2 (2000), 87–101; Adrian Piper, "Passing for White, Passing for Black," *Transition* 58 (1991), 4–32. David R. Roediger, *Towards the Abolition of Whiteness: Essays on Race, Politics, and Working Class History* (London:

Verso, 1994); David R. Roediger, *The Wages of Whiteness: Race and the Making of the American Working Class* (London: Verso, 1991); Mike Hill, ed., *Whiteness: A Critical Reader* (New York: New York University Press, 1997); Kalpana Seshadri-Crooks, *Desiring Whiteness: A Lacanian Analysis of Race* (London: Routledge, 2000); Vron Ware, *Beyond the Pale: White Women, Racism, and History* (London: Verso, 1992); Robert Young, *White Mythologies: Writing History and the West* (London: Routledge, 1990).

34 Toni Morrison, *Playing in the Dark: Whiteness and the Literary Imagination* (New York: Vintage Books, 1993), 44.

35 Ibid., 38.

36 Ibid., 37–38.

37 Ibid., 90.

38 On whiteness studies also see Richard Dyer, "White," *Screen* 29, no. 4 (1988), 44–64; Richard Dyer, *White* (London: Routledge, 1997); Peter Erickson, "Seeing White," *Transition* 67 (1995): 166–85, and "'God for Harry, England, and Saint George': British National Identity and the Emergence of White Self-Fashioning," in *Early Modern Visual Culture: Representation, Race, and Empire in Renaissance England*, ed. Peter Erickson and Clark Hulse (Philadelphia: University of Pennsylvania Press, 2000), 315–45; Viktoria Schmidt-Linsenhoff, "Bild- und Textlektüren zu Geschlechtermythen den Kolonialismus," in *Weiße Blicke*, 8–18; Angela Rosenthal, "Die Kunst des Errötens. Zur Kosmetik rassischer Differenz," in *Das Subjekt und die Anderen*, ed. Karl Hölz, Viktoria Schmidt-Linsenhoff, and Herbert Uerlings (Berlin: E. Schmidt, 2001), 95–118; and Rosenthal "*Visceral* Culture: Blushing and the Legibility of Whiteness in Eighteenth-Century British Portraiture," in *Art: History: Visual: Culture*, ed. Deborah Cherry (Oxford: Blackwell's, 2005).

39 David Bindman, *Ape to Apollo: Aesthetics and the Idea of Race in the Eighteenth Century* (London: Reaktion Books, 2002); Albert Boime, *The Art of Exclusion: Representing Blacks in the Nineteenth Century* (Washington, D.C.: Smithsonian Institution Press, 1990); Magali M. Carrera, *Imagining Identity in New Spain. Race, Lineage, and the Colonial Body in Portraiture and Casta Painting* (Austin: University of Texas Press, 2003); Beth Fowkes Tobin, *Picturing Imperial Power: Colonial Subjects in Eighteenth-Century British Painting* (Durham: Duke University Press, 1999); Simon Gikandi, *Slavery and the Culture of Taste* (Princeton/Oxford: Princeton University Press, 2011); Darcy Grimaldo Grigsby, *Extremities: Painting Empire in Post-Revolutionary France* (New Haven: Yale University Press, 2002); Michael Harris, *Colored Pictures: Race and Visual Representation* (Chapel Hill: University of North Carolina Press, 2003); Ilona Katzew, *Casta Painting: Images of Race in Eighteenth-Century Mexico* (New Haven: Yale University Press, 2004); Kay Dian Kriz, *Slavery, Sugar, and the Culture of Refinement: Picturing the British West Indies 1700–1840* (New Haven: Yale University Press, 2008); Kay Dian Kriz and Geoff Quilley, eds., *An Economy of Colour: Visual Culture and the Atlantic World, 1660–1830* (Manchester: Manchester University Press, 2003); Maurine D. McInnis, *Slaves Waiting for Sale: Abolitionist Art and the American Slave Trade* (Chicago/London: The University of Chicago Press, 2011); Nicholas Mirzoeff, *An Introduction to Visual Culture*, 2nd ed. (New York: Routledge, 1999), especially ch. 3, "Slavery, Modernity and Visual Culture;" Catherine Molineaux, *Faces of Perfect Ebony: Encountering Atlantic Slavery in Imperial Britain* (London/Cambridge: Harvard University Press, 2012); Felicity Nussbaum, *The Limits of the Human: Fictions of Anomaly, Race, and Gender in the Long Eighteenth Century* (Cambridge: Cambridge University Press, 2003); Elizabeth L. O'Leary, *"At Beck and Call": The Representation of Domestic*

Servants in Nineteenth-Century American Painting (Washington, D.C.: Smithsonian Institution Press, 1996); Alan Trachtenberg, *Reading American Photographs;* Brian Wallis, "Black Bodies, White Science;" Kathleen Wilson, *The Island Race: Englishness, Empire and Gender in the Eighteenth Century* (London: Routledge, 2003); Marcus Wood, *Blind Memory: Visual Representations of Slavery in England and America* (New York: Routledge, 2000). Kimberly N. Pinder's edited collection *Race-ing Art History* (New York: Routledge, 2002), although more general in scope, is also pertinent for these questions.

40 See especially *Representing Slavery: Art, Artefacts and Archives in the Collections of the National Maritime Museum*, ed. Douglas Hamilton and Robert J. Blyth (Aldershot: Lund Humphries, in association with the National Maritime Museum, 2007); *Art and Emancipation in Jamaica: Isaac Mendes Belisario and His Worlds*, ed. Tim Barringer, Gillian Forrester, and Bárbaro Martínez-Ruiz; with essays by Stephen Banfield [et al.]; with contributions by Graham C. Boettcher [et al.] (New Haven: Yale Center for British Art in association with Yale University Press, 2007). A recent issue of *Slavery and Abolition* (29, no. 2, June 2008), edited by Celeste-Marie Bernier and Judie Newman, critically engages the practices of memoralization enacted by recent representations of slavery in public art and museums (especially in view of the 2007 bicentenary of the abolition of the slave trade in Britain).

41 For an essay that is unusual in its focus on portraiture under slavery see Richard J. Powell, "Cinqué: Antislavery Portraiture and Patronage in Jacksonian America," *American Art* 11, no. 3 (1997): 48–73. The portrait of Cinqué is discussed by Toby M. Chieffo-Reidway in this volume. While this book was going to press we did not have the opportunity to properly consult *Slavery in Art and Literature. Approaches* to *Trauma, Memory* and *Visuality*, ed. Birgit Haehnel and Melanie Ulz (Berlin: Frank & Timme, 2010), which had just been published.

42 Darby English, "This Is Not about the Past: Silhouettes in the Work of Kara Walker," in *Kara Walker: Narratives of A Negress*, ed. Ian Berry and Darby English (Cambridge, Mass.: MIT Press, 2003), 140–67, especially 154–56.

43 Cf. Viktoria Schmidt-Linsenhoff, "Koloniale Körper – Postkoloniale Blicke," in *Den Körper im Blick: Grenzgänge zwischen Kunst, Kultur und Wissenschaft*, ed. Beat Wyss and Markus Buschhaus (Munich: Wilhelm Fink, 2008), 97–117.

44 Pareja was Velázquez's assistant. He was first recorded as working in Velázquez's studio in the 1630s, where he ground colors and prepared the canvases. See Carmen Fracchia's essay in this volume.

45 Victor I. Stoichita in *Velázquez* (Barcelona: Galaxia Gutenberg; Madrid: Fundación Amigos del Museo del Prado, 1999), 206–7, 367–81; Víctor I. Stoichita, "La imagen del hombre de raza negra en el arte y la literatura españolas del sigolo de oro," in *Herencias indígenas, tradiciones europeas y la mirada europea/Indigenes Erbe, europäische Traditionen und der europäische Blick*, ed. Helga von Kügelgen (Frankfurt am Main: Vervuert; Madrid: Iberoamericana, 2002), 275–77. See also Luis Méndez Rodríguez, "Esclavos y pintores en la Sevilla de Velázquez," in *En torno a Santa Rufina: Velázquez de lo íntimo a lo cortesano* (Seville: Fundación Focus-Abengoa, 2008), 211, 371.

46 See Pliny the Elder's book 35 (¶¶ 4–14) of his *Naturalis Historia* dedicated to portraiture.

47 Moreover, the subtle modeling of complexion and flesh color, as well as the pathetic facial expression, recall Peter Paul Rubens' study of a *Head of an African Man* (1613/14). On Rubens's study see Birgit Haenel, "Der dunkle Schatten of der weißen Seele," in *Projektionen. Rassismus und Sexismus in der Visuellen Kultur*, ed. Annegret Friedrich et al. (Marburg: Jonas Verlag, 1997), 150–63, especially 159.

48 Martin Postle, "*The Captive Slave* by John Simpson (1782-1847): a rediscovered masterpiece," *British Art Journal* 9, no. 3 (March 2009), 18, 22–3.

49 At the conference *Invisible Subjects? Slave Portraiture in the Circum-Atlantic World (1630–1890)*, October 2004, Dartmouth College, Hanover, N.H., Marcia Pointon drew attention to the expression of "capturing" a portrait as relevant to our discussion on slave portraiture. See her essay in this volume as well as Richard Brilliant, *Portraiture* (Cambridge, Mass: Harvard University Press, 1991).

50 Martin Hoyles, *Ira Aldridge: Celebrated Nineteenth-Century Actor* (London: Hansib, 2008); Herbert Marshall and Mildred Stock, *Ira Aldridge: The Negro Tragedian* (Carbondale: Southern Illinois University Press, 1968); Gwendolyn DuBois Shaw, *Portraits of a People*, 174 and 175.

51 Simpson exhibited his painting three times. *The Captive Slave* was first shown at the London Royal Academy of Arts in 1827, where the catalog entry included a line from William Cowper's antislavery poem, *Charity* (II, 138–41): "But ah! What wish can prosper, or what prayer / For merchants rich in cargoes of despair." A year later the work was shown both at the British Institute in London, and subsequently under the title *The Captive* at the Liverpool Academy. Postle, "The Captive Slave," 18.

52 Cf. Shaw, *Portraits of a People*, 49.

53 For a repertoire of runaway slave advertisements see Lathan A. Windley, *Runaway Slave Advertisements: A Documentary History from the 1730s to 1790*, 4 vols. (Westport, Conn.: Greenwood, 1983); Gabino La Rosa Corzo, *Los cimarrones de Cuba* (Havana: Editorial de Ciencias Sociales, 1988); and Benjamín Nistal-Moret, *Esclavos, prófugos y cimarrones: Puerto Rico, 1770–1870* (Río Piedras: Editorial de la Universidad de Puerto Rico, 1984).

54 Shane White and Graham J. White, "Slave Hair and African-American Culture in the Eighteenth- and Nineteenth-Centuries," *Journal of Southern History* 61 (1995), 45–76. See also the mid-nineteenth-century report by Frederick Law Olmsted, *The Cotton Kingdom: A Traveller's Observations on Cotton and Slavery in the American Slave States: Based upon Three Former Volumes of Journeys and Investigations by the Same Author*, ed. Arthur M. Schlesinger (New York: Knopf, 1953), 162–65.

55 European's first contact with the western African population expressed astonishment about the diversity of hairstyles. See John K. Thornton, *Africa and Africans in the Making of the Atlantic World, 1400–1680* (Cambridge: Cambridge University Press, 1992), 230; White and White, "Slave Hair," 51.

56 White and White, "Slave Hair," 49.

57 On the social significance of hair, see Kobena Mercer, "Black Hair/Style Politics," in *Out There: Marginalization and Contemporary Cultures*, ed. Russell Ferguson, Martha Gever, Trinh T. Minh-ha, and Cornel West (Cambridge, Mass.: MIT Press, 1990), 247–264; Angela Rosenthal, "Raising Hair," special issue on "Hair," *Eighteenth-Century Studies*, 38, no. 1 (2004), 1–16; Penny Jolly, *Hair: Untangling a Social History* (Saratoga Springs, N.Y.: Frances Young Tang Teaching Museum, Skidmore College, 2004).

58 Unknown artist, *Flora's Profile*, 1796, silhouette, cut paper and brown ink with bill of sale, 14 × 13 (35 × 56 × 33 cm), unsigned, Stratford Historical Society, Stratford, Conn.

The full text of the bill of sale reads as follows:

> Know All Men by these Present that I
> Margaret Dwight of Milford in the County of
> New Haven & State of Connecticut for the Con-
> sideration of Twenty Five Pounds S(terling) money

Received to my full satisfaction of Asa
Benjamin of Stratford in Fairfield County
in Sd (said) State have Bargain'd & sold & do
by these Present Bargain Sell & Deliver
unto this Benjamin a certain Negro
Wench named Flora to have and to hold
Sd Negro Wench to him the Sd Benjamin
his Heirs & Assigns forever & I do by these
Present bind myself & my Heirs Executors or
Administrators firmly by these Present
to warrant & defend the Sd Wench from
all Claims or demands Whatsoever
In witness whereof I have hereunto
set my hand & Seal this 13th Day of December
1796

Present

Abm DeWitt Margaret Dwight

19 years old

"An account book kept by a relative of Mrs. Benjamin records Flora's death on '31 August' in a list of 'people who died in 1815.'" See Guy C. McElroy, *Facing History: The Black Image in American Art, 1710–1940* (San Francisco: Bedford Arts Publishers in association with the Corcoran Gallery of Art, Washington, D.C., 1990), 10.

59 Gerda Mraz and Uwe Schögl, *Das Kunstkabinett des Johann Caspar Lavater* (Vienna: Böhlau, 1999); Bindman, *Ape to Apollo*; Ladislas Bugner, ed. *The Image of the Black in Western Art* (Fribourg: Office du Livre and Cambridge, Mass.: Harvard University Press, 1976–); and Julio Caro Baroja, *La cara, espejo del alma. Historia de la fisiognómica* (Barcelona: Galaxia Gutenberg/Círculo de Lectores, 1987).

60 Shaw, *Portraits of a People*, 49.

61 We borrow the term "oppositional gaze" from bell hooks. See her "The Oppositional Gaze: Black Female Spectators," *Black Looks: Race and Representation* (Boston, 1992) 115–31.

62 Kevin Bales, *Disposable People. New Slavery in the Global Economy* (Berkeley: University of California Press, 1999), 23. See also his *Understanding Global Slavery: A Reader* (Berkeley: University of California Press, 2005). However, a recent report from the Council of Hemispheric Affairs (COHA) suggests that in 2010 in Mexico alone there were 100,000 women and children trafficked into the United States, for an estimated revenue of $6.6 billion (cf. Melissa Graham, "Mexico's New War: Sex Trafficking," http://www.coha.org/mexico's-new-war-sex-trafficking). The U.S. State Department's "Trafficking in Persons Report (TIP)" can be found at http://www.state.gov/g/tip/rls/tiprpt/. Both sites accessed July 2013.

63 Cf. http://topics.nytimes.com/top/opinion/editorialsandoped/oped/columnists/nicholasdkristof/index.html. Accessed July 2013.

64 Emmanuel Levinas, *Totalidad e infinito*, trans. Daniel Guillot (Salamanca: Ediciones Sígueme, 2002), 201–61.

65 Cf. http://video.nytimes.com/video/2009/01/03/opinion/1194837193498/the-face-of-slavery.html. Accessed July 2013.

Part I

VISIBILITY AND INVISIBILITY

ONE

SLAVERY AND THE POSSIBILITIES OF PORTRAITURE

Marcia Pointon

My purpose is to chart some parameters for a discussion of portraiture in relation to subjects as slaves, or slaves as subjects, and to speculate on ways of addressing the challenging topic of slavery and portraiture. Since modern plantation slavery (though this was and is by no means the only form of slavery) involved the subjugation by Europeans of non-Europeans, this essay focuses on how European traditions of portraiture were negotiated in order to accommodate (or not) the black slave. Specific historical case studies are a vital way of opening the topic up to examination in ways that will constitute a significant new departure for the study of portrait representations. However, in this account I hope not to lose sight of the tangible and actual while endeavoring also to extrapolate some general principles. In recent years attention has increasingly been paid to the topic of portraiture in relation to slavery. For my argument, notable are Susan Dwyer Amussen's book *Caribbean Exchanges*[1] and Peter Erickson's article "Invisibility Speaks."[2] Amussen offers a useful survey of seventeenth-century portraits that include black servants. While drawing attention to the fact that these servants were property, she also stresses that these paintings are subject to visual conventions and that they leave many historical questions unanswered, including documentary evidence that the black children depicted existed and were part of the household for whom the portrait was commissioned. Erickson's approach is one of practical criticism. He tries to establish taxonomic definitions of race that are then mapped onto models of historical development. This is a highly problematic teleological argument, especially as it is underpinned by the notion of positive and negative interpretations based on a humanistic set of assumptions that are unsustainable unless by an empathetic critique as opposed to an analysis of the discursive regimes within which different notions of "humanness" have been historically formulated.[3] By focusing primarily on

1.1. Anonymous artist, *Elihu Yale, the 2nd Duke of Devonshire, Lord James Cavendish, Mr. Tunstal, and a Page*, ca. 1708. Oil on canvas. Yale Center for British Art. Gift of the 11th Duke of Devonshire, B1970.1.

the eighteenth and nineteenth centuries, my intention is to unpack the tricky relationship between two concepts, "slavery" and "portraiture," each highly charged and significant in terms of cultural politics. I propose, therefore, to start with two very different eighteenth-century instances that bring together a slave and a visual image that may be classed as a portrait.

At the outset, we need to pause and consider this word "portrait" and recognize the tendency in our own time to expand what historically was understood quite specifically to embrace the notion of a representation of any human subject, imaginary or actual. For example, the Fogg Art Museum in 2004 had a display titled "The Portrait" in which an explanatory panel asserted: "the term portrait is understood here in a wide sense as the visual representation of the human individual." By contrast I take the word portrait in its modern sense (as opposed to the use of the term common until the late seventeenth century to describe any representation of items in the world as seen) strictly speaking to mean an individual known to have lived depicted for his or her own sake. Some might add that a portrait properly speaking should aim to represent body *and* soul, or physical *and* mental presence. These definitions may prove overly restrictive with respect to the difficult category of slave portraits, but they are a good starting point.

The first of the two images I want to discuss is an oil-on-canvas portrait now in the collection of the Center for British Art at Yale University (Fig. 1.1). It purports to show from left to right Lord James Cavendish, third son of the Duke of Devonshire (born after 1673, died 1751); Elihu Yale, a merchant and founder of the university that bears his name; William Cavendish, 2nd Duke of Devonshire (1672–1729); the Duke's black page, who wears a slave collar with a padlock and is shown preparing to refill the glasses (Fig. 1.2); and an unidentified white man.[4] The page is dressed in livery, a miniature version of adult clothing, his coat strikingly lined in red with matching buttons, fashionably elongated buttonholes, and cuffs. In contrast with this Western metropolitan style is not only his silver collar but also the white turban that emphasizes his skin color, as also does the pale grey of his coat. The red of the coat's trimmings resonates with Lord James's dress, binding this small boy into the coloristic economy of the group. The figures in the right background seem to be children and could be those of the second Duke, but although the painting as a whole lacks finesse of execution, this particular group is especially crude in handling and appears very separate from the rest of the composition. One child, however, wears red, which provides a coloristic link to the page, who is situated immediately below; this underscores (intentionally or not) the difference between this playful group of children and the page in his solitary work among the adults. The portrait has generally been thought to have been commissioned to commemorate the signing of the contract for the marriage between Lord James Cavendish and Elihu Yale's daughter Anne, which took place in 1708.[5] However, as there is no sign of a marriage contract and the bride is absent, considerable doubt must be raised about this.

1.2. Detail of Figure 1.1 (page). Anonymous artist, *Elihu Yale, the 2nd Duke of Devonshire, Lord James Cavendish, Mr. Tunstal, and a Page*, ca. 1708.

On one level little is remarkable either about this portrait or about the uncertainties surrounding it; the latter are merely the impedimenta attendant upon a pictorial archaeology when the passage of time has erased the circumstances and the material conditions of the events the portrait records. I can add little to the scant information provided by archivists and catalogers, though we might note that the marriage between the daughter of an American-born merchant of Welsh origins until recently resident in India and a member of one of England's most powerful and wealthy families must, however great her dowry, have been a noteworthy occurrence.[6] Yale was a nabob who had returned from India in 1699 with an immense personal fortune, and it has been suggested that he commissioned the portrait to celebrate his own social ambitions for which the betrothal of his daughter was the vehicle.[7]

I want to draw attention to the fact that in a group portrait where there are three named figures there are also several figures who are nameless, and who are not included in the painting's title as generally given. The artist is also unidentified, and therefore nameless. Leaving aside for the moment the children in the background, the representation of the black servant, as part of an identifiable group of individuals, I infer to be a portrait.[8] But even this can be by no means certain. This recognition of something having portrait-like conviction – and yet lacking a name – has been taken up as an issue for black people's history by artists such as Fred Wilson in *Mining the Museum*.[9] Secondly, it has been assumed that this black child, generally referred to as a page, belonged to the Duke of Devonshire because he is standing next to him. Thirdly, it is worth remarking that this painting, in the collection of the Yale Center for British Art, is rarely shown, a fact that is symptomatic of the problematic relations of institutions to their funding and sponsorship histories. All these inferences begin to suggest something of what Marcus Wood has called "the utterly problematic nature of the visual representation of slavery."[10]

1.3. William Hoare, *Job, Son of Solliman Dgiallo, High Priest of Bonda in the Country of Foota, Africa*. Etching, inscribed in pencil (apparently autograph) "Guglielmus Hoare ad vivum pinxit et sculps 1734" (William Hoare painted it from life and etched it 1734). British Museum, London. © Trustees of the British Museum, London.

The second image is an etching that was produced to accompany the publication in 1734 of Thomas Bluett's *Some Memoirs of the Life of Job, the Son of Solomon, the High Priest of Boonda in Africa* (Fig. 1.3). This head-and-shoulders we can now be certain was etched after a fine portrait by William Hoare (1706–99; Fig. 1.4; Plate 2) as the original painting,

1.4. William Hoare of Bath, *Portrait of Ayuba Suleiman Diallo, called Job ben Solomon (1701–73)*, 1733. Oil on canvas, 76.2 × 64.2 cm. OM.762. Orientalist Museum, Doha. On long-term loan to the National Portrait Gallery, London.

inscribed and dated on the stretcher 1733, has recently appeared on the art market.[11] In a feigned oval, Hoare has depicted in remarkable detail the bone structure, the intelligent features, and the half smile of his sitter. There is no sense here of a stereotypic portrait representation, and great care has been taken with the skin tones and with the sitter's compellingly lucid gaze. His white gown and turban serve to enhance the sheen of the skin, the reflections, and the whites of the eyes, while the red of the Qur'an that hangs round his neck and in the upper part of his turban reinforce the sense of warmth of personality that the portrait conveys. The etching was well known and was reproduced as half of a double portrait alongside William Sessarakoo,[12] in *The Gentleman's Magazine* in June 1850. The subject of this portrait, and of the etching after it which helped make its subject famous, was the well-educated son of a Muslim Fula (Pulo) ruler in the Gambia, who, on a journey away from home for the purpose of selling slaves to European dealers, was himself kidnapped and sold into slavery. Sent to Maryland he escaped from the tobacco plantation where he had been sent to work and wrote a letter in Arabic that he tried to send to his father. On account of a series of mishaps the letter got only as far as England, where it aroused the curiosity of antiquarians and those whose humanitarianism had been stimulated by the popular novel by Aphra Behn, *Oroonoko*, the story of an African prince sold into slavery (published in 1688). Job's letter was sent to Oxford for translation, and eventually, in 1733, Dgiallo (to use his family name) was purchased and brought to England. He learned English and, with his devout religious behavior, his long curly hair, and his dignity, became an object of interest in learned circles, including that of Sir Hans Sloane, whose collections would form the basis of the British Museum.[13] Like Omai, forty years later, he was presented at court.[14] Less than two years after his arrival he was finally given his freedom and his passage home. His is, it is claimed, "the first widely documented case of an African going back home."[15]

Although Dgiallo's story has been retold countless times over the centuries, it is extremely rare for anyone to discuss his portrait.[16] Moreover, virtually everything we know about Dgiallo derives from the account of Bluett, who traveled with him from Maryland and taught him English on the ship. Bluett's declared reason for writing his book is that Job (who is always referred to by his first name) asked him to, as did Job's benefactors. He claims that he "resolved to communicate to the World such Particulars of the Life and Character of this African Gentleman as I think will be most useful and entertaining; intending to advance nothing as Fact, but what I either know to be such or have had from Job's own Mouth, whose Veracity I have no reason to doubt."[17] Bluett explains the system under which Job acquired his full name: "Hyuba, Boon Salumena, Boon Hibrahema"[18] (Job son of Solomon son of Abraham), which is reproduced in the etching, in what we are invited to perceive as Job's own hand. In a section of his book on Job's person and character, Bluett describes Job as tall and straight-limbed with a pleasant countenance and hair that was "very different from that of the Negroes commonly brought from *Africa*."[19]

Job was reluctant to sit for his portrait and possessed, we are told, "an aversion to Pictures of all Sorts" that was "exceedingly great."[20] Bluett tells his readers:

> It was with great Difficulty that he could be brought to sit for his own. We assured him that we never worshipped any Picture, and that we wanted his for no other End but to keep us in mind of him. He at last consented to have it drawn. ... When the Face was finished, Mr. Hoare ask'd what Dress would be most proper to draw him in; and upon Job's desiring to be drawn in his own Country Dress, told him he could not draw it, unless he had seen it, or had it described to him by one who had; Upon which Job answered, If you can't draw a dress you never saw, why do some of your Painters presume to draw God, whom no one ever saw.[21]

We may infer that the head-and-shoulders format obviated the need for sartorial detail although it might also be noted that the subject wears a red Qur'an, which is emphatically suspended from a cord round his neck.

Bluett's conclusion, namely, that Dgiallo's story demonstrates that there is something sublime and even godlike in a benevolent disposition towards strangers, and that hospitality is part of the English character, we may pass over. What I wish to draw attention to is, firstly, the genre of portrait frontispiece, secondly, the question of the portrait subject's will (which here arises when his sponsors are allegedly obliged to persuade Dgiallo to sit), thirdly, that his appearance as described by Bluett is measured by the ways in which it is different from that of a Negro, the word used in the text, thus indicating a hierarchical taxonomy, and, fourthly, the way in which the author's explanation of the subject's origins and of the portrait is strategically designed to support the truth effect of the narrative (a process that has been described as constructing a history recuperated from diverse sources of the author's own subjectivity).[22] Bluett thus creates an eyewitness ethnographic account that ultimately tells us more about the literary aspirations of the author than about the unfortunate Dgiallo. Technically, the portrait of Dgiallo may not appear admissible as a "slave portrait" because its subject knew at the time of the sitting that he would attain his freedom. It offers, nonetheless, a reminder that, though we might wish for a form of unequivocal visual evidence in the portrait, slave portraits may be more about process and contingency than about absolute conditions. Notwithstanding his status at the moment of portrayal, Dgiallo aroused interest and sympathy precisely because of the fact that slavery was intrinsic to his story as told. We need to be aware that in dealing with images we are often, as here, dealing with overlapping and sometimes conflicting discourses.

In short, these two images (one for which we have much circumstantial evidence, and the other for which we have very little) stage for us a range of possibilities that might form an agenda of sorts, one that may help us to draw a framework for the conceptualization of "slave portraiture" as a genre, for its figurative contingencies and specificities. The portrait of Elihu Yale and companions posits the question of visibility and naming: the recognition and acknowledgement of what features in any image are determined by the cultural and political context of the moment of viewing so that what we may recuperate even at a strictly empirical level is fairly arbitrary. Here, for instance, we inherit an assumption that the page belongs to the Duke because of their proximity in the composition. It might in this, and similar instances, be useful to adopt Leo Steinberg's word "oblivion."[23] Oblivion is not ignorance nor yet is it suppression: It might be said to involve a failure of some kind, a psychic incapacity to see what is there to be seen. The organizing schemas of Art History and Museology describe this boy of non-European (and I use this term in its most stereotypical form) appearance as a "page"; he is certainly a servant and must surely have been purchased. Elizabeth O'Leary has remarked with respect to colonial North America that nearly all bound workers and slaves were called servants, including transported debtors and convicts.[24] A reference to a black female servant in the will of Lady Ann Harvey (probate 1737) is significant in that it indicates that it is misleading to make general assumptions about the relations between black servants and the families for whom they worked. Lady Harvey made provision for "my black girl Lovey Longwell" by leaving her the substantial sum of £100 in trust, under the control of Harvey's granddaughter, Mrs. Elizabeth Courtney: "Lovey Longwell may receive the interest thereof as it shall yearly grow due and the said principal sum of the hundred pounds I order to be payd her whenever she shall marry to an advantage and to the good liking of my granddaughter."[25] In the absence of in-depth primary research into the precise identities of slave children represented in portraits, and in the light of the slave collar worn, we must view the child in the Yale-Cavendish portrait as, at the very least, "slave-like."[26] About his identity and status we know nothing, but we might reasonably infer that it is his presence in a portrait that contains a rare "likeness," as it would have been termed in the period, of the founder of a great American college that accounts for the relative invisibility of this painting within that institution. We may also guess that this black page had no say in the inclusion of his portrait within the group, raising again the question of the will of the subject. It might be reasonable to invoke here the idea of *ritratti rubati* (stolen portraits) coined in 1678 by Giulio Cesare Malvasia to denote images of individuals taken without their consent, without their knowledge, and even in opposition to their wishes.[27]

Whether portraits occur at all depends on the significance placed by a given society on its individual members. We might add that not all of its members get to be portrayed and that portraits invariably have an intended audience. In both my examples it is clear that the audience is not the colonial subject. Dgiallo is portrayed for the benefit of learned English gentlemen, and we would be unlikely to know the name of the page even were he not black; valued family servants were sometimes represented for their own sakes in named portraits, but the occurrence was rare.[28] Nor in the case of vast numbers of portraits of wealthy free men and women are we able to affix a name to a face; the stores of galleries and of dealers, not to mention private attics and street markets, are awash with paintings and photographs of now nameless European subjects. However, these are images that once *did* have names, for which individual subjects sat but which have through time become detached from their recorded identities. The depiction of subjects who may reasonably be assumed to have actually lived and who, *ab initio*, were of interest often (although not always) for their condition or their physical make-up rather than for their individuality was frequently confined to slaves and marginalized subjects such as the insane.

When the Swiss-born naturalist Louis Agassiz (1807–73) commissioned photographic representations of a black slave named Jack (a given slave name) to further his ethnological theses, he requested views from front, back, and side.[29] It is precisely the "objectness" that is a feature of these daguerreotypes that inspired Carrie Mae Weems (b. 1953) to recuperate "Jack" in her 1993 *Sea Islands* series.[30] Roland Barthes's fixation in *Camera Lucida* (1980) on Richard Avedon's photograph of William Casby (which Barthes entitled *WILLIAM CASBY, BORN A SLAVE*) (Fig. 1.5) is articulated as a revelation about a new experiential order of proof of the past. But his claim that Casby's portrait lays bare "the essence of slavery," as a masque in the Greek theatre "is absolutely pure," as well as the way the photograph is presented in the book with Barthes's gloss to accompany it, tells its own cautionary tale of how portraits may be appropriated for essentializing narratives.[31] To be sure, the construction of the insane as marginal differs from the marginality of slaves in representation. Imagery of slavery is often explicitly tied to abolitionist discourse, whereas there is little evidence of the use of visual data in the interests of liberating the insane. But the clinical gaze that determines the treatment of the insane subject informs also the slave portrait. William Casby's portrait comes to us not on account of his character or anything he did but simply because he had been a slave. In the case of the famous portraits of the insane by Théodore Géricault, particular individuals are known to have sat, but because their names have been "lost," the images have always been known by the condition from which these subjects were diagnosed as suffering.[32] One way of addressing the problem of whether such images are in fact portraits is to ask what function they served. This is true also, surely, of the images of black subjects in John Gabriel Stedman's *Narrative of a five years' expedition against the Revolted Negroes of Surinam* (1796)[33] where – the representation of Stedman and his native wife, and Kwasi, excepted – the images are mostly designed to show a condition and not an individual, and as such do not, I suggest, constitute portraits.

Portraiture is by no means a universal phenomenon as the clash of cultures that is manifest in Dgiallo's recounted objection to sitting for his portrait evinces. When portraiture does occur it indicates the centrality of being seen within politics and society, and suggests the invention of codes and forms of

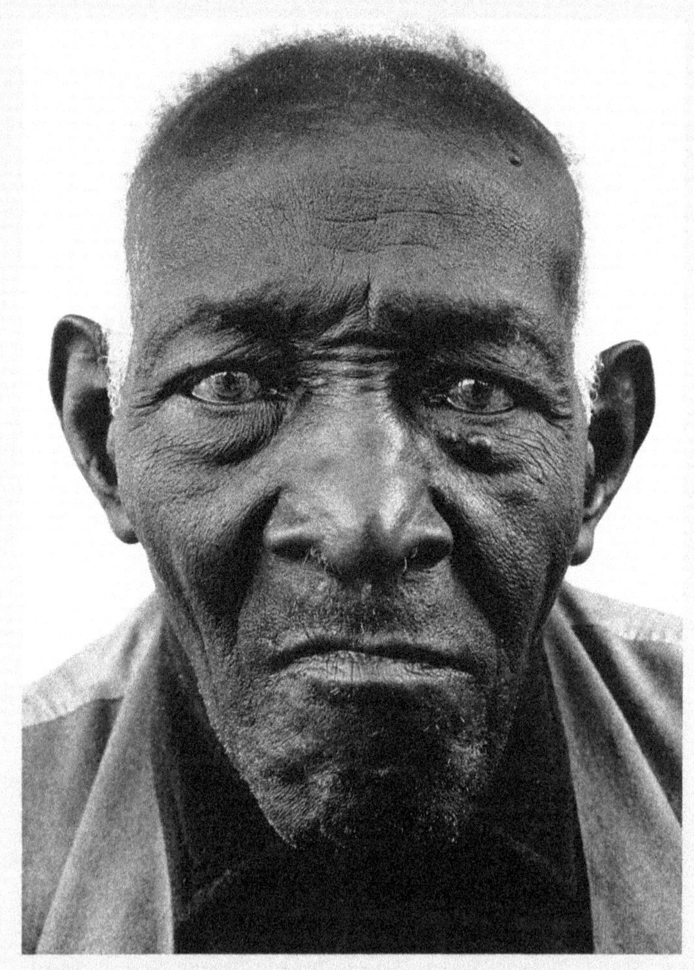

*"The mask is meaning,
insofar as it is absolutely pure . . ."*

R. Avedon: William Casby, Born a Slave. 1963

visual rhetoric through which a society theatricalizes itself. The etched portrait of Dgiallo exemplifies the forging of an identity from pre-existing conceptual orders – in this case the engraved portrait frontispiece that first occurs in the tradition of the Lives of Famous Men[34] – to accommodate something different. It is a type that was deployed regularly through the nineteenth century as a way of authenticating slave narratives.[35] The symbiosis of portrait and biography is inflected in the way in which each medium tends to be proselytized by reference to the other. Thus, "a good biography is like a good portrait," recently stated one biographer; "it captures the essence of the sitter by being much more than a likeness. A good portrait is about history, philosophy, milieu."[36] The engraved portrait, especially when accompanied by a signature (naming and writing as marks of civilization), usually, however, shows the subject when they have ceased to be a slave. Thus an engraved portrait of John Anderson in senatorial pose signed "Yours truly John Anderson," testimony to the subject's literacy and civility, prefaces *The Story of the Life of John Anderson, the Fugitive Slave* (1863).[37] Dgiallo, however, was technically still a slave in 1733 at the time of his portrait, though he had been released from slave labor. He is endowed with some of the features of a Romantic *bandito* in the manner of the seventeenth-century Italian artist Salvator Rosa (known as "Savage Rosa"), whose works were popular in eighteenth-century England. Dgiallo may also have been Europeanized to accord with the author's perception of him as a princely person, who differs in appearance from other African slaves. The fact that the portrait is taken in spite of the subject's reservations serves to remind us that the phrase "capturing a likeness" used even today by people taking photographs of their relatives is a telling one: The portrait process, per se, replicates patterns of authority that have wider resonance. Portraiture as an art form plays out technologies of power and their attendant patterns of anxiety in its modes of production and in its acts of communication.

If we look at the great historiographic landmarks in writing on the genre of portraiture, they seem to have little to offer on what David Bindman has rightly called the oxymoron of slave portraits.[38] Pliny's invaluable disquisition on Antique portraits,[39] drawn upon extensively by art historians like James Breckenridge and Richard Brilliant, established both the prevalence of portraits in the Ancient World (for Greeks the portrait comprised the whole body whereas the Romans invented the portrait bust) and their functions in relation to genealogical power and State governance.[40] Pliny also makes clear the connections between portraits of humans and cults of divinity. These characteristics,

1.5 (*on facing page*). Richard Avedon, *William Casby, born into slavery, Algiers, Louisiana, March 24, 1963.* Photograph © The Richard Avedon Foundation. Image and text as they appear in Roland Barthes's *Camera Lucida: Reflections on Photography* [1980] (New York: Hill & Wang, 1981; repr. 1993).

according to writers such as John Pope-Hennessy, Marianna Jenkins, Loren Partridge and Randolph Starn, underpin the great European portraits of the sixteenth and seventeenth centuries in which the search for immortality and the principle of emulation – portraits of virtuous men as inspiring high endeavors – are paramount.[41] With the work of literary scholar Stephen Greenblatt (who draws upon anthropologists such as Clifford Geertz), the emphasis is upon self-consciousness about the fashioning of human identity as a manipulable, artful process. The centrality of the portrait genre, whether in the Protestant north, about which Joseph Koerner has written illuminatingly,[42] or in the Catholic south is summed up in Greenblatt's assertion on self-fashioning, that autonomy is not the sole or central issue. The power to impose a shape on oneself is an aspect of the more general power to control identity.[43] Although portraiture may have variant functions in non-Western cultures, and although representations of named individuals (monarchs) in Europe before 1400 are not primarily concerned with individuality, in the early-modern period in Europe the rise of the portrait has been ineluctably associated with changing concepts of the individual and his or her identity in relation to the social.

In seventeenth- and eighteenth-century Europe, academies promulgated the hierarchy of genres in which the portrait is positioned at second rank on account of the fact that it concerns man as an individual, not "Man" as a generality, and because the requirements in the portrait of at least some degree of likeness are inimical to notions of the Ideal. Aristotle's *De Anima* (I), in contrast to Plato's rejection of the physical world, proposed that the only way in which we can apprehend the immaterial is through its impact on the material world of the senses. Commentaries on Aristotle throughout the sixteenth century address portraiture as an oscillation between mimesis and something superadded. Phrases such as *da natura* and *viva viva*, used to describe Raphael's *La Fornarina* (Fig. 11.8), are countered by Lomazzo's insistence in 1584 on quality, discretion, grandeur, and other concepts that are summed up in the *rittrati intelletuali*.[44]

In the eighteenth century, Joshua Reynolds was more categorical: "Beauty in each species of being is an invariable one."[45] However, at the same time as immutable laws like this, rejecting relativity, were adumbrated in learned societies and publications across Europe and North America, what we have learned from Foucault to call the archaeology of knowledge generated a dynamic in empirical, positivist recording and valuation of particularities and their concomitant celebration of all forms of subjugated life.[46] Social mobility led to a greater diversity within portraiture as an art form in Europe, especially in England and North America from the early years of the eighteenth century. The Earl of Fife remarked in 1798: "Before this century very few people presented themselves to a painter except those who were of great families, or remarkable for their actions in the service of their country," but now the field had become greatly extended because almost everybody who could afford twenty pounds wanted their portrait painted.[47] The appearance of portraits of individuals of non-European origin are at one level a further manifestation of this widening field, as in the work of William Hodges or in the famous portraits of the Tahitian Omai. It is to historians such as Kathleen Wilson, literary scholars such as Harriet Guest, and art historians such as Dian Kriz and Geoff Quilley that we owe a body of insightful interpretative work in this area.[48] But, though his life was certainly shaped by colonial adventurism and his representation might be said to correlate with discourses of slavery and subjugation, Omai was a free man and had never been a slave.

Postmodernism transformed the agenda for portraiture. Methodologies deriving from social history, semiotics, anthropology, and psychoanalysis from the late 1970s changed our ways of addressing portraits whether as images or as artifacts. The portrait became a focus of analysis in many media, including photography, among writers such as Harry Berger, Wendy Steiner, and Abigail Solomon-Godeau.[49] The paradox of the portrait (along with the still life) as the genre through which abstraction was first articulated has not gone unnoticed. The low genres and those in which materiality is valued are precisely those in which the rules of art and art's legibility are challenged – as with early Braque and Picasso.[50] This is, perhaps, analogous to the paradox of the slave portrait, suggesting that the portrait's apparently conceptually circumscribed boundaries may serve as a mask for innovation in times of adventurism, conceptual or otherwise. Given that likeness to the model, similitude, verism, are central to portraiture, how can the portrait be reconciled with abstraction? And similarly, if the slave officially has a subjugated identity, how can he or she be configured in a genre, the languages of which were coined to bespeak fictions of a sovereign individuality? Portraiture is poised between resemblance and transfiguration, between objectification and psychosocial concepts such as identity. Its semantic origins betray its connections to mimesis or imitation. The Latin verb *portraho*, meaning to reproduce or copy, leads in the Middle Ages to the French *pourtraire*, English "portray," and German *porträtieren*. The related Latin verb *retraho* leads to Italian *ritratto* and *ritrarre*, and the Spanish *retrato* and *retratar*, in their meaning of "copy" in use since the early sixteenth century.

I shall change tack here and propose that we bear in mind the close historical relationship between the notion of a portrait and that of a copy or imitation, a relationship that was spectacularly sidestepped by theories of Classicism and of Modernism. It would be possible to propose an extremely wide field for an enquiry into slave portraits, one that acknowledged the ways in which both portraiture and slavery as traces of memory and forms of visual encoding are metamorphosed in a wide range of contemporary art, as, for example, with Kara Walker, whose sometimes controversial black silhouettes (see Fig. I.4) against a white space invoke the heritage of Southern slavery as well as the context of Victorian bourgeois home entertainments.[51] Whatever the merits of such a wide set of parameters, they would not help in establishing how we might address portraits of slaves per se. I propose, therefore, for the remainder of this essay to focus on questions relating to portraits, power, and identity in relation to subjects who have ostensibly no social, legal, or political power (though they may have other kinds of power) and in whom the problematics of identity common to all portraits are already overwritten by their condition as slaves.

Central to these matters is on the one hand the question of belonging, and on the other that of doubling. Likeness is the *sine qua non* of portraiture, and, if the story of the Corinthian maid who drew her lover's profile on the wall of her father's house is to be believed, portraiture is the origin of painting.[52] Likeness is also, however, an immeasurable component. The trope of the subject painted in a manner so lifelike that their portrait deceives and entrances viewers is common from Antiquity to the present day, as the annual BP Portrait Awards at the National Portrait Gallery in London, and their critics, testify. Equally there is the *Vanitas* aspect of portraiture, the legacy of Christianity, which inherited the seventh commandment of Judaism against the making of graven images.[53] This may be treated flippantly, as when it is remarked that it matters not whether Michelangelo's portrait of a Medici looks like the subject since he will soon be dead and then no one will be able to judge,[54] or may generate deep-rooted written and unwritten laws as to what may or may not be depicted. In non-conformist Protestant sects such as Calvinists, Unitarians, and Quakers, portraiture – though less problematic than other kinds of representation – presented difficulties because of the implied glorification of the subject.[55] Only imagery that could be understood to be factual, informative, and didactic was acceptable. Typically, a portrait of the Quaker abolitionist Mary Lloyd (1795–1865) shows her holding a book, the cover of which is turned to the viewer. Readily legible is the inscription on that cover: "The Chain is broken. AFRICA is free. Aug 12 1834."[56] Engraving, with its utilitarian and transcriptive associations, was favored above painting that was deemed superfluous and ornamental. Quaker homes in the nineteenth century were alleged by a Quaker writer to have contained only three images, all engravings: Benjamin West's *William Penn's Treaty with the Indians*, the abolitionists' diagram of the slave ship, and a view of Ackworth School in Yorkshire founded in 1779 by the Quaker Doctor John Fothergill.[57] It is no accident that print is the medium in which the most celebrated portraits associated with slavery have come down to us. Medium might, in fact, be one possible yardstick in seeking overall grounds for an historical analysis of slavery and portraiture.

If likeness is immeasurable, how is a subject's identity constructed in a portrait image? One answer is that it is the space the subject is shown to inhabit and the material attributes represented within that space alongside him or her that articulate identity. This may readily be shown by taking a deliberately chosen canonical work such as Holbein's *Ambassadors* and asking what we know of these two individuals; we turn for information not to their faces, however remarkably drawn these may be, or to other parts of their bodies, but to the habitus – the environment which shapes the subject, which they reciprocally shape, and in which they are represented – itself a shaping process.[58] This is a painting that has been exhaustively analyzed in terms of its iconography, with recent writers drawing attention to the imperial and expansionist themes mobilized by the globe and the naming of Africa thereon.[59]

Holbein's intricate weaving of an environment that offers information on the two ambassadors and their world is a function of representing the individuality of a human subject. Each (free) human subject is understood to be unique, and the problem is how to represent him or her as such. Whereas we may admire a Chardin still life and feel we know the very vessels portrayed, what we respond to is a generic class of object with which we are familiar. It does not matter whether or not we ever saw that pot, we simply *feel* that we did as a consequence of a remarkable technique of painting. The portrait painter, however, must make us feel that we are seeing a particular individual, one whom we might have known. Jean-Paul Sartre, in 1940 (long before Barthes), coined the phrase "expressive likeness" for something that acts seemingly magically even when the subject is dead;[60] or as we might now say the issue of resemblance to the original is bypassed in the production of a truth-effect with which the imagination of the beholder engages. Recorded responses to this sense of communication with the depicted dead are legion, and it is this quality that is lacking in, for example, funerary portraits that serve as substitutes or doubles for the physical body – leaving the spirit to its afterlife – as with Egyptian pharaohs.

The word "place" richly signifies in European languages in relation to human subjects, as in the *place* one inhabits and perhaps even possesses in the legal sense, and as a position (or place) in the geopolitical and social hierarchies, as in "knowing one's proper *place*." From Edward Said to Jacques Derrida,[61] the importance of belonging to a place has been explored, as have the ways of simulating that belonging. It is through place as a receptacle that portraiture's link to the order of the "real" (its concern with model and likeness) is mythicized. To see this in process, I will turn to what is one of the best known and most widely disseminated representations of a black subject, the engraved portrait of Phillis Wheatley, celebrated as the "first published woman of African descent,"[62] which appeared as the frontispiece to her *Poems on Various Subjects, Religious and Moral* (London: 1773) (Fig. 1.6).

Vincent Carretta states that Wheatley's portrait was added to her book at the suggestion of her patron, the Countess of Huntingdon, and that it may have been "engraved after a painting by Scipio Moorhead, the subject of her poem, 'To S.M. a Young *African* Painter, on Seeing his Works.'"[63] As with all the portraits published as frontispieces to slave narratives – both Solomon Northup and William Grimes are cases in point – by the time Phillis Wheatley's portrait came before the public she was no longer a slave.[64] It is customary to reproduce these frontispieces as illustrations in academic books about slavery, and to have them on the screen as PowerPoint images while a lecturer speaks, but they are very seldom discussed *qua* image. An exception is Carretta, who compares the frontispiece portraits of Olaudah Equiano (1789; Fig. 6.9), Phillis Wheatley (1773), and Ignatius Sancho in Sancho's posthumously published *Letters* (1782).[65] Carretta is at pains to point out that only Equiano looks out at the viewer and to establish the standing of this portrait of "a *gentleman* in his own right" by contrast with Wheatley whose "frontispiece is as modest as her status."[66] In fact, it is not at all unusual for portrait subjects to be shown in profile in the eighteenth century, though it is more customarily found in a group portrait. We might take as an example a Grand Tour portrait by John Singleton Copley (Fig. 1.7) in which Mrs. Ralph Izard is shown in profile with her arms and hands in almost exactly the same position (in reverse) as those adopted by Wheatley in the portrait by this unknown artist. Indeed, one might readily argue conversely that Wheatley's position at the right of the image space and gazing upward (understood by Carretta as a contemplative pose) implies an interlocutor on the other side of the table; it is all too easy to make empathetic assumptions about visual representations of the subjects that are the objects of our study. I shall take a different approach and pay attention to how place is mythicized in Wheatley's portrait. Apart from Wheatley herself, the portrait depicts a small circular table, an ink well, pen, sheet of paper, small book, and a chair on which Wheatley is seated of which we see only the curved back. As with other portraits attached to slave narratives, the reproduced signature of the writer acts as visual guarantee of the authenticity of authorship.

The convention of the vignette format for frontispieces means that the oval frame in which her name and ownership are inscribed encloses the subject. The format intensifies attention on the material details depicted and thus serves also to remind us that this is a synthesis of elements constructed with the purpose of enhancing the subject and situating her within a familiar network of signs. To be seated at a table is often, for a woman, a sign of leisure, not labor; another

1.6 (*on facing page*). (After Scipio Moorhead?), *Phillis Wheatley, Negro Servant to Mr. John Wheatley, of Boston*. Frontispiece and title page to Phillis Wheatley, *Poems on Various Subjects, Religious and Moral* (London: printed for A. Bell, 1773). PML 77263. Pierpont Morgan Library, New York. Photo: Pierpont Morgan Library/Art Resource, New York.

Phillis Wheatley, Negro Servant to Mr. John Wheatley, of Boston.
Published according to Act of Parliament, Sept.r 1st, 1773 by Arch.d Bell,
Bookseller No. 8 near the Saracens Head Aldgate.

1.7. John Singleton Copley, *Mr. and Mrs. Ralph Izard (Alice Delancey)*, 1775. Oil on canvas. Museum of Fine Arts, Boston. Edward Ingersoll Brown Fund, 03.1033. Photograph © 2013, Museum of Fine Arts, Boston, Mass.

portrait by Copley, of Lady Wentworth, painted in 1765,[67] shows her seated on a chair with a curved back at a small circular table (on which she has a pet squirrel). Small round tables are part of women's domestic space in the eighteenth century; they are used for playing cards, sewing, or writing letters. In one of Gravelot's fine engravings after Francis Hayman for Samuel Richardson's novel *Pamela* (Fig. 1.8), the eponymous heroine has risen at the entry of Mr. B. She holds a pen in her hand, and on the small circular table behind her lie an inkwell and another quill pen. In short, rather than an instantaneous glimpse of a young woman of African descent pausing to think while writing a poem, what is being constructed with Wheatley's portrait is an identity through place and its accoutrements, an identity that mythicizes the subject as belonging to a world of eighteenth-century female gentility. The portrait also connects her to the type of the woman of letters, but the verbal inscription does not permit us to forget that this is also a world in which she is a servant. Although the portrait and the book, which it prefaces, bespeak Wheatley's accomplishments as a poet, there remain the visual and verbal traces of her servitude that underscore the gulf that actually existed between herself and the Countess to whom she dedicated her book.

Of course, there have been times when the simulation of place as a site for mythicization – and hence for identity that transcends questions of likeness – has been repudiated. One thinks, for example, of certain portraits by Rembrandt van Rijn, or Jacques-Louis David, where the habitus of the subject is indeterminate and the subject is posed against a background remarkable for its painterly qualities but devoid of identifiable motifs; we understand this as a deliberate ploy serving to displace the place of living onto a place of thinking, so that the subject appears autonomous. We are invited to understand that these individuals inhabit places of their own making that are cerebral, moral, and psychic. With slave portraits a difference emerges in the matter of habitus. If a slave belongs to another, he or she cannot be associated with any place other than that of the owner or master. Slaves (like servants) are socially marginal – and so are children. None has autonomy. Unlike the ambassadors Jean Dintville and Georges de Selves in Holbein's painting, each signifies the place of an other, a master/father. With a slave child, it may have been perhaps relatively easy to accommodate him or her into a portrait because, apart from their value as an ornamental acquisition (about which Dabydeen and Amussen have written),[68] and setting aside portraits devoted exclusively to children, the slave child was immediately outside the conventional place of belonging by virtue of the fact that they were not adult. Perhaps the strange otherworldly afterthought appearance of the children in the group

1.8. Hubert Gravelot after Francis Hayman, *Mr. B reading Pamela's letter*. Etched illustration to Samuel Richardson's *Pamela* (London, 1742), vol. I, p. 4. British Museum, London.© Trustees of the British Museum, London.

1.9. *Solomon in his Plantation Suit.* Lithograph by Coffin, frontispiece to *Twelve Years a Slave. Narrative of Solomon Northup, a citizen of New York, Kidnapped in Washington City in 1841, and rescued in 1853 from a cotton plantation near the Red River in Louisiana* (New York: C. M. Saxton, 1859). Yale University, Beinecke Rare Book and Manuscript Library.

portrait featuring Elihu Yale with which I opened can be explained by the need to further differentiate their place in representation – to ensure the idealized place they occupy is not the socially marginal space of the clearly defined black page but a place at a further remove, materially and spiritually, from the genteel adult events of the foreground.

For the European, subject identity is displaced from likeness to habitus through the production of a *factish,* to borrow Bruno Latour's term for something that unites the evidential value of the fact with the fabrication of the fetish.[69] Once freed, like Phillis Wheatley, a slave could be represented as assimilated into a European habitus, but for the slave subject, the habitus is either nonexistent or borrowed. Thus Northup's 1859 account, dedicated to Harriet Beecher Stowe, has a lithographed frontispiece showing *Solomon in his Plantation Suit* (Fig. 1.9), sitting on a bench at a cottage door with a broom, barrel, and planks of wood nearby. The cottage door motif connects it directly to Stowe's novel *Uncle Tom's Cabin,* published seven years earlier with a frontispiece showing the cabin door in front of which children crawl and gesticulate. This in turn derives from the many times reproduced (in etching and engraving) painting by Thomas Gainsborough *A Cottage Door,*[70] an exemplary trope of the European eighteenth-century rustic ideal.

So where is identity constructed? Although descriptions of subjects' physiognomies are a commonplace of post-Lavater biography,[71] what is special in

Bluett's account of Dgiallo's appearance is the comparative taxonomy that he applies. This was, of course, as Bindman has established,[72] by no means unusual, but I want to propose that we consider the possibility that physiognomic scrutiny as a mechanism for identification works as a substitute for habitus in the case of slave portrait subjects. Ironically this means a return to the "objectness" that originally belonged to the general concept in Western culture of "portrait" as a *thing* represented.[73]

In this context we should consider also the question of medium that I raised earlier. Agassiz's commission for photographs of the slave "Jack" might tempt us into the notion that somehow photography as a new medium in the nineteenth century offers a more faithful likeness – restoring the link between image and subject that I have been at pains to disassemble. By contrast, I would argue that photography is not in this context generically different from techniques of engraving (such as stipple) that were exploited to indicate flesh color. Photography serves to focus on surface, physiognomy, and the materiality of the subject as object. By this I mean that the surface of the face is itself rendered as the place/space the slave inhabits; the substitution of face for place through this maneuver produces the slave *itself* as habitus. It is to this that Barthes was responding so dramatically in his reaction to Avedon's photograph of a man once a slave.

I want, finally, to turn to the question of doubling, to ask what the implications of this might be for portraits of slaves or slaves in portraits. The relationship that is central to the experience of portraiture runs between subject and viewer. We may here be talking about a viewer who is also a subject of the portrait, a viewer who is connected in social relations to the portrait subject, or a viewer who does not and cannot have any communication with the subject outside of the portrait. In all these instances, including the last (in the case of historical portraits), the viewer (in which we may include the artist) is drawn, through the recognition of a human other, into, at some level, envisioning him- or herself as duplicated or reproduced – as doubled. The tensions and psychodynamics of portraits revolve around this dialectical relationship that scholars have variously tried to define in terms of performance, of Lacanian mirroring, or of Marxian power relations. So how might it work if the portrait subject is a slave and the viewer a free man or woman? Dgiallo's portrait was, we may recall, executed not for Dgiallo himself, who, presumably, never saw it again once he had returned to Senegal, but for the Europeans who had adopted his cause.

The most famous version of the dangers and complexities of human subjects in relation to their reflections is the story of Narcissus as told in Ovid's *Metamorphoses*. In invoking Narcissus, I wish to set aside Freud's annexation of the Narcissus legend to define a kind of sexuality, and also to ignore Lacan's mirror phase through which the child is deemed to recognize itself as a person separate from the mother by seeing his or her image reflected in the mirror's surface or, I take it, within the mirroring surface of the expressive maternal face. This is a severance that forms in Lacan's account the core of self-consciousness. Ovid's story of Narcissus involves the subject who sees himself as someone else, an unfamiliar person, and though he admires what he sees, the experience destroys him.[74] Life flickers in the water, but it is only a semblance which art – in its mimetic mirroring functions – reproduces. Mirrors are dangerous, and the theme of the destructiveness of portraits (by no means confined to Oscar Wilde's *The Picture of Dorian Gray*, 1891) is rooted in this narrative. When we think of Lacan we think of an enhanced mirror image; I want to contemplate a mirror that diminishes or reduces.[75]

The process of doubling is then a potentially destructive one to the subject. Dgiallo's reluctance to have his portrait made is attributable to his Islamic faith, but the Narcissus story should alert us to other ways in which the powerful dialectic of doubling works in portraiture. In commissioning a portrait of Dgiallo his patrons effectively held up a mirror to their subject who was already a subject in the sense that he was subject to their will. The abolitionist medallion asks "Am I not *a* Man and *a* Brother?" Dgiallo, on the other hand, is a particular named and identified man. Marina Warner has pointed out that the motif of the imperiling mirror occurred chiefly in stories about savages: The instrument of revelation, a glass, could capture and subdue wild things and bring them within the compass of civility – usually disempowered.[76] A much retold Medieval Bestiary fable indicates how "the hunter should cast a mirror in the path of the animal, and the tigress, passing by, would see herself therein reflected in little, and, by mistaking her reflection for her cub, would stop in her tracks to succour the nursling. The hunters would then be able to drop a net on her and capture her."[77] In this account, the mirror is a diminishing device, an instrument of domination, forcing upon the subject an understanding of a second and different self, a process that tames and civilizes its subject. In Warner's words "the mirror image is a kind of captivity, antithetical to freedom." She sees it as no accident that when Magellan set off to sail around the world he included in his provisions hundreds of small pieces of mirror destined to be gifts to new peoples, the Amazons and the wild folk, they expected to encounter.[78]

Domination, as many writers on post-colonialism have testified, is a matter of ambivalence. We recognize the complex empirical and historical problems associated with the idea of slave portraits – problems of status, function, audience, and authenticity. A consideration of portraits of slaves seems thus unavoidably to raise also the question of masters. It seems, then, that the portrait is a site in which it may be possible to recognize vividly played out the dialectical as well as the material conditions of slavery. In his *Introduction to the Reading of Hegel,* Alexander Kojève explores the relationship between master and slave. Of course, these terms are for him a metaphor for the interrelations of labor and desire. However, I would like to conclude with the notion that the portrait in its capturing and securing functions (artistically, socially, and psychically) presents something of the dilemma and paradox of the master–slave relationship that Kojève proposes: What he terms the tragedy of the struggle for mastery of the master over the slave. This is structured through the dependency of the master upon the slave for recognition in the struggle of what he terms the two self-consciousnesses. The master must not destroy the slave because, if his adversary dies, the other can no longer recognize him, but the recognition is one-sided because he does not recognize the humanity of the slave. Therefore, he is recognized by a thing.[79]

In its focus upon physiognomic and taxonomic specificities at the expense of habitus, the slave portrait displays a quality of "thingness," a quality that may be tempered insofar as the slave is translated into freedom. The portrait, operating as a regulative device, *seems* to secure the evidential existence of the slave and, through its place in the order of representation, thus to secure also the mastery of the master. This mastery is, of course, an illusion, for the cultural survival of the representation demonstrates, on the one hand, the historical necessity of objectifying the adversary and, on the other, the ultimate impossibility of deploying imagery in the interests of destroying autonomy. This is nowhere more amply demonstrated than in the capacity of images to generate an afterlife, of which this essay forms necessarily a part.

Notes

I would like to thank Susanne von Falkenhausen and Martha Buskirk for their insightful reading of this essay in draft.

1 Susan Dwyer Amussen, *Caribbean Exchanges: Slavery and the Transformation of English Society, 1640–1700* (Chapel Hill: University of North Carolina Press, 2007), see especially ch. 7, "If Her Son Is Living with You She Sends Her Love."

2 Peter Erickson, "Invisibility Speaks: Servants and Portraits in Early Modern Visual Culture," *Journal for Early Modern Cultural Studies* 9, no. 1 (spring/summer 2009), 23–61.

3 Erickson's account adopts a mechanistic methodology reliant on formalist analysis resulting in ekphrastic excursions and ahistorical conclusions. Visual evidence is treated as an archive of data regardless of its genre and function. Thus sketches are compared with finished paintings, studies of unidentified subjects are treated as portraits, a Gainsborough self-portrait is compared with the artist's portrait of Sancho, and there is disregard for the allegorical content of paintings that include black figures. At one point he proposes that even if black figures are absent in a painting, if they are more culturally available, they may be tacitly factored in. By whom, one must ask, and how?

4 The identification of this figure in 1886 as a lawyer, Mr. Tunstal, and the object he is holding as a marriage contract has been convincingly challenged in an unpublished master's thesis by Baird Jarman, now of Carleton University. I am most grateful to Baird for sending me a copy and allowing me to refer to his work. The figure's informal pose and physical closeness to Elihu Yale in the portrait make it more likely, it has been suggested, that this figure is David Yale, nephew of Elihu and at one time his intended heir. Given the grouping of figures and the background detail, the assumption has been that the black boy belongs to the Cavendish family and that the "conversation" is taking place at Chatsworth.

5 Typescript catalog of paintings at Chatsworth, 1933. Elihu Yale died in 1734. I am grateful for the dates given in this and the preceding notes to Charles Noble LVO, Keeper of the Devonshire Collection at Chatsworth House.

6 On the Yale family history see Hiram Bingham, *Elihu Yale: The American Nabob of Queen Square* (New York: Dodd, Mead & Co., 1939).

7 Ibid.

8 This Anglo-American rendering of a slave child/servant belongs within the tradition of fashionably dressed, usually male, African slave children – which had been seen in European fancy portraiture for several centuries by this point in time. For more on this theme, see David Bindman's essay in this volume and Amussen, *Caribbean Exchanges*.

9 Baltimore 1992; see L. G. Corrin, *Mining the Museum: An Installation by Fred Wilson* (Baltimore: Maryland Historical Society and New York: New Press, 1994).

10 Marcus Wood, *Blind Memory: Visual Representations of Slavery in England and America 1780–1865* (Manchester: Manchester University Press, 2000), 4.

11 The National Portrait Gallery failed in its attempt to prevent export of this work. However, the purchaser (the Qatar Museums Authority) has made it available on long-term loan to the London gallery.

12 William Ansah Sessarakoo was the son of a wealthy African trader; he was sold into slavery but released in Barbados and brought to London. He was the inspiration for William Dodd's poem "The African Prince" (1749).

13 A letter about Dgiallo from Joseph Ames to William Bogdani (17 November 1733) was published in *The Correspondence of the Spalding Gentlemen's Society 1710–1761*, ed. D. Honeybone and M. Honeybone (Lincoln Record Society,Woodbridge, Suffolk, Boydell Press, 2010), 81–82. The spelling of Dgiallo's name used in my text follows the inscription in his etched portrait, that is, the spelling known in the eighteenth century.

14 The South Sea Islander Omai (Omiah) traveled to England in 1773 with Captain Cook. His portrait by Sir Joshua Reynolds was exhibited at the Royal Academy in 1776. Many observers wrote about him, including Fanny Burney and Thomas Cowper.

15 Cf. Thomas Bluett, *Some Memoirs of the Life of Job, the Son of Solomon the High Priest of Boonda in Africa* (London: for Richard Ford, 1734), and Sylviane A. Diouf, *Servants of Allah: African Muslims Enslaved in the Americas* (New York: New York University Press 1998), 164. For the background to Job's story, see Douglas Grant, *The Fortunate Slave: An Illustration of African Slavery in the Early Eighteenth Century* (London: Oxford University Press, 1968).

16 See, for example, Francis Moore, *Travels into the Inland Parts of Africa ... with a particular Account of Job Ben Solomon, a Pholey, who was in England in the year 1733* (London: E. Cave, 1738); J. C. Hall, *Interesting Facts connected with the Animal Kingdom* (London: Doncaster, 1841); Gretchen Gerzina, *Black England: Life before Emancipation* (London: John Murray, 1995); Stephen Farrell,

Melanie Unwin and James Walvin, eds., *The British Slave Trade: Abolition, Parliament and People* (Edinburgh: Edinburgh University Press 2007); Jocelyn Hackforth-Jones, ed., *Between Two Worlds: Voyagers to Britain 1700–1850* (London: National Portrait Gallery, 2007). I am grateful to Dr. Lucy Peltz for allowing me to read through the vast file of information she has accumulated on William Hoare's portrait in support of the National Portrait Gallery's bid to save it from export.

17 Bluett, *Some Memoirs*, 10.

18 Ibid., 12.

19 Ibid., 46.

20 Diouf, *Servants of Allah*, 77, states that the etched portrait shows Dgiallo as "a quintessential Pulo with long hair and wearing a white turban, a white BOUBOU, and an Islamic gris-gris pouch" and that his reservations about the portrait sitting demonstrate his "insistence on cultural integrity."

21 Bluett, *Some Memoirs*, 50–51. On attitudes to portraiture in Islam, see Thomas W. Arnold, *Painting in Islam: A Study of the Place of Pictorial Art in Muslim Culture* (New York: Dover, 1965).

22 Keith Sandiford, "Envisioning the Colonial Body: The Fair, the Carnivalesque and the Grotesque," in *An Economy of Colour: Visual Culture and the Atlantic World 1660–1830*, ed. Geoff Quilley and Kay Dian Kriz (Manchester: Manchester University Press, 2003), 15.

23 As used in Leo Steinberg, *The Sexuality of Christ in the Renaissance and in Modern Oblivion* (New York: Pantheon, 1983).

24 Elizabeth O'Leary, *At Beck and Call: The Representation of Domestic Servants in Nineteenth-Century Painting* (Washington, D.C.: Smithsonian Institution, 1996), 10.

25 London: National Archive (Public Records Office), Prob. 11/702 quire 147, fols. 276–78, signed 11 November 1737. The entire will is transcribed in Marcia Pointon, *Strategies for Showing: Women, Possession and Representation in English Visual Culture 1665–1800* (Oxford: Oxford University Press, 1997) 323–24.

26 David Bindman, *Ape to Apollo: Aesthetics and the Idea of Race in the Eighteenth Century* (London: Reaktion, 2002), 42.

27 Quoted in Luigi Grassi, "Lineamenti per una storia del concetto di rittrato," *Arte Antica e Moderna* 13/16 (1961), 486.

28 See *Servants* (London: National Portrait Gallery, 2003).

29 The photographer was J. T. Zealy, reproduced in Mary Warner Marien, *Photography: A Cultural History* (Upper Saddle River, N.J.: Prentice Hall and London: Laurence King Publishing, 2002), 40–41.

30 See Kate Linker, "Went Looking for Africa: Carrie Mae Weems," *Artforum* 31 (February 1993), 79–82.

31 Roland Barthes, *Camera Lucida*, trans. Richard Howard (London: Vintage, 1982), 34 and 79.

32 The five portraits of the insane, painted by Géricault for his friend Dr. Georget, the head of the Salpetrière Hospital, were discovered abandoned in a worm-eaten chest in 1863; they are now in the Musée de Gand, the Musée du Louvre, the Musée de Lyon, the Collection Reinhart am Römerholz at Winterthur, and the Springfield [Mass.] Museum of Fine Arts.

33 John Gabriel Stedman, *Narrative, of a five years' expedition, against the Revolted Negroes of Surinam, in Guiana, on the Wild Coast of South America; from the year 1772 to 1777: elucidating the History of that Country, and describing its Productions, Viz. Quadrupeds, Birds, Fishes, Reptiles, Trees, Shrubs, Fruits, & Roots; with an*

account of the Indians of Guiana, & Negroes of Guinea, 2 vols. (London: J. Johnson, 1796).

34 See Francis Haskell, *History and Its Images: Art and the Interpretation of the Past* (New Haven: Yale University Press, 1993), ch. 1.

35 See Wood, *Blind Memory*, 130–31, on *Narrative of the Life and Adventures of Henry Bibb, an American Slave, Written by Himself* (1849). However, Wood suggests (wrongly in my view) that this type originates only in 1789 with Olaudah Equiano's *Interesting Narrative of Olaudah Equiano, or Gustavus. Vassa the African, Written by Himself* (London: printed for the author, and G. G. J. and J. Robinson and Charles Stalker, 1793).

36 Ben Pimlott, "Picture this ...," *Guardian* (28 August 2004), 22.

37 *The Story of the Life of John Anderson, the Fugitive Slave*, ed. Harper Twelvetrees, Chairman of the John Anderson Committee (London: William Tweedie, 1863), frontispiece. See also, for another similar example, *Narrative of the Life of Frederick Douglass an American Slave* (1845), ed. Benjamin Quarles (Cambridge, Mass: Harvard University Press, 1960).

38 See David Bindman's essay in this volume. See also his *Ape to Apollo*.

39 Pliny's observations are to be found in his *Natural History*. For easy access see K. Jex-Blake, trans., and Eugénie Sellers, ed., *The Elder Pliny's Chapters on the History of Art* (Chicago: Ares Publishers, 1976), especially "Bronze Statuary" and "Sculpture in Marble."

40 James D. Breckenridge, *Likeness: A Conceptual History of Ancient Portraiture* (Evanston, Ill.: Northwestern University Press, 1968); and Richard Brilliant, *Gesture and Rank in Roman Art* (New Haven, Conn.: The Academy, 1963).

41 John Pope-Hennessy, *The Portrait in the Renaissance* (London: Phaidon and New York: Bollingen Foundation, 1966); Marianna D. Jenkins, *The State Portrait: Its Origin and Evolution* (New York: College Art Association of America, 1947); Loren Partridge and Randolph Starn, *A Renaissance Likeness: Art and Culture in Raphael's Julius II* (Berkeley: University of California Press, 1979).

42 Joseph Koerner, *The Moment of Self-portraiture in German Renaissance Art* (Chicago: University of Chicago Press, 1993).

43 Stephen Greenblatt, *Renaissance Self-Fashioning from More to Shakespeare* (Chicago: University of Chicago Press, 1980), 1.

44 Cited in Grassi, "Lineamenti," 481–83.

45 Joshua Reynolds, *Discourses on Art*, ed. Robert R. Wark (New Haven: Yale University Press, 1975), Discourse IV.

46 Michel Foucault, *The Archaeology of Knowledge* (1969), trans. A. M. Sheridan Smith (London: Tavistock Publications, 1972).

47 *Catalogue of the Portraits and Pictures in the Different Houses Belonging to the Earl of Fife* (1798; copy in Society of Antiquaries Library, London, inscribed 1796), introduction, n.p., quoted in full in Marcia Pointon, *Hanging the Head: Portraiture and Social Formation in Eighteenth-Century England* (New Haven: Yale University Press, 1993), 2.

48 Kathleen Wilson, *This Island Race: Englishness, Empire and Gender in the Eighteenth Century* (London: Routledge, 2003); Quilley and Kriz, *Economy of Colour*; Harriet Guest, "Curiously Marked: Tattooing, Masculinity, and Nationality in Eighteenth-Century British Perceptions of the South Pacific," in *Painting and the Politics of Culture: New Essays on British Art 1700–1850*, ed. John Barrell (Oxford: Oxford University Press, 1992), 68–90.

49 Harry Berger Jr., *Fictions of the Pose: Rembrandt against the Italian Renaissance* (Stanford: Stanford University Press, 1999); Abigail Solomon-Godeau, *Photography at the Dock* (Minneapolis: University of Minnesota Press, 1991); Wendy Steiner, *Exact Resemblance to Exact Resemblance: The Literary Portraiture of Gertrude Stein* (New Haven: Yale University Press, 1978).

50 On this see Marcia Pointon, "Kahnweiler's Picasso; Picasso's Kahnweiler," in *Portraiture: Facing the Subject*, ed. Joanna Woodall (Manchester: Manchester University Press, 1997), 189–202.

51 See, for example, the installation *Insurrection!* at the New York Guggenheim Museum in the year 2000 and at the Boston Museum of Fine Arts in 2008. On Kara Walker see Jerry Saltz, "Kara Walker: Ill Will and Desire," *Flash Art* 29, no. 191 (November–December 1996), 82–86.

52 There are several accounts of this event including that in Pliny's *Natural History*, Book IX. For a convenient summary of the literature on the Corinthian maid see Ann Bermingham, "The Origin of Painting and the Ends of Art: Wright of Derby's *Corinthian Maid*," in Barrell, *Painting and the Politics of Culture*, 135–66.

53 Deuteronomy 5:6–21.

54 In Lorne Campbell, *Renaissance Portraits* (New Haven: Yale University Press, 1990).

55 On Calvinism and portraiture see Wayne Craven, *Colonial American Portraiture: The Economic, Religious, Social, Cultural, Philosophical, Scientific, and Aesthetic Foundations* (Cambridge: Cambridge University Press, 1986).

56 Location and artist unknown, photo Friends' House Library, London, reproduced in Marcia Pointon, "Quakerism and Visual Culture," *Art History* 20, no. 3 (1997), 414.

57 See Thomas Clarkson, *A Portraiture of the Christian Profession and Practice of the Society of Friends*, 3rd ed. (London: Blackie, 1869), 81–82.

58 I am appropriating here Pierre Bourdieu's term from *Distinction: A Social Critique of the Judgement of Taste*, trans. Richard Nice (London: Routledge and Kegan Paul, 1986), ch. 3. Although Bourdieu's "habitus" is a sociological concept tied to economic and class positionality, I want to suggest a notion based on the construction and representation of individuality.

59 Peter Erickson, "Invisibility Speaks" has much to say on this, but see also Ann Rosalind Jones and Peter Stallybrass, *Renaissance Clothing and the Materials of Memory* (Cambridge: Cambridge University Press, 2000), ch. 2.

60 Jean-Paul Sartre, *L'Imaginaire*, quoted in Grassi, "Lineamenti," 479.

61 I am thinking here of Edward Said's *Orientalism* (1978; Harmondsworth: Penguin, 1985), and of Derrida's discussion of Khōra in Jacques Derrida, *On the Name* (1993), trans. David Wood et al. (Stanford: Stanford University Press, 1995), 89 and passim.

62 Phillis Wheatley, *Complete Writings*, ed. Vincent Carretta (Harmondsworth: Penguin, 2001), introduction.

63 Vincent Carretta, "'Property of the Author': Olaudah Equiano's Place in the History of the Book," in Vincent Carretta and Philip Gould, eds., *Genius in Bondage: Literature of the Early Black Atlantic* (Lexington: University of Kentucky Press, 2001), 136. On Phillis Wheatley and Scipio Moorhead see Eric Slauter's essay in this volume.

64 *Twelve Years a Slave. Narrative of Solomon Northup, a citizen of New York, Kidnapped in Washington City in 1841, and rescued in 1853 from a cotton plantation*

near the Red River in Louisiana (New York: C. M. Saxton, 1859); *Life of William Grimes the Runaway Slave brought down to the present time, written by himself* (New Haven: published by the author, 1855). For a heavily annotated edition of Grimes, see William L. Andrews and Regina E. Mason, eds., *Life of William Grimes, the Runaway Slave* (Oxford: Oxford University Press, 2008). I am grateful to Regina Mason for an email about her notes on the authorship of the portrait. The portrait of Grimes was a wood engraving by Lockwood Sanford after a daguerreotype by Henry Wells, both with businesses in New Haven. So it had gone through two interpretative procedures before reaching the page (see Andrews and Mason, *Life of William Grimes,* 112, notes 115 and 116).

65 It was engraved by Bartolozzi in 1781 after the portrait from life by Thomas Gainsborough.

66 Carretta, "'Property of the Author,'" 136. On the frontispiece see also Gwendolyn DuBois Shaw's essay "'On Deathless Glories Fix Thine Ardent View': Scipio Moorhead, Phillis Wheatley, and the Mythic Origins of Anglo-African Portraiture in New England," *Portraits of a People: Picturing African-Americans in the Nineteenth Century* (Seattle: University of Washington Press, 2006).

67 Sold by New York Public Library at Sotheby's New York, November 30, 2005, lot 4, sale N08134; nineteenth-century wood engraving, British Museum.

68 David Dabydeen, *Hogarth's Blacks: Images of Blacks in Eighteenth-Century English Art* (Mundelstrap, Denmark: Dangaroo Press, 1985); Amussen, *Caribbean Exchanges.*

69 Bruno Latour, *Pandora's Hope: Essays on the Reality of Science Studies* (Cambridge, Mass.: Harvard University Press, 1999), 270–74.

70 The painting is in the Huntington Art Collections, San Marino, California; it was etched and reproduced in *A Catalogue of Pictures by British Artists in the Possession of Sir John Felming Leicester,* Bart, in 1821, and further reproduced many times thereafter.

71 The reference here is to the widely disseminated work of Johann Caspar Lavater, *Essays on Physiognomy,* trans. Thomas Holcroft (London: G. G. J. and J. Robinson, 1789).

72 Bindman, *Ape to Apollo.*

73 This return to likeness might be understood as a form of what Homi Bhabha calls "mimicry," when he proposes that colonial discourse is split into two attitudes towards external reality: one taking reality into consideration, the other disavowing reality and replacing it by a product of desire that repeats and rearticulates reality as "mimicry." See Homi Bhabha, "Signs Taken for Wonders: Questions of Ambivalence and Authority under a Tree Outside Delhi, May 1817," in Henry Louis Gates, Jr., ed., *"Race," Writing, and Difference* (Chicago: University of Chicago Press, 1986), 163–84.

74 *The Metamorphoses of Ovid,* trans. M. M. Innes (Harmondsworth: Penguin, 1955), book iii.

75 Lacan's famous lecture on the mirror phase, delivered in 1949, is reprinted as chapter 1 in *Écrits: A Selection,* translated from the French by Alan Sheridan (1977; London: Tavistock, 1982).

76 Marina Warner, "Psychic Time; or The Metamorphosis of Narcissus," in Christopher Bucklow, *If This Be Not I* (London: British Museum and Grasmere: Wordsworth Trust, 2004), 7–8.

77 Ibid.

78 Ibid.

79 Alexandre Kojève, *Introduction to the Reading of Hegel: Lectures on the "Phenomenology of Spirit,"* assembled by Raymond Quesneau, ed. Allan Bloom, trans. James H. Nichols, Jr. (New York: Basic Books, 1969), 12–22.

TWO

SUBJECTIVITY AND SLAVERY IN PORTRAITURE

FROM COURTLY TO COMMERCIAL SOCIETIES

David Bindman

A small number of European portraits from the sixteenth to the eighteenth century have survived in which Africans or those of African descent are the primary subject, but in an infinitely greater number they are present but visually subordinate to a European male or female, or a child of either sex. The genre of master/mistress accompanied by an adoring servant/slave was essentially invented by the great Venetian artist Titian, and the first identifiable example is the portrait of Laura Dianti, Duke Alfonso of Ferrara's mistress, painted in the 1520s (Fig. 2.1).[1] The sitter is shown in a radiant blue dress, accompanied by a small, probably male, black attendant in an elaborately striped garment, who looks up adoringly at his mistress, who in turn rests her left hand on his shoulder affectionately. The adoring look expresses the subordination of the child to the main subject of the picture, whose whiteness of skin is set off by his darkness. His presence also indicates the superior status of the sitter, as well as her ease with a subordinate, who in this case would probably have accompanied her everywhere.

The representation of blacks in portraiture was not, as is often supposed, simply a function of empire or the slave trade. Though the slave trade was a necessary condition for the acquisition of black domestic slaves, they were acquired often by wealthy inhabitants of countries not directly involved in the trade. On plantations black slaves were economic units, organized into gangs and compelled to carry out hard and repetitive work until they could no longer do it. At European courts, on the other hand, were found only small numbers of blacks, their primary role being to contribute an exotic note to the theatricality of court life. This theatricality was based on the paradox that court societies were both self-enclosed yet acutely conscious of being observed by those outside the court. In the ill-fated court of Charles I, for example, the ceremonial heart of court

2.1. Titian, *Laura Dianti*, 1523–25. Oil on canvas. Kisters Collection, Switzerland. Photo: Alinari/Art Resource, New York.

life was the masque in which an elaborate drama was acted out for the court itself, in allegorical praise of the monarch. In many masques the allegorical hero, embodying the nation in his highest spiritual existence, was played by the king himself, making the point that in a court only the king was in possession of full subjectivity; even the grandest aristocrats were only servants in his presence. By "full subjectivity" I mean here not the "truth" of a singular inner life in its plenitude but the visual fictions by which an entity is projected as possessing a sovereign, coherent, and self-contained individuality. Though the audience was the court itself, knowledge of the masque was conveyed through ambassadors and printed texts, and ordinary people and petitioners were allowed access to processions and some ceremonies.

Africans at the grander European courts and sometimes in the smaller ones might be ambassadors from African countries, members of the court bureaucracy, dancers, acrobats, and musicians, and slaves and servants both to the household and to individuals, male and female. As body servants and grooms they could signify the "Turkish" splendor of the court, and its reach beyond Europe. The Ottoman court was seen as the most splendid and worthy of emulation in its ceremonies, and the role of black slaves was much commented on in Europe. Aaron Hill in *A Full and Just Account of the Present State of the Ottoman Empire* (1709) notes that slaves are everywhere at the court including the harem, yet it was possible to be both a slave and of high rank, and slaves were not necessarily black. People were bought as slaves in every country and educated to servitude from youth or infancy, though blacks invariably were slaves.

Blacks in Europe could act as a foil to the civility of the court, and in this they shared the role with others from outside Europe, and in some cases from within Europe. The full subjectivity allowed only to princes could be replicated in aristocratic households on a smaller scale. There are many portraits in which a prince or high-ranking courtier is accompanied by a black horse groom in a turban who gazes at the commanding figure of his master with awe, and portraits of noble women whose child body servants are equally rendered open-mouthed by their beauty. These black children, both male and female, were nameless and in many cases did not exist outside the painting. They are almost always dressed in exceptional finery and with turbans, but their role was not always given to blacks. It could also be given to dwarfs and those from the Indian subcontinent; it was only necessary that they be obviously different in physical type from the principal subject of the painting.

It is not coincidental that the presence of black attendants in paintings should originate at a court, for that was to be the primary home for elaborately dressed black pages well into the eighteenth century. They also begin to accompany aristocratic males in the sixteenth century, the first portrait that we can identify being Paris Bordone's *Portrait of a Man in Armor with Two Pages* (ca. 1555–60),[2] in which the subject is shown accompanied by two elegantly dressed boys, one black, holding the soldier's helmet, and the other white. Here the boys are adolescent and are properly described as grooms for they are usually associated with horses engaged in hunting or, as in this case, in battle.

Influential though they were to become in the seventeenth and eighteenth centuries, such portraits are relatively rare in the sixteenth century. The influence of the Laura Dianti portrait was transmitted through an engraving after it produced ca. 1600,[3] and by the time of Rubens and Van Dyck black pages become reasonably common in courtly portraits produced in Italy and the northern countries, though it should be emphasized that they are less common than white pages, or indeed dwarfs and buffoons. Perhaps the most spectacular portrait of a woman with a black page is of Marchesa Elena Grimaldi Cattaneo by Van Dyck (1623), from the artist's period in Genoa.[4] The black page follows behind her, shielding her from the sun with a large parasol. He is clearly an adolescent, not a child, and he brings an exotic and dramatic note to the scene that sets it apart from the other grand female portraits of the artist's Genoese period.

Such portraits, usually on a more modest scale, sometimes of family groups with a black attendant, are common throughout Europe in the seventeenth century, and they are far from exclusive to slave-trading countries, though in countries such as England, France, and Holland they would have been easier to obtain. If in most countries in the seventeenth century the presence of black pages in supporting roles in portraits remained tied to the court, in Holland and England, as commerce began to separate rank from class and create a wealthy

2.2. Joshua Reynolds, *Paul Henry Ourry*, ca. 1748. Oil on canvas. Saltram, Devonshire, U.K. Photo: National Trust/Art Resource, New York.

bourgeoisie, so the possession of slaves began to spread beyond the court, first in Holland, then in England. In Joshua Reynolds's portrait from around 1748 of the naval officer First Lieutenant Paul Henry Ourry (Fig. 2.2), the subject is a gentleman and naval officer, emphatically not a courtier.[5] He gazes commandingly into the distance, oblivious to the exotically dressed black boy's admiring gaze. The boy provides a vivid, exotic, and polychromatic foil to the relative austerity of the sailor's figure, and his skin color, a rich olive brown, is set off strikingly against the near white of his hat and shirt ruffle, and against his master's ruddy features. The portrait is a celebration of Ourry's prowess as a sea captain. It was commissioned by the go-ahead trading port of Plympton on the Devon coast, and the presence of the black servant suggests the new horizons opening in the time of an emergent British empire through trade in distant and exotic lands, which brought riches and new knowledge to the nation under the aegis of such gallant sailors. It is not coincidental that the painting is broadly contemporary with the composition of the song *Rule, Britannia!* with its refrain: "Britons never, never, never shall be slaves!"[6]

Eighteenth-century portraits, whether they are of male or female sitters or contain male or female black servants, evoke more clearly than in earlier centuries through their visual rhetoric a series of ever-expanding binary oppositions: Europe/Africa, subject/object, white/black, free man/captive, owner/slave, civility/savagery, and so on. Yet the actual relationship between master/mistress and slave/servant was inevitably fraught with contradictions, which may or may not be visible in the paintings. In the Ourry portrait the slave/servant had one primary – perhaps *the* primary – element of identification as a subject: a name of his own, Jersey,[7] though its Englishness makes it clear that it was one imposed by the owner or master/mistress.

The terms "slave" and "portrait" constitute together an oxymoron, a contradiction in terms, for a portrait such as that of Ourry has as its defining purpose the affirmation of the sitter's subjectivity, autonomy, and integrity. He exercises with confidence – even arrogance – the "freedom" enjoyed by Britons but denied by definition to slaves. The painting is not by a strict definition a *portrait* of the black boy, though it may represent him convincingly. Whether or not he was a slave in the legal sense might be possible to find out if the relevant family legal papers have survived, but he is certainly constituted in the painting as one by his emphatic difference from his owner or master. In late-seventeenth- and early-eighteenth-century examples of this kind of portrait the black boy often wears a conspicuous slave collar, as in, for instance, Godfrey Kneller's portrait of Sir Thomas Lucy in Household Guards' uniform of 1680.[8] The black figure is a groom, and his slave status is clearly emphasized by the silver collar around his neck, which would have been both ornamental and a precaution against escape, for they were irremovable without a key and were usually inscribed with the owner's coat-of-arms or address. As such portraits became current in

2.3. Gerard Hoet after Godfrey Kneller, *Frederick Duke of Schonberg*, ca. 1689. Mezzotint. British Museum, London. © Trustees of the British Museum, London.

more bourgeois circles in the eighteenth century the page's subordination is figured as "natural," even voluntary, as if he became a slave because of his awe-struck admiration for the portrait's subject.

Though there were free blacks in Europe, who had either been freed or were descended from freed slaves, Jersey's youth suggests he was owned rather than employed, and it is most likely that he was acquired in the course of a naval expedition to acquire slaves for the West Indian or American plantations. Even so there could be a fine line between slavery and indentured labor in real life, and between a slave and a servant or groom in portraits. We need to be particularly sensitive to period here, for there was an enormous difference in the perception of slavery between the first and second half of the eighteenth century; if the conspicuous ownership of finely dressed slaves was still a sign of elevated status in the late 1740s, by the 1760s it was in the process of being discredited by the abolition campaigns, though there are some surprising later examples by Reynolds that will be discussed below.

We need also to be clear that such portraits do not provide a simple template of master/slave relations in England at the time they were painted. Black slave/servants appear in only a minority of portraits of that time, and they do not represent an index of the availability of black slaves, or even prove that the sitter owned one, for they may be fictive, or provided by the painter. Godfrey Kneller inserts a black horse groom in his portrait of Frederick Herman, Duke of Schonberg (1615–90), commander-in-chief of the British forces in Ireland (Fig. 2.3), and a very similar one in his portrait of the Duke of Marlborough (ca. 1689).[9] The mezzotint version of the latter by John Smith is taken from the same copper plate as the one after the Schonberg portrait, but with the head of the principal subject altered in the plate.[10] Such an example might suggest that the black pages in these paintings are fictive, copied from other paintings. But they could be taken from posed figures of black servants owned or employed by the painter, as in the case of a drawing by Godfrey Kneller (Fig. 2.4),[11] which shows a black youth, almost certainly drawn from life, in an attitude not dissimilar from that of the groom in the Schonberg and Marlborough portraits.

The conjunction of relatively soberly dressed subject and exotic African boy in Reynolds's Ourry portrait belongs, as we have seen, to a familiar typology of a ruler or person of high status, whether male or female, that originated in courtly representation and courtly theatricality. The context of the Ourry portrait is, of course, both socially and physically remote from court life, but in eighteenth-century England there was even among the trading community, some of whom might have aspirations to join the rural gentry, nostalgia for the life of the Stuart court and the patrician ease of Van Dyck's portraits. This was encouraged by portrait painters such as Reynolds and Gainsborough, who saw in their great seventeenth-century predecessor an artist who had achieved supreme mastery and had received recognition from the highest in the land. Even as portraiture in England became independent of the court, it continued to confer dignity on sitters through courtly accessories and attributes, among which we can count black pages, grooms, and body servants.[12]

2.4. Godfrey Kneller, *Two Studies of a Black Page*, 1685–90. Black chalk, touched with white, on blue-gray paper. British Museum, London. © Trustees of the British Museum, London.

Gainsborough seems never to have painted a black page in any of his portraits, but he was, of course, the author of the celebrated portrait of the black musician and writer

Ignatius Sancho, painted in Bath in 1768. Sancho belonged to a small number of blacks in Britain who managed to break free of their servitude and make a position for themselves in the intellectual world of the time (Fig. 2.5).[13] Reynolds, on the other hand, depicted black servants on several occasions in his mature career (the portrait of Ourry is an early work). Their seeming celebration of a relationship based on slavery is hard to reconcile with Reynolds's close connections with abolitionist circles through his friendship with Bennet Langton (1737–1801), called by Thomas Clarkson a "friend of humanity [who] lamented over the miseries of the oppressed Africans, and over the crimes of their tyrants

2.5. Thomas Gainsborough, *Ignatius Sancho*, 1768. Oil on canvas. National Gallery of Canada, Ottawa. © National Gallery of Canada, Ottawa.

2.6. Joshua Reynolds, *John Manners, Marquess of Granby*, 1766. Oil on canvas. Collection of the John and Mable Ringling Museum of Art, the State Art Museum of Florida, a Division of Florida State University. Bequest of John Ringling, SN389. © John and Mable Ringling Museum of Art, Sarasota, the State Art Museum of Florida.

as friend to morality and religion."[14] Clarkson noted that at a dinner to raise support for his anti–slave trade campaign, "Sir Joshua Reynolds gave his unqualified approbation of the abolition of this cruel traffic."[15] Two of the portraits, of John Manners, Marquess of Granby (Fig. 2.6), and Count Schaumburg-Lippe, belong to the mid-1760s, when the painter was absorbed in the whole question of the Great Style and the need for heroic painting.[16] The portrait of Schaumburg-Lippe follows a continental pattern in depicting a turbaned black groom bringing up the horse to the Count, who stands in imperious isolation.

2.7. Guilaume du Mortier, *Antonio Emanuele Ne Vunda*, 1608. Etching. Private collection.

In the Granby portrait, painted to commemorate Granby's victory against the French at Vellinghausen in 1761, the black groom, wearing a jeweled turban with a feather, is also associated with the horse against which he leans. His head and his hand in motion are painted with an uncommon vividness that contrasts his excitement in the battle with his master's calmness and command. Instead of looking adoringly toward the Marquess, he turns suddenly to look into the distance, as if he has seen something alarming, forgetting momentarily to show the expected servility and deference.

In the few cases before the nineteenth century in which blacks were granted the full subjectivity of a professional portrait, they had come directly from Africa and were believed to have been of princely rank, whatever that might mean in the African context. The early-seventeenth-century ambassador of Kongo to the Papacy known as Antonio Emanuele Ne Vunda was the subject not of a portrait in the usual sense but of memorializations that included portraits of him (Fig. 2.7).[17] He was on his way to Rome as the guest of the Pope, who was interested in converting the Congo to Christianity, but he was shipwrecked and died soon after being visited by the Pope himself. A monument was proposed for Santa Maria Maggiore, and two engravings exist that might be connected with different schemes for it, both foregrounding his portrait.[18] The first shows him as a European gentleman in a Spanish style, only the darkness of his skin indicating his African origins. The other proposal, as it happens closer to the one adopted, emphasizes his "savagery," showing him carrying a bow and arrow with a battle scene below; nonetheless he is fully articulated as a person with name, position, and rank, who has made a choice to follow the true faith.

The painted portrait and the mezzotint after it of William Ansah Sessarakoo by Gabriel Mathias made in London in 1749 had more to do with the urban world of commerce than with court life, but it is essential to the romance that surrounded Sessarakoo's visit to London that he was, in the words of a newspaper, "A Young African Prince, Sold for a Slave." Sessarakoo was, in fact, the son of a wealthy West African slave trader who had been sent by his father on a Grand Tour of Europe.[19] Unfortunately he fell victim to the treachery of his ship's captain, who sold him into slavery, from which he escaped by means, it was assumed, of the superior resourcefulness of his rank, but in reality because the British government wished to keep on good terms with his father. This exploit made him an instant celebrity in mid-eighteenth-century London, and his aura of romance was essentially constructed from two popular tales of the day: *Inkle and Yarico*, which tells of an unscrupulous English trader who sells his black mistress into slavery because her pregnancy has made her worth twice as much, and *Oroonoko*, an African prince of immaculate aristocratic bearing, who is also sold into slavery, but overcomes it through nobility of character.[20]

The extended inscription on the mezzotint after Mathias's painting, "William Ansah Sessarakoo Son of John Bannishee Corrantee Sinnee of Anamaboe and of Eukobah Daughter of Ansah Sessarakoo King of Aquamboo & Niece to Quishadoo King of Akroan. He was sold at Barbadoes as a slave in Year 1744 Redeem'd at the Earnest Request of his Father in the year 1748, and brought to England," makes much of Sessarakoo's royal ancestry and his redemption from slavery, and he is presented in the portrait as a gentleman in an elaborately brocaded jacket with a hat under his left arm. It is not clear whether he is wearing a wig, but his hair is very black and straight and not frizzy. Some stereotypical emphasis is placed on the prominence of the lips, but the pose and brocade define him as a person of rank and social distinction, for his dress, despite its elaboration, is not at all comparable to Jersey's exotic apparel in the Ourry portrait.

If a tragic tale was necessary to make Sessarakoo famous enough to be worthy of a portrait in fashionable London, Africans were occasionally able to reach such an honored position in continental European courts. The most prominent "Hofneger" was Angelo Soliman (ca. 1721–96),[21] who achieved a high position at the grandest European court of all, the Imperial court in Vienna, and was the subject of a fine portrait, known from a mezzotint by J. G. Haid (Fig. 2.8). Soliman had been brought as a slave from Africa and after service for a Sicilian nobleman entered the service of the Vienna court in 1733, following

2.8. Johann Gottfried Haid after Johann Nepomuk Steiner, *Angelo Soliman*, ca. 1750. Mezzotint. Menil Collection, Houston. Photo: Janet Woodard, Houston.

his conversion to Catholicism. His abilities and physical presence enabled him to reach a prominent position, and his standing was confirmed by marriage to a wealthy and well-connected general's widow, Magdalena Christina Kellerman. He became a member of the Masonic lodge *Zu Wahren Eintracht* (To True Harmony), to which Mozart and Haydn belonged. His portrait by Johann Nepomuk Steiner is a fascinating mélange of conflicting signifiers. His turban identifies him as a servant, but he is elegantly dressed in a fur-edged jacket, and he faces the viewer as if addressing a fellow courtier. His Africanness is signified by the landscape with a palm tree and two pyramids in the distance, but rather than savage Africa, it is Egypt that is evoked, the Egypt of ancient and hidden truths, and an ancient harmony hinted at in *The Magic Flute* (*Die Zauberflöte*) by his Masonic companion Wolfgang Amadeus Mozart. If the Turkish and African attributes identify him as a "stranger," he is nonetheless presented in full self-possession, engaging as an equal with the observer of his portrait as befitting his rank at court.

It might seem self-evident that the European-wide campaigns for the abolition of the slave trade of the 1770s and later would have killed off the courtly traditions that allowed for portraits in which blacks are subordinated to their white masters and mistresses. However, as we have seen in the case of Reynolds's mature portraits, connections that might seem obvious with hindsight were not always made at the time. I would argue that the abolition campaigns did not in themselves put an end to portraits with slaves, but rather that these portraits were rejected because of a sea change in European ideas of human difference, of which abolitionism was only an aspect. The highly influential Enlightenment morphologies of Linnaeus and Buffon, developed in the mid-eighteenth century, though they preserved a sense of European superiority, were based on the ancient idea that each continent had its own separate inhabitants who were descended from the original human tribe dispersed at the Fall. Their work opened up the possibility that human beings could be classified across the whole world broadly by methods used already to classify animals and plants. The question was how: by biological difference, skin color, or physiognomy?

Physiognomy, through the study and measurement of the human skull, was eventually to triumph as the principal index of what was defined as "racial" difference.[22] For more thoughtful artists this made their profession more rather than less problematic, for they were faced, especially by Johann Caspar Lavater's highly influential volumes on physiognomy in which he diligently reproduced objections to his theory, with a plethora of different possibilities. This ferment comes clearly to the fore in a fascinating little etching by the Berlin printmaker Daniel Chodowiecki, who, apart from making many portrait etchings himself, had provided illustrations in the 1780s both for Lavater's *Physiognomy* and

2.9. Daniel Chodowiecki, *La Cervelle d'un peintre*, 1792. Etching. Private collection.

for a book by Johann Friedrich *Blumenbach* that summarized his new racial categories.[23]

The etching is dated 1792 and is entitled *La Cervelle d'un peintre* (Fig. 2.9).[24] The French word *cervelle* in the eighteenth century was normally used to indicate the brain in the physical sense, rather than the mind, which would have been *le cerveau*. In the etching the painter's brain is made up of a jumble of different physiognomies, human and animal, some in profile, some in full face, some serious, some caricatured. The head prominently in the center is an ideal Greek one, an Apollo with a straight profile from forehead to nose. At the far left an African head is superimposed on that of a boar, perhaps signifying wildness, but some of the human-animal connections are more comic than serious, such as the pompous bewigged figure on the right who is implicitly compared to a cockerel, turkey, and duck. The head beneath him appears to be a Jew, and a grinning skull refers both to mortality and to the importance of the skull in defining character and type, while the presence of animals refers both to the traditional physiognomical comparison of animal and human types and emotions and to the weighty issue of the categorical division between animals and humanity.

The nonhierarchical juxtaposition of these diverse heads suggests something other than a binary opposition between Europe and the rest of the world, or a simple polarity between civility and savagery, or even human and animal. It hints also at the world of a commercial city, such as late-eighteenth-century Berlin where the artist lived, in which different people jostle in the street, ostensibly on equal terms. Only the ideal stands above the bustle as the antique head does in the print, but even Apollo has difficulty in asserting himself in this crowd. One might also see in the print a reference to the equalizing effect of the French Revolution, a matter of intense interest in the liberal and sophisticated circles in Berlin to which Chodowiecki belonged. Of course, Berlin continued to have a powerful court culture, and Chodowiecki's own enlightened circle was a small one, but the fundamental revision of human nature implied in the print rapidly undermined many courtly assumptions, despite vigorous attempts to reassert them in the nineteenth century.

The portrait with accompanying black servant disappeared almost everywhere in Europe after 1800, except in Russia where there are notable examples by Karl Briullov (1799–1852), especially his large portrait of Countess Giulia Pavlovna Samoilova, which surprisingly dates from as late as the 1830s.[25] The lack of such portraits elsewhere did not result in a surge in portraits of individual blacks, which still remain rare in the early nineteenth century, despite some prominent examples. There is, however, an increase in the scientific and artistic study of black typologies. Art students in all European academies were now brought up on Pieter Camper's diagrams of human racial skulls published internationally in the 1780s and 1790s,[26] which sought to depict accurately the "essential" characteristics of each racial or ethnic type.

I want to end, however, by returning to a methodological issue raised by this brief account of portraiture in relation to slavery. Images – and this no doubt applies equally to texts – not only reflect their own period but also work within conventions inherited from an earlier and what might be a completely different period. Thus conventions, as with the representation of black servants within a portrait, that arose in a context of court absolutism can continue to resonate and even be revived in what we now want to define as a commercial society, such as eighteenth-century England. Such conventions can be refigured and made to survive in the fictions of representation as they do in manners, clothing, and even morality. Hence we have to be aware of the inherited conventions or language of each medium of expression we consider, and this is where specialists in each field come into their own. Art historians used to be criticized, not unjustly, for their excessive concern with "influence," but it remains a corrective to the facile assumption that every aspect of a work can be related directly to the larger history of each period. This is not meant to be an argument against interdisciplinarity, but simply to say that ultimately it can be successful only if it is based on the specialized insights and knowledge of individual disciplines.

Notes

1 See Paul H. D. Kaplan in David Bindman and Henry Louis Gates, Jr., eds., *The Image of the Black in Western Art* (Cambridge, Mass.: Harvard University Press, 2010), vol. III.1, 107–10.

2 Ibid., *Pages and Other Attendants*, 126, fig. 55.
3 Ibid., 109.
4 Jean Michel Massing in David Bindman and Henry Louis Gates, Jr., eds., *The Image of the Black in Western Art* (Cambridge, Mass.: Harvard University Press, 2011), vol. III.2, 223, fig. 144.
5 For modern accounts of the painting see Nicholas Penny, ed., *Reynolds* (London: Royal Academy of Arts with Weidenfeld and Nicholson, 1986), no. 11, 173–74; David Mannings, *Sir Joshua Reynolds, Complete Catalogue* (New Haven, Conn.: Yale University Press, 2000), no. 1372; and David Bindman in Bindman and Gates, *The Image of the Black*, vol. III.3, 135–38.
6 Written by James Thomson and included in *Alfred: An English Masque*, with music by Thomas Arne, 1740, and premiered in London in 1745.
7 Penny, *Reynolds*, 173.
8 J. Douglas Stewart, *Sir Godfrey Kneller and the English Baroque Portrait* (Oxford: Oxford University Press, 1985), 24, 26 no. 44; Bindman in Bindman and Gates, *The Image of the Black*, vol. III.1, 259, fig. 141.
9 Bindman in Bindman and Gates, *The Image of the Black*, vol. III.1, 259–62, fig. 144.
10 British Museum, no. 1935.0413.147.
11 See Lindsay Stainton and Christopher White, *Drawing in England: From Hilliard to Hogarth* (British Museum, 1987) no. 141.
12 In reality Van Dyck depicted black attendants in only less than a handful of cases. For paintings by Van Dyck that include black servants and pages see Susan J. Barnes, Nora de Poorter, Oliver Millar, and Horst Vey, *Van Dyck, A Complete Catalogue of the Paintings* (New Haven: Yale University Press, 2004), 2:43, 2:45, 3:102.
13 Hugh Honour, *The Image of the Black in Western Art* (Houston: Menil Foundation, 1989), vol. 4.1, 30; Bindman, "Am I Not a Man and a Brother? British Art and Slavery in the Eighteenth Century," *RES* 26 (Fall 1994), 71, fig. 3.
14 Thomas Clarkson, *History of the Rise, Progress, and Accomplishment of the Abolition of the African Slave Trade*, 2 vols. (London, 1808), I:220.
15 Ibid., I:253. See also Karen C. C. Dalton, "Images of Africans and Abolitionism in Eighteenth-Century England," paper delivered at the "Looking Back with Pleasure" Conference, University of Utah, Salt Lake City, 27–28 October 1989, 5.
16 Mannings, *Reynolds*, no. 1198; Martin Postle, *Joshua Reynolds: The Creation of Celebrity*, Tate Britain (London, 2005), 104; E. K. Waterhouse, *Painting in Britain, 1530–1790* (Harmondsworth: Pelican, 1978), 221–27.
17 Paul H. D. Kaplan in Bindman and Gates, *The Image of the Black*, vol. III.1, 160–67.
18 Ladislas Bugner, *L'Image du Noir dans l'art occidental*, vol. 3, part 1: *XVIe siècle*, Menil Foundation, Paris, 1992 (unpublished), 141–46.
19 Gretchen Gerzina, *Black London: Life before Emancipation* (New Brunswick, N.J.: Rutgers University Press, 1995), 11–12.
20 Bindman in Bindman and Gates, *The Image of the Black*, vol. III.3, 4–5.
21 Peter Martin, *Schwarze Teufel, edle Mohren* (Hamburg: Junius, 1993), 232–40.
22 David Bindman, *Ape to Apollo* (Ithaca, N.Y.: Cornell University Press, 2002), 201f.
23 *Beyträge zur Naturgeschichte* (Göttingen: Bey Johann Christian Dieterich, 1790).

24 Wilhelm Engelmann, *Daniel Chodowicki's sämmtliche Kupferstiche* (Leipzig: Engelmann, 1857), no. 696.
25 Kaplan in David Bindman and Henry Louis Gates, Jr. eds., *The Image of the Black in Western Art*, vol. IV.2 (Cambridge, Mass.: Harvard University Press, 2012).
26 See Bindman, *Ape to Apollo,* 204–5.

THREE

LOOKING FOR SCIPIO MOORHEAD

AN "AFRICAN PAINTER" IN REVOLUTIONARY NORTH AMERICA

Eric Slauter

Scipio Moorhead was a young man held in slavery in Boston in the 1760s and 1770s, one of approximately five thousand enslaved persons of African descent in Massachusetts on the eve of the American Revolution. In 1773 Phillis Wheatley, a neighbor and fellow slave, published a poem addressed to Moorhead, whom she described as a "young *African* Painter"; it is her only surviving poem directed to another black person as well as her only poem about art. Literary and art historians have sometimes speculated that Moorhead produced a drawing or painting upon which a well-known London engraving of Wheatley is based (Fig. 3.1), but no direct evidence substantiates the attribution, no other works have come to light, and the materials for narrating Moorhead's life are few. The fact that someone wrote a poem to him is the only thing that truly distinguishes the archival traces left by or around this particular person from the traces of many other enslaved persons whose lives remain largely invisible to us.

What follows is an experimental portrait. In the past few decades scholars have learned to recognize agency and resistance under slavery, to chart the contours of life for free black women and men, and to trace the complex and multidirectional transmissions of culture between blacks and whites. Even still, synthetic composite sketches rather than depictions of individuals dominate the historical literature surrounding the American Revolution. While we are fortunate to have contemporary narratives from a small number of black persons themselves, the records assembled primarily by whites in the eighteenth-century – an archive of births and deaths, of baptisms and sales, of forced migrations and voluntary escapes – make it easier to talk of typical lives or ordinary lives than to recount actual lives.[1] To put Scipio Moorhead at the center of a narrative one has to balance the ordinary and the extraordinary, find the individual within parameters set by typical experience, and focus on the meaning and place of slavery at the

Publiſhed according to Act of Parliament, Sept.r 1st, 1773 by Arch.d Bell,

Bookſeller No. 8 near the Saracens Head Aldgate.

historical moment in which he lived and served. Doing so illuminates a complex matrix of personal choices and larger social forces, and it offers a new perspective on one slave society on the eve of emancipation. To be sure, that perspective is not identical to Scipio Moorhead's. The archives will not allow for a real recovery of his point of view, but they do make it possible to render the life of one individual more visible than it has been and to offer some suggestions about what looking might have meant to him.

On 11 June 1760, a group of white Bostonians presented a black child they called Scipio Sarahson to an Anglican minister for baptism.[2] While it is possible to reconstruct fundamental facts about the white players in this ceremony, and even about the setting in which it took place, the child at its center remains largely invisible. King's Chapel, a stone building sometimes called the masterpiece of the first architect of British America, may itself have been partially constructed by unfree black laborers. Once inside the building, social conventions segregated black and white parishioners. In the recent past numerous whites had brought children of African descent to Rev. Henry Caner for baptism. Thomas Hase, one of Scipio's sponsors, was a cordwainer or shoemaker; he held the title to a pew in King's Chapel and had served as a witness at the infant baptisms of at least two other slaves before Scipio Sarahson, including Rev. Caner's own slave Pompey; six years later Caner would baptize Hase's slave Crispin. Scipio's other sponsor was Sarah Parsons Moorhead, a published poet who had occasionally taught children how to draw, paint, and embroider.[3] Sarah Moorhead was married to the pastor of the Presbyterian Church, Rev. John Moorhead. The surviving baptismal record describes Scipio Sarahson as "a Negroe Servant to Revd John Morehead," but in late colonial New England a "Negroe Servant" was synonymous with a slave. Sarah and John owned Scipio.

How did this young person come to be in King's Chapel on that June day, to be in the possession of the Moorheads, to be called "Scipio" at all? Scipio Sarahson was one of over 400 people baptized in Boston in 1760, but records of baptisms accumulated and annually published in newspapers did not (as records of burials did) break the numbers down by skin color or by age. In the middle of the eighteenth century, whites in New England often imagined and even justified slavery as a temporal exchange for the spiritual comfort of Christianity. Baptizing slaves seemed to make slavery more comfortable for white slaveholders too, though they often nervously went out of their way to note that baptism did not alter a black person's legal status.[4]

Scipio Sarahson's baptismal record indicates that he was baptized as a child rather than as an infant, but although the distinction had some theological

3.1 (*on facing page*). (After Scipio Moorhead?), *Phillis Wheatley, Negro Servant to Mr. John Wheatley, of Boston.* Frontispiece and title page to Phillis Wheatley, *Poems on Various Subjects, Religious and Moral* (London: printed for A. Bell, 1773). PML 77263. Pierpont Morgan Library, New York. Photo: Pierpont Morgan Library/Art Resource, New York.

importance, it does not provide a precise age. Scipio Sarahson may have been a newborn, or he may have been a few years old. One document from 1774 refers to him as a "Negro young man;" another from January 1775 calls him a "Negro Lad." He may have been as young as twelve in early 1773, when Phillis Wheatley, then about nineteen, addressed him as a "wondr'ous youth" and "a young *African* painter."

His origin is as unclear as his age. Scipio (spelled "Sipeo" in some records, a clue to contemporary pronunciation) was one of the names most frequently given to newly imported black male slaves by white masters in New England in the middle of the eighteenth century. The names of classical worthies and gods that white masters gave to black men in eighteenth-century British America – Scipio, Cato, Caesar, Bacchus, Pompey, Neptune, Nero, and Jupiter were the most common such names in Boston – marked even baptized slaves as pagan or pre-Christian and served to ironize the power dynamic between slaveholders and slaves. The first name suggests that Scipio Sarahson was a newly imported African, but slave traders often avoided transporting infants. In 1795 an aging white Bostonian recalled one cargo of slaves, "between 30 and 40 years ago, which consisted almost wholly of children," and it is possible that the child baptized in 1760 was part of this remembered shipment.[5] But given the presence of a surname on the record it seems unlikely that this young person had just emerged from the hold of a slave ship, as Phillis Wheatley herself did in June 1761.

Sarahson may have been a misspelling of "Saracen," indicating that he was an Arab or a Muslim, but this designation does not seem to appear in other available records. It is possible that the Moorheads may have intended the name ("Scipio Saracen"), which yoked two forces (Roman and Arab) that had conquered the city of Carthage in North Africa, as a kind of classical joke. More likely, the name was an ascribed matronymic, a way of indicating that this child was Sarah's son. Perhaps – and it can only be speculation – he was the son of a "Sarah negrowoman" who was admitted by the Overseers of the Poor to the Boston Almshouse in February 1760 and who died there two and half years later. Either this Sarah arrived without a last name or the overseer in charge of her case refused to record one, a fact that may signal either that Sarah had long been a free black or that she had recently been abandoned by a white slaveholder who wished to remain anonymous in the archives. There is no indication, however, that Sarah arrived with or gave birth to a child, though the absence of such a record may say something about the record keepers. White children of a certain age who became inmates of the Almshouse were apprenticed out for a limited term, but the copious archives of the Overseers of the Poor in Boston say little about what happened to black children.[6] It is entirely possible that some black children were sold or, more likely, given away for unlimited terms to white families who could afford to support them. But, then, there is really no reason, short of desire for genealogical certainty under a system that consciously confounded it, to associate Scipio Sarahson with this particular Sarah or to imagine that the Moorheads took this young person in from the Almshouse.

It is just as likely that the Moorheads took Scipio Sarahson from the house of a slaveholding neighbor. The newspapers of Boston in this period regularly feature advertisements by whites for black infants and children who were easier to give away than to support. The child baptized as Scipio in June 1760 may have been the "likely Negro Child about a month old" advertised as "To be given away" in the *Boston Evening Post* in January. (The description of this as a "likely" black child was not meant to suggest racial uncertainty but rather, in the period vocabulary, that this child was healthy.) But again there is little reason to attach the child in King's Chapel in June to this particular advertisement. Scipio may have been the person advertised as "a Negro Child to be given away" in the *Boston Evening Post* in February; or he may have been the "likely Negro Child to be given away" advertised in the *Boston Gazette*. The only child specifically identified as male in the first six months of 1760, a "Fine Negro Male Child to be given away" advertised in February in the *Boston Weekly News-Letter*, may very well be the same child baptized in June.[7] The newspapers offer possibilities, not certainties.

Newspaper printers served as intermediaries who helped match prospective slave takers with would-be slave givers.[8] In 1748 Sarah Moorhead had advertised her services as an art instructor in Thomas Fleet, Sr.'s *Boston Evening Post*, and so perhaps the Moorheads approached the current printers of that paper, Fleet's sons Thomas and John, and were put in touch with the owners of one of the children advertised in January and February 1760. No other advertisements for male children appeared between March and the baptism in June, but of course it is just as possible that the Moorheads arranged to take possession of Scipio in a private transaction from a neighbor or a member of the congregation of the Presbyterian Church, or that they took the child off someone's hands before an advertisement could be published. And it is also possible that the Moorheads purchased Scipio in an advertised or unadvertised auction, at an estate sale, or from another family.

If Scipio came out of the household of a family known well by the Moorheads, John and Sarah may have also known Scipio's mother. Her owners may have worshiped at John Moorhead's church, and the last name Sarahson in the baptismal record may have served to shield the identity of a white family who offered the little boy to the Moorheads. And if the white Moorheads knew Sarah, it is of course possible that her son grew up in contact with his birth mother. All of this is possible, but even imagining such a possibility risks discounting the division of families and the archival gaps that slavery traded upon. Absent other documents – a bill of sale, or a record in a journal or letter – Scipio's exact origins remain a mystery, a status that slaveholders such as the Moorheads may have preferred.

Surviving archives make it much easier to sketch basic facts about the family Scipio served. Familiarly called "Jonny Moorhead," Scipio's master was born near Belfast, Ireland, in 1703 but educated in Scotland. Part of a small wave of Scotch-Irish migration, he arrived in Boston in 1727 or 1728, helped convert a barn on Long Lane into a meeting house (a designated meeting house was constructed in 1744), and was officially installed as the minister of the Presbyterian Church in 1730. That same year he married Sarah Parsons, an Englishwoman, and they had three children in the 1730s, two sons and a daughter. John and Sarah's daughter, Mary Moorhead, remained single and with her parents until John's death in December 1773 and Sarah's death a year later. Mary, to whom Phillis Wheatley would direct her first poem published after her own emancipation, an elegy on the death of John Moorhead, was twenty-eight when Scipio entered the household, and it is likely that she helped raise Scipio.[9]

John Moorhead probably interacted with black people on a daily basis, even before Scipio came into his house in 1760, but his relations with Boston's black population remain hazy. In 1742, during the religious revivals historians have termed the "Great Awakening," he wrote to an associate in Glasgow about the wave of conversions "amongst Indians, Negroes, Papists, and Protestants of all denominations," but the surviving records of his own church show that he baptized fewer blacks than other churches and officiated at fewer marriage ceremonies between blacks than some of his colleagues. The paucity of the records may, however, be more indicative of the lower social and economic status of Moorhead's congregation, for he was a minister primarily to Irish immigrants, who were themselves less likely to own slaves.

By all accounts, even his eulogist's, John Moorhead was an easily angered person. One early biographer described him as "a man of distinguished talents, and eminent for his piety; but subject to a natural temperament so excitable as frequently to lead to rash and impudent acts and expressions."[10] A nineteenth-century genealogist noted that Moorhead's "ardent and impulsive temper often led him into embarrassments."[11] Contemporaries played jokes on the aging Moorhead, largely to watch him become flustered.[12] Later memorialists dwell on comic moments in which Moorhead seemed to compromise his own authority or to display his incompetence when he tried to seem learned.[13] His fiery temper, a stereotype about the Irish but still a constant theme among contemporaries and later biographers, almost certainly made him a difficult master.

Two contemporary artists rendered John Moorhead, and these images may have been ones that Scipio Moorhead knew well. In 1749 Boston painter John Greenwood produced an oil painting of the minister, a painting that may have hung in either the church in Long Lane (constructed in 1744) or in the Moorhead home near Fort Hill (acquired in 1747). And in 1751 the Boston engraver Peter Pelham ventured that enough subscribers would pay five shillings for an engraving of Moorhead to risk the expense of making a mezzotint portrait, one of the first half dozen such engravings produced in the colonies. Inclusion in Pelham's series of mezzotints depicting Boston clergymen was a testament of sorts to John Moorhead's successful integration into Boston's English society, to his visual equality with Pelham's other subjects – men such as Rev. Henry Caner, the Anglican minister who baptized Scipio, or Rev. Edward Holyoke, the president of Harvard College, who owned a copy of Pelham's *John Moorhead.*[14] But examined side by side with Pelham's other images of Boston clergy – as they might have been at James Buck's print shop, on the walls of a wealthy Bostonian's home, or even seen by Scipio at the Moorhead's – certain distinctions become apparent: Although the images of Anglican and Congregationalist ministers are almost indistinguishable from a certain distance (each wears a similarly august wig and sumptuous robe), Pelham depicted Moorhead in a plain coat and modest wig. The caption to the print describes Moorhead as "Minister of a Church of Presbyterian Strangers at Boston in New England," a description that signaled that he and his congregation continued to remind themselves and be reminded by others of their incomplete assimilation.

As a "stranger" – and especially as an Irishman – John Moorhead faced exclusion and derision from members of Boston's English society, but his rank as minister allowed him to interact with the most powerful men in the colony. Blacks in Boston faced similar obstacles – exclusion, derision, satire, and caricature – though of course they often faced it from within the institution of slavery, and they faced it from Irish immigrants as well. It is impossible to know if the exclusion John must have felt helped him to identify and sympathize with a black slave such as Scipio, or if John Moorhead, easily angered and frustrated in his attempt to place himself "on the same Footing" with other whites, took out his frustrations on Scipio Moorhead.[15]

The sarcastic tone Sarah Parsons Moorhead strikes in some of her poetry, the surviving examples of which are all addressed to ministers, suggests that Scipio's mistress might have been more than able to hold her own with her sometimes verbally challenged husband.[16] One of perhaps only two surviving copies of her 1744 *Poem in Honour of the Reverend Mr. Whitefield* was sent from a minister in Scotland to a minister in Boston, which suggests that the poem may have been printed in Scotland and that Sarah (like her husband) had discovered a transatlantic audience as a result of the religious revivals in her community.[17] Signing her poems as a "Female Friend" and as a "Gentle Woman," Sarah Moorhead managed to employ the marginal status of female voices in midcentury Boston to make distinctly public points. An art educator as well as a poet, she may have instructed Scipio Moorhead in ways that allowed him to use (or to imagine using) his own voice as an entrance into the public sphere of revolutionary Boston.

We know little about Sarah Moorhead beyond her poetry, but one document suggests that she may have suffered during Scipio's childhood – and perhaps her entire life – from a form of mental illness. A notice in a newspaper in 1763, printed when Scipio Moorhead was probably two or three years old, observed that Sarah had "at Times been delirious for several Years past, and is now observably so." The Moorhead family asked "Shopkeepers and other Persons" to show "Kindness" and not to give Sarah "any Countenance in contracting of Debts."[18] This public notice to creditors may have signaled that the household was in dire straits, both emotionally and financially; it may also suggest that Scipio's care fell increasingly on Sarah's daughter Mary.

In the 1740s and 1750s, to help supplement John's income as minister, Sarah Parsons Moorhead offered lessons in visual arts: In 1744 she taught President Holyoke's son Edward how to paint on glass and how to paint a coat of arms on canvas; by 1748 (after the Moorheads had moved into a new home, and her children were teenagers) she was publically advertising in the *Boston Evening Post* that "Drawing, Japanning, and Painting on Glass, [were] taught by Mrs. Sarah Moorhead" at her home "at the Head of the Rope-Walks, near Fort Hill." In the 1750s she may have instructed young women in embroidery.[19] Recently two antiques dealers who specialize in American women's textiles discovered a canvas-work picture inscribed under the original sand liner with the name "Sarah Moorhead." Very few such pictures are signed, but the dealers have determined that almost certainly the picture (similar to others produced in the 1750s) was drawn by rather than stitched by Sarah Parsons Moorhead.[20] We do not have any known examples of the "Japan-work" of Sarah Moorhead (or of her students), but a vogue for "japanning" in the furniture trade emerged in Boston in the 1740s, part of that city's flirtation with emerging Atlantic and Pacific markets and of its desire to mimic the fashions of London. Sarah Moorhead's lessons helped young women (and clearly some young men) participate in these larger enterprises; she may very well have helped Scipio Moorhead to participate too.

Though her politics are difficult to reconstruct, Sarah may have joined with John as a motivating force in her community for the patriot cause. In June 1770, as boycotts of British goods helped mobilize and politicize ordinary consumers, a Boston newspaper reported that "another voluntary Spinning Match" was held "at the Rev. Mr. Moorhead's in this Town, when between 50 and 60 Daughters of Liberty engaged in that laudable Employment, and spun 193 Skeins, chiefly of fine Linen Yarn."[21] Though large and open to the public, the spinning match took place at the Moorhead house in the South End rather than at the Presbyterian Church. Sarah Moorhead may have organized and overseen this act of patriotic virtue and industry; some of the contestants may have been her students. We might picture Scipio Moorhead, then about ten, in the household on that day, helping with the preparations, attending to John and Sarah, counting skeins of yarn. But it is of course impossible to know what a young slave would have made of the talk of liberty and self-denial that must have been spoken throughout the day by both men and women, some of them slaveholders.

Outside the white family, Scipio may have turned to a few local black artists for instruction or inspiration. In the 1760s Scipio might have found a mentor of sorts in Pompey Fleet, a slave in the household of the Boston publisher Thomas Fleet. Pompey Fleet's woodcuts (Fig. 3.2) for *The Prodigal Daughter*, made around 1750, may have been copied from a lost English source; they were subsequently recopied by other engravers (including a young Isaiah Thomas, who later wrote about Pompey in his *History of Printing in America*). The story of *The Prodigal Daughter* concerns a young girl who conspires with Satan to poison her parents, only to expire herself before she is miraculously resurrected at her own funeral, but the images are of art historical interest because the signature "P.F." represents one of the first signed American illustrations. But in a society in which white slave holders sometimes branded their own initials into the flesh of black slaves and also anxiously worried about vulnerability to slave poisoners, Pompey Fleet's initials (taken as ascription of ownership or pride of authorship) and the poisoning theme of the story itself might have taken on other meanings.[22]

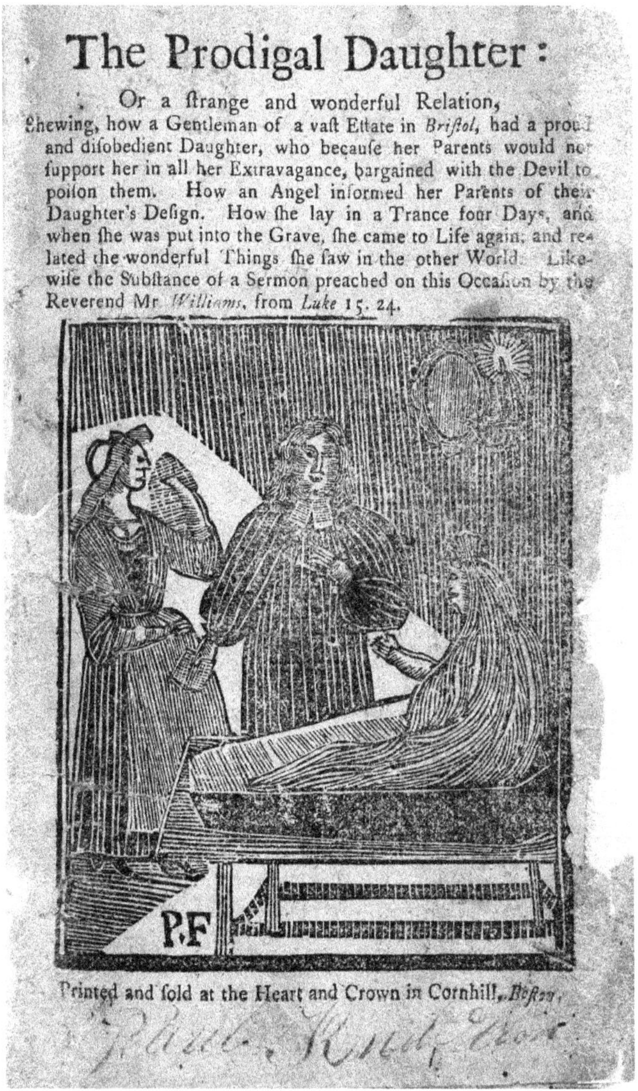

The Prodigal Daughter:

Or a ſtrange and wonderful Relation,

Shewing, how a Gentleman of a vaſt Eſtate in *Briſtol*, had a proud and diſobedient Daughter, who becauſe her Parents would not ſupport her in all her Extravagance, bargained with the Devil to poiſon them. How an Angel informed her Parents of their Daughter's Deſign. How ſhe lay in a Trance four Days, and when ſhe was put into the Grave, ſhe came to Life again, and related the wonderful Things ſhe ſaw in the other World. Likewiſe the Subſtance of a Sermon preached on this Occaſion by the Reverend Mr *Williams*, from *Luke* 15. 24.

Printed and ſold at the Heart and Crown in Cornhill, *Boſton*,

3.2. P.F. (Pompey Fleet). Title page of *The Prodigal Daughter*, ca. 1750. Woodcut. Courtesy, American Antiquarian Society, Worcester, Mass.

It is tempting to think that Scipio learned from Pompey Fleet, but there were perhaps still other black visual artists in Boston. A curious notice appeared in a Boston newspaper in early 1773. Placed by or for "a Negro Man whose extraordinary Genius has been assisted by one of the best Masters in *London*," the advertisement invited readers to a watchmaker's shop near the Town House where a free black portrait painter had set up shop and where he "takes Faces at the lowest rates."[23] This notice, which ran for three weeks in January, seems to trade on the confusion Boston readers might have about what sort of "master" a "Negro Man" might have; in this case it refers to an art instructor rather than an owner. Curious white Bostonians may have ventured to the watchmaker's shop where this free black portraitist displayed "Specimens of his Performances," and they may have patronized him, but the visual and textual record of this painter consists solely of the notice.

The African-born poet Phillis Wheatley, probably five years older than Scipio Moorhead, had numerous documented ties to the Moorhead family, and she seems to have positioned herself as a mentor of sorts. John Moorhead subscribed his name alongside six ministers and ten other "respectable Characters in Boston" to attest "To the Publick" (and especially to skeptical readers in Britain and the British colonies) that Wheatley had actually written the poems published in her 1773 collection of *Poems on Various Subjects, Religious and Moral.* When Phillis's owner John Wheatley was sick in early 1773, John Moorhead visited him "almost every Day." The first poem Wheatley published after her emancipation in late 1773 was *An Elegy to Miss Mary Moorhead, on the Death of Her Father, The Rev. Mr. John Moorhead.* Printed "from the Original Manuscript" and sold by a loyalist printer, the broadside poem was addressed both "to his Offspring, and his Church" and was almost certainly given away as a keepsake memorializing the deceased minister. Wheatley may have known John Moorhead well, but the poem offers little evidence; she invokes his "Friendship" twice in the poem, but both times in reference to his now "hapless Church," a Church to which she did not belong.[24]

To all of these documented ties can be added speculative ones: It seems likely that two women who had both published poems about George Whitefield – Sarah Parsons Moorhead in 1744 and Phillis Wheatley in 1770 – would have found something to talk about, but it is curious that Wheatley's *Elegy* does not address or even allude to Sarah. Nineteenth-century biographies of Wheatley often note that she assumed the expected posture of inferiority when visiting white households, sitting at a table set apart from whites, and so it is possible that she did not interact at all with Sarah Parsons Moorhead.[25] But whatever the connections may have been, and though he too is not mentioned in the *Elegy,* it is clear that Wheatley knew Scipio Moorhead.

It is in fact only from Phillis Wheatley's poem that we have any knowledge that Scipio Moorhead was a painter. A manuscript note left in pencil by Daniel O'Connor, a white reader, in his copy of Wheatley's *Poems on Various Subjects* indicates that Wheatley's poem "To S.M. a young *African* Painter, on seeing his Works" was addressed to Scipio Moorhead, a black "servant whose genius inclined him that way."[26] O'Connor employed the standard New England euphemism for a slave, just as the baptismal record did. Addressed to "a young

African Painter" and prompted by "seeing his Works," the poem tells us precious little about either artist or artworks. Though some readers have tried to deduce Scipio Moorhead's general subject matter and even the topics of particular paintings from references in the poem, Wheatley does not really focus on any of "his Works."[27] The poem demands attention for another reason: "To S.M. a young *African* Painter, on seeing his Works" is Wheatley's only surviving poem addressed to another black person, and it is also her only poem explicitly about artistic creation.

Wheatley's poem resembles and can be read as a contribution to the genre of poems on paintings and painters, a genre found in colonial British America only in the forty or so preceding years. Though she might have seen similar poems in British magazines, it is possible that she knew one colonial poem firsthand: the Reverend Mather Byles's "To Mr. Smibert on the Sight of his Pictures." Byles (who Sarah Parsons Moorhead gently satirized in a manuscript poem in 1753) composed his poem in 1730 to mark the first exhibition of paintings in Boston; it was subsequently published in newspapers in Boston, Philadelphia, and London and reprinted in 1744 in Byles's book collection *Poems on Several Occasions*.[28] Phillis Wheatley was certainly familiar with Byles himself, who had joined John Moorhead in attesting to the authenticity of Wheatley's poetry. In poems on specific painters, colonial poets celebrated the way in which painters such as Smibert had civilized what had been "a barb'rous Desert" and the permanence that itinerant artists gave to mortal subjects, producing paintings that could "live" and "breathe" even after the person depicted had ceased to do so.[29]

In the first half of her own poem, Wheatley praised the "*African* painter" in precisely these terms. Wheatley begins with a conventional celebration of the artist:

To show the lab'ring bosom's deep intent,
And thought in living characters to paint,
When first thy pencil did those beauties give,
And breathing figures learnt from thee to live,
How did those prospects give my soul delight,
A new creation rushing on my sight?
Still, wond'rous youth! each noble path pursue,
On deathless glories fix thine ardent view:
Still may the painter's and the poet's fire
To aid thy pencil, and thy verse conspire!
And may the charms of each seraphic theme
Conduct thy footsteps to immortal fame!
High to the blissful wonders of the skies,
Elate thy soul, and raise thy wishful eyes.
Thrice happy, when exalted to survey

That splendid city, crown'd with endless day,
Whose twice six gates on radiant hinges ring:
Celestial *Salem* blooms in endless spring. (1–18)

The second half of the poem upends the conventions employed by poets such as Byles to immortalize the creative and godlike powers of artists, offering instead a classic Calvinist indictment of the value system that might lead such an artist to treasure his or her own "Works." Who cares, she seems to ask, if a painting outlasts the sitter, since the real contest for permanence concerns the afterlife?

Calm and serene thy moments glide along,
And may the muse inspire each future song!
Still, with the sweets of contemplation bless'd,
May peace with balmy wings your soul invest!
But when these shades of time are chas'd away,
And darkness ends in everlasting day,
On what seraphic pinions shall we move,
And view the landscapes in the realms above?
There shall thy tongue in heav'nly murmurs flow,
And there my muse with heav'nly transports glow:
No more to tell of *Damon*'s tender sighs,
Or rising radiance of *Aurora*'s eyes,
For nobler themes demand a nobler strain,
And purer language on th' ethereal plain.
Cease, gentle muse! the solemn gloom of night
Now seals the fair creation from my sight. (19–34)

Within the conventions of Wheatley's own verse, the sentiment was predictable. The turn in the poem from the misery of this world to the beauties of the next (so prevalent in poems such as her *Elegy* on John Moorhead) is, more or less, what readers had come to expect and even desire from Wheatley.

In April 1784, *The Armenian Magazine*, an organ of the Wesleyan Methodist Church published in London, printed a variant version of Wheatley's poem "To S.M." Appearing possibly without her knowledge, the 1784 poem allowed the poet a greater degree of visual pleasure than the original by revising the opening:

When first thy pencil did these beauties give,
And breathing figures learnt from thee to live;
A new creation met my wondéring sight,
And filléd my ravishéd bosom with delight. (1–4)[30]

The new poem conceived of the poet as a different kind of spectator, one whose body (rather than whose soul) registered the effects of seeing the painter's works. The poem was also shorter by eight lines, most of which were trimmed from the description of the afterlife in the second stanza. But perhaps most crucially, the poem appeared anonymously. For a poem to be published without reference to Wheatley's status as a black person was an unusual thing for Wheatley.[31] Perhaps the subject and collegiality of the poem itself marked the poem as the product of a fellow "African." Or perhaps it was a sign – prompted by the Methodists' own radical ideas about spiritual equality – that the poem should be appreciated for its own merits and power, and not be treated as an index of the capability of its maker's "race."

With the possible exception of the portrait of Wheatley (see Fig. 3.1) that served as the frontispiece to her *Poems*, works by Scipio Moorhead have not survived or have not yet been identified; and no contemporary testimony links the image of Wheatley to Scipio Moorhead.[32] The famous frontispiece to Wheatley's 1773 collection could be taken as representing "deep intent" and "thought," those virtues celebrated in Wheatley's poem, but any attribution is provisional at best; and at worst, as art historian Gwendolyn DuBois Shaw has recently observed in a fascinating reading of the Wheatley frontispiece, attributions of that image to Scipio Moorhead often miss the ways in which the revolutionary and unprecedented portrait of a black female writer can serve as "valuable visual evidence of a heterocultural Atlantic world."[33] We may never know who drew Phillis Wheatley, though we do know some of the circumstances around the frontispiece portrait of Wheatley.

The representation of Wheatley was designed in part to effect visually what the attestation effected verbally, to guarantee the poems as the product of a young black woman. The Countess of Huntingdon, the Methodist patron of Wheatley and numerous other black Christians, suggested that the Wheatley family arrange to have an image taken in Boston to be engraved in London (an enterprise she believed could be "easily done" and would "contribute greatly to the Sale of the book," a fact that might materially help Wheatley). The Boston booksellers Cox and Berry advertised the book proposal in April 1773 and noted that it would be "adorned with an elegant Frontispiece, representing the author." Andrew Bell, Wheatley's London publisher, included engraved frontispieces only two other times, and neither resembles the Wheatley portrait; and Bell registered the frontispiece engraving for copyright on 1 September 1773, nine days before he registered the book.[34]

There is certainly reason to suspect the attribution, which seems to have been made first in the twentieth century and perhaps most positively only in the 1980s by the Wheatley scholar William H. Robinson.[35] It is curious that nobody at the time seized upon the image as the work of an "*African* Painter," but perhaps the idea that an image used to authenticate Wheatley's blackness had itself been produced by another black person would have strained credibility. The Bostonian John Boyle observed in January 1774 that Wheatley's *Poems* had been published in London "with a Frontice-piece representing the Author," noting that Wheatley had not been away from Africa for more than six or eight years. If it were known in Boston that the image originated from another slave, wouldn't Boyle surely have said so?[36] And, when abolitionists in the nineteenth century revisited Wheatley's biography, wouldn't they have mentioned that the familiar image of Wheatley had been engraved after a drawing by an "*African* Painter"?

The only anecdote about the image that seems to have made its way into print in the early nineteenth century focused exclusively on Phillis Wheatley's then owner, Susannah Wheatley. As Phillis Wheatley's biographer in the 1830s noted:

> During her stay in England, her poems were given to the world, dedicated to the Countess of Huntingdon, and embellished with an engraving, which is said to have been a striking representation of the original. It is supposed that one of these impressions was forwarded to her mistress, as soon as they were struck off; for a grand niece of Mrs. Wheatley's informs us that, during the absence of Phillis, she one day called upon her relative, who immediately directed her attention to a picture over the fire-place, exclaiming – "See! look at my Phillis! does she not seem as though she would speak to me."[37]

The engraved portrait above the Wheatley fireplace may have derived from an original by Moorhead, but (in spite of Susannah Wheatley's purported exclamation) it does not seem as though "her Phillis" would speak. The portraitist presents Wheatley in profile in a moment of arrested composition, with covered ears and seemingly unavailable for conversation. As many commentators have noted, this is a revolutionary image. No portrait of a black male author produced in the next decade insisted on depicting an act of composition, but perhaps no portrait of a man needed to show its author in an act of composition. Even still, as historian Laurel Thatcher Ulrich has observed of John Singleton Copley's American paintings, white women were represented exclusively as readers rather than as writers.[38] But for all of its revolutionary import, the image figures Wheatley's dependent status in a number of ways: the bound and covered hair; the visible sources of her physical support (her arm, her elbow, the table, the chair) and of intellectual or spiritual support (the book); the invisible source of inspiration that seems to lie just outside the picture plane, suggesting an attentive mode of dictation as much as creation. Intriguingly, a woodcut reduction of the frontispiece image (Fig. 3.3), produced for the title page of a 1782 almanac published

BICKERSTAFF's
BOSTON
ALMANACK,
For the Year of our REDEMPTION, 1782.
Being the Second after Leap-Year; and the Sixth Year of INDEPENDENCY. Fitted for the Meridian of BOSTON, N. E. Lat. 42′ 25° N. Long. from London 69′ 27° W.
Wherein may be found all Things necessary for this WORK.
To which is added, A SCALE of DEPRECIATION, and a great Variety of other entertaining Matter.

TIME is the Effect of Motion, born a Twin,
And with the World did equally begin;
Time like a Stream that hastens from the Shore,
Flies to an Ocean where 'tis known no more.
All must be swallow'd in this endless Deep,
And Motion rest in everlasting Sleep.
DRYD. OVID.

BOSTON: Printed by E. RUSSELL, at his Printing-Office in Essex-Street, near Liberty-Stump, South-end. (Pr. 7d. Single)

3.3. *Phillis Wheatley*. Title page of *Bickerstaff's Boston Almanack*, 1781. Woodcut. Courtesy, American Antiquarian Society, Worcester, Mass.

by Ezekiel Russell, one of Wheatley's first (and in her lifetime, last) Boston publishers, eliminates many of the picture's props. Here the intense black ink of the sitter's skin and the white space of the paper render a caption unnecessary, even to those readers who presumably never saw the 1773 London engraving.

Reconstructing what white Bostonians saw is difficult enough, but it is impossible to know exactly what works of art Scipio Moorhead had seen. He may have known the portraits by Greenwood and Pelham of John Moorhead; and he probably knew some of the images associated with students of Sarah Parsons Moorhead. But beyond those, a speculative catalog of works he had seen might include the most famous scene of dictation in colonial painting: the profile of John Wainwright, with a pen and a ledger book, attending to the

3.4. John Smibert, *The Bermuda Group (Dean Berkeley and His Entourage)*, 1728–39. Oil on canvas. Yale University Art Gallery, New Haven, Conn. Gift of Isaac Lothrop.

3.5. John Singleton Copley, *Mrs. Richard Skinner (Dorothy Wendell)*, 1772. Oil on canvas. Museum of Fine Arts, Boston. Bequest of Mrs. Martin Brimmer, 06.2428. Photograph © 2013, Museum of Fine Arts, Boston.

words of Bishop Berkeley in John Smibert's *The Bermuda Group (Dean Berkeley and His Entourage)* (1728–39). Smibert's painting (Fig. 3.4) was easily the largest and most famous painting in Boston in this period. While Smibert lived, the painting remained in the artist's studio, where it exerted an influence on contemporary painters such as Greenwood; after his death, the painting passed to Smibert's wife and then son, and remained within Smibert's family and his former studio until the late 1770s. Smibert's biographer describes the studio, a second-floor room in a townhouse, as "a virtual museum," a destination for "residents of Boston and culturally minded vistors to the city." It is possible that Scipio Moorhead joined other local painters such as John Singleton Copley in studying Smibert's copies of old masters and original works like *The Bermuda Group*.[39]

It is also possible that Scipio Moorhead had a familiarity with the portraits painted by John Singleton Copley himself, especially the images of preoccupied female sitters executed in the early 1770s, such as *Mary Charnock* (1770–71), the mother of John Greenwood, the artist who made the 1749 painting of John Moorhead. No documents link Scipio Moorhead with Copley, but the white Moorhead family knew Peter Pelham (Copley's stepfather, who had engraved the image of John Moorhead), was familiar with the family of President Holyoke (one of Copley's sitters; Sarah instructed his son in painting on glass, and Holyoke possessed a copy of Pelham's engraving of Moorhead), and had some acquaintance with Paul Revere (whose earliest silver work was produced for John Moorhead's Presbyterian Church). If Scipio Moorhead drew the image of Phillis Wheatley, perhaps he played on some of Copley's evolving conventions for figuring preoccupation. Copley would recycle the props and gestures of *Mary Charnock* – the gateleg table, the chair, and the thoughtful averted gaze of the sitter – for other commissions in the next few years, including his image of Dorothy Wendell Skinner (Fig. 3.5) in 1772.

3.6. John Singleton Copley, *Boy with a Flying Squirrel (Henry Pelham)*, 1765. Oil on canvas. Museum of Fine Arts, Boston. Gift of the artist's great-granddaughter, 1978.297. Photograph © 2013, Museum of Fine Arts, Boston.

All of Copley's paintings of preoccupied sitters of the early 1770s recall his 1765 portrait of his half-brother Henry Pelham (Fig. 3.6), exhibited in London in 1766 as *Boy with a Flying Squirrel*. Like the portrait of Wheatley, it is a profile, the only one done in Copley's American period. Produced in the midst of the controversy in Boston over the British Parliament's attempts to tax colonists under the proposed Stamp Act of 1765, and exhibited in London in 1766, Copley's portrait gave London viewers a way of allegorizing the dependent relationship between the British colonies (here figured as the squirrel) and Britain itself (the boy): that the best colonial policy resembled a turned head (what Burke would call "salutary neglect" a few years later); that the colonists labored hard and for themselves (evidenced by the patience of the squirrel with the nut); that the colonists did not pretend to a species equality with the parent country, and could be managed with a loose chain. Such a relationship of careless care could

3.7. Jonathan Spilsbury after Mason Chamberlin, *The Reverend Mr. Samson Occom*, 1768. Mezzotint on laid paper. Hood Museum, Dartmouth College, Hanover, N.H. Gift of Mrs. Robert White Birch.

hardly be called (as the Stamp Act had been) a form of "slavery" since it was in the service of the development of the colonies themselves.

3.8. John Singleton Copley, *Paul Revere*, 1768. Oil on canvas. Museum of Fine Arts, Boston. Gift of Joseph W. Revere, William B. Revere, and Edward H. R. Revere, 30.781. Photograph © 2013, Museum of Fine Arts, Boston.

Wheatley's pose differs in important ways from these figures, who (as in *Dorothy Wendell Skinner* quite literally) seem to point only toward themselves. If Wheatley's portrait exemplifies a new emphasis on preoccupation in Copley's portraiture of the 1760s and early 1770s, in another sense it resembles contemporary portraits figuring occupation, all of which depict men. Consider, for instance, the way that Mason Chamberlin's London portrait *Samson Occom* (1768) represents him in a moment of arrested reading and interpretation. Occom preached in Rev. John Moorhead's church in Long Lane in 1773 and stayed overnight with the Wheatleys. One of Wheatley's first letters, now lost, was addressed to Occom, and her most severe critique of white slaveholders, published in almost a dozen New England newspapers in 1774, was a letter to Occom.[40] It is within the bounds of possibility that Scipio Moorhead had seen the 1768 mezzotint engraving made by Jonathan Spilsbury after Chamberlin's painting (Fig. 3.7).

He may have also seen what has become the most famous occupational portrait of the period – one employing a counter top if not a table top – Copley's *Paul Revere* from 1768 (Fig. 3.8). In a gesture similar to Wheatley's, Revere cradles his chin with his right hand, suggesting (as has been often noted) an equivalence between his own head and the as yet unengraved teapot in his left hand. The teapot offered a metaphor for mixture as well as an icon of British loyalism, and both of these associations might have informed the depiction of Phillis Wheatley. Returning to the Wheatley frontispiece, a close viewer can see that the shoulder of Wheatley's chair mimics her shoulder, a fact that attests to the anthropological imperative in the decorative arts of the eighteenth century, but the image also hints at continuity between Wheatley and the chair. One implication of the image, produced in part from its flattening perspective, is that the chair functions as a handle and Wheatley as a vessel not unlike a teapot. But if the image figured Wheatley as an object, perhaps collapsing the difference between servant and tea service, it may have done so in the name of Wheatley's own neoclassical poetics: The claim that she mixed received elements (the book before her; the muse above her) to produce something new, that her work stems from nurture as much as nature, made Wheatley appealing to contemporary and later abolitionists.

Was Wheatley a revolutionary subject or a counter-revolutionary object? In the strictest sense, as a slave and a writer in 1773 she was both. But if the maker of the image did wish to comment on her objecthood, perhaps he did so with the consent of the sitter. Perhaps it was a joke between servants about their status as pieces of property, the belongings of the white Wheatleys and the Moorheads, during a moment of intense rhetoric about liberty. But this may be too much for the image to bear: Perhaps it was simply the work of a twelve- or thirteen-year old "*African* Painter." Or perhaps it wasn't.

We have ample testimony of how white contemporaries understood black people such as Scipio Moorhead and Phillis Wheatley as objects; we need to know more about how free and enslaved black people living in the last years of slavery in Massachusetts worked to de-objectify themselves.

The outlines of Phillis Wheatley's life after emancipation in December 1773 are known, but little can be said about Scipio Moorhead's existence after the death of John Moorhead that same month. A week after John's death Mary Moorhead, "singlewoman," was appointed as one of the two administrators for her father's estate. John Moorhead had died without a will, and Mary's first task was to create an inventory of his possessions. According to the document presented to the court on 10 January 1774, John Moorhead's estate was valued at just over £295. The list of thirteen items failed to list the contents of the individual rooms in the household but offered rough estimates of the value of furnishings and other belongings. The inventory showed that Moorhead owned one hundred acres of undivided land in the province of New Hampshire. The largest concentration of wealth, almost a third of the estate, was in his library. Considered together, the furniture in the kitchen, parlor, and two chambers (none of it enumerated) came next, with an appraised value of approximately £63. The third-most valuable item was "a negro young man named Scipio" who was valued at £40, about three times as much as the land in New Hampshire.

During 1774 Mary seems mostly to have cared for her dying mother, but she arranged for an auction of the most valuable property, the books, in late spring. She hired Robert Gould, whose business in 1774 consisted mostly in liquidating the luxury goods of deceased Bostonians and in selling off the possessions of people "leaving the province immediately." Departing loyalists were leaving in such numbers that the market was glutted, driving prices down. John Moorhead's library represented a third of the value of the estate; to Moorhead and perhaps the family the books were social capital. But most of the books

To be Sold by Public Auction, on
Thurſday next, at Ten o'Clock in the Forenoon, all the Houſe-Furniture belonging to the Eſtate of the Rev. Mr. *John Morehead*, deceas'd, conſiſting of,

TABLES, Chairs, Looking-Glaſſes, Feather Beds, Bedſteads and Bedding, Pewter, Braſs, ſundry Pieces of Plate, &c. &c.—A valuable Collection of Books,—Alſo, a likely Negro Lad——The Sale to be at the Houſe in Auchmuty's Lane, South-End, not far from Liberty Tree. The Goods to be ſeen the Day before the Sale. On Thurſday next, at Ten o'Clock, A. M.

By B. CHURCH.

3.9. Auction notice, *Boston Gazette*, 2 January 1775. Courtesy, American Antiquarian Society, Worcester, Mass.

didn't find buyers at the 26 May auction, and the mood at the Moorhead home must have been one of great disappointment and anxiety. Valued at almost one hundred pounds, the auctioneer Gould realized for the family a mere £17, and even then two purchasers returned books for refunds. Many books remained unsold. Mary sent some of these to a different auctioneer in early 1775 and seems to have arranged for a private sale that did not find buyers in either of the auctions.[41] In the end, she disposed of them all, but the failure of the books to sell in the first auction may have had repercussions for Scipio.

Scipio must have remained in the household between the deaths of John and Sarah, perhaps helping with what Mary described for the Court in early 1775 as the "extraordinary nursing of Mrs. Moorhead." Sarah Moorhead died in the middle of December 1774, and on 2 January 1775, the *Boston Gazette* (Fig. 3.9) carried a notice that Benjamin Church would auction the remaining moveable goods belonging to the Moorheads:

> To be sold by Public Auction, on Thursday next, at Ten o'Clock in the Forenoon, all the House-Furniture belonging to the Estate of the Rev. Mr. John Morehead, deceas'd, consisting of Tables, Chairs, Looking-Glasses, Feather Beds, Bedsteads and Bedding, Pewter, Brass, sundry Pieces of Plate, &c.&c. – A valuable Collection of Books, – Also, a likely Negro Lad – The Sale to be at the House in Auchmuty's Lane, South-End, not far from the Liberty Tree. The Goods to be seen the Day before the Sale.

An account made to the probate court before the distribution of the estate shows that the "likely Negro Lad" was Scipio Moorhead, though the record refers to him as "a Negro man, named Scipio." The account does not specify how much each item realized, but Church was able to give the estate a total of £205 for the sale of these goods.[42]

The sale of a person as the last item in an inventory of household goods "not far from the Liberty Tree" must have struck black and some white contemporaries as the height of hypocrisy. "Moses and the Prophets!" one Massachusetts author exclaimed when he reproduced this very advertisement in a newspaper in 1856 as a typical example of revolutionary inconsistency: *"A human being to be sold as a SLAVE, not far from LIBERTY TREE, in 1775!"*[43] To readers who discovered this advertisement in the middle of the nineteenth century the gruesome inventory must have seemed indicative of the compromises of the revolutionary generation, but to readers in 1775 it was perfectly common. The verbal and visual rhetoric of freedom was omnipresent in the pages of the newspaper that advertised the sale of Scipio and the rest of the Moorhead property, but so too was the reality of the business of chattel slavery.

Why did Mary Moorhead, the woman to whom Phillis Wheatley addressed her first poem after her own emancipation, sell Scipio Moorhead? During this period numerous white slaveholders made provisions in their wills for the emancipation of slaves, but John Moorhead did not make a will. If he had left one, John Moorhead may have ensured that Scipio passed to Mary rather than have emancipated him; he may have felt Scipio was too young to be on his own or had not yet served a term that would compensate for what some called "prime cost," the cost of raising him to adolescence.[44] Or John Moorhead may have stipulated, as others sometimes did, that Scipio be sold but that the slave be allowed the "liberty" of choosing a new master if more than one buyer came forward. Selling Scipio to help provide for Mary and Sarah may very well have been John Moorhead's intention.

Just over forty, unmarried, and having lost both of her parents in the last year, Mary Moorhead may have decided that she could not afford to keep and provide for a slave valued at £40; when she died two years later her own estate was appraised at just £50. She might have thought of putting an advertisement in the paper, as another slaveholder did in June 1774, to see if anyone might want to lease him; she could have used the money to support Scipio and herself.[45] But she was not the only member of the family, and by far she was the poorest. She split the estate with a married couple named Ann Agnes Willson and Alexander Willson. Alexander Willson, a mariner, was described in court records as Moorhead's "only son," and Mary's will from 1776 refers to the couple as "my Brother Alexander Morehead and my Sister Ann Agnes Willson." Alexander seems to have been Mary's cousin, not her brother. The Willsons could bank on inheriting three-quarters of the estate. They might have arranged to purchase Scipio at the January 1775 auction, but Alexander was himself in debt at the time. A memo attached to Mary's list of administration charges notes that John Moorhead had promised to pay a debt of Alexander's that totaled "upwards of £50 Dollars" and that the two administrators, Mary and a ropemaker named William McNeill, had discharged this debt without drawing on the estate.[46] The three beneficiaries may have agreed that trying to hold a slave in a moment of revolutionary insurrection was a risky business decision; in the current climate they may have sold Scipio because they felt that they could not hold onto him.[47]

Scipio Moorhead was rarely captured in the archives that whites compiled in the eighteenth century, and he disappears from sight in January 1775. After the auction he may have served a new master, or he may have taken the chance that many other enslaved black men took in Boston in 1774 and 1775: He may have taken flight. On the other hand, at fifteen he was young but not too young to serve as a soldier and may have joined with the estimated 150 blacks who fought on the side of the colonies at Bunker Hill in April 1775. His name does not appear in subsequent tax records collected in Boston, or on early census reports for Massachusetts or neighboring northern states; he was not recorded in registries of black Loyalists who left Boston on a trajectory that would take some of them to New York, Nova Scotia, London, and finally Sierra Leone.[48] Scipio was one of the most popular names for male slaves, and a new owner would have given Scipio Moorhead a different last name in January 1775. If he joined the ranks of the newly emancipated in the 1780s, he may have given himself a new name; of course, he may have emancipated himself well before 1783. We may never know if Scipio Moorhead produced the famous image of Phillis Wheatley or if he outlived slavery in Massachusetts, and we will certainly never know what looking meant to him. But if we hope to recapture the lived experience of the coming of the Revolution and the end of slavery, we need to look for figures such as Scipio Moorhead, and we need to try to look with them as well.

Notes

This essay would not have been possible without the help and advice of librarians and archivists at the Newberry Library, the Andover-Harvard Theological Library of the Harvard Divinity School, and the Massachusetts State Archives. For strategies, suggestions, and information, I am especially grateful to Wendy Bellion, Vincent Carretta, Max Cavitch, Richard Dunn, Craig Fehrman, Kate Haulman, Jane Kamensky, Catherine E. Kelly, Margaretta Lovell, Meredith McGill, Fran O'Donnell, Mark Peterson, Daniel Richter, Sarah Rivett, Joseph Roach, Chernoh Sesay, David S. Shields, Robert Blair St. George, Paul Staiti, John Tyler, Michael Warner, and Alfred F. Young and to audiences at the Colonial Society of Massachusetts in Boston in 2003, the American Studies Association meeting in Atlanta in 2004, the McNeil Center for Early American Studies at the University of Pennsylvania in 2005, and the Yale Americanist Colloquium in 2010. I dedicate this essay to the memory of Al Young.

1 For large-scale studies of African-American agency, see Sylvia R. Frey, *Water from the Rock: Black Resistance in a Revolutionary Age* (Princeton: Princeton University Press, 1991); Philip D. Morgan, *Slave Counterpoint: Black Culture in the Eighteenth-Century Chesapeake and Lowcountry* (Chapel Hill: University of North Carolina Press, 1998); Ira Berlin, *Many Thousands Gone: The First Two Centuries of*

Slavery in North America (Cambridge, Mass.: Harvard University Press, 1998) and *Generations of Captivity: A History of African-American Slaves* (Cambridge, Mass.: Harvard University Press, 2003); Jennifer L. Morgan, *Laboring Women: Reproduction and Gender in New World Slavery* (Philadelphia: University of Pennsylvania Press, 2004); David Brion Davis, *Inhuman Bondage: The Rise and Fall of Slavery in the New World* (New York: Oxford University Press, 2006); Gary Nash, *The Forgotten Fifth: African Americans in the Age of Revolution* (Cambridge, Mass.: Harvard University Press, 2006); and Cassandra Pybus, *Epic Journeys of Freedom: Runaway Slaves of the American Revolution and their Global Quest for Liberty* (Boston: Beacon Press, 2006). For recent studies centered on individuals, see the essays collected in *Genius in Bondage: Literature of the Early Black Atlantic*, ed. Vincent Carretta and Philip Gould (Lexington: University Press of Kentucky, 2001); Joanna Brooks, *American Lazarus: Religion and the Rise of African-American and Native American Literatures* (New York: Oxford University Press, 2003); John Saillant, *Black Puritan, Black Republican: The Life and Thought of Lemuel Haynes, 1753–1833* (New York: Oxford University Press, 2003); Randy J. Sparks, *The Two Princes of Calabar: An Eighteenth-Century Atlantic Odyssey* (Cambridge, Mass.: Harvard University Press, 2004); Vincent Carretta, *Equiano the African: Biography of a Self-Made Man* (Athens: University of Georgia Press, 2005); Jon Sensbach, *Rebecca's Revival: Creating Black Christianity in the Atlantic World* (Cambridge, Mass.: Harvard University Press, 2005); Gretchen Holbrook Gerzina, *Mr. and Mrs. Prince: How an Extraordinary Eighteenth-Century Family Moved Out of Slavery and into Legend* (New York: Amistad, 2008); and Joyce Lee Malcom, *Peter's War: A New England Slave Boy and the American Revolution* (New Haven: Yale University Press, 2009).

2 This project has benefited from the genealogical work of Annie Haven Thwing (1851–1940), recently made available on CD-ROM as *Inhabitants and Estates of the Town of Boston, 1630–1800; and The Crooked and Narrow Streets of Boston, 1630–1822* (Boston: New England Historic Genealogical Society and the Massachusetts Historical Society, 2001). My citations to Thwing are by record number: for example, Scipio Sarahson (Thwing 9950).

3 *Boston Evening Post*, 25 April 1748.

4 See William D. Piersen, *Black Yankees: The Development of an Afro-American Subculture in Eighteenth-Century New England* (Amherst: University of Massachusetts Press, 1988), 26, 53–54.

5 Quoted but not attributed in Jeremy Belknap, "Queries Respecting Slavery, with Answers," *Collections of the Massachusetts Historical Society* 2 (1795), 197.

6 Boston Overseers of the Poor Records, 1733–1925, Massachusetts Historical Society, Microfilm edition, reel 8, Almshouse records, 1735–1911: Records of admissions and discharges, November 9, 1758–April 27, 1774; and List of children bound out of the Almshouse, April 21, 1756–January 20, 1790.

7 As many as four children were advertised as "To be given away" in Boston papers in the first half of 1760: (1) "a likely Negro Child about a Month old" in the *Boston Evening Post*, 14 and 21 January 1760; (2) "A Negro Child to be given away" in the *Boston Evening Post*, 4, 11, and 18 February; (3) "a likely Negro Child" in the *Boston Gazette*, 4, 11, 18, and 25 February; and (4) "A Fine Negro Male Child to be given away" in the *Boston Weekly News Letter*, 7 February, and also in the *Boston Gazette*, 25 February. On giving away children, see Piersen, *Black Yankees*, 26–27.

8 On the rise of slavery and print culture in New England, see Robert Desroches, Jr., "Slave-for-Sale Advertisements and Slavery in Massachusetts, 1704–1781," *William and Mary Quarterly*, 3d ser., 59 (July 2002), 623–64.

9 For basic biographical information on the Moorheads, see *New England Historical and Genealogical Register*, 4 (1850), 197; 12 (1858), 235; 21 (1867), 41; 31 (1877), 54; Justin Winsor, *The Memorial History of Boston, 1630–1880*, 4 vols. (Boston: James Osgood, 1881), 2:514 and 3:129; and Ethel Stanwood Bolton, *Immigrants to New England, 1700–1775* (1931; Baltimore: Genealogical Publication Co., 1979), xxx. For the births of Parsons, Mary, and John, see *Boston Town Records*, 24:204, 208, 218. For William, baptized on 28 December 1736, see Arlington Street Church Records, Andover-Harvard Theological Library, Harvard Divinity School, bMS 4/2 (3), Records of Baptisms and Marriages, 1730–1772.

10 Edward L. Parker, *The History of Londonderry, N.H.* (Boston: Perkins and Whipple, 1851), 131; and see *New England Historical and Genealogical Register* 8 (1854), 180.

11 *New England Historical and Genealogical Register* 12 (1858), 235.

12 For John Adams's report of a joke played on Moorhead by contemporaries in October 1772, see *Diary and Autobiography of John Adams*, ed. L. H. Butterfield et al., 4 vols. (Cambridge, Mass.: Harvard University Press, 1961), 2:65.

13 Lucius M. Sargent, *Dealings with the Dead, by a Sexton of the Old School*, 2 vols. (Boston: Dutton and Wentworth, 1854), 1:389; Winsor, *Memorial History of Boston*, 2:514, citing Caleb H. Snow, *History of Boston* (Boston: A. Bowen, 1825), 222.

14 For the copy of Pelham's *John Moorhead* that belonged to Edward Holyoke, see *American Historical Prints, ... from the Collection of Ambassador and Mrs. J. William Middendorf II* (New York: Sotheby Parke Bernet, 1973), 6.

15 John Moorhead, "To His Excellency Thomas Hutchinson," *Boston News-Letter*, 28 March 1771.

16 Sarah Moorhead published "Lines ... Dedicated to the Rev. Mr. Gilbert Tennent," *New England Weekly Journal*, 17 March 1741 (reprinted by Benjamin Franklin in *General Magazine and Historical Chronicle*, 1 [April 1741]: 281–82); *To the Reverend Mr. James Davenport on his Departure from Boston, ... By a Female Friend* (Boston: Charles Harrison, 1742). See *American Women Writers to 1800*, ed. Sharon M. Harris (New York: Oxford University Press, 1996), 319–22. She also wrote "To the Revd Mr Byles Upon his Enquiring about a Leather Belt," 29 May 1753, Massachusetts Historical Society, Miscellaneous papers. I thank David S. Shields for this reference.

17 Copy at the Newberry Library.

18 *Boston Post Boy*, 31 January 1763.

19 See "Diary of Edward Augustus Holyoke," *The Holyoke Diaries, 1709–1856*, ed. George Francis Dow (Salem, Mass.: Essex Institute, 1911), 37 (24 April, 13 and 18 August 1744). For Sarah Moorhead's advertisement, see *Boston Evening Post*, 25 April 1748.

20 [Sarah Moorhead], Canvaswork picture, Boston, 1750–60, silk and wool on canvas, 17 × 14 3/8 inches; described in Stephen and Carol Huber, "Sarah Moorhead Canvaswork Picture," *Antiques and Fine Art* (2003); www.antiquesandfineart.com/articles/article.cfm?request=97, accessed 25 August 2003.

21 *Boston Evening Post*, 11 June 1770.

22 On Pompey Fleet, see Isaiah Thomas, *The History of Printing in America*, 2 vols. (Worcester, Mass.: Thomas, 1810), 1:295; Sinclair Hamilton, *Early American Book Illustrators and Wood Engravers 1670–1870*, vol. 1 (Princeton: The Library, 1958), xxix; Cliford K. Shipton, "Report of the Librarian," *Proceedings of the American Antiquarian Society*, new ser., 61 (1959), 229.

23 *Boston News-Letter*, 7, 14, 21 January 1773. Some speculate that the portraitist was Scipio Moorhead. See Robinson, *Phillis Wheatley and Her Poems*, 32, 274 n.; and Romare Bearden and Harry Henderson, *A History of African-American Artists: From 1792 to the Present* (New York: Pantheon, 1992), x.

24 *An Elegy to Miss Mary Moorhead, on the Death of Her Father* ... (Boston: William M'Alpine, 1773), lines 69, 8, and 12. For the relation of the Wheatleys and the Moorheads, see Susannah Wheatley to Samson Occom, 29 March 1773; Phillis Wheatley to John Thornton, 1 December 1773 (but with postscript after 3 December); and Phillis Wheatley to John Thornton, 29 March 1774, in *The Poems of Phillis Wheatley*, ed. Mason, 6–7, 201 (see note 30 below).

25 On Wheatley's respect for social distinctions, see Margaretta Odell's 1834 "Memoir" reprinted in Robinson, *Phillis Wheatley and Her Writings*, 432–34.

26 Daniel O'Connor, marginal notes in Phillis Wheatley, *Poems on Various Subjects* (London: A. Bell, 1773). Copy held by the American Antiquarian Society.

27 See, for instance, Samella Lewis, *African American Art and Artists*, 3rd ed. (Los Angeles: University of California Press, 2003), 11–12.

28 J. A. Leo Lemay speculates that Mather Byles, "To Mr. Smibert on the Sight of his Pictures," was published in a now lost issue of the *Boston Gazette* in January 1730; it was reprinted in the *American Weekly Museum* (Philadelphia), 19 February 1730, and in the *Daily Courant* (London), 14 April 1730; it was available in book form in Mather Byles, *Poems on Several Occasions* (Boston: Kneeland and Green, 1744), 89–93. See J. A. Leo Lemay, *A Calendar of American Poetry ... Through 1765* (Worcester, Mass.: American Antiquarian Society, 1972), 24.

29 See [Dr. T.T.], "Extempore: On Seeing Mr. Wollaston's Pictures in Annapolis," reprinted in Carl Bridenbaugh, *The Colonial Craftsman* (New York: New York University Press, 1950), 101. On the *ut pictura poesis* genre, see Lemay, *Calendar of American Poetry*, xxv–xxvi. Lemay catalogs six American poems on painters between 1730 and 1765; Wheatley likely also knew British examples.

30 [Phillis Wheatley], "To S.M. a young *African* Painter, on seeing his Works," *Armenian Magazine*, 7 (July 1784), 225. Scholarly editions of Wheatley's complete writings (which print numerous variants of her published and unpublished poems) do not reprint this variant; Julian D. Mason, Jr., and Vincent Carretta both note the variant. See Phillis Wheatley, *The Collected Works of Phillis Wheatley*, ed. John C. Shields (New York: Oxford University Press, 1988); *The Poems of Phillis Wheatley*, ed. Julian D. Mason, Jr., rev. ed. (Chapel Hill: University of North Carolina Press, 1989), 105; and Phillis Wheatley, *Complete Writings*, ed. Vincent Carretta (New York: Penguin, 2001), 182.

31 The *Armenian Magazine* published one original Wheatley poem, "An Elegy on Leaving ------------" (attributed, first printing) in July 1784; and the magazine reprinted "To T.H. Esq; on the Death of his Daughter" (unattributed, 1773 version) in February 1784, the variant "To S.M" (unattributed) in April 1784, "To the Right Honourable William, Earl of Dartmouth" (attributed, variant of 1773 not identical with variants reprinted in the editions of Carretta or Shields) in July 1784, "On the Death of J.C. an Infant" (unattributed, variant of 1773) in November 1784, and "On Imagination" (unattributed, variant of 1773) in December 1784. Not all of these are recorded in Vincent Carretta's edition of Wheatley's *Complete Writings*, but see his excellent notes (esp. 102–3, 178, 181, 182). One of these poems was a direct reprinting from the 1773 volume, one was a first printing, and four were variants. Wheatley was connected to a transatlantic Methodist network, centered around Selina Hastings, the Countess of Huntington, but so far as I know, no one has traced exactly how Wheatley's poems (especially variants and unique items) ended up in the *Armenian Magazine*. For Wheatley and Huntingtonian Methodism, see David Grimsted, "Anglo-American Racism and Phillis Wheatley's 'Sable Veil,' 'Length'ned Chain,' and 'Knitted Heart,'" in *Women in the Age of the American Revolution*, ed.

Ronald Hoffman and Peter J. Albert (Charlottesville: University Press of Virginia, 1989), 338–444.

32 In a footnote to Wheatley's poem "To S.M.," Robinson notes that "Dr. Dorothy Porter Wesley, curator emerita of the Moorland-Spingarn collection at Howard University, reports that, in 1945, the antiquarian Charles Heartmann offered for sale an original pen and ink portrait of Phillis, dated 1774 (which may have been the model for W. E. Braxton's pen and ink drawing of Phillis that was printed in Charles Johnson, ed., *Ebony and Topaz Collecteana* (for the National Urban League in 1927)).... In 1947, Dr. Porter received a letter from a dealer in early Americana, offering for sale a penciled portrait of Phillis, which, the dealer believed, was the portrait on which the engravings in Phillis's 1773 volume was based" (Robinson, *Phillis Wheatley and Her Poems*, 274–75).

33 Gwendolyn DuBois Shaw, "'On Deathless Glories Fix Thine Ardent View': Scipio Moorhead, Phillis Wheatley, and the Mythic Origins of Anglo-African Portraiture in New England," in *Portraits of a People: Picturing African Americans in the Nineteenth Century* (Seattle: University of Washington Press, 2006), 29. On Phillis Wheatley's portrait also see Marcia Pointon's essay in this volume.

34 For Huntington's suggestion, see the letter from Captain Robert Calef to the Wheatleys, dated 5 January 1773, and quoted in William Henry Robinson, *Phillis Wheatley and Her Writings* (New York: Garland, 1984), 31. Significantly, the letter from Calef (dated 7 January 1773, and which reports the dialogue between Achibald Bell and the Countess of Huntington) was extracted within another letter from Susannah Wheatley to Samson Occom (dated 29 March 1773); Susannah Wheatley's letter reminds Occom "not [to] forget to write to the revd Moorhead. He is very kind to Mr. Wheatley & visits him almost every Day." The letter is reprinted in full in *Poems of Phillis Wheatley*, ed. Mason, 6–7, 155 n. 30. For engravings in Bell's publications, see an engraved portrait of Edward Hitchin in Samuel Brewer, *A Covenant God the Believer's Never-Failing Friend* (London: J. Buckland, C. and E. Dilly, and A. Bell, 1774); G. Burder, engraving of a graveyard scene after George Wright in George Wright, *Solitary Walks*, 3rd ed. (London: W. Otridge; J. Buckland; G. Keith; Kitchin and Co.; S. Chandler; and A. Bell, 1775), frontispiece. Neither resembles the portrait of Wheatley. For copyright registrations, see Roger E. Stoddard, *A Library-Keeper's Business*, ed. Carol Z. Rothkopf (New Castle, Del.: Oak Knoll Books, 2002), 64.

35 For twentieth-century attributions, see Shaw, "On Deathless Glories," 28–29. William H. Robinson suggests "That Mrs. Wheatley engaged Scipio Moorhead, black artist and servant to the Reverened and Mrs. John Moorhead of Boston's Long Lane Presbyterian Church, to paint Phyllis's picture is most probable but undocumented" (Robinson, *Phillis Wheatley and Her Writings*, 31).

36 Boyle, "Journal of Occurrences," January 23, 1774, in *New England Historical and Genealogical Register* 84 (1930), 372.

37 B. B. Thatcher, *Memoir of Phillis Wheatley* (Boston: Geo. W. Light, 1834), 25–26; see also Odell, *Memoir and Poems of Phillis Wheatley* (Boston: Geo. W. Light, 1834), 18. Thatcher's version was marketed to children.

38 Laurel Thatcher Ulrich, "Furniture as Social History: Gender, Property, and Memory in the Decorative Arts," *American Furniture* (1995), 39–68.

39 I am grateful to Paul Staiti for suggesting parallels between the image of Wheatley and the scribe in Smibert's *Bermuda Group*. For the provenance and location of the painting, see Saunders, *John Smibert*, 123–24, 171–73.

40 See *Letters and Diary of John Rowe, Boston Merchant 1759–1762 [and] 1764–1779*, ed. Anne Rowe Cunningham (Boston: W. B. Clarke, 1903), 248. For Occom and the

Wheatleys, especially Susannah, see Robinson, *Phillis Wheatley and Her Writings*, 13–14, 112–13; and *The Collected Writings of Samson Occum, Mohegan*, ed. Joanna Brooks (New York: Oxford University Press, 2006), 96–98, 106–7.

41 *Boston News-Letter*, 12 December 1773.

42 See John Moorhead (docket number 15527), Administrator's Account (17 March 1775), Suffolk County Probate Record Book, 74:355.

43 Indeed, in the nineteenth century, the conjunction of a slave auction near the liberty tree made this particular advertisement worthy of citation. See Winsor, *Memorial History*, 2:485, citing Sargent, *Dealings with the Dead*, 1:150–51. Lucius M. Sargent's articles were originally published in the *Boston Evening Transcript*.

44 For examples, see *Boston Evening Post*, 20 March 1775, and the will of Margaret Alford (Thwing 48083), written in 1770, which stipulated emancipation for four slaves because "I am not satisfied in my mind of the right we have by the Law of God to make slaves of Negros." On "prime cost," see Samuel Swift's notice about his slave Scipio in the *Boston News-Letter*, 5 July 1770.

45 For the example referred to in the (loyalist) paper Mary Moorhead subscribed to, see "To be Sold or Let, a Healthy Negro Man, about 40 Years of age," *Massachusetts Gazette*, 9 June 1774.

46 See John Moorhead (docket number 15527), Account and Distribution (17 March 1775), Suffolk County Probate Court Record Book, 74:355–56; and Mary Moorhead (docket number 16115), Will (dated 5 April 1776; probated 17 January 1777), Suffolk County Probate Court Record Book, 76:25.

47 Mary Moorhead made no allowance for Scipio in her 1776 will. Alexander Willson died in 1785; he did not make a will, but by 1785 slavery had been declared unconstitutional in Massachusetts, and so no human being would appear as an item on the inventory of his estate. See Mary Moorhead (docket number 16115), Will (dated 5 April 1776; probated 17 January 1777), Suffolk County Probate Court Record Book, 76:25; for Alexander Willson's probate records, see docket number 18460.

48 I am grateful to Chernoh Sesay for looking for Scipio Moorhead in late-eighteenth-century Boston tax records.

late 1. Diego Velázquez, *Juan de Pareja*, 1650. Oil on canvas. Metropolitan Museum of Art, New York. Purchase, letcher and Rogers Funds, and Bequest of Miss Adelaide Milton de Groot (1876–1967), by exchange, supplemented by ifts from friends of the Museum, 1971. Photo: Malcolm Varon. © Metropolitan Museum of Art/Art Resource, New York.

Plate 2. William Hoare of Bath, *Portrait of Ayuba Suleiman Diallo, called Job ben Solomon (1701–73)*, 1733. Oil on canvas 76.2 × 64.2 cm. OM.762. Orientalist Museum, Doha. On long-term loan to the National Portrait Gallery, London.

Plate 3. Andrés Sánchez Galque, *Portrait of Don Francisco de Arobe and his sons Don Pedro and Don Domingo*, 1599. Oil on canvas. Courtesy of El Museo de América, inventory 69, Museo Nacional del Prado, Madrid, no. 4.778.

Plate 4. Juan de Pareja, *The Calling of Saint Matthew*, 1661. Oil on canvas. Museo Nacional del Prado, Madrid.

Plate 5 (*top*). William Hogarth, *Captain Lord George Graham, 1715–47, in his Cabin*, ca. 1745. Oil on canvas. National Maritime Museum, Greenwich, London, BHC2720.

Plate 6 (*bottom*). José Nicolás de Escalera, *Familia del Conde de Casa Bayona* (Family of the Count of Casa Bayona), 1770s. Oil on canvas. Church of Santa María del Rosario, Cuba. Photo: Ramsés Hernández Batista.

Plate 7. Albert Eckhout, *African Woman and Child*, 1641. Oil on canvas. National Museum, Copenhagen.

Plate 8. Charles Henri Joseph Cordier, *Negro of the Sudan in Algerian Costume*, 1856–57. Oxidized silver-plated bronze and onyx-marble. Musée d'Orsay, Paris, inv. no. RF 2997. Photo: Amaudet. Réunion des Musées Nationaux/Art Resource, New York.

Plate 9. Marie-Guilhelmine Benoist, *Portrait d'une Négresse* (Portrait of a Negress), 1800. Oil on canvas. Musée du Louvre, Paris. Photo: Thierry Le Mage/Réunion des Musées Nationaux/Art Resource, New York.

Plate 10. Nathaniel Jocelyn, *Portrait of Cinqué*, ca. 1839–40. Oil on canvas. Whitney Library, New Haven Museum and Historical Society, New Haven, Conn.

Plate 11. José Correia de Lima, *O Retrato do Intrépido Marinheiro Simão, Carvoeiro do Vapor Pernambucana* (The Portrait of the Intrepid Mariner Simão, Coalman of the Steamship Pernambucana), ca. 1854–55. Oil on canvas. Museu Nacional de Belas Artes/ Instituto Brasileiro de Museus/Ministério da Cultura, Rio de Janeiro. Photo: Jaime Acioli.

Part II

SLAVE PORTRAITURE, COLONIALISM, AND MODERN IMPERIAL CULTURE

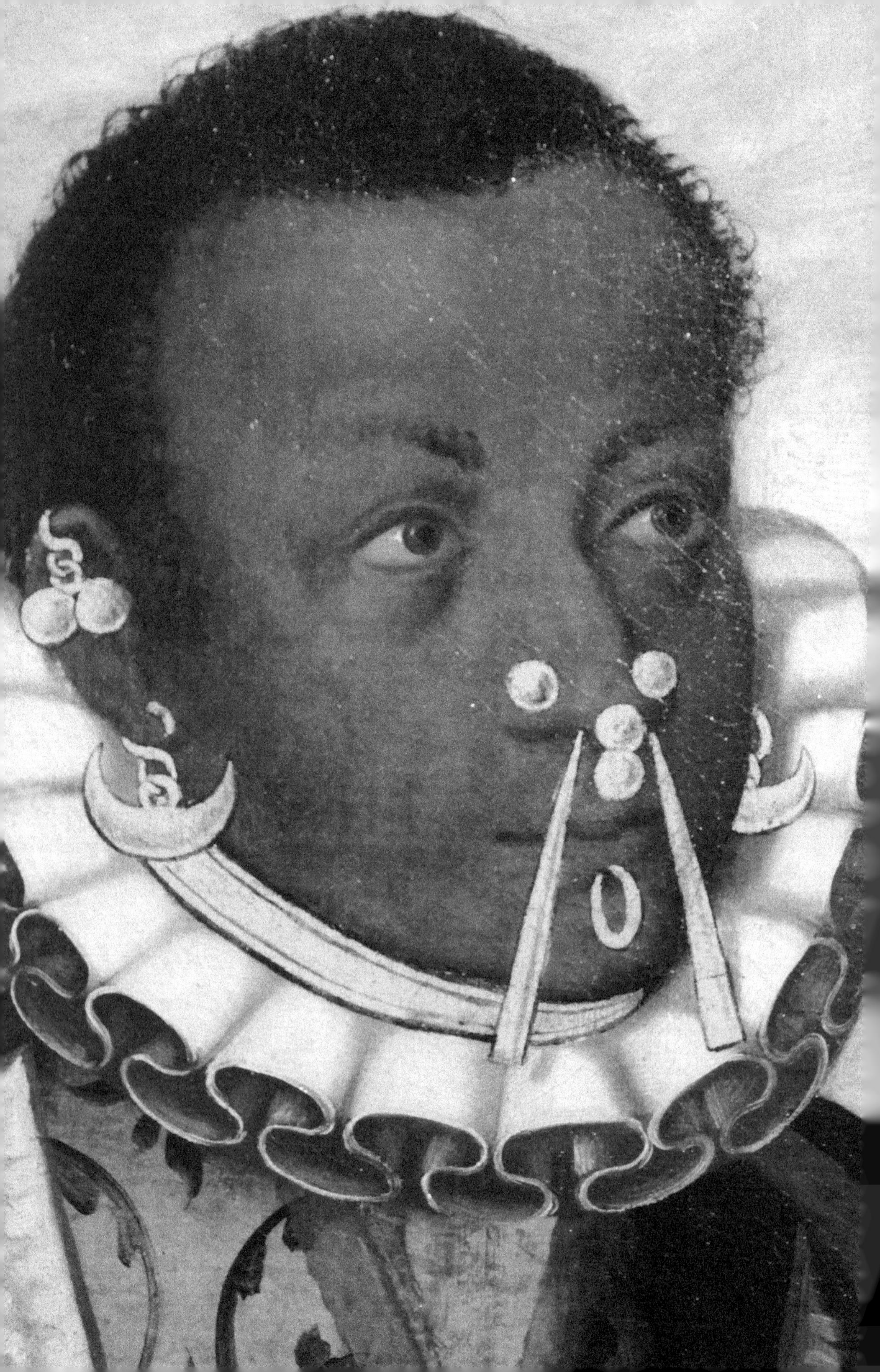

FOUR

THREE GENTLEMEN FROM ESMERALDAS

A PORTRAIT FIT FOR A KING

Tom Cummins

> ... in particular I send to your Royal person the portraits of captain Don Francisco de Arobe, and Don Pedro and Don Domingo his sons, mulatto leaders of Esmeraldas along with a short account of this event as it seemed to me that your Majesty would like to see something so new and extraordinary.[1]
>
> Juan del Barrio y Sepúlveda to Philip III, 12 April 1599

> As it seemed that your majesty would like to see these barbarians painted who until now have been invincible and being a very extraordinary thing, I sent them [their portrait] with the letter and this memorial to your majesty.[2]
>
> Juan del Barrio y Sepúlveda to Philip III, 15 April 1600

> ... the first among the leaders of said province was the captain Don Francisco de Arrobe and his sons of whom last year 1599 I sent to your majesty their portrait along with the said papers and relations.[3]
>
> Juan del Barrio y Sepúlveda to Philip III, 15 October 1600

> The doctor Juan del Barrio y Sepúlveda, Judge of The Royal Audience of Quito had this (portrait) made at his own expense in the Year 1599, for His Majesty Philip (III) Catholic king of Spain and the Indies.[4]
>
> Inscription of the painting by Andrés Sánchez Galque, *Portrait of Don Francisco de Arobe and his sons Don Pedro and Don Domingo* (1599)

Perhaps all representations engender and are engendered by desire. However, genres of representation have and provoke differing desires. Portraits, especially painted portraits, engender and are engendered by particular desires and emotions, often by those of the subject: the desire to remember and to be remembered; to be present when absent through time and/or space: to be seen and to see.[5] But the texts above, which come from a portrait and several letters penned by the man who commissioned it, suggest that a portrait can be about a different set of desires, bordering on anxieties and longings that have as much to do with the portrait as an object as it does with the subject of the portrait. That is, the patron wants the portrait to be seen and be appreciated by a specific individual, but neither is the subject of the portrait. Yet the portrait is also about the fixing of the ambiguity of its subject, an issue of political and social identity that was important to both the patron and the specific viewer. At the same time, this portrait as a painting presents its subject for whom the issue of their political and social identity is differently understood and desired. These differences in which ambivalence and ambiguity are at the nexus between patron, subject, and viewer are based upon historical conditions only possible in the New World. They, the historical conditions, are on display in the portrait as both resolved and unresolved. This simultaneity of seemingly irreconcilable states of being as a constituent part of the portrait is based on numerous related factors, but certainly one of them is the fact that the portrait was painted by an artist whose own social and political identity is altogether different from all the other parties concerned. The portrait therefore presents a historical dialectic that is called forth by all of the participants of its creation: the patron, a Spanish high official; the artist, an Indian painter; and the subject, three independent mulattos, not slaves but not legally free, an escaped slave and his two descendants. Finally the portrait is part of a larger set of communications between a colonial official and his king. It is intended to negotiate their relationship. But a portrait is radically different than a set of written documents, even when they are produced simultaneously and in relation to each other and with a common purpose. What is it, then, that can be supposed and desired of a portrait, and what can a portrait portray above and beyond those suppositions? Or simply, why does this portrait seem so important at all, at least to its patron? And what of the artist and the sitters?

The portrait was painted in 1599 in Quito, a major colonial city and seat of an *audiencia* (regional court) in the vast Viceroyalty of Peru. It was commissioned by Juan del Barrio y Sepúlveda, a judge in that court, and it was painted by the native Quiteño artist Andrés Sánchez Galque.[6] It depicts in three-quarter-length three mulatto gentlemen from the coastal province of Esmeraldas: Don Francisco de Arobe and his two sons, Don Pedro and Don Domingo, who had come to the highland city of Quito in 1599 (Fig. 4.1, Plate 3). Once finished, it was sent to the court of Philip III, where it was received and remained in the royal collection, until its transfer to the Prado Museum in the nineteenth century. This part of its

4.1. Andrés Sánchez Galque, *Portrait of Don Francisco de Arobe and his sons Don Pedro and Don Domingo*, 1599. Oil on canvas. Courtesy of El Museo de América, inventory 69, Museo Nacional del Prado, Madrid, no. 4.778.

history is recorded in part by the two numbers that appear in white and orange on the canvas and that come from different royal inventories.[7]

The portrait is full of textual and visual play that presents the parallel histories: that of its own production and that of Don Francisco and his two sons. They are, in fact, juxtaposed so as to be kept separate. For example, the painted Latin text outlines the relation of production and anticipated reception (Fig. 4.2): "The doctor Juan del Barrio y Sepúlveda, Judge of the Royal Audience of Quito, had this (portrait) made at his own expense in the Year 1599, for His Majesty Philip (III) Catholic king of Spain and the Indies." The golden initial letters and beautiful chancellery script appear against a white background as if this were a document distinct from the painted image of the three men. This illusion is furthered by the elaborate cartouche painted to appear like a gilded frame and to look as if it hangs, suspended from the canvas itself. This visual slight of hand, almost a trompe l'oeil, disassociates not only the Latin text but its content as well from the rest of the composition and thereby places the names and therefore the persons of the king and Juan del Barrio y Sepúlveda in a different realm from the pictorial space of the subjects of the portrait, dangerous and uncivilized individuals.

The textual address of del Barrio y Sepúlveda is about his participation in the creation of the image for the king. He commissioned and paid for it. The materiality of the portrait as a thing to be paid for is made apparent against the illusion of the image itself. The artist also makes manifest through Latin his

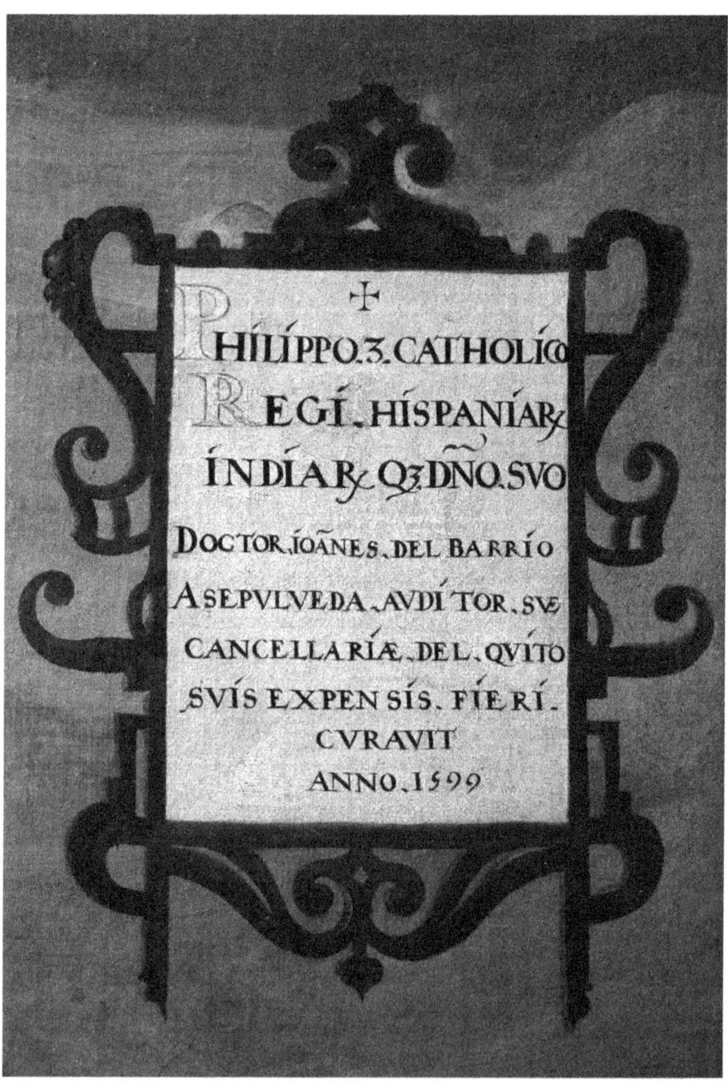

4.2. Detail of Figure 4.1 (cartouche). Andrés Sánchez Galque, *Portrait of Don Francisco de Arobe and his sons Don Pedro and Don Domingo*, 1599.

participation in the physical creation in the painting, which is signed: "Andrés Sánches Galque native of Quito, made it" (*AR SHS GA-Q nl. de qto ft*). A different text in a different script and language identifies the subjects of the portraits: Don Francisco, 56 years of age, center; Don Pedro, 22 years of age, left; and Don Domingo, 18 years of age, right. The use of the term "Don" is neither innocent nor accidental. It is a mark both of the unique history of independence that the various mulatto communities had gained from Spanish authority during the sixteenth century and of a syntagmatic chain of visuals signs that lead ultimately to the portrait of Don Francisco and his sons. To understand the links in this chain, it is important to trace them to their genesis. Few histories of image creation have such a profound and specific origin.

GENESIS

Twenty-two years before Sánchez Galque created the portrait with the title *Don* so prominently placed before the names of the three gentlemen, a crucial event took place in 1577 on the north coast of Ecuador (Fig. 4.3). In a written account of the event by one of the participants, a set of verbal, visual, and textual exchanges are described that detail the bestowing of the honorific title *Don* on a leader of an independent community in Esmeraldas. The encounter took place between Miguel Cabello de Balboa, an ex-soldier and priest, and Alonso de Illescas, an African and escaped slave. Their interaction initiated a chain of symbolic acts and visual forms that ultimately come to reside in the portrait. Hence it is important to recount briefly this history of Alonso as it led up to this event.

Alonso de Illescas was an African born in Cabo Verde, present-day Senegal, where he was captured by slave traders and eventually brought to Spain, where he was bought by the Sevillian merchant Alonso de Illescas. In 1553 the slave Alonso de Illescas found himself aboard his master's ship bound from Panama to Lima when it floundered in the rough seas off the coast of Esmeraldas, just at the equator. It was there that the slave, Alonso de Illescas, fled with others to the interior. Alonso established the first independent community of escaped slaves, Indians, and mulattos, which would soon grow in size and number. Their independence was a threat to the Spanish on many counts. First, their community

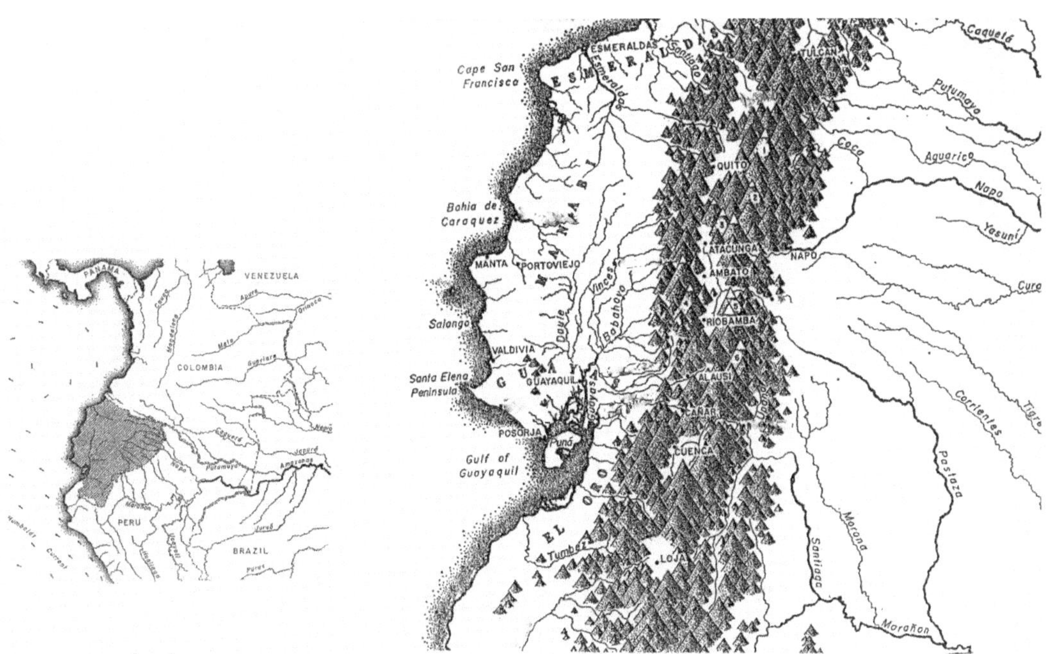

4.3. Modern map of Ecuador. Photo: Author.

was outside the authority and rule of the crown. Second, the mulatto communities were able to resist repeated incursions from the capital city of Quito to establish a port and easier entrance to Quito, which was in the highlands. Third, the establishment of an independent maroon community provided a safe haven for future escaped slaves. As these communities grew in number and strength they first overwhelmed the weakened indigenous communities and either killed them, enslaved them, and/or intermarried with them. Their offspring became a community of mulattos, a term that continued to be used to define them well into the seventeenth century. Finally, this autonomous community posed a lethal threat to the whole of the Viceroyalty of Peru by potentially providing safe harbor for English and Dutch marauders. Thus when news arrived in 1576 that Alonso had rescued several Spaniards who had been shipwrecked and who would have otherwise perished in the mangrove swamps of the region, it was seen as an opportunity to approach him and to bring him and his community under the suzerainty of colonial authority. It was with this threat in mind that Cabello de Balboa set off from Quito to meet with Alonso de Illescas on the humid and very hot coast of Esmeraldas.

Cabello de Balboa vividly describes his first encounter in a mangrove swamp. He writes in the third person of how the Spaniards stood on the shore where they had built a chapel the night before to celebrate the Nativity of the Virgin in September 1586 and awaited the arrival of the mulattos by canoe. He then shifts his account to reported speech, a type of textual portrait, writing that he addressed the approaching Alonso saying: "Come, señor Don Alonso Illescas, enjoy the good and mercy that God Our Lord and his majesty offer you on this day."[8]

Alonso from the prow of his canoe responds, "I call myself Alonso and I don't have the title Don." Cabello de Balboa replied to Alonso saying, "The king can give and place the title Don as you will come to understand shortly, if you come to shore."[9] Later that day King Philip II did grant Alonso the title of Don, and he made him governor of the territory. The king, Philip II, accomplished this gift of Don by the fact that Cabello de Balboa carried with him a *real provisión* bearing the royal seal that not only pardoned Alonso de Illescas of past transgressions but also made him governor of the area. The document was read word for word, and then taking the hand of the "new and negro governor" (nuevo y negro gobernador) and holding the *real provisión* "and looking at the seal" (y mirando el sello) said, "These are the coat of arms of the king my lord whom you well know" (Estas son las Armas del rey mi señor que bien conozcas). Kissing the document Alonso then put it over his head saying "Lord vicar, I commend to you my head and the heads of my sons and companions as to our Lord father; our land and all that is in it is of his Majesty and from now on, in his royal name, I give my obedience and that of those who are in my charge the mulattos who reside within nine or ten leagues of my house."[10]

This exchange was typical in its ritual form. The king's presence and power were made manifest through the appearance of his seal, and it conferred the rights and privileges recorded within the document to whomever it was given. In exchange the recipient paid symbolic obedience by placing himself under the king's power by physically placing the image over his head.[11] However, in this instance the men, Spaniards, Africans, and mulattos, looking at the image and ritually moving it over their bodies, acknowledged the remarkable career of the escaped slave Alonso de Illescas and his companions. But just as important, he and the other escaped slaves understood the symbolic power of the image as something ambiguous and dangerous as it passed over Alonso's head. Many, if not all, of them bore other earlier images on their bodies, marking a different kind of authority, the marks of slavery that had been burned onto them.[12]

Alonso's rise to power in Esmeraldas began by marrying the daughter of the local cacique, Chilnindauli, and after killing his father-in-law he took control of the area. This history is well known through both Cabello de Balboa's account as well as a rich set of other documents.[13] What is important here is the narrative tone used by Cabello de Balboa as it provides, from the point of view of the Spaniards, a clear historical representation of Alonso de Illescas and his group as well as other mulatto communities in Esmeraldas. Alonso's rise to power in the area is described in terms of ruthlessness and treachery. One passage suffices to give the tone. It relates how Alonso de Illescas and the others fell to fighting among themselves such that only seven men and three women remained:

> Seeing that they were now so few, they agreed upon a pact that only they and the devil would be able to imagine, and it was to get rid of (most of) the few friends they had, because there were always only a just few natives from the area with them, and not to leave alive any more than a small number of them who they could easily control, (and) they put the plan into action with such cruelty as could only be believed of such soulless and barbarous people.[14]

I want just to stress a characterization used by Cabello de Balboa as I will return to it at the end of this essay: that the mulattos of Esmeraldas are seen not just as barbarous people, that this is a categorical term used throughout the Americas for Indians as well as Africans. They are characterized also as soulless people. Their alliance with the crown and Alonso's kissing and raising of the real provision over his head in exchange for the title Don temporally redresses this categorization, but it also underscores the fact that Don Alonso and his descendants were only marginally under control of Spanish sovereignty, that they had won their independence. And, in fact, the conferring of the title Don on Alonso Illescas was only skeptically accepted by the mulatto community, or at least that is how Cabello de Balboa imagined it. He wrote a fictional dialogue in which Don Alonso is asked by some of his Indian companions:

> Who is it that moves you so that you would give up the freedom you have labored so hard to obtain and stop being your own master in order to place yourselves in servitude and be enslaved? ... How can you trust these Christians since you know that their inclination is to take everything for themselves? ... Do you think that it is for virtue's sake that they have brought these gifts (titles) for you other than as a baited hook by which to catch you? Forget about placing yourselves in the hands of your enemies for your past deeds will not be forgiven and you will not be able to do more than cry in vain, and if not for yourself, do it for us, father and we will love and obey you as such, don't pay us back by bringing our women and children to these bearded ones. You and your son-in-law would be punished as malefactors and your children as slaves and we would never be free. Don't do this thing you mean to do, if you don't want to end your life and ours in perpetual agony.[15]

Cabello de Balboa's text is remarkable as it assumes the narrative voice of the mulattos and Indians as they discuss the potential treachery of the Spanish and their begging of Don Alonso to refuse the king's gift and mercy. It also conceives of Alonso's subjection to the King of Spain as a renewed threat of enslavement, if not as a new form of bondage. This hostility and cynicism by the mulattos and Indians reads almost as if Cabello de Balboa sympathetically understands the reasons for their worry. But it is not that. He writes this text after he realizes that his political and religious mission has failed, and Alonso does not return to meet him again. Retreating to Quito, he places blame for that failure in the voices of the untrusting Indians and mulattos.

The Making of the Portrait

Uneasy relations continued to exist between the mulatto communities and the Spanish authorities in Quito. Not only was Esmeraldas rich in gold and a potential new port of entry, but there was a pool of labor there as well. These resources brought repeated Spanish attempts to "pacify" the area, but little was accomplished, and many expeditions ended in utter disaster. Nonetheless negotiations continued with these ungovernable "gobernadores" and "Dons" to "pacify" them. Thus twenty-two years after Alonso de Illescas had met with Cabello de Balboa, a related, but different group of mulattos came to Quito, led by their leader Don Francisco de Arobe and his two sons. Don Francisco was the son of an African slave and a Nicaraguan Indian who had fled from a boat traveling from Nicaragua that stopped in Bay of San Mateo in 1553, and like Don Alonso, he fled inland, first joining with Alonso and then forming an independent community. Don Francisco and his sons had come to Quito in recognition of another treaty that had been signed between them and Juan del Barrio y Sepúlveda. It was in recognition of this occasion that del Barrio y Sepúlveda commissioned the Indian artist Andrés Sánchez Galque to paint their portrait.

We do not know for certain why this Spanish judge selected this native artist to paint so important a portrait, a portrait to be sent to the king. But one can surmise that Barrio was judicious in making his decision and that he went about finding the best artist available. Unfortunately, we know only a little about the painter. He was trained in Quito, perhaps in the Colegio de San Andrés under the tutelage of the Flemish Franciscan Fray Jodoco Ricke. However, the colegio closed in 1581, and the artistic training of the natives shifted to the cloister of Santo Domingo, under the direction of Fray Pedro Bedón, a criollo born in Quito in 1556. There are two reasons to suppose that Sánchez Galque more closely followed the training of Bedón than Ricke. First, Bedón formed in 1588 an important confraternity of Nuestra Señora del Rosario de los Naturales (Our Lady of the Rosary of the Natives) in the monastery of Santo Domingo in Quito. His drawing of the Virgin of the Rosary appears on the initial page or frontispiece for the membership book of the confraternity in the Church of Santo Domingo (Fig. 4.4). This Mannerist image is more than just a beautiful drawing that initiates the membership book. It is a fundamental part of how Bedón imagined three confraternities united in common devotion, each with a discrete racial membership composed of Spaniards, criollos, Indians, and Africans. Galque was a prominent member of the confraternity and became *prioste* (steward) in 1605. At some level, therefore, Sánchez Galque worked closely with Bedón in furthering the aims of the brotherhood.

4.4. Fray Pedro Bedón, *Virgin of the Rosary*, 1588. Pen and ink with color wash. Library of the Monastery of Santo Domingo, Quito. Photo: Author.

Bedón himself had trained in Lima with an Italian Mannerist painter and sculptor, the Jesuit Bernardo Bitti, and his Mannerist influence is evident in Bedón's drawing of the Virgin of the Rosary. The sharp line, chiseled features, and exaggerated and expressive gestures are characteristic of the style learned from Bitti.[16] As José de Mesa and Teresa Gisbert pointed out some forty years ago, it is Bedón's style that informs Andrés Sánchez Galque's painting.[17] Although there are few known works of his, one small devotional painting depicting Christ at the column with Saint Peter is also signed by him and dated 1605 (Fig. 4.5).[18] Like the portrait of Don Francisco and his sons painted ten years earlier, the place of production, Quito, is placed after the artist's name (Fig. 4.6), and also

4.5. Andrés Sanchéz Galque, *Christ at the Column with Saint Peter*, 1605. Oil on canvas. Courtesy of Museo de Arte Virreinal Charcas, Sucre.

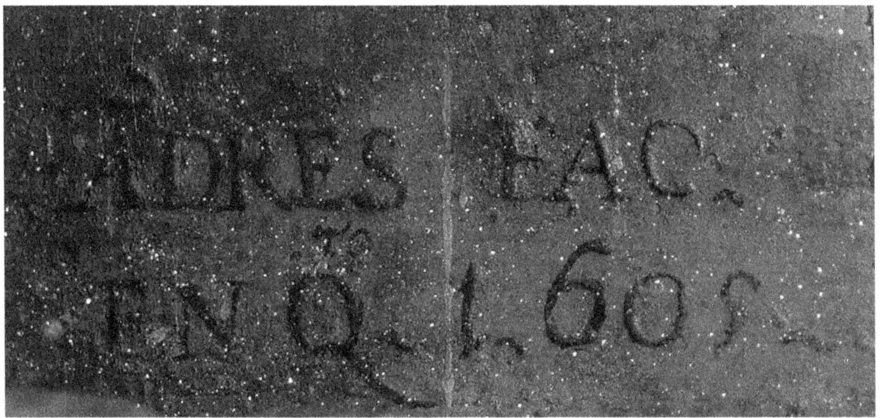

4.6. Detail of Figure 4.5 (signature). Andrés Sánchez Galque, *Christ at the Column with Saint Peter*, 1605.

like the portrait, this devotional painting displays Mannerist traits. Christ's body is elongated, and his delicately painted fingers are similar to those of Don Pedro and Don Domingo in the portrait. The point is that Sánchez Galque is one of only a very few painters in Quito besides Bedón to sign his paintings, which is recognition of the desire to register the presence of this artist, through his name, in the painting. The commission of Sánchez Galque by del Barrio y Sepúlveda for so momentous a portrait clearly recognizes the stature of this artist among his peers.

Once, however, Sánchez Galque the Indian artist was asked to paint the portrait, he was confronted with something rather unique. And so we can imagine him, standing before his subjects, the three fictive descendants of Don Alonso. This painting by Sánchez Galque, unlike his others, is truly remarkable. It is not only that it is the oldest surviving signed portrait from South America and that it is a group portrait of three sitters, Don Francisco de Arobe, and his sons Don Domingo and Don Pedro, about whom we know a great deal both before and after the portrait was painted. It is also a portrait of tremendous originality and integrity. Sánchez Galque goes beyond the desires of his patron, who requested the painting of these men in order to provide visual proof of his prodigious accomplishments as a faithful civil servant. He will present himself through his painting and signature before a king whom he will never see on a continent that he will never visit. So what are the thoughts and issues that confront Sánchez Galque as he prepares to render the mulatto leaders from San Mateo on the Ecuadorian coast in Esmeraldas into an image? Remember that the term "mulatto" in the sixteenth century refers to the offspring of native Americans and Africans and therefore is an entirely new category of being without a traditional pictorial genre of representation to which Galque has any recall.

There is not even a fixed textual description that signals any physical identifying features. Yet, Galque has been commissioned, perhaps in part because he was an Indian himself, to paint the group portrait in Quito to commemorate that in 1597 the mulattos had been "re-pacified" and had become fully Christian under the efforts of the chief judge of the Audiencia, Juan del Barrio y Sepúlveda, and the Mercedarian missionary Diego de Torres. This achievement was deemed worthy enough by Barrio y Sepúlveda to commission the portraits to be sent to Philip III in Madrid. The accompanying letter written by Barrio to the king explains his actions:

> As it would seem Your Majesty would like to see these barbarians depicted, who up until now have been invincible, and being something very extraordinary, I send them (in this portrait) with its letter and this memorial to your majesty. They are well disposed and agile men normally adorned with golden necklaces flat around the neck and nose rings, earrings, lip plugs and ring piercings on their chin and buttons in their noses and still others in their checks, all of gold – and the Indian leaders of the province as well as a few others wear the same adornments and white chain linked necklaces or strings of beads that they wear at their neck over their dress (and) they say that they are (made of) the teeth of fish or from shells. Normally they wear other adornments of less elegant and artistic manufacture. Usually they carry in their hands small spear throwers and three or four darts made of ironwood although without very sharp blades. They are all painted (in this portrait) very faithfully as they are and as they usually appear except for their dress that, which since they have made peace and have given obedience to your majesty through the *toma de posesión*,[19] and placed (themselves) under the mercy of the royal crown, they wear as appears in the portrait. As they are not civilized people (gente política) and their land which is hot they wear no more than mantas and shirts as do the rest of the Indians. They have good minds and are very cunning and astute; they understand the Spanish language although they speak it awkwardly. They have been great warriors against the heathen Indians of other heathen provinces. They are greatly feared by them (the Indians) because they kill many of them and those that they capture become their slaves over whom they rule with terrible firmness and cruel punishment. They have never been made subject to (the authority) of the Spanish. This Don Arobe has always treated the Spaniards who are washed up on shore well, which is mentioned in the petition that he presented in Quito when he made peace and offered himself as a faithful servant to his majesty.[20]

There are several critical elements of del Barrio y Sepúlveda's text that need explication and analysis because the letter is remarkable in voicing what he believes the portrait both to be and to represent. First and foremost, there is his presumption that the king would want to see the barbarians Don Francisco and his sons depicted in a portrait. He is, perhaps, following here the precedent set by the Viceroy of Peru, Francisco de Toledo, who in the 1570s sent a set of portraits of the Inca kings to Philip II. The Inca portraits, however, were imaginary historical portraits, whereas the Quito portrait was of a living sitter. Second, del Barrio y Sepúlveda reasons that the king would want to see the portrait of the three gentlemen as they are "cosa muy extraordinaria." A straight translation is "a very extraordinary thing." However, this phrase has, perhaps, an expected resonance in regard to certain objects from the Americas in the royal collections in Spain. "Exotic objects" brought from the Americas for royal viewing were kept in the late sixteenth century in the Escorial, and they were inventoried at the time of Philip II's death under the category of "cosas extraordinarias."[21] The objects listed in this inventory were extremely varied, coming from Mexico, Brazil, China, and Peru. Some were the most important political symbols of the Inca, and others were pieces of wood from Brazil. Although the portrait of Don Francisco and his sons entered into the collection of paintings and not the collection of "cosas extraordinarias," del Barrio y Sepúlveda's description of the face adornments and the kinds of weapons they carry classify some of what is represented in the portrait within the category of "cosa extraordinaria". In this sense, it is perhaps important that del Barrio y Sepúlveda does not actually refer to the portrait in the letter but rather to the persons of Don Francisco and his sons. They are something extraordinary, and he sends them ("los embia"), not it (the portrait). Of course, he means the portrait, but like the royal portrait that makes present the king, del Barrio y Sepúlveda makes present before the king the three mulattos who he has brought under the control of his majesty, transformed now into extraordinary "objects." It is as if the liminal condition in which the mulattos lived until that point (oscillating between an antagonistic juridical recognition of their freedom and a perpetual threat of enslavement) was resolved in the portrait by subjecting them symbolically to a condition of "thingness." They become objects of display offered to the king by his judge. Their portrait will come to stand for them in a system of colonial symbolic exchange.

Equally important is that although they may appear "as they are" perhaps in terms of their physiognomy, clothes, and body ornament, they do not appear to be anywhere in particular. That is, the three-quarter-length composition of the portrait and its neutral background work visually to disembody Francisco de Arobe and the others from a recognizable connection to any real physical space, meaning that they are not necessarily to be imagined standing on the same surface or even be in the same room as the artist or the viewer. Now, these are common enough conventions for portraiture, but here they create a distance between the viewer and the subject, perhaps a colonially racialized distance, that Sánchez Galque manages to factor into the portrait. The composition itself is unusual. The Spanish genre of sixteenth-century portraits rarely includes three figures.[22] Nor are there any known portraits of slaves or escaped slaves from the Americas. Yet, it is not altogether convincing. No matter how the volume of their bodies presses close to the picture surface or how vivid and tactile the texture of their clothing appears, the viewer is arrested from engaging with them. There is something too startling in the faces as they appear above the ruffled collars and in the black hands as they emerge from the ruffled cuffs holding spears. But here one could pause to ask if the faces may appear startling in some fashion to us because there are so very few portraits of mulattos from the sixteenth century, and that this is an attribute projected onto the portrait. Perhaps, but the category of mulatto is itself a colonial racial construct of the sixteenth century.[23] This is the first generation in the Viceroyalty of Peru, and in this politicized ethnogenesis created out of slavery and conquest there is newness, ambiguity, and anxiety among all.

So how is Sánchez Galque to create an image to be recognized as being that of a mulatto that is not seen as an Indio or a *negro*, escaped slave, but free? What are the traits or signs that can be factored into the portrait to signal this particular form of ethnogenesis? Can skin color be a marker here? It is insofar as one can see dark faces, that they clearly signify not European, although Don Francisco sports a graying and sparse goatee (Fig. 4.7).

They are darker than Indians are, and their hair is curled and short rather than straight and long (Figs. 4.8 and 4.9). In appearance, one might see them as Africans, but they are not. But then again, how do the faces not signify African or Indian? There is no exact degree of color or physical features that can be securely called upon to convey that they are neither and to convey that they are both. How is one to read into the figures the progenitors and descendants of a community of slaves made free by their own will?

First of all, Sánchez Galque creates in the painting an inner structure that may be said to no longer be a window into a place the viewer might imaginatively penetrate. There is a barrier behind which the three men stand. For example, there is absolutely no recession into the picture. That is, the three figures may appear in the immediate foreground. However, the horizontal structure of the composition, the verticality of the spears held forward, and the rhythmic use of color create this sense of barrier and distance. Even gesture and its meaning are unsettled as a code for understanding between viewer and subject. The hats held in their hands are to be read through courtly etiquette and as such address the spectator. But the gestures do not necessarily register as being meaningful to the subjects, but are a part of constant ongoing negotiations of signs. These are not their normal clothes, so how can the tipping of the hat mean to Don Francisco what it does to the king? The act cannot possibly be read as a form of

4.7. Detail of Figure 4.1 (goatee). Andrés Sánchez Galque, *Portrait of Don Francisco de Arobe and his sons Don Pedro and Don Domingo*, 1599.

reciprocity of meaning. These are pictorial conventions that are not fully convincing in the colonial painting, in part because what kind of men these men are is not clear, not in their representation, not in their race, not in their political belonging.

So, how is the king as the ultimate spectator of all subjects "to see them as they really are?" As the letter notes, the clothes and the gestures are not theirs

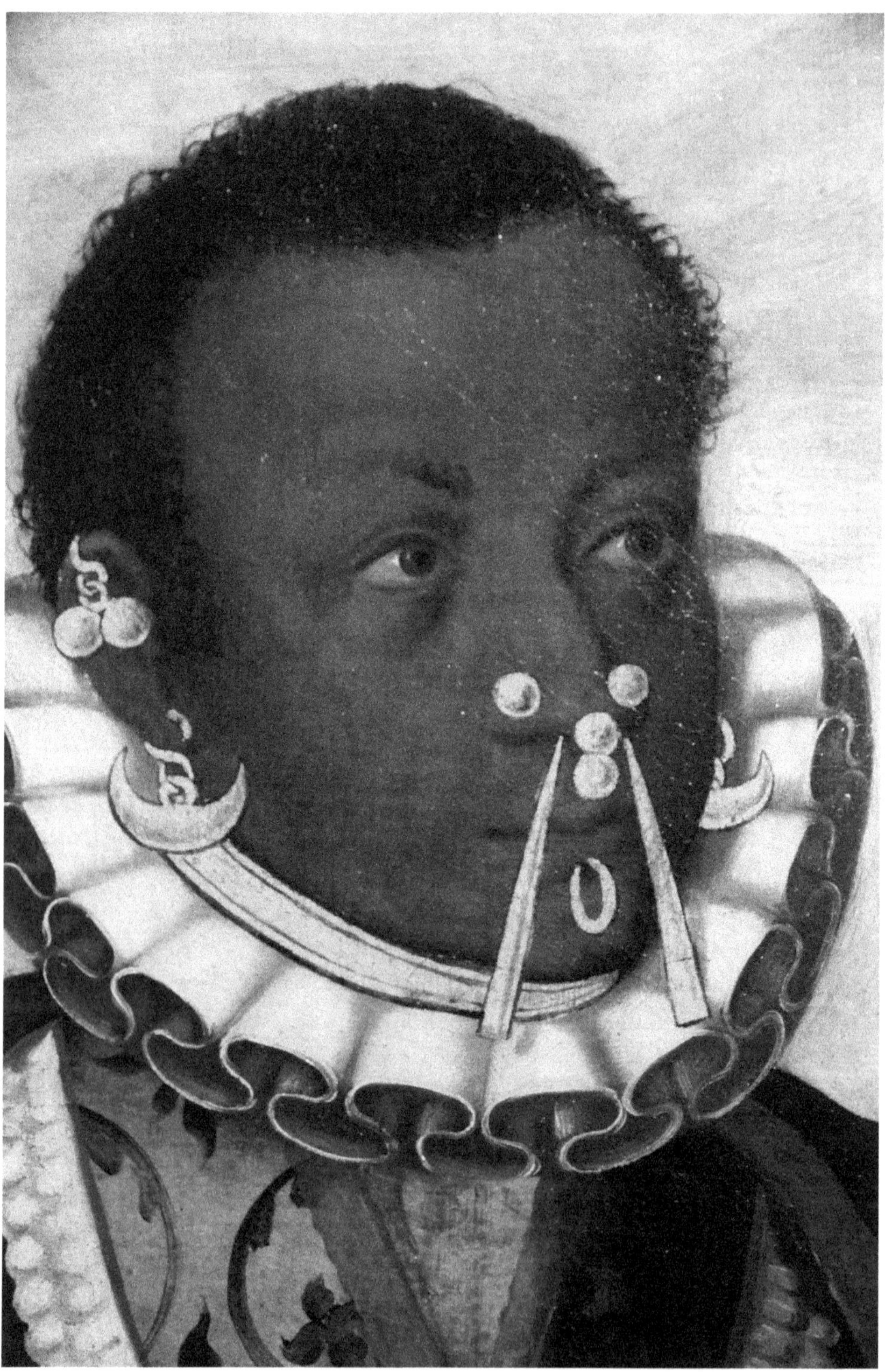

4.8. Detail of Figure 4.1 (Don Pedro's face). Andrés Sánchez Galque, *Portrait of Don Francisco de Arobe and his sons Don Pedro and Don Domingo*, 1599.

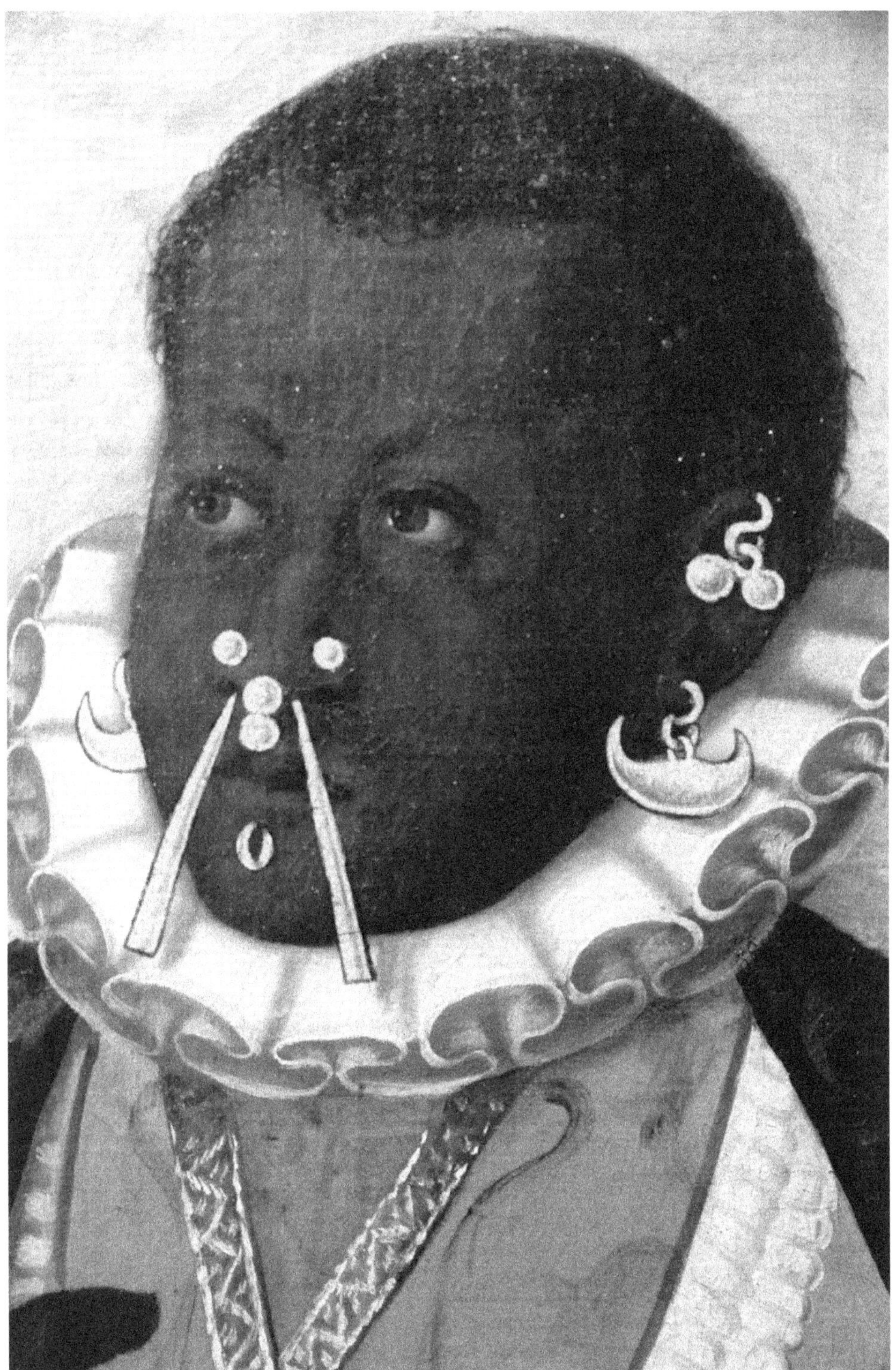

4.9. Detail of Figure 4.1 (Don Domingo's face). Andrés Sánchez Galque, *Portrait of Don Francisco de Arobe and his sons Don Pedro and Don Domingo*, 1599.

and almost disguise who they really are. What we do know is that the king is not seeing "gente política." Nor is he seeing the faces or hands of Indians or Africans. They are neither and they are both; they are mulattos.

Painting here seems to fail as a demonstrative medium because color cannot convey the subtleties of colonial race as it expands beyond binary definitions. Moreover, although Spain had perhaps greater racial diversity than most other European nations, the mulatto is a new and unstable category, outside any clear recognition other than being dangerous, a theme that seems to underlie, I believe, the accompanying letter to the painting as well as the painting itself. This first generation of mulattos is new to everyone, patron, artist, subject, and public.

To understand what Sánchez Galque accomplishes in this painting, it is important to read the very first characterization of Esmeraldas by Cabello de Balboa in his "Verdadera descripción y relación larga de la Provincia y Tierra de las Esmeraldas," in which, among other things, he treats the history of Don Francisco and the other mulattos and how they came to be in Esmeraldas and from which the history of Alonso de Illescas is recorded. He begins in the first chapter, however, by simply describing the geography of Esmeraldas, at the end of which he writes:

> There is much gold in the area and we had news of the tremendous mines of it such that it was hard to give credit to it except that it becomes believable when you consider the quantity of gold that the Natives wear on themselves, adorning their ears, noses, wrists and legs with it, also around the throat from top to bottom.[24]

Now, one might regard this as a standard Spanish description in which they see only the gold that the natives wear rather than the natives themselves. However, if one reads from a second document that describes the arrival of nineteen Indians from Esmeraldas in Quito in 1606 or seven years after the portrait was painted, we can understand that Cabello de Balboa's description is, perhaps, not just a trope, and we can also begin to understand what Sánchez Galque has consciously or unconsciously done to convey that his sitters are mulattos. The first part of this set of documents relates the testimony of Indians on the coast who came to Quito to testify that the mulattos from Esmeraldas had raided some of their villages and had killed a number of inhabitants. The document begins like many other mundane bureaucratic documents by specifying place and time. But then it immediately takes a descriptive turn unlike other documents: "the Niguas from Alloqui province of the coast have come to this city before his majesty nineteen Indians, their faces are encrusted and (their) ears and noses hang with nose rings and earrings that seem to be of gold and silver."[25] That is, the scribe interjects himself here with a personal observation of wonder and gives notice to the reader that the faces of these nineteen Indians are studded with ornaments of gold and silver. These are the same elements del Barrio y Sepúlveda uses to describe the extraordinary appearance of Don Francisco de Arobe and his sons.

There are, of course, Indians everywhere in Quito. Sánchez Galque himself is an Indian, but it is clear that the residents of Esmeraldas look different, and not because they are physically different. They are culturally different with faces studded with gold. And it is this, the gold set off against the black faces of Don Francisco and the others, which Sánchez Galque manages, I believe, to factor into his portrait as the sign of miscegenation. This handling of ornament and facial characteristics enlivens the figures in an extraordinary way. One is drawn past the rich textiles and other elements to gaze at these men in a kind of wonderment, an emotion expressed in del Barrio y Sepúlveda's letter to the king. One recognizes these three men as not Africans and not Indians but as mulattos, but not as a natural fact that can be easily rendered through color and design but as something cultural.

It is more than likely that Don Francisco and the others appeared before Sánchez Galque wearing these adornments, as del Barrio y Sepúlveda's accompanying letter so clearly emphasizes. But they shine and stand out in the painting, the golden sculpted forms against darkened surface of the individualized features of the three faces, as does the excessiveness of their new, rich clothing, and this too is a mix of European brocades, Asian silks, and Andean ponchos with necklaces of coastal shells. And in seeing this excessiveness, it is important to remember that the portrait was to be sent to the king. Their faces and their bodies, as they appear adorned here, transgress the king's law. In 1571 a royal *cédula* (decree) expressly prohibited black people, whether slaves or free, and mulattos from wearing gold, pearls, or silk.[26] But how else than by marking their bodies by multiple codes that transgress sumptuary laws could the presence of the mulatto be envisioned? What of the spears, then? They certainly did not have to be depicted holding them. They are tipped with another metal, also glistening in counterpoint to the coastal gold work on their faces. Perhaps they were weapons given to them by the Spaniards, a point to which I shall return, but it is also possible that they had carried the weapons with them to Quito because, as Cabello de Balboa notes, the Indians on the coast learned to use a bellows and iron for their spear tips from the "negroes."[27]

One wonders how the artist Andrés Sánchez Galque, an acculturated Indian at the margins of Spanish power, may have regarded his mulatto sitters. The commission itself recognizes his more elevated place within colonial Quito. His signature in Latin places him within the civilized space of erudition and civility. His portrait seems to tease out a talent that engages almost in empathy, even admiration, with his sitters. Even more, perhaps there is a longing for something now lost forever to a native resident of Quito, a native who participates in a religious confraternity and practices the art of painting.

Conclusion

In a *Relación* written to the Viceroy by Friar Hernando Hincapié, another Mercedarian friar resident in San Mateo in 1606, the friar complains that Don Francisco de Arobe as governor of San Mateo would not go to sea with Spaniards who were in pursuit of other mulattos who had raided the Indian villages of Contongo and Bolo, among others, killing the men and taking captive the children and women. The friar then says, "I tell all this to your honor so that you may see how unfaithful they (the mulattos) are and how disloyal he (Don Francisco) is even after all that you spent on them in shirts of brocade and mantas and wine that they drank when they came to Quito." Fray Hincapié then goes on to say, stressing that they are not "christianos de corazón" (sincere Christians), that they are all drunkards, especially Don Pedro, who threatens the Spaniards with boastful and ribald taunts. Finally he writes that "the Indians sleep with the mulattas and the mulattos sleep with Indian women, and for this reason all those who are born are mulattos and so in a few years there will be no Indians just mulattos such that even the devil won't know what to do with them."[28]

This is more than just a deprecating comment by the friar; for him, Don Francisco and the other mulattos are not even fit as the object of the devil's desire. Mulattos appear here not at the margins but completely outside the colonial Christian universe of evangelical engagement between Indian and Spaniard. They are imagined not to have citizenship in either of San Augustine's two cities. They are not "gente política" as Barrio emphasizes in his letter accompanying their portrait. They are not part of the polis. That is, even if they tipped their hat to the devil, he wouldn't know what to do, not even to perhaps say: "Look, a mulatto." They are as soulless in 1606 as they were in 1570 when Cabello de Balboa described them.

But if instead of reading these documents and imagining Don Francisco and his sons through this constant characterization, one looks again at the portrait of the three mulattos painted by an Indian to be sent to the king of Spain, then one might imagine something different. Perhaps one sees them as "they really are," men who had to make out of the New World their own world, and therefore were independent, or as Cabello de Balboa wrote: "andaban solos subjetos a su voluntad (subject to their own will)." As such, they were always a threat to the Christian order of colonization. The king through his various representations could make them Dons and governors, but that offer, as in any gift, expected a return. In this case it was fealty and obedience, terms that are longingly used in all the documents sometimes as goal and sometimes as having been momentarily achieved. The portrait seemingly fixes this achievement, as del Barrio y Sepúlveda's letters implore.

But in truth, the mulattos never entered fully into the expected reciprocity of citizenship. Their history in America, descending from escaped slaves, imbues them with a desire for independence and well-earned cynicism. And that finally is what seems somehow to add up in Sanchéz Galque's portrait, a fierce independence. It seems consciously or unconsciously factored into the pose and gestures that resolve into a composition that gives both an authority and strength to Don Francisco. First, one realizes that his sons, Don Pedro and Don Domingo, do not look out at us. Their gaze does not meet that of the viewer. Their attention is given over to what is in the painting, not outside of it. Their eyes are turned upward, looking toward the center and thereby defining the space where Don Francisco, their father and leader, stands. Moreover, the extraordinary nose adornments worn by the two sons are identical, whereas those worn by Don Francisco are distinct. These features form a bilateral frame that strengthens the center of this tripartite composition.

Only Don Francisco appears in full view. His sons are behind him, and they hold their spears loosely. Don Francisco's voluminous body presses forward, and he grips his weapon with all fingers tightly clasped around it. The spears and the way they are held may be purposeful elements to intensify their appearance or reputation as fierce warriors, but the weapons that Don Francisco and his son are shown holding are not those that are described in del Barrio y Sepúlveda's letter. The spears in the portrait are more European, and the weapons that del Barrio y Sepúlveda says the mulattos normally carried were small darts, three or four, and a spearthrower. This description seems based on fact, for it is clear that in the ethnogenesis of the mulattos, they adopted not only the clothes and golden adornments of the coastal communities but also their weapons. A ceramic figurine from the Jama-Coaque tradition (circa 500 B.C.) illustrates almost precisely del Barrio's description of their normal weapons (Fig. 4.10). The figurine holds three darts in his left hand and reaches back to launch a fourth dart propelled through the aid of a small spearthrower held between the palm and thumb. In the portrait, these weapons would not have had the menacing presence that the long steel tip spears have, neither as weapons nor as compositional elements.

From the center of the composition, Don Francisco looks out at the viewer in a fixed and determined, almost icy stare. It is a stare that borders on the magisterial, similar to royal portraits as well as those of viceroys and bishops. Whether it was the intent of the artist or it was the sheer presence and will of the sitters or somewhere in between, we can never know. But for all the various signs of mixture that Sánchez Galque factors into the painting, there is a compositional and gestural coherency that goes beyond simple pictorial conventions and gives tremendous vigor, strength, and integrity to the figures, above and beyond their mere presentation to the king as del Barrio y Sepúlveda so desired.

4.10. Jama-Coaque warrior figurine, 500 B.C.–500 A.D. Mold and modeled ceramic with post-fired paint. Courtesy of Museo Antropológico Banco Central del Ecuador, Guayaquil, acquisition no. GA-1-2872-85. Photo: Author

This visual presentation of self-possession is also something very different than all the descriptive qualities that del Barrio y Sepúveda notes in his letters. He pays detailed attention to their dress and adornments as well as their ferocity and barbarity. But these are signs of their barbarity, which has been overcome through his diplomacy. This is what he wants the king to see and understand: that the descendants of runaway slaves have been finally, if not re-enslaved, at least re-subjected. And it is through these figures that he desires that the king might also recall del Barrio y Sepúlveda, old and forlorn, as a still trusted and loyal servant of the crown who has rendered a great service to his majesty.

Sánchez Galque, of course, depicts all of the luxuriousness of the brocades and silks that had been given to Don Francisco and his sons to wear. He also carefully and beautifully delineates their gold earrings, nose rings, lip plugs, and shell necklaces that del Barrio repeatedly describes. Here, then, he is able to render in the portrait del Barrio y Sepúlveda's desire to show his king something extraordinary ("cosa extraordinaria"). But Sánchez Galque achieves something else by composing three figures within a pictorial space that unifies them in their being free, not just from being slaves, but from the society that would, given the chance, enslave them again. They have shed the marks of enslavement burned on their bodies; they stand in the garments offered freely to them by Spaniards in the hope of appeasement. They also stand free and capable of commanding their own history. Sánchez Galque stands between them and that history, asked to paint them as subjects of the crown, but as an artist he supersedes that mundane task to produce a most remarkable painting as it is seen today. In 1600 we do not know how it was seen, least of all by the king. It certainly did not fulfill del Barrio's desire to be released by his majesty from his tasks as the oldest judge and civil servant in Quito. He died in service in the Americas, and Don Francisco and his sons returned to Esmeraldas, where they held sway, independent of the authority that tried to lay claim to them, just as they appear in their portrait.

Bibliography of Archival Sources

Archivo General de las Indias, Sevilla

Varias Cartas de Juan del Barrio y Sepúlveda to Philip III and Response by Philip III

03–14–1596–05–25–1599

Quito 9, R.33, folios 1r–19r

Cartas de Audiencia

Asiento Hecho con Don Alsonso Sebastián de Illescas mulato Principal de la provincial de las Esmeraldas y canapés. Reducidas al servicio del Rey Nuestro Señor.

9–07–1600

Quito, 9 R. 3 N. 25, folios 1r–4v

Carta de Juan del Barrio y Sepúlveda to Philip III

12–04–1599

Quito 9r, 2n. N15

Cartas de Audiencia folios 1r–2v

Carta de Juan del Barrio y Sepúlveda. Oidor de la audiencia de Quito, a S.M.

15–04–1600

Quito 9r.r.3, n.21, C1–32n. N15 1V–2V

Cartas de las Indias

Carta del Rey a la Audiencia de Quito

07–11–1602

Quito 209, L., Folio 155r–155v

Jowdy-Duque de Infantado Mircofilm Collection Southern Methodist University

Conde de Montesclaros Papers, Roll 2, Libro 15

Expedientes 6–7 Esmeraldas 1605–1607

Relación quese hace a su excelencia señor de Monterrey Visorrey destos reinos del matança y cabtiverio que hizieron los mulatos de las Esmeraldas en los pueblos de cotongo bolo y Calavilij . . . y lo sucedido despues 1606.

Notes

1 "en particular envoi a Vuestra real persona los retratos de capitan Don Francisco de arobe y don pedro y don domingo sus hijos mulatos principales de las dichas Esmeraldas con una breve relacion deste subcesso por parecerme que su majestad

gustaria ver una cosa tan Nueva y extraordinaria." Letter from Juan del Barrio y Sepúlveda to Philip III, 12 April 1599, AGI Quito 9r, 2n. N15 Cartas de Audiencia, Folio 1r.

2 "Por parecerle Vsta Magestad gustaría ver aquellos barbaros retratados (que hasta agora ansido invensibles) y ser cossa muy extraordianria los embia con sus carta y este memorial al Magestad." Letter from Juan del Barrio y Sepúlveda to Philip III, 15 April 1600, AGI Quito 9, R3, N.21 1, 2, 3, Cartas de las Indias, Folio 1r.

3 "el primero de los mas principales de la dha provincial fueron el capp. Don Francisco de Arrobe y sus hijos que el dcho ano proximo pasado de 99 con los dchos papeles y rrelaciones, enbio retratados a Vm." Letter from Juan del Barrio y Sepúlveda to Philip III, 15 October 1600, AGI Quito 9, R3, N25.1, Folio 1r.

4 "Philippo 3 Catholici Regi Hispaniar Indiar. Qz dno. Sv. Doctor Joanes del Barrio A Spulveda Audito Suae Cancellariae del Quito Suis Expensis Fieri Curavi Anno 1599." Inscription of the painting by Andrés Sánchez Galque, *Portrait of Don Francisco de Arobe and his sons Don Pedro and Don Domingo*, 1599, fig. 4.1.

5 One need only think of Alberti's famous characterization of painting through portraiture as having a "divine force which not only makes absent men present, as friendship is said to do, but moreover makes the dead seem almost alive. Even after centuries they are recognized with great pleasure and with great admiration for the painter. . . .The face of man who is already dead certainly lives a long life through painting." Leon Battista Alberti, *On Painting*, trans. John R. Spence (New Haven: Yale University Press, 1956), 63.

6 On Sánchez Galque see José Gabriel Navarro, "Un Pintor Quiteño: un cuadro admirable del siglo XVI en el Museo Arqueológico Nacional, Madrid," *Archivos* (1929), 1–30. On Peruvian portraits see Nenita Ponce de León Elphick, "Memory, Presence, and Power: The Social Life of Peruvian Portraits," Ph.D. diss., Harvard University, 2007.

7 The painting also appears in the 1747 inventory of paintings of Felipe V and Isabel Farnesio with the number 769. Angel Aterido et al., *Inventarios Reales: Colecciones de Pinturas de Felipe V e Isabel Farnesio,* vol. 2 (Madrid: Fundación de Apoyo da la Historia del Arte Hispánico, 2004), 135.

8 "Llegué señor don Alonso Illescas, goce del bien y merced que Dios Nuestro Señor y su majestad le hacen en este día." Miguel Cabello de Balboa, "Verdadera descripción y relación larga de la Provincia y Tierra de las Esmeraldas," in *Obras* (Quito: Editorial Editorial Ecuatoriana, 1945 [1583]), 37.

9 "Alonso me llamo yo, y no tengo don." Cabello de Balboa replies to Alonso saying, "El rey que puede da y pone el don como mas largamente entendará, venido que sea a tierra." Ibid.

10 "señor vicario, mi cabeza y las de mis hijos y compañeros os encomiendo como a Señor padre; la tierra y cuanto en ella hay, es de su Majestad y desde luego, en su real nombre, os doy la obedencia mía y de los que están a mi cargo los mulatos (que residen nueve o diez leguas de mi casa)." Cabello de Balboa, "Verdadera descripción," 37.

11 For a discussion of the symbolic nature of the king's seal and its relation to portraits in the Andes see Joanne Rappaport and Tom Cummins "Between Images and Writing: The Ritual of the King's Quilca," *Colonial Latin American Review* 7, no. 1 (June 1998), 7–32.

12 African slaves in the seventeenth century were branded on the right breast with a royal brand using a capital "R" (for *real*). See Fredrick Bowser, *The African Slave in Colonial Peru 1524–1650* (Stanford: Stanford University Press, 1974), 82–83.

13 Cf. Adam Szadszdi, "El trasfondo de un cuadro: 'Los Mulatos de Esmeraldas' de Andrés Sánchez Galque," *Cuadernos prehispánicos* 12 (1986–87), 93–142; Kris Lane, *Quito 1599: City and Colony in Transition* (Albuquerque: University of New Mexico Press, 2002), 27–51; and Charles Beatty Medina, "Caught between Rivals: The Spanish-African Maroon Competition for Captive Indian Labor in the Region of Esmeraldas during the Late Sixteenth and Early Seventeenth Centuries," *The Americas* 63, no. 1 (July 2006), 113–36.

14 "Tenidos a quedar en tan pequeño número, acordaron un dectro que solo ellos y demonio lo pudiera imaginar y fue dar fin y remate de aquellos sus pocos amigos, que siempre fueron pocos los naturales de aquella parte de tierra y no dejar vivos a más de aquella cantidad que ellos pudiesen subjetar buenamente; el cual decreto se puso en ejecución con tanta crueldad, como se puede creer de gente desalmada y bárbara." Cabello de Balboa, "Verdadera descripción," 19–20.

15 "¿Quién te mueve ahora soltar las manos la libertad que con tanto trabajo has adquirido, y dejar el estado de Señor y meterte de tu voluntad en el de esclavo y siervo?. . . como te confías de estos cristianos, pues, sus condiciones tan inclinidas a aplicarlo todo para si . . . crees tú, por ventura que esos dones que te traen, esos que hayan venido, que es por otra cosa, sino el sebo puesto en anzuelo para pescarte? Aparta tu pensamiento de entregarte a las manos de tus enemigos, porque no te venga el arrepentimiento de haberlo hecho, cuando no puedas hacer más que llorar en vano, y si por ti no lo hicieres hazlo por nosotros, por padre, y pues te obedecemos y amamos como a tal, no nos lo pagues con entregarnos a nuestras mujeres e hijos en las manos de esto barbudos. Mira que a tí y a tu yerno castigarán como a malhechores y tus hijos quedarán esclavos y nosotros jamás libres; no hagas tal cosa como la que piensas hacer, si no quieres acabar tu vida y la nuestras en perpetuo y doloroso llanto." Cabello de Balboa, "Verdadera descripción," 53–54.

16 See José de Mesa and Teresa Gisbert, "The Painter, Mateo Mexía, and His Works in the Convent of San Francisco de Quito," *The Americas*, 16, no. 4 (Apr. 1960), 385–86, 392–93; José María de Vargas, *Biografía de Fray Pedro Bedón* (Quito, 1965), 37–41, 91–95.

17 Ibid.

18 Another small devotional painting attributed to Sánchez Galque is in the Luis Álvarez Urquieta collection in Santiago, Chile.

19 The *toma de posesión* was the legal investiture of authority by the colonial state of a local community's leader. It entailed among other symbolic acts that the newly installed chief wear Spanish-style clothes; see Thomas Cummins, *Toasts with the Inca: Andean Abstraction and Colonial Images on Quero Vessels* (Ann Arbor: University of Michigan Press, 2002), 302–3.

20 "Por parecerle VM gustaria ver aquellos barbaros retratados (que hasta agora ansido invençibles) y ser cossa muy extraordianria los embia con sus carta y este memorial a VM – son hombres bien dispuestos agiles y muy sueltos acostumbran traer de ordinario argollas de oro llanas al cuello y las narigueras, oregeras, beçotes y sortijas en la barba y botones en las narizes y aun otros en los carrillos // todos de oro – y los indios principales e yndias de la dicha prouinçia y algunas otras ussan tambien de la dicha gala = y los collares cadenas o sartales blancos que traen al cuello sobre vestido disen son dientes de pescados y otras conchas suelen traer otros de otra hechura no tan galanos ni artifiçiosos. Traen de ordinario – lançillas en las manos y tres y quarto dardos de Madera rejia y aunque sin hierros mui agudos. Van todos rretratados mui al propio como son y andan de ordinario- ecepto el vestido que luego que dieron la paz y obidiençia a V.M. y dellos se tomo la posession y fueron puestos

en V. rreal corona se les dio como de sus retratos lo uno y lo otro pareçe. Porque no son gente politica y en su tierra ques caliente no traen mas que mantas y camisetas como los demas yndios. Tienen buen entendimiento y son muy astutos y sagaces entienden la lengua española aunque hablan torpemente. An sido grandes guerreros contra yndios de otros prouinçias ynfieles. Temenlos mucho porque matan muchos y de los que cautivan se siruen como esclauos con gran señorio y son terribles determinados y crueles en el castigo = Jamas an podido ser sujetados de españoles – Este don Françisco de Arobe a tratado siempre bien a los españoles que an llegado por la mar a aquella costa y a los que se an alli perdido y lo que dije cuanto a esto // y los que an entrado a le conquistar en la peticion que presento en nuestra real audiencia quando dio la paz y se offreçio por vassallo de VM es como lo rrefiere cuyo testimonio va con la dicha relaçion y otros papeles." Carta de Juan del Barrio y Sepúlveda, oidor de la Audiencia de Quito to Philip III, 12 April 1599, AGI Quito 9r, r.3, n.21, C1–C32n. N15 Cartas de Audiencia, Folios 1V–2v. This text was partially published in *Arte Colonial de Ecuador* (1985), 147–48.

21 See F. J. Sánchez Cantón, ed., *Inventarios Reales Bienes Muebles Que Pertenecieron a Felipe II,* Archivo Documental Español, vol. XI (Madrid: Real Academia de La Historia, 1959), 332–42.

22 See María Kusche, *Retratos y Retratadores: Alonso Sánchez Coello y sus competidores Sofonisba Anguissola, Jorge de la Rúa y Rolán Moys* (Madrid: Fundación de Apoyo a la Historia del Arte, 2003). It is possible that Sánchez Galque based his composition on a print source such as the details of both the "Roman Emperors" and "The Royal Relatives of Maxmilian I" on *Arch of Honor* made in the workshop of Albrecht Dürer. Figures are composed in units of three, in three-quarter length, and with the two side figures behind and looking toward the central figure; see Larry Silver, *Marketing Maximilian: The Visual Ideology of a Holy Roman Emperor* (Princeton: Princeton University Press, 2008), 54–55, fig. 55, and 78–79, fig. 31. I thank Lorenzo Pericolo and Susan Dackerman for pointing me in the right directions.

23 In the sixteenth century the Spanish word "Mulato" refers to the offspring of an African and a native American as defined in a royal ordinance of 1568; see Jack Forbes, *Black Africans and Native Americans* (London: Blackwell, 1988), 173. Garcilaso de la Vega Inca (in *Primera parte de los comentarios reales,* 1611) uses it this way in a chapter entitled "Nombres nuevos para nombrar diversas generaciones" (Madrid: Nicholas Rodríguez Franco, 1723), 339–40. Mulato is the term that is used in all the documents referring to the subjects of Andrés Sánchez Galque's portrait. The identity of the subjects in terms of their race becomes confused over time so that Don Francisco and his sons are termed "Negros Indios" in the 1747 inventory of paintings owned by Philip V and Isabel de Farnesio. Miguel A. Bretos calls them "zambos," a term that is never used in any of the historical documents related to this painting; see M. Bretos "From Prehispanic to Post Romantic: Latin American in Portraits, 500 B.C.–A.D. 1910," in *Retratos: 2,000 Years of Latin American Portraits* (New Haven: Yale University Press, 2004), 34.

24 "Hay mucho oro en la tierra y tuvimos noticia de muchas soberbias minas dello y tales que acobarda el crédito, matoma algún ánimo, cuando considera lo mucho que traen sobre si los naturales, adórnanse con ella las orejas y narices y muñeca y piernas, ansi en la garganta del pie arriba." The quote continues: "en el senogil, traen al cuello collares hechos de una lámina de oro median en grosor de tres dedos de ancho, usan ansi mismo chagualas en el pecho y frente, de hechura de patenas y tales que hay algunas que pesan veinte y aun trienta pesos de oro; esmeraldas no vimos ninguna, procuran aquellos negros y sus compañeros si pudiesen el haberlas en la tierra." Cabello de Balboa, "Verdadera descripción," 6. "...right below the

knee, they wear around the neck necklaces of gold plate of a thickness of three fingers wide, they also wear in a similar fashion *chagualas* on the chest and forehead, in the form of patens and such that there are some that weigh twenty and even thirty gold *pesos*; we did not see any emeralds, which those blacks and their comrades would procure if they had them in the land."

25 "Los niguas de allorquni, provincia de la costa an venido a esta ciudad ante su majestad diez y nueve yndios, enbixadas los rostros y los narices y orexas colgadas narigueras y orexas de metal que parece ser de oro y plata." "Relación quese hace a su excelencia señor de Monterrey Visorrey destos reinos del matança y cabtiverio que hizieron los mulatos de las Esmeraldas en los pueblos de cotongo bolo y Calavilij ... y lo sucedido depues 1606," Folio 6r.

26 *Recopilación de leyes ... de Indias,* libro V, título 8, ley 40, folio 167; libro vi, título VI, ley 7, folio 218; libro VIII, título IV, folios 284–87; libro VII, título V, folios 290–91.

27 "Después que entraron los negros en aquella provincia de Porete y Tacames, que comenzaron a usar fragua ... traen algunos hierros agudos en sus dardos." Cabello de Balboa, "Verdadera descripción," 14.

28 "[D]igo a vmd todo esto por que vmd vea quan poco fieles son y quan mal aplicado es. Lo que con ellos se a gastado en camisetas de tamanese y ficcadas y mantas y botixajas del vino que beiuieron en essa ciudad (Quito) quando ay estuvieron"; "... y asi los yndios tratan con las mulatas y los mulattos con las yndias y por esta rrazon los que nacen todos son mulattos y de aqui a pocos años abra en esta tierra yndios sino mulattos que el diablo no se pueda averiquar con ellos." "Relación que se hace a su excelencia señor de Monterrey Visorrey destos reinos del matança y cabtiverio que hizieron los los mulatos de las Esmeraldas en los pueblos de cotongo bolo y Calavilij ... y lo sucedido depues 1606," Folio 4r.

FIVE

METAMORPHOSES OF THE SELF IN EARLY-MODERN SPAIN

SLAVE PORTRAITURE AND THE CASE OF JUAN DE PAREJA

Carmen Fracchia

The Afro-Hispanic slave Juan de Pareja depicted himself in his ambitious painting *The Calling of Saint Matthew* in 1661 (Fig. 5.1, Plate 4), eleven years after his master Diego Velázquez immortalized him in a superb portrait (Fig. 5.2, Plate 1). These two Spanish portraits are an exception in the context of early-modern European art theory and visual production, as this study will show.[1] In the first European treatise on portraiture since antiquity, *Do tirar polo natural*, written in Portuguese in 1548 and translated into Spanish in 1563, the theorist and painter Francisco de Holanda conceived portraiture "as an imitation of God's work of creation" and accordingly categorized portraiture as the most dignified genre among the arts.[2] Holanda considered portraiture in its social context and consequently established the genre's ethics and functions. The essence of the genre was the worthy sitter's prestige on either moral or intellectual grounds.[3] The restricted nature of portraiture, which was associated with the Spanish Court and urban cultures, was reiterated by the Spanish lexicographer Sebastián de Covarrubias in his *Tesoro de la lengua castellana o española* (1611). Here he defined the subject of the portrait as a "principal persona" whose portrayal will be remembered for posterity.[4] In the first Spanish art treatise of the seventeenth century, *Diálogos de la pintura* (1633), the painter and theorist Vicente Carducho, who was Velázquez's rival at the Habsburg Court, bitterly complains about the abuse of portraying ordinary people as noblemen, and he gives the advice to depict them at least with their professional attributes.[5] His views relegated the genre of portraiture to a secondary place, in contrast to the Spanish painter and art theorist Francisco Pacheco in his *Arte de la Pintura* (1649). This major treatise, which was completed in 1640 by Velázquez's father-in-law, elevated the dignity of the genre of portraiture in early-modern Spain by associating the notion of "inventiveness" to the genre, alongside the traditional requirement of "imitation."[6] Pacheco's defense

5.1. Juan de Pareja, *The Calling of Saint Matthew*, 1661. Oil on canvas. Museo Nacional del Prado, Madrid.

of the innovative values of portraiture was paramount for *El Museo Pictórico y Escala Óptica* (1715–24) by Antonio Palomino de Castro y Velasco, where the notions associated with the genre of portraiture, such as "likeness" and "faithful description" as visual "truth," were given greater relevance.[7] The main function of the genre of portraiture in early-modern Spain was the immortalization of the worthy elite with the implicit moral understanding that there could be no room for the portrayal of a slave.

In this study I intend to explore the role of visual discourses with regard to the construction of the subjectivity of the slave in early-modern Spanish painting by analyzing the self-portrait of the former slave Juan de Pareja (ca. 1606–70) and by relating it to the portrait of the slave Pareja by his celebrated master Velázquez (1599–1660). It is, however, important, before we address both portraits, to clarify from the outset the social status of Juan de Pareja as a slave since there is still a persistent confusion about his condition.

When Pareja painted his self-portrait in Madrid he had technically been a free man for eleven years, but he was still a slave when Velázquez depicted him and publicly exhibited his portrait on 19 March 1650 in Rome.[8] Eight months later, on 23 November 1650 and still in Rome, Pareja was legally granted freedom from slavery. The publication of the notarial document "Donatio Libertatis" confirms Antonio Palomino's claim that Pareja was Velázquez's slave: It notifies that Diego

Velázquez, resident in Rome, granted freedom from captivity to his "schiavo Joannes de Parecha."[9] The Italian document clearly states that Pareja's freedom will be applicable in Spain but that he should serve his master for another four years. Manumission was not very common in Spain, and it did not necessarily

5.2. Diego Velázquez, *Juan de Pareja*, 1650. Oil on canvas. Metropolitan Museum of Art, New York. Purchase, Fletcher and Rogers Funds, and Bequest of Miss Adelaide Milton de Groot (1876–1967), by exchange, supplemented by gifts from friends of the Museum, 1971. Photo: Malcolm Varon. © Metropolitan Museum of Art/Art Resource, New York.

exempt the domestic Afro-Hispanic slave from his previous condition.[10] In fact, after the death of Velázquez, Pareja worked for his master's son-in-law the Court painter Juan Bautista Martínez del Mazo (1605–67) until his death.[11]

The manumission document certainly resolves the ambiguity of Pareja's status as a slave, which was current for most of the twentieth century after the publication in 1932 of a document dated 12 May 1630 in which a "Juan de Pareja" asked the mayor of Seville permission to go to Madrid for four months to carry on his studies as a painter with his brother Joseph.[12] The publication of Pareja's document of manumission in 1983 shows, as Montagu rightly states, that the painter Juan de Pareja in the 1630 Sevillian document was not Velázquez's Afro-Hispanic slave.

In the Italian document Pareja is treated like anyone else mentioned in Roman baroque legal documents in which his father's name and place of birth are given.[13] We learn that Velázquez's slave was born in Antequera in the diocese of Málaga in Andalusia and that his father was Juan de Pareja. These biographical notes also correct the earliest historiographical claim that Velázquez's slave was from Seville and confirm that in accordance with Spanish practice his parents too were slaves.[14] Velázquez had a special relationship with Pareja, since he trusted his slave to sign many legal documents as his witness from 1634 to 1653 in Spain and in Italy.[15]

Pareja's ethnicity or color is not specified in the Italian document.[16] However, these matters are mentioned in the Spanish artistic historiography, mainly based on Pareja's biographer Antonio Palomino de Castro y Velasco (1655–1725), also known as the "Spanish Vasari."[17] He lived in Madrid from 1678, only eight years after Pareja's death and eighteen years after Velázquez's. In his *El Museo Pictórico y Escala Óptica*, Palomino dedicated Life 128 to Juan de Pareja's biography, which is essentially centered on the paradoxical nature of being a slave and a painter. Palomino defines Pareja's ethnicity and color "of a *Mestizo* Breed ... he was of an odd Hue" and describes his mechanical activities suited to a slave: "to grind his [Velázquez's] Colors and prepare the Canvas, and other servile Offices belonging to the Art and about the House."[18] There is no doubt that Pareja's biography addresses the theoretical polemic about the nature of painting as a liberal activity, only practiced by freemen: "his Master [Velázquez] (for the Honour of the Art) wou'd never suffer him to meddle with Painting or Drawing."[19] Thus, the art theorist had to construct a legend in which Pareja practices the art of painting in secret: "[Pareja] he being very handy and ingenious, and taking all opportunities of his Masters Absence and passing whole Nights in study when he might have taken his rest, he came to do Things very worthy of esteem."[20] Palomino also needs to justify Velázquez's attitude toward his slave assistant:

> and in order to prevent the effects of his Master's Resentment, which he apprehended would necessarily follow upon the Discovery, he made use of

> the following Stratagem. He had observed that whenever the King (*Philip* IV) came down to the Apartments to see *Velasquez* paint, and chanc'd to see any Picture set up against the Wall, his Majesty wou'd turn it, or order it to be turn'd to see what it was. Upon this *Pareja* resolv'd within himself to set up a small Piece of his own painting against the Wall, and to place it so, as to make seen to have been left there undesignedly. The King no sooner saw it, but he turn'd it about, and at the same Time *Pareja*, who waited for the Opportunity, fell on his Knees and humbly begg'd his Majesty to interpose between him and his Master, without whose Consent he had presum'd to learn the Art and wrought that Piece.[21]

Palomino's myth states that Pareja's clandestine activity ended with the slave's freedom thanks to the intervention of the king, after the monarch claimed to Velázquez that a person "who had such a Talent, cou'd not be a Slave."[22]

It is obvious that Palomino's legend signifies that the case of the Afro-Hispanic Juan de Pareja at the Spanish Court, where the "free" artist managed to forge a career as a painter, is an extraordinary and exceptional phenomenon in early-modern Spain.[23] Freedom from slavery in Palomino's biography of Pareja justifies and reconciles the contradictory nature of being a slave and a painter who was considered "eminent in Painting." This claim allows Palomino to praise Pareja's portraits ("Our *Pareja* had a most singular Ability in painting Portraits"), some of which he had the occasion to see. Palomino finds these portraits "superlatively good" and in the manner of his master so that Pareja's portraits are, in his opinion, sometimes thought to be by Velázquez.[24] However, the writer makes sure that his readers are still aware of Pareja's condition as a slave when he claims that his artistic success was achieved despite "the disgrace of his nature."[25]

Palomino does not mention Pareja's *The Calling of Saint Matthew*, in which the former slave painter depicts himself. In Spanish art historiography, this large painting was first acknowledged as Pareja's by Juan Agustín Ceán Bermúdez in 1800.[26] The striking feature of Pareja's three-meter-long oil painting on canvas is without doubt his self-portrait (Fig. 5.3). Pareja portrays himself as a contemporary Spanish gentleman with his sword and positions himself at the extreme left margin of the painting beneath the window with his head against a halo-like golden plate. He is the only figure who is looking straight at the viewer, while most of the other personages are involved in the religious event of the calling of Saint Matthew. In the most surprising way Pareja chooses to conceal his ethnic difference by constructing himself as a European nobleman. He makes sure that his audience is aware of his transformation and his authorship by holding a piece of paper that he signed and dated: "Jo.°de Pareja F[ecit].1661."

If we relate Pareja's self-portrait to Velázquez's depiction of Pareja as an Afro-Hispanic man, it is evident that Pareja chose to Europeanize his own features,[27] since Velázquez could not have Africanized a "worthy" European sitter without lowering his social status in imperial Spain, where there is documented evidence of the association of the word and color "black" with the social condition of a "slave."[28] In Velázquez's canvas the Afro-Hispanic slave is already depicted by following the conventions of formal portraiture, restricted to the upper echelons of Spanish society, without any details or accessories that might define Pareja's status as a slave. In a surprising way, the only protagonist is Pareja's gripping gaze, which totally dominates the canvas and engages the viewer. By contrast the former slave's self-portrait as a Spanish nobleman is embedded in a religious narrative.[29] The astonishing difference in the physical appearance of Pareja in the two portraits questions the visual effect of the living likeness of the sitter, which is a key traditional feature of the genre of portraiture. The specific quality of "likeness" together with the notion of visual "truth" as "faithful description" of the sitter is reiterated by Palomino when he tries to explain the origin of the portrait of the slave Pareja by Velázquez:

5.3. Detail of Figure 5.1 (Pareja's self-portrait). Juan de Pareja, *The Calling of Saint Matthew*, 1661.

> When it was decided that Velázquez should make a portrait of the Sovereign Pontiff [Innocent X], he wanted to prepare himself beforehand with the exercise of painting a head from life; and he made one of Juan de Pareja, his slave and a painter himself, with such likeness and liveliness that when he sent it with Pareja for the criticism of some friends, they stood looking at the painted portrait and the model with admiration and amazement, not knowing which one they should speak to and which was to answer them.[30]

Palomino reintroduces the concept of likeness as visual "truth" when he links the story of the portrait of the slave Pareja to the success of Velázquez's career in Rome:

> Of this portrait (which is half-length, from life) a story is related by Andreas Schmidt, a Flemish painter now at the Spanish court, who was in Rome at the time. In accordance with the custom of decorating the cloister of the Rotunda (where Raphael of Urbino is buried) on Saint Joseph's day [19 March], with famous paintings, ancient and modern, this portrait was exhibited

> It gained such universal applause that in the opinion of all the painters of the different nations everything else seemed like painting but this alone like truth. In view of this Velázquez was received as Roman Academician in the year 1650.[31]

Palomino no doubt raises the uniqueness of the Pareja portrait by echoing an ancient story when he refers to the confusion made between the sitter and the portrait.[32] The Spanish theorist, however, inverted the facts regarding Velázquez's membership in the Roman Congregazione dei Virtuosi in the church of Santa Maria della Rotonda (Pantheon), since his entry to the Roman Academy is documented before he exhibited his *Juan de Pareja*. Velázquez became a member of the Academy on 13 February 1650, a condition that allowed him and all new members to exhibit their work on 19 March to celebrate the confraternity's protector.[33]

The portrait *Juan de Pareja* was exhibited outside the Pantheon on the portico facing the main square, and according to contemporary sources the paintings were hung against Oriental carpets, which covered the columns.[34] In this context, the effect of the portrait of a black slave might have sparked the early-modern European visual fantasy of the orientalized black, which had circulated since the fifteenth century in the depiction of the black Magus in the *Adoration of the Magi*.[35]

Although we cannot take Palomino's construction of the legend of Velázquez's portrait of Pareja at face value, his story is nevertheless a signifier of the extraordinariness of the portrait of a black slave in the restrictive genre reserved for the immortalization of a worthy sitter. The subject of the portrait *Juan de Pareja* is exceptional in early-modern Spain, where the scarce visual representation of black slaves is symptomatic of the position they occupied in the imperial social order. *Juan de Pareja* is the only known portrait of a black slave in early-modern Spain.[36] In this work, Pareja is represented as an Afro-Hispanic gentleman before he was made free from slavery in 1650, which could also be seen as his master's homage to his trusted slave and disciple. Pareja could not therefore have been depicted as a painter, since only a free man could be an artist. Nor could he be painted as a gentleman, since his social reality as a slave would not have qualified him as an individual worthy to be portrayed for posterity. Velázquez's choice of a non-European subject at the papal court would have signified the visualization not only of the imperial power of Spain, but also his challenge to his own virtuosity as a portraitist. The function of *Juan de Pareja* was to heighten Velázquez's social status and self-promotion. In fact, it is interesting to notice that when Velázquez painted his slave in Rome he was also struggling in social terms. He was not considered an intellectual artist by the early-modern Spanish elites. Painting in Spain during this period was still classified as a craft and not as a liberal art; therefore even as a royal portraitist at the Habsburg

Court, Velázquez was thought to be an artisan. This is the main reason why it is believed that he aspired to the ranks of the nobility.[37] Velázquez was planning to improve his own social status by becoming a member of the powerful military Order of Santiago, but the main obstacle was that the order's rules forbade membership to painters or to those "who themselves, or whose parents or grandparents, have practiced any of the manual or base occupations ... by manual or base occupation is meant silversmith or painter, if he paints for a living."[38] Thus, when Velázquez was in Rome for the second time with his slave (1648–50),[39] he did not hesitate to seek the support of his sitter Pope Innocent X for the complicated process of the order's investigation of his genealogy and social condition as an artist. He was admitted to the Order of Santiago on 28 November 1659 after a lengthy procedure: 148 witnesses, rejections by the Council of Military Orders, and two papal dispensations to "excuse the unproven nobility" of the Court artist. Velázquez's new status freed the artist from paying taxes but more importantly enhanced his identity in a society regulated by the state policy of "purity of blood," which demanded sworn certificates for the practice of any profession. This statute had been established since the first expulsion of the Jews in 1492, with the result that only "old Christians" were allowed into the professional ranks. The purity of blood policy, which placed "the faith at the apex of the Spanish hierarchical order," created a caste society in Spain and in the New World.[40] Thus, one could argue that in early-modern Spain, both the Andalusian painters, the slave Pareja and his master Velázquez, were equals only from the theoretical and professional points of view. However, in social reality their legal status was radically different: Pareja was a slave and Velázquez was an artist slaveowner. It was a widespread practice for artists to own one or two slaves in their workshop, as did the painter-theorists Carducho and Pacheco.[41]

The ambivalent status of painting in Spain gave a particular boost to the production of self-portraiture.[42] Spanish artists used this powerful visual genre of self-fashioning to make statements about their own social aspirations.[43] Velázquez portrays himself as a nobleman in the act of painting in his celebrated *Las Meninas* in 1656 (Fig. 5.4), while Pareja depicts himself as a Spanish gentleman in his *The Calling of Saint Matthew* of 1661. Both painters with their similarly textured hair, hairstyle, and moustaches are positioned on the extreme left of their large and ambitious compositions. In a society obsessed with the policy of "purity of blood" it is perhaps not surprising that the perception of Velázquez's ethnic origin had been questioned. In 1950 the Spanish art historian Juan Antonio Gaya Nuño echoed previous claims that Velázquez with his Portuguese and Andalusian descent had "ethnic African features." While he stated that the painter did not conceal his physical appearance in his self-portrait in *Las Meninas*, painted three years before his knighthood, Gaya Nuño failed to notice Pareja's own transformation in his Prado painting.[44] The functions of both self-portraits are obviously different. While Velázquez aimed to improve

5.4. Diego Velázquez, detail of *Las Meninas* (Velázquez's self-portrait), 1656. Oil on canvas. Museo Nacional del Prado, Madrid.

his social standing through the noble activity of painting, Pareja intended to be a painter in order to be perceived as a freeman. The former slave follows the earlier exceptional example of the Afro-Hispanic poet and humanist Juan Latino (1518?–ca. 1594), whose writings became his legitimate weapon "to be accepted as a free man."[45] In his Prado canvas Pareja, who had certainly been working as a painter for several years before painting his self-portrait,[46] followed Velázquez's Roman portrayal of him as a gentleman and, as previously mentioned, furthered the process of self-idealization by choosing to Europeanize his features.[47] In his self-portrait Pareja is making his own social statement as a free man and claiming his talent as a history painter by inserting himself in a large religious composition, with life-sized figures, where he could display his anatomical skills and the use of the rhetorical language of gestures.

In order to deconstruct the subjectivity of the former slave painter in *The Calling of Saint Matthew* it is necessary to address the visual and religious context in which Pareja depicts himself. The Afro-Hispanic artist embedded himself as a secondary character in the precise moment of the calling of the apostle and evangelist Matthew. This episode is related in the Gospel of Matthew (9:9): "As Jesus was walking along, he saw a man called Matthew sitting at the tax booth; and he said to him, 'Follow me.' And he got up and followed him."[48] "Jesus saw a man called Matthew at his seat in the custom house, and said to him, 'Follow me,' and Matthew rose and followed him."

Although the depiction of *The Calling of Saint Matthew* was very popular in the Low Countries during the fifteen and sixteenth centuries, there is no doubt that Pareja had in mind the composition of the painting of the same subject (1599–1600) by Caravaggio in the Contarelli Chapel of the church of San Luigi dei Francesi in Rome.[49] Unlike Caravaggio's paintings, Pareja's work was not part of a religious decoration.[50] The commissioner and function of the Prado painting are not known. It is significant, however, that Pareja's painting was restricted to the powerful monarchic audience. The canvas was displayed in royal quarters before it was lost from sight in the basement of the Prado Museum:[51] The fleur-de-lis, symbol of the Farnese family, at the bottom right of the canvas clearly indicates that this work belonged to the collection of Queen Elizabeth Farnese (1692–1766), wife of Philip V of Spain (1683–1746),[52] which was inherited by their heir, King Charles III of Spain (1716–88), who had it displayed in his dressing room in the royal palace of Aranjuez, near Madrid.[53]

Pareja has set the calling of Saint Matthew in the narrow space of a tax office. The room is enhanced by a column wrapped in a red curtain, which unevenly divides the room in two, and also on the right by an open window with a balustrade, which allows a view of a landscape. Tax officials and members of the public among whom Pareja included himself are gathered at a table, which occupies most of the painting to the left of the column, while on the right the holy group stands against the large window. Matthew is seated in front of the column at the desk unusually covered by an oriental carpet where symbols of material wealth are displayed before him: a purse with loose coins and jewellery.[54] Matthew is looking toward Christ with a surprised expression and pointing to himself in wonder at his call to follow him. He is depicted as an orientalized Jew dressed with a turban, soft fur, silk, and jewellery, while Christ and his disciples are barefoot and wearing simple timeless robes. As in the Caravaggio painting, two other men are sitting at the table: Closer to the saint is a bespectacled bookkeeper who pauses and looks up from his work at the moment of Christ's entrance, while the client sitting at the corner of the table is viewed in profile and from behind. He is holding a document while looking at the miraculous event and is dressed as a contemporary knight with his sword and a feathered hat. Pareja inserts himself on the left of the elegant client. He is standing below the window next to another man with a moustache who is looking outside the picture. Both men are wearing contemporary but not everyday Spanish dress. The gentleman Pareja directs his gaze back to the spectator, establishing the only bridge between the painted scene and the viewer. In the background, between Matthew and the bespectacled bookkeeper is a young page holding a large folio volume, and behind him is a group of four figures: On the left is a man with a turban, who looks in surprise at the central event, and next to him is another man counting his golden coins, at which a youth behind his left shoulder is peering. Slightly separate from this group is the only visibly black slave of the composition, who probably belongs to one of the scribes or taxpayers represented in the painting (Fig. 5.5).[55] The young African slave is standing by the column, behind and above Matthew's head, and has his face pierced by the divine light, which crowns the apostle's turban. On the right of the picture in the foreground is Christ summoning Matthew and a group of three disciples: Saint Peter and Saint Andrew, who are distinguishable from the third follower by the white divine light of grace above their heads. Christ is lit not only by a holy white halo and white light but also by the two main sources that illuminate the tax office: on the left from the open window above Pareja's head and at the back from the large window with balustrade. The room is also crowded with other symbols of material culture, like account books, sheets of paper, and gilded urns, but the most significant for our discussion is the painting *Moses and the Serpent* hanging on the wall of the tax office in the background, to which I will return.[56]

5.5. Detail of Figure 5.1 (Saint Matthew and the African slave). Juan de Pareja, *The Calling of Saint Matthew*, 1661.

The religious narrative of *The Calling of Saint Matthew* in which Pareja embedded himself raises some fundamental questions: What is the significance of the black African slave, Saint Matthew, Moses, and Christ vis-à-vis Pareja's self-portrait in this religious-genre painting? What is the significance of the visual parallels that Pareja establishes between himself and these figures?

We first need to start by questioning Matthew, the central figure of the religious scene. Matthew was, as the painter depicts him, a Jewish tax collector known as Levi before he followed Christ.[57] He collected custom duties for the Romans and was therefore viewed as a social outcast by the devout Jews. Christ, for whom Matthew left all behind, would totally transform his despised social existence. He would become an apostle and one of the four evangelists. Jacobus de Voragine in the *Golden Legend* recalls the manner in which Matthew responded to Christ's call: "When Christ called him, he quit his customhouse immediately to become a follower of Christ and nothing else, not fearing his superiors though he left his accounts unfinished."[58] There are no obstacles to deter the apostle from his new identity or second nature: "Who shall separate us from the love of Christ? Shall tribulations? Or distress? Or famine?"[59] The "quickness with which he [Matthew] obeyed" as well as his generosity, humility, and submission, were all qualities demanded from Afro-Hispanic slaves in the household manuals of early-modern Spain.[60] The calling of Matthew signifies the transformation of Levi through his calling. In the *Golden Legend,* Saint Ambrose, Doctor of the Church, explains that "Matthew now followed Christ, happy and supple, and exulted, saying: 'I no longer carry in me a publican, I no longer carry Levi, I put off Levi after I put on Christ.'" This is a clear indication of the apostle's "new nature" acquired after leaving all behind, even his previous self, so that Ambrose makes Matthew claim, "I hate my race, I flee from my past life, I follow you alone, Lord Jesus, you who heal my wounds."[61]

It is clear that in the *Golden Legend* following Christ erased Matthew's own self and his past as a marginal individual to allow a transformation of his better self. This process of self-effacement and transformation of the self by the power of Christ immediately reminds us of Palomino's claim that the former slave and painter Pareja acquired a second nature. Palomino states that Pareja's new identity was forged partly due to his bondage to his master Velázquez and subsequently to Velázquez's own family, to his "honest" thoughts and to his eminence in painting. Even in spite of the "disgrace of his nature," Pareja could become a new being by the process of Christianization of the self.[62] His biographer also claimed that Pareja's qualities belonged to the soul and that "souls are of the same color and made in the same workshop."[63] Thus, on religious grounds Palomino whitens Pareja's freedom and existence.[64] In the social reality of slavery, conversion to Christianity was the passport for the "natural" acculturation of slaves in the Spanish Empire. The Church never opposed slavery, and slave auctions in Spain were first held on the steps of the Cathedral of Seville, before slaves were distributed into the main Spanish cities and into the New World.[65] Nor did the early-modern Spanish establishment and intellectuals ever question the legitimacy of either the existence of slaves, or the practice of slavery, or the lucrative workings of the slave market.[66] It is easy to imagine that Pareja could have identified with Matthew, not only because conversion to Christianity was the key to freedom from spiritual slavery, but above all because Matthew was the apostle of Ethiopia, as Pareja reminds his audience when he decided to place the only African man in the painted scene behind the apostle.[67] In the early-modern European social imaginary Ethiopia was associated both with classical antiquity, where the word Ethiopian was used with reference to black people,[68] and with Christianity, since Ethiopia was considered the first Christian nation and "the promise of Christian universality."[69]

In *The Calling of Saint Matthew* Pareja also establishes a direct relationship between Matthew and Moses by positioning the latter in the painting *Moses and the Serpent*, which hangs above the apostle's head (Fig. 5.6). Not only does Pareja depict Moses and Christ as wearing the same robes and colors, but he also positions himself at the other end of the table, mirroring Christ. It is interesting that Pareja represents Moses as the liberator of the Israelites from slavery in Egypt, where Matthew also preached. *Moses and the Serpent* depicts the story of the Exodus from Egypt when God tired of the Israelites' complaints and set on them poisonous snakes. Moses prayed for his people, and on God's command he made a serpent of brass, which he fixed to the top of a pole. All those who gazed on it were safe from the poisonous snakes (Numbers 21:4–9). This story foretold the healing effect of Christ's death and resurrection. In the New Testament, John the Evangelist (3:13–15) explains that as the Israelites were saved by looking at the bronze serpent at the top of the pole, so all those who gaze at Christ on the cross will be saved and enjoy eternal life. Catholic doctrine interprets John's comparison as an exaltation of Christ's life. Pareja depicts Moses as a liberator of the enslaved Jews from Egypt and in line with Catholic doctrine; he also represents him as the precursor of Christ as the liberator of humanity.[70] The apostle Matthew, who is positioned between Moses and Christ, is seen as the instrument

5.6. Detail of Figure 5.1 (scene depicting Moses). Juan de Pareja, *The Calling of Saint Matthew*, 1661.

of Christ's liberation in Ethiopia, with his divine light shining upon the face of the young black slave standing behind him. It is as if the bright divine light erases, illuminates, and whitens the slave's features. In my opinion, this motif is a signifier of the conversion of the Ethiopian by the apostle, which foretells Pareja's own self-whitening. The painter positions himself opposite Christ, and in this way he refers to himself as a biblical Ethiopian and subsequently as a free man. Thus, Pareja makes it clear to his audience that Matthew, the African slave, and he himself belong to the first Christian nation, which became the first site for "old Christians" and not early-modern Spain.[71] Therefore, biblical Ethiopians are older and purer than "old Christians" in Spain. In the religious narrative of *The Calling of Saint Matthew,* Pareja's self-portrait defies the core of the state policy of purity of blood in Imperial Spain and subverts the very essence of portraiture whereby the sitter should be readily identified. The biblical claim legitimizes the former slave's self-representation as an "old Christian," a Spanish gentleman, a free man, and subsequently a painter. Christianity was for Matthew and the black neophyte a place of spiritual inclusion and social acceptance. By associating himself with Matthew, the painter and black slave Pareja becomes an example of assimilation to the Spanish Empire, where the black slaves who were converted to Christianity did not awaken, any suspicion, unlike the *Moriscos* and *Conversos.*[72]

Pareja might well have been aware of the earlier whitening process of the Afro-Hispanic humanist Juan Latino, which is viewed by Fra-Molinero in the context of the conversion of the Ethiopian as an example of assimilation in early-modern Spanish society.[73] The religious link between black slaves and biblical Ethiopians is seen by the Spanish literary critic as a liberating process for black people in early-modern Spain and as marking a difference with the Christianization of the Jews and Moors in Spain, where both their religions were seen as enemies of the State. By identifying with the Ethiopians, Latino and Pareja, both black Christians, detach themselves from black Muslims.

While in the 1650 portrait *Juan de Pareja* Velázquez depicted his slave as a proud Afro-Hispanic gentleman, it is legitimate to question why Pareja fashioned himself as a European man when the religious context in which he embedded himself in his painting would have justified his metaphysical or metaphorical process of whitening. The former slave could have followed Velázquez's example in his *Kitchen Maid with Supper at Emmaus* (Fig. 5.7). Pareja, after all, reappropriated his master's juxtaposition of the image of a slave with a sacred scene in the background. In his ca. 1618 Sevillian *bodegón,* Velázquez justifies the acculturation of the anonymous female slave by positioning her in the center of the composition, at her workplace adjacent to the room where the Supper at Emmaus is taking place.[74] The dignity of Velázquez's slave is firmly contextualized in the spiritual realm, even if her features have not been Europeanized. The crucial issue, however, is that Velázquez lowers the gaze of the female slave. The slave's

5.7. Diego Velázquez, *Kitchen Maid with Supper at Emmaus*, ca. 1618. Oil on canvas. National Gallery of Ireland, Dublin.

own subjectivity has been denied, and her viewer could define her mainly by the color of her skin in a society where the word "black" signifies "slave." Thus, the challenge for Pareja is the construction of his own subjectivity from within the religious discourse of early-modern Spain. How could he create a pictorial illusion that could clearly convey his status as a man free from slavery?

One also has to remember that since the first decade of the sixteenth century viewers were aware of the rules of physiognomy, defined by Pomponious Gauricus in *De sculptura* (1504) as "a way of observing by which we deduce the qualities of souls from the features of bodies."[75] This approach to portraiture, widespread in early-modern Europe, presented another real problem for Pareja. In my opinion, the former slave, as Latino before him, was aware that the blackness of his skin would have always reminded his audiences of his enslavement, as did the skin color of Velázquez's kitchen maid. How to reconcile, in visual terms, the theoretical claim that a painter is a free individual and not a slave? There is no doubt that viewers of Velázquez's portrait *Juan de Pareja* would have had a different approach. Its extraordinariness is that Pareja's master paid any attention to his slave by breaking the invisibility of black people in the artistic milieu and elevating him into the realm of high art. Eleven years later when Pareja decided to depict himself he was a "free" man, but how could the former slave convey to his Spanish audiences the reality of his new identity? Could the color of the skin of the Afro-Hispanic painter signify freedom from slavery? Was Pareja's written statement of his pictorial authorship in *The Calling of Saint Matthew* enough to prove his identity as a painter, and therefore as a free man? Was Pareja's own association with biblical Ethiopia powerful enough to overcome the early-modern European rules of physiognomy?

Pareja had to make sure that his audiences perceived him as a painter and therefore as a free man like his masters Velázquez and Juan Bautista Martínez del Mazo. There is no doubt that the former slave painter had to resort to a visual strategy to convey his own statements. In my opinion, Pareja might have been aware of the whitening of an African man in the popular prints representing the *Baptism of the Ethiopian by Saint Philip*, where the only clue to the ethnicity of the African neophyte could be found in the written inscription below the image (Fig. 5.8). The Ethiopian baptized by the apostle Philip was none other than the eunuch whom Saint Matthew met in Ethiopia. According to the *Golden Legend* Matthew "was given hospitality by the eunuch of Queen Candace, whom Philip had baptized."[76] The "eunuch" or prime minister of the Queen of the Ethiopians was converted to Christianity through the instrumentality of the apostle Philip. While Philip was on the road leading from Jerusalem to Gaza he was overtaken by a chariot in which sat a royal official from Ethiopia who was reading a passage from Isaiah (53:7–8). Philip explained to him the passage, which prophesied the humiliations and death of Christ, with the result that the African asked to be baptized (Acts 8:27).

The seventeenth-century European prints depicting the *Baptism of the Ethiopian by Saint Philip* contradict the popular Renaissance concept of the impossibility of changing the color of the skin of the African man, as referred to in the popular emblem LIX "*Impossibile*," in the *Emblematum liber* of Andrea Alciati, published in 1531: "Why are you washing an Ethiopian in vain? Ah, desist / No one can illuminate the darkness of black night."[77] In 1995, Jean Michel Massing deconstructed this paradigm in two instances. In the first engraving of the *Baptism of the Ethiopian* by Claes Jansz Visscher after an etching by Jan Joris van Vliet the image of the African man is identifiable, but according to the inscription below, his soul has been whitened by the sacrament of baptism: "Here Philip washes the Ethiopian and, recalling the prophecies, removes the blackness not of his skin but of his soul." In the engraving of the same subject by Michel Lasne, after Aubin Vouet (see Fig. 5.8), the eunuch has been transformed into a white European neophyte, and he can be identified only by the Latin epigram below the image: "You are not washing the Ethiopian in vain. Do not stop. The water poured by the priest can illuminate the black night."[78] In these early-modern European prints the whitening of the soul and skin of the black neophyte is seen, as Massing rightly claims, as a miracle performed by Saint Philip, "a case of 'successful' Ethiopian bath."[79]

In early-modern Spain, Pareja had to find a space in which he could construct himself as an Afro-Hispanic painter in order to be accepted as a free man. After all, in theory a slave could not be recognized as a painter. Therefore he had to proclaim his freedom via his own profession by resorting to the visual idiom of high art. The popular prints of the *Baptism of the Ethiopian* provided Pareja with the right visual motif, which he adopted to fashion himself in the Prado painting.

In *The Calling of Saint Matthew* Pareja's subjectivity was construed through the links established between himself, Matthew, Moses, and Christ in order to reinforce his own freedom from spiritual slavery. His religious association with Saint Matthew, apostle of Ethiopia, justifies Pareja's freedom, his being a painter, his own self, and his existence. However, the blackness of his skin gave away to his audience his former condition of enslavement and the impossibility of his social freedom from slavery, with the consequent problem of his being accepted as a freeman and as a painter. As Matthew had to erase his publican past through

5.8. Michel Lasne after Aubin Vouet, *Baptism of the Ethiopian by Saint Philip*, 1640. Engraving. British Museum, London. © Trustees of the British Museum, London.

his conversion, Pareja had to attenuate his ethnic difference by Europeanizing himself through his association with Matthew's friend, the Ethiopian baptized by Philip. In this way Pareja chose to become Candace's eunuch as interpreted by the white seventeenth-century European gaze: as a miracle performed by Saint Philip, who succeeded in whitening not only the soul of an African man, but also his physical appearance. Thus, the seventeenth-century Spanish Catholic audience who was ruled by the policy of purity of blood could grasp Pareja's new identity as a painter and therefore as a free man in spite of subverting the genre of self-portraiture. In this way Pareja could claim his artistic freedom only one year after the death of his master Velázquez. One has to remember that the status of former slaves was not very different from their previous condition. In fact, in spite of his legal freedom in 1650 and the death of his master in 1660, Pareja was still at the service of Velázquez's descendants. *The Calling of Saint Matthew* became Pareja's manifesto of his own new position as a subject. Paradoxically, Pareja's self-portrait is also homage to his own master. In psychoanalytical terms, his partial identification with Velázquez's self-portrait in *Las Meninas* could be interpreted as part of a mourning process, which would justify the temporary metamorphoses of Juan de Pareja.[80]

In early-modern Spain, portraiture, as this study showed, was conceived as a visual code to preserve and glorify the memory of a worthy sitter.[81] For obvious social reasons a slave was not considered a "worthy" subject for a portrait. Although the "worthless" subject of Velázquez's portrait was used by the court painter to advertise his own art and social status, this extraordinary work subverts the elitist essence of the genre of portraiture coined by the art theorists in early-modern Spain since it fulfills the genre's main function of immortalizing its sitter.[82] Thus, the portrayal of the enslaved embraced and at the same time undermined the constrictions of the genre of portraiture. The inherently contradictory nature of slave portraiture drove the former slave painter Juan de Pareja to the peak of his artistic and intellectual abilities when he decided to depict himself in order to proclaim his own subjectivity. His gaze invites the viewer into a history painting that justifies his existence as a free religious man; the piece of paper he is holding in his hand to assert his authorship documents his professional freedom because a painter whose memory will be preserved could not be a slave; and in the most surprising way, the metamorphoses of his own self cleanses the stigma of manumission to reclaim his social status as a free man. Pareja's self-portrait embedded in his masterpiece *The Calling of Saint Matthew* is a celebration and a justification of his being his own master painter at the Habsburg Court in Madrid, at the center of the Spanish Empire.

Notes

Thanks to Peter Abrahams, Emilio Fracchia, Alison Hilder, Aurelia Martín Casares, Agnes Lugo-Ortiz, Jennifer Montagu, Javier Portús Pérez, Angela Rosenthal, and Barry Taylor.

1 See Ladislas Bugner, Jean Devisse, and Michel Mollat, eds., *The Image of the Black in Western Art*, 2 vols. (Fribourg: Office du Livre, 1979), 2; Carmen Fracchia, "(Lack of) Visual Representation of Black Slaves in Spanish Golden Age Painting," *Journal of Iberian and Latin American Studies* 10, no. 1 (June 2004), 23–34, and "Constructing the Black Slave in Early Modern Spanish Painting," in *Others and Outcasts in Early Modern Europe: Picturing the Social Margins*, ed. Tom Nichols (Aldershot: Ashgate, 2007).

2 Lorne Campbell, *Renaissance Portraits: European Portrait-Painting in the Fourteenth, Fifteenth and the Sixteenth Centuries* (New Haven: Yale University Press, 1990), 195, n. 18.

3 Miguel Falomir, "Los orígenes del retrato en España. De la falta de especialistas al gran taller," in *El retrato español: del Greco a Picasso*, ed. Javier Portús Pérez (Madrid: Museo Nacional del Prado, 2004), 80.

4 See the definition of *retrato* by Sebastián de Covarrubias, *Tesoro de la lengua castellana o española* (1611), ed. Martín de Riquer (Barcelona: Horta, 1987), 908: "la figura contrahecha de alguna persona principal y de cuenta, cuya efigie y semejanza es justo quede por memoria a los siglos venideros." See also Javier Portús Pérez, "Varia fortuna del retrato en España," in Portús Pérez, ed., *El retrato español*, 21, 43, 95.

5 Pérez Sánchez, "Velázquez y el retrato barroco," in Portús Pérez, *El retrato español*, 182–3, and Portús Pérez, "Varia fortuna del retrato en España," 29–30, 43.

6 Portús Pérez, "Varia fortuna del retrato en España," 29–30.

7 Ibid., 20, 24–25, 30.

8 See "Life of Velázquez," translated from Antonio Palomino de Castro y Velasco, *El Museo Pictórico y Escala Óptica* (1715–24), 3 vols. (Madrid: M. Aguilar, 1947), in Enriqueta Harris, *Velázquez* (Oxford: Phaidon Press, 1982), 3:209. This exhibition took place during Velázquez's second visit to Rome (1648–50). Juan Agustín Ceán Bermúdez, *Diccionario histórico de los más ilustres profesores de las Bellas Artes en España*, 6 vols. (Madrid: Imprenta Viuda de Ibarra, 1800), 4:50, believes that Pareja also accompanied his master during his first trip to Italy (1629–31).

9 Jennifer Montagu, "Velázquez Marginalia: His Slave Juan de Pareja and His Illegitimate Son Antonio," *Burlington Magazine* 125 (1983), 684.

10 Aurelia Martín Casares, *La esclavitud en la Granada del siglo XVI: género, raza y religión* (Granada: Editorial Universidad de Granada, Diputación Provincial de Granada, 2000), 435–69.

11 Montagu, "Velázquez Marginalia," 684.

12 Ibid., 684. For the transcription of the document, see *Corpus Velazqueño. Documentos y Textos*, ed. Ángel Aterido Fernández, 2 vols. (Madrid: Ministerio de Educación, Cultura y Deporte, 2000), 1:87.

13 I am extremely grateful to Dr. Montagu for having clarified to me that the remarkable thing about the manumission document is that Pareja as a slave was not treated differently from a free Italian man.

14 Antonio Palomino de Castro y Velasco, "Juan de Pareja," in *El Museo Pictórico y Escala Óptica* (1715–24), 3 vols. (Madrid: M. Aguilar, 1947), 3:960; Ceán Bermúdez, *Diccionario*, 50.

15 See Aterido Fernández, ed., *Corpus Velazqueño*, 1, and Montagu, "Velázquez Marginalia," 684. I am very grateful to Dr. Aurelia Martín Casares, who clarified to me that it was not common that a slave could read or write and therefore to appear as a witness in legal documents in early-modern Spain. The Spanish anthropologist believes that this is an indication of the special relationship between master and slave.

16 I am also grateful to Dr. Montagu, who assured me that in Roman baroque legal documents the absence of an ethnic definition of the subject would be normal practice.

17 Palomino was named Royal Painter in 1688: see Jonathan Brown, *The Golden Age of Spain* (New Haven: Yale University Press, 1991), 288, 302–4.

18 Quotations in English from Palomino's "Life of Juan de Pareja" are taken from Antonio Palomino de Castro y Velasco, *An Account of the Lives and Works of the Most Eminent Spanish Painters, Sculptors and Architects, and Where their Several Performances are to be Seen. Translated from the Museum Pictorium of Palomino Velasco* (London: printed for Sam. Harding, on the pavement in St. Martin's-Lane, 1739), 73. For the original version, see Palomino, "Juan de Pareja," 960: "de generación mestizo, y de color extraño" and "moler colores, y aparejar algún lienzo, y otras cosas ministeriales del arte, y de la casa."

19 Palomino, English translation, "Life of Juan de Pareja," 73; Palomino, original version,"Juan de Pareja," 960: "Velázquez (por el amor de su arte) nunca le permitió, que se ocupase en cosa, que fuese pintar, ni dibujar." In Spain this polemic about painting as a liberal art was still alive during the eighteenth century, since this activity was considered a craft until the end of the previous century. See Alfonso E. Pérez Sánchez, "El retrato clásico español," in *El Retrato*, ed. Fundación Amigos del Museo del Prado (Barcelona: Galaxia Gutemberg, 2004), 228.

20 Palomino, English translation, "Life of Juan de Pareja," 73–74; Palomino, original version, "Juan de Pareja," 960: "él [Pareja] se dió tan buena maña, que a vueltas de su amo, y quitándoselo del sueño, llegó a hacer de la Pintura cosas muy dignas de estimación."

21 Palomino, English translation, "Life of Juan de Pareja," 74; Palomino, original version, "Juan de Pareja," 960: "Y previniendo en esto el disgusto forzoso de su amo, se valió de una industria peregrina; había pues observado Pareja, que siempre, el señor Felipe Cuarto bajaba a las bóvedas, a ver pintar a Velázquez, en viendo un cuadro arrimado, y vuelto a la pared, llegaba Su Majestad a volverlo, o lo mandaba volver, para ver, qué cosa era. Con este motivo, puso Pareja un cuadrito de su mano, como a el descuido vuelto a la pared: apenas lo vio el Rey, cuando llegó a volverlo; y a el mismo tiempo Pareja, que estaba esperando la ocasión, se puso a sus pies,y le suplicó rendidamente le amparase para con su amo, sin cuyo consentimiento había aprendido el arte, y hecho de su mano aquella pintura."

22 Palomino, English translation, "Life of Juan de Pareja," 74–75; Palomino, original version, "Juan de Pareja," 960: "No se contentó aquel magnánimo espíritu real con hacer lo que Pareja le suplicaba, sino que volviendo a Velázquez, le dijo: *No sólo no tenéis, que hablar más de esto; pero advertid, que quien tiene esta habilidad, no puede ser esclavo.*"

23 See Palomino, original version, "Juan de Pareja," 961, who claimed that after Pareja's liberation he still served his master and his master's daughter: "todo lo restante de su vida sirvió, no sólo a Velázquez . . . sino después a su hija, que casó con Don Juan Bautista del Mazo," and Palomino, English translation, "Life of Juan de Pareja," 75: "*Pareja* was so honourable as to continue not only to serve *Velasquez*, as long as he liv'd, but his Daughter after him." The Afro-Hispanic poet Juan Latino (1518?–ca. 1594) was a previous notable exception of a successful black humanist and latinist in early-modern Spain, see Baltasar Fra-Molinero, "Juan Latino and His Racial Difference" in *Black Africans in Renaissance Europe*, ed. Thomas F. Earle and Kate J. P. Lowe (Cambridge: Cambridge University Press, 2005), 326–44.

24 Palomino, English translation, "Life of Juan de Pareja," 75. Palomino, original version, "Juan de Pareja," 961: "Tuvo especialmente nuestro Pareja singularísima habilidad para retratos, de los cuales yo he visto algunos muy excelentes, como el de José Ratés (Arquitecto en esta Corte) en que se conoce totalmente la manera de Velázquez, de suerte, que muchos lo juzgan suyo." Palomino mentioned Pareja's portrait of *The Architect José Ratés Dalmau* (ca. 1660–70, Valencia, Museo de Bellas Artes).

25 Palomino's comments were not translated in the 1739 English biography of Pareja. See Palomino, original version, "Juan de Pareja," 961: "[Pareja ha] llegado a ser eminente en la Pintura (no obstante la desgracia de su naturaleza)."

26 Ceán Bermúdez, *Diccionario*, 52.
27 Carl Justi, *Velázquez y su siglo*, trans. Pedro Marrades (Madrid: Espasa-Calpe, 1953), 578, was the first art historian to notice and compare the visual differences in both representations of Juan de Pareja.
28 See Aurelia Martín Casares, "Free and Freed Black Africans in Granada in the Time of the Spanish Renaissance," in *Black Africans in Renaissance Europe*, ed. T. F. Earle and Kate J. P. Lowe (Cambridge: Cambridge University Press, 2005), 248–49.
29 In Spain, artists, like Pareja, start depicting themselves in religious altarpieces and paintings as secondary figures from the first half of the sixteenth century: see Juan Antonio Gaya Nuño, *Autorretratos de artistas españoles* (Barcelona and Buenos Aires: Argos, 1950), 16–25.
30 Palomino refers to Velázquez's *Pope Innocent X*, 140 × 120 cm, which is in Galleria Pamphili, Rome. See Antonio Palomino de Castro y Velasco, "Life of Velázquez," 209. For an interesting approach to this portrait and Palomino's legend see Victor I. Stoichita, "El retrato del esclavo Juan de Pareja: semejanza y conceptismo" in *Velázquez* (1999), 367–81.
31 Antonio Palomino de Castro y Velasco, "Life of Velázquez," 209–10.
32 Enriqueta Harris, *Velázquez* (Oxford: Phaidon, 1982), 146–47, and Portús Pérez, "Varia fortuna del retrato en España," 17–52.
33 Julián Gállego, *Velázquez* (Madrid: Museo del Prado, 1990), 390–91. The Academy of Virtuosi or confraternity of artists was founded in 1542 in the Pantheon by canon Desiderio d'Adiutorio in 1542; see Ludwig Freiherr von Pastor, *Storia dei Papi dalla fine del mediovevo*, trans. Angelo Mercati, 17 vols. (Rome: Desclée & Ci. Editori Pontifici, 1959), 5:736.
34 Everett Fahy, "A History of the Portrait and Its Painter," *Metropolitan Museum of Art Bulletin* 29 (1970/71), 472.
35 Bugner, Devisse and Mollat, *Image of the Black in Western Art*, 161–253 and Fracchia, "(Lack of) Visual Representation," 25.
36 See note 1 above.
37 Jonathan Brown, *Velázquez: Painter and Courtier* (New Haven: Yale University Press, 1986), 251–52.
38 Quoted in ibid., 251.
39 See note 8 above.
40 Claudio Lomnitz-Adler, *Exit from the Labyrinth. Culture and Ideology in the Mexican National Space* (Berkeley: University of California Press 1992), 263.
41 See Julián Gállego, *El pintor, de artesano a artista* (Granada: Universidad de Granada, 1976), 85; Fracchia, "(Lack of) Visual Representation," 30, n. 16.
42 Portús Pérez, "Varia fortuna del retrato en España," 50–51. See Gaya Nuño, *Autorretratos de artistas españoles*, for the history of self-portraits by Spanish artists.
43 For the genre of self-portraiture, see Richard Brilliant, *Portraiture* (London: Reaktion, 1991), ch. 2, and Campbell, *Renaissance Portraits*, 209, 215–17.
44 Gaya Nuño, *Autorretratos de artistas españoles*, 22–23.
45 See Fra-Molinero, "Juan Latino and His Racial Difference," 330.
46 The earliest signed painting by Pareja is dated 1658, before the death of his master: *The Flight into Egypt* (1.68 × 1.25 cm, oil on canvas, Sarasota, FL, John and Mable Ringling Museum of Art); see Juan Antonio Gaya Nuño, "Revisiones sexcentistas: Juan de Pareja," *Archivo Español de Arte* 30 (1957), 276, and Anthony F. Janson, ed., *Great Paintings from the John and Mable Ringling Museum of Art* (New York: John and Mable Ringling Museum of Art, 1986), 113.

47 Campbell, *Renaissance Portraits,* 14, claims that the "degree of idealization [of the sitter] is measurable when there exist two approximately contemporary portraits of the same sitter by different artists."

48 *English New Revised Standard Version: The Holy Bible: with Illustrations from the Vatican Library* (London: HarperCollins, 1996).

49 See Basi Yamey, *Art and Accountancy* (New Haven: Yale University Press, 1989), 66.

50 It would be obvious to assume that Pareja saw this work when he went to Rome with Velázquez not only because of the great fame and controversy surrounding Caravaggio's three paintings of the life of Saint Matthew, but also because the French church was located in the same neighborhood as the national church of the Spanish, San Giacomo degli Spagnoli. For the history and bibliography of the decoration of the Contarelli Chapel, see Helen Langdon, *Caravaggio: A Life* (London: Chatto and Windus, 1998), 170–79.

51 Pareja's *The Calling of Saint Matthew* is still invisible to the public since it is kept in the basement of the Prado Museum, except for a brief time during the museum exhibition *The Spanish Portrait: From El Greco to Picasso* (October 2004–February 2005). See Portús Pérez, "Varia fortuna del retrato en España," 50, fig. 20.

52 I am very grateful to Dr. Javier Portús Pérez, who with great knowledge showed me Pareja's painting and pointed out the Farnese motif. This painting was inventoried in 1746 in the Farnese collection at the royal palace of San Ildefonso de La Granja. See Pedro de Madrazo, *Catálogo descriptivo e histórico del Museo del Prado de Madrid. Escuelas Italianas y Españolas* (Madrid: Rivadeneyra, 1872), 513.

53 Ceán Bermúdez, *Diccionario,* 52. See also the transcription of Charles III's inventory in the palace of Aranjuez in Aterido Fernández, ed., *Corpus Velazqueño,* 2:670. See also Madrazo, *Catálogo,* 513.

54 Campbell, *Renaissance Portraits,* 135; the Oriental rug is according to Campbell a "indication of the sitters' affluence." Dr. Portús pointed out to me that this Dutch iconographic motif is rarely used in Spanish paintings.

55 In early-modern Spain the word "black" was used to signify "slave."

56 I am grateful to Dr. Portús, who suggested that Pareja' s *Moses and the Serpent* was based on "Jusepe" Leonardo's painting on the same subject. See Alfonso E. Pérez Sánchez, *Pintura barroca en España: 1600–1750* (Madrid: Cátedra, 1992), 249. José Leonardo's painting is in the Museum of the Real Academia de Bellas Artes de San Fernando, Madrid.

57 See Mark 2:14 and Luke 5:27.

58 Jacobus de Voragine, *The Golden Legend,* trans. William Granger Ryan, 7 vols. (Princeton: Princeton University Press, 1995), 2:186.

59 Ibid., 187–88.

60 Spanish household manuals gave instructions on how to treat slaves and their obligations: see Vicente Mexía, *Saludable instrucción del estado del matrimonio* (Córdoba: Juan Baptista Escudero, 1566), fols. 237v–242r. See also Fracchia, "(Lack of) Visual Representation," 27.

61 Voragine, *Golden Legend,* 187.

62 Palomino, original version, "Juan de Pareja," 961: "[Pareja] Y por esta noble acción [servitude], como por haber tenido tan honrados pensamientos, y llegado a ser eminente en la Pintura (no obstante la desgracia de su naturaleza) ha parecido digno de este lugar ... por sus honrados procederes, y aplicación, se labró un nuevo ser, y otra segunda naturaleza." Palomino's comments were not translated in the 1739 English biography of Pareja. See also Stoichita, "El retrato del esclavo Juan de Pareja," 375–79.

63 Palomino, original version, "Juan de Pareja," 961: "el ingenio, habilidad, y honrados pensamientos, son patrimonios del alma; y las almas todas son de un color; y

labradas en una misma oficina." Palomino's comments were not translated in the 1739 English biography of Pareja.

64 Stoichita, "El retrato del esclavo Juan de Pareja," 377–78. With reference to Palomino's life of Pareja, Stoichita cites Juan Latino as a previous example of a slave who was made free thanks to royal intervention, and his subsequent assimilation is viewed as a case of metaphysical whitening of the African in the Golden Age of Spanish literature.

65 Fracchia, "(Lack of) Visual Representation," 28.

66 On Spanish political thought on slavery see Martín Casares, *La esclavitud en la Granada*, 65–89.

67 Voragine, *Golden Legend*, 184 recalls: "Matthew the apostle was preaching in Ethiopia in a city called Nadaber" and in Egypt.

68 The terms Ethiopian and Indian were interchangeable when used to refer to black people. See Jean Michel Massing, "From Greek Proverb to Soap Advert: Washing the Ethiopian," *Journal of the Warburg and the Courtauld Institute* 58 (1995), 182, and Fra-Molinero, "Juan Latino," 337.

69 Fra-Molinero, "Juan Latino," 330, 331, 344. In early-modern Europe Ethiopia was intended as synonymous with Africa, although geographically it refers to the north-eastern area of the continent.

70 I am very grateful to Dr. Emilio Fracchia, who assisted me in the Catholic interpretation of these religious scenes.

71 Fra-Molinero, "Juan Latino," 339.

72 Ibid. In Spain *Moriscos* and *Conversos* are the respective designation for Muslims and Jews converted to Christianity.

73 Ibid.

74 The anonymity of the subject is a common feature of all Velázquez's *bodegones* (this term signifies the combination of still-life and genre in a kitchen scene or tavern) made in Seville before 1623, when he moved to the court of Philip IV in Madrid. See Mulcahy, *Spanish Paintings in the National Gallery of Ireland*, 80; Davies and Harris, *Velázquez in Seville*, 128–29, 132–39; Fracchia, "(Lack of) Visual Representation," 24–28. For the Dublin painting and Velázquez's *The Kitchen Maid* (Art Institute, Chicago), without the religious background, see also Fracchia, "Representación de la esclavitud negra en la España imperial y la problematización del par "original-copia" in *Original-Copia ... Original?*, ed. Gabriela Siracusano (Buenos Aires: CAIA, 2005), 269–79; T. J. Tiffany, "Light, Darkness, and African Salvation: Velázquez 's *Supper at Emmaus*," *Art History* 31, no. 1 (2008), 33–56.

75 The quotation is cited in Campbell, *Renaissance Portraits*, 27.

76 Voragine, *Golden Legend*, 184.

77 Ibid., 185. Alciati, *Emblematum liber* (Augsburg, 1531), fol. E3r.

78 Massing, "From Greek Proverb to Soap Advert," 188–91.

79 Ibid., 190.

80 I am very grateful to Mrs. Alison Hilder for her useful comments and for her psychoanalytical interpretation of the temporary metamorphoses of Juan de Pareja.

81 See note 3 above. For the early-modern Spanish concept of visual code see Fernando Bouza, *Communication, Knowledge and Memory in Early Modern Spain*, trans. Sonia López and Michael Agnew (Philadelphia: University of Pennsylvania Press, 2004).

82 *Juan de Pareja* remained invisible to large audiences until 1971 when it came into the possession of the Metropolitan Museum of New York. Velázquez's portrait previously belonged to Italian and British private collections. See *Metropolitan Museum of Art Bulletin* 29 (1970/71), 475.

SIX

OF SAILORS AND SLAVES

PORTRAITURE, PROPERTY, AND THE TRIALS OF CIRCUM-ATLANTIC SUBJECTIVITIES, CA. 1750–1830

Geoff Quilley

The historical association of black Atlantic communities with the sea has centred overwhelmingly on the image of black Africans forcibly transported in slave ships to the plantation culture of the Americas and the Caribbean. As W. Jeffrey Bolster has noted, this is an image that reinforces the belief "that blacks were acted on, rather than acting; that blacks aboard ship sailed as commodities rather than seamen."[1] While not ignoring the horrific reality of the Middle Passage, Bolster is concerned to shift the focus by drawing attention to the degree of agency among the black maritime community in the early-modern Atlantic. This is an important intervention, which has been pursued by subsequent scholars, most recently Marcus Rediker and Peter Linebaugh; but it draws attention also to a major discrepancy between early-modern modes of representation and the social history of the circum-Atlantic world.[2]

For the prevailing stereotype of black people as commodities is largely reinforced within the arena of visual representation: It has frequently been observed that on the rare occasions when blacks do appear in painting, prints or sculpture, it is usually as servants (often enslaved) in portraits, where they double as markers of the superiority of white culture, as figures who seem "to exist to reproduce blackness for and somehow also to produce the whiteness" of their master or mistress.[3] Though represented in portraiture, therefore, they are not represented as portraits, but as attributes of the principal subject of the portrait. There is little sense of black agency in terms of self-representation, whether in portraiture or in any other form of visual media or genre.

In this sense, there is a significant overlap between the representation of blacks in portraits and the visual representation of sailors, whether black or white, though I must stress immediately that this is not to imply by any means that lower-deck or other sailors were slaves or suffered any similar condition of servitude as that which was the norm for the millions transported from Africa to the Americas during this period. Yet, for the eighteenth century there was a significant discursive overlap between slavery and seamanship that needs to be acknowledged. This was played out most conspicuously in sailors' complaints about their working conditions and environment, particularly in relation to the discourse around the practice of impressment.[4] In contrast to the evidence provided by Bolster's documentation of black subjectivities in the Atlantic maritime world, visual culture, particularly what may be termed "high art," appears to serve to strip the identities of those significant groups, communities and classes of people, who (per)formed the material, economic circulation of labour and goods that embodied the development of circum-Atlantic capitalism: slaves, sailors, dock workers and other sections of the labouring classes. With regard to the study of visual culture and the particular themes of this book, on the one hand this has resulted in an overwhelming preponderance of scholarly focus upon a handful of images featuring black sailors – notably John Singleton Copley's *Watson and the Shark* (Fig. 6.1) and Géricault's *Raft of the Medusa* (Fig. 6.2); on the other hand it comprises an expropriation of portraiture (as a genre

6.1. John Singleton Copley, *Watson and the Shark*, 1778. Oil on canvas. National Gallery of Art, Washington, D.C., Ferdinand Lammot Belin Fund, 1963.6.1. Image courtesy of the Board of Trustees, National Gallery of Art, Washington, D.C.

6.2. Théodore Géricault, *The Raft of the Medusa*, 1819. Oil on canvas. Louvre Museum, Paris. Photo: Scala/Art Resource, New York.

and medium) from certain categories of subject – or, to put it another way, a disbarring of certain categories of individual from the genre of portraiture – that is a function of the genre itself and is, furthermore, contained and indexed or signalled within the genre or particular work. In this sense, one of the social and ideological functions of portraiture in the eighteenth century was to confer or assign subjectivity to a particular person or social category, and conversely, through the confines of the genre, to define and delimit the nature of subjectivity across a broad social spectrum according to bounds of propriety set in part by the portrait genre itself. To participate in portraiture as part of a privileged "scopic regime" was to mirror and confirm one's own subjectivity as a viewer before the subjectivity portrayed in the image.[5]

It is, I would argue, not insignificant that blacks in the eighteenth century, when they were visually represented at all, were frequently depicted as sailors; and this, as I shall explore in this essay, was primarily because of these issues of subjectivity that underpin the representation of both blacks and sailors. Before proceeding further, it is worth dwelling on Copley's *Watson and the Shark*, since, although not a portrait as such, it exemplifies many of the issues that I want to consider, through its inclusion of the prominent, though problematic, figure of the black sailor.

Despite the painting's overt primary meaning as a straightforward rescue narrative, commemorating the youthful Brook Watson's escape (minus a leg) from a shark while swimming in Havana Harbour in 1749, its disconcerting and elusive lack of semiotic closure centres around the ambiguous identity of the black sailor. He is at once visually and narratively contradictory, in ways that the other figures in the painting are not. He is at the apex of the composition, yet furthest from the centre of the action. Equally, in the rope that forms the linking line between him and Watson, he holds a key to the youth's salvation, yet he lets it hang loosely between his fingers as though having no use for it. In short, he is at once central and peripheral to the pictorial and narrative structure of the composition. The uncertainty is compounded by the lack of any clear indicators of his identity: Is he enslaved or a free black? Is he passive or active, noble or ignoble, heroic or subversive? The location of Havana Harbour complicates matters further: Is he British, Spanish or French colonial? The image gives us no secure way of knowing. His ambiguity, and its latent potential threats, were certainly not lost on contemporary reviewers at the painting's exhibition in 1778:

> It would not be unnatural to place a woman in the attitude of the *black*; but he, instead of being terrified, ought, in our opinion, to be busy. He has thrown a rope over to the boy. It is held, un-sailor like, between the second and third fingers of his left hand, and he makes no use of it.[6]

As this viewer found, it is impossible to assign the black sailor any clear sense of subjectivity and agency: He is "un-sailor like," in contrast to the other figures, whose roles and attitudes are made explicit. By subjectivity I refer here not only to the fictional projection of the uniqueness of an inner life, but to the visualization of a self-possessed and autonomous individuality. I want to suggest in this essay, therefore, that subjectivity and its indeterminability are crucial to the representation of both blacks and sailors in this period, and that, consequently, the consideration of sailors might illuminate aspects of the portrayal of black slaves. In particular, I shall explore the relation between subjectivity and property vis-à-vis the genre of portraiture, in order to analyse the areas of overlap and the significant differences in visual depiction between sailors and slaves, and what in turn these reveal about the visualization more generally of slaves and slavery in this period.

In the case of portraits where the black servant or slave is shown accompanying his or her master or mistress, the servants are individually represented but in such a way that it disqualifies them from being assigned the subjectivity that their own presence in the picture functions to bestow upon their master, who thus constitutes the proper subject of the image.[7] William Hogarth's painting *Captain Lord George Graham, 1715–47, in his Cabin* (Fig. 6.3, Plate 5) does precisely this, though in a rather more complex manner, in that the black servant is just one of several figures ranged around the seated Graham who in various ways refer to him as the subject of the picture. Extremely unusual in being a conversation-piece set in the great cabin of a ship, it appears to be a commemorative painting celebrating Graham's recent promotion to the command of the *Nottingham*.[8] It plays upon the stereotypical reputation of sailors for raucous drinking, music-making and irreverence: The composition echoes *A Midnight Modern Conversation* (Fig. 9.5), and similarly Graham's cap is askew and the laughing steward brings in a duck on a platter but spills the gravy down the back of Graham's clerk or advisor seated in front of him. The latter thereby becomes the butt of a joke (he is a sitting duck?); he is also alone in being out of keeping with the music-making going on among the rest of the group. There thus appears to be a tension between this seemingly serious-minded figure with his book, which he has given up reading or reciting, and the musicians who drown him out with their "catch," probably a popular nautical ballad, to which Graham is evidently more inclined to listen.

The picture also plays – though, it must be added, in a nonpejorative way – upon eighteenth-century stereotypes of black people, above all their renowned love of music, especially drumming (Fig. 6.4). African music and dance were also conventionally associated with lewdness and sensuality.[9] This perhaps complements the likely erotic charge of the song.[10] On the other hand, the black servant's pipe and drum might be taken to be in competition with the singer, in the same way that the latter is comically parodied by the dog in the foreground howling and joining in the cacophony. The black's drumming might therefore be associated with the dog's noise rather than the singer's music, assigning to the black's contribution to the performance a bestial rather than a refined character,

6.3. William Hogarth, *Captain Lord George Graham, 1715–47, in his Cabin*, ca. 1745. Oil on canvas. National Maritime Museum, Greenwich, London, BHC2720.

an idea supported by his being placed on the same axis as the wig-wearing pug who appears to be conducting the performance. The fact that Graham, it seems, would rather listen to this than his bookish associate further complicates the possible proximity between the sailor and the slave, at least in terms of their supposed coarseness. There are clearly many levels on which this elusive picture may be interpreted. However, in any case the black servant, through the nature of his music-making, is represented as sensual and unrefined, qualities that provide a visual sympathy between him and his master (and thus presumably fit him even more appropriately for a life at sea).[11] In relation to Graham, therefore, he stands in a subsidiary but significant position, acting as a reference back to his seated master, who remains the undisputed central focus of the composition. He also stands apart from the remaining figures in the group: firstly from the other two principal figures ranged around the table with Graham, but also from the steward, who is moving towards the table, is in the light of the window, and directly grins out at the spectator. Instead, despite the considerable sympathy with which he is portrayed (and, for example, being better dressed than the steward), the black servant is in the shadow, behind, and if he is looking at anything, it appears to be at the gravy dripping down the clerk's back. Despite its complexities, therefore, *Captain Lord George Graham in his Cabin* still follows the established convention for such portraits, where the black servant functions as a foil to the central subject and subjectivity of the white master, and where the servant is represented but does not represent him or herself, and is not portrayed (in the sense of being a portrait). Thus the subjectivity of the master or mistress is produced by contrast with its negative, the absence of subjectivity in a person that is owned.

6.4. Detail of Figure 6.3 (black servant). William Hogarth, *Captain Lord George Graham, 1715–47, in his Cabin*, ca.1745.

A parallel, though different, strategy of expropriation is observable in relation to the sailor, whereby questions of propriety and genre are brought to the fore. A recurrent feature of late-eighteenth- and early-nineteenth-century caricature of Jack Tar involves his confrontation in some way with portraiture, and thus with the representation of subjectivity. In this imagery, the relationship of the sailor to

6.5. George Woodward, engr. Roberts, *A Sailor Sitting for his Miniature*, ca. 1800. Coloured etching. National Maritime Museum, Greenwich, London, PAF3848.

the genre of portraiture is always problematic and conflicted. While the sailor is shown, unlike the black slave or servant, with often a significant degree of forthright self-determination and agency, the narrative that frames the dialogue between the sailor and portraiture is such as to undercut his apparent right to that subjectivity. So that the sailor finds himself, as it were, not so much the subject *of* the genre as subjected *to* the genre in a way that questions his claims to participate in it. A brief examination of some examples will clarify this.

An early-nineteenth-century print by George Woodward, *A Sailor Sitting for his Miniature* (Fig. 6.5), provides a stark presentation of the encounter between the sailor and the portrait-painter as one of comical but irresolvable conflict and misunderstanding. What interests me here is how it posits the encounter between the lower-deck seaman and portraiture as one of crisis, and how that crisis is centred on the unclassifiable nature of the sailor, a figure who hovers between being subject and non-subject, slavish labourer and free spirit, who fitted none of the usual patterns of patrician-plebeian relations of eighteenth-century society and was thus a mirror to a host of contradictions and dialectics around the relation of freedom to slavery that, as David Brion Davis has demonstrated, ran through the heart of the Enlightenment.[12]

The joke at face value (so to speak) is a very simple one, of incompatible contrasts, between the effete and (surely) effeminate city elegance and refinement of the miniaturist and the gruff, weather-beaten but manly brutishness of the sailor. The artist's refinement is epitomised in his own portrait representation, in profile (a "noble" format associated with coins and medals), which is contrasted with the full-face openness and "Henry the Eighth" pose of the sailor's portrait, displaying his frank but unashamed ugliness, warts and all (or, rather, syphilitic sore and all – his Poll's "hearts delight" as he calls it, openly and impolitely drawing attention to the existence of the large black mark on his face and, worse, implying the means of its derivation). The scene thus satirizes both the artist and the sailor, but the comedy is achieved solely at the sailor's expense through stipulating that his gruesome visage is an entirely inappropriate subject for the portrait miniature (which is also a genre associated traditionally with gentility and aristocracy, or at least gentry). If this were not enough, the dialogue reinforces the sailor's being the butt of the joke by infantilizing him. Despite the authoritative and imperative mode of his speech, in which he makes one demand after another of the artist, he concludes on a note of ignorance and perplexity, in his implicitly questioning conditional: "If you can get my hulk, head and stern into that there little bit of ivory, d-n me, but I think you would be able to tow a seventy-four through one of the cock boat Arches of London Bridge." In other words, his plain-spoken literalness is applied to such an extent that it exceeds the norms of adult rationality and reverts to a child-like or "primitive" worldview that is unable to accommodate the illusions of scale and dimension that underpin picture-making: So, he cannot believe that his gross physical bulk can be contained or reproduced within the space of a small piece of ivory. Likewise, the satirist employs a device that is typical of the characterization of the sailor at this period, whether in the visual arts, in literature or in theatre: that is, his adoption of nautical jargon for every social situation and level of discourse, however far removed from the environment of the ship and therefore inappropriate. So the sailor refers to himself as "hulk, head and stern" to metaphorize his body into the fabric of a vessel.[13] A similar strategy is apparent in other satirical representations of tars confronted with portraiture, where the sailor is unable, linguistically and epistemologically, to step outside the confines of the ship, and where the portrait, both as artefact and genre, stands for all the values of polite culture to which he is thereby excluded. *Sailors in Westminster Abbey* (Fig. 6.6) shows a pair of red-faced, bullish tars, dressed in their best onshore clothes, before the statue of Shakespeare, whose elevated, philosopher's pose points up the vulgarity of the sailors'. Shakespeare points to the first line of verse, "The Cloud Capt. Towers," and in response the sailors point back, comically but asininely misconstruing the line of poetry according to their own limited seafarers' understanding and according to the conventions of recording the names of vessels and their commanders: "Captain Towers!! who the Devil can this Capt. Towers be? Rot me if I ever heard of his Name or that of the Ship." Despite the affectionate buffoonery with which the tars are characterized here, whereby not only are they unaware of Shakespeare but they also assume that the statue is a portrait of Captain Towers, commander of the ship *Cloud,* their encounter with the genteel culture of portraiture (in this case further complicated by being a retrospective, historical portrait of an iconic cultural figure) serves to reemphasize their distance from that gentility and their intrinsic incapability of ever participating in it. As many commentators remarked throughout the eighteenth century, the sailor was a breed apart, who when he was working was at sea and out of sight to polite society, and when ashore had such distinctive modes of life and language – that were generally characterized by grossness

6.6. Anonymous artist, *Sailors in Westminster Abbey*, 1804. Coloured etching. National Maritime Museum, Greenwich, London, PAF3816.

and riotous behaviour – that he was virtually a foreigner in his own country.[14] Daniel Defoe's attitude to seamen's antisociality was typical:

> 'Tis their way to be violent in all their motions. They swear violently, drink punch violently, spend their money when they have it violently ... in short, they are violent fellows, and ought to be encourag'd to go to sea, for Old Harry can't govern them on shoar.[15]

There was thus a conventional association of sailors with social transgression, brutality and criminality, that was summed up in Dr. Johnson's celebrated comment:

> His negro servant, Francis Barber, having left him, and been some time at sea ... it appears ... that his master kindly interested himself in procuring his release from a state of life of which Johnson always expressed the utmost abhorrence. He said, "No man will be a sailor who has contrivance enough to get himself into a jail; for being in a ship is being in a jail, with the chance of being drowned." And at another time, "A man in a jail has more room, better food, and commonly better company."[16]

This also points to an intrinsic lack of freedom as part of the condition of the tar that might be comparable to enslavement, an association enhanced both implicitly by Johnson's comments being made in connection with his black servant, and also more generally by the cultural attribution to the sailor of a naturally violent, savage character.

The violence of the sailor is reproduced in Woodward's satire in his ugliness, aggressive posture and gigantic scale in comparison to his counterpart (his giant size also reinforces the joke over his not fitting into the ivory miniature), as well as the threatening tone of his language. And the incommensurable gulf that this produces between him and the polite society personified in the miniaturist is likewise reproduced compositionally in the emphatic vertical line made by the curtain and the table leg. This is exactly centrally placed, only slightly interrupted by the sailor's foot, and in effect divides the scene into two pictures: on the left the elegant, light world of the artist, and on the right the windowless environment of the sailor, complete with his standard attributes, pipe and punch bowl. The essential message of the satire is that these two worlds are antithetical and unbridgeable: The sailor's face and all that it stands for cannot, in the end, be contained in the form of the miniature. However, the larger point is also that this disparity between his literal, seaman's perception and the miniaturist's art of sophisticated deception is the sailor's problem, not the artist's. The aesthetics of the eighteenth-century portrait could have no means of comprehending the problematic and unclassifiable distinctiveness of the sailor, who was not a subject in the sense demanded by the portrait genre. The only logical conclusion is Defoe's, to render the sailor invisible by not representing him in portrait format – which is, of course, precisely what we find in eighteenth-century visual culture, the nonportrayal of the tar in any humanistic manner, or in any way whereby he might be included within the parameters of genteel politeness. His social otherness is manifested as exclusion from polite modes of eighteenth-century visual representation. The final point of the satire, then, is that such a scene as that depicted is unthinkable (except in a satirical print such as this). While he could be represented almost endlessly in caricature or stereotyped on the stage, the lower-deck sailor did not meet the criteria for inclusion within the genre of portraiture, not only because of his class status as a labourer (neither is he portrayed in the manner in which even black servants, such as Lord George Graham's, could be), but also because of his otherness, and consequently the problematic elusiveness of his subjectivity.

In this respect there is another significant aspect to the dichotomy between artist and sailor in this caricature. For the opposition between them is also one of property. While the artist's status and individuality are marked by his possessions, from his tasteful gown and drapes to his palette and brushes, the instruments of his profession, the sailor has nothing except the luxurious and ephemeral commodities of consumption: tobacco and punch. This again conforms to the prevailing stereotype of the eighteenth-century tar: His lack of property was frequently cast as a proverbial disdain for the ownership of things, other than transient commodities of pleasurable consumption – sex, booze and tobacco. As this print, and innumerable others like it, imply, the sailor's wages were supposed typically to be spent on such bodily gratification rather than on permanent possessions. On the one hand, this propertyless state supported the identification of the tar as a free spirit, the simple but untied man of the world; on the other it aligned him with the bonded condition of the slave, whose lack of personal ownership of material things was a precondition to their person being owned by someone else. This likewise conformed to the economic condition of the tar as a unit of labour currency, transferable between vessels of different kinds and adaptable to many different manual tasks, who was paid in wages to be redeemed at the end of the voyage, whenever that might be. His condition (theoretically, at least, if not in actual practice) as pure unit of labour depended on his being unhampered by "tools of the trade," as other professionals, artisans or labourers were, and uncommitted to any particular location or specialized work. In short, it depended upon his having no property as a labourer, in the double sense of his having no possessions to speak of that were proper to his work (in contrast, for example, to carpenters', butchers' or even field-hands' implements) and in turn having no single skill or role that was "proper" to him as a labourer.

There thus seems to be implied in this print a correspondence between the tar's invisibility – at least, his ineligibility to be made visually representable through the medium of portraiture – and his lack of property; and upon this correspondence hinges the question of his subjectivity, or rather the lack of it. *A Sailor Sitting for his Miniature*, therefore, presents the very idea of including sailors within the social scope of portraiture as a crisis, in which the questioning of the sailor's compatibility with the practice and genre of the portrait also amounts to a questioning of his claims to subjectivity, in a manner similar to the denial of subjectivity of the slave in portraiture.

Jonathan Lamb has made the important connection between property and subjectivity, centred on the dual etymological sense of "own," meaning both "to possess" and also to be distinctively individual, on one's "own."[17] Tracing the discourse of property from the seventeenth-century social philosophies of Thomas Hobbes and John Locke, Lamb argues that the eighteenth-century relation of property to identity (of both people and things) rested on two principal elements. Selfhood was formulated on the one hand by what one could legitimately claim as possessions (one's property) and on the other by what was intrinsic to the individual person or object (one's properties); thus, for example, stone has properties that are special to it, which make it not wood, metal nor any other material and which distinguish it as such. Both these senses of owning were predicated on a fundamental element of narrative, in that "ownership of a thing and the narrative of how it came to be owned are intertwined elements which combine ultimately into the narratives of self and nation – biography and history."[18] The identity of anyone or anything, therefore, is determined by what is proper to it. And here, of course, to complicate matters further, the term "proper" has a moral value to do with "propriety"; as Lamb notes, for Hobbes the terms "property" and "propriety" were interchangeable. The logic of this is that the abandonment or loss of a governing principle of property must conclude with madness and derangement (as opposed to "arrangement" where things are in their "proper" place). Things unconstrained or undefined by being owned must necessarily be able to assume the properties of other things *ad libitum*:

> Failure to own a thing properly licenses things to act and speak independently. Such a failure of ownership is represented in a number of ways:
>
> 1) As a failure of propriety, the loss of what is becoming or in keeping with humans in their relations with things.
> 2) As the loss of personal identity, a species of madness when we are so far beside ourselves we can no longer give a true narrative of our selves, or what we own.
> 3) As the loss of authority and justice, for the right to property is lost along with the ability to account for things we called our own.
>
> In such circumstances, things are liberated from their owners and truth is merely what each dispossessed, vainglorious or infatuated individual imagines it to be.[19]

Tellingly, therefore, Tom Rakewell in the final plate of Hogarth's *The Rake's Progress* (Fig. 6.7) is visually represented in his ultimate and complete madness as stripped, utterly naked, even down to his wig: His loss of mind and thus the loss of his capacity to own himself is rendered as the loss of every article of property that he once so coveted and that up until this point has defined the very principle of his self-identity. He is at once possessed and dispossessed, or perhaps better, possessed through being dispossessed: that is, his loss of every kind of property results in his being inhabited by a self other to him. And with this scene, of course, the Rake's narrative of himself ends.

This reciprocity between property and subjectivity has important implications for the representation of both slaves and sailors, not least in terms of race and ethnicity. African slaves, notoriously, once they reached the Americas and were sold as goods, were frequently renamed, sometimes with a classicized moniker such as Gustavus Vassa that imposed upon them an identity for their new status as property. This was also a fundamental method of erasing as far as possible any trace of their African identity and the memory of the Middle Passage that described the means by which they arrived at their new place

6.7. William Hogarth, *The Rake's Progress*, 1735. Etching and engraving. British Museum, London. © Trustees of the British Museum, London.

and condition. In a contradictory sense, therefore, to the logic of Hobbes and Locke, plantation slaves in the Americas were rendered *as* property through the sublimation of the narrative of how they came to be owned. Hence (in part at least) the intractable problems posed by the Atlantic slavery system for Enlightenment philosophy, and also the current, postmodern scholarly concern with diasporic, black or circum-Atlantic identity, whereby slaves, like sailors, have become repositioned as a central component of the fluid, mobile community that circulated the interstitial spaces of the early-modern Atlantic maritime world.[20]

As many scholars have recently documented, blacks, both enslaved and free, formed a significant component of that mobile lower-deck community. And they were certainly not immune to caricature, as the image *A Milling Match Between Decks*, from 1812 (Fig. 6.8), demonstrates. Undoubtedly, the most celebrated black sailor was Olaudah Equiano, who was, of course, also renamed following his transportation to the Americas, first as Jacob and Michael, then under physical coercion as Gustavus Vassa. His book, *The Interesting Narrative of the Life of Olaudah Equiano, or Gustavus Vassa, the African, Written by Himself* (first published 1789), is above all else a proclamation of self-ownership, charting as it does the author's hard-won, entirely self-motivated transition from captive slave to free citizen. It is very significant, therefore, that as the frontispiece to volume 1 Equiano reproduced his own portrait (Fig. 6.9).[21] In a roundel format taken from an original painting by the miniaturist William Denton (who was

6.8. William Elmes, *A Milling Match Between Decks*, 1812. Hand-coloured etching. Courtesy of the Lewis Walpole Library, Yale University, New Haven, Conn.

also one of the book's original subscribers), engraved by Daniel Orme and published by Equiano himself, it shows him fashionably dressed, directly engaging the viewer as an equal, and pointing to the Bible he holds in his left hand. This is conspicuously marked as being open at Acts, chapter 4, verse 12, a highly important passage that Equiano highlights in his book as the crucial spur to his attainment of revelation.

It is while reading this passage from Acts, during yet another voyage, this time to the Mediterranean, and also during crises of faith and personality, when Equiano is beset by the blaspheming and immorality of his fellow crew, that revelation comes to him. This also figures as the resolution to an internal mental struggle over the means of salvation:

> Reflecting on my past actions, I began to think I had lived a moral life, and that I had a proper ground to believe I had an interest in the divine favour; but still meditating on the subject, not knowing whether salvation was to be had partly for our own good deeds, or solely as the sovereign gift of God; in this deep consternation the Lord was pleased to break in upon my soul with his bright beams of heavenly light; and in an instant as it were, removing the veil, and letting light into a dark place, I saw clearly with the eye of faith the crucified Saviour bleeding on the cross on mount Calvary.[22]

Revelation comes amidst the uncertainty whether salvation is achieved as the result of good deeds or as the exclusive gift of God. Equiano's crisis over salvation is thus also related to the issue of property and narration, or self-ownership: Does salvation result from what one can narrate of oneself – one's "*own* good deeds" (my emphasis) – or from God as some property bestowed? In this sense, his gift of revelation parallels his grant of manumission earlier in the book, which is also partly earned through his own good deeds as a merchant trading on behalf of his master, but able to generate some small business on his own account. This provided sufficient funds for him to buy his freedom, but his official manumission had still to be granted, as a form of gift, by his master, a Montserrat Quaker, Robert King.[23]

Equiano's story, therefore, is also the tale of his journey towards God. His enforced voyage from Africa to the West is metonymically transfigured into a voyage towards subjectivity and self-ownership through revelation. Accordingly, complementing the portrait frontispiece to volume 1, the frontispiece to the second volume shows a shipwreck, *Bahama Banks. 1767.*[24] This similarly refers to a lengthy "survivor sub-narrative" in the book recounting his providential rescue after being wrecked on a Caribbean desert island, which is again emphasized as a critical moment en route to finding God.[25] This message is reinforced in the caption to the print, which quotes from the Book of Job.

6.9. Daniel Orme after W. Denton, *Olaudah Equiano or Gustavus Vassa the African*, 1789. Stipple engraving. Frontispiece to Olaudah Equiano, *The Interesting Narrative of the Life of Olaudah Equiano, or Gustavus Vassa, the African, Written by Himself* (London, 1789). National Maritime Museum, Greenwich, London, ZBA2657 and British Library, London, UK/© British Library Board. All Rights Reserved/The Bridgeman Art Library.

The *Interesting Narrative* is also a narrative of things, which assume significant character at critical junctures in the book and serve to allegorize the author's course towards liberty. Throughout the book there are regular references to objects such as shackles and whips that are the instruments of torture and servitude. More particularly, once Equiano is enslaved, his life is increasingly determined by objects from which he is alienated and over which he is unable to exert any control: On the contrary, the narrative unfolds according to the degree to which things control him. In other words, the narrative of his being enslaved is underpinned by his relation to property and is determined by the extent of his ability or inability to narrate himself in terms of his own property, in the sense both of objects external to him and of qualities inherent to his own person. Herein, of course, lies the narrative's structural tension: For, once enslaved, he becomes no longer his own person, but is himself an object of (someone else's) property. It is worth examining this in a little more detail for it casts further light on the portrait frontispiece.

The book opens with an account of the author's childhood in an innocent, pastoral – and implicitly nobly savage – region of the northwest African interior. Here there is essentially no need for property or commerce: "As we live in a country where nature is prodigal of her favours, our wants are few and easily supplied ... we have few manufactures.... In such a state money is of little use."[26] It is from this state of grace that he is kidnapped and taken to the coast to be bartered and shipped across the Atlantic. As he nears the coast his relationship to things becomes one of growing alienation and instability, culminating with his first sight of a slave ship, an object so far removed from his control or understanding that he concludes that it must be worked by magic.[27]

On arrival in the Americas things assume a threatening aspect: The other property of his master, in the form of material goods and luxury items, is endowed with human attributes – things can take on a life of their own – and function as potential spies upon Equiano, himself now also property. When summoned into the house to fan his sleeping master, the objects in the room exert control over him. The implication is that his own state of being owned entails an unavoidable inability "to own a thing properly," which "licenses things to act and speak independently." Immediately prior to going to the task of fanning his master, he comes face to face with a stark demonstration of how under slavery things exert power over people: A black woman slave was "cruelly loaded with various kinds of iron machines; she had one particularly on her head, which locked her mouth so fast that she could scarcely speak; and could not eat nor drink." Then he enters the room where his master was sleeping:

> The first object that engaged my attention was a watch which hung on the chimney, and was going. I was quite surprised at the noise it made, and was afraid it would tell the gentleman any thing I might do amiss: and

> when I observed a picture hanging in the room, which appeared constantly to look at me, I was still more affrighted.[28]

Aside from the metaphorical status of the clock and picture as signifiers of the hegemonic techniques of time-control and surveillance central to plantation slavery, Equiano's mystified encounter with them exemplifies his fraught relation to things and the central but unstable discourse of property that underpins his narrative of himself.[29]

The elusiveness of property continues when, as a merchant acting on behalf of his master, he accumulates a small amount of money and goods for himself, but is disappropriated of these by white thieves, in ways that are contrary to any sense of natural justice but are unable to be redressed by a black slave.[30] This inversion of property and propriety extends also to the black body itself, Equiano lamenting the fate of free blacks who are kidnapped and sold back into slavery.[31]

Perhaps the most striking incident of a thing with a life of its own is Equiano's encounter with a "talking book," a recurrent trope among slave narratives.[32] This occurs during the same period of wonderment and fear on his arrival in the West and reiterates the figuration of things assuming the subjectivity of his master:[33]

> I had often seen my master and Dick employed in reading; and I had a great curiosity to talk to the books, as I thought they did ... for that purpose I have often taken up a book, and have talked to it, and then put my ears to it, when alone, in hopes it would answer me; and I have been very much concerned when I found it remained silent.[34]

Equiano's "concern" at the silence of the book exactly corresponds to his distress at his slave status and his absence of subjectivity. As Henry Louis Gates Jr. has written: "Of course the book does not speak to him. Only subjects can endow an object with subjectivity; objects, such as a slave, possess no inherent subjectivity of their own. Objects can only reflect the subjectivity of the subject, like a mirror."[35]

The fact, therefore, that in the book's frontispiece Equiano represents himself, firstly, as a portrait and, secondly, in possession of a book – and not just any book, but the Bible – doubly announces his own subjectivity as a free citizen: The frontispiece is "both the first and last illustration of the trope of the 'talking book' that the author uses to emphasize the significance of literacy and acculturation in his autobiography."[36] The autobiographical reference to the passage from Acts further announces that this book has indeed spoken to him: literally so in Equiano's account of his revelation. In contrast to the sailor having his miniature taken in Woodward's satire, Equiano's qualification to be fitted into that "little piece of ivory"[37] is entailed entirely in his self-ownership, and in the public articulation of his subjectivity, as he proffers, before God.

However, his declaration of subjectivity before God, rather than before any earthly authority, sidesteps any issue concerning the precise identity of that subjectivity. Despite writing in English for primarily an English audience, Equiano's title to the book prominently announces him as "The African" and prioritizes his African name over his western one. On the one hand, as one critic has written, such bicultural identity enabled Equiano to avoid the pitfall of "becoming either totally co-opted by or totally alienated from the Western socio-cultural order."[38] On the other, it renders his autobiography a truly circum-Atlantic production and leaves his sense of home, belonging, and what is his own as free-floating: What is Equiano's property, apart from the Bible shown in the portrait, the portrait itself and the book it illustrates, and where his property belongs are still uncertain issues, transcending national boundaries.

In one sense, this refers back to Equiano's "other" identity, that of the sailor, whose antipathetic relation to property left him ambiguous in terms of race or nation: He was at once the wild rover with a girl in every port but also the ancient mariner, cursed to wander the earth unendingly. On the one hand, this reflects the actual ethnic heterogeneity of the Atlantic maritime world, populated by a protean mass of classes and cultures from Europe, the Americas and Africa. On the other, the sailor's lack of racial or national fixity cannot be simplistically passed off as merely a reflection of a preexistent socioeconomic "reality." For it is also an issue of representation. As caricatures such as *A Sailor Sitting for his Miniature* indicate, the tar's features are presented as brutish and unclassifiable: dark, weather-beaten, pock-marked complexion, bulbous nose, protruding forehead, a shock of unkempt hair, thick lips. These were conventionally visual signs of the savage or degenerate and further confuse the issue over the sailor's race. His, so to speak, free-floating identity is at a fundamental level tied to an absence of narration about what he "owns," both in the sense of what he possesses (or not) and what he may legitimately narrate about himself. Furthermore, as a sailor labouring at sea, he has, almost by definition, no territory that is "proper" to him. In short, he is not attributed a nation through narration.[39]

In another sense, however, the sailor's relation to property, and therefore the construction of his subjectivity, was markedly different from that of the African slave. I want to turn here to a set of drawings made by a naval lieutenant on a voyage related to the Atlantic slave trade in the mid-1770s to consider this further.

Between 1774 and 1777 *HMS Pallas* made a series of voyages to the West African coast, the purpose of which was to survey and report on the forts and factories then under British control. Among the officers, as second lieutenant on at least two and possibly three of these voyages, was Gabriel Bray. As a committed amateur artist, Bray made numerous watercolour drawings of both the places and people visited and also of daily life on board ship.[40] As such they are unique in their representation of lower-deck life at sea at this period. More pertinent to the subject in question, their portrayal variously of Africans, Europeans and other ethnicities, of slaves or potential slaves, un-enslaved Africans and naval employees, is deeply ambiguous and interpretatively problematic with regard to the representation of identity. Considered from the perspective or problematic of portraiture, rather than simply of documentation, these drawings have a value of great importance in what they reveal about the efforts and failures of articulating or defining clear identities in the flux of the eighteenth-century circum-Atlantic world.

Bray presents this maritime world in all its multifaceted variety, and it is remarkable that in the set of drawings the portrait plays a highly important role. Thus, he provides scenes made prior to the voyage's departure of port and dockyard personalities and locations; genre and portrait depictions of life on board the *Pallas,* from head-and-shoulder renditions of fellow sailors to improvisatory "snapshots" of figures sleeping, eating or playing; coastal profiles of the forts that were the object of inspection; and facial profiles of Africans that are "ethnographic" in character.[41] As a group the drawings comprise something of a visual log of the voyage, charting it from its inception to its conclusion. At the most fundamental level, therefore, this sequence of drawings represents a narrative of Bray's own participation in the mission and his place in it, as an assertion of subjective identity.

Bray's work on these voyages was also of direct, material consequence to the metropolitan government debate over commercial policy for the West African coast and the trades linked with it, notably the slave trade. With other officers he produced directly observed written reports on British forts and factories that formed some of the material for official treatises criticizing and recommending policy in the region.

In this sense, Bray's official work on the African coast was essentially all to do with ownership: ownership of the forts, which entailed competing colonial proprietorial claims against rival European imperial powers, and therefore ownership of the trade they were designed and built to support, the slave trade, which comprised the dispropriation from individuals of their own selves, to render them as property. Who owned what on the coast of West Africa, between the competing claims of European trading nations, African kings and chiefs, independent agents and dealers (both European and African) and the enslaved, was literally up for grabs. The mid-century trader John Hippisley summarized the situation thus:

> The Gold-Coast trade [was] carried on almost entirely by the Fantees, a people exceedingly intelligent and tenacious of their rights; – insomuch,

> that they would laugh in a person's face who should tell them, *That by an English act of parliament they have liberty to trade with whom they think proper.* It is a liberty they have *constantly taken*, as the undoubted right of a free people; *so free*, that upon the slightest disgusts they often *make very free with the chiefs themselves.* – Here it may be asked perhaps, Why, if there is so little influence, we keep forts in the Fantee country? We answer, *Merely because the Dutch do*, who, if we were away, would find it worth their while *at any expence* to oppose the independence of the Fantees, – an independence which hitherto these Negroes have preserved by the jarring interests of the Europeans settled among them.[42]

Hippisley wrote this in support of the erection of a fort at Cape Apollonia, which was later the subject of one of Bray's coastal profiles. Bray also produced two drawings of the Fante, one concentrating on their style of hair and headdress, in common with the majority of his drawings of native Africans (Fig. 6.10), but the other showing them as somehow independent subjects.

In the face of this delicate, precarious balance between ownership and influence, Bray produced many portrayals of his fellow sailors, which comprised a form of self-portrait also, an assertion of the sailor as subject in a context where the meanings of subjectivity were in flux. Perhaps it is not surprising, therefore, that two of the most important drawings produced by Bray at this time were self-portraits (Figs. 6.11 and 6.12). Their similar date (March–April 1775), composition, palette and careful addition of spandrels to create an elliptical roundel format suggest that they were conceived as a complementary pair, which is supported by their iconography, where themes of self-examination and self-fashioning are brought to the fore. One shows Bray in the act of painting

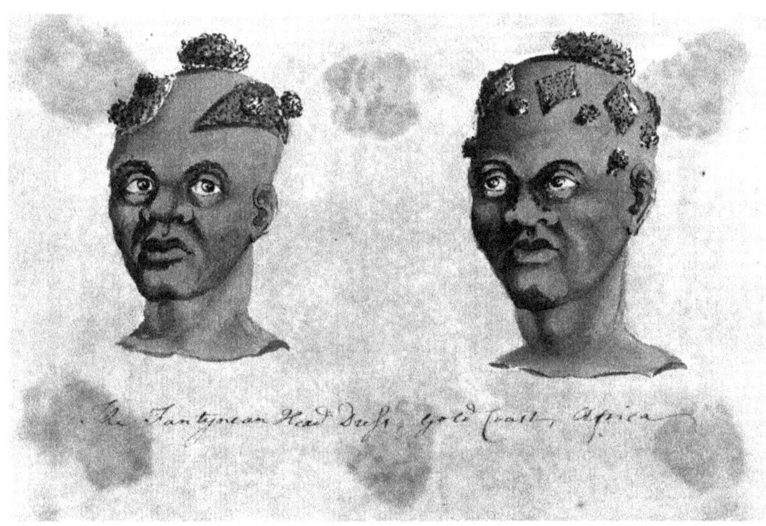

6.10. Gabriel Bray, *The Fantyman Head Dress, Gold Coast, Africa*, March 1775. Watercolour. National Maritime Museum, Greenwich, London, PAJ2040.

in his drawing-book, crouched over a green baize-covered desk with his palette and colour blocks ranged before him; in the immediate context of this voyage, it is a representation of himself in the act of being the artist rather than the sailor (except insofar as he is in the act of painting a ship, perhaps his own ship, his own voyage), and in the act of representing his own subjectivity. The other shows him shaving, seated at the same table but this time before a mirror – presumably the same mirror he used to see himself painting – where he is halfway through the careful scraping away of the lather and stubble from his face. The mirror is placed on its stand with its back to the viewer, so that an immediate rapport is presented between mirror and image, whereby in order to decode the image the viewer is required at some level to identify with Bray looking at his reflection. Yet, at the same time such identification is also denied since Bray in

6.11. Gabriel Bray, *Lieutenant Gabriel Bray Sketching in Watercolours*, April 1775. Watercolour. National Maritime Museum, Greenwich, London, PAJ2025.

6.12. Gabriel Bray, *Lieutenant Gabriel Bray Shaving*, March 1775. Watercolour. National Maritime Museum, Greenwich, London, PAJ2024.

the image does not return the gaze as would someone looking in a mirror. The artist-viewer identity is left floating, creating an uncertainty around the self that is represented in this pair of self-portraits. The reciprocity between the two pictures is strikingly rich. The self-portrait painting at once advertises the painted artifice of the self-portrait shaving, its quality as produced artefact, while the acts of painting and shaving are rendered as similarly delicate and meticulously careful tasks that are treated as equivalent. The semantics of each painting are amplified by reference to the other. Painting, they seem to suggest, was for Bray just as much an act of self-fashioning as shaving, with its direct control over physical appearance – which perhaps explains Bray's adoption of this extraordinary conceit in the first place.

For the iconography of the self-portrait shaving is extremely rare.[43] For obvious reasons it poses significant practical difficulties, the overcoming of which displays not just a developed artistic subjectivity but also a considerable degree of virtuosity. There could be various ways of interpreting this picture. The blade might be taken as a reminder of the latent potential violence of the sailor's life. Shaving might alternatively be seen as a reference to the sailor's self-sufficiency, for which he was renowned: He is shaving himself rather than being shaved by a barber. It is certainly an image of self-control, not just in the careful dexterity with which the blade (and by extension, the brush) is handled, but also in a wider cultural sense. For beards were linked in eighteenth-century theories of the body with sexuality and sexual excess, and shaving was also taken as a mark of distinction from a "savage" state.[44] To depict himself shaving, therefore, is to distance himself both from the stereotypical tar as a figure of uncontrollable sensuality (and therefore a lower order of being) and also from the Africans whom the voyage encountered and who frequently figured in Bray's drawings. This choice of subject might also indicate a degree of narcissism: Bray was evidently sensitive to personal grooming and appearance, both his own and that of others. Hence his drawings of Africans focus primarily on their hairstyles, while his own exuberantly fulsome head of hair is not just carefully top-knotted but also pictorially delineated with great attention.

This, however, also points to a degree of ambiguity in the drawings. For Bray's attention to his own hair renders him curiously feminized, a character that is enhanced by his parallel practice of watercolour painting, an art-form typically associated with genteel young ladies. In addition, his interest in hairstyle might rather align him with, than distance him from, the Africans of his drawings, who clearly share a similar interest. The self-portraits, then, do not offer such a clear-cut articulation of identity and subjectivity as might at first appear to be the case.

Nonetheless, however else we might read this picture and its pendant, it represents above all else a degree of self-absorption. This is entirely consistent with the extremely complex and problematic relations of selfhood to property that underpinned the construction of subjectivity in the fluctuating, uncertain spaces of the circum-Atlantic world. In these self-portraits Bray not only represents himself on his own, but also as owning himself, through a narrative of his property, his painting implements, and through the reciprocal act of self-fashioning, the clarification of his own facial features and the properties of his persona. Painting allows him to depict himself shaving, and shaving also becomes a form of self-portraiture, the shaping and articulation of the face. Through the mutual acts of painting and shaving, scrutinizing himself in the mirror for both practices, Bray reveals himself to himself. In doing so he also proclaims ownership of himself in a manner denied the slave, which, notwithstanding the parallels between their conditions, points up the fundamental differences between them.

6.13. Anonymous artist, *Her Mistress's Clothes*, ca. 1815. Watercolour on ivory. National Maritime Museum, Greenwich, London, ZBA2436.

A contrast can be made here with the extraordinary and problematic painting *Her Mistress's Clothes* (Fig. 6.13). This, like Bray's self-portraits, also involves the visual rhetoric of the mirror to reveal ownership of the subject. However, in this case it does not affirm self-ownership, but the opposite.

Though obviously of a later date than Bray's drawings, this appears to be something of a generic iconography.[45] It may be related, therefore, to similar long-standing imagery such as that of "Labour in Vain" or "Washing the Ethiopian"; it no doubt shares a similar proverbial significance.[46] While the "Labour in Vain" motif asserts the futility of washing the black body, whose colour can never change, the message of *Her Mistress's Clothes* centres on "the proverbial sow's ear that cannot be made into a silk purse": Dressing the black woman in fine clothes, it suggests, is a vain gesture, for she will never be beautiful, unlike her white companion, whose beauty the dress enhances rather than mocks.[47] In this regard the image is closely related to the conventional use of the black slave in portraiture to serve as a foil highlighting the beauty of the white mistress. Yet, the intimate proximity of the two faces, and the disturbingly forceful manner in which the white girl clasps the black to force her to look at herself in the mirror, as well as the cross-dressing theme, all render this image much more problematic than the conventional white mistress–black slave portrait.

In her bizarre gesture of holding the black girl's chin (which might remind us of Equiano's shock at the sight of the black woman loaded with an "iron machine" that "locked her mouth"), the porcelain-complexioned white beauty holds the other's face as though it were a mask. This sense of interchange and doubling between the two heads is reinforced by their exactly similar hairstyles, making this picture comparable to John Raphael Smith's extraordinary pastel *A Woman Holding a Black-Face Mask* (ca. 1794–1800), which plays upon the relativities and slippages between whiteness and blackness as indexes of beauty.[48] *Her Mistress's Clothes*, therefore, contains an implicit – and no doubt unintended – questioning of how black-white subjectivities are produced and represented within the wider contexts of slavery and circum-Atlantic exchanges. This amounts to a questioning also of whiteness and blackness as absolute, fixed values, even at the same time as the image functions to reify such fixity: Its "double consciousness," to revert to W. E. B. DuBois's phrase, is the destabilization of the apparently unproblematic demarcation between whiteness and blackness that the picture presents on its surface.[49] In this sense, it is, just as much as Bray's drawings, an image emanating from a truly circum-Atlantic culture.

The stark difference between Bray's self-portraits and *Her Mistress's Clothes* is the difference between the sailor and the slave. It is a difference between self-fashioning and being fashioned, between self-ownership and being owned, between the assertion of subjectivity and the enforcement of objecthood. For, if nothing else, the black girl is being cruelly instructed that "Only subjects can endow an object with subjectivity.... Objects can only reflect the subjectivity of the subject, like a mirror."[50] Fine clothes, the property of the white mistress, do not as objects themselves confer subjectivity upon her other property, the slave girl. Forcing her to look in the mirror, therefore, is to compel her to contemplate her own objectivity: The mirror and the slave share a similar status (and, it might be added, a similar colour).

However, in their unstable ambiguities over the relation of subject to object and over how subjectivity is produced in relation to the eighteenth-century discourse of property, both *Her Mistress's Clothes* and Bray's images share more than appears at first sight. As Equiano's narrative and portrait demonstrate, the discourse of property was not itself ideologically stable, but it is of pivotal importance in the analysis of slavery and portraiture. In these images, it emerges in the respective relationships of the slave-girl and the artist to the mirror; while in caricatures of the sailor having his portrait taken the status of property and property-ownership underpins the uncertain relation between the sailor and the artist, that points to a closer proximity of the property-less sailor to the slave than to the artist. Proximity becomes congruence in Hogarth's highly sympathetic rendition of the black sailor: Yet, what results in this figure is a near-illegibility, as he floats ideologically between notions of property and liberty, self-possession and objecthood, subjectivity and servitude. All these images pertaining to sailors and slaves offer different but complementary profiles of the face of the sea and severely problematize the production and meanings of portraiture in the eighteenth-century circum-Atlantic world, insisting that a much wider range of references and questions be invoked in approaching this complex area of study.

Notes

My thanks to Angela Rosenthal, Agnes Lugo-Ortiz, and Philip Morgan for their helpful comments on earlier drafts of this essay.

1 W. Jeffrey Bolster, *Black Jacks: African American Seamen in the Age of Sail* (Cambridge, Mass.: Harvard University Press, 1997), 2.

2 Peter Linebaugh and Marcus Rediker, *The Many-Headed Hydra: Sailors, Slaves, Commoners and the Hidden History of the Revolutionary Atlantic* (London: Verso, 2000).

3 Joseph Roach, *Cities of the Dead: Circum-Atlantic Performance* (New York: Columbia University Press, 1996); see also Hugh Honour, *The Image of the Black in Western Art*, vol. 4: *From the American Revolution to World War I. Part 1: Slaves and Liberators* (Cambridge, Mass: Harvard University Press, 1989); David Dabydeen, *Hogarth's Blacks: Images of Blacks in Eighteenth-Century English Art* (Manchester: Manchester University Press, 1987); and Angela Rosenthal's and Agnes Lugo-Ortiz's introduction to this volume.

4 See especially Emma Christopher, *Slave Ship Sailors and Their Captive Cargoes, 1730–1807* (Cambridge: Cambridge University Press, 2006); Marcus Rediker, *Between the Devil and the Deep Blue Sea: Merchant Seamen, Pirates and the Anglo-American Maritime World, 1700–1750* (Cambridge: Cambridge University Press, 1987), 32–34, 45–50, 213, 226. For the way this discourse was played out in popular visual culture, see *The Press Gang or English Liberty Display'd*, 1770 (British Museum: BM Satires 4410), James Gillray, *The Liberty of the Subject*, 1779 (BM Satires 5609).

5 Peter de Bolla, *The Education of the Eye: Painting, Landscape and Architecture in Eighteenth-Century Britain* (Stanford: Stanford University Press, 2003).

6 *General Advertiser, and Morning Intelligencer*, 27 April, 1778, 4. My thanks to John Bonehill for this reference.

7 See especially Dabydeen, *Hogarth's Blacks*.

8 Ronald Paulson, *Hogarth*, 3 vols. (New Brunswick, N.J.: Rutgers University Press, 1992–93), 2:176–77.

9 See, for example, Hans Sloane's comment, that "The *Negros* are much given to Venery, and although hard wrought, will at nights, or on Feast days Dance and Sing; their Songs are all bawdy, and leading that way": Sloane, *Natural History of Jamaica*, 2 vols. (1707–25), 1:xlviii, cited in Kay Dian Kriz, "Curiosities, Commodities and Transplanted Bodies in Hans Sloane's *Voyage to ... Jamaica*," in Geoff Quilley and Kay Dian Kriz, eds., *An Economy of Colour: Visual Culture and the Atlantic World, 1660–1830* (Manchester: Manchester University Press, 2003), 93. See also the accounts cited in Roger D. Abrahams and John F. Szwed, *After Africa: Extracts from*

British Travel Accounts and Journals of the Seventeenth, Eighteenth and Nineteenth Centuries Concerning the Slaves, their Manners and Customs in the British West Indies (New Haven: Yale University Press, 1983).

10 It is possibly "Farewell my Judy," according to the catalogue entry for the painting on the National Maritime Museum's website: http://collections.rmg.co.uk/collections/objects/14194.html (accessed December 2012).

11 It perhaps also implies a sympathy with Hogarth himself, who surely has included a self-reference in the form of the bewigged dog, being his own pug, Trump.

12 David Brion Davis, *The Problem of Slavery in the Age of Revolution, 1770–1823* (Oxford: Oxford University Press, 1999).

13 See Geoff Quilley, "Duty and Mutiny: The Aesthetics of Loyalty and the Representation of the British Sailor c. 1789–1800," in *Romantic War: Studies in Culture and Conflict, 1789–1815*, ed. Phil Shaw (Aldershot: Ashgate, 2000), 80–109.

14 See N. A. M. Rodger, *The Wooden World: An Anatomy of the Georgian Navy* (London: Fontana Press, 1988), 15.

15 Peter Earle, *Sailors: English Merchant Seamen, 1650–1775* (London: Methuen, 1998), 13.

16 James Boswell, *Life of Johnson*, ed. R. W. Chapman, introduced by Pat Rogers (Oxford: Oxford University Press, 1998), 246.

17 Jonathan Lamb, unpublished paper presented at the conference *The Maritime in Modernity*, Center for the Study of the Novel, Stanford University, 29–30 April 2005. I am extremely grateful to the author for providing me with a copy of his paper and for allowing me to quote from it.

18 Ibid.

19 Ibid.

20 See particularly Roach, *Cities of the Dead*, and Paul Gilroy, *The Black Atlantic: Modernity and Double Consciousness* (Cambridge Mass: Harvard University Press, 1993).

21 See Vincent Carretta, *Equiano the African: Biography of a Self-Made Man* (Athens: University of Georgia Press, 2005), 287–92, who points out the frontispiece's place within an established iconographic tradition involving religious figures.

22 Olaudah Equiano, *The Interesting Narrative of the Life of Olaudah Equiano, or Gustavus Vassa, the African, Written by Himself*, ed. Werner Sollors (New York: Norton Critical Editions, 2000), 143–44.

23 There is much more that could be discussed on the parallels between Equiano's revelation and enslavement, not least that between his vision of Christ crucified and the tortures inflicted on the slave body: see Marcus Wood, *Slavery, Empathy and Pornography* (Oxford: Oxford University Press, 2002).

24 Carretta, *Equiano, the African*, 292.

25 Equiano, *Interesting Narrative*, 111–21.

26 Ibid., 24.

27 Ibid., 40. Vincent Carretta, of course, has now cast doubt on the authenticity of Equiano's account of his birth and upbringing, but what concerns me here is the place of the frontispiece within the narrative *qua* narrative, notwithstanding its possibly fictionalized construction. See Carretta, *Equiano, the African*, xiv–vx, and Carretta, "Questioning the Identity of Olaudah Equiano, or Gustavus Vassa, the African," in *The Global Eighteenth Century*, ed. Felicity Nussbaum (Baltimore: Johns Hopkins University Press, 2003).

28 Equiano, *Interesting Narrative*, 44.

29 My thanks to Sarah Monks for her helpful insights on this aspect of Equiano's narrative.

30 Equiano, *Interesting Narrative*, 75–76, 80–81, 82–83, 86–87.

31 See, for example, his account of Joseph Clipson: ibid., 90.

32 See Henry Louis Gates, Jr., "The Trope of the Talking Book," in Equiano, *Interesting Narrative*, 361–67.

33 Ibid., 364.

34 Equiano, *Interesting Narrative*, 48.

35 Gates, "Trope of the Talking Book," 366.

36 Caretta, *Equiano, the African*, 290.

37 We should remember that Equiano's portrait was engraved after a painting by a miniaturist, which could easily have been done on ivory.

38 William L. Andrews, "The First Fifty Years of the Slave Narrative, 1760–1810," in *The Art of Slave Narrative*, ed. John Sekora and Darwin T. Turner (Macomb: Western Illinois University Press, 1982), cited in Angelo Costanzo, *Surprizing Narrative: Olaudah Equiano and the Beginnings of Black Autobiography* (Westport, Conn.: Greenwood Press, 1987), 46. See also Carretta, *Equiano, the African*, 292–94.

39 Homi K. Bhabha, ed., *Nation and Narration* (London: Routledge, 1990).

40 See Roger Quarm, "An Album of Drawings by Gabriel Bray RN, HMS *Pallas*, 1774–75," *The Mariner's Mirror* 81, no. 1 (1995), 32–44; Geoff Quilley, "The Lie of the Land: Slavery and the Aesthetics of Imperial Landscape in Eighteenth-Century British Art," in *Representing Slavery: Art, Artefacts and Archives in the Collections of the National Maritime Museum*, ed. Douglas Hamilton and Robert J. Blyth (Aldershot: Lund Humphries in association with the National Maritime Museum, Greenwich, 2007), 118–35.

41 In this respect, they resemble the drawings of Pacific Islanders and other non-European peoples encountered on Cook's voyages, made by Sydney Parkinson, William Hodges and John Webber; see Rudiger Joppien and Bernard Smith, *The Art of Captain Cook's Voyages*, 4 vols. (New Haven: Yale University Press, 1985–88).

42 (John Hippisley), *Essays. I. On the Populousness of Africa. II. On the Trade at the Forts on the Gold Coast. III. On the Necessity of Erecting a Fort at Cape Apollonia* (London, 1764), 26–27.

43 I am aware of no examples prior to the twentieth century. The closest eighteenth-century images are the self-portraits by Jean-Etienne Liotard, showing him with and without his "oriental" beard; see Angela Rosenthal, "Raising Hair," *Eighteenth-Century Studies* 38, no. 1 (2004), 1–16.

44 Ibid. My thanks to Angela Rosenthal for elucidating this point.

45 There are at least two, almost identical versions of this image, this of the early nineteenth century, the other of 1845 by the American artist Harriet Cany Peale; see Helen Weston, "'The Cook, the Thief, His Wife and Her Lover': LaVille-Leroulx's *Portrait de Négresse* and the Signs of Misrecognition," in *Work and the Image*, ed. Valerie Mainz and Griselda Pollock, vol. 1: *Work, Craft and Labour: Visual Representations in Changing Histories* (Aldershot: Ashgate, 2000), 53–74; Elizabeth O'Leary, *At Beck and Call: The Representation of Domestic Servants in Nineteenth-Century American Painting* (Washington, D.C.: Smithsonian Institution Press, 1996), 140–43.

46 On the "Labour in Vain" iconography, see Jean Michel Massing, "From Greek Proverb to Soap Advert: Washing the Ethiopian," *Journal of the Warburg and Courtauld Institutes* 58 (1995), 180–201.

47 O'Leary, *At Beck and Call*, 143.

48 See Angela Rosenthal, "*Visceral* Culture: Blushing and the Legibility of Whiteness in Eighteenth-Century British Portraiture," *Art History* 27, no. 4 (2004), 585.

49 W. E. B. DuBois, *The Souls of Black Folk: Essays and Sketches* (Chicago: A. C. McClurg & Co., 1903), 3; and Gilroy, *Black Atlantic*.

50 Gates, "Trope of the Talking Book," 366.

SEVEN

BETWEEN VIOLENCE AND REDEMPTION

SLAVE PORTRAITURE IN EARLY PLANTATION CUBA

Agnes Lugo-Ortiz

Preliminaries: On the Troubles of a Religious Spectacle

> Wanting, on a Maundy Thursday, to arouse humility through the ceremony of the day, the first Count of Casa Bayona washed the feet of twelve slaves from his Sugar mill, he sat them at the table and served it, be this because other poor people did not make themselves available, or because he believed that in doing so with his slaves that he humbled himself more and offered a better example, but it did not happen like that, because taking advantage of the good deed and of the gift of their master, the slaves later refused to work. It was necessary to use some force, when it was clear that leniency and persuasion were useless. Then, at once, they raised their heads, they instigated others to revolt, they rose up, attacking that Sugar mill and others that were nearby, and it was necessary for the Government to pacify them with weapons, at the cost of much blood and some lives.
>
> "Representation issued by Diego Miguel de Moya and signed by almost all sugar mill owners of this jurisdiction – Havana, 1790"[1]

Few known episodes in the history of Cuban slavery display such a degree of eccentricity and theatrical elan as the one protagonized by the religiously devout first Count of Casa Bayona (1676–1759) and his apostolic slaves on that fateful Maundy Thursday of 1727. Yet, hardly any details concerning this mimetic performance have been fully unearthed. What particular circumstances incited Bayona to incarnate himself in the divine role of Christ? On what basis were his slaves selected, and what was the slaves' understanding of this bizarre conscription that placed their master at their feet while seating them at his table? And if they actually refused to work, as the above 1790 document claims, was this refusal indeed related to the symbolic inversions enacted in the ritual performance of the Last Supper? What we do know, however, is that once their revolt was extinguished – a revolt that destroyed Bayona's sugar mill and was probably led by the enslaved apostles themselves – the Count did not turn the other cheek, as his Christian role would have demanded, but he instead unleashed his vengeful wrath in a vicious slave hunt. He commanded that the rebellious apostles, once caught, not only be publicly executed but that their heads be placed on tall pikes in plain view – like monumental portraits – for the visual consumption and moral edification of the other slaves – a truly horrific lesson in humility and subservience and one that the 1790 documentary account significantly concealed.[2]

The remarkable theatricality and visuality of these extraordinary events – and the intensity with which the bodies both of the master and of the slaves appear to be performatively figured, transfigured, and de-figured through the enactment of a sacred narrative (the sacrifice of the Eucharist, on the one hand) and through a brutal and spectacular punishment of beheading (on the other) – seem to mark a cultural limit. It conveys a moment of troubling and intractability in the languages and traditional frameworks within which a fraction of an emergent Cuban colonial planter class attempted to formalize and endow with meaning the constitutive asymmetries in the relationship between masters and slaves, as well as its own claims to local political authority at a key juncture in the development of the large slaveholding plantation system on the island.

This planter class, a dynamic and extremely ambitious proto-bourgeois Criollo elite, came into being in the decades preceding the eleven-month-long British occupation of Havana of 1762, a brief interlude during which Spanish commercial restrictions were lifted and Cuban trade in goods and slaves thoroughly liberalized.[3] The group became progressively eager to modernize the technological infrastructure of the colony, persuade the metropolis to moderate mercantilist restrictions, and set the foundations for the development of large-scale sugar production geared toward the international market system based on the unrestricted flow of African enslaved labor. Their power and prestige would fully flourish toward the turn of the nineteenth century by cunningly taking advantage of the vacuum left in world supplies of cane sugar due to the financial collapse and hostile political isolation of Haiti following its 1791 Revolution.[4]

Closely tied to one another by joint economic ventures and by familial/affective bonds and structures of sociability, these emergent elites were no less eager to acquire the symbols of status and prestige necessary to articulate and anchor their ever-increasing social and economic power. Anxious to rationalize production and maximize investments, and to energetically engage in the fluid monetary dealings of North American and transatlantic trade, they keenly strove to endow themselves with the hidebound symbolic accoutrements of the most rancid land-based aristocracy. In the half-century that preceded the

1810 beginning of the wars for independence from Spain across the Americas, Cuban planters had pushed to secure 104 titles of nobility, second only to the Viceroyalty of Peru (118 titles) and slightly superceding those held in the powerful, centuries-old courtly culture of the Viceroyalty of New Spain (103 titles).[5] Their predicament, however, was that instead of serfs bonded to their lords by an implicit, however illusory, pact that exchanged loyalty for protection, one grounded on the image of eternity created by centuries of genealogical recognition, these newly made Cuban would-be-lords rather dreamed of a capitalist fiefdom supported by the coerced and anonymous service of uprooted foreign-born slaves. Cuban historian Manuel Moreno Fraginals had called them a *sacarocracia* – a sugar aristocracy.[6]

The performance staged by the first Count of Casa Bayona on that Maundy Thursday in 1727 was indeed symptomatic of the uneasy transactions through which a sector of that planter class erratically attempted to symbolize the transition from the small-scale patriarchal and semi-mechanized sugar mill, prevalent on the island until the mid-eighteenth century, to the large capitalist-oriented slaveholding plantation system (or *ingenio*). Their figuring of this transition, as well as their claims to local sovereignty, were articulated through languages and practices of a soon-to-be Ancien Régime. As Natalie Zemon Davis reminds us, the act of "playing Christ" by washing the feet of the poor on Holy Thursday "had long been a practice of European monarchs, including the king of Spain, and of bishops in the Old World" and all over the Americas.[7] Thus, Bayona's performance appears to be a local rearticulation of these practices, an imitation of an imitation. In this doubly mediated event the Count imitated Catholic kings and bishops in their imitations of the Christian story, and through that doubling, the *abatimiento* (the embattlement and humiliation) of his body and personhood enacted, in an apparent paradox, an identification with an absolutist conception of vertical power and authority. More than a carnavalesque "ritual of inversion" (where subject positions are switched, potentially effecting a dislocation in the structures of thought and feeling), seen from the perspective of the master, this performance suggests a solemn ritual of incorporation, one in which Bayona's own subject position as a slave-master was to be indulgently confirmed by appropriating the languages and self-fashioning practices of royalty and ecclesiastical hierarchy.

It is difficult to historically ascertain to what extent this performance indeed had the power to transform the structures of thought and feeling of the diverse players involved, particularly by investing slaves with an unprecedented sense of self, agency, prestige, and entitlement that could have enabled the revolt that ensued and the religious irreverence that, according to documents, they defiantly displayed afterwards. What is clear, though, is that Bayona's act reveals not just the kind of mimetic gestures by which these colonial elites imagined their relatively newly acquired position of grand masters and their will to local sovereignty. Most intriguingly, it also displayed their trust in the possibility of inciting a consenting, subordinate subjectification ("to arouse humility through the ceremony of the day") among their slaves through the embodied/performative interpellation of a metaphysical language. At this point in time – when small-scale patriarchal sugar mills had not fully developed into the impersonal, mass enterprise of the late-eighteenth-century plantations, neither in economic nor in ideological terms, and many decades before the 1791 events in Haiti – it still seemed feasible to envision performative fantasies conveying the illusion of a harmonious slaveholding world based on language acts, the dream of a tension-free coexistence between masters and slaves and of a joyful and redemptive enslavement. To be sure, this "trust" in no way foreclosed the possibility that the failure of such fantastic attempts could be resolved in a spectacle of torture, as the outcome of the events of Maundy Thursday tragically demonstrates.[8]

7.1. José Nicolás de Escalera, *Familia del Conde de Casa Bayona* (Family of the Count of Casa Bayona), 1770s. Oil on canvas. Church of Santa María del Rosario, Cuba. Photo: Courtesy of Centro Nacional de Conservación, Restauración y Museología (CENCREM), Havana, Cuba.

7.2. Detail of Fig 7.1 (slave). José Nicolás de Escalera, *Familia del Conde de Casa Bayona*, 1770s. Photo: Ramsés Hernández Batista.

The Slave Head: Between Performance and Portraiture

It was precisely at the edge of this juncture that Cuba's foremost eighteenth-century visual artist, the Criollo José Nicolás de Escalera (1734–1804), painted what Cuban art historians have identified as the earliest oil portrait of a man of color deemed to be a slave produced in the Spanish Caribbean during the colonial period. This is the full-bodied and rather voluminous figure that appears seated in the lower right of the triangular canvas of the *Familia del Conde de Casa Bayona* (*Family of the Count of Casa Bayona*) (Fig. 7.1, Plate 6, and Fig. 7.2). Dating from the mid-1770s, the painting was made expressly for Santa María del Rosario, a church located on what once were the Bayona family's properties on the outskirts of Havana.[9] Although occupying, by a slight margin, the lowest register in a hierarchically organized group, the presence of the black (or rather mulatto) figure in the canvas is astonishingly prominent. Seated alone on one step, with one

7.3. William Dobson, *Portrait of John, 1st Lord Byron (ca. 1600–52)*, ca. 1643. Oil on canvas. Tabley House Collection, University of Manchester, UK. Photo: Bridgeman Art Library.

of his legs comfortably flung over the other, he rests an elbow on his raised knee while his elevated right hand supports his contemplative face – evoking the pose of an enlightened thinker.

Escalera's work significantly deviates from the conventions of European courtly slave portraiture [studied or alluded to in this volume in the Introduction (Figs. I.1 and Fig. I.2) and in essays by David Bindman (Figs. 2.1–2.3, 2.6), Marcia Pointon (Figs. 1.1, 1.2), and Geoff Quilley (Fig. 6.3, Plate 5)] in which enslaved Africans are frequently propped up as pages, appearing in positions of admiring subordination to their masters, and often aligned in analogical relations with animals (as in William Dobson's famous *Portrait of John, 1st Lord Byron (ca. 1600–52)*, ca. 1643, Fig. 7.3). These conventions are ostensibly at work, as well, in the first slave portraits associated with the emergent plantation economies of the southern British colonies of North America (particularly in the Catholic-settled territory of Maryland, although not exclusively). In these works the local colonial gentry, similar to their Cuban counterparts, enacted cultural languages of a European aristocracy (to which many of their first colonists belonged) to symbolize their recently acquired power as slaveholding landowners and to produce the fantasy of a "courtly plantation."[10] Some notable examples include Gerard Soest's representation of the founder of Maryland, *Portrait of Cecilius Calvert, Second Lord of Baltimore, with grandson and attendant*, circa 1670 (Fig. 7.4) and, especially, Justus Englehardt Kühn's *Portrait of Henry Darnall III*, circa 1710 (Fig. 7.5). In both of these images, slaves appear as shadowy presences, as somewhat impertinent intruders in a scenario where the masters affect indifference (literally turning their backs) to an existence upon which their own position as subjects of power depends, both in socioeconomic terms as well as with regard to the asymmetries visualized in the canvas. Iconographically, the no less courtly portrait of Escalera's pensive slave could not be, at first glance, more emphatically different.[11]

Escalera's commission to paint this family portrait more than twenty years after the events of Maundy Thursday was envisioned by his main patron, José Bayona y Chacón – the above-mentioned first Count of Casa Bayona whose religious fervor had led to the 1727 transformation of a slave's head into an equally aestheticized spectacle of death and terror through decapitation. This intriguing and rather uncanny coincidence invites, I would like to suggest, a historical inquiry into the relationships between the performance of a slave's body as a site of mutilation and punishment and the rather exceptional inscription of his face and full-length body as a site of individualized visual identification and supposed selfhood in portraiture: between the lived drama of death and the static

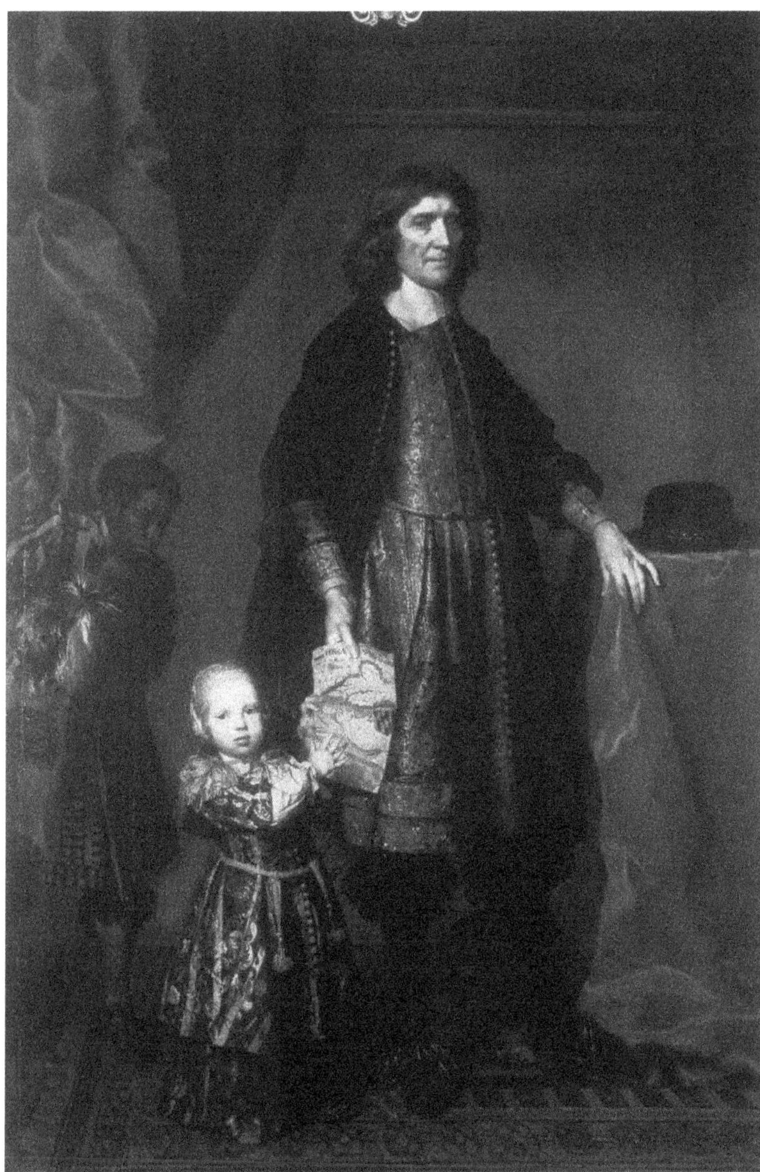

7.4. Gerard Soest, *Portrait of Cecilius Calvert, Second Lord of Baltimore, with grandson and attendant*, ca. 1670. Oil on canvas. Courtesy of Enoch Pratt Free Library, Maryland's State Library Resource Center, Baltimore.

visual fiction of immortality, between the contingency of rotting flesh and the illusion of transcendence that portraiture had conventionally conveyed.[12]

Although I have described the slave heads that were placed on pikes on that fateful Maundy Thursday in 1727 as "monumental portraits," the terrifying representational logic of slaveholding violence actually forecloses the possibility for these heads to function as portraiture. This macabre form of visualization strived to make these spectacular heads become "faceless." It endeavored to obliterate them as the rhetorical signifiers of singular subjectivities, to have them stand in instead for an annihilated body, for an exemplary amputated corpse. This is an inversion of what Gilles Deleuze and Félix Guattari, in their critique of the metaphysics of the subject, have identified as the privileged signifying status that the face has acquired over the rest of the body in Western cultures. The face is produced, they say, when the head ceases to be coded by the body "so that the body, head included, has to be decoded and has to be overcoded by something" we call "the face" – which is the dominant representational logic of Western portraiture (even in its avant-garde dislocations). That act of overcoding the body by the face is what Deleuze and Guattari have called "facialization."[13] In the representational logic of slaveholding violence, it is the head that is overcoded by the body (through a process of commodification that transformed the African captive into an enslaved being – into an entity for labor, reproduction, and punishment), and facelessness the process by which subjecthood, however elusive and unstable it may be, was denied.

7.5. Justus Englehardt Kühn, *Portrait of Henry Darnall III*, ca. 1710. Oil on canvas. Maryland Historical Society, Baltimore. Bequest of Miss Ellen C. Daingerfield.

The heads on the pikes were, more accurately put, anti-portraits – ones intended to produce traumatic dissociative identifications and to destroy any sense of agency or self-asserted emancipatory will among captive witnesses. What was, then, the relationship between the anti-portrait, the spectacular facelessness produced in the wake of the events of Maundy Thursday 1727, and the rhetorical facialization of Escalera's slave portrait of the mid-1770s, one that so forcefully deviates from the conventions of courtly plantation slave portraiture in other areas of the Americas? Was slave portraiture in this instance, and in a proto-Foucauldian inversion, a mechanism wielded to establish an imaginary bridge between violence/coercion, discipline, and subjectification by permanently "hanging the head" (to borrow the witty phrase coined by Marcia Pointon in her study of eighteenth-century British portraiture) on the aestheticized surface of a canvas?[14] And isn't this, after all, a rather intractable proposition, for it is quite probable that the slaves who used the church may have seen in the auratic portrait of their kin (if indeed that was what they perceived) a force "other" than the frozen and obedient entity iconically envisioned by their masters? What follows here is an attempt to reconstruct, from the crumbling traces left in the slaveholding archive, some of the terms and contexts that ungirdled the passage from the performative violence of physical beheading to the apparently redemptive restitution of the slave's body and face in portraiture: the early seigniorial response on the part of a master to the threat of slave rebellion, the urban scenario and structures it mobilized, the renewed sacred narratives it visually deployed, and their points of legendary inflections and illegibility. It is an attempt to move between the structural and discursive conditions that enable such a representation and the possible contingencies that underwrote it.

Slave Insubordinations and Seigniorial Foundations

Nicolás de Escalera's *Family of the Count of Casa Bayona* was part of the decorative program designed for the new and larger church that the first count, José Bayona y Chacón, planned to construct during the mid-1750s in place of the small parochial structure he originally built upon the ashes of the sugar mill (known as the Ingenio Quiebrahacha, Corral Xiaraco) and that was destroyed in the 1727 slave rebellion. The construction of the new church and the design of the visual program for its interior ultimately belonged to a more complex and ambitious foundational project the Count had initially envisioned after the 1727 events. So threatening was this revolt said to have been that it almost reached the capital city of Havana, placing in danger not just the property and life of the masters but those of the Spanish colonial authorities as well. Bayona took advantage of the panic and anxiety produced by the rebellion to submit a petition to the king of Spain requesting permission to found a *señorío*, a seigniorial or feudal city, on the site of the destruction on his property. He proposed that this *señorío* – to be devoutly dedicated to Santa María del Rosario (Virgin Mary of the Rosary, the patron saint of the Dominican order) – serve as a protective shield against future slave uprisings ("to prevent and curb the uprisings of black slaves," as the petition put it) by creating a numerically significant defensive enclave of white population in a region that was located barely five leagues, or about fifteen to twenty miles, from Havana.[15]

In his 1728 petition, submitted via *scriptor* to the king of Spain, Bayona puts forward the urgent reasons for the foundation of the *señorío* (the second to be established on the island), among which the threat of slave rebellions, and specifically the revolt of 1727, appears explicitly as one of its major justifications:

> suffering the pain and inconvenience of having the slaves of the ... sugar mill rebel, with firearms and machetes that ... they stole [from him] and ... creating commotion among the slaves from the neighboring sugar mills, who rising up with a good amount of munitions *did much and serious damage, death and sacrileges, stealing the sacred robes and vessels,* and placing this city [Havana] and its dwellers in great concern because of the universal slave rebellion that was feared, and that would have occurred if it were not for the promptness with which groups of infantry, cavalry, and countrymen came to help, destroying, killing and arresting those slaves they managed to capture alive. (My emphasis)[16]

Bayona's account semantically conveys the cumulative horror of the events through syntactical contiguity. By placing the robbery and profanation of the religious vestments and sacramental objects at the same level of signification with the loss of human lives and the wounding of bodies, his account conceives slave rebellions as not only endangering the life and property of the masters and the survival of the colonial order itself represented by Havana. These also entail an equally worrisome threat of symbolic disarray, an inadmissibly violent dislocation of the (sacred) signs. Be this the expression of a sincere and fearful piousness (Bayona indeed was a highly devout Catholic, tertiary of the Dominican order, and founder of the Brotherhood – *cofradía* – of the Holy Sacrament) or a dramatic rhetorical game to elicit the solicited grants from the Crown, the fact remains that the slave revolt is staged here as a metaphysical irreverence, one that underwrites the destruction of the masters' being not only through bodily annihilation but also by transgressing the languages and signs that sustained the order of their world. The *señorío* was structurally designed to contain this polyvalent threat. It endowed Bayona with administrative, military, and judicial powers over his properties and the people who inhabited them, securing the sort of semifeudal authority and prestige he had long sought, and consolidating the title of nobility he acquired in 1723.[17]

By the mid-eighteenth century throughout the Spanish-American empire, as José Luis Romero has argued, the baroque concept of *ciudades hidalgas* (noble cities) that inspired urban development during the first two centuries of colonial rule was progressively receding and giving way to the emergence of *ciudades criollas* (creole cities), that is, cities organized around triumphant bourgeois commercial principles rather than upon seigniorial hierarchical values.[18] It is, then, significant that the foundation of Santa María del Rosario was envisioned under the rubric of a fading seigniorial paradigm. The city was to be hierarchically organized around a main square where the church and the houses of the town's founders (*los principales*) were to be located. The square was also to serve as the point of origin for eight streets that were to emanate from its corners toward the periphery, setting the lines for the future expansion of the city and anticipating its highly stratified development.

The church was the central architectural element of the colonial *ciudad hidalga* and of Bayona's *ciudad condal*. It also supported the ambitions of the enlightened and reformist Bishop Pedro Morell y Santa Cruz, who at the time was involved in a systematic campaign to address the influx of non-Catholic religious beliefs to Cuba brought about by the intensification of the African slave trade (crucial for the explosion of the sugar industry on the island) and the challenges it posed to evangelization.[19] Thus, the project for the reconstruction of the church must be seen as integrally linked to the programmatic containment of African spiritual practices brought about by the trade.

By 1760, the construction of a new and more magnificent church had already started under the direction of the architect José Perera, marking the beginning of the short-lived golden age of Santa María del Rosario, one that lasted barely thirty years. The British occupation of Havana in 1762 delayed the project somewhat, but the church was finally completed in 1766, after the death of the first count of Casa Bayona (in 1759) and under the supervision of the successor to his title, his brother-in-law and cousin Francisco José Chacón y Torres (1712–79), as the first count left no legitimate descendants.

The new building was assigned the self-important name of Iglesia Parroquial de Santa María del Rosario, Catedral de los Montes Extramuros de la Siempre Fiel Ciudad de La Habana (Parochial Church of Santa María del Rosario, Cathedral of the Hills Beyond the Walls of the Always Faithful City of Havana) and is still commonly known as "la catedral de los campos de Cuba" ("the cathedral of the Cuban countryside"), insofar as it is indeed one of the most complex and attractive religious structures built in Cuba during the colonial era.

The church was decorated with numerous paintings that were placed in the main altar and its two side chapels, as well as along the six lateral altars that flanked the nave. Most of these paintings were executed by José Nicolás de Escalera, who had benefited from the preferential patronage of the first count of Casa Bayona and his family since the 1750s.[20] Bayona's sponsorship enabled Escalera to secure important commissions in Havana during that period, including a request for religious images for the convent of San Felipe Neri and a gallery of portraits (now lost) for the Real y Pontificia Universidad San Gerónimo de La Habana, ruled by the Dominican order and of which the first count was co-founder in 1728. Although the paintings for Santa María del Rosario date from the 1770s, Cuban art historians have not doubted that given Escalera's patronage relationship with Bayona – the main force behind the initial plans to reconstruct the church – the first count and his wife must have entrusted him with this commission before the count's death in 1759.[21] Escalera painted the main altar depicting Saint Thomas Aquinas, Saint Raphael Archangel, Saint Vincent Ferrer, Saint Domingo of Guzmán, and Saint Francis of Assisi, as well as scenes of the Holy Trinity, Saint John Nepomucemo, and Saint Francis of Paula in the lateral altar devoted to Christ Crucified; the images of the Annunciation, Saint Anna, and Saint Joachim in the altar of Saint Joseph; and finally, the coherent narrative program dedicated to the Virgin, Santa María del Rosario, and to the foundation of the Dominican order to which the portrait of the family of the first count of Casa Bayona with his slave belongs.

A Tale of Divinely Ordained Hierarchies

Family of the Count of Casa Bayona conforms to the centuries-old Catholic practice initiated in the Renaissance of having the donor's image painted in churches. Unlike the only other known slave portrait painting extant in the Spanish colonial Caribbean from this period – where the enslaved subjects appear as pious supplementary figures, apparently carrying the offerings for the nun devotee, as in the Puerto Rican José Campeche's *Exvoto de la Sagrada Familia* (Exvoto of the Holy Family), 1778–80 (Fig. 7.6) – the portrait of Bayona's today unidentified and thus nameless slave belongs to a complex group of four large triangular-shaped oil paintings on canvas. These occupy each of the four pendentives located in the spandrels at the cross-axis of the church, below the dome that hovers in the area just in front of the altar (Fig. 7.7). While Campeche's exquisite exvoto was singularly designed for individual private devotion (its miniature portable scale is an index of its domestic/intimate function), Escalera's exceptional work is of monumental proportions and was destined for public view in a church that was not only used by white Criollos. It was also the site for the evangelization and ritual staging of the baptisms and marriages of the local slave population – parochial records make this fact abundantly evident.[22]

Aesthetically affiliated to the Murillesque style that prevailed within much of Spanish-American colonial religious painting during the eighteenth century and well into the nineteenth, Escalera's canvases visually articulate a miraculous tale: the story of the origin of the rosary associated with the legendary apparition of the Virgin to Santo Domingo de Guzmán, the thirteenth-century Spanish priest who founded the Dominican Order. Also known as the Order of the Preachers, the Dominicans played a crucial role in the Christianization of the Americas from early colonial times, leaving, as well, a major imprint on the art of the period. Escalera's painted narrative has a semi-chronological structure that begins with the depiction of the glorification of Santo Domingo through his vision of the Virgin and ends with a moment of temporal semiclosure in the portrait of the family of the first count of Casa Bayona with his slave gathered in reverence around a sculptural image of Santo Domingo. Thus, questions of language and conversion, and of the spiritual transformation of subjectivity

7.6. José Campeche, *Exvoto de la Sagrada Familia* (Exvoto of the Holy Family), ca. 1778–80. Oil on wood. Colección del Instituto de Cultura Puertorriqueña, San Juan, Puerto Rico.

through the introjection of "the Word," appear at the core of this cycle, as do questions concerning the transmission of divinely ordained authority.[23]

In its chronological structure each of the four canvases of the cycle is synthetically emblematic of a distinct instance in a process of becoming – moving from heaven to earth, from the realm of the sacred toward a secular and self-referential contemporaneity mediated by (fetishistic) sainthood. These images are: (a) *Glorificación de Santo Domingo* (*Glorification of Santo Domingo*) (Fig. 7.8 and Fig. 7.7, Point A); (b) *La Rosaleda de Nuestra Señora* (*The Rose Garden of*

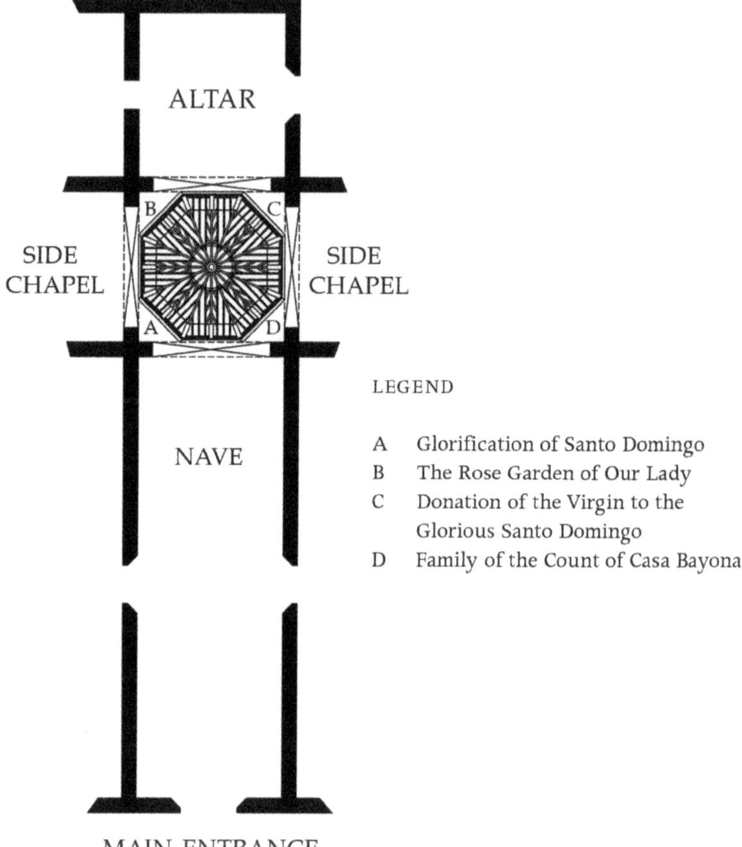

7.7. Schematic floor plan, Church of Santa María del Rosario, Cuba. Drawing courtesy of Nguyen Rodríguez Núñez.

Our Lady) (Fig. 7.9 and Fig. 7.7, Point B), (c) *Donación de la Virgen al Glorioso Santo Domingo* (*Donation of the Virgin to the Glorious Santo Domingo*) (Fig. 7.10 and Fig. 7.7, Point C), and (d) *Family of the Count of Casa Bayona* (Fig. 7.1, Plate 6, and Fig. 7.7, Point D).

Chronologically, this visual narrative moves clockwise, from left to right when facing the altar, as if signaling not only temporal progression but also a sense of eschatological mystery and concealment – for its beginning and end points (Fig. 7.7, Points A and D) are not immediately visible to the viewer who enters through the main door of the church. The first canvas of the cycle, *Glorification of Santo Domingo* (Fig. 7.8 and Fig. 7.7, Point A), depicts the apparition of the Virgin to Santo Domingo under the heavenly surveillance of God the Father and God the Son. This image is followed by two liminal, spatiotemporal instances in which the mediation and transmission between the sacred and the earthly are brought together through the intensified phenomenon of sainthood, *The Rose Garden* (see Fig. 7.9 and Fig. 7.7, Point B) and *Donation of the Virgin to the Glorious Santo Domingo* (Fig. 7.10 and Fig. 7.7, Point C). Finally, the

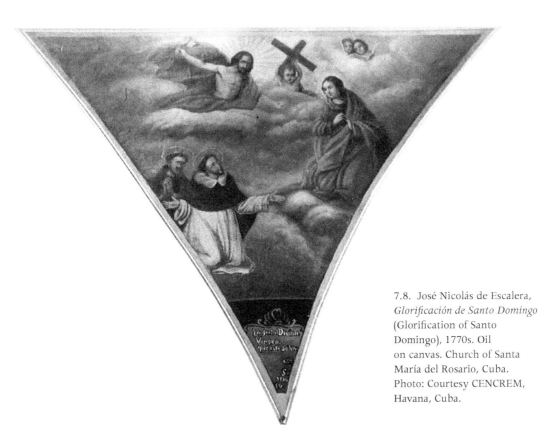

7.8. José Nicolás de Escalera, *Glorificación de Santo Domingo* (Glorification of Santo Domingo), 1770s. Oil on canvas. Church of Santa María del Rosario, Cuba. Photo: Courtesy CENCREM, Havana, Cuba.

7.9. José Nicolás de Escalera, *La Rosaleda de Nuestra Señora* (The Rose Garden of Our Lady), 1770s. Oil on canvas. Church of Santa María del Rosario, Cuba. Photo: Ramsés Hernández Batista.

7.10. José Nicolás de Escalera, *Donación de la Virgen al Glorioso Santo Domingo* (Donation of the Virgin to the Glorious Santo Domingo), 1770s. Oil on canvas. Church of Santa María del Rosario, Cuba. Photo: Author.

chronological dimension of the cycle ends with the *Family of the Count of Casa Bayona* (Fig. 7.1 and Fig. 7.7, Point D). At this moment of closure, a now hieratic image of Santo Domingo has completely displaced the Virgin in the mediating role with the mundane, becoming the ultimate vehicle of sacred transmission by holding the rosary, in an act of anointing, over Bayona's head, his family, and his slave – marking the culminating point (contemporary and self-referential) in a story of sacred endowments.[24]

While the story made visible in the chronological arrangement of these canvases has an unequivocal teleological character (with a relatively discernable progression from beginning to end points), the circular structure of the spandrels troubles, without undermining, its purported linearity, making any episode in the cycle both a potential starting or ending point depending on the contingent reading and position of the viewer. A temporal structure in which any point can be made either a moment of closure or the mark of a new beginning – both carrying the promise to mobilize a new time – corresponds allegorically and philosophically to the logic of redemption. Thus, with medieval flare, the conjunction of the architectural design of the church with the chronological narrative articulated in the visual program of its pendentives coalesces in one pictorial experience: linearity and circularity, progression and repetition, teleology and redemption, history and allegory. Within the chronological narrative, the presence of the slave in the lowest area of the final canvas, punctuating moments of spatial and temporal closure in a story that visually goes from high (i.e., the heavenly images of God the Father and God the Son in *Glorification of Santo Domingo*) to low – from the sacred to the mundane, from the transcendental to the contemporary – could be then understood as the eschatological instance that reopens the cycle toward a new beginning in its architectural circularity. The slave is the capillary figure through which the movement of history as a repetitive and teleological immobility is symbolically recycled, the fulcrum on which the scaffold of a divinely ordained world appears to rest.

Redemption and Rationality

Like other canvases in the sequence, *Family of the Count of Casa Bayona* is also stratified along a vertical compositional structure. The family group is hierarchically placed around the sculpted image of Santo Domingo de Guzmán, who is represented here like an apparition in full flesh, but with a paler complexion than the Criollos – which gives him a slightly ghostly aura. He occupies the upper register, placed atop a pedestal against the dark background of a monumental interior with arches. Given the specular and self-referential structures and themes of the cycle, these likely refer to a church or, even more probable, a cathedral. Santo Domingo extends his right arm, ostensibly to display a rosary, for the devotion of the pious family gathered around him. With his other hand he supports the open Holy Scripture and a white lily branch, one of his iconographic accoutrements, symbol of virginal purity. While, due to a lack of documentation, the specific names and full identities of most of the individual figures portrayed in this painting cannot be unequivocally ascertained, one may safely assume (considering the historical and thematic contexts of the work, in which ideas of hierarchical transmission and foundation are so central) that the figure receiving the grace of the rosary to the immediate left of Santo Domingo is a posthumous and idealized portrait of the first count of Casa Bayona, founder of the aristocratic dynasty.[25]

Most family members gathered around him direct their attention to the saint, the women occupying the lower register of the composition on the left and the slave seated in a contemplative pose across from them and just below a group of men. Although the slave occupies by a slight margin the lowest register in the family hierarchy, he appears notably prominent, evoking, as mentioned earlier, the pose of an enlightened thinker. Indeed, with his upward gaze, he appears in a contemplative, reflective attitude, absorbed in the apprehension of the saintly presence and the transmission of the sacred Word. Significantly, the saint's book opens directly toward the face of the slave, whose attentive eyes, in turn, meet the evangelizing offering. Unlike the irreverent rebels of the 1727 Maundy Thursday uprising, this slave willingly, and rationally, acquiesces to divine interpellation.

While most of the male Criollos are dressed in finely tailored European fashion or ecclesiastical garb, the black servant wears an open white shirt with rolled-up sleeves that display his arms, muscular and strong due to hard physical labor in service – we assume – to this family (see Fig. 7.2). He is a man in his prime with a full shock of shortly cropped brown hair and cleanly shaven face. His hat is respectfully removed and placed under his left arm. The brown cloak wrapped around his lower body and flipped up over part of his back conceals his thighs but accentuates through the striking tonal contrast the white stockings that dress his ankles and the black silver-buckled shoes.

The only figures bearing rosaries in this scene, apart from Santo Domingo, are the women and the slave. The women have theirs around their wrists and the slave around his neck. It is not far fetched to see here an analogy between rosary and chains, as if this was marking both a point of devotional excess in their subjection to the divinely sanctioned hierarchy and, in the case of the slave, the metaphorical shedding of his material shackles for the symbolic ones of the rosary to now primarily serve God instead of man. Indeed, this mulatto does not appear to be a regular plantation slave but one invested with the accoutrements of culture and civilization – a domestic and domesticated servant whose body, although ostensibly present, is not yet the object of an intrusive gaze and who appears at ease in this community. His prominence in the scene even threatens to eclipse the ecclesiastical figure seated behind him in an armchair at the right of the canvas, who may possibly be Juan Francisco Chacón y Rodríguez de Paz, dressed in a white surplice with a mortarboard in his right hand, perhaps displaying his status as chancellor of the Universidad de San Gerónimo de La Habana. The slave is decidedly not the object, or more exactly put, the victim of the intrusive gaze that we later find in anthropological photographic portraits of slaves made, for instance, by Joseph Zealy in South Carolina for Louis Agassiz during the early 1850s (see Fig. I.3) or, indeed, in some of the commercial *cartes-de-visite* made by Christiano Junior in Brazil around 1865.[26] His body, which clearly is a body for labor (as is evidenced by his muscular arms and their sense of physical strength in inescapable contrast to the relatively small body-frames of most of the Criollo men portrayed), nonetheless seems to simultaneously conceal its bodiliness under the loud cultural decorum of clothing. Or to say it with and against Deleuze and Guattari, his head is overcoded by a highly culturalized body that, through that culturalization, marks itself as a face. There is a fiction of agency in his disposition. Here he appears not just as a culturally written entity, but also fully as a subject of reason whose subordination to the divinely ordained familial hierarchy is an act of understanding, not of coercion. In a semi-Aristotelian twist, he displays the virtue of the slave, which is rational obedience and self-control.[27] Thus, the shadow of punishment has vanished from the horizon of pictorial insertion in favor of rational submission, one induced through the subjectifying power of (divine) language. The image itself visualizes the performative power of that language in what appears to be a renewed and forceful attempt to displace the traces of its 1727 failure. The slave has now, through a fiction of redemptive understanding, been frozen in an eternal pose of rather oxymoronic "rational awe," peacefully enthralled within the transcendental webs of his divinely ordained subjection.

The Legend of the Slave and the Count

What would have secured a slave (or a recently freed slave, if that was the case) such a prominent position among an aristocratic Criollo-Christian community of this sort? Who was he? And what has led art historians to assert that the social condition of this figure was indeed one of enslavement, particularly when his anomalous dignified demeanor so remarkably deviates from the short-lived, but significant, iconographic tradition of slave portraiture that emerged in the "courtly plantation" cultures of the Americas in the eighteenth century? One of the greatest challenges faced by scholars of slave-portraiture is to avoid the pitfall of exclusively seeing these kinds of representation as acts of symbolic enslavement without interrogating the micro-contingencies that made the portraits possible and that further complicate their signification. The question is not only what broader social structures and discursive conditions enabled the entrance of the slave into the dignified realm of slave portraiture, but also why this particular slave is represented and not any other. Such an inquiry into "the particular" need not lead to a liberal narrative of individual uniqueness or to indexical traps flowing from impossible attempts to recover the slave as an "original presence." It can, however, forestall the rather tautological inclination to read such objects exclusively within the restrictive interpretive frame of "subjection" and disallow us from engaging, in consequence, in a potential, and regrettable, act of hermeneutic re-enslavement.

If the master's archive has left practically no traces that would permit us to confidently identify the particulars of most of the white "sitters" that appear in this portrait, even fewer have been found on the presence of the black servant. Oral tradition, nonetheless, offers us a series of puzzling narratives and legends that have been crucial to the reception of this work and to a potential understanding of the conditions that enabled the entrance of this particular slave (and not any other) into the ennobling sphere of representation in oil portraiture and its specific discourses of subjectification.

According to a legend that has been orally transmitted to posterity, the first count of Casa Bayona was healed of an ailment by this slave.[28] The story relates that both the slave and the master suffered from gout, and through experimentation, or perhaps through herbal knowledge associated with Afro-Cuban religious practices, the slave discovered the medicinal properties of some waters near the manor that ameliorated the pain of the disease.[29] He shared this knowledge with his master, who, in exchange, distinguished him with special considerations. Decades later, in return for the gift of health (for the restitution of the master's body, so to speak), the slave received a dignified entrance into the realm of visual representation – the image of his body as transcendence in Escalera's painting. In some versions of this legend the slave is also granted his freedom as a reward for the master's cure (thus linking emancipation and representation).

No less than with written documents, oral narratives of this sort cannot be taken at face value. However, the painting itself seems to provide evidence about the plausibility of some aspects of this account, for the slave's prominent display of his ankles and his shoes, which emerge dramatically from the folds of his brown cloak, calls attention to the main visible physical locus of gout: the feet. This ostentatious display of the shoes is certainly a mark of distinction (as they were luxury items that most plantation slaves never possessed), but it also could be a celebratory sign of the slave's capacities to overcome illness. Gout is a medical condition characterized by attacks of acute inflammatory arthritis that leads to swollen joints, the base of the big toe being most commonly affected and making it extremely uncomfortable to wear shoes. That the slave is shown here wearing his could be seen as a boisterous indication of his exceptional prowess, his power to overcome the challenges of the mortal body through reason and local knowledge, thus making him worthy to enter the fictions of immortality granted by portraiture. His healed master, by contrast, is only a bust, symbolically liberated from the painful weight of the body.

Akin to Kwasi, the internationally renowned healer famous for his exact (and politically instrumental knowledge) of the medicinal properties of the flora and fauna of Surinam, and who was memorialized in the engraved portrait made by William Blake for Stedman's 1796 *Narrative of a five years' expedition against the Revolted Negroes of Surinam* (see Fig. 9.3),[30] the legend regarding Escalera's painting suggests how the authority that slave healers commanded from masters enabled a different sort of symbolic exchange between masters and slaves mediated by portraiture. Quite literally, the slave, the one who within the logic of chattel slavery is not the owner of his own body but who nonetheless is conceived as pure "bodiliness," seems to be allowed into the transcendental and dignifying realm of portraiture in oil (not just as a shadow) at the moment when he is able to restore the contingent materiality of the master's body. The Hegelian inversion suggested by the legend is delightful. It is at the juncture in which the master feels his own bodiliness (thus collapsing his fantasies of a self-determined and sovereign consciousness), when he feels the precariousness of his own fragile material existence, that a different kind of material and symbolic exchange with the slave is made possible, enabling in consequence the potential for recognition, representation, and transcendence.[31]

This legendary tale, regardless of its possible factual veracity, is indeed indicative of the meaning-making operations through which such a relatively anomalous presence in the history of Cuban portraiture has come to be popularly understood. But most importantly, by calling our attention to a probable and absolutely contingent factor (i.e., the healing of the master's body by the slave as a reason for his appearance in the portrait), the legend also opens up an imaginary field within which to consider an intricate series of particularities in a master-slave relationship that move both within and beyond the structural and ideological factors ostensibly at work in the painting.

If the portrait is, as discussed above, the closing instance of a genealogical narrative geared toward the symbolic legitimation of seigniorial authority (in the context of a broader and deliberate socioeconomic project), the presence of the slave is not only, then, the fulcrum on which the scaffold of a divinely ordained world rests, but also the element that evokes its frailty and potential unsettling, an instance of fugue. The legend brings to the fore the bodiliness of the master, his vulnerability to suffering and death, and his ultimate entanglement with the will and irreducible difference of the slave – that is, his fragility despite his position as a subject of power. Nevertheless, the painting assuages such a potential disruption by enforcing, in no uncertain visual terms, the image of a transcendentally harmonious and rationally grounded subjection.

On Reuniting the Head and the Body

The sociohistorical, urban, and ideological/narrative webs within which the head of the slave appears to have momentarily shifted from a performative site of exemplary mutilation and faceless subjection (its predominant condition under the material and symbolic logic of chattel slavery) to one of exemplary representation and subjectification in portraiture are thick and, at points, elusive. Both the foundation of Santa María del Rosario as well as the slave portrait inscribed in the pendentive painting of its church are associated with a disciplinarian imperative and the aspiration to establish a new social order. Fear and anxiety are nominally at the root of the racially homogeneous and caste-based initiative to build this urban shield against slave insurrections. But so are the desires on the part of an emergent Creole and proto-bourgeois planter class to advance claims to local power (subtly elusive of the central colonial administration) and to endow themselves with accoutrements of legitimacy that could be culturally legible and individually experienced: the prestige of a superior nobility produced by the semiotics of aristocratic pyrotechnics; an embodied sense of "place in the world" for all members of the community enabled by a hierarchical and intentionally virtual urban design; and the allure of an immobile and divinely ordained hierarchy underwritten by the fictions of eternity provided by genealogical lineages and ecclesiastical sanction. The Cuban planter classes, at this initial stage of their energetic projection into the world market system, were most decisively engaged in making the performance of their status fully intelligible and visible. In the case of Santa María del Rosario, this procured intelligibility had as an intractable *conditio sine qua non* an attempt at historical erasure, the creation of an instrumental tabula rasa: the triumphal vanishing of all traces of the memory of slave resistance, of their ultimately untameable refusal to be subordinated. Such attempts against memory or, to say it more accurately, such attempts to elaborate an elision of memory through a new and visible order are also part, in this instance, of the conditions of possibility for the incorporation of the slave into the realm of portraiture. Thus, whereas the foundation of Santa María del Rosario and its urban design tried to emphatically sublimate the memory of slave resistance into a highly codified and controlled new order immune to such disturbances, the summoning of the slave's head within the visual program of the church seems to point to not just a heightened act of narrative displacement but, most acutely, to the persistence of a will to re-emplot and re-stage that head within a new religious tale. This tale was built with and against the traces of the master's past failure to incite obedient subjection through performative embodiment, as well as the traces of the horrors of the monumental anti-portraits with which that failure culminated. It was also built (in its legendary dimensions) upon contingencies that bring to the fore, on the one hand, the master's vulnerability as a subject of power, his condition as a mortal being, and on the other, the dream of an enslaved existence moved by bonds of love and allegiance, and in which the slave, far from seeking the annihilation of his master, tends to the healing of his body.

No longer a character in a history of human violence, this narrative visually relocates the slave both within an aristocratic familial structure and at the culminating moment of a sacred account. As an element in a genealogical tale, the slave on the canvas now appears removed from the experiences that Orlando Patterson has described as characteristic of the enslaved condition: natal alienation (i.e., the violent detachment from the webs of kinship) and cultural estrangement (i.e., the shredding through coercion, vulnerability, and dishonor of symbolic referents that make the world intelligible).[32] Bestowed with grace and embracing the Christian teachings that once eluded him, placed within a familial world, and portrayed with full bodily integrity, in this visual story the slave's head – as if in an ultimate act of redemption enabled by representation – seems to have finally found the totality of being, whether moral/intellectual, cultural, or physical, it once brutally lost.

Abbreviations

AHN Archivo Histórico Nacional, Madrid
AGI Archivo General de Indias, Seville
ANC Archivo Nacional de Cuba, Havana

Notes

Doing research in Cuba is often a challenge for American and Puerto Rican academics given the ongoing political impasse between the island and the United States and the anachronistic and misguided U.S. embargo. I have been fortunate to count on the support of extraordinary Cuban colleagues who, at key moments, have made my work there possible. They are too many to be listed here, but among them I would like to especially single out Raida Mara Suárez Portal, Director of Patrimony of the City of Havana, for her years-long, unyielding confidence in my work and for her friendship. I would also like to thank the excellent Cuban photographer Ramsés Hernández Batista and María Mercedes García Santana, director of the Centro Nacional de Conservación, Restauración y Museología (CENCREM), for their help in securing some of the images for this essay, and Orelvis Rodríguez Morales, Coordinator for Patrimony and Development at the CENCREM, for his passion for the work of Escalera and for sharing, with such generosity, his work. I am also thankful to Nguyen Rodríguez Núñez for his elegant design of the floor plan illustrations of Santa María del Rosario and to Miguel Amat for assistance with photographs. This essay has benefited from the careful, patient, and loving critical readings of Angela Rosenthal and Diane Miliotes. To the two of them goes my greatest gratitude. Any shortcomings of the essay are, of course, my sole responsibility.

1 "Queriendo un Jueves Santo, el primer Conde de Casa Bayona excitar la humildad en la ceremonia del dia, labó los pies a doce esclavos de su Ingenio, les dio la mesa y sirvio a ella, ó por que no se lo proporcionaron otros pobres, ó por que creyó que con sus siervos abatía mas su persona y se les recomendaba mejor pero no le sucedio así, por que abusando aquellos del beneficio y del obsequio de su señor, se resistieron despues a trabajar. Fue preciso usar de alguna fuerza, quando se experimentó inutil la blandura y la persuasion. Entonces ellos de una vez levantaron la serviz, convocaron otros á tumulto, se sublevaron, insultaron aquel Yngenio y otros colindantes, y fue necesario que el Gobierno los aplacase con armas, á costa de mucha sangre y algunas vidas." ["Representación extendida por Diego Miguel de Moya y firmada por casi todos los amos de ingenio de esta jurisdicción – Havana, 1790"]. Spelling and ungrammatical syntax in the original. ANC, Junta de Fomento, Legajo 150, no. 7405. These events were first recorded in contemporary Cuban historiography by Manuel Moreno Fraginals in his now classic study *El ingenio. El complejo económico social cubano del azúcar,* 3 vols. (Havana: Comisión Nacional Cubana de la UNESCO, 1964), 1:49; and by Leví Marrero, *Cuba: Economía y sociedad Vol. 10. Azúcar, ilustración y conciencia (1763–1868) (II)* (Madrid: Editorial Playor, 1984), 224. According to Marrero, another copy of the document is in AGI, Estado 7. In this essay, all subsequent references to *El ingenio* will make use of the single-volume edition published by Editorial Crítica (Barcelona) in 2001, in which the account of the events of Maundy Thursday appears on page 99. All translations are mine in collaboration with Diane Miliotes, unless otherwise noted. Tomás Gutiérrez Alea's excellent film *The Last Supper* (Havana, 1976) was loosely based on these events and on Moreno Fraginals's account of this historical period in *El Ingenio.*

2 Moreno Fraginals describes the conclusion of these tragic events in the following terms: "Slave hunters brought this very Christian act to an end by capturing the black runaway slaves and nailing on twelve tall pikes the heads of the slaves before which his Excellency Señor Count of Casa Bayona had humbled himself." ["El cristianísimo acto lo finalizaron los rancheadores cazando a los negros cimarrones y clavando en doce lanzas las cabezas de los esclavos ante los cuales se humillara el Excelentísimo Señor Conde de Casa Bayona."] Moreno Fraginals, *El ingenio,* 99.

3 Criollo in this historical context means a person of Spanish descent born in the Americas, thus someone viewed as white.

4 Cf. Moreno Fraginals, *El ingenio*, 5–141.

5 Cf. Paul Rizo-Patrón Boylan, *Linaje, dote y poder. La nobleza de Lima de 1700 a 1850* (Lima: Pontificia Universidad Católica del Perú, 2000), and Nora Siegrist, "La hidalguía en Buenos Aires en el siglo XVIII. Concepto sobre su alcance en los actos positivos," *Procesos Históricos. Revista Semestral de Historia, Arte y Ciencias Sociales* 9 (enero 2006), 1–25, 20, and 21.

6 Moreno Fraginals, *El ingenio*.

7 Natalie Zemon Davies, *Slaves on Screen. Film and Historical Vision* (Cambridge, Mass.: Harvard University Press, 2000), 66.

8 Religious performances played a fundamental role in processes of evangelization in the Americas since the sixteenth century. Cf. Carolyn Dean in her *Inka Bodies and the Body of Christ. Corpus Christi in Colonial Cuzco, Perú* (Durham: Duke University Press, 1999), and Diana Taylor, *The Archive and the Repertoire. Performing Cultural Memory in the Americas* (Durham: Duke University Press, 2003).

9 Cf. Loló de la Torriente, *Estudio de las artes plásticas en Cuba* (Havana, 1954), ch. II: "Nicolás de la Escalera. Primeros Monumentos"; Guy Pérez Cisneros, *Características de la evolución de la pintura en Cuba* (Havana: Dirección General de Cultura, Ministerio de Educación, 1959), 34–39; Isabel Fernández Sáinz, "Nuestra pintura colonial," *Revista de La Universidad de Havana* 1, no. 66 (1968), 61–65; Martha de Castro, *El arte en Cuba* (Miami: Ediciones Universal, 1970), 30–31, 35–39; three texts by Adelaida de Juan: *Introducción a Cuba: Las Artes Plásticas* (Havana: Instituto del Libro, 1968), 30, *Pintura y grabado coloniales cubanos* (Havana: Editorial Pueblo y Educación, 1974), 10, and *Pintura cubana. Temas y variaciones* (Mexico City: Universidad Nacional Autónoma de México, 1980), 21–23; Guillermo Sánchez Martínez, "Un pintor cubano del siglo XVIII: José Nicolás de la Escalera y Domínguez," *Revista de la Biblioteca Nacional José Martí*, vol. 1 (enero-abril 1981), 143–52; Jorge Rigol, *Apuntes sobre la pintura y el grabado en Cuba* (Havana: Editorial Letras Cubanas, 1982), 60–61; Jorge R. Bermúdez, *De Gutenberg a Landaluze* (Havana: Editorial Letras Cubanas, 1990), 101–14; Olga López Núñez, "Notas sobre la pintura colonial en Cuba," in *Pintura europea y cubana en las colecciones del Museo Nacional de Havana* (Madrid: Fundación Cultural MAPFRE Vida, 1998), 49–73, 53, and "Un pintor habanero, José Nicolás de la Escalera, 1734–1804," *Espacio Laical*, espaciolaical.net/contens/08/0846.pdf; and Orelvis Rodríguez Morales, "Apuntes sobre Nicolás de Escalera Tamariz," *Patrimonio y Desarrollo. Boletín Digital del Centro Nacional de Conservación y Museología de Cuba*, no. 6 (2010), 4–6; and "Acercamiento a la posible identificación de los personajes de la obra *Santo Domingo y la Noble Familia de Casa Bayona* del pintor cubano José Nicolás de Escalera Tamariz" (unpublished manuscript; I thank the author for sending me a copy of his work still in progress but that has already unearthed important information for our understanding of Escalera's painting).

10 Cf. Elisabeth L. Roark *Artists of Colonial America* (Westport, Conn.: Greenwood Press, 2003), and Elizabeth L. O'Leary, *"At Beck and Call." The Representation of Domestic Servants in Nineteenth-Century American Painting* (Washington, D.C.: Smithsonian Institution Press, 1996); especially ch. 1, "The Custom of the Country: The Colonial Era," 7–34.

11 On the notion of "shadow" in slave portraits see Alex Bontemps, *The Punished Self: Surviving Slavery in the Colonial South* (Ithaca: Cornell University Press, 2001), especially Part 1, "Spotlights and Shadows."

12 This holds true until the avant-garde dismantled portraiture's mimetic pact in the first decades of the twentieth century and which has recently been taken to new points of nonfigurative radicality, for example, in the DNA portraits of South African photographer Gary Schneider.

13 Gilles Deleuze and Félix Guattari, "Year Zero: Faciality" in *A Thousand Plateaus. Capitalism and Schizophrenia*, trans. Brian Massumi (Minneapolis: University of Minnesota Press, 1987), 167–91.

14 Marcia Pointon, *Hanging the Head. Portraiture and Social Formation in Eighteenth-Century England* (New Haven: Yale University Press, 1993).

15 "[O]bviar y refrenar las sublevaciones de los esclavos negros"; "Expediente sobre la fundación de Santa María del Rosario, Cuba" (1733), AHN Santo Domingo 381. Cf. Leví Marrero, *Cuba: Economía y sociedad Vol. 6. Del monopolio a la libertad comercial (1701–1763) (I)* (Madrid: Editorial Playor, 1978), 50–53. Louis Pérez, Jr., suggests that a total of about 300 slaves were involved in this revolt. See his *Cuba: Between Reform and Revolution* (New York: Oxford University Press, 1988), 65. These slaves were mostly new arrivals from Africa. Also see Luisa María Martínez O'Farrill, who explicitly confirms the number: "La esclavitud en el término municipal de Santa María del Rosario" (in *Boletín PMD* 20/05/2008, www.arnac.cu/Boletin/pdfbol/b4.pdf).

16 "padecido el quebranto y contratiempo de habérsele levantado parte de los negros de la labor del ... ingenio, con las armas de fuego y de corte que ... [le] robaron y ... hecho conmoción de los demás negros de los otros ingenios de la comarca que sublevados y bien municionados *hicieron en los campos muchos y graves insultos, muertes y sacrilegios, hurtando las vestiduras y vasos sagrados,* poniendo a esta ciudad [Havana] y sus moradores en gran cuidado por la universal conmoción de negros que se temió, y se hubiera experimentado a no haber acudido con prontitud al reparo, con destacamentos de infantería, dragones y gente del país, que los avanzaron y destruyeron, matando y prendiendo todos los que se pudieron aprisionar vivos." "Expediente" (1733), AHN Santo Domingo 381. Also cited by Leví Marrero in *Cuba: Economía y sociedad*, 6:50.

17 On the establishment of the *señorío* of Santa María del Rosario, see AHN Santo Domingo, 381 (also in AGI Santo Domingo 380 and 381), Marrero, ibid., 50–53, and Pablo Fornet Gil, *La ciudad diminuta. Estudio urbanístico de Santa María del Rosario* (Havana: Editorial de Ciencias Sociales, 1996), especially 7–15. On Bayona's nobiliary titles, see Francisco Santa Cruz y Mallén, *Historia de familias cubanas*, Tomo I (Havana: Editorial Hércules, 1940); Rafael Nieto y Cortadellas, *Dignidades nobiliarias de Cuba* (Madrid: Ediciones Cultura Hispánica, 1954); and Leví Marrero, *Cuba: Economía y sociedad, Vol. 8. Del monopolio a la libertad comercial (1701–1763) (III)* (Madrid: Editorial Playor, 1978), 140–42.

18 José Luis Romero, *América Latina: Las ciudades y las ideas* ([1976] (Mexico City: Siglo XXI, 2001), especially chapter 3, "Las ciudades hidalgas" (69–118), and chapter 4, "Las ciudades criollas" (119–72). Useful for the organic relationships between urban designs and intellectual formations in Latin America is Angel Rama, *La ciudad letrada* (Hanover, N.H.: Ediciones El Norte, 1984).

19 Among the many reforms introduced by Morell y Santa Cruz in the mid-eighteenth century was the recognition and institutional intrusion of the Catholic Church in the life of the African *cabildos*. Since the sixteenth century, the Spanish Crown allowed enslaved Africans to form their own autonomous social organizations according to ethnicity. These organizations, known as *cabildos de nación,* became bedrocks for the rich development of Cuban syncretic spiritual beliefs. However, in 1755, Morell, weary of the threat African religious and cultural autonomy could pose to the hegemony of Catholicism, made the African *cabildos* official by transforming them into *ermitas*, chapel parishes, led by Catholic priests. On the Christianization of *cabildos*, see Marrero, *Cuba*, 8:157–61. On the uneven success of the attempt, see Fernando Ortiz, "Los cabildos afrocubanos," in *Etnia y sociedad* (Havana: Editorial de Ciencias Sociales, 1993), 54–63, and especially *Los negros brujos* (Miami: Colección Ébano y Canela, 1973). On Morell y Santa Cruz see Juan Martín Leiseca, *Apuntes para la*

historia eclesiástica de Cuba (Havana: Talleres Tipográficos de Carasa y Ca., S. en C., 1938), 101–15; Eduardo Torres-Cuevas and Edelberto Leiva Lajara, *Historia de la Iglesia Católica en Cuba (1516–1789)* (Havana: Ediciones Boloña, Publicaciones de la Oficina del Historiador de la Ciudad, 2007), 381–418; Francisco de Paula y Coronado's preface to his edition of Pedro Morell y Santa Cruz's *Historia de la Ysla y Catedral de Cuba* (Havana: Imprenta Cuba Intelectual, 1929).

20 Cf. Martínez, "Un pintor cubano del siglo XVIII," 146.

21 It must be pointed out, however, that no document has yet been found to support this art historical consensus, even though the bases for this conjecture are firmly grounded. I also subscribe to this opinion until evidence to the contrary is identified.

22 Cf. Libros de Matrimonios and Libros de Bautizos in the Archivo Parroquial de Santa María del Rosario, 1733 onward. I am grateful to Father Santiago Fernández Sánchez for graciously hosting my research at his parish.

23 The fact that the only one of the four canvases signed by Escalera was the family portrait indicates that it was thought of as the closing moment of a cycle that was conceived as a whole. I thank Orelvis Rodríguez-Morales for pointing out the location of the signature in his unpublished manuscript "Acercamiento a la posible identificación... "

24 The almost illegible inscription at the bottom of the triangular canvas partly reads: "La Virgen predicó y enseñó la devoción del Rosario, fácil medio para (illegible) la Divina Misericordia" ["The Virgin preached and taught the devotion of the Rosary, an easy means to (illegible: perhaps 'conseguir' or 'recibir') Divine Mercy."

25 For a discussion of the possible identity of the sitters see Rodríguez Morales, "Acercamiento..."

26 Cf. Brian Wallis, "Black Bodies, White Science: Louis Agassiz's Slave Daguerreotypes," *American Art* 9, no. 2 (summer, 1995), 39–61, and *Escravos brasileiros do século XIX na fotografia de Christiano Jr.*, Edição organizada por Paulo Cesar de Azevedo e Mauricio Lissovsky; Textos de Jacob Gorender, Manuela Carneiro da Cunha, Muniz Sodré (São Paulo: Ex Libris, 1988).

27 Cf. Aristotle, *Politics*, Book One.

28 This legend has been passed on for generations among *rosareños* and has been recorded by scholars of Escalera's work (Pérez Cisneros, de Juan, Rigol, Bermúdez, Rodríguez Morales). It was also recounted in the pamphlet published by the Patronato Restaurador of Santa María del Rosario after the restoration of the church in 1942 (quoted in Pérez Cisneros, 38), and transmitted through time to the descendants of the first count of Casa Bayona, José María Chacón y Calvo and Juan O'Naghten (who is still living and is the eighth count of Casa Bayona). I am grateful to Eusebio Leal (historian of the city of Havana) and to Mr. O'Naghten himself for this information.

29 The fundamental study on the uses of herbs, plants, and animals in Afro-Cuban religions is still Lydia Cabrera's *El monte* [1954], 9th ed. (Miami: Ediciones Universal, 2006).

30 For a detailed discussion of Kwasi's portrait see Susan Scott Parish's contribution in this volume.

31 This statement, of course, does not pretend to have general validity with regards to the practice of slave portraiture, but only to be historically specific to Escalera's piece. Toni Morrison's beautiful reading of the relationship between the crippled sadistic mistress and her young slave in Willa Cather's *Sapphira* would be an example of how bodily frailty does not lead in all cases to recognition. See her *Playing in the Dark: Whiteness and the Literary Imagination* (New York: Vintage Books, 1993).

32 Orlando Patterson, *Slavery as Social Death* (Cambridge, Mass.: Harvard University Press, 1982), 1–14 and 17–101.

Part III

SUBJECTS TO SCIENTIFIC AND ETHNOGRAPHIC KNOWLEDGE

EIGHT

ALBERT ECKHOUT'S *AFRICAN WOMAN AND CHILD* (1641)

ETHNOGRAPHIC PORTRAITURE, SLAVERY, AND THE NEW WORLD SUBJECT

Rebecca P. Brienen

The Dutch painter Albert Eckhout lived and worked in Brazil from 1637 to 1644, during a period when the northeastern settlements of the Portuguese came under the control of the Dutch West India Company (WIC). The economy of colonial Dutch Brazil, centered at the coastal city of Recife, was based on the cultivation and export of sugar, which relied on a constant influx of enslaved West Africans. As a result, the population of the Dutch colony displayed the same heterogeneous mixture of Europeans, Africans, and Indigenous Americans that one could encounter in many locations throughout the Atlantic world during this period. Portuguese planters, Dutch and German soldiers, merchants, and employees of the WIC walked the streets of Recife with colonized Tupinamba from the mission settlements, people of mixed racial background, and enslaved men and women of African ancestry.

During his seven years as court artist to the Dutch colony's governor general, Count Johan Maurits van Nassau-Siegen, Eckhout created hundreds of natural history drawings, twelve monumental still lifes, and an extraordinary group of eight life-size paintings that feature the various ethnic groups present in the colony.[1] As one of the first trained European painters in the Americas, Eckhout's work, like that of his fellow Dutch artist in Brazil, the landscape painter Frans Post, has long been of interest to scholars of the European expansion, but art historians concerned with colonialism, slavery, early-modern science, and the construction of race have only recently begun to exploit the rich visual materials that these artists left behind. In the first half of this essay, I discuss Eckhout's ethnographic series as a general introduction to a more focused consideration of his paintings of Africans, which have become central images in the ongoing scholarly debate about the artist and how his works should be interpreted (Fig. 8.1,

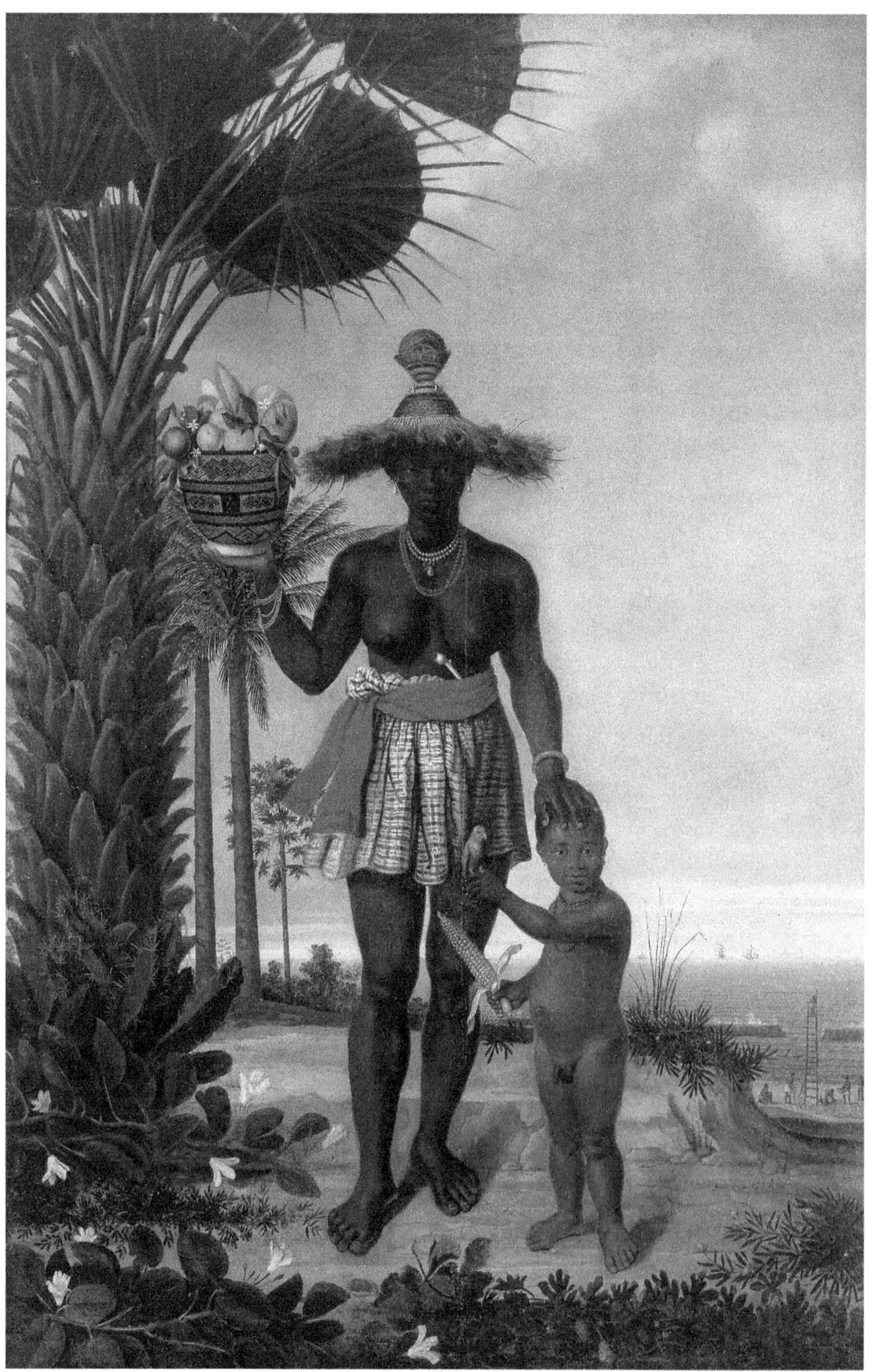

8.1. Albert Eckhout, *African Woman and Child*, 1641. Oil on canvas. National Museum, Copenhagen.

Plate 7, and Figs. 8.2, 8.6 and 8.7). Eckhout's painting *African Woman and Child* (1641), a highly complicated image that addresses slavery and representation among its many themes, will be the focus of this essay. I conclude with a discussion of Eckhout's oil study of a young black woman, *Woman on Beach*, upon which the main figure in this painting appears to be based (Fig. 8.3).[2] One of the underlying questions that concerns me here is to what degree it is possible to interpret

8.2. Albert Eckhout, *African Man*, 1641. Oil on canvas. National Museum, Copenhagen.

8.3. Albert Eckhout, *Woman on Beach*, ca. 1641. Oil on paper. Jagiellonian University Library, Kraków. Photo: Author.

these images as portraits, as representations of a specific enslaved historical subject who was forced to pose for the artist in his Brazilian studio.

This study highlights the difficulties one faces in attempting to locate subjectivity in paintings that have traditionally been understood to function as ethnographic imagery. By exposing Eckhout's final painting to be a highly constructed work of art, I draw attention to the painter's process of erasing the woman as a singularity to create both the slave and the ethnic type.

Albert Eckhout's Ethnographic Portrait Series

As an expression of both colonial control and the increasing attention to classificatory systems present in early-modern natural history, Albert Eckhout painted a remarkable series of eight life-sized paintings of the different ethnic groups (including people of mixed race) present in Brazil for his patron, Governor General Johan Maurits van Nassau-Siegen.[3] This cycle of paintings includes four images of Brazilian Indians (a Tapuya man and woman and a Tupinamba man and woman), a mulatto man and a mameluco (half Tupinamba/half European) woman, and finally an African man and woman. Casta paintings produced in Spanish America in the eighteenth century demonstrate a similar impulse to map colonial humanity, but there are some important distinctions (Fig. 8.4).[4] First, Eckhout's series is unique (unlike the multiple series of casta paintings that were produced) and was probably made with a particular site in mind – most likely the primary Brazilian palace of colonial governor Johan Maurits van Nassau-Siegen, although others have argued for a European location.[5] Furthermore, casta paintings focus attention squarely on heterosexual pairs and their offspring as examples of the different ethnic groups in New Spain and the mixtures possible between them. In contrast, Eckhout's images do not, generally speaking, emphasize reproduction and include only two children. Indeed, the common assumption that Eckhout's series was displayed in male-female pairs has been called into question by the possibility that the paintings were originally divided into a male group and a female group and hung on opposite sides of a room.[6] The use of text on casta paintings, which identifies both the parents and their offspring as examples of particular racial types or mixtures, indicates that these works are self-conscious products of Enlightenment-period systems of human classification. The text on Eckhout's paintings, by contrast, is limited to the artist's signature, the date, and the location, which together attest to their veracity as works of art made *in situ* and "after life," but gives no information about the people and things depicted.[7] Finally, excluding early

8.4. Anonymous artist, *Las castas*, eighteenth century. Oil on canvas. Museo Nacional del Virreinato, Tepotzotlán, Mexico. Photo: Schalkwijk/Art Resource, New York.

works in the genre, in particular those by Manuel Arellano during the eighteenth century, casta paintings increasingly take the form of genre scenes and mini-domestic dramas, while Eckhout's works are static, lack a clear narrative, and more specifically draw on the iconography of portraiture and early-modern ethnographic imagery.

Ethnographic Imagery and the Ethnographic Portrait

The paintings in Eckhout's series are most frequently referred to as "ethnic portraits" or "ethnographic portraits" in the literature, terms that need some discussion and perhaps defense.[8] Generally speaking, figural representations with an ethnographic agenda identify and represent aspects of a particular culture that can be distilled into visual form; they highlight broadly shared characteristics of the group, not unique qualities of the individual. Such images frequently highlight social activities that were exclusive to or were considered typical of the group under consideration. Examples from the sixteenth to seventeenth centuries include the rituals surrounding birth, death, war, and marriage, the characteristics of which were understood by early-modern Europeans as evidence of the sophistication and degree of civilization a people had achieved. Whereas representations of feasts, rituals, and battles often require many figures, ethnographic types (which occur in male and female versions) distill all of the information thought to be essential about a people, social group, or gender into a single figure. It should come as no surprise that such images, which largely circulated in printed form as illustrations to travel accounts, atlases, and costume books, focus on aspects that can be represented, such as markings on the skin and other types of bodily ornamentation, clothing and jewelry, and hair style. For example, the illustration to Pieter de Marees' *Description of the Gold Coast of*

8.5. Pieter de Marees, *How the Women Comport Themselves*. Woodcut. Illustration in chapter 7 of *Description of the Gold Coast of Guinea*, 1602. Royal Library, The Hague.

Guinea (*Beschrijving en historisch verhaal van het Gouden Koninkrijk van Guinea*, 1602) displays the variety of women to be found in Elmina in Ghana (then called the Gold Coast of Guinea), from a well-dressed city-dwelling mulatta slave to an almost naked woman from a rural area (Fig. 8.5). Ethnographic types such as these generally feature single adult (sexually mature, but youthful) figures standing in a static frontal pose. The most common format displays male and female pairs (presumably a couple), which may be pictured separately or may appear together in the same image. These formal characteristics were largely established in sixteenth-century publications, such as Cesare Vecellio's 1590 *Habiti antichi et moderni di tutto il mondo* and Abraham de Bruyn's 1581 *Omnium pene Europae, Asiae, Aphricae atque Americae Gentium Habitus*, although no one would mistake these woodcut prints of national types for portraits.

While Eckhout's changes to this formula in format and medium are clear, it is nonetheless useful to draw attention to them. Unlike prints, which are generally small in size and limited to black and white, in Eckhout's work the oil-paint medium, the naturalistic style, the life-size format, and the direct gaze of the figure out of the canvas give each of his depicted "specimens" the illusion of subjectivity – in other words they look like formal portraits of real people.[9] Like the portraits made by his seventeenth-century Dutch contemporaries, the figures in Eckhout's paintings are convincing because they have been carefully constructed in order to impart this effect. Both portraits and ethnographic portraits do similar types of work and attempt to "convince their viewers of something about their sitters, their character, and their social position," although the moral qualities or characteristics presented in the ethnographic portrait are highly generalized.[10] Despite the widely held belief that the primary function of a traditional portrait is to reproduce the features of an individual, the tendency toward convention and typing are as strong in this mode of representation as in ethnographic imagery.

Although the language of sixteenth-century ethnographic illustration clearly influenced many of Eckhout's pictorial decisions, these images (taking the woodcuts in Vecellio as a classic example) display a universal body type and show little or no interest in documenting complexion. In contrast, Eckhout's paintings demonstrate his clear interest in physiognomy, which places his work at the beginning of a more self-consciously "racial" approach to figural representation and ethnographic imagery (in terms of creating a distinct phenotype), which can be traced from the mid-seventeenth century forward. Even some printmakers around this time begin trying to reproduce the varieties of skin color that could be observed among non-European peoples; nonetheless, skin color would not develop into an essential marker of racial difference until the end of the eighteenth century.[11]

In spite of the specificity of detail that Eckhout's paintings display, it is always essential for the viewer to remember what is a central, but unstated, characteristic of such representations: the fact that the people or groups depicted in them did not create, commission, or in any way control their appearance in these works of art. This is not an example of "ethnic self-ascription"; paintings like these were made for the visual consumption of someone else, generally a white male European subject.[12] As such these paintings testify to the imbalance of power between the maker of the image, his patron, and the person depicted, something that has also been noted by scholars of nineteenth-century anthropological photography.[13]

Interpreting Eckhout's Ethnographic Series

In a letter written almost forty years after the ethnographic series was completed, Eckhout's patron, Johan Maurits, described the paintings as images of the *wilde natien* (savage peoples) under his authority in Brazil, which gives us insight into the larger ideological project of the original program, but no information about the specific works of art.[14] It is nonetheless clear that the figures included in Eckhout's ethnographic "collection" were in part intended to reproduce, by means of representative examples or types, the diversity of the local population. Europeans are not included as any of the primary figures, and they are pictured in the backgrounds of only two paintings. They are nonetheless implicitly present not only as the ideal against which the peoples depicted were measured but also as the principal shapers and consumers of the images.[15] These paintings also document (especially if we pair them with Eckhout's twelve still-life paintings of colonial fruits and vegetables and his *Tapuya Dance,* as was likely intended) a large number of the plants and trees to be found in Brazil. Eckhout's close study of nature is revealed, for example, in his representation of the papaya tree in the painting of the mulatto man, which remarkably includes both male and female parts.[16] Nonetheless, one would expect that if the painter had been attempting to achieve a complete portrait of Brazil's natural diversity, he would have included a greater variety of animals in his paintings, which are limited to only a few, namely, a European (?) dog, a dead snake, a small hummingbird, two blue crabs, a tarantula, a toad, and two guinea pigs. The animals traditionally associated with Brazil and the New World, such as parrots, monkeys, armadillos, and alligators, are curiously absent, excepting the small lovebird held by the young boy in Eckhout's painting of the African woman.[17] Instead of presenting a comprehensive view of Brazil's plants and animals to complement Eckhout's presentation of ethnic types, it seems better to assume that backgrounds and the objects (including plants and animals) that surround each man and woman were carefully selected to complement and comment upon the primary figure represented.[18]

In an essay from 1979, historian Ernst van den Boogaart was the first to argue that the paintings of the Tupis and the Tapuyas in Eckhout's ethnographic series were conceived in opposition to each other, setting up a dichotomy of savage and civilized Indians (Figs. 8.6 and 8.7).[19] According to this interpretative model, which has dominated subsequent scholarship, Eckhout's series "illustrates Dutch rule" over the native Amerindian population and functions as a visual justification for the civilizing presence of the Europeans, who are able to "improve" the Amerindians by introducing them to European dress, weapons, and customs.[20] The body parts she carries, his "deforming" facial decorations, their nude but unheroic bodies, the dangerous animals that accompany them, and their wild surroundings all serve as evidence of the Tapuya's primitive and undesirable status. This is contrasted with the Tupis who cover their genitals with clothing (thus, more "European" in appearance) and are shown with useful or harmless animals, as well as pictured within peaceful and cultivated landscapes that include a white colonial presence.[21]

Van den Boogaart and his followers, most importantly anthropologist Peter Mason, have extended this interpretive model to the series as a whole, creating a "triad of civility": The "savage" and naked Tapuyas are the least civilized of the group, followed by the "halfway decently dressed" Tupi Indians in the middle, with the mixed-race couple occupying the highest level available to non-Europeans.[22] According to this model, the mestizos have a more attractive and refined appearance than the other ethnic groups pictured in the series; they are "decently dressed," look more "European," and carry and wear objects (such as his musket and rapier or her jewelry) that give additional evidence of their superior degree of "civility" in comparison to the Amerindians and the Africans.[23] Their position above the rest of the figures is based on the fact that their fathers are Europeans, although none of these scholars suggests that Eckhout's series endorses miscegenation.

While Mason has gone some distance in bringing attention to the colonial discourse of race, gender, and sexuality present in these works of art, the overarching interpretive model has fundamentally remained the same. Although this model is largely convincing, it is nonetheless highly problematic because it allows for only three levels of civility for the four pairs of figures, somewhat inelegantly solving the problem by placing the Tupis and the Africans on "more or less the same level."[24] But how should one interpret Eckhout's paintings of Africans in this series, whose highly complex representations are inadequately accounted for within this tripartite system? Before addressing this question in detail, it is important to closely study the works of art in question, in particular Eckhout's *African Woman and Child*, certainly the most complex image in the entire series.

ECKHOUT'S *AFRICAN WOMAN AND CHILD*

In Eckhout's painting the main figure, a tall, powerfully built woman with smooth dark brown skin, stands in front of a coastal landscape; small fishing figures are visible along the shoreline to the right, and four European ships sail

8.6. Albert Eckhout, *Tupinamba Woman*, 1641. Oil on canvas. National Museum, Copenhagen.

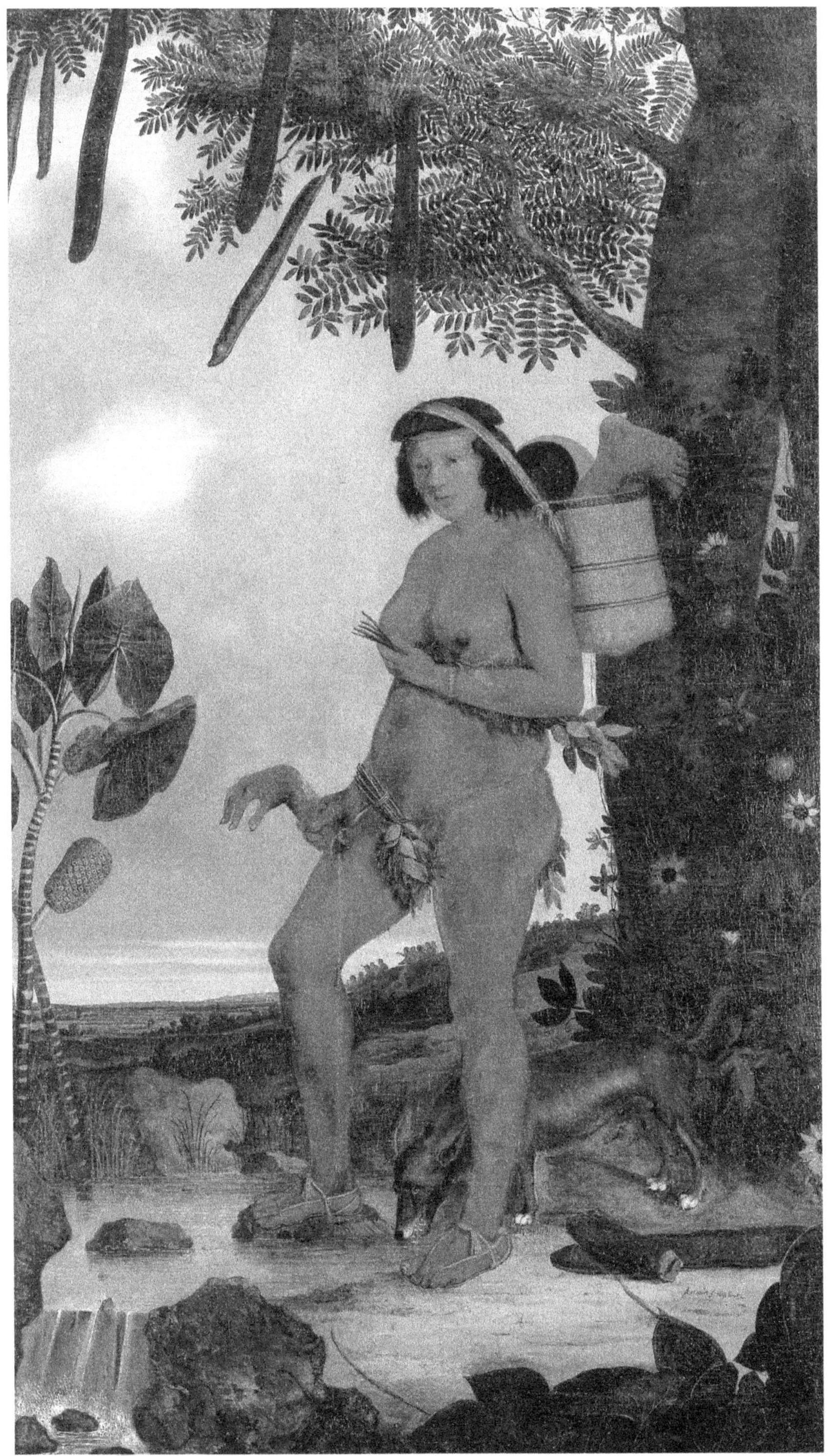

8.7. Albert Eckhout, *Tapuya Woman*, 1641. Oil on canvas. National Museum, Copenhagen.

in the deep background along the horizon (Fig. 8.1). Her most extraordinary attribute is a tall and elaborate woven hat, which is decorated with teeth and a thick fringe of peacock feathers. A small white pipe is tucked into a red sash, which serves to hold a short blue and white striped skirt around her waist.[25] Double ropes of white pearls and red coral beads curve around her neck, echoing the form of her full exposed breasts. The richness of these necklaces is complemented by her bracelets and the elegant pearl earrings with small red bows that adorn her ears. The nude young boy at her side, who wears strands of black pearls around his neck and small gold hoops in his ears, is presumably her son, although his skin color is somewhat lighter than that of his mother.[26] A small, brightly colored red and green love bird perches on his left hand, and he uses his right hand to point an ear of shucked corn between his mother's legs, a gesture that is unmistakably sexual.[27] This emphasis on fecundity, sexuality, and prosperity is reinforced by the woman's cornucopia-like basket, which overflows with ripe fruit, including bananas, oranges, and lemons.

Given the extraordinary multiplicity of attributes, this description seems to pose as many questions as it answers: How exactly is one supposed to interpret this image? Contemporary documentation regarding the Brazilian reception of Eckhout's ethnographic series is limited to Zacharias Wagener's *Thierbuch*, an illustrated manuscript from around 1641.[28] A German with a background in cartography, Wagener's services in the WIC eventually led to his appointment as chief notary and butler to the colonial governor, Count Johan Maurits.[29] In his *Thierbuch*, Wagener made copies of the figures from Eckhout's paintings and complemented each with a descriptive text.[30] It is therefore not surprising that this work has often been used as a key to the "true meaning" of Eckhout's ethnographic series.[31] But much in the same way that historians of art recognize that emblem books, while useful, are not infallible sources for unlocking the symbolic meaning of objects in seventeenth-century Dutch paintings, it is important to remember that Wagener's descriptions were written for his drawings, which were made for his personal use and introduce many changes, additions as well as deletions.

New World Slaves?

Wagener labels his copies of Eckhout's paintings of Africans "black man" and "black woman," drawing upon the Portuguese terms that were in use among WIC employees in Brazil.[32] In the text accompanying his image of the man, Wagener states "these blacks are brought to Brazil from Africa," naming Guinea, Angola, and Cape Verde as the main areas of origin.[33] He explains that the Africans have "great wars between themselves, using swords, shields and long assagai."[34] The captives taken during these wars are then sold as slaves to the Portuguese in Africa and then to Dutch traders, who in turn sell them to the sugar plantation owners in Brazil, who treat them very badly. Wagener's figures are stockier in build and less elegant than Eckhout's, which seems to be less the result of ideology than artistic skill. For our purposes, the most significant change he introduces is a brand above the "Negra's" left breast in the form of a crowned M – generally thought to be the monogram of Johan Maurits (Fig. 8.8). This detail is in keeping with Wagener's description of slavery in the Dutch colony that accompanies this image, in which he impassively states: "Our people, like the Portuguese, recently decided that it would be a good idea to put certain signs or marks on men, women, and children."[35] The child, whom Wagener also includes in his copy, shows no signs of having been branded. Wagener's version of the African man is also unmarked.

While it may seem convenient to assume that Eckhout's paintings of Africans show slaves as well, such a simple explanation is undermined by the complexity of these images. These representations simply do not fit easily into the visual tradition for slavery as it existed in the sixteenth and seventeenth centuries, most commonly manifested in representations on maps, in travel accounts, and in natural history publications. Examples include the engravings of Africans in the mines of New Spain in de Bry's edition of Benzoni (part V, 1594) and the woodcuts of slaves in Dutch Brazil in Piso and Marcgraf's 1647 *Historia naturalia Brasiliae*. These images all favor anonymous male slave types, whose primary attributes are their youthful, well-muscled bodies (the Greco-Roman

8.8. Zacharias Wagener, *Molher Negra* (Black Woman). Watercolor on paper. Illustration in *Thierbuch*, ca. 1641. Kupferstich-Kabinett, Staatliche Kunstsammlung, Dresden.

ideal), closely cropped hair, and near nudity, which is relieved only by a simple white loincloth. This is also true of the images of slaves painted by Frans Post, Eckhout's fellow Dutch painter at Johan Maurits' Brazilian court. Nor can the striped cloth they wear be used to fix their status, because images from the seventeenth century show free and enslaved West Africans wearing the same kind of cloth.[36] Indeed, in prints and paintings by European artists from the seventeenth century, the most common color worn by enslaved men and women in Brazil is white. While the varieties of skin color observable among the world's peoples could be reproduced with greater or lesser degrees of accuracy by painters, European printmakers from this period had not yet made skin color a central feature of ethnographic illustration, nor could it be used to distinguish those who were enslaved from those who were free.

If we extend this discussion to paintings produced in Europe around this time, the enslaved Africans encountered are of a clearly different type. One extremely unusual example is the 1632 *Rape of a Negress* in the Musée des Beaux-Arts, Strasbourg, by Dutch artist Cristiaen Gillsz. van Couwenburgh, who was active at the Stadhouder's court in The Hague during the period that Eckhout was in Brazil.[37] This painting shows an appalling scene of three young white men who are about to rape a naked, struggling, and clearly terrified black woman on a bed. Pornographic, not ethnographic, in intent, this image highlights the sadistic pleasure taken by the young men and, by extension, the implied viewer in the powerlessness of the victim. This violent fantasy of black female subjugation and denigration is nonetheless distant from Eckhout's painting in both content and intent. In Couwenburgh's large-scale theatrical production, which may have been considered humorous to contemporary audiences, the black woman wears only a kerchief on her hair and displays no other distinct attributes or ornaments. Her masculine, even animal-like form and flat black skin color appear to have little in common with the woman in Eckhout's painting, whose dark brown skin displays subtle modulations in tone and whose body, while strongly muscled, is idealized and eroticized to a much greater degree.

More common in Europe at this time, especially in England and the Dutch Republic, are the anonymous young boys depicted in still-life paintings and as attendants or pages in portraits of aristocratic women, as seen in Adrian Hanneman's circa 1654 *Portrait of Mary Stuart with a Black Attendant* at the Mauritshuis in The Hague, among many other examples from the period.[38] Applying this visual tradition to Eckhout's painting *African Woman and Child* would require the naked boy to function as the enslaved page and the woman to take on the role of the white female subject, an uneasy fit at best. In her recent book on Eckhout, Denise Daum has nonetheless argued that by referencing this mode of aristocratic portraiture, Eckhout distances his work from the discourse of slavery by granting the African woman the illusion of subjectivity, which is reinforced by her life-size representation and the painter's respectful attention to her black skin and physical beauty.[39] While I am not convinced that Eckhout intentionally meant to associate his painting with this type of portraiture, I agree that his representation of the African woman is a largely positive one.

There is no question that slavery is referenced in Eckhout paintings (the models were almost certainly slaves), but it is one of several overlapping and competing themes. Like the New World slaves in the prints addressed above, Eckhout's Africans are attired in a similarly skimpy manner, which serves to expose large expanses of their toned, well-muscled bodies. Representations of slave women in the Americas become more common toward the end of the seventeenth century, and a number of these images show muscular enslaved women wearing jewelry, including pearl necklaces. See, for example, the woman in the print *Negers speelended op Kalabasses* (Blacks Playing Calabashes) in Johan Nieuhof's account of Dutch Brazil, *Gedenkweerdige Brasilianese zee- en lant-reize* (Amsterdam, 1682).[40] Nonetheless, the jewelry worn by Eckhout's woman – her pearls and gold bracelet – and her other attributes – the colorful woven basket and impressive hat – find no parallels in depictions of South American slaves. To adequately explain the presence and function of these objects, one must look beyond images of slaves to other types of representation – specifically to allegorical as well as ethnographic images of Africans.

ECKHOUT'S SOURCES

Eckhout may have been familiar with Pieter de Marees's 1602 *Description of the Gold Coast of Guinea*, an influential early account of a Dutch voyage to West Africa.[41] In de Marees' illustration of Capo Lopo Gonsalves (Cape Lopez), for example, a half-nude, jeweled woman and a small child stand in the center of the image (Fig. 8.9). To her right is a man wearing a loincloth and carrying both a spear and an elephant tusk. Unlike the woman, his position is made clear in the text. As noted by de Marees, this figure is "a common inhabitant as he goes about every day and trades with foreigners, bringing elephant tusks for sale."[42] Earlier in the text, de Marees discusses weapons made by the Africans along the Gold Coast, and he specifically mentions a large sword with a "fish" skin scabbard decorated with a large red shell. His description matches almost perfectly the ceremonial sword with the ray skin scabbard with a reddish oyster shell that forms the primary attribute of the man in Eckhout's painting.[43] Scholars have determined that this is an Akan sword from the Gold Coast of Guinea.[44]

The illustrations in de Marees were made by artists in Europe, and they are based on idealized European models rather than personal observation. Eckhout, by contrast, lived in Brazil for more than six years, which afforded him ample opportunity to closely observe people of African ancestry, many thousands of whom were forcibly imported to work on the colony's sugar plantations during this

8.9. Pieter de Marees, *The Inhabitants of Capo Lopo Gonsalves*. Woodcut. Illustration in *Description of the Gold Coast of Guinea*, 1602. Royal Library, The Hague.

short period. While the athletic build of his *African Man* (Fig. 8.2) is not a fundamental departure from the printed tradition for slaves or Africans in early-modern ethnographic representation, the attention to detail in the man's face, including his large, expressive brown eyes whose whites have a strong yellowish cast, suggest that Eckhout used a real model, most likely a slave in Brazil. The hairstyle he wears – worn long in a more European manner rather than closely cropped as was typical in images of black men – is quite unconventional. It nonetheless appears to be a peculiarity of the Dutch tradition; we also see it on contemporary images of black slaves in Brazil made during the period of Dutch occupation.[45] With respect to the background, it appears that Eckhout manufactured a West African location by including a date palm tree, shells from the Atlantic coast, and most importantly an elephant tusk, an unambiguous reference to the trade in ivory that is also seen in the de Marees illustration and on maps of Africa from this period. Eckhout's African man wears a loincloth like the merchants and traders in de Marees' text, but his impressive sword could only have been in the possession of a high-ranking tribal leader, contributing to the work's contradictory effect.

The woman in Eckhout's painting may also be compared to the one depicted among the inhabitants of Cape Lopez in the de Marees illustration. In both images the women have exposed breasts, wear elaborate jewelry and a short skirt, and are accompanied by a nude male child. In the painting, her attributes also connect her to the visual tradition for the personification of Africa as one of the four parts of the world. Comparison to the woodcut illustration of Africa from the 1644 Dutch edition of Cesare Ripa's *Iconologia* (1603) demonstrates the overlapping areas with respect to iconography. This woodcut highlights the figure's dark skin color and curly hair, and simplifies her clothing to a short skirt, leaving her breasts entirely exposed.[46] She also holds a cornucopia filled with grain. It should be noted that pearls and especially red coral are common in other representations of the personification of Africa from this period.[47] In Eckhout's paintings, however, there is additional pictorial emphasis on sexuality, most obviously demonstrated by the ear of corn pointed toward the woman's vagina. Beginning in antiquity, many travelers wrote about the fertility of the continent of Africa – which explains why in Ripa's original illustration (and the 1644 Dutch version), Africa carries a cornucopia. This assumption of fecundity was extended to Africa's indigenous animals as well as its peoples, many of whom were described as oversexed. Allegedly eyewitness testimonies, which often addressed the sexual proclivities of Africans, were reproduced in travel accounts and reached a wide, literate audience throughout Western Europe during the early-modern period. Readers of de Marees's text, for example, were probably not surprised to read his account of the women of Cape Lopez, whom he calls "very much inclined to unchastity and whoredom," further suggesting that "in particular they like to fornicate with a foreigner, which they consider a great honor."[48] De Marees also singles out the men for shameful practices, asserting that "a man will present his Wives to foreigners who come there."[49]

A Natural Pair?

That Eckhout's African man in the painting is supposed to be understood as the husband or partner of the African woman is an assumption worth examining in greater detail. Do the figures in Eckhout's ethnographic series really form pairs as in traditional Dutch seventeenth-century portraiture? Does the series function as a sort of Noah's ark of colonial humanity? Support for this interpretation may be found on the decorative borders of period maps, which frequently include ethnic types, often in male-female pairs. Closer examination of Eckhout's paintings of Africans nonetheless disrupts this seemingly obvious notion. It is true that the man and woman each wear clothing of the same type of blue and white striped cloth, but the other objects of material culture they hold and wear come from different parts of western Africa. Viewers were supposed to recognize that each was African, but the man with his Akan sword and spears demonstrates his ties to Guinea. As pictured in an African setting, he cannot yet be identified as a slave, which may explain why Wagener did not brand him like the woman. Warrior, noblemen, trader – his attributes offer a number of different possibilities, which together suggest that his role here is in part allegorical; he represents this region of the Gold Coast and the economic interests that the Dutch had there.

Unlike the man, the woman is not connected to Guinea, but to Angola by means of her attributes, especially her basket and hat, and possibly her striped skirt as well. The Dutch became increasingly involved in this region because of their conquest of Portuguese Brazil. When the quality and number of slaves imported from Guinea proved inadequate, the WIC moved southward, and in 1641 they conquered Luanda in Angola, the most important port city in the West African slave trade. Competing African rulers from this region, such as the king of the Congo and the Count of Sonho, sent ambassadors to both Dutch Brazil and the court of the Dutch stadholder Prince Frederik Hendrik in The Hague during the years that followed. In Eckhout's corpus of oils on paper (Jagiellonian Library, Kraków) there is a small group of costume studies of Africans – perhaps inspired by one of these visits – in which the male figures wear conical hats that display patterns similar to those seen on the African woman's hat and basket. Gifts offered to Johan Maurits by these Congo delegates were not limited to silver platters and other costly but inanimate objects, but in 1642 even included 200 African slaves.[50] Because Eckhout's paintings of Africans are dated 1641, her basket and hat could also represent objects acquired during the conquest of Luanda that year. The basket has been identified as Bakongo, and her hat may have been produced in the area around Sonho, near the kingdom of the Congo, in what today is northern Angola and the lower Congo region. Peacock feathers, which are prominently featured on her hat, were objects of trade in the region, and they also appear on headdresses of warriors, as seen in illustrations to Portuguese explorer Duarte Lopez's account of the Congo, published by the Italian Filippo Pigafetta as *Relatione del reame di Congo* (1591).

This framework of trade, conquest, slavery, and the ritual of the gift becomes especially important when one realizes that Eckhout's African woman stands against a South American – specifically Brazilian – coastline. Unlike the date palm that frames the African man and asserts his African location to the viewer, the large wax palm tree on her right and the papayas behind her are indigenous to South America. Close inspection of the painting further reveals a group of Tupinambas, a Brazilian indigenous group allied with the Dutch, fishing along the shoreline in the deep background on the right. Even the clay pipe she wears at her waist may be read as a sign of both her location and her ethnicity. Beginning in the seventeenth century, blacks in the New World are increasingly associated with pipes and smoking, which become one of their main attributes.[51] A contemporary connection between smoking and a debauched lifestyle, especially for women and low-life types such as soldiers, makes this detail consistent with the emphasis on sexuality addressed above.[52]

As argued by Peter Mason, carefully rendered artifacts generally demonstrate the "authenticity" of the ethnographic portrait, and that holds true for most of the images in this series. But here, in a way that is quite remarkable, her multinational array of attributes serve instead to highlight the African woman's hybridity. Her cultural identity is formed through the deliberate intermingling of her various attributes. For example, her African basket is filled with tropical fruits grown in Brazil, and a European pipe is tucked into the waistband of her African striped skirt. The coral beads around her neck and her hat signal an African provenance, but her pearl earrings with red bows and pearl necklace are also worn by elegant young women in seventeenth-century Dutch genre paintings. Unlike many European artists, who created improbable mixtures of unsuitable attributes in order to make their ethnographic images more exotic and exciting, especially to the uninitiated, Eckhout made this mixture of European, American, and Indian attributes appear acceptable if not entirely natural for his patron, the governor general of Dutch Brazil.

REINTERPRETING ECKHOUT'S ETHNOGRAPHIC SERIES

While van den Boogaart's "levels of civility" model is quite convincing when applied to the Tupis and the Tapuyas alone, it is nonetheless clear that the Africans cannot occupy the same level as the Tupis. I have suggested elsewhere that in order to properly account for his images of Africans, Eckhout's series requires a fourth level of civility; yet the complexity of these images defies easy placement into such a framework and even calls into question the usefulness of applying such an interpretative model to the series as a whole. Indeed, with their expensive, finely wrought attributes (her jewelry, hat, and basket, his sword, shield, and spears) Eckhout's Africans, despite their half-clothed state, seem far closer in terms of "civility" to the mameluca, who also wears beautiful jewelry, and the mulatto man, who similarly carries fine weapons, a gun and a rapier, albeit both European in manufacture. Eckhout's *Mulatto Man* is also subtly connected to his *African Woman and Child,* because both paintings include papaya trees and European ships along the horizon. It must furthermore be noted that there is no clear indication that the mulatto man, who was by definition the offspring of a European man and a black woman, was not intended to represent a slave.[53] He is shown guarding rather than laboring in the sugar field behind him. As Wagener notes, most mulattos were slaves, inheriting that status from their mothers, and many were employed in the Portuguese and Dutch colonial armies. Yet the painting of the African woman stands apart from the rest of the representations in this series, including the African man and the mixed race couple, because of her extraordinary multiplicity of attributes and lack of a stable ethnic or social identity.

Viktoria Schmidt-Linsenhoff has asserted that the figures in Eckhout's ethnographic series (along with the blacks represented in Fran Post's idealized images of plantation life) can be read as images of free colonial subjects in a "virtual Dutch Brazil *without slavery,*" a problematic thesis on a number of levels.[54] Eckhout was the painter of a colonial governor general, who was also an agent of the Dutch West India Company. The purpose of the colonial enterprise is to know, understand, and often denigrate subject peoples in order to better rule and utilize them; neither African is painted as a typical New World slave, yet slavery is central to the meaning of each. Eckhout's image may be read as a sympathetic response to African beauty and dark skin color, but this sympathy is double-edged. Eckhout's African woman has much in common with the main character in Isaac Teale's poem "Sable Venus; An Ode" (1765), in which a black African queen of love dazzles her white male audience with her beautiful face and body as she travels from Africa to the New World. This poem and the well-known engraving that illustrates it were reproduced in volume II of *The History, Civil and Commercial, of the British Colonies in the West Indies* (1801, first published without the engraving in 1793), written by Jamaican slave holder and merchant (and member of Parliament) Bryan Edwards. As Robert Young has noted, this poem and the image (see Fig. 11.9) that accompanies it represent the "fantasy of a Black Botticellian Venus, triumphantly riding her chariot from Angola to Jamaica to be enthroned by enraptured, desiring colonists."[55] As Schmidt-Linsenhoff noted, in Eckhout's painting, the African woman is equally cut off from the brutal realities of New World slavery.[56]

The ultimate message of Eckhout's painting *African Woman and Child* seems to be that the prosperity of the colony is embodied by this woman, who is caught midpoint in her transition from African to African American and from free woman to slave. As such this painting is central to proper understanding of the series as a whole, which is not simply a representation of ethnic types or colonial subjects or even a visual demonstration of the need for and benefits of the European colonial presence. Rather the cycle taken as a whole testifies to the stability and prosperity of the colony under the benevolent leadership of Johan Maurits van Nassau-Siegen. The importance of African slaves to achieving this goal – a subject of constant discussion and concern to Johan Maurits and his contemporaries – is made manifest in this work of art.

Eckhout's Drawing of a Woman of African Ancestry in Brazil

But what can be said about Eckhout's drawing (see Fig. 8.3), upon which this figure was almost certainly based?[57] Does it shed any additional light on our interpretation of Eckhout's painting? Using oils on prepared paper, Eckhout carefully painted a standing female figure, whom he positioned against a sketchy coastline that includes sand, water, and a stormy sky, but no plants or other signs of life. Her hair, worn very short, is a startling burnt orange color, and her skin is a warm golden brown. Instead of a basket, she holds a grayish object, about the same size and shape as a human skull, aloft in her right hand. Her few attributes are limited to this odd object and her short, blue and white striped skirt. Although relatively simple and rather small in size (36 cm by 24 cm), this casual sketch is a remarkably powerful and haunting image, primarily because of the intensity of the main figure's expression as she stares directly out at the viewer. Eckhout created a large number of drawings in oils in Brazil, but this is one of the few documented cases in which he used one as a study for a painting.[58]

Although Eckhout likely used this drawing as a source for his painting, there are more differences than similarities between the two images. The areas of overlap result in a fairly short list: Each image displays a partially clothed female of color in her childbearing years; both women wear a short skirt of striped cloth; and each is positioned in a standing frontal pose with the right arm holding an object aloft. Neither woman has any marks or blemishes on her skin. But little else is the same; the woman in the oil study is not pictured with a hat, a basket, fine jewelry, or a child. In addition, her skin color does not match the dark brown color of the main figure in Eckhout's painting; rather, her skin color is the same as that of the Tupinamba woman and the African woman's child, who may or may not be of mixed race.[59] The woman in the drawing also has a slighter, more youthful figure with smaller breasts; she lacks the powerful shoulders and muscled arms of the African woman in Eckhout's painting, whose stronger, more masculine physique testifies to her capacity for hard physical labor, with the child signaling her ability (real or hoped for) to reproduce. But perhaps the most important difference is not related to background, attributes, or body type, but rather to facial expression – the passive expression on the face of the African woman in the painting versus the confrontational expression on the face of the woman in the oil study.

The physical beauty of Eckhout's model and her intense facial expression serve to both attract and repel the viewer. Most likely a slave, the woman stares out from the page, her expression sullen, almost angry, her gaze disruptive. This sketch, unencumbered by the requirements of a formal, finished image, records disturbing signs of the model's face to face encounter with the artist and its unequal relationship of desire and power. For example, her breasts, small and delicate in form, are lighter in color than the surrounding skin, suggesting that Eckhout made her expose them specifically for this image. Similar signs of exploitation, if not violation, may be seen in the series of slave portraits commissioned by Louis Agassiz in the late nineteenth century, which served to document "authentic" African types on a South Carolina plantation for the new science of anthropology.[60] In his photograph of Delia, for example, one can see how her dress, visible at the bottom of the daguerreotype, was roughly pulled down around her waist in order that the photographer could both see and reproduce the size and quality of her breasts as indicators of her gender, age, and ethnic group.

Other examples of ethnographic voyeurism in Eckhout's work include a remarkable drawing of a seated naked man, possibly albino, of African descent in Brazil (Fig. 8.10), a work that is unique in his oeuvre and has received little attention from scholars.[61] Although the artist has focused his attention on the seated man's ruddy face and the tight curls of his short yellowish hair, it

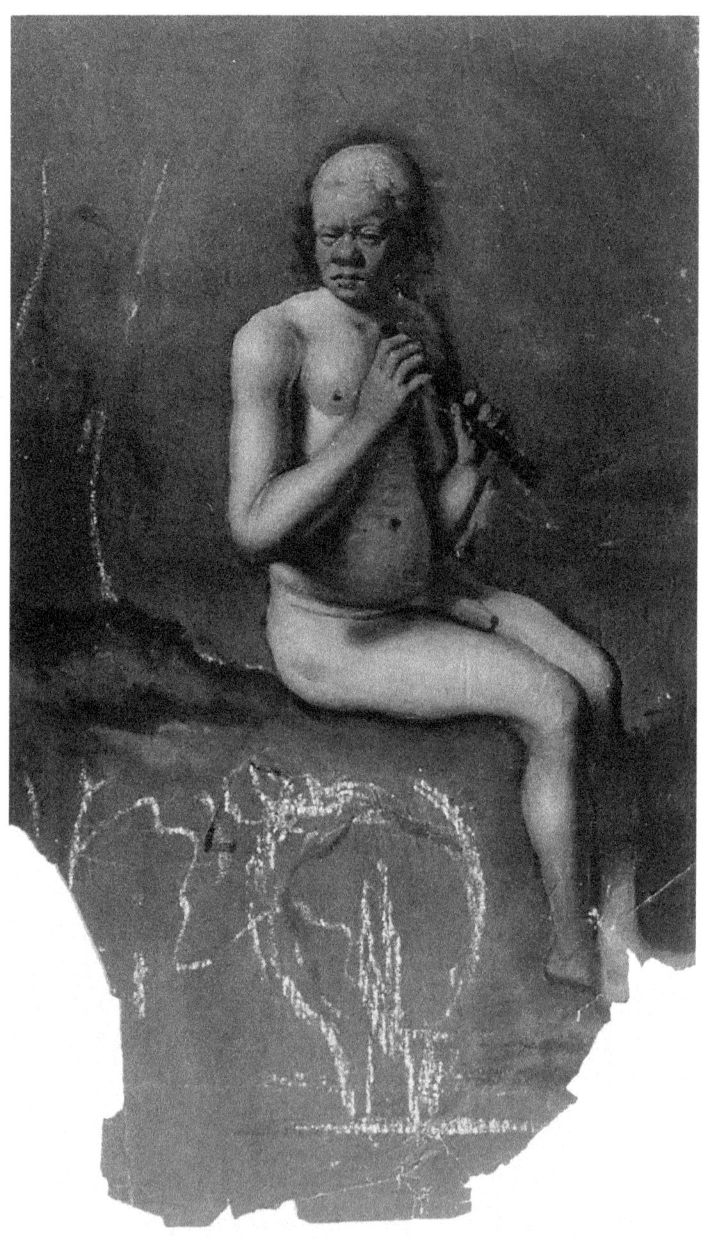

8.10. Albert Eckhout, *Albino Man of African Descent*, ca. 1641. Oil on paper. Jagiellonian University Library, Kraków. Photo: Author.

is difficult to overlook his penis, which is completely exposed and positioned alongside his thighs, one imagines to give the viewer a sense of length. It is possible that Eckhout may have imagined this figure to be a shepherd or perhaps a licentious follower of Pan in a pastoral composition that was never completed. This is the only representation of the albino slave. He holds a pipe for music, and the white chalk outlines of Angolan fat-tailed sheep are visible in the foreground. Nonetheless the lack of a developed narrative or visual framework for this figure calls attention to his status as a natural history curiosity. But the artist has also humanized him, and he, like the woman on the beach, denies the easy objectification of his naked body. His narrowed eyes and admittedly hostile expression challenge and confront the painter, and by extension us, as we gaze upon him.

In the completed ethnographic portrait, the African woman also looks out of the canvas, but the complexity of emotions – fear, anger, and perhaps even a degree of resignation – that Eckhout recorded during his encounter with his model are gone; she has been reduced to a mannequin, a dressed-up body from which a real woman can no longer be distinguished. In the informal oil drawing, she does not welcome our attention; she is made available and vulnerable. Although the painter recorded her oppositional attitude, this is not like Couwenburgh's image of sexual degradation. Instead, by granting her the ability to look back, the viewer can imagine her not as a yielding, passive object but a thinking, feeling subject. Eckhout's simple yet powerful oil study exposes the rawness of the physical encounter between the male European painter and the female New World slave. This tension, however, has no place in the final painting. Made docile and static, albeit exotic, the disruptive presence of Eckhout's model is buried under a multitude of attributes and associations. She has become fit for visual consumption by the colonial governor, WIC employees, and visiting officials and ambassadors. The oil study nonetheless serves to remind us of the colonial reality, with its uneasy mix of ethnic groups, its latent violence, and its unequal relationships of power and desire. Eckhout did not record the name of this woman, but his image allows a visual echo of her presence to persist.

NOTES

This essay is a revised version of a paper presented in 2004 at the conference "Invisible Subjects? Slave Portraiture in the Circum-Atlantic World (1660–1890)," Dartmouth College, Hanover, N.H. While it contains new material and observations, it also draws on two of my earlier publications. See "Albert Eckhout's Paintings of the *wilde natien* of Brazil and Africa," *NKJ (Nederlands Kunsthistorisch Jaarboek/Dutch Yearbook of Art History,* Alternative Worlds), (2002): 107–37, and chapter 5 in *Visions of Savage Paradise: Albert Eckhout, Court Painter in Colonial Dutch Brazil* (Amsterdam: Amsterdam University Press, 2006). See also my dissertation, "Art and Natural History at a Colonial Court: Albert Eckhout and Georg Marcgraf in Seventeenth-Century Dutch Brazil" (Northwestern University, 2002). The traditional title "Negro Woman" goes back to the Portuguese label (Molher Negra) given by Zacharias Wagener to his circa 1641 watercolor copy of Eckhout's painting (discussed later in this essay). See also Rebecca P. Brienen, *Albert Eckhout: Visões do Paraíso Selvagem: Obra Completa* (revised and expanded edition of *Visions of Savage Paradise)*, Rio de Janeiro: Capivara Press, 2010.

1 I have excluded the lost painting of Johan Maurits with Brazilians (Tupinambas) and the *Tapuya Dance* (no date) from this discussion. See chapter 6 in *Visions of Savage Paradise*.

2 In his recent work on exoticism, cultural anthropologist Peter Mason understood this oil study as a flexible model or framework for the creation of other paintings in Eckhout's series. He suggests that the image prepares "the way not for one composition but for a series of compositions ... [which] implies a high degree of indeterminacy, a relatively unspecific form that becomes increasingly specific through the addition of further detail

(the jewelry, the child, the vegetation, the basket, etc.)." See Peter Mason, *Infelicities: Representations of the Exotic* (Baltimore: Johns Hopkins University Press, 1998), 44–45.

3 Although the Swedish botanist Carolus Linnaeus was the first scientist to include human beings with animals in his 1735 *System of Nature,* Eckhout's paintings and early-modern maps both demonstrate that human classificatory systems were already present (although without a clearly articulated "scientific" basis) in the seventeenth century. See Valerie Traub, "Mapping the Global Body," in *Early Modern Visual Culture: Representation, Race, and Empire in Renaissance England,* ed. Peter Erickson and Clark Hulse (Philadelphia: University of Pennsylvania Press, 2000), 44–97.

4 Recent important publications on casta paintings include Magali M. Carrera, *Imagining Identity in New Spain: Race, Lineage, and the Colonial Body in Portraiture and Casta Paintings* (Austin: University of Texas Press, 2003), and Ilona Katzew, *Casta Painting: Images of Race in Eighteenth-Century Mexico* (New Haven: Yale University Press, 2004).

5 There is some debate among Eckhout scholars regarding the site where the paintings were actually made. Those who believe that they were created in Europe suggest that the signatures and dates on the paintings were added later. For a discussion of both sides of the debate, see my *Visions of Savage Paradise,* especially chapters 1 and 6.

6 In all of the paintings of the men, the light falls from the left; in all of the paintings of the women, except the African woman, the light falls from the right. The idea that all of the men and women form "mating" pairs is also challenged by the fact that the "mixed" pair is made up of a mameluca and a mulatto and by the fact that Eckhout's African man and woman each reference different regions of western Africa.

7 The labels currently applied to the paintings are derived from seventeenth-century descriptions of the works (by Johan Maurits van Nassau-Siegen and Zacharias Wagener) and inventories (made after 1654 when they entered the collection of the king of Denmark).

8 Denise Daum has recently argued, following Viktoria Schmidt-Linsenhoff, that Eckhout's paintings are better called "ethnographische typenportraits," because this term brings better attention to the ambivalence of their construction and makes clearer the fact that these images are not portraits of individuals but of ethnic groups. See Denise Daum, *Albert Eckhouts 'gemalte Kolonie': Bild- und Wissenproduktion über Niederländisch-Brasilien um 1640* (Marburg: Jonas Verlag, 2009), 106–7.

9 Many scholars have called attention to Eckhout's naturalistic style and his ability to create representations that appear to be both realistic and unmediated. See Paul Vandenbroek, *Beeld van de andere, vertoog over het zelf* (Antwerp: Koninklijk Museum voor Schone Kunst, 1987); Peter Mason, "Portrayal and Betrayal: The Colonial Gaze in Seventeenth-Century Brazil," *Culture and History* 6 (1989), 37–62; and most recently Viktoria Schmidt-Linsenhoff, "Rhetorik der Hautfarben: Albert Eckhouts Brasilien-Bilder," in *Zeitsprünge. Forschugen zur Fruhen Neuzeit* 7 (2003), 286–312.

10 Ann Jensen Adams, *Public Faces and Private Identities in Seventeenth Century Holland: Portraiture and the Production of Community* (Cambridge: Cambridge University Press, 2009), 25.

11 This trend is especially evident in printed images of Africans. See the illustrations to Johann Theodor de Bry's *India Orientalis* (collection of travel accounts related to the East and Africa) and to Johan Nieuhof, *Gedenkwaerdige zee en landtreize* (1682).

12 See Peter Hulme, *Colonial Encounters, Europe and the Native Caribbean, 1492–1797* (London: Methuen, 1986), 57.

13 See Brian Wallis, "Black Bodies, White Science: Louis Agassiz's Slave Daguerreotypes," *American Art* (summer 1995), 39–61. As he argues, "the typological photograph is a form of representational colonialism" (54).

14 See Johan Maurits van Nassau-Siegen, letter of 26 July 1679, to Resident Le Marie in Copenhagen, Archive of Johan Maurits (A4), 1477, Koninklijk Huisarchief (KHA).

15 Van den Boogaart, "The Slow Progess of Colonial Civility: Indians in the Pictorial Record of Dutch Brazil, 1637–1644," in *Imagen del indio en la Europa Moderna* (Seville: CSIC, 1990), 403. Europeans are present in the backgrounds of the paintings of the Tupinamba man and the Tupinamba woman. In the former, they ride in a boat and observe Indian women bathing, and in the latter a man and woman appear on the balcony of their plantation house and look out over their lands. For a complete discussion of these works, see chapter 4 in my *Visions of Savage Paradise.* The European presence is also made clear in the backgrounds of the *African Woman and Child* and the *Mulatto Man,* whose seascapes include European ships. In her recent essay, Schmidt-Linsenhoff pays considerable attention to the white gaze and how it determines the meaning of the varieties of skin color depicted in the paintings (see note 10 above). She does not address the internal gaze of control exerted by the white colonists in the backgrounds of the works mentioned above.

16 As noted by Whitehead and Boeseman, *A Portrait of Dutch 17th Century Brazil: Animals, Plants, and People by the Artists of Johan Maurits of Nassau* (Amsterdam: North Holland, 1989), 71.

17 Nonetheless, Eckhout's oil sketches include multiple examples of these and other types of South American animals. Eckhout's *Tapuya Dance,* which may have been part of the same decorative cycle along with Eckhout's twelve still lifes and his eight ethnographic portraits, does include an armadillo.

18 Vandenbroek argues that this manner of presentation transforms the people – alongside the plants and animals – into natural history study material. See Vandenbroek, *Beeld van de andere,* 38. According to Peter Mason, "The close juxtaposition of animals and humans in the Eckhout paintings may also imply some kind of mental bracketing in which the colonial I is separated off from the exotic, animal-like, primitive Other." See Mason "Portrayal and Betrayal," 53.

19 See Ernst van den Boogaart, "The Dutch West India Company and the Tarairiu 1631–1654," in *Johan Maurits van Nassau-Siegen, 1604–1679: A Humanist Prince in Europe and Brazil* (The Hague: Johan Maurits van Nassau Stichting, 1979) 519–38, and "The Slow Progress of Colonial Civility: Indians in the Pictorial Record of Dutch Brazil, 1637–1644," in *La Imagen del Indio en la Europa Moderna* (Seville: CSIC, 1990). This interpretive framework has been followed and expanded upon by subsequent authors, including Paul Vandenbroek, Peter Mason, and myself.

20 As Mason has noted, to be "civilized" means to be "docile and amenable to European domination." See his "Portrayal and Betrayal," 45.

21 The hairstyle and facial hair of the man demonstrate a European influence. He also wears shorts and carries a European knife.

22 Mason, "Portrayal and Betrayal," 49.

23 Van den Boogaart states: "They are decently dressed albeit barefoot"; "The Slow Progress of Colonial Civility," 402. See also Bodo-Michael Baumunk, "Von Brasilischen fremden Völkern. Die Eingeborenen-Darstellungen Albert Eckhouts," in *Mythen der neuen Welt. Zur Entdeckungsgeschichte Lateinamerikas,* ed. K. H. Kohl (Berlin: Fröhlich & Kaufmann, 1982), 192. Mason argues that the image of the Mameluca conveys a "more Europeanised sensuality" ("Portrayal and Betrayal," 55).

24 Van den Boogaart "The Slow Progress of Colonial Civility," 402.

25 Technical analysis by Danish researchers has demonstrated that the stripes in her skirt were originally blue, not black as they currently appear.

26 There has been a general assumption in the literature that the lighter skin color automatically means that the child is of mixed race. This need not be the case.

Eckhout may have assumed that black children attained the dark skin of their parents over time; he may have observed such differences in skin color among the members of the colony's community; or he may have adhered to the theory that skin color is based on the quality and duration of one's exposure to the sun.

27 This gesture – both phallic and erotic – has been recognized as such in the literature. See Baumunk, "Von Brasilischen fremden Völkern," 188–99, and Mason, "Portrayal and Betrayal," 37–62.

28 See C. Ferrão and J. P. M. Soares, eds., *Dutch Brazil: "The Thierbuch" and "Autobiography" of Zacharias Wagener*, vol. 2 (Rio de Janeiro, 1997). Unless otherwise indicated, all subsequent references to the *Thierbuch* will use this edition.

29 Later he became "opperhoofd" of the VOC (Dutch East India Company) factory at Deshima.

30 Scholars who believe that Eckhout made his paintings in Europe argue that Wagener based his drawings on lost preparatory studies, not on the finished oil paintings on canvas.

31 See, for example, the catalog for the 2004 Eckhout show at the Mauritshuis, Quentin Buvelot, ed., *Albert Eckhout: A Dutch Artist in Brazil* (The Hague: Maurtishuis, 2004). Wagener's captions for his watercolors are reproduced in conjunction with Eckhout's paintings.

32 He writes "Omen Negro" and "Molher Negra" (the Portuguese are "homen negro" and "mulher negra"). See Wagener, *Thierbuch*, 218.

33 Ibid., 174.

34 Ibid.

35 Ibid., 175.

36 For images of free Africans wearing striped cloth, see Ezio Bassani, ed., *Un cappuccino nell'Africa nera del seicento: I disegni dei Manoscritti Araldi del Padre Giovanni Antonio Cavazzi da Montecuccolo* (Milan: Associazione "Poro," 1987). There has been much recent work on West African cloth production (styles, materials, etc.) and their consumption of European cloth in the seventeenth century. Evidence suggests that checkered and striped cloth was made locally and imported from abroad. The slaves in Nieuhof wear striped cloth, but these images may have been influenced by Eckhout's paintings.

37 See Diane Wolfthal, *Images of Rape: The "Heroic" Tradition and Its Alternatives* (Cambridge: Cambridge University Press, 1999), 189–92.

38 On the iconography of the black page see also David Bindman's and Marcia Pointon's essays in this volume.

39 Daum, *Albert Eckhouts "gemalte Kolonie,"* 85.

40 Elmer Kolfin notes that jewelry becomes a common attribute of slave women in the eighteenth century; he reproduces this image in his study of slave imagery from Surinam. See his *Van de slavenzweep en de muze: twee eeuwen verbeelding van slavernij in Suriname* (Leiden: KITLV, 1997).

41 Pieter de Marees, *Beschryvinhe ende historische verhael van het Gout koninckrijck van Gunea anders de Gout-Custe de Mina genaemt liggende in het deel van Africa*, ed. S. P. L'Honore Naber (The Hague: M. Nijhoff, 1912). Unless otherwise indicated, translations into English will come from the following edition: *Pieter de Marees, Description and Historical Account of the Gold Kingdom of Guinea*, trans. Albert van Dantzig and Adam Jones (New York: Oxford University Press, 1987).

42 De Marees, *Description and Historical Account*, 236.

43 Van Dantzig and Jones were the first to note the similarity of this description to both the sword in the painting and the African sword owned by Johan Maurits, now in the collection of the National Museum in Copenhagen.

44 See Doran Ross, "The Iconography of Asante Sword Ornaments," in *African Arts* 9 (1977), 16.

45 Barbara Berlowicz, conservator at the National Museum of Copenhagen, has demonstrated that this hairstyle is original and does not represent overpainting from a later period. Conversation with Barbara Berlowicz at the National Museum conservation lab in Denmark, 1999.

46 In earlier illustrations, there is no attention to Africa's skin color, and she wears an elephant hat (as discussed in Ripa's description).

47 For an authoritative discussion of the iconography of the four parts of the world, see *Reallexikon zur Deutschen Kunstgeschichte*, part V (Stuttgart: Alfred Druckenmuller Verlag, 1967), 1108–1202. A fairly exotic personification of African with a turban may be seen in Frans Francken II, *Allegory on the Abdication of the Emperor Charles V at Brussels, October 25, 1555*, ca. 1636, in the Rijksmuseum.

48 This description of Capo Lopo Gonsalves is largely borrowed from Linchoten's *Itinerario*.

49 De Marees, *Description and Historical Account*, 238.

50 In 1642 Dom Garcia, the king of the Congo, made a gift to Johan Maurits of 200 slaves and a silver platter, now used as a baptismal patter in the Evangelische Nikolai-Kirchengemeinde in Siegen. This platter is discussed in *Zo wijd de wereld streekt* (The Hague: Stichting Johan Maurits van Nassau, 1979), 147, fig. 166.

51 See Ivan Gaskell, "Tobacco, Social Deviance, and Dutch Art in the Seventeenth Century," in *Looking at Seventeenth Century Dutch Art*, ed. Wayne Franits (Cambridge: Cambridge University Press, 1997), 68–77. I thank E. Kolfin for pointing out the connection between pipes and black slaves during the early-modern period.

52 Ibid., 75.

53 Contemporary definitions did not include the possibility that the father could be black and the mother white, although that undoubtedly occurred.

54 Schmidt-Linsenhoff, "Rhetorik der Hautfarben," 297. She correctly notes that Eckhout's Africans do not work. She also argues the same for Frans Post's Africans, which is more problematic, because in the painting *View of Itamaraca* (1637), a black slave is shown attending to a horse and another carries fruit. In his painting the *Ox Cart*, the slaves are also shown working. In addition, there are the many images of slaves associated with sugar mills in Frans Post's oeuvre. I had already noted in 2002 that the Africans in Eckhout's Africans are not pictured as New World slaves. See also Daum's critique of this (*Albert Eckhouts 'gemalte Kolonie,'* 85).

55 Robert Young, *Colonial Desire: Hybridity in Theory, Culture, and Race* (London: Routledge, 1995), 158.

56 Schmidt-Linsenhoff, "Rhetorik der Hautfarben," 297.

57 See Mason, *Infelicities*, 44–45.

58 Eckhout also used an image of a costume study in oils of an African as a reference for his final painting. Eckhout's chalk drawings of fruits and vegetables were used as studies for his still life paintings, and there are several other drawings of Indians that can be connected to images in the ethnographic series. All of these drawings are in Kraków at the Jagiellonian Library.

59 According to seventeenth-century climatological theory, he may simply be lighter because he was born in Brazil. Accounts of travel to Africa also assert that black babies are born "reddish" like the Brazilians. Indeed, his color matches that of the Tupinamba as they are pictured in Eckhout's series.

60 Wallis, "Black Bodies, White Science."

61 Discussed by Thomas Thomsen in *Albert Eckhout, Ein Niederlandisher Male und sein Gonner Moritz der Brasilianer ein Kulturbild aus dem 17. Jahrbundert* (Copenhagen: Ejnar Munksgaard, 1938), and most recently by Schmidt-Linsenhoff, "Rhetorik der Hautfarben."

NINE

EMBODYING AFRICAN KNOWLEDGE IN COLONIAL SURINAM

TWO WILLIAM BLAKE ENGRAVINGS IN STEDMAN'S 1796 *NARRATIVE*

Susan Scott Parrish

The goal of this volume is to place what appear to be two mutually exclusive phenomena into critical conversation with each other in order to understand the actual and historical nature of their connection. This volume asks whether portraiture, which developed in tandem with European concepts of individual human secular identity, was a genre that could not have as its subject an enslaved person who was by law deprived of self-ownership. My analysis will focus on two engravings produced by William Blake from the watercolors John Gabriel Stedman made in the Dutch colony of Surinam between 1772 and 1777. Stedman served as a captain in a Scottish regiment that was engaged by the Dutch to suppress the insurgency of the maroons. Maroons were escaped slaves who lived in small mobile units just beyond the plantations and who periodically raided these plantations for captives and booty. One engraving shows a group on a march through wilderness terrain; the African figures represented here inhabit an indeterminate zone between slavery and freedom. The other engraving exhibits a former slave of African descent who won his freedom by masterfully aligning himself with colonial self-interests.

Both of these engravings are portraits, I want to argue. Unlike aristocratic and genteel portrait paintings made in Europe that included enslaved, highly assimilated or exotically costumed, and often juvenile Africans, whose function was by contrast to establish the civility and prestige of the more important white and named subject of the portrait, these images of Africans made in the volatile, slave-majority, colonial settings of the Caribbean rim document the possibilities of African self-determination and self-fashioning. Not only were the conditions of slavery more intense in the Americas than in Europe, but these conditions were at their most explosive in colonies like Surinam. The average sugar estate there had a slave population of 228, a number 17 times that of tobacco plantations in Virginia and Maryland. The overall ratio of Africans to Europeans was 25 to 1, but reached the disparity of 65 to 1 in plantation districts. It was not only a racially polarized society, but was, by the later eighteenth century, in the words of one contemporary European observer, "the theater of a perpetual war" between European authorities (including, as their agents, both white and black foot soldiers) and African maroon resisters. Because the extreme brutality of this society and its proximity to a dense tropical jungle made various forms of marronage chronic and destabilizing, there were paradoxically both more chances of death but also more paths to liberty in Surinam than in North American mainland colonies. Blake's engravings of slave torture and martyrdom are well known; less well known are his portraits of tactical resistance.[1]

Recent theorists of portraiture outline a number of factors that are typically present in the genre: an intended reference to or copy of a particular and identifiable person, a subject's participation in or even initiation of the image-making situation, and a rhetorical staging of identity for an anticipated audience. Along with these features, according to Marcia Pointon in her essay in this volume, "it is the space the subject is shown to inhabit and the material attributes represented within that space alongside him or her that articulate identity." Pointon, borrowing from Pierre Bourdieu, calls this the subject's "habitus." This is a "site for mythicization – and hence for identity that transcends questions of likeness." In other words, a rendering of the sitter's material environment does not so much copy his or her unique individuality as participate in the sitter's material staging of broader social practices of taste. Pointon argues that "for the slave subject, the habitus is either nonexistent or borrowed": "If a slave belongs to another, he or she cannot be associated with any place other than that of the owner or master."[2]

Bourdieu used the term "habitus" in a 1979 study of France to designate the complex process by which an individual's social, and specifically economic, position manifested itself in material taste and bodily practice, such that group identity is confirmed and perpetuated through relatively unconscious individual disposition. What seems so strikingly different about individuals in a colonial slave society, though, is how volatile were categories of identity or status and how they were tied inextricably to issues of race and powers of environmental control. Modern European concepts such as class are inadequate for understanding identity in such a setting. For the slave subject in Surinam, habitus as defined in modern European terms would have been "borrowed." If the concept of habitus could be stretched, however, to include not only consumer behavior in a global market, but also the control over one's physical environment through nature knowledge – a category more germane to the society under consideration – one would find that representations of Africans in Surinam did visualize the places out of which subjects made identity.[3]

In the two images under consideration here, Stedman and Blake depart from the more typical representational idiom of the *Narrative* in which the slave figures are sources of sympathetic and erotic stimulation. Critics have rightly responded to the rhetoric of white imperial sympathy in the text and engravings by revealing its false consciousness. Marcus Wood, for example, in analyzing the frontispiece image (engraved by Franceso Bartolozzi) (Fig. 9.1), argues that because of the manner in which this image "simultaneously sentimentalizes, sexualizes and trans-sexualizes the body of the black victim at the moment of death," we ought to see it as having "pornographic elements." Moreover, the accounts and images of slave abuse are "sentimental artifacts ... designed to be enjoyed ... as fantastic spaces, or spaces for fantasy." While I agree with Wood's reading of these images, I think it is important to reckon with those representations of Africans in the *Narrative* that are not meant to elicit an eroticized pity. The first image I will analyze was intended by Stedman, in its watercolor version, to be an image of *European* suffering at the hands of better adapted Africans, and their more expert territorial tactics. In Blake's engraving, it ends up being a portrait of superior African environmental control. The second image reflects on and satirizes the shape this African environmental mastery takes once removed from the tropical forest. When the subject's mastery of place turns into a mastery of European cultural codes, he becomes the target of visual satire.[4]

Before turning to the engravings by Blake that portray this alternate, and even resistant, territorial experience and nature-knowledge of New World Africans (hence providing that verifying habitus often present in portraiture), I need to explain the nature of that territorial experience more thoroughly. Without such information – information Blake no doubt received verbally from Stedman's face-to-face and written narration as well as from his original watercolor – we will not be able to comprehend Blake's engravings. I use the phrases "New World Africans" and "Diasporic Africans" as necessary short-hand terms, behind which was a complex and uneven process of retention, assimilation, and syncretization. Africans who arrived in the Americas came from a multitude of geographical and hence cultural locales in West and Central Africa; moreover, the Middle Passage shuffled these groupings into a heterogeneous mix, which were vulnerable to still more change upon arrival in the Americas. Most historians agree, however, that retentions, though dynamically syncretized, would have been strongest in concentrated large slave or maroon societies found in Jamaica, Brazil, and Surinam.[5]

Historians of plantation slavery in the Americas have asserted that enslaved Africans did have an experience and knowledge of their environment – a sense of place – that was distinct from the Euro-Americans whom they served. Colonials not only perceived this alternate African experience, but they made

"From different Parents, different Climes we came,
At different Periods;" Fate still rules the same.
Unhappy Youth while bleeding on the ground;
'Twas Yours to fall—but Mine to feel the wound.

9.1. Franceso Bartolozzi. Frontispiece from John Gabriel Stedman, *Narrative of a five years' expedition against the Revolted Negroes of Surinam* . . ., 2 vols. (London: Printed for J. Johnson . . . & J. Edwards, 1796). Engraving. Special Collections Library, University of Michigan, Ann Arbor.

use of African environmental knowledge in manifold ways: Africans worked as territorial guides, as experts in rice culture, as collectors of specimens, and as healers adept in the use of local plants. Their various forms of expertise were not only understood locally but were also recorded in transatlantic letters as well as printed in books and scientific journals published in European centers. Inasmuch as artists working or traveling in the Americas understood this colonial epistemic situation, they could represent that habitus out of which the once-alien Africans had formed their identities. Africans' connections to their new environments did not only, potentially, create a sense of belonging to a spiritually ripe place, but also could enable them to produce knowledge that afforded them varying degrees of agency. Because Africans brought with them a cultural conviction about heeding and knowing their immediate environment, they were able to broach and manipulate to their own ends this initially alien natural world.[6]

Africans in the Americas were more typically associated with those aspects of nature deemed "hidden" or "secret" because their labor and dwelling conditions put them closer to sequestered parts of the landscape not typically accessed by white colonial writers. In the Caribbean, maroon communities and short-term runaways knew the mountainous retreats of their islands. In a letter sent from Jamaican planter James Theobald to the Royal Society of London's president, Earle of Macclesfield, in 1757, Theobald described how maroons would emerge from their "scarce acceptable retreats" to plunder plantations. Bryan Edwards, in his 1796 *Observations ... on the Maroon Negroes of the Island of Jamaica*, wrote that "the Spanish inhabitants are said to have possessed, before the attack, about fifteen hundred enslaved Africans, most of whom, on the surrender of their masters, retreated to the mountains, from whence they made frequent excursions to harass the English." They "skulked about the skirts of remote plantations ... [and] knew every secret avenue of the country; ... nor had anything to lose, except life, and a wild and savage freedom." According to Stedman, the Cottica rebels' settlement in Surinam was "naturally surrounded by a broad infoardable Marsh or Swamp which prevented all Communication except by private paths under water known only to the Rebels"; a separate settlement of rebels, surrounded "by Ma[r]shes, Quagmires, mud, and water, is such that it fortifies them, from any attempts of Europeans whatever, nay they are even Indiscoverable by negroes, except by their own, So thick and impenetrable is the forest on that Spot, and overchoaked with thorns-briers, and underwood of every Species."[7]

Not only maroons, but also plantation slaves came to be associated with the cane breaks and woods "far from the plantation houses and the routes of the slave patrols," where their magical religious practices were carried out in secret. In Virginia, slaves gathered in the woods, marshes, and swamps away from the "prying eyes of white owners or overseers," and came to know these areas "more intimately than did their masters." In the Carolina low-country, "whites even recognized that slaves were sometimes more familiar with their property than they themselves were" because of both planter absenteeism as well as the nature of slave labors. For slaves involved in rice culture, which relied heavily on inland swamp irrigation systems, knowledge of swamp territory would have been strong. Moreover, the river networks running between plantations and connecting interior territories to ports were best known to those people of African birth or descent who worked the boats, bearing tobacco, indigo, rice, messages, and people, and who brought skills of river navigation with them from Africa. John Michael Vlach has described slaves' intimate knowledge of the nonpublic byways of the plantation grounds and the inter-plantation territory; in particular, he writes that "the black system of place definition positively embraced the random and meandering givens of the natural world." Virginia historian Rhys Isaac calls this phenomenon "an alternative territorial system."[8]

Slaves used in patrols came likewise to an intimate knowledge of the woods: In his 1774 description of Jamaica, Edward Long observed that West Indian blacks "are remarkable, like the North American Indians, for tracking in the woods; discerning the vestige of the person, or party, of whom they are in quest, by the turn of a dried leaf, the position of a small twig, and other insignificant marks, which an European would overlook." Africans used in patrols also used this territorial knowledge to further their own interests. According to the Dutch Captain Ernst Godfried Hentschel who led an anti-maroon expedition consisting of 500 men in Surinam in 1755, enslaved patrol guides used their knowledge of the woods and their awareness of the value of their labor to resist his authority and undermine the success of the campaign against the maroons. "In the morning," he wrote, "when the march ought to have begun, there were 22 Negroes missing, bearers as well as musketeers.... These negroes have shown themselves very unwilling on several occasions, and when they were seriously put to work several of them threatened to run off into the forest at the first opportunity. Daily, most of the negroes show increasing reluctance to march farther." "The runaways are constantly swarming around us, yelling out to us that we shall never get to the top of the mountain at the fourth village.... The runaways aim mostly at the whites, seldom shooting at Negroes.... The Negro musketeers ... will not go out ahead, and when attacked, they go hide, and then it takes hours of effort to get them together again. The bearers are even cleverer. They throw their burdens to the ground and run and hide, so that a considerable amount of provisions is lost." Moreover, "the Negroes hide the food in the secondary growth and go back to get it later. They all provide themselves with food and say that if the commander does not march back to Paramaribo, they will be able to find the way by themselves." In fact, it was customary throughout the eighteenth century for 50 percent of the slaves on larger expeditions to desert.

Not only could slave guides and porters gain freedom through desertion, but they could, if they proved themselves trustworthy, gain manumission to become Rangers. Stedman wrote that in the midst of one campaign in 1773, he was "obliged to make Slaves to Soldiers." In 1772 the colonial government formed the elite "Neeger Vrijcorps," or, Corps of Rangers, by purchasing and freeing plantation slaves.[9]

The campaigns against the maroons that Stedman participated in between 1772 and 1777 were, according to the Prices, "characterized by the colonial troops' criss-crossing, more or less blindly, vast expanses of treacherous forests and swamps, with the maroons – through an efficient system of spies and lookouts – almost always remaining at least a step ahead, and often setting fatal ambushes for their pursuers." It was only the Ranger Corps who, in the words of Stedman, figured out "and discovered to the Europeans" "by their indefatigable efforts" how to penetrate the Cottica rebels' marshy stronghold via "underwater Paths of Communication," even though several were "shot and drowned in the execution." On another occasion, in June of 1773, one maroon group, signaled by their spies, laid in ambush for the colonial troops: "no sooner were these unfortunate Men got in the Swamp till near theyr armpits than their black Enemies rushed out from under Cover and shot them dead at pleasure in the water." On the superior orientation of the black Rangers over the European troops, Stedman wrote: "*one* of these free negroes ... was Preferable to half a Dozen White men in the *Woods* of Guiana, which Seemed their natural Element, While it was the bane of the Europeans."[10]

It was just such a history of these forests and swamps – used to hide rebel strongholds and resistant slave porters and musketeers, deciphered by black Rangers, and suffered through by ill-adapted colonial forces – that Stedman and Blake sought to represent in the engraving I would now like to consider: *March thro' a swamp or Marsh in Terra-firma* (Fig. 9.2). Stedman describes the scene of the engraving in a way that reflects just such an agonistic relation between disoriented European troops and a South American forest environment well manipulated by the maroons and well navigated by slave guides:

> The First Figure Represents *Col. Fourgeoud* Preseded by a negro Slave as a Guide, to give Notice when the watter is too Deep, And followed by some of his Officers and Private Marines, Wading through the Marsh in a heavy shower of Rayn till Above Their Middles, and Carrying their Ammonition & their Accoutrements Above their Heads as they Can, to Prevent them from Dragging through the Swamp While in the Offing may be seen how the Slaves Carry the Burdens, And in What manner sometimes the rebel Negroes fire on the Troops, out of the Palm trees &c And which Situation of Marching is Certainly the most Dangerous in Surinam where they may be Attacked from under the Surrounding Bushes, without being Able to

9.2. William Blake, attributed, after J. G. Stedman, *March thro' a swamp or Marsh in Terra-firma.* Engraving from John Gabriel Stedman, *Narrative of a five years' expedition against the Revolted Negroes of Surinam …*, 2 vols. (London: Printed for J. Johnson … & J. Edwards, 1796), vol. 1, facing page 104. Special Collections Library, University of Michigan, Ann Arbor.

> Return the fire more than once, Since in such a Depth of Watter no Soldier Can Load his Musquet Without Wetting the Lock, And Who generally is Already too much Animated by the heat of the Action.

Stedman's commander, Colonel Fourgeoud, is the most pernicious figure in Stedman's *Narrative*. Pitiless, precipitate, and tyrannical, Fourgeoud is the character against whom Stedman develops his own signal trait of manly sympathy.[11]

Interestingly, a watercolor similar or identical to the one Blake worked from was given by Stedman to Fourgeoud as a present. Fourgeoud sent it on to the Prince of Orange (a personal friend) and the Duke of Brunswick "as a Proof of What he and his Troops Underwent in Surinam." Stedman worked hard while in Surinam to sustain his patronage network (both military and social) through gifts of watercolor portraits. In his private diary and his *Narrative* (printed twenty years after the fact), however, he repeatedly criticized the plantocracy and military commanders. Presumably, then, Blake or Stedman changed the expression on Fourgeoud's face to depict what Stedman wanted publicly to convey about his military master. The portrait of Fourgeoud was meant originally to convince those rulers in the distant metropole of their countrymen's suffering on the front lines of empire; it was a portrait of white military martyrdom rhetorically presented to elicit relief. If, in the frontispiece, the white soldier suffers *on behalf of* his black victim, in this image the white soldiers are buffeted by the combined assaults of forest and black foe. Consequently, the engraving is necessarily a portrait of African territorially based subterfuge.[12]

Unlike the place information at the bottom of the frame of other portraits in the *Narrative* that barely anchors subjects in their environments, the swamp, woods, and rain-crossed sky in this image leave no flat whiteness against which to objectify figures: Here is environmental overload. In such a place, it is the African figures, both slave and rebel, aligned along that vertical axis characteristic of the tropical forest, who fit in. The rebels, shooting from above, in the upper left segment of the image, are camouflaged by the palm leaves; shot issuing forth from their muskets is indistinguishable from – even allied with – the rain as both assault the troops. The bearer (whose kind Hentschel found "even cleverer" than the black musketeers at hiding and generally confounding the expedition) is hard to distinguish visually from the bushes behind him. The guide is likewise camouflaged by Blake's placement of the dark outgrowth of bushes, which seem aberrantly to obtrude into the marsh almost for that very purpose. In contrast to this subtle visibility, the European soldiers, by virtue of their white skin, shirtfronts, and pants, stand out from the densely plaited environment and are hence easy targets. The ligneous ropes or *nebees*, which appear to form a protective canopy above the soldiers' heads, are in fact, Stedman tells us elsewhere, poisonous. Rather than an assertion of superior technology, the soldiers' muskets instead serve visually to pen the four white foreground figures into a restrictive parallelogram. While Fourgeoud's hand seems to command the slave guide by virtue of its being raised (hierarchically) above his head, the tip of his finger cannot break the vertically oriented axis of African environmental control, which does in fact occupy the uppermost regions of the forest canopy. Even though the choice to render Fourgeoud in stark profile could suggest a classical tradition of the honorific medallion (perhaps evident in the original watercolor), Blake instead uses the profile (as well as the pinched and fervid facial expression) to forestall our sympathy with the human thus portrayed, much as he does in his engraving of the debauched and tyrannical "Planter in his Morning Dress." The figure just behind and to the right of Fourgeoud I believe to be Stedman himself; it bears such a likeness to Stedman's frontispiece self-portrait. Significantly, he is also rendered in profile, but one that is diametrically opposed to Fourgeoud's; his handsome youthful face and flowing curls are reminiscent of medallions of the Apollo Belvedere, inviting our admiration rather than our criticism.[13]

Though the slave guide seems positioned under the very hand of authority, his better conditioned eye, his body's superior familiarity with the environment, and his linkage with a hidden network of rebels ironize the peremptory hand above him. Though his expression is oriented around an upward-turned gaze, it is absent of the quality of supplication placed into the eyes of black servants, pages, novitiates, and other supposed devotees of white mastery one sees everywhere in the pictorial representations of diasporic Africans in this period. His eyes – unlike the misdirected gazes of the soldiers – are no doubt searching out other rebels secreted aloft in the palms. His body, though placed in the lowest segment of the frame, is also closest to us, and in a sense draws us in more than the other faces, which are turned in profile, bisected by a musket, or positioned in the distance. Last, the fact that we see his presumably naked (and hence potentially erotic) body only from the chest up turns his figure into a bust, which, like the classical medallion, served to honor the body depicted rather than objectify or satirize it.[14]

Describing the painter George Robertson's 1770s images of Jamaica, Geoff Quilley remarks of the engraved version of *A View in the Island of Jamaica* (1778), that "it is remarkable how at home [the enslaved Africans] appear in this threatening environment." This does not, however, according to Quilley, amount to a critique of the Africans' displacement to the Caribbean plantation locale; rather the image allows "the picturesque" to obviate or deflect thinking about the politics of slavery. In Blake's and Stedman's image of the anti-maroon expedition in swamp territory, by contrast, the artists portray the Africans' better habitation in this environment in order to display diasporic Africans' strategies of resistance to colonial authorities. Africans understood that it was especially through the mastery of the terrain not circumscribed by plantation borders that offered them some measure of control over their lives, if not absolute freedom.

In this engraving, not only do we see a surreptitious territoriality that eludes the presumably panoptic visual control of colonial power, but we see Africans taking on the prime position for surveillance. The two figures in the trees mark out their human targets before firing, perhaps informed ahead of time by an "efficient system of spies and lookouts." In the swamp, it appears to be the slave guide who has the most potential for visual awareness – for decoding the optics of this encounter. If we come to comprehend his gaze rightly – that it is not one of supplication but rather of surveillance – and we manage to discover the camouflaged marksmen in the trees, Blake and Stedman will have taught us better tactics of identification than the soldiers possess. Unlike the frontispiece, which encourages us – oxymoronically – to *feel for* the dead African, this image trains us to *think like* a live and strategically dominant African. Much like Herman Melville's later novella *Benito Cereno* (1855), which slyly tests its readers' powers of detection and reveals the befogged dangers of liberal sympathy, this engraving works against the very dynamics of voyeuristic and erotic sympathy encouraged in the *Narrative's* engravings of black suffering.[15]

The other Blake/Stedman image I want now to consider shows an African figure who parlayed his comprehension and manipulation of the natural world into not only manumission but even transatlantic prestige (Fig. 9.3). That this prestige provoked satire on the part of Stedman and Blake is of particular interest. The subject of this portrait seems to have gone by the name Kwasimukamba at his birthplace on the coast of Guinea circa 1690. After being captured and brought to Surinam as a slave sometime around 1700, he became known to his masters and fellow slaves as either Kwasi or, more importantly, Gramman (or Greatman) Quacy. By the end of his turbulent life, when he was a free man living in his own planter's house in Paramaribo with his own three slaves, he received letters from such places as the Hague and Uppsala addressed "To the Most Honorable and Most Learned Gentleman, Master Phillipus of Quassie, Professor of Herbology in Suriname."[16]

What we know of Kwasi's history, we know on the one hand from European sources, in particular Stedman and Hentschel, and on the other hand from late-twentieth-century descendants of escaped slaves, the Saramaka, who earned their freedom through armed struggle and negotiations with colonial authorities in 1762 and who have memorialized their "first-time" through oral transmission. Kwasi was a principal healer and diviner for both slaves and colonials in Surinam, and, Stedman tells us, he got the name of a "*Loocoman*, or *Sorcerer*, among the vulgar Slaves, [so that] no Crime of any Consequence is Committed at the Plantations but *Graman* Quacy ... is Sent for to Discover the Perpetrator." The slaves have so much "Faith in his Conjurations" that he need only look them in the face for the guilty party to admit his or her crime. He "not only has done a Deal of Good to the Colony but fill'd his Pockets with no inconsiderable Profits ... while his Person is Adored & Respected like a God."

9.3. William Blake after J. G. Stedman, *The celebrated Graman Quacy*. Engraving from John Gabriel Stedman, *Narrative of a five years' expedition against the Revolted Negroes of Surinam . . .*, 2 vols. (London: Printed for J. Johnson . . . & J. Edwards, 1796), vol. 2, facing page 348. Special Collections Library, University of Michigan, Ann Arbor.

Stedman dismisses Kwasi's *obias* (protective charms) as mere "trash" made up of "Small Pebles, Egg Shells, Cut-hair, Fish bones &c.," but also calls them "Artful Contrivances" and demonstrates their efficacy in colonial policy by describing the "Barbacued hands" of two maroons recently brought in by black Rangers emboldened like "bull dogs" by Kwasi's charms.[17]

Kwasi had such power over Africans on the plantations because they believed him to have a special knowledge of and hence control over the *pharmacosm* of Surinam. As explained earlier, Africans had brought with them from across the Atlantic, in dynamic and uneven ways, a belief that the natural and spiritual worlds were wholly intertwined, that the natural world possessed both toxins and antidotes, and that this world was neither inert nor beyond human mediation. They believed that certain adept humans could control such a spiritually infused cosmos either to harm or heal, to foresee the future, or to divine hidden truths about the past. Kwasi, more than any other figure within Surinam plantation culture in the second half of the eighteenth century, was understood to possess such powers.[18]

Not only did Kwasi understand how to operate within the Africans' *pharmacosm*, but he also grasped how to advance himself within transatlantic Enlightenment science. Kwasi knew that his European masters were foremost dedicated to turning the natural realm in Surinam into commodities that could be traded within a world market and hence needed to control the heated resistance of the enslaved and maroon populations in Surinam; he perceived too their interest in placing natural specimens into a universal system of organization. Around 1730, Kwasi came to understand the healing properties of the roots of a local tree. In 1761 a Swedish immigrant, Mr. D'Ahlberg, wrote a letter to his famous countryman, Carolus Linnaeus, telling him of Kwasi's discovery of the root that was esteemed "for its Efficacy in strength'ning the stomach, Restoring the Appetite &c." Linnaeus named the tree *Quassia amara* in the African's honor. In Surinam, where it became a major pharmacological export, it was called "Quassiehout" or "Kwasi-bita." Kwasi was rewarded for his various works by his colonial masters: Around the time of his root discovery in 1730, he was given a golden breastplate with the inscription "Quassie, faithful to the whites" by a member of the Suriname Council and became the slave to Governor Mauricius in 1744. Then, Stedman continued: "by his insinnuating temper and industry this negro not only Obtained his Freedom from a State of Slavery time out of mind, but by his Wonderful artifice & ingenuity has found the means of Acquiring a verry Competant Subsistance." The governor sent Kwasi to The Hague in 1776 to pay a visit to Willem V, Prince of Orange, where the prince gave him, according to Stedman's diary, "a broad gold-laced coat & hat, with a white feather, a large gold medal, a gold-headed cane, & silver gilt hanger. The fellow had two chests of wine, & all free."[19]

"Qwacy might have even Amassed Riches," Stedman continued in his *Narrative*, in a more derogatory tone, "were he not in other Respects an indolent dicipating Blockhead, whereby Which he at last Fell into a Complication of Loathsome disorders of Which the Leprosy is one & which is ... incurable forever." Despite this, Stedman took Kwasi to be "one of the most Extraordinary Black men in Surinam, or Perhaps in the World." Stedman tells of the day when "the Celebrated Graman Qwacy ... Came to Show me his Coat, Gold medal, &c., Which he had got in a Present from the Prince of Orange." After this verbal description of Kwasi, Stedman offered that "Having taken a Portrait of this Extraordinary man with his Gray Head of Hair, & Dress'd in his Blew & Scarlet with Gold Lace, I here take the Liberty in the Annex'd Plate to Represent him to the Curious Reader." In this image, Kwasi would have been about eighty-six.[20]

To the Saramaka, Kwasi's story is not one of ambiguous "artifice & ingenuity" tempered by opportunistic loyalty. His is a story of unmitigated betrayal. Kwasi's encounter with the Saramaka took place beginning in 1754 on the Baakawata, a tributary of the Suriname River about three months' journey upriver from Paramaribo. Kwasi came to them of his own design pretending that he was their close friend and that he wanted to know the secret of their chief Ayako's *obia* that made him invulnerable. Ayako deceived Kwasi by telling him that "his power resided in the small stand of sugar cane" planted behind his house. Kwasi left the Saramaka and went back to the city, only to return months later with a force of 500 men. The Saramaka tell that their ancestors slew all the soldiers except for Kwasi, whom Ayako grabbed and "stretched his ear out hard.... then sliced it cleanly off! He said, 'Take this and show it to the white folks.'" "Kwasimukamba said, 'This is one hell of a thing for Kwasimukamba of Tjedu! When a person's ear is cut off, his face is spoiled!' And he left for the city." The modern Saramaka believe that Kwasimukamba is the reason "you must not trust them with a single thing about the forest. City people! They fought against us along with the whites." If you look closely at Blake's image of Kwasi, you will indeed not be able to find his right ear.[21]

Of these incidents, Kwasi related to colonial authorities that he had been kidnapped by the Saramaka in 1754 while looking for plant medicines on Cassewinica Creek and used as a servant for about a year. Returning downriver to the plantations putatively to help the Saramaka find more captives, Kwasi was trusted by them as a kind of guide because he knew the plantation territory so well; he used this opportunity to escape from inter-African bondage back into plantation slavery. He promised to lead the whites up the Suriname River, but cautioned that the runaways have "instructions to poison all the rivers and creeks if the whites are seen to be coming." Captain Hentschel, the leader of this 1755 expedition, told yet a different story: He reported that the runaways, rather than disfiguring but ultimately sparing Kwasi, instead "cursed [him] hideously" and demanded that the soldiers turn over "two kegs of gunpowder and the guide Kwasi." After many casualties on *both* sides, according to Hentschel, the colonial forces and Kwasi returned to the city.[22]

How should one read these conflicting accounts of Kwasi's life and dealings with various figures in the eighteenth-century Atlantic world? Most important for this volume, does his being recognized as not only an African *dresiman* (curer) and *lukuman* (diviner), but also a transatlantic Enlightenment virtuoso, as well as a key politico-military operative make this representation of Kwasi a portrait, and, if so, what kind of a portrait? Stedman himself calls this engraving a "portrait" and specifically invites "the Curious Reader" to view his (and Blake's) handiwork. Summoning the metropolitan reader's curiosity suggests that Stedman viewed Kwasi as a kind of unique specimen. In the engravings, Blake presented many of the figures as singular specimens – a black Ranger, a European marine, Stedman's mulatto "wife" Joanna, an Arrowauka female, a wealthy planter – and their placement in relation to the horizon line accentuates this quality. In all these engravings, the horizon cuts laterally across these subjects' ankles or calves, implying that these figures spring from and are hence indicative of this opulent and debauched colonial environment. However, the absence of any background from the calf upward invites the viewer to inventory each body's features for signs of the curious social formation that was Surinam. Do the environments of these particular images amount to that thick material description or habitus that, according to Pointon, serves, paradoxically, to invent and authenticate presence in portraiture?

The architectural and land features behind Kwasi do indeed give more relevant contextualizing information than they do in the other images. The map of Paramaribo that Stedman provides indicates that the building to our left is the governor's mansion, while the structure on the right is Fort Zelandia; the small figures that Kwasi's heel risks squashing and that his sword appears to cut through are the "Society" (or local colonial) soldiers marching in formation. The placement of Kwasi's body between political and military structures of governance exhibits the fact that he has the indispensable corps of black Rangers "under his Command" and that he "has done a Deal of Good to the Colony" by keeping plantation slaves in line and guiding expeditions against the maroons. While he relies on the patronage of Dutch colonial rule (symbolized architecturally here), the colonial authorities rely upon the power he possesses within and over the Africans' *pharmacosm*.[23]

We know from Stedman's narration that Kwasi is, in part at least, staging his own person in this encounter. Kwasi has "Pay'd [Stedman] a visit" "to Show [him] his Coat, Gold meddal, &c.," perhaps knowing that Stedman has been making watercolors of people and estates in Surinam for years and giving many of them as tokens of gratitude to various European hosts along the way. While the other specimen subjects typically avert the gaze of the viewer, Kwasi's eyes court and beseech the viewer's favor. Just as Stedman's description of Kwasi

9.4. William Blake after J. G. Stedman, *A Coromantyn free Negro or Ranger armed*. Engraving from John Gabriel Stedman, *Narrative of a five years' expedition against the Revolted Negroes of Surinam* . . ., 2 vols. (London: Printed for J. Johnson . . . & J. Edwards, 1796), vol. 1, facing page 80. Special Collections Library, University of Michigan, Ann Arbor.

is poised between a reifying admiration ("wonderful" "Extraordinary") and a dismissive reproach ("indolent dicipating Blockhead"), the artists' figuration both memorializes Kwasi as a curiosity and satirizes him. Kwasi has dressed himself in the tokens of his successful and self-empowering assimilation, but the fact that the engraving freezes Kwasi's temporary genuflection and hat-doffing at greeting into a permanent posture of ingratiation essentially robs Kwasi of the authority that the narrative and the habitus has already established that he indeed possesses.[24]

While the free black Ranger of another Blake engraving (who, the narrative tells us, would have "Adored & Respected [Kwasi] like a God") stands in a slightly stiffened contrapposto posture, and renders the viewer inconsequential by not acknowledging his or her gaze as he looks over the viewer's right shoulder (Fig. 9.4), Kwasi's entreating face and bending knees instead prop up the viewer's own sense of authority. The motion of Kwasi's form is not compensated for by a stabilizing leg (as in the Apollo Belvedere, or in Sir Joshua Reynolds' *Lord Middleton* (1762) and *Omai* (1776) portraits). If anything, his physical imbalance connotes the reeling, inebriated foreground figure of William Hogarth's *A Midnight Modern Conversation* (1732/1733) (Fig. 9.5). Hogarth's engraving portrays a milieu of excess, where the rectilinearity of the room's architectural features are tumbled askew by the tipping this way and that of the various bodies, especially in the foreground. Stedman, from the critical distance of London of the intervening decades, and of his new posture as a "man of feeling," saw Surinam as a milieu similarly imbalanced by debauched patterns of behavioral excess. Kwasi, the "indolent dicipating Blockhead," who could profit to the point of dissipation off his allegiance to the whites, was a telling symptom of such imbalance.[25]

9.5. William Hogarth, *A Midnight Modern Conversation*, 1732/1733. Etching and engraving. British Museum, London. © Trustees of the British Museum, London.

We cannot know the nature of Blake's own imaginative contribution to this engraving because the original watercolor has been lost, but we do know that both Stedman and Blake were surrounded by a visual and theatrical culture of political satire in 1790s London. Although Blake accused a contemporary of having his "Eye ... perverted by Caricature Prints, which ought not to abound as much as they do," widely disseminated satirical prints left their mark on Blake during the period when his Prophetic Books were exploring the fallen world and he was working on Stedman's *Narrative*. While "caricature" for Hogarth or "burlesque" for Henry Fielding involved the over-reduction of a person to one salient, indicative, and even grotesque feature, both satirists strove instead for a more inclusive rendering of "Character," which could "show the whole man as a thinking and feeling being." A satirical print, David Bindman has argued, works by a logic of "unmasking." It "pretends to conceal its intentions." A satirical print ultimately subverts its apparently complementary or neutral rendering of physiognomy to reveal the hidden, flawed side of character, and hence "show the whole man" as the sum of his two sides. Stedman's and Blake's portrait of Kwasi also works by a chiasmus of legitimation and de-legitimation: It identifies the structures that ground Kwasi's authority, but then sets Kwasi's body into a frozen ingratiating motion. Stedman and Blake force Kwasi to qualify his own prestige.[26]

Not only did this satirical visual culture influence the artists, but there is a good chance that the stage also provided them with the popular comedic character of Harlequin through which to view Kwasi. In the earlier part of the century, Harlequin, the sly, black-masked servant of sixteenth-century Italian *commedia dell'arte*, became famous on the London stage through his association with the Faust legend in *The Necromancer, or, Harlequin Doctor Faustus* of 1723 (and in revival for decades thereafter), which was, according to theater historian John O'Brien, "certainly one of the most commented-upon phenomena in the public sphere." Harlequin Faustus was a "con artist who indeed might have begun his career as that most compelling and threatening of early eighteenth-century rogues, the bad apprentice." Harlequin provided entertainment through broad physical comedy; his was a body of tricks and transformations. Not only would he change form and shape, but he would transform fellow characters into animals and objects. People went to see Harlequin Faustus because he represented a kind of magic of metamorphosis unique to the theater. In the late 1720s, actor-manager Luigi Riccoboni speculated in print that Harlequin's black mask derived from "African slaves captured by Roman armies in wars of conquest and brought back to the seat of empire." At midcentury, this figure was recognizable as both a kind of indigenous English rogue, but also as an alien "sable sorcerer" with either continental or African features. By the end of the century, Harlequins were easily identifiable as Africans: *Harlequin Mungo* was staged in

1789 and *Furibond, or Harlequin Negro* in 1807. For both Blake and Stedman, the story of an African who was taken into slavery and brought to Surinam, who was a powerful practitioner of both magical arts and modern science (like Faust before him), who sold out his countrymen for personal advancement, who traveled to the seat of empire to perform for royalty, and who seemed to represent a mobile and protean embodiment – this story would no doubt have called to mind the popular London phenomenon of Harlequin. The artists, in echoing this theatrical persona, rendered Kwasi's opportunistic assimilation to European civility and modernity as a comically diabolical performance. In many ways, Kwasi is a compelling link between the urbane, European, eighteenth-century Harlequin figure and the early-nineteenth-century American plantation minstrel figure of Jim Crow, as popularized by the white performer Jim Rice (Fig. 9.6). In Blake and Stedman's Kwasi, we see the eerie imposture of the too-clever servant being exported to the plantation colony; he is not yet being made to dance and sing to belie his labor and his fury. Rather, Kwasi is made to play the faux gentleman to show how unnatural African power is revealed to be when it leaves the wilderness habitus.[27]

9.6. Anonymous artist, *Mr. T. [Thomas Dartmouth] Rice as the Original Jim Crow*, early 1830s, publ. by E. Riley. Lithograph engraving. pfMS Thr 556 (157), Harvard Theatre Collection, Houghton Library, Harvard University, Cambridge, Mass.

Stedman's reaction to another powerful Afro-Surinam figure may shed some light on his attitude toward Kwasi. In the diary he kept while in Surinam in the 1770s, Stedman describes getting into a "dispute with a damned impertinent fellow, a Capt. of the Owca negroes, called *Fortune Dago-So*," who had come to ask for money at the house of Captain and Mrs. Mackneal while Stedman was their dinner guest. When "*Capt. Fortune*" remarked on Stedman's own impertinence, Stedman "was incensed to hear so much from the mouth of a *bush-negro*, and replied him with the most threatening language he ever heard in town before." Later, when Fortune kissed Stedman's hand, Stedman "was much satisfied, and promised him 4 *bitts* next day." Stedman opposed the "unmanly submission" the colonials exhibited to "those black gentlemen," the maroon leaders: "The negroes are no fools, and in return presume impertinence, trying dayly to keep the *Whites* more and more in awe of their long beards and silver-headed staves, whom they will at last, at this rate I'm afraid, try in futurity to extirpate all together, and make the English, American, prophecy true, that they shall need no more to send for slaves to the coast of Guinea. N.B. Their number is incredible, and all are armed." Though his syntax is confusing, Stedman is here foreseeing the future "extirpation" or at least enslavement of the outnumbered white population. Stedman understood not only the licentious debauchery of white power in Surinam but also the tenuousness of that very power.[28]

In 1776 Stedman paid another maroon leader, Captain Bonny, the respect of imitating the design of a house Bonny had built on newly cleared land in the forest. "Now the negroes having found, by long experience, that such a ground, where the timbers are new fallen, exacerbates sulphureous and other poisonous and pernicious vapors," Bonny had raised his house and particularly his bed a number of feet above the ground to avoid such vapors. Stedman is comfortable acknowledging the superiority of African knowledge of wilderness territory, won by their "long experience," and particularly when this knowledge remains outside of Paramaribo, keeping a safe pastoral distance from the town. Stedman and Blake represent the superior nature-knowledge of the Africans in the engraving of the swamp march, laying bare the ill-placed European military hubris shown in the tropical forest. However, when Africans, empowered by their knowledge and control over the Surinam *pharmacosm* and territory, display their symbols of prestige "in town," Stedman turns his derision and satire upon them: standing down Fortune Dago-So until "satisfied" by his show of submission or turning the grounds of Kwasi's authority – the habitus that confers presence – into a stage for his obsequy. Within the representational logic of their respective images, the "slave" guide in the swamp has more authority than the "free" and "celebrated" Graman Quacy.[29]

Stedman understood the volatility of subject positions in Surinam. While opportunities for advantageous self-fashioning among African "Atlantic creoles" occurred throughout the Americas in the early era of slavery (when categories of servitude were still porous), by the late eighteenth century such transformations were more restricted to acts of violent rebellion and collusion in slave majority Caribbean and South American locales. Stedman understood how important was knowledge of the natural environment to any subject's viability and power in the colony. Stedman valorized such a state of potent comfort in the forest when it came to maroon subjects who stayed in their "retreats," or slave guides or Rangers who navigated these zones. When Africans who gained power through the Surinam *pharmacosm* tried to parlay that power in European terms, especially in the capital of Paramaribo – when they became "city folks" to use the Saramakan construct – Stedman's admiration for such figures deteriorated. Stedman could grudgingly accept being surpassed by Africans in the forest and even begin to assimilate himself to their place-adaptive inventions, but when free Africans began to cut figures of authority grander than his own in the city and in the larger Atlantic world, Stedman reacted with satirical fire in his writing. As he consulted with Blake during the engraving process, Stedman no doubt communicated these attitudes to Blake, who himself could draw upon a late-eighteenth-century London public culture of satire and entertainment for his models.

Together, Stedman and Blake practiced a form of Romantic containment of African authority to the forest environment. In attesting to European martyrdom in that forest, they – remarkably – fashioned a portrait of African optical and territorial mastery that challenged their viewers' habits of identification. However, in their portrait of Kwasi "in town," they qualify not only the authorizing power of the wilderness habitus, but also of the urban habitus that continued to confer upon Kwasi his prestige; they do this by a kind of physiological satire whereby Kwasi's courtliness is arrested off-balance and made risible. Rather than working to "show the whole man" as the sum of his two sides, as the product of an inner complexity, to return to Bindman's definition of the satirical portrait, the fissure in this image is not within Kwasi's character; instead, it is between a built environment that anchors authority and a bodily bearing that betrays unredeemable artifice and off-kilter "indolence." In this way, paradoxically, portraiture, *even when* conferring habitus, can make its subject less than a "whole man" by taking complexity out of the person and displaying it, instead, in and as a broader irony of history and geography.[30]

NOTES

Passages from my book *American Curiosity: Cultures of Natural History in the Colonial British Atlantic World* (2006) appear with kind permission of the University of North Carolina Press.

1 David Bindman argues that "Black servants in grand portraits and in satirical paintings invoke nature's tribute to culture and savagery's tribute to gentility"; they contribute to the "aesthetic presentation of power"; *Ape to Apollo: Aesthetics and the Idea of Race in the Eighteenth Century* (London: Reaktion Books, 2002), 42, 38. Of such portraits, Joseph Roach argues in *Cities of the Dead: Circum-Atlantic Performance* (New York: Columbia University Press, 1996) that "what these representations accomplished ... was the accommodation of exotic accounts of Atlantic superabundance and sacrifice into the normalizing regimes of whiteness" (131). Richard Price and Sally Price, Introduction to John Gabriel Stedman, *Narrative of a Five Years Expedition against the Revolted Negroes of Surinam* (Baltimore: Johns Hopkins University Press, 1988), xiv; this edition takes as its source Stedman's authoritative 1790 manuscript, which was then heavily edited to make it more politically palatable, against Stedman's wishes, when published in London in 1796: John G. Stedman, *Narrative, of a five years' expedition, against the Revolted Negroes of Surinam, in Guiana, on the Wild Coast of South America; from the year 1772 to 1777: elucidating the History of that Country, and describing its Productions, Viz.*

Quadrupeds, Birds, Fishes, Reptiles, Trees, Shrubs, Fruits, & Roots; with an account of the Indians of Guiana, & Negroes of Guinea, 2 vols. (London: Printed for J. Johnson ... & J. Edwards, 1796). David de Ishak Cohen, *Essai Historique sur la Colonie de Surinam* (Paramaribo, 1788), quoted in the Prices' Introduction, xiv. For more on the nature and extent of Blake's engravings of slaves, see Anne K. Mellor, "Sex, Violence, and Slavery: Blake and Wollstonecraft," *Huntington Library Quarterly* 58, nos. 3 and 4 (1996), 345–70; Anne Rubenstein and Camilla Townsend, "Revolted Negroes and the Devilish Principle: William Blake and Conflicting Visions of Boni's Wars in Surinam, 1772–1796," in *Blake, Politics, and History*, ed. Jackie DiSalvo, G. A. Rosso, and Christopher Z. Hobson (New York: Garland, 1998), 273–98; Marcus Wood, "John Gabriel Stedman, William Blake, Francesco Bartolozzi and Empathetic Pornography in the *Narrative of a Five Years' Expedition against the Revolted Negroes of Surinam*," in *An Economy of Colour: Visual Culture and the Atlantic World, 1660–1830*, ed. Geoff Quilley and Kay Dian Kriz (Manchester: Manchester University Press; New York: Palgrave, 2003), 129–52; and David Bindman, ed., *Mind-forg'd Manacles: William Blake and Slavery* (London: Hayward Gallery, 2007).

2 Marcia Pointon, "Slavery and the Possibilities of Portraiture," Chapter 1 in this volume. See also Richard Brilliant, *Portraiture* (Cambridge, Mass.: Harvard University Press, 1991).

3 Pierre Bourdieu, *Distinction: A Social Critique of the Judgement of Taste*, trans. Richard Nice (Cambridge, Mass.: Harvard University Press, 1986).

4 Wood, "John Gabriel Stedman," 133, 146. See also David V. Erdman, "Blake's Vision of Slavery," *Journal of the Warburg and Courtauld Institutes* 15, nos. 3/4 (1952), 242–52, and Tassie Gwilliam, "'Scenes of Horror,' Scenes of Sensibility: Sentimentality and Slavery in John Gabriel Stedman's *Narrative of a Five Years Expedition against the Revolted Negroes of Surinam*," *English Literary History* 65, no. 3 (1998), 653–73. Gwilliam argues that Stedman's use of sentimentality to domesticate and palliate the love story between himself and the slave woman Joanna pushes both "narrator and narrative into unsustainable extravagance and unsought self-confrontation" (653).

5 Sidney W. Mintz and Richard Price, "The Birth of African-American Culture," in Timothy E. Fulop and Albert J. Raboteau, eds., *African-American Religion: Interpretive Essays in History and Culture* (New York, 1997), 46.

6 Judith A. Carney, *Black Rice: The African Origins of Rice Cultivation in the Americas* (Cambridge, Mass.: Harvard University, 2001); Peter H. Wood, *Black Majority: Negroes in Colonial South Carolina from 1670 through the Stono Rebellion* (New York: Knopf, 1974), 30, 59–62, 120–22; Lorena S. Walsh, *From Calabar to Carter's Grove: The History of a Virginia Slave Community* (Charlottesville: University Press of Virginia, 1997), 63; Sharla M. Fett, *Working Cures: Healing, Health, and Power on Southern Slave Plantations* (Chapel Hill: University of North Carolina Press, 2002); Susan Parrish, *American Curiosity: Cultures of Natural History in the Colonial British Atlantic World* (Chapel Hill: University of North Carolina Press, 2006), ch. 7.

7 James Theobald to the earl of Macclesfield, read 5 May 1757, *Royal Society Letters and Papers*, III, 244; Bryan Edwards, *Observations on ... the Maroon Negroes of the Island of Jamaica ...* (1796), in Richard Price, ed., *Maroon Societies: Rebel Slave Communities in the Americas* (Garden City, N.Y.: Anchor Press, 1973), 230, 233–34; Stedman, *Narrative*, 84.

8 See Edward A. Pearson, *Designs against Charleston: The Trial Record of the Denmark Vesey Slave Conspiracy of 1833* (Chapel Hill: University of North Carolina Press,

1999), 25–26; quote on 25; Walsh, *From Calabar to Carter's Grove*, 13, 50, 111; on the prohibition of such meetings after slave rebellions, see 33; Joyce E. Chaplin, *An Anxious Pursuit: Agricultural Innovation and Modernity in the Lower South, 1730–1815* (Chapel Hill: University of North Carolina Press for the Institute of Early American History and Culture, Williamsburg, 1993), 266–76; See Carney, *Black Rice*, 86–88; W. Jeffrey Bolster, "African Roots of Black Seafaring" in *Black Jacks: African American Seamen in the Age of Sail* (Cambridge, Mass.: Harvard University Press, 1997), ch. 2; see John Michael Vlach, *Back of the Big House: The Architecture of Plantation Slavery* (Chapel Hill: University of North Carolina Press, 1993), 1–17, 231, on slaves' intimate knowledge of the nonpublic byways of the plantation grounds and the inter-plantation territory, 14; Rhys Isaac, *The Transformation of Virginia, 1740–1790* (Chapel Hill: University of North Carolina Press for the Institute of Early American History and Culture, Williamsburg, 1982), 52–53.

9 Long, *History of Jamaica*, 408; he added: "I have known some white Creoles not less expert at this art, which they acquired, as they said, by frequently ranging the woods after wild hogs, or runaways"; Hentschel, *Journal*, in Richard Price, *To Slay the Hydra: Dutch Colonial Perspectives on the Saramaka Wars* (Ann Arbor, Mich.: Karoma, 1983), 106, 116, 119. Stedman, *Narrative*, 639, 153, 632.

10 Stedman, *Narrative*, editors' introduction, xxvi, 85, 107, 396.

11 Stedman, *Narrative*, 402. Geoffrey Keynes, in his *Bibliography of Blake* (New York: Grollier Club, 1921; reprint, 1969), attributes this engraving to Blake despite the lack of signature: of this and two other unsigned plates. Keynes writes: "there can be no doubt that they are his work" (242); this plate is dated 1 December 1794.

12 Stedman, *Narrative*, editors' introduction, xci, note 36c. The 1796 printed version repeatedly toned down Stedman's hatred for and criticism of Fourgeoud; see *Narrative*, editors' introduction, lix.

13 Stedman, *Narrative*, 192. Pointon argues that the profile creates distance between the viewer and subject, allowing either for immortalization as in Roman medallions or for criticism if the portrait has a satirical component; *Hanging the Head: Portraiture and Social Formation in Eighteenth-Century England* (New Haven: Yale University Press, 1993), 95, 107.

14 On the importance and function of portrait busts in classical memory and the making of the neoclassical, Augustan public sphere, see Pointon, *Hanging the Head*, 7.

15 Geoff Quilley, "Pastoral Plantations: The Slave Trade and the Representation of British Colonial Landscape in the Late Eighteenth Century" in Quilley and Kriz, *An Economy of Colour*, 114, 116. In *The Practice of Everyday Life*, trans. Steven F. Randall (Berkeley: University of California Press, 1984), Michel de Certeau refutes Michel Foucault's analysis of the dynamics of power (represented through the apparatus of the panopticon) by proposing the daily, numerous, and almost invisible tactics by which humans evade centralized institutions' spatial strategies of domination (xix, 30). In this image, Blake is showing even more than tactical resistance; instead he shows how the Africans become the panoptic power within the forest space.

16 Stedman, *Narrative*, 666; this summary of Graman Quacy's life is derived both from Stedman (581–84) and from the Prices' note (666).

17 Stedman, *Narrative*, 581–82, 584.

18 Religious historian Theophus Smith in his *Conjuring Culture: Biblical Formations of Black America* (Oxford: Oxford University Press, 1994) coined the term "pharmacosm" or "pharmacopeic cosmos" to describe the way that African-American cultures in the nineteenth and twentieth centuries read the Bible through their Africa-retained practices of conjure. I am using it for this earlier period because

I think it aptly describes the African spirit-infused sense of a nature open to the magical practices of a human adept. On cosmologies brought from West and Central Africa and the methodological issues involved in considering cultural retentions, see Albert J. Raboteau, *Slave Religion: The "Invisible Institution" in the Ante-bellum South* (New York: Oxford University Press, 1978), 3–42, 49, 59, 85; John Thornton, *Africa and Africans in the Making of the Atlantic World, 1400–1800*, 2nd ed. (Cambridge: Cambridge University Press, 1998), 209–21, 283–88; Sidney W. Mintz and Richard Price, "The Birth of African-American Culture," in *African-American Religion: Interpretative Essays in History and Culture*, ed. Timothy E. Fulop and Albert J. Raboteau (New York: Routledge, 1997), 46.

19 Stedman, *Narrative*, 582. In 1869, the colony exported 245,622 kilos of *Quassia amara* for medicinal purposes and to be used in English beer. See Richard Price, *First-Time: The Historical Vision of an Afro-American People* (Baltimore: Johns Hopkins University Press, 1983), 155; *Journal of John Gabriel Stedman, 1744–1797, Soldier and Author: Including an Authentic Account of His Expedition to Surinam in 1772*, ed. Stanbury Thompson (London: Mitre Press, 1962), 185.

20 Stedman, *Narrative*, 581–82, 584.

21 The late-twentieth-century Saramaka, in interviews carried out over a course of about twenty years starting in the 1960s with anthropologists Richard and Sally Price, told a number of stories about their "first-time." One in particular, which Richard Price calls "Kwasimukamba's Gambit, 1755" bears the kernel of their philosophy of mistrust of the outside world – of whites, of Creoles and "city people." Price, *First-Time*, 153–55; Richard Price, *Alabi's World* (Baltimore: Johns Hopkins University Press, 1990), 33; on Kwasi's missing ear in the Blake engraving, see the Prices' note in Stedman, *Narrative*, 666, and the note on 636 in which the Prices comment that "the maiming and sending back of a traitor – a slave siding with the whites against the Maroons – is an important theme in Maroon historiography."

22 "Kwasi's Intelligence Coup" (1754), testimony taken from Kwasi and included in full in Price, *To Slay the Hydra*, 87; see Ernst Godfried Hentschel, "Captain Hentschel's Journal" (1755) in Price, *To Slay the Hydra*, 116, 120, 109, 114–15; see also Price, *First-Time*, 157, 158.

23 Stedman, *Narrative*, 582.

24 In his journal Stedman records making and giving watercolors of acquaintances in Surinam and of their estates; see *Journal of John Gabriel Stedman*, ed. Thompson, 162, 164, 185–86, 189.

25 Stedman, *Narrative*, 581–82.

26 David Bindman, *William Blake: His Art and Times* (London: Thames and Hudson, 1982), 26, 25; Bindman, *Hogarth* (New York: Oxford University Press, 1981), 107.

27 John O'Brien, *Harlequin Britain: Pantomime and Entertainment, 1690–1760* (Baltimore: Johns Hopkins University Press, 2004), 94, 108, 129. See also Roxann Wheeler, "Colonial Exchanges: Visualizing Racial Ideology and Labour in Britain and the West Indies," in Quilley and Kriz, *An Economy of Colour* 37. On the figure of Jim Crow, see Eric Lott, *Blackface Minstrelsy and the American Working Class* (Oxford: Oxford University Press, 1995); he argues that minstrelsy both acknowledged and disavowed the economy's reliance on the labor of the body by "invoking the black male body as a powerful cultural sign of sexuality as well as a sign of the dangerous, guilt-inducing physical reality of slavery but relying on the derided category of race finally to dismiss both"; in short, minstrelsy represented "a major effort of corporeal containment" (118).

28 *Journal of John Gabriel Stedman,* ed. Thompson, 179.

29 Ibid., 195.

30 On the comparative freedoms of the "charter generations" of African "Atlantic creoles," see Ira Berlin, "From Creole to African: Atlantic Creoles and the Origins of African-American Society in Mainland North America," *William and Mary Quarterly,* 3rd ser., 53, no. 2 (1996), 251–88.

TEN

EXQUISITE EMPTY SHELLS

SCULPTED SLAVE PORTRAITS AND THE FRENCH ETHNOGRAPHIC TURN

James Smalls

It Was a Very Good Year

In the year 1848, the French sculptor Charles Henri Joseph Cordier (1827–1905) chose to submit a bust of a former African slave to the Salon. The impact of *Saïd Abdallah, de la tribu de Mayac, Royaume de Darfour* on the Salon jury, the critics, and the general public was extraordinary (see Fig. 10.1). Many regarded the portrait as a tour de force in its profound political and aesthetic immediacy, serving not only as a kind of trophy to congratulate and pronounce to the world France's wisdom in abolishing slavery, but also giving visual and ideological support to the future Napoleon III's policies of assimilation, foreign expansion, and cultural influence.[1] The *Saïd Abdallah* bust was to be the beginning of a long, successful, and calculated career path that rested on Cordier's technical abilities as a professional craftsman and portrait sculptor, his knack for taking advantage of opportune political moments, and his entrepreneurial acumen. He tirelessly solicited support from the State for his ambitious projects. As well, it did not hurt that he became fast friends with the Count Alfred-Emilien de Nieuwerkerke, director of Fine Arts. It was through Nieuwerkerke's influence that Cordier would soon come to receive choice government and private commissions.

Between 1848 and 1870, Cordier earned his reputation by specializing in sculptural busts of *types raciaux* fashioned in elaborate amalgams of precious and semiprecious materials. At the time, *la sculpture ethnographique* or *la sculpture anthropologique*, as it was termed, had relatively few expert practitioners and was deemed limited as a genre by some contemporary observers. Cordier's sculptures were different from prior ethnographic works, however, in that they employed an approach combining scientific realism with classical idealization,

10.1. Charles Henri Joseph Cordier, *Saïd Abdallah, de la tribu de Mayac, Royaume de Darfour* (Saïd Abdallah of the Mayac Tribe, Kingdom of Darfur), 1848. Bronze. Laboratoire d'anthropologie, depot du FNAC, inv. no. 27051–1977–207, Musée de l'Homme, Paris.

stoic restraint with a Romantic exuberance. As a result, he amassed around him a small coterie of admirers, the most significant of whom was the critic Théophile Gautier (1811–72), who detected something new, invigorating, and progressive in Cordier's work.

In his *Mémoires*, Cordier not only recounted the circumstances surrounding the creation and exhibition of *Saïd Abdallah*, but also referenced the importance of 1848 for his success as an artist: "A superb Sudanese arrived at the studio. Within a fortnight I did his bust and sent it to the Salon, feeling quite sure that it would be accepted. Just then the Revolution of 1848 burst out, and the jury was democratically elected. Trembling, I got up my nerve to send in the Sudanese bust anyway, and it was a revelation to the art world. . . . My genre had the freshness of something new, revolt against slavery, the budding science of anthropology, widening the circle of beauty by showing that it existed everywhere."[2]

Cordier's romanticized recollection reveals much about the sculptor's perception of his own relationship to art and society but discloses little about this "superb Sudanese." His cocky yet cautious position regarding the fallout from the events of 1848 suggests that he understood the implications and ideological significance of locating a black slave presence in a work of art at that crucial moment in France. Based on his own account, the sculptor regarded himself as a kind of creative messiah and harbinger of progress – one who, by sheer force of will, courage, and talent has singlehandedly transported the lowly slave to a new level of aesthetic and cultural achievement. Indeed, that very process of inspiration and revelation required the bestowal, if not the imposing, of both scientific and Eurocentric aesthetic paradigms onto the individualized slave.

As Cordier's bust exemplifies, the historical, political, and ideological significance of 1848, along with the slave image and slavery itself as a visualizable concept, were to weigh heavily on the imagination of the French artistic and scientific communities. As well, Cordier's choice of subject in 1848 indicates that the slave portrait was intrinsically politicized due to the context out of which such likenesses were fashioned – namely, within the historical parameters of and the discourses over slavery, abolition, and colonialism. Indeed, Cordier's bust underscores my contention that there is no such thing as a politically neutral (even when aesthetically alluring) representation of an *esclave* (slave), *nègre* (negro), or *noir* (black).[3] This is to say that, given the historical and ideological contextual weight of the sculpted portraits considered in the following pages, any shift of meaning that accompanies their transformation from representation of a particularized individual into a universalized ethnographic type – a shift that seems to occur consistently in the nineteenth-century French context – is inherently and inevitably charged with political content and intent. Throughout this account, then, the slave presence is one that says much about

Western aesthetics, science, and racialized discourse, and in most instances, very little or absolutely nothing at all about the slave as individual. With the works of Cordier and others, the slave himself or herself is automatically rendered equivalent to political and ideological discourse unique and specific to French identity and national concerns. It was through the dispute over slavery and abolition with its political, cultural, and representational fallouts that the French nation was able to grapple with its own identity crisis both before and after 1848.

Although the year 1848 was important to Cordier's decision to specialize in ethnographic sculpture, his subsequent success was due to the fact that his sculptures spoke directly to Napoleon III's ambitions for French colonial infiltration and expansion. Key to the emperor's plans was his doctrine of assimilation, which had begun under the Second Republic (1848–52) and was intensified under the Second Empire (1852–70). The principle of assimilation was designed to uphold, propagate, and reinforce French republican ideals. In the process, all of the paradoxes and contradictions associated with French colonialism and the murky concept of "race" were also upheld and propagated. The doctrine of assimilation "assumed that the institutions and society based on the 1789 French Revolution were so admirable that the colonies must model themselves on France."[4] Under Napoleon III, the precept was applied primarily to Algeria but also to other overseas colonies such as Martinique, Guadeloupe, and Réunion. His plan was never fully realized, however, thus becoming a stumbling block to the emperor's designs for complete subjugation of France's colonial possessions and French political and cultural influence in them. The ultimate failure of assimilation spoke to Napoleon III's error in oversimplifying and romanticizing the character of those to be subjugated. As well, he underestimated the intense resistance to colonization by the indigenous populations he sought to subdue. Resistance did not, however, stop the emperor from supporting artists such as Cordier whose work assisted in the promotion of his colonial ambitions.

Cordier's sculptures are concrete visualizations of the Second Empire's assimilationist desires in that they attempt to collect, study, and integrate as many different racial groups and types as possible into a single, unified Eurocentric vision of beauty as sign of successful incorporation (read subjugation) of the racial/ethnic other. By tapping into and exploiting contemporary science and classicizing aesthetics, Cordier's works reinforced Napoleon III's goal to promote multiracialism and interculturalism into Western, that is, specifically French-defined, dictates of culture and society. At the same time, his art was put to use to perpetuate the idea of a French "progressive" scientific and humanitarian spirit based on a deceptive platform of international understanding and mutual cooperation. Moreover, as we shall see, the imperatives of assimilation itself were manifested in the eclectic and technical manner in which Cordier pieced together his figures. In the overall process, the slave's individuality and

10.2. Jean-Baptiste Pigalle, *Le Nègre Paul*, ca. 1760. Terracotta. Musée des Beaux-Arts d'Orléans. © Musée des Beaux-Arts d'Orléans, cliché François Lauginie.

agency were conveniently neutralized for the ultimate expediency of French national distinction and for the sculptor's egocentric identity.

For the racial and exotic aspects of his *Saïd Abdallah* bust, Cordier had at his disposal a few precedent examples from which to draw. One such model was a terracotta bust by the eighteenth-century French sculptor Jean-Baptiste Pigalle representing *Le Nègre Paul* (Fig. 10.2).[5] The portrait was executed around 1760 and depicts the young black slave of Thomas-Aignan Desfriches, an amateur painter, draftsman, and art collector from Orléans.[6] The Desfriches family was involved in the trade in colonial goods, including the slave trade. One unusual characteristic of this work that sets it apart from other representations of black slaves or servants during the period is that Pigalle's black figure is given a name and is not rendered completely anonymous, as was typically the case with the slave portrait. Nevertheless, we know nothing of Paul's biography except that he was brought to Orléans along with other colonial merchandise by Desfriches's brother, who had been a captain in the merchant marine. The emphasis in the bust is on a strong demarcation of ethnic facial features and on the display of exotic costume.

Le Nègre Paul constitutes visual testimony to the fact that Africans and colonial blacks were frequently brought to Europe to work in upper-class and middle-class households, sometimes appearing in art works "as part of a complex ritual of display of ... ostentatious wealth the bourgeoisie accumulated through African slave labor on Caribbean plantations."[7] Prior to the temporary abolition of slavery in 1794, the laws governing the legal status of colonial slaves brought onto French soil were ambiguous. However, once in France, a slave's status changed to that of servant, and he or she could legally petition for manumission. As was the case with all other imported slaves, Paul had to have been registered and his status confirmed and recorded by the French authorities. Thus, Paul is not a paid model but a *négrillon,* who, in all likelihood, had very little or no say at all in his presentation. Here a turbaned black page is presented as visual sign of materialist indulgence and colonial possession, and is intended not to reference the person of Paul, per se, but the social status and

10.3. Jean-Antoine Houdon, *Buste d'une négresse*, 1781. Bronze. Musée de Soissons, Soissons. © MINETTO Michel; © Musée de Soissons, Soissons.

power of Paul's owners, who, in creating a portrait of him, were following the vogue in eighteenth-century European aristocratic society of creating visible self-reflexive signs of wealth, prestige, and command over dark laboring bodies. The work is significant in the context of the sculpted slave portrait in that it demonstrates that even when the sitter is specifically named in a work's title and is rendered with highly descriptive physiognomic detail, the individuality of the one represented becomes secondary if not irrelevant.

Pigalle's piece was not the only prior example of a slave presence in sculpture from which Cordier would have been influenced. Other artists, such as Jean-Antoine Houdon and Simon-Louis Boizot, created sculpted slave portraits, although these tended not to be the main thrust of their artistic output. The slave image for these sculptors served a distinct function having little to do with probing the subjectivity of the slave and more to do with identifying and positioning themselves as artists in the highly politicized contemporary moment. The *Buste d'une négresse* (1781) (Fig. 10.3) by Houdon and a sculptural group entitled *Moi égale à toi. Moi libre aussi* (1794; La Rochelle, Musée du Nouveau Monde) by Boizot are works of both ethnographic interest and political focus produced during the late eighteenth century in France. Houdon's bust is a prime example of how the imaging and the imagining of the slave could be conscientiously advanced to the political benefit and strategic ideological positioning of the artist himself in times of social and political stress or crisis.

Houdon's *négresse* was exhibited in the Salon of 1781 and listed in the catalog as a "plaster bust of a Negress in imitation of antique bronze."[8] The work was completely ignored by the critics, and, although the portrait was obviously particularized, no attempt was made to identify the sitter. We know from documented sources, however, that Houdon modeled his bust while working on an elaborate fountain group in the late 1770s, representing "two lifesize figures, one in white marble, & the other [in a material] imitating a Negress."[9] In it, the black woman was placed in the role of servant pouring water over a central white female bather, thus attending to her mistress's physical needs.[10] Houdon's black servant had been cast in lead, and it has been noted that his use of this material to distinguish the black figure from the white one was highly original for the period and is perhaps without precedent.[11] Cordier would later exploit such use of materials for chromatic effect as a way to approximate the skin color of racial types.

Upon completion, the bather and the black attendant were acquired as fountain figures by the king's cousin, the duc de Chartres (later duc d'Orléans) who, in 1779, installed them in his exotic English garden at Monceau near Paris.[12] In November 1793 the duc de Chartres was guillotined, and his property fell into neglect. One year later, the fountain figures were confiscated by the Commission temporaire des arts, and the head of the *négresse* was recorded lost. However, from a plaster copy of the original lead statue, Houdon recast in bronze the smiling *négresse* bust in 1794. The figure's "wistful expression, the large, deeply cut eyes with the lids half closed, the broad nose and full lips between which the teeth are visible,"[13] as well as the detailed treatment of the hair, indicate that Houdon had worked from a live model, the specifics of whose biography, typical of most slave portraits, remain unknown to us.

Houdon's decision to recast the head in 1794 is significant. During the 1789 Revolution, Houdon had been criticized for his seeming lack of loyalty to the revolutionary cause. To assuage any doubts about his allegiance, he recast the *Buste d'une négresse* in a patriotic context by adding on the base of the bust the following inscription: "Given Freedom and Equality by the National Convention 16 Pluviôse, year two of the French Republic, One and Indivisible."[14] As was the case with Cordier's *Saïd Abdallah* bust, the date in which Houdon decided to recast his black subject was politically volatile. Houdon's move corresponded with the National Convention's vote, in 1794, to abolish slavery in all French colonies. The transformation of the sculptor's *négresse* from its *ancien régime* status as emblem of black servitude or enslavement to white aristocratic privilege, to symbolic representative of republican sentiments by literally the stroke of a pen, sums up the significance of slavery and the slave subject as convenient means of political and ideological positioning by the artist. By penning his inscription in the crucial year of 1794 – during the most radical phase of the revolutionary process – Houdon conscientiously transformed a black woman showcased with particularized racial features from slave into an icon of French enlightened democracy. Clearly the move was expedient for Houdon, who, like most artists of the period working within a highly politicized context, rightly anticipated the gesture as a means of sparing himself the trauma of the guillotine.

"LE PLUS BEAU NÈGRE . . ."

The actual relationship between Saïd Abdallah and Cordier remained murky in the art-historical record only until very recently. It was believed previously that this "superb Sudanese" who suddenly materialized in the studio was perhaps a visitor on a diplomatic mission to France from the region of Darfur in eastern Africa. Indeed, Cordier's business acumen and seemingly effortless finesse in making connections in the art and government administrations would have afforded him ready access to such foreign dignitaries as well as to political leaders, noted scientists, and cultural personalities. However, recent scholarship has determined the identity of the sitter as Seïd Enkess, a former slave who had become a popular artist's model in Paris.[15] Enkess's identity is highly germane to Cordier's aesthetic and political agenda and to the debates within anthropological circles at the time.

In 1847, one year prior to the appearance of the *Saïd Abdallah* bust, there was a debate raging among members of the Ethnological Society of Paris regarding "the distinctive characteristics of the white race and the black race"[16] in discerning beauty and ugliness. These discussions pitted the staunch abolitionist Victor Schoelcher against Victor Courtet de l'Isle, a conservative theoretician of racial hierarchies who ranked races according to their relative beauty or ugliness based on their physical representatives.[17] Joining these debates were Armand d'Avezac, the anthropologist Armand de Quatrefages de Bréau, and Pierre-Marie Dumoutier, a noted phrenologist who used precise measurements from life casts and skulls to arrive at his own conclusions on comparative racial types. Courtet's racial argument can be summed up in his own words: "[T]he more beautiful the characteristic representative of a race, the more advanced the civilization of this race; the uglier the representative, the more imperfect the civilization. As to the idea that I have of relative beauty and ugliness, it is that which anyone can easily conceive, taking on the one hand, as a point of comparison, the character of Apollo or that of Minerva, and on the other hand, the character closest to that of the brute."[18]

In his rebuttal to Courtet's claims linking race and subjective standards of beauty, Schoelcher accused Courtet of confusing objective science with racial politics as a way of proving the inequality of the races. D'Avezac, joined by Dumoutier, used two life casts from two different African men to prove the weakness of Courtet's position (Figs. 10.4 and 10.5). D'Avezac concluded that "the distinction that M. Courtet would like to establish with regard to the slave races is not sufficiently substantiated. The Society, right now, has before its eyes a bust that presents to the highest degree all the traits of ugliness and degradation attributed to Negroes. This bust is, however, that of a free man, a member of the Ewe race and one of the best families of the Yebou nation. It is the bust of Ochi-Fekoué"[19] (see Fig. 10.4).

The bust of Ochi-Fékoué was compared with a second life cast about which Gustave d'Eichthal, secretary of the Ethnological Society of Paris at the time, concluded: "[t]he two casts that the Society has here before its eyes are themselves new proof of the importance of typological representations. One of these figures, as has already been noted, a true depiction of Negroid ugliness, is that of an individual who is a member of one of the most civilized races of Africa. The other cast, an example of Negroid beauty, is that of Seïd Enkess, a member of some reputedly barbarian tribe of Upper Sennar [Sudan]. This is an important contrast for the theory linking the physical type with civilization"[20] (see Fig. 10.5).

Enkess had appeared before the Ethnological Society sometime after 28 February 1847 in a session in which he gave information about his identity, the circumstances that brought him to Paris, and his profession as "a painter's model."[21] His life cast had been made shortly before the Society's meeting of 25 June 1847. Based on his own account, Enkess was a former slave born into the Mayac Tribe in the African Kingdom of Darfur and eventually was brought to

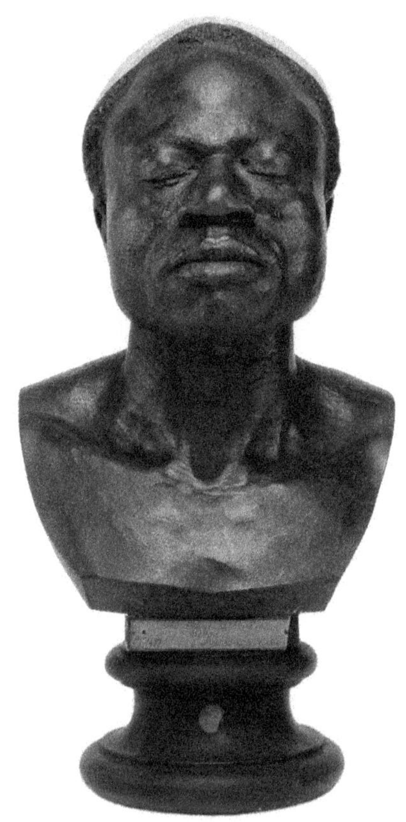

10.4. *Ochi-Fékoué*, Life cast, 1847. Patinated plaster. Musée de l'Homme, Paris.

Europe about 1838 by Prince Galitzine. These biographical tidbits, in addition to the close likeness of Seïd's life cast to Cordier's bust, confirm that Enkess was indeed the model for *Saïd Abdallah*. Enkess's appearance before the Ethnological Society in 1847 suggests that Cordier's association with him was not as accidental as the sculptor had led us to believe in his *Mémoires*. Not only had Enkess become an artist's model by the time Cordier met him, but, already from 1847, he had been designated as the most beautiful "specimen" of his race by influential members within anthropological circles.

Perhaps one reason why Cordier considered his bust of Saïd Abdallah as "a revelation" to the art world was because, relatively speaking, very few blacks were available as artist's models in France at the time.[22] This created a situation in which the black subject for art became a rarefied commodity, and the black presence in art, thus being unique, was noteworthy and highly valued both aesthetically as well as politically. As a model, Enkess was in demand by artists of high reputation and fame. It is therefore not farfetched to suggest that it was perhaps in the studio of his mentor and friend, François Rude (1784–1855), where Cordier must have first encountered Enkess in 1846 – the year in which the sculptor first entered into his master's studio as a student.

In contrast to Enkess's status as representative of "la beauté nègre" (Negro beauty), the identity and life cast of Ochi-Fékoué as evidence of "le laideur nègre" (Negro ugliness) are just as intriguing. It was Armand d'Avezac who provided a detailed account of his research on this particular African. As it turns out, Ochi-Fékoué was a merchant traveler in Africa when he was captured and sold into slavery (it is unclear by whom). He was then transported to Brazil where he was baptized under the Christian name Joseph.[23] As had been the case with Enkess, Joseph also arrived in Paris sometime between 1836 and 1838 with his master and soon gained his freedom. He then worked as a servant in Paris before returning to Brazil and before Cordier could meet him.[24]

Cordier's success in 1848 prompted him to devise a way to exploit further his popularity as a specialist in ethnographic portraiture. For the Salon of 1850, he decided to recast his *Saïd Abdallah* bust and exhibit it under a new title, *Nègre de Timbouctou* (Negro from Timbuktu). The calculated change of title transformed

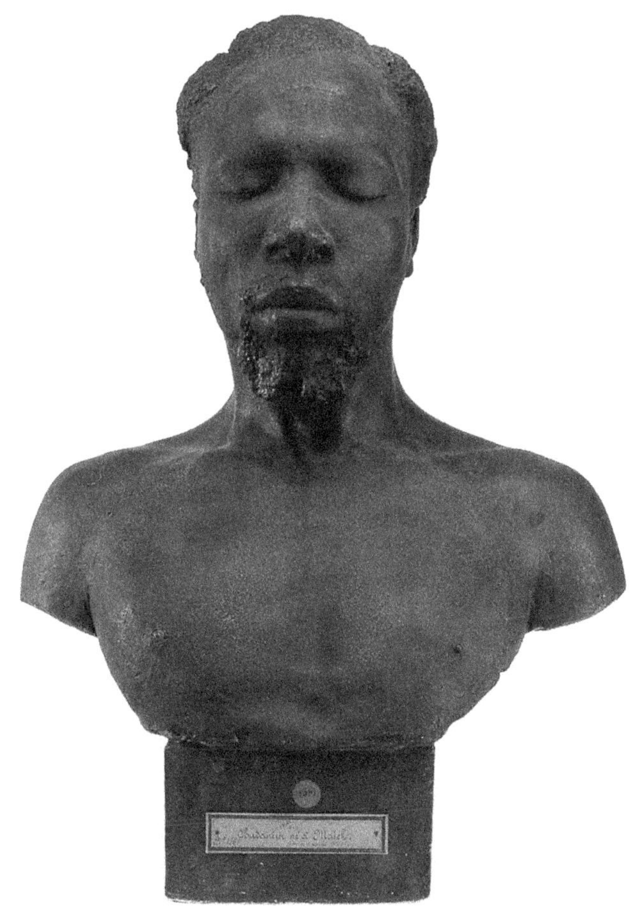

10.5. *Seïd Enkess*, Life cast, 1847. Patinated plaster. Laboratoire d'anthropologie, Musée de l'Homme, Paris.

10.6. Charles Henri Joseph Cordier, *La Vénus Africaine* (African Venus or *Négresse des colonies*), 1851. Bronze. Laboratoire d'anthropologie, depot du FNAC, inv. no. 27051–1977–214, Musée de l'Homme, Paris.

the portrait of a unique (former) slave individual into an aesthetically stunning generic "specimen" of racial and cultural difference. Cordier's move operated to generalize the various geographical regions found on the vast African continent and lump them into a single undifferentiated category – "Afrique." Clearly, with the transformation of his *Saïd Abdallah* bust into a *Nègre de Timbouctou*, Cordier demonstrated an acute awareness of a fine line between the particularized slave portrait and the ethnographic portrait as generic specimen of a type. The slippage back and forth across this fine line was achieved by way of convenient change of title or, in some cases, by placement of the work in a particular spatial or political context for reasons of expediency. Racial and ethnographic types could be fashioned in such ways so to appeal to an eclectic array of aesthetic as well as political tastes and, in the process, bolstered the artist's own prestige and artistic identity.

In the 1851 Salon, now under the title *Nègre de Timbouctou*, Cordier's portrait of Saïd Abdallah (Seïd Enkess) was exhibited alongside a companion piece titled *Négresse des colonies* (Fig. 10.6). This practice of pairing male and female "specimens" of a racial or ethnic group became Cordier's standard practice. Like *Nègre de Timbouctou*, the *Négresse des colonies* was given a generic title indicative of a broad racial and geographical designation, thus blurring or collapsing the distinction between a universalizing racial type and the naming of a specific individual. Such a move speaks strongly to the relevance of the slave as raced representative, whose biological and biographical presence is unfixed and easily transformed into a floating signifier of the ideological and political construction "race." With both works, Cordier employed an exaggerated realism in the details of the facial features and costumes. The woman exhibits thick and fleshy lips, a broad, flat nose, coarse locks of hair, and ethnographically detailed jewelry. Both figures are also draped in African clothing conscientiously arranged to fall in a classicizing manner. The black woman's elongated neck, serious expression, and concentrated gaze impart an air of solemnity and intelligence. The fleshy form of her torso beneath the drapery is palpable. Her upper body is rendered in such a way so to suggest, as if depicted in an imaginary full figure, a relaxed contrapposto stance characteristic of classicized statuary. The bringing together of two seemingly disparate yet complementary aspects – painstaking ethnographic realism in the figure's countenance coupled with hints of classical refinement in the torso and clothing – was an eclectic stylistic formula for which Cordier became known in the art world. This was a practice that also satisfied Napoleon III's assimilation doctrine and the colonialist's need to claim knowledge over and to incorporate the racial and cultural "other" into Western aesthetic paradigms.

In his critique of the Salon of 1857, and six years after the first appearance of Cordier's *Négresse des colonies* (Fig. 10.6), the influential art critic Théophile Gautier decided to bestow upon that work a new title – *La Vénus Africaine*. He chose the title because of his stated admiration for Cordier's ethnographic approach and his love of the Venus theme. In his enthusiastic reception of the work, Gautier discerned the masterful alliances the sculptor made in the piece among art, science, industry, and classicizing aesthetics.[25] That Cordier's *Vénus* was a black African and not a lily-white goddess of love points to Gautier's willingness to go along with the sculptor's "altruistic" program of incorporating a particularized black slave presence into the aesthetic and mythological pantheon of Eurocentric culture.[26]

A noteworthy feature shared by both *La Vénus Africaine* and its complementary male pendant is an imposing of Western concepts of beauty and nobility onto images of peoples from non-Western races and cultures as a means to impart an aura of "civilization" and successful assimilation into a Western aesthetic upon them. This is particularly noteworthy with *La Vénus Africaine* in which the Western, Eurocentric concept of the Greek goddess of love has been grafted onto the image of an ethnographically detailed *Africaine* – creating what at first glance would seem to be an oxymoronic confluence.[27] This process was, no doubt, viewed by Cordier and his contemporaries as an act of ennoblement or even as an act of abolition itself – that is, a representational means of demonstrating that racial others could be liberated from their believed uncivilized status, rescued from their assumed "ugliness," and made as beautiful and as noble as were the ancients themselves. On the other hand, such a manipulation could also be viewed as a "violation" in its erasure of the newly emancipated slave's individual humanity by the imposing of an objectifying Eurocentric ideal upon them. So, in the process of elevating the black slave woman to the level of goddess, Cordier and Gautier also manage to silence and erase her by speaking through and for her. The slave is denied personhood, even if specifically named in the work's title, and becomes a broad signifier of what one contemporary scholar has called the "vagueness of the negress' geography," likened to "la superbe Afrique."[28] This process of muting black subjectivity has also been viewed as the result of the gendered and sexualized "metaphoricity" of the

Venus theme coupled with processes of artistic and racialized "objectness" that allow for and explain the feasibility of the black Venus theme.[29]

The Ethnographic Turn

In 1846, two years before revolutionary upheaval in France and the subsequent abolition of slavery, Charles Baudelaire wrote a brief essay entitled "Why Sculpture Is Tiresome."[30] In it he decried the limitations of sculpture over painting, arguing that the former medium had become conservative and monotonous in its redundant mimicry of ancient works of art. Sculpture, in his view, lacked modern inspiration. Likewise, both Théophile Gautier and Emile Zola often expressed their lament over the pitiful state of contemporary sculpture. In their critiques these writers advocated that sculptors embrace the ethnographic. Ethnography was, in their view, the direction that sculpture had to take in order to be lifted out of its mediocrity and aesthetic doldrums.[31]

Ethnographie as a legitimate science in France was a distinct product of the nineteenth century and was dominated by a small number of individuals who were, on average, politically and socially well served by Napoleon III's regime. Ethnography became a source of inspiration for sculptors particularly in the 1860s. It was originally an offshoot of *ethnologie,* which, in turn, was a branch of anthropology. *Ethnologie* and *ethnographie* are not the same, although both terms were used interchangeably in the early nineteenth century. Whereas ethnology tended to consider issues such as origins and development of language and customs, for example, ethnography insisted on precise scientific methods of measuring and classifying "knowable" physical facts. In his sculptures, Cordier confuses ethnology and ethnography in that he simultaneously concentrates on recording observable physical differences between racial "specimens" while supplying the ethnologist with visual information to ponder such things as clothing and hairstyles. In his works, unique physical features are associated with specific individuals and are rendered simultaneously as universal characteristics of entire racial and ethnic groups. The ethnographic, as opposed to ethnological, dimension of Cordier's enterprise is underscored by his insistence on venturing into the field to gather physical evidence firsthand, and yet his use of the ethnographic portrait for political maneuvering and aesthetic classification speaks directly to the ethnological.[32]

Although Cordier became an associate member of the the Société d'Anthropologie de Paris, founded in 1859 by the renowned anthropologist Paul Broca (1824–80), his approach to the ethnographic was at odds with that organization's leader who considered art in general and Cordier's work in particular to foster unscientific and fictional constructs of ideal rather than "real" racial types.[33] Thus, although positioning himself as an artist with a serious scientific mission, Cordier found himself at odds with the "hard-core" world of science during the Second Empire. Cordier did, however, attempt to legitimate his program of combining idealizing aesthetics and science by explaining his sculptural method in terms as factual as possible in an address to the Society on 6 February 1862:

> I sculpted these busts from life by employing a geometric procedure that guarantees the exactitude of likeness, dimensions, and forms. . . . I take my models as much as possible from their respective countries and I proceed as any artist would in representing a true likeness of the race. First of all, I examine and compare my subjects with a large sampling of individuals from the same race. I study the form of their heads, the features of their faces, the expression of their physiognomy. I charge myself with seizing the common characteristics of the race that I want to reproduce. I appreciate these characteristics in their entirety as well as in their details. . . . I then conceive of an ideal or rather a type for each of these characteristics. Then, by grouping all of these partial types, I constitute in my mind an assembled type in which is united all the special beauty of the race that I am examining.[34]

Buried in Cordier's rationalized approach to the ethnographic is the point that, as a discourse, ethnography produces meaning that complicates its assumed function as an instrument of scientific knowledge and the objective fixing of the other in time and space.[35] Ethnography and the sculptor's assessment of his role in it confront the problem of who has control over the construction and naming of otherness and difference. As both a notion and an act, ethnography brings into view the subjective position of the outsider as cultural commentator and critic. The tendency to marginalize yet romanticize ethnographic otherness, legitimated through science and the imposing of Western aesthetics, is what Cordier's sculptures both constitute and promote. They exploit the slave as liminal subject and ideal serving as reflexive stand-in for the artist-anthropologist's own interests and desires. The subjectivity of the slave him- or herself is diminished, if not voided.

Colorful (Im)Personalities: Evacuation and the Polychromatics of Race

Cordier was the first sculptor of the nineteenth century to link successfully polychromy and ethnography. His skill at (re)fashioning the materials of sculpture, combined with his powers of ethnographic observation and description, made his busts some of the most visually captivating of the period. He never painted his pieces but rather pieced them together in technically complex arrangements of differently colored stones and semiprecious materials. Based on his own words, Cordier viewed himself as a social and artistic maverick who was singlehandedly responsible for using color in the discovery and revelation to the world of a dormant beauty in different races.[36] Although Cordier's ethnographic busts dazzled the public with their combination of ethnographic realism and polychromatic effects, they were, for the most part, condemned by several conservative critics as being crassly decorative and highly commercial. There was a hint of truth to such criticism, for indulgence in polychromy also reflected the Second Empire's materiality and middle-class lust for the luxurious. Heated debates ensued about the social and aesthetic merits and pitfalls of the use of color in both sculpture and architecture.[37]

Cordier's interest in applying color to his sculptures had been whetted by the eighteenth-century discoveries of antiquities at Herculaneum and Pompeii, the fragments of the frieze from the Mausoleum at Halicarnassus, unearthed in 1856, and the Prima Porta Augustus, discovered in 1863.[38] Perhaps most significant for the colonial and racial implications of his work was the fact that Cordier's penchant for using color in his portrait busts was stimulated by discoveries of abundant onyx quarries in the Oran region of Algeria (a vast province conquered by the French in 1847) abandoned since antiquity and reopened in 1842. Like most sculptors, Cordier harbored an intense passion for learning about new materials and their properties. He kept apprised of advances in geology and mineralogy, and became quite knowledgeable in the field of chemistry – learning the various means to attain chromatic nuances through oxidation processes and through the application of different patinas. These techniques were used to delineate not only the differing hues and textures of fabric, but also the skin tones of his racial and ethnic types. His expertise in these areas, coupled with his close personal connections with important scientists, businessmen, and government officials, fostered his ability to acquire, primarily through generous state funding, the large quantities of precious and semiprecious materials needed for his work.

It is important to note that Cordier's use of polychromy is not simply of aesthetic importance, but also carries with it a dimension significant to his conceptual approach to racial knowledge and to the problematizing of the intersubjective relationship between the slave and the artist. There can be no denying that the historical and discursive alliances among race, polychromy, and aesthetics manifest themselves acutely in Cordier's pieces and operate to "provoke new readings and meanings for the sex and gender identification of ... [the slave] ... body."[39] As an ideological sign and gesture for the social and political positioning of the artist himself, Cordier's use of color in general, but in particular skin color, operates as a crucial site of inscription, representation, and control. His employment of color nuances emphasizes the visibility of signs of difference in which the point of referential comparison is the unseen white male body and its attendant signs and codings of mastery (through aesthetic and technical manipulation) and superiority over the slave body.[40] Moreover, the racialized codings behind Cordier's artistic enterprise become more pronounced in the nineteenth-century colonial context where racial differentiation and its idealization were both linked to democratic or humanitarian ideals and legitimated by the believed "truth" of science.

In an 1854 letter to Achille Fould, then the Director of Fine Arts and the Minister of State, Cordier requested that the French government subsidize a six-month trip to Algeria so that he could gather ethnographic evidence with the goal of reproducing "a beautiful collection of busts … which will have a picturesque and interesting effect at the Universal Exposition" slated to be held the following year.[41] His request was granted, and the result was a series of thirteen busts representing Arabs, Kabyles, Black Africans, Jews, Moors, and other ethnic types fashioned out of onyx, semiprecious attachments, and enameled jewels. Two years later, in 1856, the sculptor once again sought and was granted funding from the French State to leave on a mission to Algeria. His request was once again approved, and, at the Salon of 1857, he exhibited eighteen portrait busts of various ethnic types, most fashioned out of a combination of marble, onyx-marble, and bronze. Of the busts exhibited, *Negro of the Sudan in Algerian Costume* (Fig. 10.7, Plate 8) was the most admired and became Cordier's signature piece. The bust was such a success that Cordier produced five replicas of it, two of which were purchased by Napoleon III in 1857 and a third acquired by the French government in 1860 for the Palace of Saint-Cloud. Each facsimile was a unique work of art in that each exhibited slight variations in its use of materials. In the Salon, these busts caused a sensation with the Salon-going public and especially with Gautier, who lauded their aesthetic panache and technical bravura.[42] With the exception of *Negro of the Sudan in Algerian Costume*, these sculptures were soon destined for display in the anthropology wing of the Muséum d'Histoire naturelle so as to provide scientists and the public with visual information on the appearance of races not usually encountered in France.[43] As objects of both science and art placed in the museum environment, Cordier's busts were explicitly intended to serve as models to lend credence to the numerous scientific theories on race and racial typologies that were in circulation at the time.

In 1860 Cordier was again recognized by his peers in being rewarded a separate gallery at the Palais de l'Industrie in Paris devoted exclusively to the display of fifty of his ethnographic pieces showcasing African, Asiatic, and European types.[44] The catalog for this exhibition, written by the critic Marc Trapadoux, lauded the technical and scientific qualities of Cordier's work.[45] As Gautier had done before him, Trapadoux promoted the sculptor as a technical, scientific, and aesthetic genius of the Second Empire. Mirroring Cordier's conceptual approach to his busts, Trapadoux described the works with an intriguing mixture of sober physiognomic detailing and romantic reverie. In reference to *Negro of the Sudan*, for example, the critic wrote:

> With his male casualness, with his widespread pride exhibited upon his traits, this figure seems like a Spartacus to me, like a Toussaint Louverture. The sentiment of human dignity, revolt against injustice, the hatred of slavery profoundly criss-crossing this noble face; the reflection

10.7. Charles Henri Joseph Cordier, *Negro of the Sudan in Algerian Costume*, 1856–57. Oxidized silver-plated bronze and onyx-marble. Musée d'Orsay, Paris, inv. no. RF 2997. Photo: Amaudet. Réunion des Musées Nationaux/Art Resource, New York.

> of an ardent soul, a flash of intelligence illuminates this stormy face that commands respect; a face which allows us to discern a loftiness and disdain that repels pity. This bust is one of the most beautiful specimens of the race.[46]

Trapadoux's praisings reflected his and his contemporaries interest in the juxtaposing of the slave, or rather, the slave ideal as automatically evoked by the representational presence of a black figure, with noble bearing and intelligence bestowed upon a "Negro countenance" through classicizing language. Indeed, in his discussion of *Negro of the Sudan*, Trapadoux himself acknowledged the classicized aspect of the piece when he described it as having the "look of a Roman emperor."[47]

The ideological effects of classicizing language did not stop here. In keeping true to form as a shrewd promoter of his ethnographic types through male-female pairings, Cordier decided, in 1861, to sculpt a female counterpart to his *Negro of the Sudan in Algerian Costume*. The *Câpresse des Colonies* (also called *Négresse des Colonies*) (Fig. 10.8) is a bronze figure with a single piece of multicolored onyx forming a classicized swath of drapery placed diagonally across the figure's torso.[48] As with *Negro of the Sudan in Algerian Costume*, this work is aesthetically powerful in its contrast between Eurocentric classicism and ethnographic realism. Although the figure's facial features were taken from the living model, her personhood has been undercut by her function both as a decorative object and as a generic racial representative of the colonies. As a "hybridized" racial type and physical specimen of an exotic other, she is presented as more noble than savage.

Cordier's goal in sculpting racial and ethnographic types was twofold: first, to align himself conscientiously with the contemporary progressive scientific movements of anthropology and ethnography, and second, to promote visually, in his own words, "l'ubiquité du Beaux."[49] Cordier's attempts to seek out and capture "Beauty" in all the scientifically classified races of man and to show that that beauty was universal carry with them serious political and colonialist implications that cannot be ignored. Although his search for beauty in other races was predicated on his understanding and acceptance of Western notions of classical aesthetics as the standard from which to judge, his search was in fact audacious for the period. In his role as harbinger of science and beauty, he boasted that "[b]ecause beauty is not the province of a privileged race, I give to the world of art the idea of the universality of beauty. Every race has its beauty, which differs from that of other races. The most beautiful Negro is not the one who looks most like us, nor the one who presents the most pronounced characteristics associated with his race. It is the individual in whom are united such forms and traits, and a face that reflects with harmony and balance the essential moral and intellectual character of the Ethiopian race."[50] Despite this

10.8. Charles Henri Joseph Cordier, *Câpresse des Colonies* (*Négresse des Colonies*), 1861. Oxidized silvered bronze, gilt bronze, and onyx-marble. Musée d'Orsay, Paris, inv. no. RF 2996. Photo: Raux/Ojéda. Réunion des Musées Nationaux/Art Resource, New York.

selfless humanitarian posture, I contend that Cordier's very approach to ethnographic sculpture constitutes a colonizing act. His busts exemplify the extent to which the act of sculpting itself was a gesture that supported France's civilizing mission through a doctrine of social, cultural, and aesthetic subjugation of the racial/ethnic other. In this process, the subjectivity and agency of those represented were necessarily subordinated and, for all intents and purposes, practically erased.

In the busts under consideration, ethnographic description and the aestheticized language of classicism simultaneously harmonize and conflict. In them, aesthetics and science operate to strip the sitter of their personhood while "ennobling" them as representatives of grand abstract ideals on which French national identity was founded and promoted. With Cordier's *Câpresse des Colonies,* for example, an aura of stoic dignity and passive compliance has been bestowed upon a black subject who substitutes as visible sign of the slave's "willing" acceptance of the civilizing process – a procedure reflective of the ultimate assimilationist and pacification intentions of Napoleon III in his desires to identify, order, and then absorb into the French empire those racially and ethnically diverse peoples encountered. Moreover, the gesture is promoted as a just and humanitarian one. In the case of the *Câpresse,* the black figure herself has been (re)constructed and restrained (or constrained) into aesthetic complacency through appropriated "colonized" materials and classified under the sanctioned weight of science. The sculpted black subject as slave becomes a conduit through which the underlying political motivations of territorial exploration, infiltration, command, and ultimate assimilation as subjugation are expressed.

10.9. Jean-Baptiste Carpeaux, *Pourquoi naître esclave?* (Why Be Born a Slave?), ca. 1868. Terracotta. Musée de la Chartreuse, Douai, no. inventaire 819. © Musée de la Chartreuse, Douai.

The *Câpresse's* classicizing visual language combined with precise physiognomic description, detailed hairstyle, and jewelry, as well as its intense polychromy, constitute a visually and conceptually intriguing counterfoil to Jean-Baptiste Carpeaux's (1827–75) 1868 bust *Pourquoi naître esclave?* (Why Be Born a Slave?) (Fig. 10.9) – a figure who is, conversely, intended to be more savage than noble.[51] Both works are related in that the same model, whose biographical details are unknown to us, may have posed for both artists.[52] Whereas Cordier's bust played into the documentary and taxonomic interests of anthropology and ethnography, Carpeaux's image – although ethnographic in its focus – played more into the popular and commercial resurgence of the slavery theme precisely two decades after abolition.

Carpeaux's bust was initially given the generic title *Afrique* and was created originally as a preparatory study for a larger project – a monumental fountain laid out between the Observatoire and the Jardins du Luxembourg, commissioned by the city of Paris for the 1867 Universal Exposition, and representing the four parts of the world (Asia, Africa, Europe, the Americas) supporting, in temporal harmony, a gigantic globe.[53] After the critical success of this monument, Carpeaux decided to exhibit only the bust of the personification of Africa in the 1869 Salon under the new title *Why Be Born a Slave?* The title of Carpeaux's bust, presented in the form of a query, was in keeping with abolitionist strategy in that it brought to mind the question "*Am I Not a Man and a Brother?*" used in the late eighteenth century as an antislavery, humanitarian slogan and engraved as title on a well-known abolitionist medallion designed by the English artist Josiah Wedgwood (1730–95) (see Fig. I.7). However, the question "Why be born a slave?" also echoes European fantasies about possession, domination, and physical control over vulnerable bodies. Carpeaux's bust demonstrates that there was a link between imperial politics and racial and sexual politics during the Second Empire – an observation underscored by the fact that Napoleon III purchased Carpeaux's bust (as well as several busts by Cordier) for the Palace at Saint-Cloud, considered by one art historian as "a virtual repository for erotic art."[54]

Whereas Cordier's *Câpresse des Colonies* downplays the eroticizing of the female body by its focus on the decorative qualities of the materials, combined with emphasis on precise ethnographic facial delineation, Carpeaux's sculpture accentuates the sensual and the erotic for dramatic effect. *Why Be Born a Slave?* underscores the artist's interest in depicting the slave's physical subjugation and victimization. The woman's tossed head, piteous facial expression, and wild hair animate the bust and assist in the imagining of a narrativized space and encounter, thus forcing the viewer to take on the position and role as slaveowner. A rope, tightly drawn around the figure's torso and gouged into her pliant flesh, highlights her exposed breast, the multiple symbolism of which I have written about elsewhere in reference to French representations of black women as figurative and literal slaves.[55]

In their own distinct ways, Carpeaux's *Why Be Born a Slave?* and Cordier's *Câpresse des Colonies* emphasize the physical possession and containment of the black female slave body. Carpeaux highlights this dramatically through the appearance of a binding rope, while Cordier places emphasis on the work's materiality as means of containing and civilizing the slave body underneath. Both works serve a decorative function and satisfy the desire to possess and study the slave captive. Simultaneously, both works encourage fantasies about the sexualizing potential of the captive/captivating slave body.

The widespread belief in black female hypersexuality was particularly strong in the medical and popular literature of this period and bears strongly on these sculpted works.[56] Ultimately, both sculptors de-personalize their slaves while constructing "race" and "sexuality" as linked categories. Cordier does so by "dressing up" the black female in classicizing garb, subduing her assumed sexual impulse, and piecing together opposing ethnic and cultural features (i.e., the African and the European) in a harmonious fashion. Carpeaux, on the other hand, "strips down" his slave to a minimum of ethnographic signs and presents her as an eroticized object of bondage. Both "dressing up" and "stripping down" are slaveowning and colonizing acts that operate to objectify and commodify. Carpeaux's bust, in particular, characterizes the paradoxical nature of racial and gender ideologies of the period in that the work accomplishes two opposing goals simultaneously: It speaks the humanitarian language of protest against human bondage as unjust, provoking outrage from its viewers, while simultaneosuly stimulating an erotic look upon the slave and thus provoking sexual fantasies of slave ownership for the viewer who is presumed to be a heterosexual male. The slave becomes a focus of simultaneous indignation against slavery and titillation for it.

Contrary to Carpeaux's bust of violent slave resistance, Cordier's *Câpresse* is static and docile. However, she too satisfies fantasies of domination and subjugation, but in a different way. Cordier contains and restrains the erotic charge of the slave through the imposing of classicizing traits and sensualizing materials. By bestowing classicizing drapery and a noble bearing onto the slave body, Cordier tames her supposed unrestrained sexuality and succeeds in his civilizing mission through a mastery over her. In addition, because Cordier's figure is smiling and her head is turned askance, she is seemingly content or passive in her role as looked at object of our aesthetic, and potentially erotic, pleasure. The implication here is that this particular unnamed black woman, extended to either slave or free blacks in general, could never achieve on their own such a level of refinement and sophistication without European assistance and insistence. Such a belief was merely one of many points of moral justification for French imperialism and colonial infiltration into different parts of Africa and the colonies.

The blatant and subtle eroticized aspects of these two works are linked with "the discourse of colonialism [which] is pervaded by images of transgressive sexuality ... and ... persistent fantasies of inter-racial sex."[57] Indeed, in the context of slavery, sex is connected with the legacy and discourse of commerce coming out of colonial encounters. Both sculptures underscore my contention that no matter how particularized or generalized the slave figure is allowed to become, it is forever locked into an ontological prison of sorts – a phenomenon that weighs on the very condition of the slave's being and that, in the postcolonial context, has been referred to as "crushing objecthood."[58] This condition speaks to the very paradox of defining the slave portrait in that it poses the problem of resolving questions of a slave's identity and subjectivity, particularly when taking into account the fact that the very definition of a portrait as an affirmation of individuality and elevated social position seems contradictory to the definition of a slave – that is, a nonsubject, an object of denigration, manipulation, abjection, an entity negated and emptied of identity, one whose subjectivity has been canceled out and evacuated by her or his very status as a slave. Through the physical and psychological destabilizing effects of racialization and colonialism, the slave becomes a locus of ambiguous and constantly shifting meaning for both the slave "person" and the slavemaster.

Shaping the processes of slave objectification and their impact on agency was the development and deployment of some weighty racial discourses launched in the nineteenth century. The beliefs of Charles Darwin (1809–82) and Joseph Arthur Comte de Gobineau (1816–82) especially, joined with positivist ideas around art and science, contributed not only to the development of nineteenth-century racist and racialist ideologies, but also to sexualizing ideas in the visualization of the slave.[59] It should come as no surprise that Cordier and Carpeaux produced their sculptures at a time when the influence of these ideologies on art and science was particularly strong.

In no way downplaying the impact of Darwinian theories on the significance of these sculpted slave portraits, the ideas of Gobineau are perhaps the more relevant here in considering how racial and sexual typologies operate within visual representation and against the potential agency of the black (mainly female) slave. Between 1853 and 1855, Gobineau published his *Essai sur l'inégalité des races humaines* in which he defined race as the determining factor in the trajectory of history. For Gobineau, history existed only as a result of the deeds and activities of the white (male) race. In his view, black people, if left on their own, would remain "immersed in a profound inertia."[60] In his writings, Gobineau was less concerned with fixing "pure" racial types and was more intrigued with issues of miscegenation, racial mixtures, and indeterminacies as the determinant of Western historical progress. Significant to the works of both Carpeaux and Cordier is that, according to Gobineau, the white male's response to the allure of black female sexuality was rooted in his mastery over her resistance to domination. Gobineau saw the black races as feminized and subordinate to white males. That is, black slave women as well as men represented for Gobineau and others like him entire continents and nations to be conquered. As I have already suggested, Carpeaux's *Why Be Born a Slave?* as well as Cordier's *Câpresse des Colonies* visualize such an attempt by white male artists at mastery and control over slave resistance. The works of both sculptors provide visual traces of Gobineau's gendered racial scheme in which the domination and subordination of the inferior "feminine" races by white males was taken as historically inevitable. Thus, the slave as subject signifies an automatic investment and inevitability in European (white male) domination over the slave's subjectivity and agency.

". . . that which has been robbed"

In his influential essay "Myth Today" (1957), Roland Barthes described an image of a black soldier saluting the French tricolor in his attempt to illustrate the cultural generation and circulation of myth.[61] He cast the black figure in semiotic terms – as an icon robbed of his unique individuality and yet exploited as a signifier full of meaning. Barthes understood that the visualization of the racial other in this way gave the black subject a deceptively cohesive identity.[62] He also realized that the history and motives of the image maker (the colonialist or "mythmaker") are also significant. The historical context for Barthes's observation was colonialism's legacy and the artist's motive was the creation of myth as a means of forgetting the interchangeability within the self/other relationship. Indeed, as David Theo Goldberg has observed, "the recognition of the self in the other remains at root an alienated identity, an 'identity-in-otherness'."[63] In the process of forging French national and self definition through the other, the artists discussed herein "drained and tamed,"[64] distanced, and made transparent the black slave. The act of "draining and taming" the slave through objectifying processes of amalgamation (science and aesthetics) not only reflects, but also constitutes, colonialist "mythmaking" practice. In the process of their fashioning, these sculpted slaves were summarily stripped of their subjectivity and agency. They became nothing more than aestheticized containers for the colonizer's ideologies and his egocentric sense of self and purpose. In order to determine the political force of the black presence in French art, which is, in essence, a slave presence, and the mythical burden of meaning that the black figure carries, one must look at these sculpted slave portraits from the point of view not of the slave-as-person (of which we are led to believe that they represent), but rather, from the vantage point "of that which has been robbed"[65] and put to productive use by and for the "mythmaker." The slaves themselves, even when and if named – such as was the case with Seïd Enkess and Ochi-Fékoué (Joseph) – were neutralized in their ability to speak and act for themselves. Ironically, it is in this mode that the slave was and remains most dynamic, passing from a recognizable element in a visual equation into a complex ideological system that speaks more of France and Frenchmen than it does of Africa and Africans. In the Barthean sense, these evacuated and "hollowed out" slave portraits have been filled in with a self-reflexive ideology that functions as "interpellation ... [a] calling up of [subordinated] subjects into an essentially bourgeois and collective psychic space."[66] They constitute "empty shells," albeit, exquisite ones.

Notes

1 Hugh Honour, *Image of the Black in Western Art* (Cambridge, Mass.: Harvard University Press, 1989), 4: part 2, 100–101. Other works in the Salon of 1848 included a plaster group of a *Cavalier Africain attaqué par une lionne* by Isidore Bonheur (brother of Rosa Bonheur) and an unspecified *Sujet d'Afrique* by Théodore Hébert.

2 See Charles-Henri Cordier, Mémoires et notes écrites par Charles Cordier, statuaire, chevalier de la Légion d'honneur, né à Cambrai le 1er novembre 1827, décédé à Alger le 19 avril 1905, 10. Original manuscript retained by the family. Facsimiles located at the Musée du Louvre archives and the Documentation du Musée d'Orsay, Paris.

3 On the history and shifting meaning of these terms in the eighteenth and nineteenth centuries, see Serge Daget, "Les Mots eclave, nègre, noir, et les jugements de valeur sur la traite négrière dans la littérature abolitioniste française de 1770 à 1845," *Revue française d'histoire d'outre-mer* 60 (1973), 511–48.

4 J. P. T. Bury, *Napoleon III and the Second Empire* (London: English University Press, 1964), 122. On the docrine of assimilation as it was conceived and implemented in the late nineteenth century, see Raymond F. Betts, *Assimilation and Association in French Colonial Theory, 1890–1914* (New York: Columbia University Press, 1961).

5 See S. Rocheblave, *Jean-Baptiste Pigalle* (Paris: Librairie Centrale des Beaux-Arts, 1919), plate 24. The word "nègre" entered into the French language in 1516 and was used rarely before the eighteenth century. It was employed with more currency as a scientific term in the French language with the development of the African slave trade and with the proposition of various racial theories.

6 On the biography of Desfriches, see Paul Ratouis de Limay, *Aignan-Thomas Desfriches: Un amateur Orléanais au XVIIIe siècle* (Paris: Librairie H. Champion, 1907). Also see Antoinette Le Normand-Romain, "Sculpture et ethnographie," in *La Sculpture ethnographique: De la Vénus hottentote à la Tehura de Gauguin* (Paris: Réunion des Musées Nationaux, 1994), 35. Also see Jean-René Gaborit, *Jean-Baptiste Pigalle, 1714–1785. Sculptures du Musée du Louvre* (Paris: Editions de la Réunion des Musées Nationaux, 1985), 92–93.

7 See Griselda Pollock, *Differencing the Canon: Feminist Desire and the Writing of Art's Histories* (London: Routledge, 1999), 287.

8 H. H. Arnason, *The Sculptures of Houdon* (New York, 1975); also see Honour, *Image of the Black*, 4: part 1, 34, note 23.

9 *Salon de 1783*, 49; Honour, *Image of the Black*, 4: part 1, 36.

10 Ann L. Poulet, *Jean-Antoine Houdon: Sculptor of the Enlightenment* (Washington, D.C.: National Gallery of Art and Chicago: University of Chicago Press, 2003), 241; cited in Marc Furcy-Raynaud, "Correspondance de M. d'Angiviller avec Pierre," part 1, *Nouvelles archives de l'art français (NAAF)*, 3d ser., 21 (1905), 238, letter of 10 January 1779. Also see Louis Réau, *Houdon: Sa vie et son oeuvre* (Paris: F. De Nobele, 1964), 1:47.

11 Poulet, *Houdon*, 243.

12 Ibid., 241.

13 Ibid., 243.

14 Ibid., 244; see Paul Vitry, "La Tête de Négresse par Houdon du Musée de Soissons," *Bulletin des musées de France* (January 1931), 7–9; and Paul Vitry, "Un Buste de la collection M. de Camondo. La Négresse de Houdon," *Gazette des Beaux-Arts* (November 1931), 307–11; also see Honour, *Image of the Black*, 4: part 1: 36, note 29. The French text reads: "Rendue à la liberté et à l'égalité par la Convention nationale

le 16 pluviôse, deuxième de la République française une et indivisible." This slogan has become part of the myth of the French Republic resulting from the French Revolution that promotes "the unitary, universalist, and inclusive nature of the Republic as polity based on individual rights" as opposed to rights founded on an acknowledgement of group differences. It has been noted that this ideal, becoming the basis for French law and legitimation for the obfuscation of race as a recognized category of difference, is paradoxical in light of French involvement in colonial slavery and the slave trade. See Herrick Chapman and Laura L. Frader, eds., *Race in France: Interdisciplinary Perspectives on the Politics of Difference* (New York: Berghahn Books, 2005), 1.

15 See Laure de Margerie, "The Most Beautiful Negro Is Not the One Who Looks Most like Us," in *Facing the Other, Charles Cordier (1827–1905) Ethnographic Sculptor,* ed. Laure de Margerie, Edouard Papet, et al. (New York: Harry N. Abrams, 2004), 13.

16 This was the title of a debate that took place in 1847 among members of the Ethnological Society. Cited by Christine Barthe, "Models and Norms: The Relationship between Ethnographic Photographs and Sculptures," in *Facing the Other,* ed. de Margerie, Papet, et al., 96.

17 See Jean Boissel, *Victor Courtet, 1813–1867, premier théoricien de la hiérarchie des races humaines* (Paris: Presses Universitaires de France, 1972).

18 Victor Courtet, *Tableau ethnographique du genre humain* (Paris: A. Bertrand, 1849). "Discours préliminaire sur les caractères et les rapports généraux des races humaines," in *Discours prononcé à la Société ethnologique de Paris,* séance du 25 juin 1847.

19 Quoted from *Nouvelles Annales des voyages de la géographie et de l'histoire séance du 25 juin 1847* (Paris: Arthus Bertrand, 1840–65) vol. 11, 388; Barthe in de Margerie, Papet, et al., *Facing the Other,* 99. Both casting from life and ethnographic photography became complementary pursuits in the recording and classification of anatomy, skull shapes, and physiognomic/phrenological types. Casting from the live or dead model was put to anthropological use as a means of capturing ethnographic particulars of the living (or recently dead) model and to preserve such details for future study and categorization. See Édouard Papet, "Ethnographic Life Casts in the Nineteenth Century," in *Facing the Other,* ed. de Margerie, Papet, et al., 127. It is important to note that Cordier was adamantly opposed to the use of life casts for creating sculpture. In his own words, life casting only "weakens the flesh and makes the body look dull." For Cordier, the talented sculptor only needed the living model, his hands, and modeling tools. Cited in de Margerie, "'The Most Beautiful Negro . . .'," in de Margerie, Papet, et al., *Facing the Other,* 27, from Charles Cordier, "Rapport de Charles Cordier: types ethniques représentés par la sculpture," *Bulletin de la Société d'Anthropologie de Paris* (1862), 65–66.

20 Quoted from *Nouvelles Annales des voyages de la géographie et de l'histoire séance du 25 juin 1847,* vol. 11, 391; Christine Barthe, "Models and Norms: The Relationship between Ethnographic Photographs and Sculptures," in *Facing the Other,* ed. de Margerie, Papet, et al., 99.

21 See "Notice sur Seïd Enkess, nègre d'une remarquable beauté qui habite Paris," *Bulletin de la Société Ethnologique* (Paris, 1847), part 1; cited in Barthe, "Models and Norms," 99.

22 See Laure de Margerie, "'The Most Beautiful Negro . . .'," in *Facing the Other,* ed. de Margerie, Papet, et al., 15–16.

23 See Armand d'Avezac, "Histoire sommaire du nègre Ochi- Fékoué-Dé, natif de Yébou, baptisé au Brésil sous le nom de Joseph," in *Notice sur le pays et le peuple des Yébous en Afrique* (Paris, 1845), 18; cited in Barthe, "Models and Norms," 112, note 30.

24 The life casts of Ochi-Fékoué and Enkess were bequeathed, in the early 1870s, by the Ethnological Society of Paris to the Anthropology Laboratory of the Muséum d'Histoire naturelle as part of that institution's national repository for the diverse collections of life casts, photographs, and ethnographic sculptures procured by the Ministry of Fine Arts and destined for scientific study and research.

25 See Théophile Gautier, "Le Salon de 1857," *L'Artiste* (22 November 1857), 2:183; also see Michael Clifford Spencer, *The Art Criticism of Théophile Gautier* (Geneva: Librairie Droz, 1969).

26 For an engaging and nuanced discussion of this work in the context of the meaningful overlay of racial, aesthetic, and sexual significance, see Charmaine Nelson, "Vénus Africaine: Race, Beauty and African-ness," in *Black Victorians: Black People in British Art 1800–1900*, ed. Jan Marsh (London: Ashgate, 2005), 46–56. Many of the ideas contained in Nelson's essay parallel and complement those I present here.

27 In her nuanced assessment of this particular work, Charmaine Nelson has designated the *Vénus Africaine* as "a true puzzle" in that both Cordier and Gautier have made her into "a revered Western mythological figure, the goddess of love, with definite connotations of beauty and Antiquity," combined with "racial definitions of Western colonialism, anthetical to all that was thought beautiful." See Nelson, "Vénus africaine," 47.

28 See Gayatri Spivak, "Imperialism and Sexual Difference," *Oxford Literary Review* 8, nos. 1–2 (1986), 228–29.

29 Nelson, "Vénus africaine," 47–48.

30 See Charles Baudelaire, *Art in Paris, 1845–1862. Salons and Other Exhibitions*, trans. Jonathan Mayne (London: Phaidon Press, 1965), 111–13.

31 During the Second Empire, Zola and Gautier regarded sculpture as the least romantic of the arts. See Théophile Gautier, *Histoire du romantisme. Notices romantiques. Les progrès de la poésie française depuis 1830* (Paris: Charpentier, 1874), 29; Ruth Butler Mirolli and Jane van Nimmen, *Nineteenth Century French Sculpture: Monuments for the Middle Class* (Louisville: J. B. Speed Art Museum, 1971), exhibition catalog, 10.

32 It is important to note here that the Ethnological Society of Paris was founded in 1839 and was modeled on several philanthropic societies formed in England and headed by antislavery activists and men of science. See Claude Blanckaert, "On the Origins of French Ethnology," in *Bones, Bodies, Behavior: Essays on Biological Anthropology*, ed. George W. Stocking, Jr., History of Anthropology 5 (Madison: University of Wisconsin Press, 1988), 18–55; also see Fred W. Voget, *A History of Ethnology* (New York: Holt, Rinehart, and Winston, 1975).

33 Francis Schiller, *Paul Broca, Founder of French Anthropology, Explorer of the Brain* (Berkeley: University of California Press, 1979), 137.

34 Quoted from Charles Cordier, "Types ethniques représentés par la sculpture," *Bulletin de la Société d'Anthropologie de Paris* [séance du 6 février] (1862), 64–66, 67–68.

35 For elaboration on the discursive complexities of ethnography, see James Clifford and George E. Marcus, eds., *Writing Culture: The Poetics and Politics of Ethnography* (Berkeley: University of California Press, 1986).

36 Cordier, *Mémoires*, 13; see also Papet, "Ethnographic Life Casts," 53.

37 Cf. Andreas Blühm, ed., *The Colour of Sculpture* (Amsterdam: Van Gogh Museum, 1996).

38 Despite physical evidence that brightly colored paint had been applied to most statuary from antiquity, conservative artists and critics insisted that classical statuary should remain white and pristine. See Blühm, *The Colour of Sculpture*, 39.

39 Nelson, "Vénus africaine," 48.

40 Cf. Charmaine A. Nelson, "White Marble, Black Bodies and the Fear of the Invisible Negro: Signifying Blackness in Mid-Nineteenth-Century Neoclassical Sculpture," *RACAR* 27, no. 1/2 (2000), 87–101.

41 See *Archives nationales* (F21 72), letter from Cordier to Achille Fould (28 January 1854).

42 Théophile Gautier, "Le Salon de 1857," *L'Artiste* (22 November 1857), 2:183–85.

43 See A. Andrei, "Galerie anthropologique et ethnographique de M. Cordier," *L'art au dix-neuvième siècle* 5 (1860), 188–89.

44 Édouard Papet, "The Polychromy Techniques of Charles Cordier," in *Facing the Other*, ed. de Margerie, Papet, et al., 83; A. Durant, "A propos de l'exposition d'agriculture – L'exposition des produits de l'Algerie au Palais de l'Industrie," *L'Art au XIXe siècle* 2 (1860), 166; Mirolli and van Nimmen, *Nineteenth Century French Sculpture*, 21.

45 Marc Trapadoux, *L'Oeuvre de M. Cordier, galerie anthropologique et ethnographique pour servir à l'histoire des races* (Paris: C. Lahure, 1860). Also see Andrei, "Galerie anthropologique," 188–89.

46 Trapadoux, *L'Oeuvre de M. Cordier*, 14–15; Andrei, "Galerie anthropologique," 188–89.

47 Trapadoux, *L'Oeuvre de M. Cordier*, 14.

48 The term *câpresse* is the feminine variant of the word *câpre*. The term was one of several racial designations used in the colonial context to classify the result of different racial mixtures. A *câpresse* was the name given to the offspring of a mulatto (*mulâtre/mulâtresse*) and a black person (*noir/noire*).

49 Laure de Margerie and Édouard Papet, "Charles Cordier (1827–1905). Sculpteur, l'autre et l'ailleurs," *La revue du Musée d'Orsay*, no. 18 (spring 2004), 8.

50 Charles Cordier, "Rapport de Charles Cordier: Types ethniques représentés par la sculpture," *Bulletin de la Société d'Anthropologie de Paris* (6 February 1862), 66.

51 Cf. Anne Middleton Wagner, *Jean-Baptiste Carpeaux* (New Haven: Yale University Press, 1986).

52 De Margerie, "The Most Beautiful Negro," 13.

53 Honour, *Image of the Black*, 4: part 1, 259–62.

54 Albert Boime, *Hollow Icons* (Kent, Ohio: Kent State University Press, 1987), 80.

55 See my essay, "Slavery Is a Woman: 'Race', Gender, and Visuality in Marie Benoist's *Portrait d'une Négresse* (1800)," *Nineteenth-Century Art Worldwide* 3, no. 1 (2004), 1–22, available at www.19thc-artworldwide.org.; Marcia Pointon, "Liberty on the Barricades: Woman, Politics and Sexuality in Delacroix," in *Naked Authority: The Body in Western Painting, 1830–1908* (New York: Cambridge University Press, 1990), 59–82; and Maurice Agulhon, *Marianne into Battle: Republican Imagery and Symbolism in France, 1789–1880* (New York: Cambridge University Press, 1981).

56 See Sander L. Gilman, "Black Bodies, White Bodies: Toward an Iconography of Female Sexuality in Late Nineteenth-Century Art, Medicine, and Literature," in *"Race," Writing and Difference*, ed. Henry Louis Gates, Jr. (Chicago: The University of Chicago Press, 1986), 223–61; Joanna De Groot, "'Sex' and 'Race': The Construction of Language and Image in the Nineteenth Century," in *Sexuality and Subordination*, ed. Susan Mendus and Jane Rendall (London: Routledge, 1989).

57 Robert Young, *Colonial Desire: Hybridity in Theory, Culture and Race* (London: Routledge, 1995), 181–82.

58 See Frantz Fanon, *Black Skin, White Masks*, trans. Charles Lam Markmann (New York: Grove Press, 1967), 109.

59 Darwin's *Origin of Species*, published in 1859, was translated into French by Clémence Royer in 1862 as *L'Origine des espèces*. The work immediately led social theorists to

propose a series of hypotheses on racial difference and made even more intimate the association between sexuality and race. See Thomas Glick, *The Comparative Reception of Darwinism* (Chicago: University of Chicago Press, 1988). On Gobineau, see Michael D. Biddiss, *Father of Racist Ideology: The Social and Political Thought of Count Gobineau* (London: Weidenfeld and Nicolson, 1970).

60 Arthur Count de Gobineau, *Essai sur l'inégalité des races humaines* (Paris: Firmin-Didot, 1853–55), II:348.

61 Roland Barthes, *Mythologies* (Paris: Editions du Seuil, 1957; reprint: New York: Hill and Wang, 1972), see esp. 109–59.

62 David Theo Goldberg, *Racist Culture: Philosophy and the Politics of Meaning* (Oxford: Blackwell, 1993), 4.

63 Ibid., 59.

64 This expression is taken from Barthes, *Mythologies*, 125.

65 Ibid., 144–45.

66 Ibid., see esp. 109–59. As noted by Jacqueline Rose, Barthes's evacuation thesis was also a "critique of the ideology of mastery, for which the visual field was seen as the predominant site." See Jacqueline Rose, "Sexuality and Vision: Some Questions," in *Vision and Visuality*, ed. Hal Foster (Seattle: Bay Press, 1988), 120.

Part IV

FACING ABOLITION

ELEVEN

WHO IS THE SUBJECT?

MARIE-GUILHELMINE BENOIST'S *PORTRAIT D'UNE NÉGRESSE*

Viktoria Schmidt-Linsenhoff

The Painting

In 1800 the Salon exhibition in Paris presented a painting by Marie-Guilhelmine Benoist (1766–1826), labeled in the catalogue *Portrait d'une Négresse* (Fig. 11.1, Plate 9).[1] The portrait shows a beautiful young woman sitting in an armchair in front of a light beige background. The sitter is turned to the right side, looking at the beholder with a turn of her head. She wears a golden earring, a headscarf – one corner falling down in a transparent cascade – and a garment from the same fine, white cloth, exposing a bare breast, shoulder and arm, and provoking the notion of the naked body under the sheet. The left hand lies relaxed on her belly, the right arm like a barrier against the space of the beholder on her lap. The blue shawl on the chair completes the Tricolor *bleu, blanc, rouge,* being the only bright colors in the almost monochrome painting. The light falling on the dark complexion of face and body modulates their three-dimensional volume in a sculpturally designed form, and the warm brown- and gold-colored reflections convey a sensitivity and transparency, which, since the sixteenth century, the European theory of painting often had declared impossible to achieve in the representation of Ethiopian complexion.[2] The expression of the face and the gaze is neutral, inviting projective identifications and contradictory descriptions in art historical literature, for example, self-conscious and proud, uneasy and sad, uprooted and isolated and so on. Though the exhibition catalogue of 1800 replaces the individual name of the sitter with a racializing type-category, the formal schema of portraiture and the treatment of the face suggest a strong notion of individuality. The striking contradiction between the painting's aesthetic claim to be a portrait and its social function – not as a portrait – is

11.1. Marie-Guilhelmine Benoist, *Portrait d'une Négresse* (Portrait of a Negress), 1800. Oil on canvas. Musée du Louvre, Paris. Photo: Thierry Le Mage/Réunion des Musées Nationaux/Art Resource, New York.

crucial to my reading. The omission of the name of a portrayed person in the exhibition catalogue was not unusual; the idea was to emphasize the art-value instead of the mechanical work of imitation, taking into account that the public would nevertheless acknowledge the identity of the sitters, who were often well known in society. This is not the case here. Nobody knew the Négresse, and even today very little is known about her biography – except for the facts that she did not commission her portrait in an elegant, Parisian interior and that she made no use of the painting for her own purpose. But if not a portrait, what sort of painting is it – an academy of a half-naked, black model, an allegorical body-image referring vaguely to slavery and liberty, or an erotic genre painting showing a modern Black Venus? What exactly is the subject matter, and who is the subject depicted?

The comparison with a portrait of a *Mulher de Bahía* (Fig. 11.2) from the mid-nineteenth century might be useful to clarify what Benoist's *Portrait d'une Négresse* is not. Though we have no information concerning the sitter, there is no doubt that we are looking at a portrait, which tells us at least something about the social status of the depicted woman.[3] The sitter had successfully appropriated the European conventions of self-performance imported by colonial elites

11.2. Anonymous artist (Brazilian School), *Mulher de Bahía* (Woman of Bahia), mid-nineteenth century. Oil on canvas. Acervo do Museu Paulista da Universidade de São Paulo, São Paulo. Photo: Hélio Nobre.

in Brazil, yet maintains her local African heritage in presenting the exuberance of the Afro-Brazilian jewelry. We can isolate different codes and layers of cultural references, carefully chosen and combined in a telling way by the sitter no doubt in cooperation with the painter. The portrait of the *Mulher de Bahía* was conceived in a completely different local context some decades after Benoist's *Négresse*. Nevertheless the paintings are related to each other, both negotiating the place in visual culture of emancipated African women in white slave-holder societies. Benoist's painting certainly was not intended to function as a substitute for a particular woman of African descent, as is the case with the *Mulher de Bahía*. Nevertheless and despite the racializing de-nomination and anonymity of the "Woman of Paris," the painter wanted to provoke a similar attitude of empathy toward the sitter and to arouse the viewer's interest in the personality of the woman and her fate, overshadowed by deportation, slavery and servitude. All expectations usually inspired by a portrait are here simultaneously aroused and disappointed.

This element of uncertainty concerning the genre of Benoist's painting unsettled its critique from the first to the most recent comment. In 1800 the anonymous author A.D.F. doubts that the painting is a portrait at all,[4] and Maud Sulter's 2002 photographic paraphrase of Benoist's *Portrait d'une Négresse* (Fig. 11.3) transforms the borrowed composition into a portrait of a well-known black woman artist.[5] The large-scale Polaroid print is a portrait of the British playwright and critic Bonnie Greer (born 1948) and was recently purchased by the National Portrait Gallery in London. The variations are significant: The bare breast is covered, and the expression and the gaze of Bonnie Greer are not "empty," but convey a strong and active personality. Maud Sulter's photographic portrait is a historical masquerade in which the sitter performs the appropriation of European images made to define and control African subjectivity. Her borrowing seems to be less a condemnation than a critical re-vision of the colonial heritage, an effort not only to reject the European gaze on African bodies in the past, but also to engage in a form of creative dialogue with images and visual patterns, whose impact on neocolonial culture today is indubitable. Maud Sulter's comment draws attention to the fact that Benoist's painting in 1800 exposes the naked body of the black woman to white viewers and that the painter's promise to articulate black female subjectivity in the European diaspora was suggested, but not fulfilled. In realizing what Benoist's painting anticipated as a future possibility, Maud Sulter in 2002 reactivates the utopian potential of the painting without ignoring the historical frame of racism and sexism in which it was conceived. My analysis of the painting follows Maud Sulter's work in two aspects. I want to emphasize the utopian potential of the highly ambivalent "false" portrait, and I want to use her method of interpictorial references.

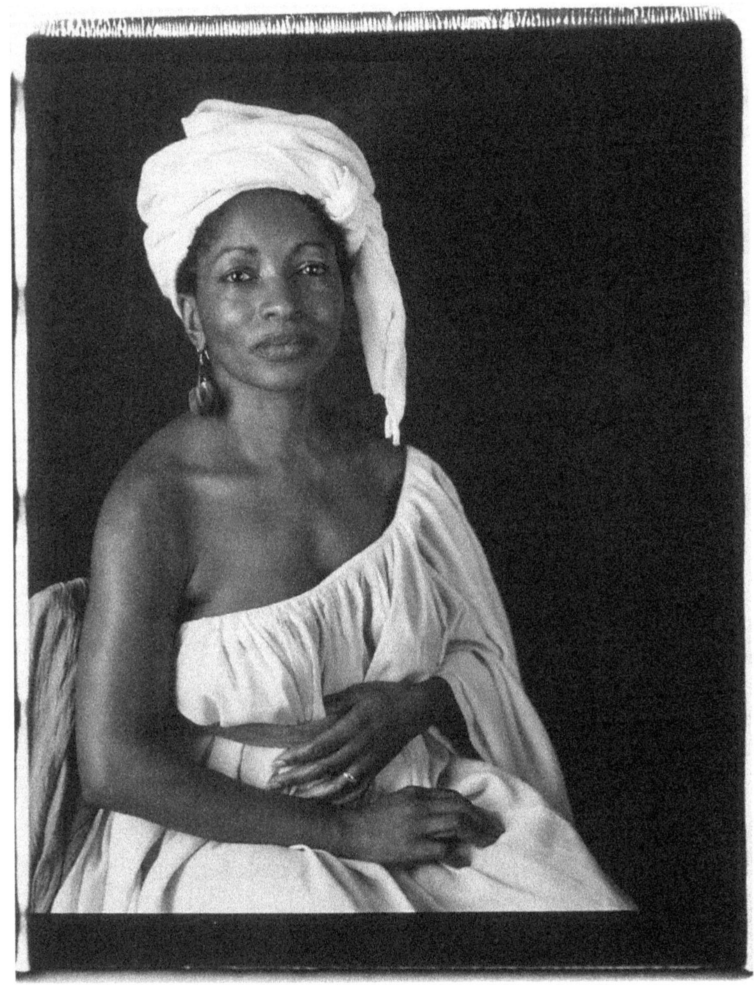

11.3. Maud Sulter, *Bonnie Greer*, 2002. Color Polaroid print. Private collection. Photo: Hood Museum of Art, Hanover, N.H.

My starting point is the paradoxical tension between the perception of the painting as a portrait of an African woman in Paris, whose individual personality is silenced and negated, and the perception of an image that looks like, but socially does not function as, a portrait. My scope is not to explain the painting as an expression of the personality of the painter or of the sitter. Though there is no visual evidence that the painting was conceived by Benoist in order to mark a certain position in ideological debates about race and gender, it was located in these textual fields in the course of its two hundred years of reception. I want to broaden the notion of visual meaning-production beyond the usual practices of iconography and the normativity of written texts, too often constrained to the scopic triangle between the painter, the sitter and the viewer. My aim is to include the latency of other images that come into the mind of the viewer while looking at Benoist's *Portrait d'une Négresse*.

The Painter and the Sitter

All we know about the *Portrait d'une Négresse* depends on our knowledge of the biography of the white woman painter, who never sold the painting, but kept it in her studio as her main masterwork.[6] The painter was born as Marie-Guilhelmine de Laville-Leroux and was brought up in a royalist family. Her father encouraged her professional development in the studios of Elisabeth Vigée-Lebrun and Jacques-Louis David. In 1786 a *Self-Portrait* of the young woman articulated an extraordinary claim for history painting. The classical drapery, the wildly waving hair and the energy of movement signify a bacchanal wildness as metaphor of a female genius. With the copy of a detail of David's history painting *Belisarius* on her easel she stands up for her teacher's stoical concept of pre-revolutionary virtue. Four years later, Benoist's history painting *Innocence between Virtue and Vice,* presented in the first revolutionary Salon exhibition of 1791, defines female republican virtue by making use of the iconography of *Hercules at the Crossroad,* the gender order of which is inverted and boldly adapted to female interests.[7] After an interruption of her career – caused by her marriage to Pierre Vincent Benoist in 1793 – the artist made her comeback in the Salon exhibition with the spectacular subject matter of the *Portrait d'une Négresse*. It is likely that the painter met the black sitter in the house of her brother-in-law Benoist-Cavay, a naval officer, who brought the woman as his former slave, servant, or mistress from Guadeloupe to Paris.[8] The emancipation of black slaves in the enlightened circles of metropolitan culture was an exception, but happened often enough to arouse the particular interest of intellectuals and to inspire literary and artistic creativity – I have in mind particularly the intellectual career of the Moorish page Soliman at the court of Vienna (see Fig. 2.8) and Ignatius Sancho in London, who was portrayed in 1768 by Thomas Gainsborough (see Fig. 2.5). The special interest in little black girls that was shown by aristocratic white women in the late Enlightenment is well known. The

11.4. Francisco Goya, *The Duchess of Alba Holding María de la Luz*, 1796–97. India ink wash. Museo Nacional del Prado, Madrid, D4183.

11.5. Sophie de Tott, *Ourika*, 1793 (?). Oil on canvas. Private collection. Reproduced in *Ourika: Madame de Duras* (Exeter: University of Exeter Press, 1998), frontispiece.

Duchess of Alba adopted an enslaved black girl whom she named María de la Luz, and she asked Goya to memorialize their affectionate relationship and the equal status held by the girl in her household (Fig. 11.4).[9] Benoist must have heard of the famous case of the little girl from Senegal, whom the governor

Chevalier de Boufflers brought from the island of Goré to Paris in 1768 as a present for his aunt, Madame de Beauvau. The success in society enjoyed by the Senegalese girl, who was educated and trained in French civilization, is documented in a portrait, possibly from 1793, by the otherwise unknown painter Sophie de Tott (Fig. 11.5).[10] The portrait, painted in a sentimental late-Rococo style, shows the Senegalese girl, wearing golden slave bracelets, adorning with flowers the bust of her first owner Boufflers in order to express her gratitude to him. After her death in 1799 she became the model for *Ourika*, the black female hero in the novel of Madame de Duras (published in 1823).[11] The engraving, showing the Senegalese slave Phillis Wheatley as author, discussed elsewhere in this volume (see essays by Marcia Pointon and Eric Slauter), gives evidence that the intellectual emancipation of enslaved African women was possible in different ways and occurred perhaps more often than is known today. Beyond this tradition of enlightened fascination with spectacular "exceptions," Benoist could be sure of public interest in her painting, relating as it did to the current debates about the reestablishment of the slave system, which had been abolished by the National Assembly in February 1794. The eight contemporary reviews of the painting with which I am familiar can be related to different positions in these debates. Three of them took the opportunity to articulate racist prejudices, repeating the topos of the natural ugliness of Africans, which no painterly skill could embellish; five of them praised the beauty of the painting in general and acknowledged the remarkable perfection of design, measuring its formal qualities in a flattering comparison with Jacques-Louis David.[12] Making the assumption that ideal black beauty in portrait painting was understood in 1800 as an argument against the reestablishment of slavery, we could appreciate the *Négresse* as an abolitionist statement by the painter. But as is well known, the contradictory relationships between slavery and beauty, social reality and painterly construction, and literary and visual discourses are more complicated. The lack of documents concerning the status of the sitter and the artist's attitude to slavery have led the scholarly approach of social-historical reconstruction into a dead end: We have to go back to the painting itself and its readings.

Critical Readings

Although the French State thought enough of Benoist's *Négresse* to purchase it after the artist's death in 1826 for the national collection of contemporary French painting in the Musée du Luxembourg, twentieth-century art historians have paid little attention to the work of women artists in general and even less to the representation of blacks. The feminist rediscovery of "forgotten" women artists since about 1970 was eager to make a scandal out of the "revealing case of Mme. Benoist."[13] Despite professional success and devotion to her profession, the artist was forced to break off her career because her husband's position in the government made it necessary for his wife to withdraw from all public activities in the art system. Feminist art historians focused on the victimization of a woman artist at the peak of her career, but they were reluctant to tackle the questions presented by Benoist's painting with regard to early feminism in the French Revolution: the power relation between two unequal women. On one hand, we have a white bourgeois painter with a Jacobin past, married to a minister in a government inclined to favor slavery; on the other hand, the black sitter, balanced in a precarious state between emancipation and servitude. The portrait embodies this power relation in a spectacular way and puts into question the notion of universal sisterhood by making visible the participation of white women artists in colonial culture – a dilemma that feminist art historians were not able to acknowledge in the 1970s.

Actually the first serious attempt at interpretation was made by Hugh Honour in 1989, when he praised the "warmly humane and noble image," sketching the painting's political context in the Parisian abolitionist circle *Amis des Noirs* and Olympe de Gouges's *Déclaration des droits de la femme*. Honour's enthusiasm for the "most beautiful portrait of a black woman ever painted,"[14] which he read as an allegorical representation of black liberty, was criticized by scholars from a postcolonial and post-feminist point of view as being too harmonizing and overly simplified. These scholars focused instead on the problematic effects of exoticism and voyeurism, which still underlie racist and sexist ideologies today. Griselda Pollock even compared the "scopic regime" of the black nude in painting with the scopic regime of the slave block, "where naked men and women were exposed to the calculating gaze of their would-be owners."[15] Once the overlapping of sexual and colonial politics and the unconscious Eurocentrism of the Western feminist enterprise were acknowledged, Benoist's painting became a privileged object of critical self-reflection, illuminating the blind spot in Western feminist theory and social movements. The painting was located in intersecting debates about slavery and women's struggle for civil rights in the French Revolution – debates which were radically changing between the Jacobin abolition of slavery in 1794 and its re-institution by Napoleon in 1802. The political participation of women of varying status in the street and in clubs after 1789 had provoked aggressive anti-feminist measures, which resulted in a breathtaking backlash against women's political rights, later fixed into law by the Napoleonic Code. It has turned out to be difficult to locate Benoist's painting with precision in the rapidly changing crossover of discourses about the roles and rights of Africans and women in the French Republic.

Of course, we may assume that Benoist read and discussed many articles and books dealing with these questions, but if we want to mark her position we can rely on no other source than the painting itself. Recent publications tend to deny any critical intention of the painter. Whereas Astrid Reuter (2000) downplays any political meaning at all, emphasizing instead the painter's personal interest in questions of style, Helen Weston, Darcy Grimaldo Grigsby and James Smalls judge the painting in the framework of feminist and postcolonial theory without seeing any positive acknowledgement of black female subjectivity.[16] Weston and Grigsby put forward the anonymity of the black model, whose individuality is denied by the painter. Weston understands the "deliberate opposing of the two identities of artist and sitter" in the signature above the sitter's hand as a strategy of the white woman painter to improve her career by means of the alterity of a black woman's image. Having identified Benoist politically with the pro-slavery interests of her husband's family, Weston sees in the painter an absolute lack of solidarity with black women. She condemns the artist for not caring about the "woman of Guadeloupe" and for exploiting the "sensational value of the figure's blackness and difference" to satisfy the "need for recognition of her own identity as a professional working artist."[17] Grigsby concedes that Benoist might have articulated a position independent from that of her relatives but understands the painting nevertheless as testimony to the post-Jacobin political backlash during the time of the Directorium. The anonymity of the sitter, she writes, stresses the "typological rather than the individual" making invisible the "black female servant or slave," concluding: "The sitter is robbed like a slave, of her person's property." Grigsby observes the transformation of a real African woman into an image of a race-type and an allegory of a continent, defining this esthetical proceeding as an "act of depletion, that is not unlike the condition of slavery itself."[18]

James Smalls's analysis – working through the dynamics of race, gender and visuality – is the most nuanced one. He explores the painting's potential to articulate "a voice of protest, however small, in the discourse of human bondage," but ultimately sees the dominance of a visual strategy of Othering, by which the painter empowers her own female "colonial Self." Smalls blames Benoist for robbing "the black sitter of her identity, her voice, and her agency in order to make a statement about the social position and power … of bourgeois and upper class white women."[19] The remarkable white headwrap, for example, signifies – according to Smalls – servitude and labor in the context of slavery, but it recalls also the Phrygian cap of liberty and a visual stereotype of Orientalism. He concludes that the headwrap "may operate as an instrument of identity and rebellion even though its very presence also serves as a signifier of difference imposed upon the sitter by a privileged white woman whose own sense of identity depended on black woman's labor, physical submission and forced anonymity."[20] Finally Smalls refers to theories of the gaze in sexual and colonial power-relations. He reconstructs a multiple network of looking, a "dialogic exchange between the artist, the sitter and the viewer," which creates shifting subject-positions and performs interracial, same-sex desire between the painter and the sitter. Though Smalls seems to appreciate the subversive potential of sexual transgression, he blames Benoist for sexualizing the black model. Benoist and her *Négresse,* he argues, both remained slaves to the hegemonic male white slaveholder culture: The image was a political failure.

Owing much to the critical readings of Weston, Grigsby and Smalls, still, I disagree with their conclusions. Their art historian's desire that the portrait should reconstruct and represent the full subjectivity of the sitter, which slavery had denied and silenced, is in itself problematic. In my view, these art historians have misunderstood the function of the image. I would argue that the painting portrays neither the individuality of the sitter nor a racial type, but a particular, precisely defined social group: French women of African descent, who had experienced slavery and in 1794 achieved French citizenship. The strong expression of individuality is not meant to express the individuality of the woman depicted, but the capacity of black French women to develop a type of individuality that is similar to, but not identical with, the type of individuality the republican culture invented for white French women. The painting does not illustrate anthropological issues about racial taxonomy (with which we know Benoist was familiar), but issues about the cultural hybridization of the French colonial-metropolitan society after abolition. It addresses the problems of internal difference and the heterogeneity of the national body, which was imagined as exclusively white and masculine – notwithstanding the declaration of human rights, the republican constitution and the abolition of slavery. The painting can be read as a visual test about the integration of emancipated former slaves into the nation: How much visual difference is tolerable, how is blackness redefined after abolition, how far can black bodies be integrated into the white national body, where are the limits of integration? Whereas the few portraits of emancipated slaves produced during the eighteenth century (like Thomas Gainsborough´s *Ignatius Sancho*; see Fig. 2.5) articulate the emancipation of African slaves in terms of their assimilation to European norms, Benoist emphasizes difference – a visual difference she teaches the beholder to appreciate and to enjoy aesthetically. The *Portrait d´une Négresse* stresses difference of appearance not as biological race-category, but as a social experience related to the production of visual meaning, which depends on the white beholder.

MOI LIBRE AUSSI

Obviously Benoist´s *Négresse* was meant to be understood as comment and answer to Anne-Louis Girodet's *Portrait du citoyen Belley, ex-représentant des colonies* (Fig. 11.6) in the Salon exhibition two years earlier.[21] Unlike Benoist's anonymous *Négresse,* this painting is a real portrait, showing the well-known black deputy of Saint-Domingue and a bust of the renowned abolitionist G. T. F. Raynal. The double portrait is built up on binary oppositions: Europe and Africa, past and future, death and life, marble and flesh, white intellectuality and black sensuality and so on. The painter does not assimilate the African

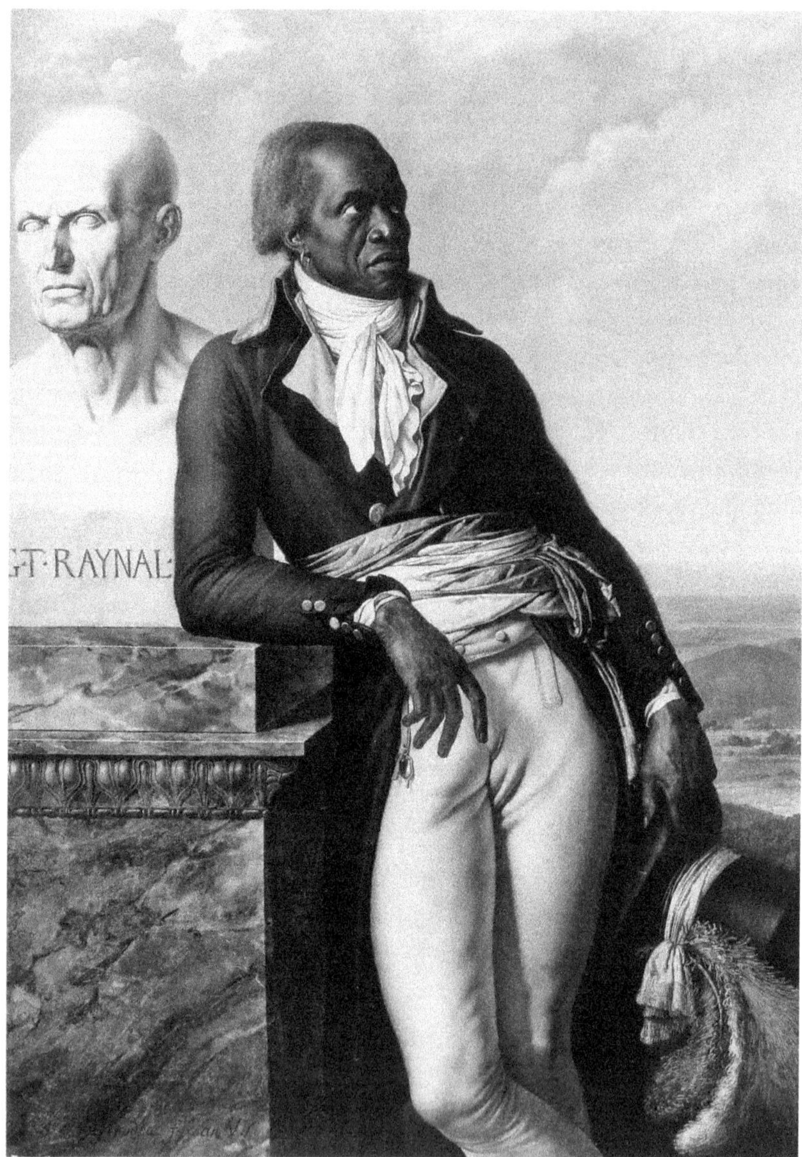

11.6. Anne-Louis Girodet de Roussy-Trioson, *Portrait du citoyen Belley, ex-représentant des colonies*, 1797. Oil on canvas. Châteaux de Versailles et de Trianon, Versailles. Photo: Erich Lessing/Art Resource, New York.

body of the black deputy, but idealizes his visual otherness, marked as sexual virility. Like Benoist's *Négresse*, the portrait of the black deputy was neither commissioned nor bought by the sitter, but kept in the painter's studio, where it functioned as testimony to the artist's avant-garde position, linking issues of classicism and slavery. Being the most successful pupil in the school of David, the homosocial dynamics of which have been described in detail,[22] Girodet struggled for independence from David, marking again his "originality" in the field of portrait-painting and outdoing David with the spectacular aesthetic of a black body. Girodet's painting deals with problems of equality and difference, esthetical and political representation of the republic in terms of an allegedly universal masculinity. The image of Belley was intended and understood by the public as an argument for the emancipation of the humble, childish *negro* as icon of a paternalistic abolition movement. Nevertheless it confirms the Jacobin dogma that only men have political agency in the public sphere, linking the questions of emancipation and integration of former slaves with traditional discourses about hegemonic and marginal masculinity, homosocial relationships and homoerotic desire.

Benoist's supplementation of Girodet's exclusively male model of emancipation is related to a parallel iconography in abolitionist image-production, distributed under the title *moi libre aussi* in various media such as copper prints, small sculptures in porcelain, etc.[23] The meaning depends on which "I" is speaking: I, the black slave, wants to be free as you are, white brother; or, I, the black enslaved woman wants to be free, as you have become after abolition, black brother. Similar to these prints, the close, interpictorial relationship between the paintings of Girodet and Benoist alludes to the metaphorical shift between feudal, colonial and sexual connotations of "slavery" common in the rhetoric of European enlightenment.[24] Much more important is the transfer of this iconography from the medium of popular image-production into the high art of portrait-painting, which in the years around 1800 was the privileged medium of self-definition and performative shaping of a new republican model of subjectivity. Employing David's patterns of portrait-painting, Girodet and Benoist are conceding republican subjectivity to former slaves, who in 1794 had become French citizens – but without conceding the sitters' right to represent themselves and to control their own image. Girodet and Benoist articulated their own visions of the future status of African bodies in the French national body. Both artists refer to traditional stereotypes of the primitive, sensual African body, turning their negative connotations into an aesthetical ideal of exoticism. I will discuss here neither Girodet's personal strategies of an aesthetic of difference, nor the possible intention of Benoist in the given context. Instead I want to investigate the complex network of references, allusions and quotations linking the *Portrait d'une Négresse* with mental and material images, exploring a broader field of interpictorial meaning production.[25]

BLACK VENUS

The studio-costume of the *Négresse*, the colors of the Tricolor and the bare breast all suggest an allegorical dimension of the body-image. Bare breasts were familiar as signifiers of personifications of the four parts of the world and of enlightened ideas, like liberty, republic, nature and so on. In Charles Grignions's engraving after Hubert Gravelot's *The Four Continents* (1740), the nakedness of Africa and America hints at their primitive state compared to Europe and Asia, and in

Boizot's print *La France republicaine ouvrant son sein à tous les Francais* (1792), the exposed breasts signify the natural legitimacy of the republic, paralleled with nature itself in the image of the Greek goddess Artemis from Ephesos.[26] The naked breast was part of mythological and allegorical masquerades in ladies' portraiture and disappeared with the increasing realism of portrait-painting about 1800. During the time of the Directorium mythological and allegorical nakedness was employed in only a few cases, mostly in portraits of *femmes galantes*, referring to the pre-revolutionary eighteenth-century tradition.[27] In 1796 John G. Stedman's *Narrative of a five years' expedition against the Revolted Negroes of Surinam* was illustrated with a print showing a bare-breasted mulatta, Joanna (Fig. 11.7). Joanna was the victimized hero of the author's sentimental love

11.7. T. Holloway after J. G. Stedman, *Portrait of Joanna*. Engraving from *Narrative of a five years' expedition against the Revolted Negroes of Surinam* ... (London: Printed for J. Johnson ... & J. Edwards, 1796), vol. 1, facing page 88.

11.8. Raphael, *Portrait of a Young Woman* (*La Fornarina*), ca. 1518. Oil on canvas. Galleria Nazionale de Arte Antica, Palazzo Barberini, Rome. Photo: Scala/Art Resource, New York.

story, following the pattern of a "colonial marriage." The meaning of the image of the bare-breasted woman, like Benoist's *Négresse*, oscillates between a courtesan-portrayal and a personification of the colony, showing the juxtaposition of sexual and colonial desire.[28] Benoist refers more directly to a composition on a higher level of the classical *beau ideal*. The pose of the *Négresse* echoes *La Fornarina*, a painting attributed to Raphael which is thought to represent his mistress (Fig. 11.8).[29] The reference to Italian Renaissance painting defines the naked breast of the *Négresse* as token of the platonic eroticism of the pure *beau ideal*. The quotation of a canonical masterwork, linked with narratives on colonial eroticism and idealism in art, tranforms the frivolous connotation of the naked breast into a discourse of high art. The location of the *Portrait d'une Négresse* at the same level as Raphael's *La Fornarina* implied a comment on the classical canon with an "Ethiopian Venus."

Since the sixteenth century the Black Venus in literature had been an ambivalent figuration of alterity, becoming more visible in art history with the expansion of the slave trade in the first decades of the seventeenth century. During the eighteenth century the figure became more popular, embodying the intersection of medical, anthropological and esthetical debates.[30] In 1756 Le Cat wrote in his widely read *Traité de la couleur de la peau humaine* (Treatise on the Color of Human Skin): "Believe me, those people have their own Venus as we have ours; and it is not up to us to decide which of these two deities, the Greek or the Ethiopian, deserves to win the prize."[31] Around 1800, different interpretations of the phantasmatic figure, which was embedded in the collective mentality, were related to different positions on the question of slavery. French slave-traders used to offer their commodities as *Venus Noirs*, and the increasing visibility of black prostitutes in the Palais Royal fascinated French genre-painting.[32] A famous British pro-slavery publication, Bryan Edwards's colonial history of the West Indies (1794), was adorned with poems and prints celebrating the middle-passage of the slave trade. Prominent among them was the image of a *Sable Venus*, which the painter Thomas Stothard had derived from Raphael's fresco

11.9. Graigner after Thomas Stothard, *The Voyage of the Sable Venus*, 1801. Engraving. In Bryan Edwards, *The History, Civil and Commercial, of the British Colonies in the West Indies* (Dublin: Luke White), 1801, vol. 2, chap. I. Goldsmiths Library, University of London.

Triumph of Galathea in the Villa Farnese in Rome and which was compared with the *Venus Medici* in Florence[33] (Fig. 11.9).

But it is not only the metaphorical shifts between art and slavery that take place on the body-image; enlightened travel-writing and scientific illustrations also reveal the multiplicity of contradictory notions embodied in the image of the Black Venus. François Le Vaillant's report *Voyage dans l'Interieur de l'Afrique* (Paris, 1790) conveys his knowledge about the crucial role of Hottentot woman in the typology of the Black Venus, which covers the whole range between seductive beauty and beastly monstrosity. He offers his readers the visual evidence and ultimate truth about the famous "tablier d'Hottentotte" as "caprice de la mode"[34] (Fig. 11.10). Some years after Benoist had presented her *Portrait d'une Négresse* in the Salon exhibition, the South African woman Sarah Bartman was presented in European capitals as *Venus Hottentotte*, living proof of the uncanny monstrosity of black female sexuality.[35] My argument is not that Benoist's *Portrait d'une Négresse* is a depiction of a Black Venus, but that the meaning of the painting draws on many facets of this contested mental image. Benoist's aesthetical and erotic acknowledgment of the female African body in high art is committed to enlightenment traditions of cultural relativism, countering anthropological and popular constructions of black, female monstrosity, which were circulated in order to legitimize the reestablishment of slavery in 1802. The figuration of a Black Venus as beautiful otherness, as an alternative to the classical ideal of Antiquity and Italian Renaissance, soon became unbearable. Ingres's painting *La Baigneuse* was on display in the Salon exhibition of 1808. This highly original composition can be read as an echo, an answer to and an inversion of Benoist's *Négresse* – celebrating the stainless whiteness of a marble-like body and dismissing the sense of living, dark flesh that Benoist had offered as a modern Venus. Ingres replaced the figure of the *Ethiopian Venus* with the figure of the odalisque, the sexually enslaved woman in the Harem. The uncomfortable memory of French black slavery in the Antilles was replaced by the lure of *white slavery* on the stage of orientalism, which dominated colonial visual culture and French colonial interests in North Africa.

11.10. Anonymous artist, *Hottentotte à Tablier*. Illustration in François Le Vaillant, *Voyage dans l'intérieur de l'Afrique* (Paris, 1790), plate VII. Photo: Author.

Republican Womanhood in French Portraiture

The most interesting aspect of Benoist's invention is the deliberate nationalization of a French woman of African descent. Benoist combines the mental image of the Black Venus and the portrait-schema developed by David after 1790, a new model of white, revolutionary upper-class womanhood. The amalgamation of the Black Venus and the visual schema of French republican womanhood generates a new image: a visual model of black French republican womanhood in a post-slavery society. The iconographic index of the French nationality of the woman of African descent consists of the colors of the Tricolor and the quotation of David's portrait-painting. Benoist's composition is conceived as a sexual and racial inversion of David's *Self-Portrait,* painted in prison after the Thermidor and kept later for some time in his studio, where Benoist probably saw it (Fig. 11.11). Benoist does not simply identify with her still-famous teacher, but links her comeback in the Salon exhibition with the Jacobin past of her teacher. The pose of the sitter and the neutral, monochrome background painted in *frottis*-technique is close to David's portrait of *Madame Trudaine,* whom he represented as an aristocratic Jacobin follower of the Revolution in 1792. The similarity draws attention to the difference: Whereas in David's portrait the introverted pose and nervous paleness signify Madame Trudaine's almost

11.11. Jacques-Louis David, *Self-Portrait,* 1794. Oil on canvas. Musée du Louvre, Paris. Photo: Gérard Blot/Réunion des Musées Nationaux/Art Resource, New York.

11.12. Jacques-Louis David, *Henriette Verninac, née Henriette Delacroix*, 1799. Oil on canvas. Musée du Louvre, Paris. Photo: Erich Lessing/Art Resource, New York.

disembodied, patriotic virtue, Benoist emphasizes the warm sensuality of a relaxed, half-naked African body, but – and this is the point – without marking the *Négresse* as lascivious or coquettish. Benoist follows closely David's sculptural and monumental concept of the female figure in his portrait of Henriette Verninac (Fig. 11.12),[36] who looks a bit like a classical pillar in an armchair and whose image Delacroix, the brother of the sitter, found "too cold" compared with the "original."[37] Benoist borrows from David the compositional and sociological schema, but she does not imitate his treatment of complexion. David painted the skin of *Henriette Verninac* as a hermetically closed surface, recalling materials like marble or porcelain, whereas Benoist painted breathing flesh; the skin seems to be sensitive and transparent to sensations coming from inside or outside. Benoist's painting makes visible that the sitter feels the warm light on her face and body, while the rouge on the face of Madame Verninac is a layer

11.13. Jacques-Louis David, *Madame Récamier*, 1800. Oil on canvas. Musée du Louvre, Paris. Photo: Réunion des Muées Nationaux/Art Resource, New York.

of sterile makeup, unable to communicate emotional and physical sensations. David originally intended to show in the Salon exhibition of 1800 the portraits of Madame Verninac and Madame Récamier together. Though he later dropped this project, we may assume that Benoist had this company in mind when painting the *Portrait d'une Négresse*. The elegantly designed neckline, the gaze over the shoulder, the exceptionally long right arm building a barrier against the beholder and the subtle balance between erotic promise and refusal – all these particular elements echo David's *Madame Récamier* (Fig. 11.13).

As is well known, the artist did not finish the painting because of a serious quarrel with Juliette Récamier, resulting in a complete rupture. David did not respond to the sitter's wishes concerning her portrait, defending his position as artist in a letter: "Madame, women have their caprices, artists have theirs, too."[38] The case illustrates the increasing influence of women in the production of their own image – an influence the "woman of Guadeloupe" surely did not have in Benoist's studio. Ewa Lajer-Burcharth stresses the importance of women in the culture of the Directorium – often described as decadence and effemination of the essentially male Jacobin revolutionary culture – and the phobic reactions to women's renewed prominence in art patronage, particularly in the field of portrait painting: As commissioners, as sitters, as motifs and even as painters, women were more visible than ever before.[39] No doubt it was due to this general condition of female presence in the post-revolutionary Salon exhibitions that Benoist could address issues of difference between women. The comparison of

Benoist's *Négresse* and David's *Madame Récamier* provokes reflections on differences between female white and black beauty and virtue, which was, in a post-abolitionist, colonial-republican society, an issue of national interest. David could expose Juliette Récamier´s intellectual and erotic liberties with the utopian potential of antiquity (if she had not been playing the role of a Greek courtesan, she could not have been portrayed in bed), whereas Benoist articulated a utopian vision of the role a former slave could play in the republic by inverting antiquity into Africanity. She exposed the real presence of a living body close to the tactile eye of the beholder, appealing less to voyeurism than to the viewer's bodily self-awareness.

The inversion of Antiquity/Africa, ideal body/real flesh, past/present provoked racist protest by two critics. The anonymous author of a "Critique en vaudeville" wrote:

> I do not know if it is a talent
> To put black upon white,
> One sees it in this painting;
> The contrast wounds the eyes,
> The more it brings out the figure,
> The more hideous the portrait appears.[40]

Jean Baptiste Boutard, author of the most detailed comment in 1800 on Benoist´s *Négresse*, claims that it is impossible for an artist to manage the color/light problems posed by attempting to paint black people.[41] Boutard emphasizes the "hideousness" of the dark figure in front of the light background, but praises nevertheless its elegance, which is not due to the black model itself but to the skill of the painter trained by David. The incoherence of the argument reveals the ideological order that Benoist's painting has disturbed. Her *Portrait d'une Négresse* subverts the hierarchy of the light/dark opposition, which throughout the eighteenth century was crucial in normative discourses about female virtue and desire, and which was negotiated in portrait-painting about 1800: The whiteness of the body image was understood as an index for female virtue, conceptualized as paradoxical reconciliation of pure chastity and seductive beauty. Beginning in the sixteenth century, countless portraits of women synthesize the virtue and beauty of the sitters by means of their whiteness, set off by contrast with black Moorish pages.[42] The fashion of the white, fluid dress shaping the body like a classical statue established the symbolism and the aesthetics of white antiquity in everyday culture. Outstanding paintings by women artists, promoting the essential whiteness of ideal womanhood in France, are Constance Charpentier's *Mélancholie* and Nisa Villers' portrait of *Mademoiselle Charlotte du Val d'Ognes*,[43] both linking the rhetoric of light and darkness with fragility and weakness, often declared as being women's nature. While the gendering of the female body by means of the hierarchy of whiteness/darkness was articulated in early-modern times through the blackness of Moorish pages and the whiteness of antiquity, about 1800 the hierarchy was applied independent of this iconography. François Gérard, for example, conceptualized his portrait of *Madame Regnault* (Salon, 1799) on the opposition of black and white without any references to antiquity. The body of the sitter appears to be made of some artificial substance, its pure whiteness completely emancipated from carnal materiality. In the Salon exhibition of 1798 Gérard had promoted an erotic-aesthetical ideal of love with the porcelain stasis of *Amor and Psyche* performing a strangely disembodied, frozen, emotionless and colorless sexuality, which Lajer-Burcharth reads as emblematic for gender politics of the Directorium. The inversion of white and black, dark and light in Benoist's *Négresse* was a critical comment on the "Leitthema" of female portraiture in French classicism, opposing the cultural ideal of female disembodiment with a black counter-image of sensual revitalization.[44]

Deformation and Signature

An anonymous reviewer wrote: "This painting has a fine tone; the color is well applied; but the design is incorrect. The left collarbone is too strongly pronounced; perhaps it is a portrait."[45] The author noticed the strange deformation of the hand and links this observation with his uncertainty about the genre of the painting, which might or might not be a portrait. I understand the not-quite-logical conjunction – the observation that the wrist is designed incorrectly and the question to which genre the painting belongs – as rationalization and disavowal of an unbidden memory of slavery. The bony ugliness of the hand is the most obvious sign of slavery and snubs the standards of grace and elegance in ladies' portraiture. The ugliness of the female hand, which looks like the split claw of an animal, recalls tropes of the beastly nature of *negroes*, the most common argument used to legitimate their enslavement. But the visual evidence of the beauty of the woman and the Davidian portrait-schema of republican French womanhood tell another story: The brutish ugliness of the black woman's hand is not innate, but the after-effect of slave-work and torture. The deformation is testimony of the sitter's biography as a slave. The beholder in the Salon exhibition of 1800 knew very well that mutilation or severing of the hand were used to punish runaway slaves from plantations. The author of the review could not have been irritated by the simple fact of seeing a visual representation of slavery: Slaves had long been visible as elegant Moorish pages in portrait paintings or as pitiable victims in popular prints of the abolition movement. What was irritating was the index of torture inserted in a representation of a republican French subject, a scar and stigma put on display in the wrong place, a visible trace of the past complicating the difficult passage from slavery to emancipation in the present.

Helen Weston first noticed the amazing likeness to David's artist's hand in his self-portrait and the emblematic position of Benoist's signature above the deformed hand of her sitter.[46] The bend of David's fingers is dictated by the brush he holds while painting his self-portrait in prison. The crippled fingers of the *Négresse* hold nothing – nor are they touching in the usual narcissistic way some cloth or shawl, a conventional motif often used by David and Benoist. The white cloth draped over the legs (and here it is completely unclear how the figure of the woman is meant to be sitting – or is she lying on a Recamière?) is painted as a flat, almost abstract rectangular field, framing like an inserted image the mutilated fist, which forms a monumental base for the signature of the white artist painted in the color of the complexion of her African sitter. The signature *Laville-Laroux femme Benoist* sums up the chronology of the artist's career: started in the name of her father, continued after an interruption with the *Portrait d'une Négresse* as wife of her husband, recalling her apprenticeship and declaring at the same time homage to and independence from David. What is the meaning of the juxtaposition of the scriptural signature and the deformed hand? The image of the hand marks a particular site in the composition, interrupting its fluent elegance with an isolated icon of pain and deformation, as a sort of break (in the sense in which Roland Barthes defines the *punctum* in photography). The combination of the written signature with the icon of the deformed hand may be read as the emblematic inscription of the artist's self in her work, a visual metaphor of female authorship.

In the seventeenth century, images of female hands in the act of drawing or painting were introduced in the iconography of the fame of women artists. A drawing by the French artist Dumonstier le Jeune isolates Artemisia Gentileschi's hand holding a brush as *pars pro toto*, paraphrasing a detail of her *Self-Portrait as Pittura* (1630), which stands in for the artist's genius (Fig. 11.14).[47] A more contemporary example is Elisabeth Vigée-Lebrun's *Self-Portrait* (1790).[48] Here the shadow of the working hand falls on the canvas, the brush touches, crossing the line between the woman who paints and the painted woman, projecting the artist's hand at work as an iconic signature into the self-reflexive meta-painting as discussed by Victor Stoichita.[49] The seventeenth-century tradition of scriptural-iconic signatures and the symbolism of the isolated hand as metaphor of artistic creativity became of increasing interest for strategies of self-presentation during the eighteenth century. The motif allowed a sophisticated reflection on the relationship between author and work, between the reality of what was represented and the representation as artefact.[50] Benoist's scriptural-iconic signature juxtaposes her own history as producer of the image with the history of the woman whose image is her work, encoded in the deformation of the fist. The concept recalls the topos that only hard work can achieve grace and easiness

11.14. Pierre Dumonstier le Jeune, *The Hand of Artemisia Gentileschi*, 1625. Drawing. British Museum, London. © Trustees of the British Museum, London.

(*spezzatura*) in art and may have autobiographical dimensions projected by Benoist into the art-theoretical commonplace.

More important, Benoist does not display the crippled fist of the emancipated slave as victimization but as a symbol of female creativity and resistance. The invention objects to paradigms of dilettantism and natural weakness, which were dominating the current debates about women artists. Benoist's inscription of white authorship in a black body-image deformed by slavery transfers the issue of women artists from the discursive field of female nature into discourses about work and resistance, sensuality and desire, deformation and biography. David, who exposed in his *Self-Portrait* the deformation of his face by a swollen cheek as metaphor for his individual genius and political failure, wrote in prison that "painters paint themselves in their art."[51] As the unfinished portrait of *Madame Récamier* can be read as David's self-representation in a particular historical moment of loss,[52] we may understand the scriptural-iconic signature of Benoist in the *Portrait d'une Négresse* as self-representation in a particular moment of colonial, gender- and art-politics, a precarious moment between utopian perspectives and failure.

Classicism and Slavery

What was the social function of the portraits painted by Girodet and Benoist, neither commissioned nor used by the sitters to articulate their post-abolition selves? Kept in the artists' studios and charged with personal and artistic self-reflections, the paintings served first of all as a self-positioning of David's pupils, challenging the authority of their teacher in their quest for independence. Any interpretation that concentrates only on social-political context and the biographies of painters and sitters risks missing the aesthetic level and its articulation of social-political meaning. Girodet and Benoist introduced slavery, emancipation and blackness as body-images and metaphors of romantic resistance against normative concepts of art and gender. Both artists inscribed onto the image of persons without control over the image-production an intensified sensuality and sexuality, encoding discriminating stereotypes with positive significations. The problematic vitality of the black bodies is not designed as wild, but as refined, sartorial luxury; their eroticism is not unconscious and raw, but expressed as self-controlled, formal elegance. The turning of discriminating stereotypes toward the positive creates new patterns of alterity within the aesthetical realm, exploiting the cultural productivity and the subversive potential of the memory of slavery. The artistic self-reflection on the tension between racial alterity and national identity lays open to question the imagined whiteness and wholeness of the French national body. The vision of internal difference and heterogeneity of the French national body offered an alternative to chauvinistic concepts of the nation. The artistic language in which this vision was articulated is nevertheless highly problematic: The idealizing inversion of racist stereotypes perpetuates them as Exoticism and Primitivism.

THE WOMAN OF GUADELOUPE

At stake is, finally, the cultural agency of the "woman of Guadeloupe," which, though not represented by the painting, nevertheless existed and certainly was articulated in other media than portrait paintings. Her lack of control over the portrait does not necessarily mean that she did not participate at all in its production.[53] We may take it for granted that the hours of work in the artist's studio were hours of intense communication between Madame Benoist and the black servant of her brother-in-law, and that the dialogue between the two women in an unequal power-relation touched the issues raised by the painting. We cannot assume that the "woman of Guadeloupe" appreciated the artist's subtle interpictorial references, or that she was interested in the strategies Benoist applied in order to position herself in relation to David and her fellow pupil Girodet as a white woman artist. But there can be no doubt that she was fascinated by the process that made her likeness appear on the canvas. The "woman of Guadeloupe" was the first beholder, judging the portrait like a mirror of her self and her self-image. We do not know whether she identified with the false mirror, but certainly she saw the emergence of a new model of post-abolitionist identity with interest, perhaps even with pleasure. The painting does not document her emotions and reflections, but we may assume that the "woman of Guadeloupe" communicated her judgement to the painter, thus entering into the definition of post-abolition femininity.

NOTES

1 Marie-Guilhelmine Benoist, *Portrait d'une Négresse*, 1800, oil on canvas, 81 × 65 cm, Paris, Musée du Louvre, Inv. Nr. 2508, signed: Laville-Leroulx, F. Benoist.

2 Katja Wolf, "Schwarz-Weiß-Malerei. Beobachtungen zum Inkarnat in Bildnissen mit Mohrenpagen," in *Die Freiheit der Anderen*, ed. Annegret Friedrich (Marburg: Jonas, 2004), 137.

3 Edward J. Sullivan, ed., *Brazil: Body and Soul* (New York: Harry N. Abrams, 2001), 273, fig. 136. Published on the occasion of the Exhibition "Brazil: Body and Soul," Solomon R. Guggenheim Museum, New York, Guggenheim Museum, Bilbao.

4 A.D.F., "Notice sur les ouvrages de peinture, de sculpture, d´architecture et de gravure exposés au Salon du Musée central des Arts, Paris l'an 8, 1800," p. 15 in Collection Deloynes, 22/626, Paris, Bibliothèque Nationale, 365. Astrid Reuter, *Marie-Guilhelmine Benoist. Gestaltungsräume einer Künstlerin um 1800* (Berlin: Lukas, 2002), 318.

5 Maud Sulter, *Bonnie Greer*, 2002, color Polaroid print, 80.4 × 56 cm, London, National Portrait Gallery. For further information see www.npg.org.uk.

6 Marie-Juliette Ballot, *Une élève de David. La Comtesse Benoist, l´Emilie de Demoustier 1768–1826* (Paris: Librairie Plon, 1914). The only modern monograph is Reuter, *Marie-Guilhelmine Benoist*.

7 For Marie-Guilhelmine Benoist, *Innocence between Virtue and Vice*, 1780, oil on canvas, 87 × 115 cm, private collection, see Viktoria Schmidt-Linsenhoff, ed., *Sklavin oder Bürgerin? Französische Revolution und Neue Weiblichkeit 1760–1830*, exhibition catalogue (Frankfurt am Main: Jonas, 1989), 419, ill. 11.15; and Viktoria Schmidt-Linsenhoff, "Herkules als verfolgte Unschuld? Ein weiblicher Subjektentwurf der Aufklärung von Marie Guilhelmine Benoist," in Daniela Hammer-Tugendhat, ed., *Die Verhältnisse der Geschlechter zum Tanzen bringen* (Marburg: Jonas, 1991), 17–46.

8 Ballot, *Une élève*, 151; and Reuter, *Marie-Guilhelmine Benoist*, 198.

9 See *Goya. Prophet der Moderne*, exh. cat. (Berlin and Madrid: Verein d. Freunde d. Nationalgalerie,) 2005, 148.

10 See Roger Little, "Madame de Duras et Ourika," in *Ourika: Madame de Duras* (Exeter: University of Exeter Press, 1998), 54.

11 *Ourika*. For further information see Roger Little, "Madame de Duras et Ourika," 54 ff. The curiosity of the Parisian public about black women is described by Samuel Baur in *Reisen einer Negerinn: Charakteristische Gemälde aus der gesitteten und rohen Welt, ein Pendant zu Voltaires Candide* (Nuremberg: n.p., 1790).

12 Reuter, *Marie-Guilhelmine Benoist*, 317–18, puts together all reviews in French.

13 Ann Sutherland Harris and Linda Nochlin, *Women Artists, 1550–1950* (Los Angeles: Los Angeles County Museum of Art, 1978), 49. See also the writings of the German feminist artist Gisela Breitling, *Die Spuren des Schiffs in den Wellen. Eine autobiographische Suche nach den Frauen in der Kunstgeschichte* (Frankfurt am Main: Fischer, 1986), 132, 170.

14 Hugh Honour, *Black Models and White Myths*, part 2 of *From the American Revolution to World War I*, vol. 4 of *The Image of the Black in Western Art* (Cambridge, Mass.: Harvard University Press, 1989), 7.

15 Griselda Pollock, *Differencing the Canon: Feminist Desire and the Writing of Art History* (London: Routledge, 1999), 299.

16 Helen Weston, "The Cook, the Thief, His Wife and Her Lover: La Ville-Leroux's *Portrait de Negresse* and the Signs of Misrecognition," in *Work and the Image: Work, Craft and Labour. Visual Representations in Changing Histories*, ed. Valerie Mainz and Griselda Pollock (Aldershot: Ashgate, 2000), 53–74; Darcy Grimaldo Grigsby, *Extremities: Painting Empire in Post-revolutionary France* (New Haven: Yale University Press, 2002), 42–63; James Smalls, "Slavery Is a Woman: 'Race,' Gender and Visuality in Marie Benoist's *Portrait d'une Négresse* (1800)," available at http://19thc-artworldwide.org/spring_04/articles/smal_print.html.

17 Weston, "The Cook," 53, 54.

18 Grigsby, *Extremities*, 60.

19 Smalls, "Slavery," 1, 4.
20 Ibid., 17.
21 Viktoria Schmidt-Linsenhoff, "Male Alterity in the French Revolution. Two Paintings by Anne-Louis Girodet at the Salon of 1798," in *Gendered Nations: Nationalism and Gender Order in the Long Nineteenth Century*, ed. Ida Blom, Karen Hagemann, and Catherine Hall (Oxford: Berg, 2000), 81–105; and Grigsby, *Extremities*, 9–63. See also Sylvain Bellenger, *Girodet, 1767–1824* (Paris: Gallimard, 2006).
22 Thomas Crow, *Emulation: Making Artists for Revolutionary France* (New Haven: Yale University Press, 1995); Abigail Solomon-Godeau, *Male Trouble: A Crisis in Representation* (New York: Thames and Hudson, 1997).
23 For versions in sculpture see Jean Métellus and Marcel Dorigny, *De l'Esclavage aux Abolitions* (Paris: Éditions Cercle d'art, 1989), 122.
24 For early feminist discourse see Schmidt-Linsenhoff, *Sklavin oder Bürgerin*, 9; and Ruth Jung in Schmidt-Linsenhoff, *Sklavin oder Bürgerin*, 80. For Mary Wollstonecraft see Weston, "The Cook," 57; and Moira Ferguson, "Mary Wollstonecraft and the Problematic of Slavery," *Feminist Review* 42 (autumn 1992), 82–102.
25 For interpictorial meaning-production see Valeska von Rosen, "Interpikturalität," in Ulrich Pfisterer, ed., *Metzler Lexikon Kunstwissenschaft. Ideen, Methoden, Begriffe* (Stuttgart: Metzler, 2003), 161–64.
26 For Hubert Gravelot's *The Four Continents* see David Bindman, *Ape to Apollo: Aesthetics and the Idea of Race in the Eighteenth Century* (Ithaca, N.Y.: Cornell University Press, 2002), 27, ill. 2. For Boizot's print *La France Republicaine* see Schmidt-Linsenhoff, *Sklavin oder Bürgerin*, 486.
27 For example, Jean Baptiste Isabey, *Mme. Tallien as Diana*, print after lost painting, Paris, Bibliothèque Nationale. The purifying effect of marble sculpture and antiquity allowed nudity in ladies' portraiture in a few cases such as Joseph Chinard, *Madame Recamier*, 1805, Lyon, Musée des Beaux Arts; and Antonio Canova, *Paolina Borghese*, 1804–08, Rome, Villa Borghese. See Georges Duby and Jean-Luc Daval, eds., *Skulptur: Von der Renaissance bis zur Gegenwart: Renaissance bis Rokoko. 15. bis 18. Jahrhundert* (Cologne: Taschen, 1999), 315.
28 John G. Stedman, *Narrative, of a five years' expedition, against the Revolted Negroes of Surinam, in Guiana, on the Wild Coast of South America; from the year 1772 to 1777: elucidating the History of that Country, and describing its Productions, Viz. Quadrupeds, Birds, Fishes, Reptiles, Trees, Shrubs, Fruits, & Roots; with an account of the Indians of Guiana, & Negroes of Guinea*, 2 vols. (London: Printed for J. Johnson ... & J. Edwards, 1796; reprint, Baltimore: Johns Hopkins University Press, 1988).
29 Soon after, the famous painting inspired Ingres's Odalisques.
30 See Viktoria Schmidt-Linsenhoff, "Das koloniale Unbewusste in der Kunstgeschichte," in *Globalisierung/Hierarchisierung. Kulturelle Dominanzen in Kunst und Kunstgeschichte*, ed. Irene Below and Beatrice von Bismarck (Marburg: Jonas, 2005), 24.
31 "Croyez-mois, ces peuples ont leur Venus comme nous avons le nôtre; & ce n'est point à nous décider laquelle des deux Divinités grecques ou Ethiopienne merite d'obtenir la palme." Claude Nicolas Le Cat, *Traité de la couleur de la peau humaine en général, de celle des nègres en particulier, et de la métamorphose d'une de ces couleurs en l'autre, soit de naissance, soit accidentellement* (Amsterdam: n.p., 1765), 7.
32 See Louis-Leopold Boilly, *The Galleries of the Palais Royal*, 1809, oil on canvas (grisaille), 50 × 63 cm, in Susan L. Siegfried, *The Art of Louis-Léopold Boilly: Modern Life in Napoleonic France* (New Haven: Yale University Press, 1995), 64, ill. 40.

33 Rosalie Smith McCrea, "Dis-Ordering the World in the 18th Century: The Duplicity of Connoisseurship: Masking the Culture of Slavery, or, *The Voyage of the Sable Venus: Connoisseurship and the Trivializing of Slavery*," Internet publication, The Society for Caribbean Studies Annual Conference Papers, vol. 3, 2002, www.scsonline.freeserve.co.uk/olv3p16.PDF. See also Felicity Nussbaum, *The Limits of the Human: Fictions of Anomaly, Race and Gender in the Long Eighteenth Century* (Cambridge: Cambridge University Press, 2003), 153.

34 Francois Le Vaillant, *Voyage dans l'Interieur de l'Afrique par le Cap de Bonne Esperance*, tome II (Paris: Leroy, 1790), 346, plate II.

35 Partha Mitter, "The Hottentot Venus and Western Man: Reflections on the Construction of Beauty in the West," in *Cultural Encounters: Representing Otherness*, ed. Elizabeth Hallam and Brian V. Street (London: Routledge, 2000), 35–50.

36 Jacques-Louis David, *Madame de Verninac*, 1799, oil on canvas, 145 × 120 cm, Paris, Musée du Louvre; in Jean-Jacques Lévêque, *L'Art et la Révolution française, 1789–1804* (Neuchâtel: Ides et Calendes, 1987), 146.

37 *David*, exhibition catalogue, no. 157, 354.

38 Ewa Lajer-Burcharth, *Necklines: The Art of Jacques-Louis David after the Terror* (New Haven: Yale University Press, 1999), 236.

39 Ibid., 251.

40 "Je ne sais si c'est un talent / De mettre du noir sur blanc, / On le voit dans cette peinture; / Ce contraste blesse les yeux, / Plus il fait sortir la figure, / Plus le portrait parait hidieux." Anonymous, "La verité au Museum ou l'oeil trompé. Critique en vaudeville sur les tableaux exposés au salon, Paris l'an 9 (1800)," in *Collection Deloyens*, 22/623, Paris, Bibliothèque Nationale, 14.

41 Jean Baptiste Boutard, "Salon de l'an VIII. Portraits peints par des femmes," *Journal des Débats*, 6. Brumaire l'an 9, 2: "Ces visages africains sont, de par la nature, si uniformément laids, qu'il est imposssible à l'art de leur donner aucune espèce de beauté; il ne prétent que foiblement a l'art du coloriste; une pareille figure ne peut ni se detacher d'un fond brun, ni se mettre en harmonie avec un fond clair: il est impossible de faire circuler l'air autour, parce qu'elle ne se prête point à la dégradation de couleur et de lumière necessaire pour produir cet effet l'artiste ne peut se faire valoir que par la pose de son modèle, et la correction de son dessin, dans les parties qui présentent du moins des formes familières à l'art; enfin, par le choix des accessoires et l'execution generale. C'est ce qu'a fait mad. Benoist; sa *Negresse* est posée avec esprit, c'est-à-dire, dans une attitude gracieuse et qui ne sort point de l'habitude des gens de sa couleur; le buste, et sur tout le bras, sont bien dessinés; la draperie qui entoure la tête, est disposé avec grace. On reconnaît dans l'exécution la (?) manière sage et le beau faire de son maitre." (Those black faces are, by nature, so uniformly ugly, that it is impossible for art to endow them with any sort of beauty; they only lend themselves feebly to the art of the colorist; such a figure cannot be distinguished against a dark background, and neither can it be placed harmoniously against a light one: it is impossible to allow air to circulate around it, because it does not lend itself enough to the gradation of color and light necessary to produce such an effect; the artist cannot but recur to the pose of her model, and to the correction of her design, in those parts that present forms that are less familiar to art; finally, by the selection of accessories and the general execution. This is what Benoist has done; this *Négresse* is posed with spirit, that is, in a graceful attitude and that is not very common among people of color; the bust, and especially the arm, are well designed; the cloth that wraps her head is arranged with grace. One recognizes in the execution the expert manner and skillful hand of its mistress.)

42 Angela Rosenthal, "Die Kunst des Errötens. Zur Kosmetik rassischer Differenz," in *Das Subjekt und die Anderen. Interkulturalität und Geschlechterdifferenz vom 18.Jh. bis zur Gegenwart*, ed. Herbert Uerlings et al. (Berlin: Erich Schmidt, 2001), 95.

43 Constance Charpentier, *Mélancholie*, 1801, Amiens, Musée de Picardie; see reproduction in Schmidt-Linsenhoff, *Sklavin oder Bürgerin?*, 419, ill. II.27; Nisa Villers, *Portrait of Mademoiselle Charlotte du Val d'Ognes*, 1800, New York, Metropolitan Museum; see reproduction in Schmidt-Linsenhoff, *Sklavin oder Bürgerin*, 131.

44 Lajer-Burcharth, *Necklines*, 280.

45 "Ce tableau est d´un bon ton; la couleur en est bien etendue; mais le dessin est incorrect. La clavicule gauche est sentie d'une manière beaucoup trop forte; peut-être est-ce un portrait." A.D.F, "Notice sur les ouvrages de peinture, de sculpture, d'architecture et de gravure exposés au salon du Musée central des Arts, An VIII," in *Collection Deloynes*, 22/226, Paris, Bibliothèque Nationale, 365.

46 Weston, "The Cook," 53.

47 See Mary D. Garrard, *Artemisia Gentileschi: The Image of the Female Hero in Italian Baroque Art* (Princeton: Princeton University Press, 1989), 63; and Joanna Woods-Marsden, *Renaissance Self-portraiture: The Visual Construction of Identity and the Social Status of the Artist* (New Haven: Yale University Press, 1998), 194–95.

48 Elisabeth Vigée-Lebrun, *Self-Portrait*, 1790, oil on canvas, 100 × 81 cm, Florence, Uffizi Gallery.

49 For the painting, see Mary D. Sheriff, *The Exceptional Woman: Elisabeth Vigée-Lebrun and the Cultural Politics of Art* (Chicago: University of Chicago Press, 1996), 234; Victor Stoichita, *Eine Kurze Geschichte des Schattens* (Munich: Fink, 1999), 101.

50 See Karin Gludowatz, *Fährten legen – Spuren lesen: die Künstlersignatur als poietische Referenz* (Munich: Fink, 2011); for its actuality in eighteenth-century painting see Claudia Denk, *Artiste, citoyen & philosophe: der Künstler und sein Bildnis im Zeitalter der Aufklärung* (Munich: Fink, 1998).

51 T. J. Clark, "Gross David with the Swoln Cheek: An Essay on Self-Portraiture," in *Rediscovering History: Culture, Politics, and the Psyche*, ed. Michael S. Roth (Stanford: Stanford University Press, 1994), 243–307. For the topological tradition see Frank Zöllner, "'Ogni Pittore Dipinge Sé': Leonardo da Vinci and 'Automimesis,'" in *Der Künstler über sich in seinem Werk. Internationales Symposium der Bibliotheca Hertziana in Rom 1989*, ed. Matthias Winner (Weinheim: Wiley, 1992), 137–60.

52 Lajer-Burcharth, *Necklines*, 303.

53 One area where the subject may have had some control over her representation is the head-tie; for the social significance of Afro-Caribbean head-ties, see Pamela Franco, "The Martinican: Dress and Politics in Nineteenth-Century Trinidad Carnival," in *Carnival: Culture in Action: The Trinidad Experience*, ed. Milla Cozart Riggio (New York: Routledge, 2004), 64–75. For more on agency through self-adornment see Richard J. Powell, *Cutting a Figure: Fashioning Black Portraiture* (Chicago: University of Chicago Press, 2008).

TWELVE

THE MANY FACES OF TOUSSAINT LOUVERTURE

Helen Weston

François Dominique Toussaint was born into slavery on 20 May 1743 on the island of Saint-Domingue (now Haiti), where his father worked on the Breda sugar plantation. Toussaint was given the slave name of Toussaint Breda. This was a common strategy for identifying slaves with their owner's property, as if they were a mere extension of that property. In Toussaint's time the plantation was owned by the count of Noé and managed by Bayon de Libertat, a man who is widely perceived in Toussaint literature as a kindly mentor who gave Toussaint the rudiments of an education and encouraged his natural skill as a horseman. By his early thirties Toussaint had gained his freedom and was himself the owner of a coffee plantation. In 1789 he is documented as having granted freedom to slaves on his plantation.

There is no single official portrait either of Toussaint Breda as a slave or of Toussaint Louverture (the name he took at the time of the slave rebellions) as a victorious general who defeated Napoleon's armies. However, there are several contemporaneous descriptions of him and some supposed "portraits" produced during his lifetime, of which there are barely two alike. Mostly he is in military uniform, and at no point is he represented on bended knee pleading for his freedom or thanking the white man for bestowing it. The only situation for which this latter form of portrayal might have been appropriate and which would have reminded us of his original slave status is the scene of his death.

Toussaint Louverture died in captivity in the fortress of Joux in the French Jura, at the age of fifty-nine, on 7 April 1803, from pneumonia and apoplexy. His death is referred to by Aimé Césaire in his poem on Louverture in *Notebook of a Return to the Native Land,* as a "white death" and Louverture as a man "alone, defying the white screams of a white death":

> What is also mine
> a lone man imprisioned in whiteness
> a lone man defying the white screams of white death
> [TOUSSSAINT, TOUSSAINT LOUVERTURE][1]

The visual representation of this imposition of a state of whiteness on the enslaved and colonized, and their defiance summoned in the face of such imposition, is, in part, the subject of this essay.

In Frantz Fanon's discussion of the social psychology of colonial rule in *Black Skin, White Masks,* he argues that in a colonial situation, where the numerically inferior alien race is dominant through access to power sources such as military force or superimposition of its culture, there is a fundamental belief that the values and institutions of the metropolitan power are better than those of the subject or colonized people. He suggests that this belief can result in an urge by the colonized to imitate or adapt to white values and reject indigenous values, to "Turn White or disappear."[2] After traveling some way down this path, in his belief in French republicanism after the promise of recognition of rights for all men born free and equal in the 1789 Declaration of the Rights of Man, Louverture, in his total commitment to leading the slaves in their fight for freedom, ultimately, in the final years of his life, refused and defied such imitation and encouraged the blacks of Saint-Domingue to do the same. At times this defiance took the form of deliberately slipping in and out of different identities, of dissimulating, pretending, in order to survive. For this practice he was certainly perceived by his enemies as a man of many faces, as hypocritical, and with the "portraits" that function as frontispieces, for example, it seems that at times almost any face would do. I am suggesting that the perceived hypocrisy or duplicity is in some way connected with the variety and quantity of supposed portraits of Louverture.

Drawing on the theories of Franz Fanon, Aimé Césaire, L. Adèle Jinadu and Adam Lively,[3] among others, I would like to argue that dissimulation can be an admirable form of defiance, especially when it is brought into play for sheer survival. This was the case in the relationship between Louverture and Bonaparte. After his entrapment by Bonaparte and imprisonment in a French fortress, Louverture, in a bid to survive, pretended to submit to the French leader and begged for Bonaparte's bestowal of his consideration.

"Bestowal" or "conferral" is a loaded word at this moment in the history of France and of Saint-Domingue/Haiti. The French word is *l'octroi,* and it is in the context of "granting" liberty or independence. There is, as both Louverture and Fanon have pointed out, a world of difference between demanding that oppressors acknowledge men's natural rights on the one hand, and, on the other, having to beg for such rights to be conferred with the expectation of gratitude and obedience from the oppressed. Much abolitionist art representing the black figure with white-imposed mask of subservience, gratitude, obedience, expresses the latter. Representations of Louverture and of the black revolutionaries' struggle for Haiti's independence more frequently express the former.

The notion of *l'octroi* had already come to the fore in the endless discussions in the National Assembly about whether to "accord" political rights to men of color, culminating in the decree of 15 May 1791. Robespierre had cut right to the core of the argument, asserting that it was not so much a question of whether or not to "accord" political rights to citizens of color, but whether to preserve such rights, since they had, of course, always had them and such rights were not the exclusive property of whites. Skin color was irrelevant. Men were men and not someone else's property.[4] Abbé Grégoire immediately wrote to the men of color following the 15 May decree, explaining that this decree was not a favor. For a favor was a privilege and a privilege was an injustice: "In securing for you the exercise of your political rights we have paid off a debt; failure to do so would have been a crime on our part and a stain on the Constitution" (of 1791).[5] By September 1791 the opposers had reneged on this decree. Ten years later, in December 1802, Louverture rebutted efforts on Bonaparte's part to bring the inhabitants of Saint-Domingue under his power. He declared, "[We want] an absolute acceptance of the principle that no man born red, black or white, can be the property of his fellow man. We are free today because we are the strongest."[6] It was not France's place to confer such freedom.

Louverture did not live to witness Saint-Domingue's declaration of independence from France in January 1804, when it became the first black republic and resumed its original name – Haiti. Nor was he the one to take credit for it or be seen and portrayed as one of those who made it happen. That honor was for his black general, Jean-Jacques Dessalines, and the mulatto Alexandre Pétion, immortalized in 1822 in *The Oath of the Ancestors* by Guillaume Guillon Lethière.[7] Without Louverture's vision and leadership, however, the slaves of Saint-Domingue might never have demanded and claimed their right to freedom and independence. The bicentenary of the death of Louverture, the "Precursor," was commemorated near Pontarlier at the fortress of Joux, where he had been imprisoned in April 1803, and his life celebrated by local communities and pilgrims from Haiti (Fig. 12.1). The poster design for these events perpetuates the perception of Louverture's role as precursor and shows him on horseback encouraging his men to follow him. It also juxtaposes him with the symbols of slavery, for on the left of him are the broken chains, now crossed with the word "Liberté," and on the right is the new coat of arms of Haiti. Across the center of the poster is a detail from a nineteenth-century print of the fortress of Joux.

12.1. "Fort de Joux, Jeudi 7 Avril 1803, Mort de Toussaint Louverture, Le Précurseur, Liberté Haïti." Publicity card for celebrations of the bicentenary of the death of Toussaint Louverture in 2003 at Pontarlier and the fortress of Joux. Photo: Janice Smarsik, Dartmouth College, Hanover, N.H.

It is surprising that no contemporary portrait was commissioned of Louverture, given his public image and extraordinary achievements, especially in the last years of his life. For he was responsible for progressively installing "black power" in Saint-Domingue: first, military power against Napoleon's forces, then economic and political power when he formulated – and declared – the island's new constitution on 8 July 1801. Louverture's constitution was declared without consultation with Bonaparte. It abolished slavery, made military service mandatory for all males of the population between the ages of fourteen and fifty-five, recognized Catholicism as the State religion, proposed ways of rescuing Haiti's economy and setting up plantations again, and permitted the importation of blacks to build up the population, but not as slave labor.[8] It also named Toussaint Louverture as Governor for Life with power to name his successor. This clearly amounted to a threat for Bonaparte, and perhaps it is not surprising that no artist in France was approached to record the features of this powerful man whom Bonaparte could not dominate. For Louverture's "arrogance" Bonaparte declared him an enemy of France and sent a military expedition of approximately 30,000 men, led by his brother-in-law, General Leclerc, to suppress Louverture and the slave insurgents. Louverure was tricked into attending a meeting with one of Bonaparte's generals on 7 June 1802, when he was captured and forced to board a ship bound for France – appropriately named *Le Héros*. His treatment under detention and his lonely death provoked a wave of anger among his troops, and under the new leadership of Dessalines and Pétion, the fighting resumed against Bonaparte's superior forces, until the latter were resoundingly defeated and banished from the island in mid-November 1803. As Laurent Dubois has appropriately expressed it, "while emancipation had been won through an alliance with the French Republic in 1794, it was preserved by the defeat of the French army in 1804.... The period between these two moments of dramatic transformation was dominated by the legendary leader, Toussaint-Louverture."[9]

In contemporaneous representation of Louverture, primarily in prints, and in the epithets attached to his name at the time, it is often in relation to Bonaparte that he is characterized, and it is this relationship of rivalry and opposition that to a large extent determines the nature of the constructed images of him. In his book *Intersubjectivity*, Nick Crossley quotes Martin Buber's contention in his work *I and Thou* that the world is "twofold" for human subjects, in accordance with their "twofold attitude" as they address others; there is "I-it and I-Thou."[10] In addressing the other in the case of a slave, they will constitute the slave as It, an object of their experience, to be used. In the second case, Thou is a subject who is in communication with us and on an equal footing. Buber uses Napoleon as the obvious example of a "demoniac thou" who is universally recognized as thou but does not ever recognize anyone else in this way. For Bonaparte, Louverture was a black slave who had simply got above himself and needed to be put down. He was the major obstacle preventing the reinstatement of slavery in France's most productive and lucrative colony. The point about Louverture and his relationship with Napoleon is that he pushed Napoleon to recognize him as an equal, as Thou. Michel-Rolph Trouillot has devoted an extraordinary essay to the idea of recognition, or rather the lack of it, as it regards the Haitian

Revolution. He argues that there was denial at the time and it was seen as a non-event, because "it was 'unthinkable' in the framework of western thought" that a crowd of slaves could overcome the armies of Napoleon. Resistance and defiance could not exist either, since to acknowledge these was to acknowledge the humanity of the enslaved.[11] If the Haitian Revolution was not to be recognized, how could there be official portraits of the man who led it?

By the time of Louverture's death liberty had been established in Saint-Domingue for nearly ten years. Liberty and racial equality had been demanded, claimed even, in a very concrete form, by slaves in revolt in 1791 and 1793 in the wake of France's universalist Declaration of the Rights of Man in 1789, which had proclaimed all men born free and equal. Slaves were thought to be members of the human race, but, as Trouillot has pointed out, there were degrees of humanity for even the strongest supporters of abolition, and the inclusion of the word "citizen" in the Declaration of the Rights of Man and Citizen already "denotes the germ of a contradiction."[12] At the time, however, liberty and the right to republican citizenship was announced by François Polverel and Léger Félicité Sonthonax to the enslaved of Saint-Domingue in 1793, although this had not in fact been their brief. Their brief had been simply to bring an end to the slave resistance. Early revolts were largely against the *grands Blancs*, the wealthy, aristocratic French plantation owners like le Comte de Vaudreuil and the Duc de Choiseul Praslin, but they were supported by radical republicans in the metropolis, including Jean-Paul Marat and Maximilian Robespierre. One of their demands was inclusion of men of color in both the assemblies in the colonies and in the metropolis. The *grands Blancs* had made their position very clear on this in letters from the 1780s to Louis XVI, requesting that only they (twenty-one of them) should represent the colonies as deputies to the Etats Généraux, on the grounds that they were all noble, all officers, all property owners, all obedient subjects and the king's submissive children:

> We have broken unexplored lands; we have constructed towns; we have almost founded an Empire. Victims of a hostile climate, we have defied death to increase your possessions, and when finally, it has been well-ackowledged that nature denied Frenchmen the physical strength to cultivate (or to work) the land under a burning sun, we have had the presence of mind to ordain labor, and we have looked to the bosoms of Africa for a country of people who are all used to this climate; we have commanded them to enrich the Metropolis and our Sovereign, and we treat them, for the sake of humanity and for own interest, like our children, despite the wrong assertions made by some new philosophers.[13]

Their slaves were their children, as they themselves were the king's children, and this double layer of infantilization appears to have been part of the automatic justification for exclusion of slaves from any consideration as representatives in the colonial or in the French assemblies.

For Toussaint Louverture any return to this Ancien Régime state was anathema. Years later, in his response to a proclamation by Bonaparte of 4 nivôse, year VIII, in which Bonaparte tried to persuade the inhabitants of Saint-Domingue that his new constitution was in their interests – "Un des premiers actes de la nouvelle législature sera la rédaction des lois destinées à vous régir" (One of the first acts of the new legislature will be to draft the laws destined to govern you) – Louverture protested, recognizing that this was imposition of "l'octroi de la charte française," the conferring of the French charter on the island's inhabitants, and he decided that Saint-Domingue should draw up its own constitution.

The revolutionary, regenerated France of the early-mid 1790s was not the enemy, just the opposite, and Louverture supported the régime that acknowledged "all men born free and equal" and proclaimed liberty, equality and fraternity as its beliefs. He was not a major player in the conflagrations and destruction of Le Cap in 1791 and 1793, although he probably supported the right to revolt. At the same time he is supposed to have helped the family of his master and protector on the Breda plantation to escape from the black insurgents (Fig. 12.2). This image is an engraving by Reiner Vinkeles showing a generic scene of a black slave protecting the white master at the entrance to his house. It could represent the black Eustache, model servant for his obedience and compliance, who also saved his master from this fate. There is no suggestion that it represents Louverture. Indeed, if this was meant to represent Louverture, he has

12.2. Reiner Vinkeles after Daniel Vrydag, *Saint Domingue, A Slave Defending His Master during the 1791 Revolt,* n.d. Engraving. Marcel Chatillon Collection. © Mairie de Bordeaux. Photo: Jean Michel Arnaud.

been turned into a man of heroically large and muscular form, in relation to the Frenchman standing just behind him. Both Louverture and Eustache tend to be mentioned in catalogue captions, however.[14]

Louverture had been freed in 1776, had become a property owner and slave owner and had fought as lieutenant general in the king's army at the head of three or four thousand blacks. By 1794 he was fighting with the French Republic, was promoted to general, fought off the English and the Spanish, and invaded the eastern part of Saint-Domingue, uniting the whole island in 1795. The following year he was made General in Chief of the armies of Saint-Domingue. Many epithets are attached to Louverture's name that probably help to fashion his appearance in an artist's imagination; he is the Black Spartacus,[15] the Precursor who led the way to freedom, the sable Mars, the Black Hercules, a new Alexander the Great. But, more importantly, the image of Toussaint Louverture is most often constructed in relation to Bonaparte. He is the Black Napoleon. His self-perception especially was, misguidedly as it turns out, as "le premier des Noirs" addressing "le premier des Blancs." If these roles of hero, leader, negotiator, freedom fighter, precursor and Napoleon's equal were part of Louverture's sense of self in the years 1799–1803, so too were his blackness and his enslaved origins. It is this sense of dual identity of black slave and Napoleon's equal that interests me, as it arises in the many constructions of his subjecthood in contemporary and later accounts of his life by French and British writers and in images of him.

Physical descriptions of Louverture vary according to the writers' relationship with Napoleon. During the Consulate period and Louverture's final years, the British thought highly of him because he was Napoleon's enemy. There were positive characterizations of him in the *Morning Chronicle,* and British artists such as John Kay represented him as authoritative and dignified as he addresses his troops (3,000 soldiers and 2,000 civilian supporters) at the peak of his power and self-confidence, on 1 February 1802 at Gonaïve, on the west coast of Haiti from the Black Mountain, knowing that Napoleon's brother-in-law, General Leclerc, was approaching with an army that vastly outnumbered Louverture's forces (Fig. 12.3). Louverture is raised on high ground looking down toward his troops set out on the right for as far as the eye can see in neat, disciplined divisions. The long low shadows of the legs indicate late afternoon and setting sun. Although we see Louverture from behind, there is no doubt that his heroic pose is based on that of the Apollo Belvedere. As Mary Evans notes in her book on John Kay, "Had L'Ouverture been a rebel against the British dominion, he would have been execrated as a trouble-maker; but since it was against the French [that the dictator of Haiti was rebelling], he became a popular hero in Britain, and as such Kay hailed him in this print!"[16] There was even a magic lantern performance in 1802 at the Lyceum Theatre, which put Bonaparte and Toussaint together, as the bad guy and the good guy, respectively.[17] The details

12.3. John Kay, *Toussaint Louverture*, 1802. Engraving. Private collection. Photo: Janice Smarsik, Dartmouth College, Hanover, N.H.

of this show are on the playbill for a Phantasmagoria show, where Bonaparte is referred to as First Consul of France and "Toussaint" as Rebel Chief.

Among Louverture's French detractors were those who idolized Napoleon in monographs at the time of Louverture's capture (1802), such as C. Y. Cousin d'Aval and DuBroca, who speak of "needing to tear away the veil of hypocrisy," especially as a Christian, and to condemn his excessive ambition; these were his main crimes. There was resentment that he imitated the religion of the Europeans; but for Louverture this was a more acceptable religion than Vaudoo, in part because the Vaudoo priests' power was felt as a threat. Excessive ambition (getting above his station) is a euphemism for the fact that he had failed to accept his place and his mask as obedient and submissive to the "excessive ambition" of Bonaparte (which involved reinstating slavery). For the frontispiece to their books, Cousin d'Aval and DuBroca used the portrait produced by Bonneville for his *Portraits des hommes célèbres de la Révolution* (vol. 4, 1802),[18] which they presumably deemed to be a wholly negative characterization, a stereotyping of the black, with thick lips and flattened nose. It bears little relation to any of the descriptions of Louverture and is close to similar negative portraits of Henri Christophe, one of Louverture's generals, later king of Haiti. Indeed, it is so close that there is probably confusion here between the two. A more plausible image comes from the description by General Caffarelli, Bonaparte's aide de camp at the fortress of Joux, at the end of Louverture's life, although he has to add a comment about dissimulation at the end. He is described as diminished, ill and undignified, as small, thin, ugly, his legs feeble and wasted. His large eyes were sunk in their sockets but were still alert and piercing. He had pronounced cheek bones, hollow cheeks, a wide but relatively long nose, a large mouth but no teeth on the upper jaw and the lower jaw was thrust forward and had long protruding teeth. Caffarelli gives us a close observation of a sick man, an individual. It is in stark contrast to the typical descriptions by contemporaneous phrenologists and taxonomists who generalized and fixated on measurable information – facial angles, cranial formation and so on. Caffarelli concludes, "He had a shifty look, full of falseness and dissimulation" – exactly what Bonaparte wanted to hear.[19]

On the other hand, Marcus Rainsford, an officer in the British service, arrested as a spy in 1799 in Saint-Domingue, also writing in 1802 about Saint-Domingue and the life of Toussaint-Louverture, describes him as having "a mind most elevated, and a disposition the most benign ... discernment in magnanimity and goodness. He was generous, affable, humane ... above all, Religion and Morality appear to receive his unfeigned support in precept and in practice.... In person he is of manly appearance, to which age is about to give a venerable aspect; his countenance is remarkably striking, but full of the most prepossessing suavity; he is a perfect black, and such a description of figure as might be supposed that of the sable Mars" (Fig. 12.4).[20] Rainsford had reason to be grateful to Toussaint (and therefore perhaps also flattering) because he had ordered Rainsford's release from prison. Regardless of this, however, this is a portrait by someone who knew him at the height of his power, rather than at the lowest depths of imprisonment and approaching death, and it should therefore be taken seriously. In this image Louverture holds a scroll; this gives him natural authority. He is a man in command, he has the power of the word. He delivers a formal address.

This is a dignified image, a noble image, and a far cry from so many of the white constructions of black heroism that depend on narratives of rescue (of whites) and self-sacrifice, and on the black body being clothed in nothing more than a loincloth, all of which we have seen in Fig. 12.2. Whether it is a close likeness to Louverture's appearance at this time is hard to assess.

Very few of the supposed "portraits" of Louverture were done during his lifetime. One of the best claims to this, however, is the *Equestrian Portrait of Toussaint Louverture on Bel-Argent,* ca. 1800, by Denis Volozan (Fig. 12.5). Volozan, originally from the area of Lyons, was from a family that owned property in Saint-Domingue, and accordingly, it seems plausible that he stayed on the

12.4. J. Bordes after Marcus Rainsford, *Toussaint Louverture.* Engraving, reproduced in Marcus Rainsford, *St. Domingo, or An Historical, Political and Military Sketch of the Black Republic with a View of the Life and Character of Toussaint L'Ouverture,* 2nd ed. (London: printed by and for R. B. Scott, 1802), illustration to page 41. Photo: British Library, London. © British Library Board, 9555.bbb.4.

12.5. Denis A. Volozan, *Equestrian Portrait of Toussaint Louverture on Bel-Argent,* ca. 1800. Pen and wash. Marcel Chatillon Collection. © Mairie de Bordeaux. Photo: Jean Michel Arnaud.

island before going on to Philadelphia ca. 1800, where he then spent the rest of his life. His image adopts a well-worn formula for the heroic equestrian portrait, following conventions of classical antiquity, Renaissance or eighteenth-century classical revival models. There is a nice irony in the thought that this relatively small sepia and wash drawing might predate Jacques-Louis David's *Bonaparte Crossing the Alps,* also of 1800. Both generals are calm on fiery, prancing white horses. There is a difference, however. Heroic equestrian portraits of rulers often present the head turned toward the spectator of the image, as is the case with David's portrait of Bonaparte. Louverture is presented by Volozan in strict profile, and by some critics it has come to be seen as an unflattering profile, sometimes referred to as "simian." There is no denying the similarity between the two portraits, especially the positioning of the legs of the horse and the strapping around the tails. The generals' uniforms are also, of course, very similar. Volozan's horse and rider are in fact closer to Van Dyck's *Prince Thomas of Savoy on Horseback* (1634), which may well have been the common source for both. If the date of ca. 1800 is accepted, then the portrait predates the declaration of independence in Haiti by three years; yet for the chief Curator of the Aquitaine Museum in Bordeaux, where the drawing is kept, it is undoubtedly a positive representation of a leader and "as a general and as the hero of Independence that he is represented here in theatrical pose, just like his horse, in the manner of equestrian statues of kings, perhaps to evoke the royal genealogy of the man."[21] The royal genealogy referred to here is the belief that Louverture was the grandson of Gaou-Guinou, an African chief of the Aradas nation on the Ivory Coast.

Both Bonaparte and Louverture were also compared to Alexander the Great during their lifetimes, and these portraits clearly refer, albeit obliquely, to Alexander taming Bucephalus, and in more general terms, to the accepted pictorial device of equating the ruler's control over his subjects with the horseman's control over the "unruly" energy and power of the animal. There is also some consensus that one of the two "authenticated" portraits that have become most closely associated with Louverture, being constantly reproduced on book covers, opera programs, frontispieces for mémoires and so on, probably derives from the Volozan portrait.[22] This is the undated lithograph by Nicolas-Eustache Maurin, published in the second volume of *L'Iconographie des contemporains depuis 1789 jusqu'à 1829* by the widow Delpech in 1832 (Fig. 12.6). Maurin was born in 1799 and was therefore only five when Toussaint died and not in a position to draw this from life, as was claimed in the book title.[23] Carlo Avierl Célius, who has made an important, in-depth study of some of the Louverture portraits, suggests that the Caffarelli description might have been the inspiration for Maurin and that both are negative characterizations, bordering on the caricatural, stereotyping of "the ugly negro," rather than being a positive representation and self-affirming.[24] Of course, any deviation from the Apollo Belvedere facial model would have been considered to be "ugly," regardless of a range of other criteria such as hair arrangement and texture, eye color or means of rendering balance and proportion of features. Again, if Volozan did this portrait from life, as would have been possible (before Louverture's arrest on 7 June 1802, departing by boat on 15 or 16 June and arriving in Brest on 12 July), it is a likely contender for the prototype from which the other profile portraits would derive, and while it does not contradict Cafarelli's unflattering description in many respects, it does represent a glorified and triumphant figure in a long tradition of heroic equestrian portraits. It is worth noting that the frontispiece to Luc Dorsinville's eulogistic publication of *Miscellaneous Official Publications–Toussaint-Louverture, général Haitian, with illustrations including portraits* (Port-au-Prince, 1953) is an adaptation of the Volozan and the Maurin. It is entitled "Toussaint Louverture inaugurant la guerre contre l'armée Française en 1802." The book is dedicated to "Son Excellence le Général de Division, Paul E. Magloire, Président de la République" and was a contribution to the official celebrations of 150 years of

12.6. Delpech after Nicolas-Eustache Maurin, *Toussaint Louverture*, 1832. Lithograph. British Museum, London. © Trustees of the British Museum, London.

independence and recognition of Louverture's role.[25] This image could not have been perceived as in any way denigratory.

But there is still a problem of perception. Is the Volozan/Maurin a racist construction? Célius argues that this appears to be the case and compares the Maurin with diagrams accompanying the theories of Petrus Camper, which at times have been interpreted as relating the African to the ape. Célius makes the point with the Toussaint portrait. Others have done the same with the *Portrait of Belley* by Girodet (see Fig. 11.6). While it is easy to draw this conclusion on the basis of a superficial glance at the diagrams of Camper, it is the case that Camper was a fierce opponent of slavery, and he explained that he was not denigrating the African in comparison with the European, nor implying a closing of the gap between the African and the ape.[26] The comparison with the Maurin portrait is not wholly convincing, since the distinguishing feature about Louverture's profile was the forward thrust of the lower lip and jaw and the long nose, not the protrusion of both lips and receding chin, as in the Camper illustration. And, significantly, it is the Maurin portrait, and not the Bonneville, that is most often used as frontispiece for books that pay homage to Louverture and construct him as hero. Likewise, a close look at the cell in which Louverture died also shows a reproduction of this portrait on the wall among tributes placed there during the bicentenary (Fig. 12.7). Interestingly, in 1853 the Maurin was reused in the *Mémoires du Général Toussaint-Louverture, écrits par lui-même pouvant servir à l'histoire de sa vie, ornés d'un beau portrait gravé par Choubard,* edited by Lepelletier de Saint-Rémy, who adds Louverture's signature and authenticates the portrait as a true likeness.[27] He claimed that it had been given by Toussaint to Roume, commissaire delegated by the Directoire government to Saint-Domingue. In comparison with the 1832 image, the Choubard has been tidied up. The lip protrusions are lessened, the mouth closed and the face is younger and in stronger profile, which has the effect of lessening the angle of the forehead in relation to the nose. The forehead slopes less, becomes more vertical. There are other slight differences in detail of the jacket and hat, but the most striking addition is the wording around the inside of the now medallion-shaped image. This reads "La Couleur de mon corps / Nuit-elle à mon honneur et à ma bravoure?" (Does the color of my body harm/obscure my honor and my courage?) These lines are an adaptation from the French version of *Othello,* Act 1, Scene V:

> What! Is this African name no more than an outrage?
> Does the color of my face obscure/blacken my courage?[28]

This text is interesting as there is an implication that black heroism is an oxymoron. The text asks, "Why should the blackness of an African call into question my courage as a man?" The difficulty comes with the conjunction of black skin

12.7. Cell in the fortress of Joux, occupied by Toussaint Louverture, showing fireplace with Maurin print, documents and floral tributes from pilgrims at the time of the bicentenary of his death. Photo: Author.

and the uniform of a superior French officer, since, as already noted, for many whites the only acceptable image of the courageous black at this time was in his "savage," "natural," unclothed state, and the only acceptable acts of heroism were the rescue of whites and the patriotic self-sacrifice for France, which France, in paternalistic role, was able to acknowledge.

As for representations of Louverture, at no point is he represented on bended knee before any other power, as if liberty were being *octroyé* as a favor, by the fatherland. True liberation and independence for Haiti was gained by slaves fighting for it, claiming it. Only false, untrustworthy liberation would come from an alien power granting freedom and independence. It was precisely this sort of subservience that would be overtly represented twenty years after Louverture's death in a lithograph by Bove, seemingly for a piece of Sèvres porcelain decoration by Jean Charles Develly (Fig. 12.8). It shows President Jean Boyer, who succeeded Péthion as president of Haiti, accepting the "granting" of independence by France brought by the emissaries of Charles X "to the acclamation of all classes of inhabitants." He is shown from behind as if about to go down on bended knee.[29] The leading Frenchman holds the document of recognition, the voice of power in this case. There are five uniformed officers on the French side opposite Boyer and just one on the other. French ships and flags and cannon are much in evidence, as are Haitian palm trees and crowds of inhabitants, men, women and children, gratefully welcoming and cheering the French. Of course, it had been more than twenty years since Haiti had won its independence. When this was eventually *octroyé* by the French on 11 July 1825,

12.8. Bove after Jean Charles Develly, *Le 11 juillet 1825. L'Ordonnance de S. M. Charles X, qui reconnaît l'indépendance d'Haïti, est reçu par le Président Boyer, aux acclamations de toutes les classes d'habitans de l'Ile,* 1825. Lithograph. Marcel Chatillon Collection. © Mairie de Bordeaux. Photo: Jean Michel Arnaud.

it came at great cost to the Haitian people. They had to pay huge indemnities to the French colonizers in recompense for their being dispossessed of their properties (which would of course include their slaves) during the rebellions. It is arguable that Haiti never recovered from this financial beating. But still in 1825

12.9. Villain (rue de Sèvres), *Le Général Toussaint Louverture à qui le Général Leclerc avait envoyé ses enfants, pour tâcher par là de l'engager à déserter la cause des noirs, les renvoie après les avoir embrassés*, 1822. Lithograph. Marcel Chatillon Collection. © Mairie de Bordeaux. Photo: Jean Michel Arnaud.

the Haitians were expected to be grateful. Jean-Claude Halpern has suggested that, even when people were against slavery and sided with the Society of the Friends of Blacks, nevertheless they would find it easier to see the conferral of liberty on the slaves by the magnanimous whites, than to have the figure of the Black Avenger emancipate himself and fail to show respect for the values of the world of the whites.[30] This speaks of fear of a black backlash and a situation out of control for the whites.

Toussaint Louverture was that Black Avenger. From his *Mémoires* and those of his son, Isaac, and others who came into contact with him, it is clear that he had a strong sense of his high status identity.[31] If there is one ingredient in portraits of him that distinguishes them from those of his black contemporary generals, it is that he is upright and defiant. He gives the orders, points the finger, he has the power of the word. It was precisely this perceived arrogance, this self-affirmation, which would be his downfall, however. He refused to wear the usual mask expected of the noble savage and formulated in sentimental literature of the earlier eighteenth century, that of the hospitable, brave, but compliant ruler, with all the Christian virtues. Unlike Oroonoko, for example, Louverture was never described as having features that would conform to European notions of beauty. On the other hand, like Oroonoko, his ebony blackness and his strength were admired. He also opposed Vaudoo and pronounced Christianity as the official religion of the island. But he was never compliant where the status of equality for himself and his fellow blacks was concerned.

There is nothing but defiance and resistance in the representation of the dilemma facing him in Villain's lithograph construction of a family scene (Fig. 12.9). Louverture, the father, here tested to the limit, as he is given a choice between having his family with him and giving up the fight for independence, or having his sons taken away from him and continuing the struggle for his fellow blacks. This is one of a series of lithographs commissioned by President Boyer in 1822 to record the crucial episodes of Haiti's history. The first recorded the encounter between Louverture and General Maitland in March-April 1798, when the former persuaded the latter to leave the island. The next shows the dramatic scene of Louverture declaring the constitution of Saint-Domingue in July 1801. The last represented his death on 23 April 1803. The moment here depicted is 9 February 1802 on the plantation at Ennery. Louverture is centre-stage, his wife and sons, Isaac and Placide, to the right. To the left stands M. Coisnon, the boys' tutor and in this instance Bonaparte's messenger. From Bernard Gainot's researches into the role of Coisnon, we know that the two boys had for some time been considered as useful hostages during their period in Paris as pupils at the Collège de la Marche.[32] The text beneath the image explains that, after receiving his sons, who had been sent from Paris by General Leclerc in an attempt to persuade Louverture to give up his campaigns against slavery, Louverture tells their tutor to take them back to France. The image has parallels

12.10. La citoyenne Rollet after Fougea, *Le Nègre armé*, ca. 1794. Stipple engraving. Marcel Chatillon Collection. © Mairie de Bordeaux. Photo: Jean Michel Arnaud.

with ancient history paintings, especially with David's *The Lictors Bring Brutus the Bodies of His Sons*, where devotion to *la patrie* has to come before devotion to family. On the wall behind it is just possible to discern the outline of a map of Haiti. Neither the pleas of his wife nor those of his sons, expressed with the kind of gravity to be found in the solemn speeches of Jean Racine's tragedies as well as in the image itself, could dissuade him from his decision: "Reprenez mes enfants puisqu'il le faut. Je veux être fidèle à mes frères et à mon Dieu" (Take my children back, since that is how it must be. I wish to be faithful to my brothers and to my God).

The lithograph by Villain shares common meaning with the *Nègre armé* of 1794, engraved by Citizenness Rollet (Fig. 12.10). Both are primarily domestic genre scenes. Both involve the principled decisions of the father to fight for freedom from slavery (here specifically in Saint-Domingue). Freedom from slavery is spelled out on the jamb of the entrance in the *Nègre armé* – "Décret de la Conv(ention) qui rend la liberté aux Hommes de couleur" (Decree of the Convention that returns freedom to Men of Color). With his rifle slung over his back and his appearance offering all the signs of a hero from ancient Rome, this man's anguish at relinquishing his son, whom he clutches to his chest, is written emphatically over his brow and in his eyes. In both works the distress of the mothers and children is similarly in vain. In stylistic terms there is reference in both works to classical Davidian images of weeping women from *The Oath of the Horatii* (1785) and *The Lictors Bring Brutus the Bodies of His Sons.*

We were aware of Louverture's detractors speaking of his "look" as shifty and of reports of his untrustworthiness, of his deceit and hypocrisy. For the most part he identified wholly with blackness, against white domination and that mixed race desire to *vivre blanchement* (to live like whites in denial of their inherent blackness).[33] Adam Lively notes Aimé Césaire's identification with Toussaint Louverture, "that great symbol of black resistance, and with the alien place of exile, where he died."[34] With the last drawing in this series of commissioned works in 1822, I want to consider the positive meaning of dissimulation in the form of assuming the "white" mask at the time of his "white" death, as Aimé Césaire calls it:

> What is mine too: a small cell in the Jura,
> The snow lines it with white bars
> The snow is the white jailer who mounts guard in front of a prison
> What is mine, a man alone, imprisoned by whiteness, a man alone, who
> defies the white screams of a white death.[35]

Whiteness, in all its forms, was the imprisonment and the death of Toussaint Louverture, as far as Césaire was concerned.[36] But, as he saw it, Louverture continued to refuse this white imposition of a mask of white death, for even while pretending to be the obedient servant, he was in fact using dissimulation as the best hope of survival. This is sometimes referred to as a "fluidity of identity." It was a question of adapting and playing with great flexibility to particular situations. In his communication with Bonaparte, Louverture slips in and out of identities of the black general, leader and soldier on an equal footing with Bonaparte, and the black slave, forcibly mastered and dominated by Bonaparte. There is, for example, a letter dated 7 October 1802, addressed to General Bonaparte, Premier Consul (not this time to "le Premier des Blancs"). In it Toussaint Louverture adopts the mask of humble respect and submission:

> The respect and the submission that I offer you are forever engraved in the depth of my heart. If I have failed to comply with my duty, it was not out of my will.... If I have failed the Constitution, it was out of the desire to serve it well. I have had the misfortune of suffering your wrath. I am one of your soldiers and the First Soldier of the Republic of Saint-Domingue. I

am today wretched, ruined, dishonored, and the victim of my service; let my situation touch your sensibility. You are grand in feelings and too just to not pronounce yourself on my destiny. I have asked General Caffarelli, your aide-de-camp, to hand my report over to you. I beg you take it into consideration.

Greetings and respect,
Toussaint-Louverture[37]

He is apologetic, and he is on his knees begging for understanding. Bonaparte insisted that if Toussaint Louverture referred to his career as a soldier and to his victories, this would be considered as an act of insubordination. So Louverture calls himself "un de vos soldats" (one of your soldiers), but then, using capital letters, he adds "Premier Soldat de la République de Saint-Domingue" (First Soldier of the Republic of Saint Domingue). Bonaparte also ordered that he use only Toussaint as his rightful (slave) name. But the letter is signed "Toussaint-Louverture." So, even at the very end, when he realized the need to adopt that mask of obedience and agreed to be subject to Napoleon's will and command, it was nevertheless done so in a spirit of noncompliance, resistance and self-affirmation and only adopting the mask as necessary gesture for survival.

In the lithograph of *La Mort de Toussaint Louverture* Villain has given him a martyr's death (Fig. 12.11). There are similarities again with David's *Death of Marat* in which many have seen a sort of pietà. The presence of Louverture's manservant, who at first was allowed to keep him company, but who was not in fact with him at the end, contributes to this idea of a pietà.[38] In this image Louverture wears a heavy, buttoned coat over plain shirt and trousers. One of the problems with his imprisonment was the removal of his military uniform. This was taken from him when he was imprisoned. It was felt as the final humiliation and affront to his dignity, since the uniform was part of the man, his role and identity as a general. He had always been reluctant to take it off. Remove the uniform and you diminish the man, symbolically reenslaving him. The general's uniform was part of what set him on a level footing with Bonaparte. Despite its absence in Villain's image, the inclusion of the manservant and the reference to pietàs invests this image of Louverture at the end of his life with dignity and with a sense that, like many great rulers, he is pronouncing his famous last words: "By overthrowing me, all that has been beaten down in Saint-Domingue is the trunk of the tree of liberty for blacks; it will grow again from the roots, because these are many and they are deeply embedded in the earth." These were not his final words but were apparently uttered as he embarked on the ship *Le Héros* taking him to France and to his death. They signal confidence in the black subject's refusal to be fashioned into a white construction of inferiority and subjection, where only white expectation would define status and identity.

12.11. Villain, *La Mort de Toussaint Louverture*, 1822. Lithograph. Bibliothèque Nationale de France, Paris, Estampes.

There is a second portrait deemed by his son Isaac (published as late as 1818) to be a likeness of Louverture (in addition to the Maurin already discussed). It was engraved after a drawing by Montfayon (Fig. 12.12) and reproduced as a frontispiece to Gragnon-Lacoste's *Toussaint Louverture...le Premier des Noirs*

12.12. After a drawing by Montfayon, *Toussaint Louverture*. Engraving. Frontispiece to Gragnon-Lacoste, *Toussaint Louverture, Général en chef de l'armée de Saint-Domingue, Surnommé le Premier des Noirs* (Paris: A. Durand; Bordeaux: Pedone-Lauriel, Librairie Féret et fils, 1877). British Library, London. © British Library Board, 10644.d.4.

of 1877. Both this and the Maurin show him in uniform, without the hat in the case of the Montfayon. This keeps the high forehead and receding hairline avoiding any unflattering profile with protruding lower jaw. Both indicate a long thin face and pointed chin. In 1990 it was the Montfayon that was used to promote the image of Jean-Bertrand Aristide in a mural painting at the time of his election to the presidency, when it was juxtaposed with a portrait of himself, as if to draw parallels between the two and the moral principles that they both held in order to break with social systems that were still based on old privileges. Two hundred years earlier the Haitian Revolution had played a vital role in the destruction of slavery. In fact, many saw Haiti as the face and symbol of redemption for the whole of the African race.[39] Making visible the many faces that accompany the name of Toussaint Louverture and understanding the reasons for which they were conceived, together with the prejudices with which they were perceived, will hopefully contribute to keeping this Revolution in the public eye and conscience.

NOTES

1 "Ce qui est à moi / c'est un homme seul emprisonné de blanc / c'est un homme seul qui défie les cris / blancs de la mort blanche / (TOUSSAINT, TOUSSAINT LOUVERTURE)." Aimé Césaire, "Cahier d'un retour au pays natal," in *The Collected Poetry*, trans. Clayton Eshleman and Annette Smith (Berkeley: University of California Press, 1983), 46–47.

2 Frantz Fanon, *Black Skins, White Masks*, trans. Charles Lam Markmann (New York: Grove Press, 1967), 100. See also L. Adele Jinadu, *Fanon: In Search of the African Revolution* (New York: Routledge & Kegan Paul, 1978), 31–33.

3 Adam Lively, *Masks. Blackness, Race and the Imagination* (New York: Vintage, 1999); Aimé Césaire, *Toussaint Louverture: La Révolution française et le problème colonial* (Paris: Présence Africaine, 1981); Frantz Fanon, *Peau Noir/Masques Blancs* (Paris: Editions du Seuil, 1952), *Les Damnés de la Terre* (Paris: F. Maspèro, 1961); trans. Constance Farrington as *The Wretched of the Earth* (New York: Grove Press, 1968).

4 On Robespierre's role in these debates see Florence Gauthier, "La Révolution française et le problème colonial: Le Cas Robespierre," in *Annales historiques de la Révolution française* 288 (1992), 169–92.

5 "Lettre aux citoyens de couleur et nègres libres de Saint-Domingue et des autres isles françaises de l'Amérique' par Grégoire, député à l'Assemblée Nationale, évêque du département de Loir et Cher, Paris, 8 juin 1791, et AP 27, 14 juin 91. Réédité dans *La Révolution française et l'abolition de l'esclavage*," 12 vols. (Paris: EDHIS, 1968) 4: document 14. Cited in Rita Hermon-Belot, "Grégoire et l'universalité des principes: Les fondements chrétiens de son combat abolitioniste," in *Grégoire et la cause des Noirs (1789–1831) Combats et projets*, ed. Yves Bénot and Marcel Dorigny (Paris: Société française d'histoire d'outre-mer, 2000), 25–36.

6 Cited in Aimé Césaire, *Toussaint-Louverture*, 278.

7 For a discussion of this painting see Helen Weston, "*The Oath of the Ancestors* by Lethière 'le mulâtre': Celebrating the Black/Mulatto Alliance in Haïti's Struggle for Independence," in *An Economy of Colour: Visual Culture and the Atlantic World, 1660–1830*, ed. Geoff Quilley and Kay Dian Kriz (Manchester: Manchester University Press, 2003), 176–95; Darcy Grimaldo-Grigsby, "Revolutionary Sons, White Fathers, and Creole Difference: Guillaume Guillon-Lethière's *Oath of the Ancestors*, 1822," *Yale French Studies* 101 (2002), 201–26.

8 See the lithograph by Villain of *Toussaint Louverture proclame la Constitution de Saint-Domingue*, one of a series of works commissioned by President Jean-Pierre Boyer in 1822 to chart and celebrate the recent history of Haiti.

9 Laurent Dubois, *Avengers of the New World: The Story of the Haitian Revolution* (Cambridge, Mass.: Harvard University Press, 2004), 4.

10 Nick Crossley, *Intersubjectivity: The Fabric of Social Becoming* (London: Sage Publications, 1996), 10–13; Martin Buber, *I and Thou* (Edinburgh: T. and T. Clark, 1958).

11 Michel-Rolph Troulliot, *Silencing the Past: Power and the Production of History* (Boston: Beacon Press, 1995), 82–83.

12 Trouillot, *Silencing the Past*, 79–83. Trouillot makes the crucial point that the Haitian Revolution has been forgotten, denied or trivialized in Western historiography. Haitian historians face "uneven power in the production of sources, archives, and narratives" (27).

13 "[N]ous avions été défricher des terres inconnues; nous avons bâti des Villes ; nous avons presque fondé un Empire. Victimes du climat, nous avons bravé la mort pour augmenter vos possessions, et quand enfin, il a été bien reconnu que la nature refusait aux Français la force de corps nécéssaire pour cultiver un sol brulé sous une zone ardente, nous avons conservé nos têtes pour ordonner les travaux, et nous avons été chercher au sein de l'Afrique un Peuple tout entier d'habitants acclimatisés; nous les avons prescrit d'enrichir le Métropole et notre Souverain, et nous les traitons par humanité et par intérêt, comme nos Enfans, en dépit des assertions erronées de quelques Philosophes novateurs." *Lettre des Commissaires de la Colonie de Saint-Domingue au Roi* (Paris: n.p., 1788), 5.

14 See Jean-Yves Boscher, "on sait en effet que le Noir Eustache ... protégea ... son maitre pendant cette révolte des esclaves.... Toussaint Louverture lui-même avait aidé et caché la famille de son protecteur en 1791" (it is known indeed that the Blackman Eustache ... protected ... his master during that slave revolt ... Toussaint Louverture himself had helped and hid the family of his protector in 1791), in *Regards sur les Antilles, Collection Marcel Chatillon*, exhibition catalogue (Paris: Réunion des Musées Nationaux, 1999–2000), 229.

15 When Abbé Raynal called for the Black Spartacus to lead the slaves to freedom in *Histoire des Deux Indes* he was actually referring to Jamaica and Guyana, not Saint-Domingue, as Trouillot points out (*Silencing the Past*, 85), and there is no proof that Louverture had read Raynal or saw his role in this way. Recent writers have nevertheless made much use of the Black Spartacus in describing Louverture.

16 Hilary and Mary Evans, *John Kay of Edinburgh: Barber, Miniaturist and Social Commentator 1742–1826* (Aberdeen: Impulse Publications, 1973), fig. 7, 64–65. Kay had depicted several known sympathizers with the French Revolution, including Tom Paine, Citizen M. C. Brown and Charles Sinclair. He also produced a caricature of William Pitt, lampooning his assumption of hostilities against the French Republic.

17 21 July 1803. An early exponent of the art of the magic lantern, Paul de Philipstal, produced the performance of phantasmagoria. See Laurent Mannoni, *The Great Art of Light and Shadow: Archaeology of the Cinema*, trans. Richard Crangle (Exeter: University of Exeter Press, 2000), 173–75.

18 This "portrait" is reproduced in Hugh Honour, *The Image of the Black in Western Art*, vol. 4, *From the American Revolution to World War I*, part 1: *Slaves and Liberators* (Cambridge, Mass.: Harvard University Press, 1989), 106–7.

19 This description is quoted in a recent article, much of which is devoted to the representations of Toussaint Louverture, by Carlo Avierl Célius, "Les Enjeux de la representation: Portraits de noirs et de mulâtres pendant la révolution à Saint-Domingue (1789–1804)," in *Negros, mulatos, zambaigos: Derroteros africanos en los mundos*

ibéricos, ed. Berta Ares Queja and Alessandro Stella (Sevilla: Publicaciones de la Escuela de Estudios Hispano-Americanos, Consejo Superior de Investigaciones Científicas, 2000), 313–59, 343. For discussion of the details of Toussaint's death and the documents related to his imprisonment in the fortress at Joux, see Roland Lambalot, *Toussaint Louverture, Prisonnier d'État au Château de Joux: Ouvrage édité en hommage à Toussaint Louverture dans le Cadre du Bicentennaire de la Révolution Française* (Pontarlier: Office du Tourisme de Pontarlier, 1989).

20 *St. Domingo, or An Historical, Political and Military Sketch of the Black Republic with a View of the Life and Character of Toussaint L'Ouverture*, 2nd ed. (London: R. B. Scott, 1802).

21 Boscher, *Regards sur les Antilles*, 232.

22 David Blake and Anthony Ward, *Toussaint or the Aristocracy of the Skin*, English National Opera at the Coliseum, first performed in 1977, revised by the composer in 1982.

23 The full title of the book is *L'Iconographie des contemporains ou portraits des personnes dont les noms se rattachent plus particlulièrement, soit par leurs actions, soit par leurs écrits, aux divers événements qui ont eu lieu en France depuis 1789 jusqu'en 1829*, 3 vols. (Paris: François Séraphin Delpech, 1832–51). The title confirms Trouillot's view that the Haitian Revolution was largely denied or seen only in so far as it affected France.

24 See note 19 above. Célius also reproduces the "portrait" of Christophe.

25 A portrait of Toussaint serves as inspiration for the real estate tycoon Mr. Walters in Frank Webb's 1856 novel *The Garies and Their Friends*, and it is tempting to think that Webb may have had a version of Volozan's painting in mind. I am grateful to one of the anonymous readers.

26 Camper's thesis on the subject was published after his death, in 1791. It was translated into English by Thomas Cogan, *The Works of the Late Professor Camper, On the Connection between the Science of Anatomy and the Arts of Drawing, Painting, Statuary etc. etc. in Two Books. Containing a Treatise on the Natural Difference of Features in Persons of Different Countries and Periods of Life …* (London, 1794), quoted in Hugh Honour, *The Image of the Black in Western Art*, vol. 4, part 2 (Cambridge, Mass.: Harvard University Press, 1989), 13–15.

27 In his book *Toussaint-Louverture, un révolutionnaire noir d'Ancien Régime* (Paris: Fayard, 1989), Pierre Pluchon, author of many works on Louverture, asserts, "Le portrait de Toussaint qui illustre la couverture de cet ouvrage a été aquarellé par Maurin et dessiné au XIXe siècle par Delpech à partir d'un document d'une veridicité indubitable. A propos de cette gravure voici ce qu'a écrit l'historien Haitien Saint Rémy: 'Le portrait de Louverture est authentique. Il fut donné par Louverture lui-même à l'agent Roume. L'original du portrait est religieusement conservé dans la famille Roume, chez M. Le comte Roume de Saint-Laurent, qui habite Paris.'" (The portrait of Tousssaint that illustrates the cover of that work is a watercolor painted by Maurin and designed in the nineteenth century by Delpech after a document of indubitable veracity. Here is what the Haitian historian Saint Rémy has written about that engraving: "Louverture's portrait is authentic. It was given by Louverture himself to the agent Roume. The original of this portrait is carefully guarded by the Roume family, at the house of the Count Roume de Saint-Laurent, who lives in Paris.") However, Maurin may have been relying largely on the Caffarelli description.

28 "Quoi! Ce nom d'Africain n'est-il donc qu'un outrage? / La Couleur de mon front nuit-elle à mon courage?"

29 In the Bibliothèque Nationale there is a lithograph by A. Choyère representing the Independence of Haiti (Qg3–fol. L'Amérique latine après 1739. M242965). It shows a crowned figure of France standing before her throne decorated with fleurs de lys, receiving a dark-skinned woman presumably representing Haiti. She wears a feathered headdress and short tunic and is simply the generic figure of the American Indian. She is about to genuflect before the monarch. Behind her are ships and above a child mercury figure with olive branch. Scales of justice can be seen in an arch above these figures. This is precisely the sort of image produced in France in the 1820s to erase any idea of the avenger and continue to insist on the generosity and graciousness of France in granting this independence.

30 In 1771 Louis Sébastien Mercier dreamed of a statue of a "negro, his head bare, his arm outstretched, with pride in his eyes and a noble and imposing demeanor." The words under the statue would read "To the Avenger of the New World!" This man, he continues, had "broken the chains of his compatriots." He had turned those "oppressed by the most odious slavery" into heroes, who had spilled the blood of their tyrants. *L'An deux mille cent quarante: Rêve s'il en fut jamais* (1770; reprint Paris, 1977), 127.

31 *Mémoires du Général Toussaint-Louverture, ecrits par lui-mêmê, pouvant servir à l'histoire de sa vie, ornée d'un beau portrait gravé par Choubard, ed. M. Lepelletier de Saint-Rémy, des Cayes, Haiti* (Paris: Pagnerre, 1853); Antoine Métral, *Histoire de l'Expédition Militaire des Français à Saint-Domingue, sous Napoléon Bonaparte, suivi des mémoires et notes d'Isaac Louverture, sur la même expédition, et sur la vie de son Père* (Paris: Edmé and Alexandre Picard, 1841).

32 Bernard Gainot, "Un projet avorté d'intégration républicaine: L'Institution Nationale des Colonies (1797–1802)," in *Le Dix-huitième siècle* 32 (2000), 372–401. This explores the lives of the sons of Belley, Lethière, Christophe and Toussaint Louverture (among others) at the Collège de la Marche in the Quartier latin in Paris, and the career of Abbé Coisnon. Louverture's children arrived there on 23 October 1796.

33 Didier Renard, "Vivre blanchement: Les hommes de couleur libres et la Révolution française," in *Les Droits de l'Homme et la Conquête des Libertés*, ed. Gérard Chianéa (Grenoble: Presses universitaires de Grenoble; Vizille: Musée de la Révolution française, 1989), 257–62.

34 Lively, *Masks*, 228.

35 "Ce qui est à moi aussi: une petit cellule dans le Jura, / une petite cellule, la neige la double de barreaux blancs / la neige est un geôlier blanc qui monte la garde devant une prison / Ce qui est à moi / c'est un homme seul emprisonné de blanc / c'est un homme seul qui défie les cris blancs de la mort blanche."

36 See note 1.

37 "Le respect et la soumission que je vous dois étaient toujours gravés au fond de mon cœur. Si j'ai péché en ferant mon devoir, c'est sans vouloir.... Si j'ai manqué en faisant la Constitution, c'est le grand désir de faire le bien. J'ai eu le malheur d'essuyer votre courroux. Je suis un de vos soldats et Premier Soldat de la République de Saint-Domingue. Je suis aujourd'hui malheureux, ruiné, deshonoré, et victime de mes services; que ma situation touche à votre sensibilité. Vous êtes trop grand de sentiment et trop juste pour ne pas prononcer sur mon sort. J'ai chargé Général Caffarelli, votre aide de camps, de vous remettre mon rapport. Je vous prie de le prendre en considération.

Salut et respect,

Toussaint-Louverture"

This letter is reproduced in Lambalot, *Toussaint Louverture au Château de Joux,* 22–23.

38 This servant was Martial Besse, born in 1759 of a white father and black mother. He trained as a soldier, became chef de brigade and went to Saint-Domingue. He was sent back to France in order to accompany Toussaint Louverture in prison. Christophe later made him a count and field marshal of his kingdom.

39 See David Nicholls, *From Dessalines to Duvalier: Race, Colour and National Independence in Haiti,* 3rd ed., Warwick University Caribbean Studies (London: Macmillan, 1996).

THIRTEEN

CINQUÉ

A HEROIC PORTRAIT FOR THE ABOLITIONIST CAUSE

Toby Maria Chieffo-Reidway

Nathaniel Jocelyn (1796–1881) of New Haven, Connecticut, occupies a singular position in the history of nineteenth-century American art for his extraordinary portrait of Cinqué (ca. 1813–79), the legendary leader of the *Amistad* rebellion of 1839 (Fig. 13.1, Plate 10).[1]

The *Cinqué* portrait went beyond the written and spoken antislavery rhetoric of the times and presented Jocelyn with an opportunity to link his role as an artist with his abolitionist and Christian beliefs. A devout evangelical Congregationalist during the Second Great Awakening, Jocelyn saw all aspects of his life, including attaining artistic acclaim and economic success, embedded in his religious convictions. Unlike other portraits of slaves or freed blacks of this period, *Cinqué* dissociated black skin and Africanness from traditional images that linked them with slavery. Rather, it directly undermined those racial stereotypes by depicting its black subject as a dignified hero. This painting presents Cinqué as a man of power, independence, and intelligence – even more provocatively, as a Christ-like figure – and registers a symbolic negotiation in which an African subject appears suspended between the cusp of freedom and a life of servitude.[2] Jocelyn also incorporated elements of New Haven's unique colonial history into the portrait, thus visually embedding the story of the *Amistad* captives into the larger American struggle against tyranny. By imbuing the portrait with an iconography rich with historical resonances and Christian symbolism, Jocelyn provided the abolitionist cause with a new visual language, superseding established boundaries of racialized identities.

The manner in which Jocelyn's portrait of Cinqué challenged Jacksonian era concepts of portraiture, along with the way it emerged as a significant icon for the abolitionist movement in the midcentury, makes it the most important paint-

13.1. Nathaniel Jocelyn, *Portrait of Cinqué*, ca. 1839–40. Oil on canvas. Whitney Library, New Haven Museum and Historical Society, New Haven, Conn.

ing of an African from that period.[3] The creation of *Cinqué* was the galvanizing event of Jocelyn's life as an artist, abolitionist, and Christian.

THE *AMISTAD* AFFAIR

The *Amistad* story began in April 1839 when the Portuguese slave ship *Teçora* and its cargo of 500 or 600 African captives set sail for Havana, Cuba.[4] The abduction of the Africans from their homeland was illegal. It was in violation of a treaty signed by Spain, its colonies, and Britain in 1817, and also of the Spanish queen's royal decree of 1838.[5] The *Teçora* avoided the British "slave patrol" warships, sailed across the Atlantic, and docked in Cuba (a Spanish colony at the time). In Cuba the slavers obtained false papers declaring their African captives to be pre-1820 subjects of Spain, who could therefore officially be sold as slaves.

The slavers sold forty-nine adult Mendi Africans (from Mendi country [Sierra Leone] on the west coast of Africa) from their "cargo" to the slave speculator José Ruiz for $450 each, and also four young children (three females and one male) to Ruiz's partner Pedro Montez. Under the cover of dark, with false passports in hand but still fearing British detection, the group then set off through Havana on foot to the dock, where they met the chartered schooner *La Amistad*. The small black vessel was built in Baltimore specifically for transporting slaves. On 28 June 1839, it set sail for the plantations of Puerto Principe, a few days voyage up the northwest coast of Cuba.[6]

On 1 July, the third evening at sail, a mutiny occurred. The Africans, unchained in the hold, rose up and killed the captain and the cook. Two sailors on the crew dove overboard and were presumed drowned. Ruiz, Montez, and Montez's young slave Antonio were the only survivors. Sengbeh Pieh (later called Cinquez or [Joseph] Cinqué), the acknowledged leader of the Mendi Africans, ordered Montez and Ruiz to sail the ship back to Africa. The two Spaniards devised a plan by which they would sail east toward Africa by day and northwest by night in hopes that they would be caught or rescued by the British.[7]

After two months of this zigzag sailing and many sightings and fruitless encounters with other ships, the *Amistad* crew and the Africans put ashore on the northeastern tip of Long Island, New York, to seek supplies. Meanwhile, due to the erratic behavior of the ship, the Brooklyn Navy Yard of New York dispatched two United States Naval vessels to find the mysterious vessel. The following day, according to historian Howard Jones:

> Lieutenant Meade on board the USS Washington saw the activity ashore and at Lieutenant Gedney's orders seized the schooner, the cargo, and the blacks. Perhaps because New York had abolished slavery, Gedney took his prize to New London, Connecticut, where slavery was legal. There he would seek salvage of the *Amistad* and its cargo, including the blacks.[8]

A significant legal debate with international overtones ensued. Myriad legal questions emerged in the following weeks: Were they African slaves, were they Spanish slaves, were they cargo, was the United States entitled to the ship and the "cargo," and what court should have jurisdiction over the case?

The incident broadened an already wide gap among differing abolitionist factions and anti-abolitionist groups. Among the abolitionists, two main variants existed: the immediatists, in favor of immediate emancipation, versus the colonizationists, who wanted gradual emancipation along with deportation of American slaves back to Africa to colonize Liberia. Jocelyn, along with his brother Simeon and William Lloyd Garrison, were counted among the immediatists.[9]

Like a clarion call, the leading immediatists seized upon the event as an over-arching template to aid their less fortunate "brethren" and to demonstrate to the country the feasibility of their abolitionist and Christianizing methods. The editor of the *Emancipator,* Rev. Joshua Leavitt, convinced a mutual friend, Roger Sherman Baldwin, to take the Africans' case. The venerable John Quincy Adams joined him.

Their strategy evolved beyond the legal arguments into an abolitionist cause célèbre. Their aim was not to make theirs a typical "abolitionist crusade," but rather to direct the public to see the Africans as kidnapped citizens of a foreign country, one untainted by American slavery. They were thus careful to keep the focus on the captives, and on a national level, the universal evils of slavery. They focused on the hypocrisy of the United States with regard to the proclamation of inalienable rights and on the inherent paradox of the system. The *Amistad* captives transformed the priorities of the New Haven and New York immediatists into larger national and even international issues of slavery. For example, the abolitionists noted that the British government took a keen interest in the case and even went so far as to "demand their [the captives'] freedom of the Spanish authorities, in case our [the United States] government should remand them over to Spain." The British insisted "upon the fulfillment of the [1817] treaty with Great Britain, by which the slave trade was declared illegal, and in consequence of which, these Africans are entitled to their freedom."[10]

On 6 March 1841, John Quincy Adams presented the case to the United States Supreme Court. According to *Colored American,* he contended "that no law was applicable to the case of his clients, save that contained in our Declaration of Independence; ... That they had gained their Independence, and we had no right to interfere with them, nor the Spanish Government the right to demand them of us." On 11 March 1841, the *Amistad* Committee announced the verdict that the captives were free "without condition or restraint."[11]

After the trial, the *Amistad* Africans became the catalyst the abolitionists needed to unify their various factions. They put their differences aside to support the freedom of the Africans and their subsequent return to Sierra Leone. Unfortunately for the abolitionists, the freedom of Cinqué and his fellow captives was not decided on the basis of their worth as human beings, deserving full human rights. Rather, it was predicated on the issues surrounding the illegality of the international slave trade. In other words, the verdict was based on maritime law, not on the unalienable rights of humankind. Nevertheless, for the abolitionists, it was read and publicized as a moral victory that highlighted the universal evils of slavery and the virtues of Christianity.

JOCELYN'S PORTRAIT MAKING

In the early nineteenth century, Philadelphia was the acknowledged center of the arts in the United States and had the longest sustained experience with art exhibition. Therefore, the immediatists and their brethren in the more northern states would have followed the lead of those in Philadelphia with respect to the advanced use of imagery for the cause. Philadelphia had a strong history of antislavery publications, which included engravings and daguerreotypes. John Sartain (1808–97), the most famous and proficient engraver in the country, lived and worked in Philadelphia. However, there was probably only one artist in the country with the unique combination of painterly skill and knowledge of and proximity to the African captives, and a deep personal commitment to abolition, qualified for the *Cinqué* commission – the religiously driven Nathaniel Jocelyn.[12]

Jocelyn was not unlike other enterprising New Englanders in the early nineteenth century. Although he received little formal art training and earned his primary living as a banknote engraver, his dream was to become a preeminent portrait painter in the new republic. For Jocelyn, *Cinqué* was a once-in-a-lifetime opportunity to marshal his artistic skill and his passion for black equality to make manifest the abolitionist ideal of the black man, free from the evils of slavery.

Jocelyn found himself with a certain latitude in painting Cinqué. Previous portraits of black subjects had dealt with them explicitly as either slaves or free. Cinqué, on the other hand, was neither; caught between two states of being, by virtue of his unique story (no portrait of a subject quite like this was to follow *Cinqué* either). Prior to *Cinqué*, the common use of abolitionist imagery (including engravings from painted portraits) was restricted to material that could be mass-produced for the edification of adults and the education of children, while also being easily mass distributed in the South. In a typical issue of an abolitionist newspaper, several columns would contain advertisements of various antislavery graphic works for sale. In the 31 May 1838 issue of the *Emancipator*, these items were found among others: *Slave Market Of America (A broad sheet, illustrating by facts and engravings, the slave market in the District of Columbia.)*; *Views Of Slavery (A lithographic print giving six different views of slavery, viz: 1. Sugar Plantation; 2. Mode of Punishment; 3. Slave Auction; 4. Wresting from a Colored Woman Her Free Papers, in order to reduce her to slavery; 5. Tearing a Little Child from Her Mother's Arms, and Selling It [sic] to a Slave-Trader; 6. Shipping Slaves for New Orleans. Price of the whole, [set of prints] only $1 per hundred; 12 cents per dozen; 12 cents, single.)*; *Southern Ideas Of Liberty*; etc.

In retrospect, Jocelyn may not have realized his portrait set a new standard. On rare occasions, a single painting breaks at every level with an artist's current style and visual language. Usually the artist recognizes the painting does not fit in with his or her oeuvre, but the artist continues to work in this new direction until the painting contains all the elements and content that it was designed to convey. *Cinqué* was that type of breakthrough portrait.

John Neagle's (1796–1865) most famous painting, *Pat Lyon at the Forge* (Fig. 13.2), is another example of a breakthrough portrait. In 1829 Neagle's painting introduced the paradigm for the genre-portrait, specifically that of the Jacksonian-era model of the common man who rose to commercial success. At the time of the portrait, Pat Lyon was a physically large, independent-minded man of fifty-seven. In his youth, he had been falsely imprisoned on a robbery charge, and after the real culprit was apprehended, Lyon nevertheless for a time remained in prison. Here similarities with Cinqué begin to emerge that shed light

13.2. John Neagle, *Pat Lyon at the Forge, (1779–1829)*, 1829. Oil on canvas. Courtesy of the Pennsylvania Academy of the Fine Arts, Philadelphia. Gift of the Lyon Family, 1842.1.

on the links between the two portraits. Both Lyon and Cinqué were imprisoned under unusual circumstances (Cinqué, although originally deemed innocent in his first appearance before the Hartford court, was nevertheless kept in jail).

Analysis of Neagle's painting of Lyon reveals artistic connections to *Cinqué*. To begin, the painting is a full-length portrait of Lyon at his forge with intense, warm color contrasts playing off the walls of the workplace. Lyon stands proud; his white shirt, loose at the neck, reveals a bare chest. His bare muscular arms direct the viewer's focus to one hand, which holds his hammer at rest, but poised for action. The "whiteness" of his head and chest are in contrast to the dark stone background of the hearth chimney. Substitute Cinqué's dark skin, reverse the background light and dark, and the remainder of the description of *Lyon* could be of *Cinqué*. Two proud men were falsely accused, vindicated, and finally able to return to their private lives – not the usual storybook ending for a black man.

Jocelyn's portrayal of Cinqué was inspired. He depicted him as a righteous, strong, and independent-minded leader – characteristics usually attributed to white men. Jocelyn's portrait single-handedly challenged nineteenth-century views of "blackness" and "whiteness." Did Jocelyn, by evoking Neagle-esque characteristics in his portrait, attempt to blur the line between "whiteness" and "blackness" in accordance with the abolitionist contention of equality between the races? Did he infuse "white" characteristics into the portrait of Cinqué?

There was no precedent for *Cinqué* in Jocelyn's earlier works, nor were there any portraits quite like it in his later paintings. Why was some of the political dynamism of *Cinqué* not used in the portrayal of white abolitionist sitters after *Cinqué*? I posit that it was physically dangerous to be an immediatist sitter for a portrait painted in an extremely innovative style and might have provided an excuse for detractors to become incensed at the implications. The sitter would have already been considered radical and incendiary by foes; one's religiously conservative constituency would not want to have the radical aspect of their abolitionist leader reinforced by a painted image. Frankly, it would not have been profitable to market a less than humble version of a white abolitionist leader at the time.[13] As will be demonstrated, the lack of any visual precedents for *Cinqué* made it acceptable to create an innovative and extreme (in its new use of strong color and historical and Biblical references) image of an African to thwart the prevailing black stereotypes.

For Jocelyn to have modified his style to a more dramatic and allegorical mode would have been ruinous to his conservative client base. Jocelyn's clients in the New Haven area (including Yale faculty) were not ready to make that aesthetic leap. Historians such as Virgil Barker have placed Jocelyn in the "Basic Average" category of midcentury portraiture. His assessment of Jocelyn is typical of historians who did not recognize the relationship of Jocelyn to abolitionism. Barker wrote, "Jocelyn's work has the academically dependable

13.3. John Sartain after Nathaniel Jocelyn, *Cinqué*, ca. 1840. Mezzotint on paper. National Portrait Gallery, Smithsonian Institution, Washington, D.C., NPG.69.66.

prosaicism which, like the humanly dependable people whom it depicts, later times usually overlook. But on one occasion Jocelyn was moved to impart to his placidly objective manner a tragic dignity; his portrait of the slave-hero Cinqué … with well drawn dark head and shoulders dramatic between light background and white drapery, is visually as well as humanly haunting."[14] Barker recognized the psychological impact of the portrait, but without addressing the nineteenth-century abolitionist mindset, he missed the opportunity to decode its ideological implications.

Perhaps the subtle layering or embedding of New England history, the use of light and costume as an allusion to Christianity for Africans, the marking of the location as New Haven by the rendition of the landscape and foliage, the use of color as a stand-in for power, and the hint of potential and past violence (which the immediatists always circled like a fire, but never got close enough to be burned) ensured the physical survival of the painting. This portrait was conceived and executed intentionally, before the court verdict was announced. The men of the Lewis Tappan circle and fellow "coadjutors" in Philadelphia, including Robert Purvis, were not opposed to the implication of a *hint* of violence in the painting (Cinqué clutching the staff) should the *Amistad* trial verdict not go their way. More than the abolitionists in New York and New Haven, the Philadelphia contingent was astute and in tune with the power of imagery in propaganda.

In New Haven, the unique convergence of the antislavery movement's aims and the *Amistad* mutiny allowed Jocelyn to advance his own skills as a painter while developing a more visible role as an abolitionist. Jocelyn emerged from this confluence with his skillful depiction of Cinqué. It was crucial to the Anti-Slavery Society's aims to replicate *Cinqué* for mass distribution. John Sartain was commissioned for this critical task.[15]

Eventually, the mezzotint of *Cinqué* by Sartain (Fig. 13.3) was added to the list of graphic works for sale in the *Emancipator*. Like Jocelyn, John Sartain was an avowed immediatist, and through his artistic skill, the quality and content of abolitionist graphics would have been significantly improved. The images were one prong of the immediatists' multipronged approach to influence the American people and spur their conscience and Christian duty from passivity to action. The engraving firm N. & S. S. Jocelyn was too invested in the lucrative banknote engraving trade to be involved in the production of the abolitionist graphics previously listed.[16] In the Jocelyn brothers' service to abolition, Simeon, a pastor, fulfilled his most important functions in the pulpit and in the leadership of antislavery organizations. Nathaniel's most important contribution was at his easel.

The Heroic Portrait

Nathaniel Jocelyn's role in developing a potent visual image of Cinqué was crucial to the abolitionist movement. The abolitionists used the plight of the *Amistad* Africans to rally their cause, and the portrait became an especially pivotal element in the fight for immediate emancipation.

As an immediatist, Jocelyn probably recognized an opportunity to fulfill the wishes expressed in his diary in 1821 – to explore artistic possibilities beyond the realm of conventional portraiture and into history and landscape painting:

> I speak of Portrait painting, not that fulmost [*sic*] inclined to that department but through this is the only hope I have of ever devoting myself to the art. Gladly, indeed would I yield myself up to Historic art or paint the seasons as they rise. This first prompted me, and I shall always study nature, as an historical painter, that should leisure or easy circumstances ever put it in my power I can turn to it with pleasure and with a mind stored with materials.[17]

Jocelyn and his fellow abolitionists William Lloyd Garrison and Robert Purvis recognized the impact Jocelyn's art could have on the abolitionist movement. The presence of the Africans in New Haven and Jocelyn's earlier study of European art provided him with both the circumstance and a "mind stored with materials" to utilize his artistic talent and expand his religious fervor into the arena of social reform.

Jocelyn's painting of Cinqué is not a didactic history painting. Rather it is an atypical portrait that contained elements of both history and landscape painting. The difficulty Jocelyn would have had in creating an *Amistad* history painting was twofold: First, the history of the African captives was yet to be completed. The outcome of their trial and their freedom or return to bondage was unknown. Second, the last thing the abolitionists wanted was to depict incensed Africans attacking Spanish sailors with machetes, gaining their freedom, and being turned loose on the streets of New Haven. Since the portrait was to be completed before the end of the trial, it is plausible that its aim was to influence the outcome in favor of the Africans and the abolitionist cause.

Jocelyn undertook a more a subtle position with his portrait of Cinqué. His image of Cinqué is one of dignity, strength, and virility – a heroic leader, not a savage warrior. This portrait was brought into even sharper relief by contrasting it with another contemporary interpretation of the affair. In 1840 Amasa Hewins (1795–1855) rose to the bait of depicting the violence and gore of the mutiny. He exhibited a 135-foot-wide canvas of *The Death of the Captain of the Amistad, Capt. Ferrer,* engraved by John W. Barber later that year (Fig. 13.4).[18] Hewins portrayed the captain and his crew being slain by the African captives. Anti-abolitionists and general audiences, not ready for an honorable depiction

Death of Capt. Ferrer, the Captain of the Amistad, July, 1839.
Don Jose Ruiz and Don Pedro Montez, of the Island of Cuba, having purchased fifty-three slaves at Havana, recently imported from Africa, put them on board the Amistad, Capt. Ferrer, in order to transport them to Principe, another port on the Island of Cuba. After being out from Havana about four days, the African captives on board, in order to obtain their freedom, and return to Africa, armed themselves with cane knives, and rose upon the Captain and crew of the vessel. Capt. Ferrer and the cook of the vessel were killed; two of the crew escaped; Ruiz and Montez were made prisoners.

13.4. John Warner Barber after Amasa Hewins, *Death of Capt. Ferrer, the Captain of the Amistad, July, 1839.* Engraving. Frontispiece of John W. Barber, *A History of the Amistad Captives* (New Haven, Conn.: E. L. & J. W. Barber, 1840). Courtesy of the Rare Book, Manuscript, and Special Collections Library, Duke University, Durham, N.C.

of Cinqué, seemed more inclined to favor an image of a stereotypical African as savage and brutal. Stereotypes such as Hewins's dominated mainstream thought and in retrospect made Jocelyn's portrait more radical for its time.[19]

During this time, Jocelyn built a reputation within the immediatist movement as the artist of choice to portray antislavery leaders such as William Lloyd Garrison, Jehudi Ashmun, William Henry Seward, and James Armstrong Thome.[20] Richard J. Powell describes the difference between an abolitionist portrait and a typical portrait of the Jacksonian era:

> Unlike traditional portraiture, it was never intended to merely hang on the wall of someone's home. Nor was it meant to hang in the hallowed halls of a government building, business establishment, or religious institution. Its original function was that of a weapon – a metaphorical weapon, but a weapon nonetheless.[21]

Furthermore, Powell makes the important point that the portraits of the abolitionist leaders were in and of themselves radical. "Their portraits, rather than functioning as markers of mainstream acceptance, glorified nonconformity, cultural and racial difference, and the willingness to take the high moral ground on social issues in the face of widespread injustice and complacency."[22]

The Portrait Commission

There are limited facts relating to the commission of the portrait. It is known that Robert Purvis, a wealthy free black Philadelphia businessman, paid $260 for the painting. (Purvis is directly quoted on the matter in a 26 December 1889 article in the *Philadelphia Inquirer*, titled "A Priceless Picture," fifty years after the commission.) The decision to commission Jocelyn to paint Cinqué most likely stemmed from Purvis's relationship with Garrison. The portrait served a dual purpose – as a personal status symbol and emotionally significant acquisition for Purvis, and more importantly, as a model for subsequent graphic replicas, offered for sale.

Purvis was deeply involved financially and emotionally with several antislavery organizations, both in Philadelphia and nationwide, and "helped launch Garrison's *Liberator*."[23] Jocelyn was a logical choice for the commission. He was an abolitionist artist with proximity to the captives in New Haven. Additionally, he and his brother Simeon were friends of Garrison. Simeon together with Lewis Tappan and Joshua Leavitt founded the Amistad Committee established to free the *Amistad* captives and return them to Africa.

There is scant data relating to the commission or the exact date of the completed portrait. There is only one direct reference that ties Cinqué to the Jocelyn family during the period in which Cinqué was sitting for him. Sarah, Jocelyn's nineteen-year-old daughter, in a fleeting casual mention, wrote in her diary: "I sent Mr. Nally *when we went for the purpose of carrying Cinquez the prisoner to his quarters* to invite Mr. Penderson [Lemuel, an engraver] to spend the evening with us – he came at a very late hour" (emphasis added).[24] This brief fragment by Sarah Jocelyn implies a casual carriage or cart ride from her father's studio without the jailer, Colonel Stanton Pendleton. If she were not returning Cinqué from her father's painting studio to the New Haven jail, why else would she be involved with the most famous of the African captives?

The only other source that some writers have seen as a reference to the portrait sitting by Cinqué is a cryptic notice published in the *New Haven Daily Herald* on 12–14 August 1839 by Jocelyn, which reads:

> The subscriber wishing when in town to be uninterruptedly engaged in the practice of his profession, during the hours from 10 A.M. to 1 P.M. and from 5 to 6 P.M. would feel greatly obliged if persons having other business with him, would call at other hours of the day. Nath'l Jocelyn.

Historian Foster Wild Rice mentions this notice as evidence of the portrait sitting with Cinqué. However, the dates of the notice are too early to be linked with the *Amistad* affair. The United States Navy did not seize the vessel *Amistad* until 26 August 1839, and the Africans were not brought to New Haven until 1 September. Since the precautions enumerated in the notice were too early for Cinqué, I contend that Jocelyn closed his studio to paint the attributed portrait of James Armstrong Thome.[25]

In August 1839, approximately twelve days after the advertisement was placed in the *New Haven Daily Herald,* the *Amistad* was seized in Long Island Sound, and on 1 September the *Amistad* captives were brought to New Haven. Jocelyn may have started Thome's portrait only to be interrupted by the *Amistad* news and a major New Haven artistic event, the use of his "rooms" for the exhibition of Thomas Sully's full-length portrait of Queen Victoria. On 4 September, three days after the captives arrived in New Haven, the New York Amistad Committee was formed. At some point between October 1839 and early 1840, the portrait of Cinqué was commissioned and in progress. The first evidence that the portrait was in development is a letter of March 1840 from Lewis Tappan to his brother Arthur that expressed a "need for a graphic replication of the portrait."[26] The painting of the Cinqué portrait must have been a gradual process because Jocelyn continued to honor previous portrait commitments from December 1839 to early 1840. There is no mention of any other portraits in progress or completed during 1840, and only *Cinqué* was alluded to by Tappan in March 1840.

December of 1840 surfaces as the month *Cinqué* was completed. Three written items lead to that conclusion: the first, Sarah's aforementioned diary entry of 15 December when she referred to "carrying Cinquez the prisoner to his quarters." The second, from 28 December, is a reference to "Cinqué's likeness" in a letter to Lewis Tappan by James B. Covey, a twenty-year-old Mendian, and the captives' Mendi language interpreter.[27] The third and most significant item is Jocelyn's daughter Frances's 30 December diary entry: "This noon Father started for Albany to paint Governor Seward's [portrait]."[28] It is unlikely that the conscientious Jocelyn would have embarked on another portrait commission so far from New Haven before completing the *Cinqué* portrait.

A flurry of activity surrounding the portrait took place in January and February 1841 just prior to the arguments before the Supreme Court petitioning for the captives' freedom. The portrait was publicly mentioned for the first time in the 24 February 1841 *Pennsylvania Freeman* printing of an article titled "Portrait of Cinque" (reference to the engraving by John Sartain). The decision by the Supreme Court to free the Africans was rendered on 9 March 1841.

An Emblematic Portrait

A close examination of the portrait will show that it was unique for Jocelyn and deviated significantly from his other portraits in several ways, including the sitter, his dress and pose, the overall coloring of the painting, and background treatment. Despite the fact that *Cinqué* was Jocelyn's only portrait of a black subject and required a new system of coloration for the painting of the flesh, the final product was a success. He depicted an African wearing a white garment and confidently holding a staff as a dignified man. His head is held erect and turned to his right – Cinqué's gaze, while fixed on a distant point, has greater implications – and he is posed in a radiant landscape. It is a moment of liminality in which the one who is threatened with enslavement looks confidently toward an indeterminate space and time for the possibility of freedom.

Affinity with Allston

A series of influences contributed to this distinctive portrait. Jocelyn admired and respected his fellow American artist, Washington Allston (1779–1843). Jocelyn in his early development as a portrait painter studied the palettes of both Gilbert Stuart (1755–1828) and Allston and concluded that "the materials in Allston's palette [are] more ample than that of Stuart. As a general palette the colours on Allston's appear to be more powerful."[29] Clearly, the *Cinqué* portrait and other works by Jocelyn are more inspired by Allston in their coloration and technique than by Stuart. Allston's influence on Jocelyn is evident in Allston's well-known affinity for Titian's Venetian color and glazing technique. Jocelyn wrote, "I have painted with tints like Allston. By those changes I learn the nature & *power of colours*" (emphasis added).[30] As David Bjelajac stated, "like

Leonardo, Titian, and others, Allston was a 'chemist' or alchemist, who applied mystical, quasi-scientific theories of color and light to painting."[31]

Jocelyn's emblematic portrait of Cinqué activates a series of religious connotations and imagery and deploys a complex body of iconographic and historical references at the service of a specific political agenda. I begin with an investigation of the use of light in the painting. There are two sources of light. The first is the sunset behind the figure, and the second falls on Cinqué's face and upper torso and continues in a vertical line down the center of his body. Powell has seen the glow on Cinqué's body as symbolic of "a divine intervention on his part," and indeed this "glow" contributes to the ethereal aura that surrounds the sitter.[32]

In so doing, Jocelyn departed from his other portraits, which appear more immediate and in which the gaze of the sitter is directed toward the viewer. Jocelyn applied a distracted gaze to Cinqué. The use of a direct gaze causes a sitter to appear more human and approachable while the distracted gaze makes a sitter seem unearthly and aloof. Cinqué's ethereal gaze places him on a different plane from the viewer, which elevates his stature and moves him into a symbolic realm. Amid this presentation, Jocelyn displayed his skill at conveying Cinqué's human and spiritual qualities. I argue that Jocelyn included in the portrait individualizing and humanizing details that personalize the sitter. For example, his large down-turned eyes project kindness, and his slightly parted mouth reveals a glimpse of a protruding front tooth.[33] These small details reinforce the human quality of a specific man, Cinqué. Through them, the viewer senses this is not a "fancy piece" (entirely painted from the imagination) or a completely allegorical interpretation of the subject.

Cinqué: *Ecce Homo*

Jocelyn has not only emulated Allston's and Titian's color and technique but Titian's religious subject matter as well. Jocelyn's portrayal of Cinqué is informed by religious allusions and is an intentional association with Christ. Jocelyn seems to be referencing the well-known Christian image known as *Ecce Homo* for *Cinqué*. Derived from John 19:4–7, the phrase "ecce homo" or "behold the man" was exclaimed by Pontius Pilate as he led Jesus before the crowd. Jocelyn was perhaps most likely exposed to Italian *Ecce Homo* paintings during his trip with Samuel F. B. Morse (1791–1872) to Europe, where he had an opportunity to view original western images of the story of Christ.

In Morse's letters there are numerous references to having seen various versions of *Ecce Homo* throughout their travels. Morse noted his purchase of a group of "loose prints" including Bellini's *Ecce Homo*.[34] Additionally, in America, copies after the Italian masters were a ready staple of exhibitions, such as at the National Academy of Design and the Pennsylvania Academy of the

13.5. Titian, *Ecce Homo*, ca. 1560. Oil on canvas. Courtesy of Brukenthal National Museum, Sibiu, Romania, 3186.

Fine Arts. The annual exhibition records of the Pennsylvania Academy of the Fine Arts listed multiple citations of various American artists' copies of Italian *Ecce Homo* paintings on exhibition.[35] For example, copies after Guido Reni were exhibited, among others such as Charles R. Leslie, *Head of Our Saviour,* 1823; Hugh Bridport, a miniature of *Christ Crowned with Thorns,* 1829; Edwin H. Darley, *Ecce Homo,* 1828; and unnamed artist, *Head of Christ,* 1835. Therefore, even if Jocelyn did not see these specific works, it is clear that audiences and other artists were familiar with *Ecce Homo* depictions of Christ.

The portrait of Cinqué has the most resonance with Titian's *Ecce Homo* (Fig. 13.5). Several variations on this theme are by or ascribed to Titian. Jocelyn's *Cinqué* wears a garment that crosses his shoulder, with a side of his torso exposed and a staff grasped in his hand, both of which are iconographical attributes usually associated with *Ecce Homo* depictions of Christ. *Cinqué* does not, however, bear a crown of thorns or a purple or red colored robe. The white cloth garment that Cinqué dons in the portrait is typical of his native dress. However, Jocelyn's use of the white garment is in contrast to the standard nineteenth-century men's clothing the captives wore during the trial and while they were in jail. In the painting, Jocelyn combines traditional African dress for adult men with the robe depicted in representations of Christ. Jocelyn is simultaneously inscribing Cinqué's cultural heritage while palimpsestically establishing a relationship to Christ's image.

Not only does Cinqué's averted gaze make him appear ethereal as discussed earlier, but by not looking directly at the viewer, his depiction seems to undermine the very nature of Jacksonian portraiture, whereby the sitter typically presents himself and confronts his audience with a direct gaze. Literally and figuratively, Cinqué, like *Ecce Homo,* is being "looked at" or "beheld" by his audience so that they could "See, What a Man." He is embodying two somewhat divergent characteristics; that is, he is being presented as a real man with unalienable rights, but at the same time he is utilized as a symbol to be studied, watched, and displayed for a greater cause. Ultimately, he is simultaneously both humanized and dehumanized.[36] The portrait and Sartain's engraving of it were coordinated to be released prior to the Supreme Court's 9 March 1841 decision to free or enslave the Africans. These images were intended to sway popular support in favor of freeing the captives. Like the message behind Titian's painting *Ecce Homo,* Cinqué was awaiting a verdict that would determine his destiny.

The Meaning of Landscape

The rare inclusion of a landscape in Jocelyn's portrait served to imbue the painting with emblematic clues to fortify his interpretation of the subject. Behind Cinqué is a vibrant sky, jagged deep gray clouds intersecting and contrasting with a brilliant red-orange sunset on the horizon. There are atmospheric blue hills in the far distance and a spalling red-faced sloping rock or hill in the middle distance. At the foot of the hill in the middle distance, there are two rocks, one large and one small, and slightly behind them and at the foot of the hill are two palm trees. Other leafy green trees frame Cinqué.

The background of the *Cinqué* portrait has been formally described, but not thoroughly interpreted, by previous scholars. Eleanor Alexander describes the background of the portrait as a contrived element of the painting. Yet although landscapes are seldom seen in Jocelyn's works, it is wrong to assume that the scenic background was entirely "artificially executed, [and] was not painted from observation or personal knowledge." If indeed Jocelyn was attempting to identify the homeland "for which Cinqué yearned," it is understandable that the background may seem contrived.[37]

13.6. *Sierra Leone North West of the Peninsula on Entering the Estuary.* Frontispiece of Rankin F. Harrison, *The White Man's Grave: A Visit to Sierra Leone in 1834,* vol. I (London: Richard Bentley, New Burlington Street, 1836). Courtesy of Smithsonian Institution Libraries, Washington, D.C.

It is difficult to ascertain whether or not Jocelyn knew what Sierra Leone, the Mendi homeland, looked like.[38] A British traveler writing in 1836 described approaching Sierra Leone by sea as "a low shore, where the heaped-up mountains ... rise like pyramids in the desert (Fig. 13.6)."[39] Clearly, this is not how the mountains are depicted in the *Cinqué* portrait. I believe that the landscape behind Cinqué refers to a location closer to the artist's home, New Haven, Connecticut – the site of the trial.

In *Cinqué*, there are two palm trees in the distance. The palm trees, clearly not indigenous to New England, are fictitious elements in the painting. Therefore, why include these two trees? One explanation is to connect Cinqué with his homeland, in which palm trees are native. Despite the myriad interpretations and the possible meanings of the palms, I contend their relationship to Christian symbolism seems to be one of the most plausible reasons for their inclusion in the background.[40]

There are also two trees that surround the sitter that I identified as elm trees based on their leaf shape, tree size, and significance to the New Haven region. Jocelyn established a regional reference to New Haven by including elm trees and a landscape familiar to residents of New Haven. In order to effectively promote this painting as antislavery propaganda, Jocelyn employed strategically placed elements to link Christian symbolism and a local freedom theme.

Historical Affiliations

I contend that the prominent hill behind Cinqué looks noticeably like the Connecticut location known as West Rock. In New Haven, East and West Rock are outcroppings that were and remain tourist attractions with historical implications. They are considered major Connecticut landmarks and symbols of the American past that evoke a sense of regional pride (Fig. 13.7). Jocelyn recognized that for the people of Connecticut, West Rock had special meaning and "the associations with [it] were regionally specific."[41] Located on the periphery of New Haven, West Rock is the more famous of the two sites. Notable for its distinctive physical beauty and grandeur as well as its important historical significance, West Rock appears in many nineteenth-century paintings.

In 1825 Morse painted a southeast view of West Rock with a radiant sunset capped by darkened clouds as a background for his portrait of Yale Professor Benjamin Silliman (Fig. 13.8). Undoubtedly, Jocelyn was familiar with this major work by his friend. Morse utilized West Rock to place Silliman at Yale in New Haven. William Kloss mentions an additional reference imbued in West Rock that is relevant to Silliman: a reference to Silliman as a man of science, particularly geology, and the author of an 1805 article specifically on the geology of West Rock.[42]

13.7. John Warner Barber, *Southeastern View of West Rock and Westville*, 1838. Wood engraving. J. W. Barber, Connecticut Historical Collections (New Haven, Conn.: John W. Barber, 1838). Collection of the author. Photo: Author.

It is possible that Jocelyn, who had not employed a sunset landscape in previous portraits, was influenced by the background sunset landscape of Morse's portrait of Silliman for the background of *Cinqué*. However, there are a few significant differences between the two depictions of West Rock. Jocelyn's West Rock does not reference the geological makeup of the rock. It was painted in less detail than Morse's to allow for a more subtle reference to the actual rock and to permit a layered interpretation of the site and its relation to the sitter. Jocelyn's interpretation of West Rock (along with the distant blue rolling mountains north of it) included the New Haven location in a manner that vaguely references an exotic land and the theme of freedom for the persecuted.

Jocelyn's sunset for *Cinqué*, appropriated from Morse, recalls a meaning reflected earlier in the century by Charles Willson Peale (1741–1827). In an August 1818 letter to his son Rembrandt, the senior Peale offers his interpretation of the sunset that he added to his portrait of his son: "In the horizon a brig theng [brightening] up emblematical that the evening of your days will be brighter than on former times."[43]

Not far along the ridge of this red cliff is an outcropping of rocks created by upheaval of the earth's crust and glacier movement. In the painting there are two rocks, prominently featured in the middle ground next to two palm trees. These rocks lean on one another and form an inner space, which became known locally as Judges Cave. Jocelyn took painterly liberties in his placement of the two rocks by situating them at the base of West Rock rather than on the ridge, where the cave is actually located. In doing so, he avoided distracting the viewer from Cinqué's face. This placement also serves to isolate the rocks as a distinct compositional element.

The inclusion of Judges Cave alludes to a particular episode in New Haven history and adds another layer of allegorical meaning to the portrait. The natural position of the rocks offered a discrete hiding place for two seventeenth-century English regicides, Colonel Edward Whalley (ca. 1615–ca. 1675) and his son-in-law, Colonel William Goffe (d. 1680). Both men were Cromwellian army officers and judicial members of the high court of justice.[44] Edward Whalley fought with distinction in Cromwell's Great Rebellion, the civil war that erupted to depose the controlling ruler Charles I, king of Great Britain and Ireland from 1625 to 1649. Among the complex issues of Cromwell's Rebellion, what is relevant here is that Whalley understood himself to be fighting for Christian liberty in an

13.8. Samuel Finley Breese Morse, *Benjamin Silliman (1779–1864) B.A. 1796, M.A. 1799,* 1825. Oil on canvas. Yale University Art Gallery, New Haven, Conn. Gift of Bartlett Arkell, B.A. 1886, M.A. 1898, to Silliman College.

attempt to create a Christian commonwealth to depose Charles I. Cromwellian rhetoric conveyed the belief in a Christian sense of liberty and a pure Church. Ultimately, Charles I was captured, brought to trial, sentenced to death, and executed in 1649. Whalley, Goffe, and John Dixwell (ca. 1607–ca. 1689) served on the High Court of Justice that sentenced the king to death. Eleven years after the death of Charles I and the restoration of the crown, the regicides feared retribution from Charles II, successor to the throne. Dixwell fled to Germany and arrived in America in 1664–65, while Whalley and Goffe sought immediate refuge in Boston and eventually in New Haven. In 1660 when Charles II took the throne, he sought vengeance for his father's conviction and organized a search for Whalley and Goffe in America.

In pursuit of the regicides, the Royal officers traced them to New Haven. The officers received no assistance from New Haven residents regarding the whereabouts of the two men and, "Fuming with impatience, the officers were forced to attend services and hear the Reverend John Davenport preach a most exasperating sermon. 'Hide the Outcasts,' the pastor read from the Scriptures, 'and betray not him that wandereth.'"[45] After receiving little help from the local townspeople, the officers returned to England angry, frustrated, and without the regicides. Whalley and Goffe had been hiding in a cave (later called Judges Cave) at the top of West Rock for about a month.[46] The people of New Haven took pride in keeping the regicides' whereabouts secret.

13.9. Profile depiction of an African man. Rock carving at Judges Cave. West Rock, New Haven, Conn. Photo: Author.

For generations to follow, Judges Cave and West Rock became popular spots for local residents as well as visitors from other regions. The Jocelyn daughters made several references to their visits to West Rock. In her 1848 diary, Elizabeth writes, "We rode up to the Rock – West rock. We spent an hour at judges cave – carving our names and others, exploring its recesses and sealing [scaling] its sides. I found my name in full on both rocks, and suppose that some 'friend of the past' carved it there."[47] And, "We took our dinner in the shade of Judge's Cave, and spent an hour or two there. The shade was so grateful that it brought to my mind that passage in Scripture 'Like the shadow of a great rock in a weary land.'"[48]

13.10. Frederic Edwin Church, *West Rock, New Haven*, 1849. Oil on canvas. New Britain Museum of American Art, New Britain, Conn. John Butler Talcott Fund, 1950.1.

Signatures and messages carved directly into the exposed surfaces of the flat rocks that lead to the entrance of Judges Cave are still clearly visible today. Many of the carvings are dated in the 1840s. Of particular interest is an outline of a profile of a male who appears to be of African descent (Fig. 13.9). This image of a shirtless male is truncated at the waist. There is a noticeable "X" carved on the right pectoral, the subject's hair is short and the nose broad. The dates immediately surrounding the carving range from 1842 to 1846. The drawing holds many intriguing possibilities. It is tempting to see in the outline carving a likeness of Cinqué. The "X" on the right side of his torso evokes the wound made by the Roman spear in Christ's side. This image might have been carved in celebration of Cinqué's freedom and return home in November 1841.

Due to West Rock's association with the regicides, the site carries important political and historical meaning and was a favorite subject for artists. Thomas Cole (1801–48) in his "Essay on American Scenery" stated: "American scenes are not destitute of historical and legendary associations – the great struggle for freedom has sanctified many a spot, and many a mountain, stream, and rock has its legend, worthy of a poet's pen or the painter's pencil."[49] He specifically cited West Rock for a future work: "The story of the Regicides Goffe, Whalley & Dixwell affords in my opinion fine subjects both for poetry & Painting. A [work] in which Goffe, on the solitary rock near New Haven, should be made to give vent to his feelings as an exile – his thoughts springing from the past & looking forward to the future."[50] Frederic Church's painting entitled *West Rock,*

New Haven, dated 1849 (Fig. 13.10) "stood as a permanent and prominent reminder of the principles upon which the new nation was founded. The peace and plenty of the present were only possible because of the struggles of the past." Carved on the wall of the cave at West Rock the regicides wrote: "Opposition to tyrants is obedience to God."[51]

POLITICAL AGENDAS

New Haveners had a long history of protecting dissenters and fugitives; for example, Thome and Garrison did so during Jocelyn's time. Some New England and Midwestern states protected fugitives from slavery by ignoring the law, just as New Haveners centuries earlier hid the regicides in Judges Cave. The immediatists saw in the trial of the *Amistad* Africans as black fugitives an obvious parallel to the fugitive slave laws. In the immediatists' view, Cinqué's role as a dissenter and a fugitive from injustice further helped white Protestant viewers to identify with Cinqué. West Rock highlights the martyrdom of fugitive Protestants, while Cinqué's clothing and pose evoke the martyrdom of Christ. Just as the judges were fighting to be free of the King's tyranny, so was Cinqué fighting for his and the other captives' freedom and release. Cinqué's plight and the Supreme Court's decision to free him would eventually provide some advancement for the antislavery cause and the future of emancipation. Jocelyn depicted Cinqué as a pillar of fortitude and an example of leadership, qualities that are emphasized by his position in front of West Rock where Whalley and Goffe once hid in their struggle for Puritan religious freedom. The abolitionists resolved to protect the freedom of the Africans. Jocelyn's hope might have been that the New Haven residents would stand by the captives just as they once did for the regicides.[52]

The portrait of Cinqué, with its Christian overtones and abolitionist theme, was considered so radical that it was denied a place in the sixth annual Artist Fund Society. The image of *Cinqué*, while associated with the *Ecce Homo* iconography, deviates from the traditional humble depiction of Christ, reflecting the growing evangelical notion of a vigorous, forceful, and dynamic Christ.[53] John Sartain, the society's treasurer (and the mezzotint artist of *Cinqué*), was planning to make Jocelyn an honorary member of the society in order to qualify him for exhibiting the portrait of Cinqué. Unfortunately, John Neagle, president of the society, and the picture hanging committee rejected Jocelyn's painting, precluding Jocelyn from election as an honorary member. The rejection letter addressed to Purvis reads:

> Dear Sir, – The hanging committee have instructed me most respectfully, to return the portrait which you kindly offered for exhibition it being contrary to usage to display works of that character, believing that under the

excitement of the times, it might prove injurious both to the proprietors and the institution.

At the same time, I am instructed to return the thanks of the society for your tender of the use of so excellent a work of art.

Respectfully, &c. J. Neagle[54]

It is important to note that Neagle was a colonizationist, who rejected many if not all of the elements in Jocelyn's radical abolitionist painting. While Neagle does not explain what he meant by "works of that character," it probably referred to the political radicalism of Jocelyn's *Cinqué* image. Neagle undoubtedly felt that the image would be an effective agent for the immediatist cause because he saw paintings as having a direct visual effect. He believed and said that an observer of a portrait "may be stirred with noble emulation ... to go and do likewise."[55] Jocelyn's painting represented an important opposing view to the colonizationist position; it would also inflame anti-abolitionist and pro-slavery feeling, thus adding to the "excitement of the times." The combination of Neagle's position as a colonizationist, the burning of Pennsylvania Hall three years earlier, and the proposed tour of the Africans all contributed to anxiety about potential mob violence, protest, and disruption of the exhibition and gallery.

Neagle recognized the artistic quality and incendiary nature of the portrait, so his letter of rejection was a direct affront to the abolitionist cause. Henry Clarke Wright responded to Neagle in a letter to the editor of the *Pennsylvania Freeman*:

Why is that portrait denied a place in that gallery? Any objection to the artist? No. – He has recently been elected an honorary member of the society; and, if I mistake not, this rejected portrait was the principal means of procuring him that honor – if honor it be. Any objection to the execution? No. The "hanging committee" themselves pronounced it an "excellent work of art." Those who are allowed to be judges in such matters rank it among the first portrait paintings of our country. Any objection to the character of Cinqué? This could not be, for portraits of military heroes have been and are displayed in the gallery. He resisted those who would make him a slave, by arms and blood. For doing this, did that committee exclude his portrait from their exhibition! Besides he has been pronounced "guiltless" in this deed by the highest tribunal of this country, and by the government of England. Was the portrait rejected because Cinquez [*sic*] is a man in whom there is no interest? This could not be, for his name and his deeds have been heralded in every paper in this nation and in England – have stirred every heart and have been the theme of every tongue. Though confined in a prison, he has been, the last eighteen months, an object of interest to the United States, to Spain, to England, and to France. – Cinqué

> will continue to be an object of interest, and his name will be the watchword of freedom to Africa and her enslaved sons throughout the world.
>
> Why then was the portrait rejected? Why? "contrary to usage to display works of that character!" "The excitement of the times!" The plain English of it is Cinqué is a NEGRO. This is a negro-hating and negro-stealing nation; a slave-holding people. The negro-haters of the north, and the negro-stealers of the south will not tolerate a portrait of a negro in a picture gallery. And *such* a negro! His dauntless look, as it appears on canvas, would make the souls of the slaveholders quake. His portrait would be a standing Anti-slavery lecture to slave-holders and their apologists. To have it in the gallery would lead to discussions about slavery and the 'inalienable' rights of man, and convert every set of visiters [*sic*] into an Anti-slavery meeting. So "the hanging committee" bowed their necks to the yoke and bared their backs to the scourge, installed *slavery* as doorkeeper to the gallery, carefully to exclude everything that can speak of freedom and inalienable rights, and give offense to men-stealers!! Shame on them! Let the friends of humanity, of justice and right, remember them during the summer.
>
> Had he looked into the future a little, J. Neagle would have sooner severed his hand from his body than have allowed it to sign his name to that note. Posterity will talk about him when slavery is abolished, as it surely will be and then all his fame, as an artist will not save him from merited condemnation.
>
> If Mr. Jocelyn is the man I think and hope he is, he will return his certificate of membership to the "Artist Fund Society," counting it no honor to belong to a society that can perpetrate such meanness and outrage.
>
> Thine.
>
> H. C. Wright.[56]

In the spring of 1841, the abolitionists planned to have the portrait exhibited simultaneously with a visit by Cinqué and some *Amistad* Africans to Philadelphia.[57] Wright exhorted his fellow abolitionists to remember the hanging committee during the tour of the Africans when he stated: "Let the friends of humanity, of justice and right, remember them during the summer." Perhaps Wright was hinting at disrupting the exhibition. The tour of the *Amistad* Africans took place after the close of the Artist Fund Exhibition with little or no notoriety.

By using a black man as his subject, placing the figure in front of a luminous sunset and landscape setting, and imbuing the elements of the painting with rich symbolism, Jocelyn was able to transcend all of his previous portraits and use *Cinqué* as an instrument of advocacy for abolitionism. His success is evidenced by the enduring nature of the portrait's "spearlike entry into the heart of American slavery."[58] Cinqué was representative of a struggle, an ongoing battle over slavery that was consuming nineteenth-century America. The commission of this painting allowed Jocelyn to create a heroic portrait that reflected his religious, moral, and political beliefs. The portrait embodied the passion of the abolitionist movement and its Christian underpinnings. Through the *Cinqué* portrait, Jocelyn was able to fulfill a lifelong ambition of artistic acclaim and realize his conviction:

> Above all; our pencils may become the champions of Religion, Morality and Virtue.[59]

NOTES

1 The significance of the *Cinqué* portrait is widely recognized by historians of American art who have written on the topic, namely, Guy McElroy, *Facing History: The Black Image in American Art, 1710–1940* (Washington, D.C.: Bedford Arts, 1990); Eleanor Alexander, "A Portrait of Cinqué," *Connecticut Historical Society Bulletin* 49, no. 1 (1984), 30–51; Richard J. Powell, "Cinqué: Antislavery Portraiture and Patronage in Jacksonian America," *American Art* 11, no. 3 (1997), 48–73; Bernard Heinz, *Nathaniel Jocelyn: Puritan, Painter, Inventor, Journal of the New Haven Colony Historical Society* 29, no. 2 (New Haven: New Haven Colony Historical Society, 1983); Foster Wild Rice, "Nathaniel Jocelyn – 1796–1881," *Connecticut Historical Society Bulletin* 31, no. 4 (1966), 97–145.

2 The *Cinqué* portrait broke with the typical image of an African in America as a stereotypically degraded individual. In Stephen F. Eisenman, *Nineteenth Century Art: A Critical History* (London: Thames and Hudson, 1994), 164–65, the contrast is made between John Lewis Krimmel (1786–1821) and Jocelyn and their depiction of Africans. I argue that the case can be made for Jocelyn being the first artist in the United States to create a major work of art with a significant African subject depicted in a favorable or noble light.

3 Richard Powell was the first to juxtapose and contrast the *Cinqué* portrait with Jacksonian-era portraiture. He published the most thorough art historical article on abolitionist portraits prominently featuring Cinqué. His article was influential in my research.

4 Wyatt-Brown, *Bertram Lewis Tappan and the Evangelical War against Slavery* (Cleveland: Press of Case Western Reserve University, 1969), 205.

5 Clifton Johnson, *The Amistad Case and Its Consequences in U.S. History* (New Haven: New Haven Colony Historical Society, 1990), 5.

6 Howard Jones, *Mutiny on the Amistad* (New York: Oxford University Press, 1987), 23.

7 Ibid., 23–29.

8 Ibid., 28–29.

9 Nathaniel Jocelyn and his younger brother, Simeon Smith Jocelyn (1799–1879) established a successful engraving firm, N. & S.S. Jocelyn, designing banknotes, maps, atlases, and book illustrations. Simeon was a well-known pastor and abolitionist.

10 Editor, *Colored American* (26 December 1840).

11 S. S. Jocelyn, et al., *Colored American* (13 March 1841).

12 To gain a greater sense of how unique the depiction of Cinqué was in 1840, one only has to look at an example of an anti-abolition tract published as late as 1866,

a year after emancipation in 1865, and consider how persistent the negative black stereotypes were. A typical volume such as *The Six Species of Men, With Cuts Representing the Types of the Caucasian, Mongol, Malay, Indian, Esquimaux and Negro. With Their General Physical and Mental Qualities, Laws of Organization, Relations to Civilization, &c.*, Anti-Abolition Tracts, 5 (New York: Van Evrie, Horton & Company, 1866) stated: "The negro is incapable of an erect or direct perpendicular position. The general structure of his limbs, the form of the pelvis, the spine, the way the head is set on the shoulders, in short, the entire anatomical formation, forbids an erect position." And, "There is no such monstrosity in the world as a 'colored man,' that is, a being like ourselves in all except color.... The negro face cannot express those higher emotions which give such beauty to the Caucasian countenance, and as nature has denied them the outward manifestation, it is no more than reasonable to suppose they do not have the emotions themselves." John David Smith, *Anti-Abolition Tracts and Anti-Black Stereotypes* (New York: Garland Publishing, 1993), 137.

13 "PORTRAIT OF W. L. GARRISON. $1 single, $10.50 per dozen, $75 per hundred," *Emancipator* (3 May 1838) (From the Jocelyn Portrait of 1833). "I am desirous to have you sit to my brother for a portrait before you leave for England. I suppose you will have but little time for the purpose, but if you can be here but one or two days he can get the likeness and finish the painting afterwards. He is now painting a portrait of Jehudi Ashmun (1794–1828) for the Colonization Society, which is to be engraved. It is my desire to engrave yours whilst you are in England, and publish the print." (Simeon Smith Jocelyn to William Lloyd Garrison, 29 March 1833, Connecticut Historical Society [hereafter CHS]).

14 Virgil Barker, *American Painting: History and Interpretation* (New York: Macmillan, 1950), 398.

15 Powell in "Cinqué," 59, states, "During this time period, it was common for well-known people such as Purvis to have their daguerreotypes taken." Interestingly, there are no known daguerreotypes of Cinqué.

16 With the exception of Simeon's engraving of Ashmun and Garrison after Nathaniel's paintings, the firm for the most part did large jobs like the atlas and maps for the Morse brothers and banknotes for many banks and stock companies.

17 Nathaniel Jocelyn, Diary, 31 January 1821, CHS.

18 There is a discrepancy as to the actual title of Hewins's mural and the wood engraving rendition by John Warner Barber.

19 A few minor works exist that fall between Jocelyn's *Cinqué* and Hewin's excesses. One example is a notable group of sketches or drawings of the Africans by a young man of seventeen or eighteen years, William H. Townsend (1822–51) (Beineke Rare Book and Manuscript Library, Yale University). He completed twenty-two extant drawings and none known of Cinqué. Townsend had a skillful ability in drawing the head and features of the Africans, and he took advantage, during the time of the trial, of the public presence and accessibility of the captives to New Haveners during the Africans' daily exercise walks on the Green. Created for unknown reasons in 1839–40, the drawings are a compassionate and natural depiction of the various members of the group. The series of drawings are straightforward renderings free of artistic pretense, political propaganda, or ulterior motives. They remain sympathetic and humanistic visions of the captives that may be the best documentary images we have of the Mendi Africans.

20 Jocelyn's brother Simeon made engravings from Jocelyn's abolitionist portraits, and they were used as fundraising tools for the cause. Also, Garrison's portrait was auctioned to raise funds for the American Anti-Slavery Society. The 1840 Thome por-

trait is attributed to Jocelyn. There is no known engraving of the portrait. (National Portrait Gallery, Smithsonian Institution, Washington, D.C.).

21 Powell, "Cinqué," 68.

22 Ibid., 49, 50. Other artists who painted abolitionist leaders include Francis Alexander, Robert Douglass, Jr., Robert Duncanson, and Patrick Reason. Abolitionist subjects include Lydia Maria Child, Prudence Crandall, Lucretia Mott, James Armstrong Thome, and Wendell Phillips. Persons of color represented in painted portraits or graphic representations include Martin R. Delany, Frederick Douglass, Henry Highland Garnett, Charles Lenox Remond, and Freeman Cary, as well as Haitian political leaders Jean-Pierre Boyer and Fabre Geffrard.

23 Ibid., 59.

24 Sarah Ann Jocelyn, Diary, 15 December 1840, CHS.

25 The description on the label of the Thome portrait published by the National Portrait Gallery suggests why Jocelyn wanted few studio visitors. Thome (1813–1873), Kentucky-born, was a traveling agent for the American Anti-Slavery Society. Thome and a companion, Horace Kimball, were conducting a study for the society on the results of slave emancipation in the British West Indies, refuting the prevailing belief among abolitionists that slavery could be eliminated only gradually because most slaves would need to be prepared for life in freedom. In late 1839, Thome fled Ohio, where he was teaching, to avoid arrest for assisting a runaway Kentucky slave in his escape to freedom. He sought refuge in Fairfield, Connecticut. Therefore, Jocelyn's mysterious advertisement for privacy may well have been written to allow him to paint the portrait of Thome in flight from warrants for his arrest. (Collection of the National Portrait Gallery, Smithsonian Institution, Washington, D.C.)

26 Powell, "Cinqué," 63.

27 Ibid., 61.

28 Frances Marie Jocelyn, Diary, 30 December 1840, CHS. William Henry Seward was a New York abolitionist and later served as Secretary of State during Abraham Lincoln's presidency as well as Andrew Johnson's.

29 Nathaniel Jocelyn, Diary, 9 February 1821 (occasional pagination, 24) CHS. Jocelyn's comments about the two palettes were made prior to visiting Stuart's studio in August 1823. His comments are based on his general observations of portraiture and experimentations with portrait coloration.

30 Nathaniel Jocelyn, Diary, 4 March 4, 1826, CHS.

31 David Bjelajac, *Washington Allston: Secret Societies and the Alchemy of Anglo-American Painting* (Cambridge: Cambridge University Press, 1997), 31.

32 Powell, "Cinqué," 54.

33 It was a prevalent custom on the West Coast of Africa for natives to extract, sharpen, and make one or more teeth protrude from the upper or lower jaw. He shared this physical characteristic with several of his fellow Mendian captives. See John W. Barber, *A History of the Amistad Captives* (New Haven: E. L. and J. W. Barber, 1840), 26.

34 Samuel F. B. Morse, Samuel Finley Breese Morse Papers (Library of Congress, Washington D.C., 1996), microfilm, box 60, reel 33, 13 February 1831, no. 98102. Contents: List of articles sent in a box to America from Italy.

35 Peter Hastings Falk, ed., *The Annual Exhibition Record of the Pennsylvania Academy of the Fine Arts 1807–1870* (Greenwich, Conn.: Sound View Press, 1988), 180.

36 This additional analysis of *Ecce Homo* was brought to light after my conversations with Angela Rosenthal and Agnes Lugo-Ortiz.

37 Eleanor Alexander, "A Portrait of Cinqué," *Connecticut Historical Society Bulletin* 49, no. 1 (1984), 44.

38 Ibid. Alexander asserts that Jocelyn was aware of illustrations from a current (nineteenth-century) geography book by Richard Lander, presumably *Records of Captain Clapperton's Last Expedition to Africa* (London: Colburn and Bently, 1830).

39 Rankin F. Harrison, *The White Man's Grave: A Visit to Sierra Leone in 1834*, 2 vols. (London: Richard Bentley, New Burlington Street, 1836), 1:24.

40 Generally, the palm tree in Christianity is a symbol of peace through authority, permanence, grace, stateliness and elegance. Here it can be seen as a symbol to equate Cinqué with unwavering faith and strength. See Psalm 92:12: "The righteous shall flourish like the palm tree."

41 Angela Miller, *The Empire of the Eye: Landscape Representation and American Cultural Politics, 1825–1875* (Ithaca: Cornell University Press, 1993), 104.

42 William Kloss, *Samuel F. B. Morse* (New York: Harry N. Abrams, 1998), 96.

43 Lillian B. Miller, ed. *The Selected Papers of Charles Willson Peale and His Family*, 5 vols. (New Haven: Yale University Press, 1983), 3:598.

44 Rollin G. Osterweis, *Three Centuries of New Haven 1638–1938* (New Haven: Yale University Press, 1964), 55.

45 Ibid., 56.

46 Ibid., 56–57.

47 Elizabeth Hannah Jocelyn, Diary, 8 November 1848, CHS.

48 Ibid., 3 June 1849. "He will shelter Israel from the storm and the wind, He will refresh her as a river in the desert and as the cool *shadow of a large rock in a hot and weary land*" (Isaiah 32:2).

49 Quoted in Franklin Kelly, *Frederic Edwin Church and the National Landscape* (Washington, D.C.: Smithsonian Institution Press, 1988), 23.

50 Christopher Kent Wilson, "The Landscape of Democracy: Frederic Church's *West Rock, New Haven*," *American Art Journal*, 18, no. 3 (1986), 37.

51 Ibid., 23.

52 Relating to abolitionists' plan to hide the captives, see Amos Townsend Jr. to Lewis Tappan, 18 January 1841, Lewis Tappan Papers.

53 A little more than a decade later, antislavery evangelist Joshua R. Giddings (1795–1864), a member of the House of Representatives (Ohio, 1839–58), was promulgating in his House speeches the idea of Christ as the "model 'agitator.'" Daniel Walker Howe, *The Political Culture of the American Whigs* (Chicago: The University of Chicago Press, 1979), 177.

54 Letter to Editor from Henry Clarke Wright, *Pennsylvania Freeman*, 21 April 1841, reprinted in *Emancipator*, 17 June 1841 (includes Neagle's letter to Purvis).

55 Robert W. Tochia, *John Neagle: Philadelphia Portrait Painter* (Philadelphia: Historical Society of Pennsylvania, 1989), 162.

56 Letter to Editor from Henry Clarke Wright, *Pennsylvania Freeman*, 21 April 1841, reprinted in *Emancipator*, 17 June 1841.

57 A. F. Williams to Lewis Tappan, 13 March 1841, Lewis Tappan Papers; cited in Powell, "Cinqué," 65.

58 Powell in "Cinqué," 68 wrote: "According to Purvis, a testament to the portrait's spearlike entry into the heart of American slavery occurred literally within months of its creation. Shortly after acquiring the portrait, Purvis gave shelter to Madison Washington, a runaway slave, who stayed briefly at Purvis's Lombard Street address, one of the 'station stops' along America's legendary Underground Railroad. Here, Washington saw Cinqué's portrait and learned of his valor. Some months later,

following Washington's return to the South and his reenslavement, Washington successfully led a revolt on board the slave brig *Creole* en route from Hampton, Virginia, to New Orleans. In an article published in the *Philadelphia Inquirer* decades later, Purvis adamantly maintained that Washington's insurrection on the high seas was inspired by having seen Cinqué's portrait and having heard Cinqué's stirring story of self-liberation."

59 Nathaniel Jocelyn to Daniel Dickinson, ca. 1818, Jocelyn Family Papers, CHS.

FOURTEEN

THE INTREPID MARINER SIMÃO

VISUAL HISTORIES OF BLACKNESS IN THE LUSO-ATLANTIC AT THE END OF THE SLAVE TRADE

Daryle Williams

The 2004–06 touring exhibition *Retratos: 2,000 Years of Latin American Portraits* introduced North American museumgoers to the comely portrait of Simão Manuel Alves Juliano, a black man who traversed an impressive arc of notoriety and visuality in the middle years of the nineteenth century.[1] On loan from Brazil's National Museum of Fine Arts, the handsomely proportioned, unsigned, and undated canvas *O Retrato do Intrépido Marinheiro Simão, Carvoeiro do Vapor Pernambucana* (Fig. 14.1, Plate 11) was attributed to José Correia de Lima (1814–57), an academic painter who taught at the Brazilian Imperial Academy of Fine Arts (founded 1826) between 1840 and 1857. Understated in comparison to the florid Spanish American baroque portraits that accompanied the portrait of Simão on its five-city tour of the United States and Mexico, *The Portrait of the Intrepid Mariner Simão, Coalman of the Steamship Pernambucana* was, nevertheless, a highlight of the fine show.

The *Retratos* catalog described the subject of the Correia de Lima canvas as the hero of the *Pernambucana*, a Brazilian steamer wrecked on the shores of southern Brazil in October 1853. This information, coupled with the rope held in the sitter's muscular right hand, might have led the viewer to understand that the intrepid mariner was one of the many men and women of color who plied the dangerous seas of the South Atlantic during the nineteenth century. Yet, *why* Simão won the honor of a stately portrait in an era of frequent maritime calamity went uninterrogated. The history of *how* this black man came to be portrayed in academic portraiture also went undiscussed. Lacking the typical gestures to curses of Ham, oriental despotism, African barbarism, racial degeneracy, or the other stock tropes of academic blacks, ethnographic "types," and popular caricature of the nineteenth century, the portrait quizzically evoked a style analogous to portraits of the great white men of the Brazilian empire.

14.1. José Correia de Lima, *Retrato do Intrépido Marinheiro Simão, Carvoeiro do Vapor Pernambucana* (The Portrait of the Intrepid Mariner Simão, Coalman of the Steamship Pernambucana), ca. 1854–55. Oil on canvas. Museu Nacional de Belas Artes/Instituto Brasileiro de Museus/Ministério da Cultura, Rio de Janeiro. Photo: Jaime Acioli.

A biographical sketch included in the *Retratos* catalog, clouded in an imprecision that has plagued much of Brazilian art historical scholarship concerning the visuality of men of color, did little to resolve the mystery of the painting. The English-language text informed the viewer that "[t]he sitter is an Afro-Brazilian sailor, who served aboard the steamship *Pernambucana*. The vessel foundered off the coast of Santa Catarina, and Simão saved numerous lives. His right hand holds a rope, a reference to his trade."[2] A similar text was included on the label that accompanied the portrait.

Simão's trade – coalman or sailor – may be a matter of detail, but the key information concerning his race-nation was woefully incorrect. Simão was born a free man around 1824 on the island of Santo Antão, Cape Verde. He spent a total of no more than fourteen months in Brazil, including the heady days immediately following the wreck of the *Pernambucana,* before returning to his homeland. Simão died of cholera in 1856 on the Cape Verdean island of São Vicente. Far from being an Afro-Brazilian, Simão was an Atlantic Luso-African. Simão, indeed, may have been one of the first black men to be rendered in Brazilian academic portraiture, as the catalog for 2000 mega-exhibition *Mostra do Redescobrimento* had suggested, but the attribution of the sitter's identity as Afro-Brazilian could be easily disproved. Equally easy to disprove is the more recent suggestion, made by the Brazilian national statistical bureau, that the Correia de Lima canvas portrays Zumbi (1655?–95), the Brazilian-born leader of the maroon community Palmares.[3]

Ample archival evidence exists to prove that Simão was neither Afro-Brazilian nor a runaway slave. He lived in the nineteenth century, long after the fall of Palmares. He was a favorite of the Crown rather than a symbol of the African's resistance to the Brazilian slavocracy. There is a curious logic, no doubt, to these mistaken identities. The Correia de Lima portrait, I argue, is a composite image of the free African mariner and a stock black, possibly enslaved, male body. The portrait, then, is marked by an aesthetic tradition that largely fixed black bodies as laborers, slaves, and runaways. Within the rarefied world of academic portraiture, a freeborn African would seem to be a nearly *impossible* subject. Contemporary art historical scholarship has let these traditions go largely unchallenged, making this particular portrait an anomaly worthy of little more than the bland description "sensitive and mysterious" proffered by one prominent Brazilian critic.[4]

As we shall see, a bramble of factual errors, incuriosity, and false assumptions has surrounded the portrait of Simão since the sitter's fleeting moment of celebrity in 1853. Yet, a careful history of these imprecisions helps us understand some of the broadest terms of the visual world in which black men and women transited in the liminal era that followed the end of the slave trade between Africa and Brazil. With diligence and serendipity, the historian uncovers in the portrait of Simão a remarkable personal history colored by the visuality of blackness, enslavement, and the subjectivity of Africans in the Atlantic world. The portrait and its sitter are, I argue, protagonists and symbols of the conflictive, contradictory processes that destroyed the slave trade, racialized blackness, and made Atlantic citizenship in the age of emancipation.

The consolidation of transoceanic steamship service and the closure of the transatlantic slave trade are the historical frames to this portrait of blackness and heroism. The documentary and visual evidence remains incomplete, but the clues are sufficient to argue that *O Retrato do Intrépido Marinheiro Simão* and a handful of complementary portraits bring to light an expansive conversation about color and virtue that circulated throughout the Portuguese-speaking Atlantic in the 1850s. The structural underpinnings of this conversation dated back to the early decades of the nineteenth century, but the confluence of technological and historical changes evident at the century's midpoint, stoked by the anxieties and opportunities produced by the end of the "infamous commerce," opened up a space for Simão to be portrayed as a subject worthy of the kind of "quality" portraiture otherwise denied the black man. The moment was fleeting, but nonetheless significant, for understanding how blackness moved across and with nineteenth-century visual culture.

THE TRAGEDY OF THE *PERNAMBUCANA*

As a portrait painted by the chair of historical painting at the Imperial Academy of Fine Arts, the Correia de Lima canvas requires a certain contextualization that begins with an otherwise unremarkable news bulletin in *Jornal do Commercio.* On 15 October 1853, the bellwether of the Rio de Janeiro press reported that the *Prince,* a British Royal Mail steamer en route from Uruguay, and the *Pernambucana,* a Brazilian passenger steamship en route from the southern ports of Rio Grande do Sul, were late in their anticipated arrivals to the capital of the Brazilian empire, a bustling, highly Africanized city of 205,000 residents, about 37 percent of which were enslaved.[5] Unbeknown to the *Jornal*'s readers, the Brazilian steamer, carrying well-heeled slaveholding elites, a British vice-consul, army veterans, and slaves for delivery, among others, had been overtaken by a wild storm on the night of 8 October. As the ship pitched in the stormy waves and the vessel split apart, pandemonium broke out among the 120-odd passengers and crew. The most dramatic accounts of the wreck would later recount that the steam engines had exploded, adding to the number of fatalities. Fact and rumor, charge and countercharge followed the bedraggled survivors as they were transported to Rio on a Brazilian naval warship cruising southern waters to intercept ships violating prohibitions on slave imports.[6]

By the time death notices, requiem masses, and official inquiries had confirmed forty-two deaths, a shipwreck mania had whipped from the towns nearest the wreck south of Laguna, to the ports of Porto Alegre and Rio, quickly spreading throughout the Atlantic by mail packet. Nearly all surviving periodicals printed in Rio in the last two months of 1853 discussed the *Pernambucana* tragedy. By early 1854, lurid news reports of castaways and heroes had been picked up in the international news sections of papers published in Lisbon, Oporto, Paris, London, and Philadelphia. By the close of the decade, the *Pernambucana* had inspired fanciful literature featuring Africans published for German and U.S.

readers. The tragedy of the *Pernambucana* was included in the revised version of Jean-Baptiste Benoît Eyriès' *Histoire des naufrages* (1859), a compendium of the greatest maritime disasters.[7]

With reports of nautical disaster on the minds and in the mouths of the *fluminense*[8] public and its correspondents throughout the Atlantic, theatrical performances, epic verse, praise poetry, sonnets, and political commentary about shipwrecks proliferated. The revivals of the tragedy *Pedro-Sem que já teve e agora não tem* (Pedro-Without Who Is Now without What He Once Had), with its showstopping shipwreck scene in the fifth act, and the ballet *O Náufrago Feliz* (The Happy Castaway) were symptoms of the mania. Poet Lerack de Sá as well as typographer Francisco de Paula Brito, whose print shop had become a literary heart of the Brazilian Court, were quick to put the *Pernambucana* to verse. The perils of maritime travel were taken up in the *Periódico dos Pobres*, a semiweekly Rio publication whose male editors serialized fictional dialogues between female cousins to comment on current events.[9] These dialogues echoed the exchange of open letters published in the main dailies that alternatively assigned blame for the fatal wreck to an incompetent crew, a negligent steamship company, and foolhardy passengers. The unpredictability of divine fortune was a recurrent theme.

Deep anxieties, no doubt, fueled public interest in the *Pernambucana* tragedy. Residents of Rio, most living within sight of the ship-filled Guanabara Bay, confronted in the wreck many unsettling indicators that the Atlantic world was being remade by steamship travel. Fast, convenient, and economical, the steamship was nonetheless a site of danger for seafarers and their material belongings. Fluminenses, moreover, confronted a land- and seascape in a process of being remade by the end of a transatlantic slave trade that had nourished the city's fortunes from the early eighteenth century, when the trade shifted from the plantations of the northeast to the mines of the southeast, through the explosive growth in trade that accompanied the residency of the Portuguese Court (1808–21) and the First Reign (1822–31), to the period of the clandestine trade, principally with Angola and Mozambique, that lasted from 1831 through the early 1850s.[10] By 1853 the southeastern coast of Brazil and the high seas beyond were, simultaneously, liberated of the scourge of the slave trade – theretofore the lifeblood of Fluminense slave society – yet deeply disturbed by the end of the trafficking in African lives and labor. The *Pernambucana* was a reminder of this anxious, transitional state, as the narrative of the tragedy had to make sense of a freeborn African hero who had recently traveled to Brazil by his own volition but who arrived in Rio de Janeiro aboard a Brazilian imperial naval vessel assigned to interdict clandestine trafficking with Africa. At the intersection of the steamship in ascendance and slave trade in decline were anxieties about what to do with the Africans who had once traveled in the holds of slaving vessels and continued to remain on the seas, stoking the fires of steamships and unloading their cargoes to make Rio into a prosperous port-city of the Luso-African-Atlantic.

Simão, the black coalman-hero of the ill-fated *Pernambucana,* confronted these anxieties head on. In his twenties, the native of Cape Verde – the archipelago that had served as the staging ground for early transatlantic slaving before declining into a generalized misery only partially ameliorated by the installation of a transatlantic coaling station at Mindelo, on the island of São Vicente – had distinguished himself during the wreck by saving thirteen passengers, swimming back and forth between shore and sinking ship. Simão's efforts to save a white woman of means, Camila Vieira da Costa, and her numerous children gained the most public comment, but the Cape Verdean was also praised for saving a war veteran. By some accounts he also rescued a female slave. These actions were so remarkable that the members of Rio's Commercial Association organized a public subscription in Simão's name. Flush with optimism that new domestic capital markets were soon to flourish in the absence of competition from the slave trade, association members raised eight *contos de réis,* a princely sum for a coalman, who would be able to acquire a large urban property or ten adult slaves. (Simão's premature death in 1856 prevented him for taking actual possession of the purse, which had been placed on ten-year deposit.)

Heralded as the "The Intrepid Mariner," Simão enjoyed an audience with the emperor Dom Pedro II on 7 November. The emperor and the hero reportedly chatted about the coalman's family in Cape Verde before the monarch awarded his guest a small purse of 400 *milréis* and an honorary medal. The emperor's act of benevolence, widely reported in news bulletins that circulated throughout the Atlantic in the regular steam sailings, would be followed by additional honors conferred by the prince regent of Portugal, the governor-general of Cape Verde, the Humanitarian Society of Oporto, and Lloyd's of London. The recognition conferred by the Portuguese monarch and colonial governor were especially noteworthy, as they helped diagram a web of honors that made Simão out to be an esteemed guest of the Brazilian monarch, a loyal subject of the Portuguese Crown, a colonial of note, and a humanitarian citizen of the high seas.

Festooned in royal medals, beneficiary of the handsome purse, and honored by the commercial elite of Guanabara Bay, the Duoro Valley, and the City of London, Simão returned to Cape Verde in early 1854 to find his homeland desolated by drought, famine, and out-migration. Cholera, carried by steamship, struck the archipelago soon after Simão's return, exacting a heavy toll on the coaling stations at Mindelo as well as the islands of Santiago and Fogo.[11] Simão succumbed to the epidemic on 5 September 1856.[12] Once the epidemic struck Brazil, 200,000 would perish.[13] Simão's death apparently passed unnoticed in the Brazilian, Portuguese, and Cape Verdean press. Yet even in death, Simão continued to enjoy an Atlantic celebrity. On his native Santo Antão, "Simão Salvador" (Simão the Savior) became a local hero of the hamlet of Ribeira Grande, where the honorific medals have been on display in the municipal chamber since the 1860s. He is also a notable of the Cape Verdean diaspora.

PORTRAITS OF A FREEBORN BLACK HERO IN BRAZILIAN SLAVE SOCIETY

Without doubt, the most enduring legacy of Simão is the Correia de Lima portrait, first exhibited at the 1859 salon. The painting has been part of the Brazilian national gallery since the mid-nineteenth century and has hung in a prominent place in the permanent installation of the National Museum of Fine Arts for years. A lithograph that anteceded the canvas, discussed below, was displayed at the grand Exposição da História do Brasil, held in Rio in 1881. The oil portrait has been loaned to several significant expositions, in the aforementioned *Mostra do Redescobrimento* (2000) and *Retratos* (2004–06) as well as *Imagem e identidade*, a major reinterpretation of the Brazilian "national" collection organized in 2002. This familiar work remains, sadly, misunderstood. But it is not necessarily beyond understanding, as we can still see many traces of a visual culture that was as familiar to Correia de Lima's contemporaries as to contemporary audiences. This visual culture draws heavily on the image of blacks laboring on ships, docks, and quays. Correia de Lima's academic mentor, Jean-Baptiste Debret, for one, filled his sketchbooks and the famed *Voyage historique et pittoresque au Brésil* (1834–39) with blacks at water's edge (Figs. 14.2 and 14.3). Studio photographers, such as João Goston (d. 1882, active after 1854), daguerreotyped black female street vendors in front of painted wharves, with miniaturized cruisers off in the distance (Fig. 14.4). Anonymous blacks appear as stock characters in the maritime-themed paintings of the Atlantic age, from John Singleton Copley's noble *Watson and the Shark* (1778) (see Fig. 6.1) to the 1789 abolitionist engraving of the slaver *Brookes* (Fig. 14.5) and the much-discussed *Slave Ship* (1840), by J. M. W. Turner (Fig. 14.6), and Géricault's *Raft of the Medusa* (1819)[14] (see Fig. 6.2). The portrait of Simão spoke quite eloquently to a visual culture that treated the waterways as a black person's space.

Less eloquent was the conversation between the visuality of blackness and virtue in the age of Atlantic slavery. The language of a portraiture of *black heroism* in Lusophone slave society was especially troubled. As news of the *Pernambucana* tragedy first circulated in Rio and Porto Alegre, a biographical sketch of "a black man," "author of various heroic acts," "native of the Cape Verde Islands, and free-born" took shape.[15] But the appropriate descriptors for *what kind* of black man – especially a black African hero – were much more elusive as the physiognomic *preto* used in the earliest printed accounts required certain modifiers to disassociate the common connotation of blackness to enslavement, beyond the pale of heroism. Thus, *O Rio-Grandense* accurately described Simão as "um preto ... e livre de nascimento," (free-born) while the

14.2. Jean-Baptiste Debret, *Les rafraichissements de l'après dîner sur la Place du Palais* (After Dinner Refreshments on the Palace Square), 1835. Lithograph after watercolor. In *Voyage pittoresque et historique au Brésil, ou Séjour d'un artiste français au Brésil, depuis 1816 jusqu'en 1831 inclusivement*, vol. 2, plate 9. Photo: f SA 6038.16, Houghton Library, Harvard University.

14.3. Jean-Baptiste Debret, *Les barbiers ambulants* (Itinerant Barbers), 1835. Lithograph after watercolor. In *Voyage pittoresque et historique au Brésil*, vol. 2, plate 11. Photo: f SA 6038.16, Houghton Library, Harvard University.

14.4. João Goston, *Negra posando em estúdio* (Black Woman Posing in the Studio), ca. 1870. Daguerreotype (?). © Instituto Moreira Salles, Rio de Janeiro.

Jornal do Commercio mistakenly presumed that he had to have been a *preto liberto* (freedman). For some, Simão could not be *preto*, hero, and enslaved.

Once Simão had been honored by the emperor and his name – curiously, solely his first name as if he were one of the first-name-only slaves and *criados* (servants) aboard the *Pernambucana*[16] – had circulated widely in the literary, nautical, women's, and political press, these earliest associations with the color of enslavement came to be superseded by the title "the intrepid mariner" and various monikers related to heroism, virtue, and valor. The lengthy, semiofficial account appearing in the 7 November edition of the *Jornal do Commercio* made no mention of color and instead described "um intrépido e benévolo marinheiro de nome Simão, natural de Cabo Verde" (an intrepid and benevolent mariner by

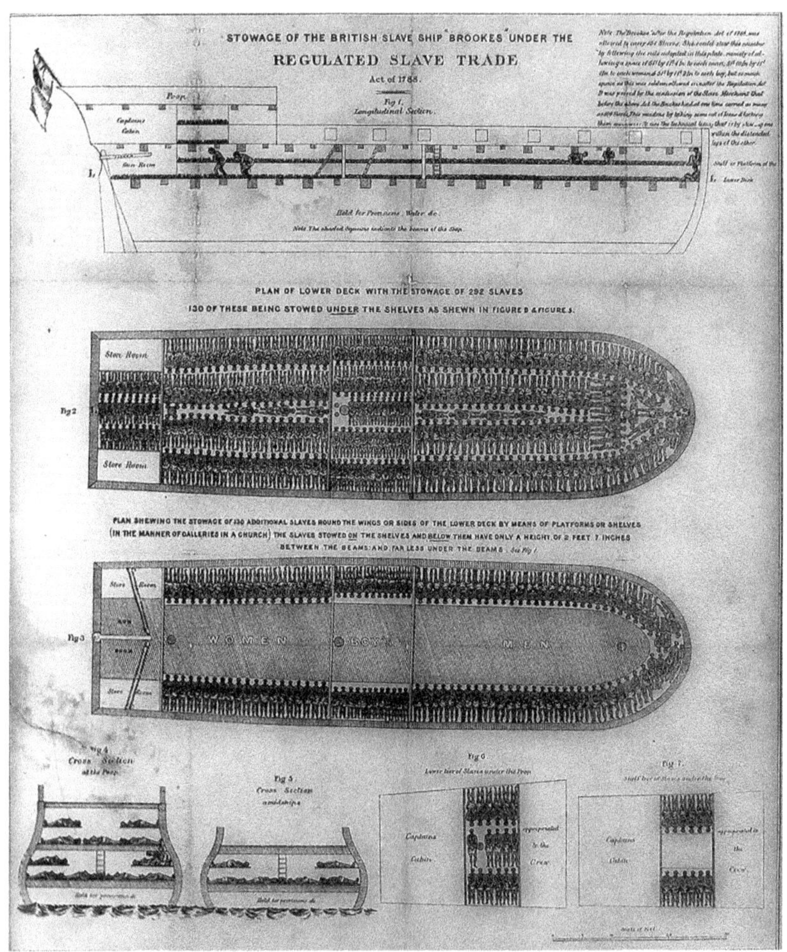

14.5. Anonymous artist, *Stowage of the British Slave Ship "Brookes" under the Regulated Slave Trade Act of 1788*, 1789 (?). Etching. Library of Congress, Rare Book and Special Collections Division, Washington, D.C.

the name of Simão, born in Cape Verde). The only color mentioned in the decree that accompanied the medal offered by the emperor was the fiery red of the ribbon upon which the medal was to hang. The decree that accompanied the honor from the Portuguese prince regent was similarly silent on skin color. It would be, in fact, Simão's fearlessness and virtue that would transcend, even erase, his blackness to render him a man of impeachable dignity. If his national origin as an "African" remained somewhat troublesome for the Brazilians, as *africano* was often shorthand for foreigner, barbarian, or contraband, his "black" color – which could stand in for both race and imputed slave status – might be overlooked by the Luso-Brazilian monarchies.

The poetry of Francisco de Paula Brito (1809–61), the freeborn mulatto printmaker, author, and theater impresario who was clearly smitten by Simão, perhaps best captured the linguistic transformation of the *preto* into the *Intrépido Marinheiro*. On 18 November, Paula Brito published a long praise poem, "SIMAO O Heroe da Pernambucana" (SIMAO Hero of the Pernambucana), in his literary magazine *Marmota Fluminense*. The poem opens with images of placid waters turning into the harrowing night of 8–9 October. The *Pernambucana* runs aground; the waves sweep away the second-in-command. Passengers scream. Suddenly, Simão, "the black fireman," "the mariner" comes to save a pregnant woman, damsels, and children. Paula Brito freely acknowledges Simão's phenotypical darkness as well as his Cape Verdean birth. But, above all else, Simão is a "homem de força e valor" (a man of strength and valor).[17]

The rub, certainly, was that Paula Brito knew that the blackness of this "black fireman" raised the spectre of enslavement, diminished rights, and lack of dignity. The poetic solution to the dilemma was twofold. On the one hand, Paula Brito connects the coalman directly to Dom Pedro, a national political figure supposedly above the nastiness of color and race prejudice.[18] On the other hand, he asserts a long-standing political claim, developed two decades earlier in publications such as the short-lived broadside *O Homem da Cor* (1833; The Man of Color), that the truly virtuous in Brazil were color-blind. Often credited as the founder of the Brazilian "black" press, Paula Brito's treatment of the color question was to simultaneously render color rhetorically irrelevant as well as to assert a political program that challenged color prejudice and racial discrimination. The concluding three stanzas of the encomium to Simão wove together these two poetic-political strategies: "Our Monarch is the first / to give

14.6. Joseph Mallord William Turner, *Slave Ship (Slavers Throwing Overboard the Dead and Dying, Typhoon Coming On)*, 1840. Oil on canvas. Museum of Fine Arts, Boston. Henry Lillie Pierce Fund, 99.22. Photograph © 2013, Museum of Fine Arts, Boston.

a sublime example, / that He makes no account / of the color of men. / If he who saves just one life / has the prize and title of glory, / he who saves *thirteen lives*, / what name will history give? / No one doubts SIMÃO / no one denies his laurels / SIMÃO accomplished divine acts / Virtue has no color."

In a juridical environment in which former slaves faced constitutionally diminished civil and political rights relative to the freeborn, and where blackness was intimately linked to slave descent – even in a fluid context in which a significant portion of the population of color was free and Brazilian born – Paula Brito's emphatic praise of Simão and the emperor had clear political overtones. If Simão – a man of color, a sailor, and an African – could win a decoration from the monarch, then all men of virtue were to be seen beyond color. At once a statement of the immateriality of color *and* an affirmation of the color of virtue, the poem was a direct critique of a legal system ripe in the contractions of securing liberal political rights to all free citizens, but circumscribing those same rights based upon the illiberal mark of birth status and prior servitude. Paula Brito's political position was in the minority among the political class, but it engaged an underlying legal-juridical problem for the Brazilian empire, particularly as the slave regime confronted the major challenge of maintaining the necessary evil and its attendant racial hierarchies while confronting a multitude of claims upon citizenship that might include blacks, including former slaves as well as Africans brought to Brazil as illegal contraband, and therefore free.[19]

Amid the chorus of praise heaped upon Simão, other voices used the *Pernambucana* episode to cast a certain level of disbelief that a black man, an African, might be capable of the virtue credited to the object of Paula Brito's poetry. Unsubstantiated allegations circulated in Rio Grande that the coalman had agreed to save passengers only upon the promise of monetary compensation. Unnamed sources had suggested that Simão had been obligated to admit to the governor (*presidente*) of Santa Catarina that he acted for financial gain.[20] The anomaly of these rumors, which were received with skepticism by the editors of *O Rio-Grandense*, suggests malice motivated by personal jealousy or ignorance. Nonetheless, the rumors punctured the notion that Simão was an unassailable man of honor.

The more direct challenge to an African man's capacity for honor surfaced in the public commentary concerning a capital punishment case brought before the authorities at precisely the same moment that shipwreck mania hit the capital. On the night of 22 October, the small-time slaveholder Francisco José da Costa Tibau entered his kitchen near downtown Rio and proceeded to beat his slave, a forty-year-old African of the Inhambane nation, from southern Mozambique, also named Simão. Both master and slave were known to drink, and in this instance, it appears that an inebriated Simão, who worked as a slave-for-hire, reacted violently to a blow from his master. After fatally stabbing Tibau seven times, Simão fled, only to be quickly apprehended, reportedly with the bloodied knife "still red and hot" in his hand.[21] News of the murder appeared in the Rio press on the eve of the first reports of the *Pernambucana*. Quickly tried by jury, the slave Simão was sentenced to death by hanging under the provisions of an 1835 law, passed in response to the Malê Revolt of that year, that allowed for capital punishment in cases in which a slave killed his master. An automatic appeal went before the Conselho do Estado, whose members let stand the death sentence.[22] The condemned Simão attempted suicide without success, and on 14 December the execution order was carried out in front of a rowdy crowd in the Largo de Moura.

The coincidence of names notwithstanding, the case of the "two Simons" – both Africans in Brazil on opposite sides of enslavement – provided various commentators the opportunity to explore the perils of Africanness in a slave society cut off from Africa but with Africans in the midst. On the one hand, the editor of the *Pacotilha* section of the *Correio Mercantil*, whose editorial position leaned critical against the slave regime, pondered the situation: "sons of the same land and the same race, courage transforms the mariner into a hero, and ire transforms the slave into an assassin. If Simão [the coalman] were a slave would he be as dedicated and heroic as he was? If Simão [the slave-for-hire] was free would he be a barbarous assassin?"[23] The unnamed author of the editorial column of the *Diário do Rio* took a different tack, implying the coexistence of Simão the hero and Simão the assassin within the same [black] body: "It's the case that evil alternates with good in this world, and on the side of virtue one need not look far to find vice and perversity."[24] Even if Simão the intrepid mariner were truly good, he carried with him an opposing Simão – enslaved, degraded, and criminal. The shadow of an evil antipode – made visible by ascendant anti-black, anti-slave, and anti-African sentiment – may have been difficult to see in the formal elements of the Correia de Lima portrait. However, the episode of the two Simons is highly suggestive that a black hero might, for many, be an *impossible* subject.

What Simão *himself* made of his blackness, his Africanness, and his heroic subjectivity remain opaque. He left no autobiography of his larger travels throughout the Atlantic. If he saw himself as an African, it remains unclear if he might have tried to present himself as some sort of universal African, like Equiano (ca. 1745–97; see Fig. 6.9), as a member of an African "nation," or as some other form of African identity. In Brazil, Simão was rather generically called an "African" without any consistent attempt to assign a "nation." Among contemporaries in Portugal, the matter of his Africanness was secondary to his legal status as a Portuguese subject. Simão's identity, in fact, anticipated the sociological dilemma of Cape Verdean immigrants in post-emancipation American societies, where the mixed-raced Cape Verdean immigrant – one of the few groups of Africans to voluntarily emigrate to the Americas prior to modern African independence – was caught between labels of local ethnicity, Portuguese citizenship, and racialized blackness.[25]

Simão's voice on this and other matters is, sadly, muffled. The existing documentation records no direct words spoken or written by the hero of the *Pernambucana*. The biographical details that began to circulate in early November surely came from him, but the quality of information never went beyond facts that could have been gleaned from an initial conversation, reprinted and repeated. We have no evidence of any familiarity with the trial and execution of Inhambane Simão. The hero Simão, who likely spoke a Cape Verdean version of Portuguese called Cape Verdean Creole, perhaps peppered with pidgin English picked up in polyglot Mindelo, was observed to have been conversing directly with the Brazilian emperor as well as the governor of Cape Verde, but we have no direct quotes or observations. Even if it is to be presumed that Simão was illiterate, and thus unable to pen his own narrative, it seems quite curious that the register of his life was *solely* taken by others, most of whom seemed more interested in the celebrity than the person. Curiously, the journalistic and archival records provide direct evidence about how Simão the assassin described himself on the witness stand, whereas the printed and manuscript documents that describe Simão the mariner give us little direct evidence to understand the tenor of his voice and the content of his speech.

The Portrait(s) of the Intrepid Mariner

Against these social conditions that silence Simão at the moment of his greatest renown, we return to the Correia de Lima portrait. The painting is an attributed likeness, but in the portrait, like in the spoken portraits produced during the shipwreck mania induced by the *Pernambucana* tragedy, Simão gives a face (and a potential voice?) to the experience of black mariners of the Portuguese Atlantic at the end of the slave trade.

O Retrato do Intrépido Marinheiro Simão, again, is quite conventional for its style and quite anomalous for its subject. The commonness of a salon-eligible oil-on-canvas portrait contrasts with the anachronism of the sitter's color. That is, the Imperial Academy of Fine Arts produced very few portraits of blacks prior to the Paraguayan War (1865–70), and even by the end of the nineteenth century, the numbers of academic black portraits was modest. The historical irony was thick, as men of color, both free and enslaved, had served as some of the first artist's models at the academy; they cleaned and guarded a building built by slaves working alongside free laborers.[26] Blacks mixed clay for sculpture classes. Black women washed the linens. Numerous academy professors were slaveholders or concessionaires of Africans liberated during the suppression of the trade. Enslaved Brazilians had intimate communion with the Academy students, and after midcentury, the Academy began to matriculate descendants of former slaves.

José Correia de Lima, who began his studies at the Academy at the age of twelve, would have been quite familiar with this history of blackness in the fine arts in Brazil. Nevertheless, his agreement to take on a black subject was highly anomalous for his generation and for his own *oeuvre* composed of countless portraits of notables, especially the emperor, and a selected number of historical and allegorical compositions.[27] The ledger books of the Imperial Academy do not record a direct payment to Correia de Lima in compensation for a portrait of Simão. It is quite plausible that Simão, who departed Rio for Cape Verde in February 1854, never came to see a canvas that is generally dated around 1855.

Newspaper reports suggest strongly that the portrait executed by Correia de Lima actually originated as a photograph that was intended for republication in the *Illustrated London News*.[28] Although an image of Simão never made it to the London periodical, the proceeds of the public subscription raised by the Commercial Association were used to pay the costs of a visit to one of Rio's many photographic studios. The photographic portrait is now lost, but it would endure as a lithograph, a line drawing, and at least two canvases available to viewers in Brazil, Portugal, Cape Verde, and France.

Simão's contact with photography was entirely consistent with the cultural and commercial tastes of the age. News of the photographic patent assigned to Daguerre and Talbot circulated throughout the Atlantic in 1839, and early experiments in photochemical image production were underway in Lisbon and Rio in the first half of 1840, when photographic equipment and images began to accompany maritime travelers between Europe and Brazil. Photographic experimentation spread to the Portuguese empire in Africa as early as 1843, in portraits of local nobility, and later became an important tool in ethnographic, scientific, and missionary work throughout the continent.[29] Thus, by the time daguerreotyping began to compete with other technologies, in the 1850s, photography had become widely disseminated throughout the Portuguese-speaking world.[30] In this early period of the history of photography, demand for the portrait fueled the commercialization of photographic visual culture.[31]

Whether Simão had any direct contact with daguerreotypists prior to his arrival in Rio remains unknown, but once a celebrity in the imperial capital, the coalman would have found it quite easy to find a photographer eager to take a portrait. At least eight daguerreotype studios were active in Rio in 1853, and itinerant photographers frequently passed through the city. Although purveyors of less expensive, reproducible photographic techniques, including precursors of the *carte-de-visite*, began to make inroads in Rio consumer culture just as Simão arrived from the *Pernambucana*, photographic portraiture still retained a close association with the skill and refinement of the daguerreotypists, who hawked their establishments as "frequented by a respectable public," where members of "high society" including the Bragança nobility might be seen. Dom

Pedro himself was a devotee of the photograph – as sitter, photographer, and collector. It is quite possible that Simão encountered a likeness of his patron during his visit to a photographic studio.

While taking in photographic portraits of such illustrious Brazilians, Simão was likely also introduced to photographic images of everyday black men and women. Like Simão, these men and women were developing intimate relationships with photography and photographers. Many of the earliest photographers in Brazil looked to the black as an appropriate subject, and by the 1850s, the black subject had emerged as an important player in the market for photographic portraiture and sale. The prolific, pioneering works of José Christiano Junior (Portuguese, 1832–1902; active in Rio 1863–67), Alberto Henschel (German, 1827–82; active in Rio 1870–78), and Augusto Stahl (Italian, 1828–77; active in Rio 1862–70) would later consolidate the market for photographic images of

14.7. Francisco de Paula Brito and Louis Thérier, *SIMÃO Heròe do Vapor Brasileiro Pernambucana* (Simão, Hero of the Brazilian Steamship Pernambucana), November 1853. Lithograph after daguerreotype (lost). Instituto Histórico e Geográfico Brasileiro, Rio de Janeiro.

blacks, but even in the 1850s, the black sitter was a regular feature in photography, sometimes as an accessory to the white sitter (e.g., black nursemaids and their white charges) and other times as one of many ethnographic "customs" and "types" so favored by foreign collectors. Victor Frond (1821–81), a French military-official-turned-photographer who resided in Brazil between 1857 and 1860, was an especially prominent pioneer of the commercialization of photographic and lithographic images of Brazilian blacks, particularly slaves.[32]

The ultimate destination of the photograph that came out of Simão's visit to the daguerreotype studio is unknown. However, a lithograph taken from the photograph was on sale at Francisco de Paula Brito's well-transited printshop as early as 16 November (Fig. 14.7). Paula Brito had enlisted the aid of Louis Thérier, an engraver contracted from a prominent French print house who had arrived in Rio in early 1853, to render the photograph into a lithograph suitable for sale. Captioned "SIMÃO Heròe do Vapor Brasileiro Pernambucana," the Paula Brito-Thérier print made no gestures toward the world of maritime disaster and selfless heroism that had been used to rhetorically portray Simão in the first two weeks of November. Rather, the composition, medium, and tone of the monochrome print evoked a physical and performative economy of masculine stature and distinction. In the engraving, Simão is seated in three-quarter profile, wearing a blazer with thin lapels, a buttoned vest, and knotted tie.[33] The chair upon which he is seated is not visible, nor the apparatus that likely held his head still during the original photographic shoot, but the print clearly followed the refined, if stiff, conventions of portrait photography of the 1850s. Sold at one *milréis* (one-quarter to one-third or the cheapest advertised price for a daguerreotype, but in excess of a day's wages for a semi-skilled laborer), the print connoted a certain compositional and economic equivalence between Simão and the commercialized images of the era's great figures.

In the daguerreotype's journey from unique photograph to reproducible print suitable for sale, one detects the arc of a production history that closely followed Euro-Brazilian tastes for serialized portraits of notable men of the age, sold by subscription. Recent scholarship on the history of the press and printmaking in Brazil has documented how Frond and S. A. Sisson, as well as purveyors of the illustrated press, satisfied a demand for lithographed portraits of the Brazilian well-heeled, selling serialized inserts for albums, known as *galerias*, of illustrious Brazilians. Portraits of the elite were also included as inserts in the periodical press.[34] The growth of this portrait market has been timed to the mid-to-late 1850s, when improved printing and engraving technologies and the growing availability of skilled labor allowed printshops to supply consumers with quality images, often with accompanying text. Thus, it is somewhat remarkable that the Simão portrait came out of Paula Brito's network of typographers, engravers, and race moralizers two years *before* Sisson's *Álbum do Rio de Janeiro moderno* (1855) and three years before Frond's arrival in Brazil. Simão's image, and several others published in *Marmota Fluminense* in 1853–54, laid the groundwork for the illustrated biographical portraits of the luminaries of Brazilian society included in the short-lived *Illustração Brazileira* (1854–55) and Sisson's monumental picto-biography of Brazilian notables, *Galeria dos brasileiros illustres*, completed in 1861.[35]

PRETA FUGIDA.

Fugio na villa da Constituição da provincia do S. Paulo, a Jeronymo da Silva Leitão, uma escrava de nome Polucena, crioula, tem os signaes seguintes: 22 annos de idade, é baixa, olhos grandes, cara redonda, bom preta, nariz chato, corpo mal feito, braços de homem e pulsos muito largos; quando caminha piza com força e tem tambem todos os dentes e muito claros. Quando fugio furtou alguma roupa, a qual tem as iniciaes do senhor e outras peças, as iniciaes A. B. L., e consta que fugira com um preto de nome Luiz, que se intitulava forro nesta villa. Dá-se 50$ de gratificação a quem a apprehender e levar á casa do seu senhor na dita villa.

COZINHEIRO.

Aluga-se um perito cozinheiro de forno e fogão, muito asseiado e fiel; na rua de Santa Anna n. 47 E, sobrado.

RETRATOS DO PRETO SIMÃO,

copiados do daguerreotypo, e lithographados na — *Empresa Dous de Dezembro* —, vendem-se a 1$, nas lojas de Paula Brito, praça da Constituição ns. 64 e 78, *loja do canto.*

Dá-se gratis aos assignantes da *Marmota*, e accionistas da Empresa.

MILITÃO Honorio de Carvalho comprou, por ordem do Sr. Firmino Alves da Cunha, e conta de Carneiro e Cunha, o meio bilhete da 69ª loteria a beneficio da casa da Misericordia desta côrte, n. 4873.

VENDE-SE um moleque de 12 annos, servindo de copeiro e com principio de cozinheiro; na rua da Quitanda n. 50, armazem.

VENDE-SE uma preta e cinco crias, um preto sapateiro, e uma preta, todos bonitas figuras, moços e sem vicios, sendo as pretas boas quitandeiras; no trapiche da Ilha das Cobras, casa do administrador.

VENDE-SE ou aluga-se a casa da rua do Cattete n. 15, com [illegible] commodo para familia; dirijão-se á mesma rua n. 25.

ALUGA-SE a casa de dous andares e armazem da rua da Misericordia n. 62, com agua dentro e sahida para o Castello; quem a pretender dirija-se á rua Direita n. 79, 1º andar.

THEATROS.

DE S. FRANCISCO.

HOJE QUARTA-FEIRA 16 DE NOVEMBRO DE 1853.

Depois da execução de uma escolhida

OUVERTURA

terá lugar a representação do sempre applaudido drama em 5 actos e 1 prologo, do Sr. L. A. Burgain:

PEDRO SEM.

14.8. Advertisements for daguerreotype studios, runaway slaves, a "sociable and loyal" cook, the Paula Brito-Thérier lithograph, and theatrical performances of *Pedro-Sem*, among others, 16 November 1853. *Jornal do Commercio*, Rio de Janeiro.

Simão, of course, was not a true peer of the "most illustrious figures of Brazil, in politics, the sciences, and letters" who came to be profiled by Sisson. Therefore, the creation and circulation of the Paulo Brito-Thérier lithograph would not follow the same path as the Sisson prints. The Brito-Thérier lithograph does not appear in any known album or *galeria*. Much to Paula Brito's chagrin, the *Marmota Fluminense* lithograph was intimately attached to the visual and textual economies of blackness that Paula Brito claimed to be irrelevant. Simão was, visually and poetically, a black man whose blackness was fundamental to his portrait.

Paula Brito contributed to this intimacy of Simão and blackness by placing classified ads for "Portraits of the *Preto* Simão, copied from the daguerreotype and lithographed" (Fig. 14.8). Sandwiched between solicitations for the hire, purchase, lease, rent, or exchange of black men, women, and children, the ads placed Simão within the commercialized world of blackness familiar to any reader of the age. The advertisement placed in the *Jornal do Commercio* appeared in a peculiar state of compositional tension, as the offer for the sale of the lithographed hero, framed in a roped border, appeared adjacent to notices for the return of a runaway slave. Even before the portrait of Simão began to circulate freely, it was already part of Rio's explosive world of commerce and sociability that traded upon blacks as commodities and criminals rather than notables and heroes.

Paula Brito worked diligently to manage the public reception of the lithograph. As early as 8 November, he issued rejoinders about the mariner's color-blind/colored valor, declaring in *Marmota* that "The Black Simão, color does make the hero, no, it is his deeds!" Shortly thereafter, the entrepreneurial typographer provided assurances that the portrait had been printed

14.9. Anonymous artist, *O preto Simão, salvador dos naufragos da PERNANBUCANA* (The Black Man Simão, Savior of the Castaways of the PERNANBUCANA [*sic*]), 1854. Pen on paper (?) after lithograph. *Revista Estrangeira*, 6, Lisbon.

on fine quality paper. Quickly, the image made its mark outside Brazil, carried to Europe sometime in late November, to reappear as a line drawing in the Parisian *L'Illustration* and the *Revista Estrangeira*, published in Lisbon[36] (Fig. 14.9).

Cross-Atlantic consumers of mass-produced illustrated literature might have found the lithograph finely rendered, but it begged the question how the viewer might understand the connection between the image of the gentlemanly Simão of the lithograph and the rhetorical projections of a robust black coalman battling ferocious waves, ferrying between land and sea to bring one more water-soaked passenger to shore. If Simão was indeed a hero for his very laborious deeds – a man made worthy by his acts – the lithograph rendered the coalman largely indistinguishable in dress, body positioning, and demeanor from very unlaborious men whose acts filled the biographical sketches of the illustrated press.

Some of Paula Brito's Fluminense interlocutors remained skeptical of the typographer's attempts to portray Simão as hero of a color-blind Brazilian society. Among them was an author writing in the *Diário do Rio de Janeiro* under the pseudonym "O Tupi," in allusion to one of Brazil's "foundational" (and "fictional") indigenous groups, published an open criticism of the Simão rage sweeping through Rio in the third week of November. "Here in my country," the author wrote, "things are taken to the extreme – it's everything or nothing; Now, it's the theme of the African Simão, and friend Paula Brito, who understands all too well this era that we are living through, has just published a portrait of the hero of the *Pernambucana*. I think right all that has been done, and much more could be done; but the truth is that the show has ended, the fashion has bust for the dutiful protection of the African Simão." "Well done!" he snorted, "a medal of honor decorates the chest of the intrepid mariner, and deserved it was. However, the Brazilian government seems to have forgotten to recognize and honor the Brazilians who founded the Lovers of Instruction Society."

Jealous of attention afforded to Simão and not the Society, and likely tired of hearing and seeing more of Simão, the writer sought to burst the bubble of valor surrounding Simão, not unlike the commentators who placed him in the continuum with Simão the assassin. The words carried a distinct tone of xenophobia, counterpoising the nativist "Tupi" against "The African Simão." That several of the romantic poets of the era – Manuel de Araújo Porto-Alegre (1806–79) and José de Alencar (1829–77) – took up the nativist theme while also proffering withering critiques of the capacities of Africans, is suggestive of the difficult terrain in which Simão might have presented the image of gentlemanly honor. Paula Brito's assertion of color-blindness, and its attendant notions of the rejection of racial discrimination, stood in counterpoise to the compelling power of white nativism.

Thus, by the time that Correia de Lima took up his portrait, both the intrepid mariner and his image had been subjected to intense scrutiny. How, precisely, Correia de Lima dealt with such scrutiny is poorly understood, but the pictorial choices made by the painter among the imagery known to be at his disposal, the subsequent contextualization of the canvas at its public debut in 1859, and the progressive "forgetting" of who exactly the intrepid mariner was, all suggest that the weight of white nativism, with its echoes of the hostility seen in the two episodes of the two Simons, was significant.

In the Correia de Lima painting, a brawny Simão has been stripped of the sartorial fineries of the earlier lithograph and turns toward the viewer in a three-quarter profile. He gazes directly outward. The upper body is framed within an oversized blue collared tunic. The buttonless placket opens widely in a "V" to reveal a hairless chest and the subtle lines of pectorals. A muscular right forearm crosses the midsection; the left arm is in repose, in shadow. A braided rope gently curves from a tightened, angled right fist toward the edge of the canvas. Simão's torso and his symbolic rope appear close in the foreground, nearly overwhelming the neck and lower face, with its thinly mustachioed lips sitting between a strong nose and square jaw. The lighting of the eyes and forehead, unmistakably belonging to a man of African descent, help to rebalance the head and frame the sweep of hair, parted above the right eye, massing into two nappy mounds. The background is nearly pure color, bearing scant figurative or symbolic elements to compete with the singular, dominant subject.

Upon close inspection, the viewer finds distinct traces of the lithograph, itself bearing traces of the lost photograph. The hair is shorter in the painting; the skin tone is lighter and richer. But the slightly uneven left eye, the dip of the right ear, and the jutting of the chin have uncanny similarities (see Plate 11 and Figs. 14.1 and 14.7). The unbalanced proportions between the contained face and the massive torso – the "anatomic incongruence" observed by Lucio Migliacco, curator for the nineteenth-century selections at the *Mostra do Redescobrimento* – suggests that the finely rendered head of the intrepid mariner has been rather clumsily grafted onto the body of another, anonymous black body.[37] Rather than an actual and complete portrait of Simão, the Correia de Lima portrait appears as a composite of a lithograph, its photographic antecedent, and generic male anatomy.

It is quite plausible that Correia de Lima had occasion to personally meet Simão, but not sufficient time to refine the portrait from multiple sittings. With a lithographic image readily available, the artist had the material suitable to render a faithful likeness of the mariner's face, while looking no further than the artist's models employed at the Academy to find inspiration for painting the body of a muscular black laborer, of which the streets of Rio were replete. But, more than a question of opportunity, I would argue that the composite portrait of Simão was a product of certain obstacles to the visual rendering of a black man's personal integrity and virtue in Brazilian slave society. In executing the portrait, Correia de Lima, whose *oeuvre* does not appear to include other portraits of men of color, surely confronted the conundrum whether a black man could be the subject of serious, academic portraiture, with its logic of singular inner worth, or whether Simão, as a black man, had to be reduced to a simulacra of virtue, a confection of rote portraiture, imperial patronage, and Paula Brito's marketeering. Or to say it differently, the question is if in rendering a portrait of a free black man Correia de Lima was able to do without the visual rhetoric of enslavement. Does the Simão of the lithograph, whose heroic deeds are sanctified by tailored clothes, reside within the Simão of the canvas, whose open chest places his visual qualities much closer to the ethnographic African "types" pioneered by the European *viajantes* and perfected by purveyors of the *carte-de-visite*? We must ask ourselves whether Correia de Lima, portrait artist of the emperor in full regalia, found it impossible to paint Simão wearing the ribbons awarded to him by monarchs and governors throughout the Luso-Atlantic. Correia de Lima, like his contemporaries, appeared to waver on the matter of whether Simão could be treated as an object of fundamental human dignity. Perhaps the visage of a black man must always sit in the shadows cast from the gallows on the Largo da Moura.

Conclusions

The disposition of the Correia de Lima portrait between the painter's death, in June 1857, and the 1859 salon, remains unclear. Art historian Donato Mello Júnior has argued that Augusto Müller (1815–ca. 1883), a colleague of Correia de Lima at the Imperial Academy of Fine Arts, had secured the portrait of Simão to hang alongside Müller's own *Retrato de Manoel Correia dos Santos, Mestre de Sumaca* (ca. 1839) (Fig. 14.10), a government-commissioned work first exhibited at the 1841 salon.[38] As Müller and Correia de Lima had been colleagues and competitors in the market for academic portraiture, the pairing of the Simão and Correia dos Santos portraits had a compelling logic as both canvases depicted common men who had distinguished themselves in maritime accidents, going on to win honorific medals from the imperial government. (In 1839, the white Correia dos Santos had successfully commandeered a ship to safety after the crew had mutinied, winning him public esteem and honorific medals.) Both portraits were sure to win the approval of the emperor, who delighted in the fine arts and the commendation of worthy subjects. The emperor had personally lent a portrait of the Portuguese navigator Magellan, painted by German artist Otto Grashof (1812–76), making his contribution to the artistic celebration of nautical heroes. The broader pictorial logic of the pairing – which placed Simão and Correia dos Santos within a visual economy of heroes – was entirely consistent with the visual economy of the *galeria* making significant inroads into elite tastes. Their key distinction, however, was that Simão and Correia dos Santos were both rendered open-chested with ropes in hand; both were quite distant from the contained physiognomy and sartorial dignity afforded the illustrious Brazilians lithographed by Paula Brito and profiled in *galerias*.[39]

Given his quick departure from Brazil, Simão had limited opportunity to see his likenesses circulate in Brazilian visual culture. Simão surely knew the Paula Brito lithograph, but it is entirely plausible that he never saw the Correia de Lima canvas. Simão had succumbed to a devastating cholera outbreak in Mindelo three years before the canvas was placed on public display in Brazil. The once famous coalman died impoverished, apparently without the dignity of a marked grave.[40] The visual imprint of Simão's transatlantic presence, nonetheless, endured. The Correia de Lima portrait has remained part of the Brazilian national collection since 1859, occasionally compelling the curators and visitors to make *something* of the anomalous portrait. The Paula Brito-Thérier lithograph has become a collector's item. Another oil-on-canvas portrait, hanging near his medals, returns Simão to the performance of gentlemanly respectfulness and dignity. There is a tantalizing possibility that Paula Brito's protégé Machado de Assis (1839–1908) and the many subscribers of *Marmota Fluminense* had occasion to look upon their personal copies of the lithograph of Simão.

In his personal travels through the Atlantic, Simão confronted and confounded a changing social and visual landscape of blackness. The social world of his upbringing, at a marginal corner of the black Atlantic, had undergone fundamental change as maritime steam traffic placed the port of Mindelo and its black laborers within a cosmopolitan network of trade, travel, and disease. Portuguese colonial policy projected onto Cape Verde the (re)assertion of metropolitan dominion in Africa in this new context of capitalism.[41] Figures such as Simão, inadvertently, played their part, affording the colonized certain opportunities to perform rituals of citizenship and imperial belonging throughout an empire trying to rid itself of enslavement.

The gradual disassociation between enslavement and empire was a peculiar subtext to Simão's journeys through the Portuguese world.[42] Within the Portuguese empire, the reforms enacted under the vigorous lead of the Marquês Sá da Bandeira mandated a slave census and transferred to colonial authorities

14.10. Augusto Müller, *Retrato de Manoel Correia dos Santos, Mestre de Sumaca* (Portrait of Manoel Correia dos Santos, First Mate of a Smack), ca. 1839. Oil on canvas. Museu Nacional de Belas Artes/Instituto Brasileiro de Museus/Ministério da Cultura, Rio de Janeiro. Photo: Jaime Acioli.

the power of tutelage (*patrono natural*) over slaves, freedmen, and their children. Additional reforms tried to extend to the colonies free soil and free womb laws that had been in place in the metropole since the Pombaline period. By March 1855, slavery was formally abolished on São Vicente, where Simão died within sight of the dirty coaling station serving the transatlantic steam traffic. A new Portuguese empire, freed from slavery yet still deeply invested in an Atlantic project that rendered Africans as colonized citizen-subjects, was in the making.[43]

A slave census would not be initiated in the Brazilian empire until 1872, following the passage of the Law of the Free Womb. But, on the western shores of the Portuguese Atlantic, Simão's moment of celebrity coincided with an upsurge in the incidents of men and women of color being counted, providing the underpinnings for claims to self-worth and citizenship. The untethering of the Brazilian and Portuguese empires to the slave trade, and the possibility that an African might be made visible, a hero rather than degraded slave or illegal contraband, was an important reflection of these changing claims.

The historical and discursive burdens of slavery remained heavy throughout the Luso-Atlantic, especially for people of color. New visual technologies such as photography carried the potential to render blacks and blackness as ethnographic curiosities and "types" beyond the pale of citizenship and moral dignity. Nonetheless, in the 1850s, while the centuries-old trade in human cargo, powered by wind and brawn, slipped into history, the residents of Rio and their cousins and correspondents throughout the Portuguese Atlantic gazed deeply into the poeticized, politicized, photographed, lithographed, and painted eyes of the coalman-hero Simão in search of a new black Atlantic. In his eyes, the "color" of slavery was strong, but so too were the possibilities to portray the blackness of beauty and virtue.

Notes

I thank Mr. Jorge Pires, former Councilman of the Câmara Municipal de Ribeira Grande, Santo Antão, and Ms. Maria José Lopes, former Director of the Instituto do Arquivo Histórico Nacional, Praia, Santiago, for their kind assistance in locating Cape Verdean source materials. Additional thanks go to the participants in the November 2005 Center for Historical Studies (University of Maryland) Faculty Work-in-Progress Colloquium, who offered feedback on the first draft of this study.

1 *Retratos: 2,000 Years of Latin American Portraits*, a touring exhibition organized by the San Antonio Museum of Art, the National Portrait Gallery, and El Museo del Barrio, with the sponsorship of the Ford Motor Company Fund.

2 *Retratos: 2,000 Years of Latin American Portraits*, ed. Elizabeth P. Benson (New Haven: Yale University Press, 2005), 182.

3 The Correia de Lima portrait is used to illustrate the Instituto Brasileiro Geográfico e Estatístico's online timeline *Brasil: 500 anos de povoamento*. The caption for the 1695 defeat of the Palmares *quilombo* implies that the portrait of Simão depicts the slain Zumbi, registering a key episode in the resistance to slavery. See http://www.ibge.gov.br/brasil500/, accessed 15 August 2007.

4 Carlos Roberto Maciel Levy, "Visitando o Museu Nacional de Belas Artes," *Jornal da Crítica*, 4 January 1998, http://www.artedata.com/crml/textos/crml9053.htm, accessed 4 December 2011.

5 Mary C. Karasch, *Slave Life in Rio de Janeiro, 1808–1850* (Princeton: Princeton University Press, 1987), table 3.6.

6 Arquivo Publico do Estado de Santa Catarina [Florianópolis] 18.158 Registros Presidência da Província, Registro Militar e da Marina, 25–26, posting from João José Coutinho to Tenente Theotonio Raymundo de Brito, 25 October 1853.

7 W[ilhelm]. O[ertel]. von Horn, *Simon: Lebensgeschichte eines Negersklaven in Brasilien: für die Jugend und das Volk erzählt* (Lahr, 1856); Frances Harriet Green, *Shahmah in Pursuit of Freedom; or, The Branded Hand* (New York: Thatcher and Hutchinson, 1858); J. B. B. Eyriès, *Histoire des naufrages; délaissements de matelots, hivernages, incendies de navires et autres désastres de mer, d'après M. Eyriès*, ed. Ernest Faye (Paris: Morizot, 1859), ch. 36.

8 The nominal distinction between *fluminenses* (residents of the state of Rio de Janeiro, including Niterói) and *cariocas* (residents of the city of Rio de Janeiro) was rare in the nineteenth century, when the Fluminense world encompassed all of Guanabara Bay.

9 *Periódico dos Pobres* (Rio), 27 October 1853.

10 Rio's relationship to the slave trade is explored in Manolo Florentino, *Em costas negras* (São Paulo: Companhia das Letras, 1997), João Fragoso, *Homens de grossa aventura* (Rio de Janeiro: Civilização Brasileira, 1998), and *O Arcaismo como projeto* (Rio de Janeiro: Civilização Brasileira, 2001). The trade is treated in Leslie Bethell, *The Abolition of the Brazilian Slave Trade: Britain, Brazil and the Slave Trade Question, 1807–1869* (Cambridge: Cambridge University Press, 1970), Robert Conrad, *World of Sorrow: The African Slave Trade to Brazil* (Baton Rouge: Louisiana State University Press, 1986), and Jaime Rodrigues, *De Costa a Costa: Escravos, marinheiros e intermediários do tráfico negreiro de Angola ao Rio de Janeiro (1780–1860)* (São Paulo: Companhia das Letras, 2005).

11 *Subsídios para a história de Cabo Verde e Guiné*, vol. 6 (1853–61) (Lisbon: Imprensa Nacional, 1911), 52–59; K. David Patterson, "Epidemics, Famines, and Population in the Cape Verde Islands, 1580–1900," *International Journal of African Historical Studies* 21, no. 2 (1988), 291–313.

12 Arquivo Histórico Nacional do Cabo Verde, Praia Cx 15, Peça 86, p. 54, Registro Civil de São Vicente, Assentos de Óbitos, Freguesia de Nossa Senhora da Luz (1851–65).

13 Donald B. Cooper, "The New 'Black Death': Cholera in Brazil, 1855–1856," *Social Science History* 10, no. 4 (1986): 467–88.

14 The *Brookes* and Turner images are discussed in detail in Marcus Wood's *Blind Memory: Visual Representations of Slavery in England and America, 1780–1865* (New York: Routledge, 2000), ch. 2.

15 *Diário Mercantil* (Rio), 25 October 1853; *O Rio-Grandense* (Rio Grande), 28–29 October 1853.

16 Among the survivors, "Claudio" and "Antonio" are explicitly listed as slaves, and "Camilo" and "Francisco" are listed as *criados da câmara* (servants or cabin boys).

17 "SIMAO O Heroe da Pernambucana," *Marmota Fluminense*, 18 November 1853.

18 The research on Paula Brito's views on the emperor as a slaveholder and monarch of a slavocracy remains to be done, but it is clear that Paula Brito saw in the emperor an august leader whose protection conferred automatic, irreproachable respect. The sole biography of Paula Brito, Eunice Ribeiro Gondim's *Vida e obra de Paula Brito* (Rio de Janeiro: Brasiliana, 1965), makes only a preliminary gesture at analyzing and contextualizing the prolific Paula Brito.

19 Hebe Maria Mattos de Castro, *Escravidão e cidadania no Brasil monárquico* (Rio de Janeiro: Jorge Zahar, 2000). For a study of the illegally enslaved's attempts to assert their legal freedom (and by extension, their rights), see Beatriz Gallotti Mamigonian, "O direito de ser africano livre: os escravos e as interpretações da lei de 1831," in *Direitos e justiças no Brasil: ensaios de história social*, ed. Silvia Hunold Lara and Joseli Maria Nunes Mendonça (Campinas: Editora UNICAMP, 2006), 127–60.

20 *O Rio-Grandense*, 20 November 1853.

21 *Folhinha dos Bons Costumes para o anno de 1855* [*Folhinha Laemmert*] (Rio de Janeiro: Eduardo & Henrique Laemmert, 1855), 152 and 159.

22 Arquivo Nacional, Rio de Janeiro Fundo Conselho do Estado [1R] Seção de Justiça, Códice 301, Vol. 2, flhs. 9–10, 29 November 1853.

23 João Luiz Ribeiro, *No meio das galinhas as baratas não têm razão: a Lei de 10 de junho de 1835: escravos e a pena de morte no Império do Brasil, 1822–1889* (Rio de Janeiro: Renovar, 2005), 194–99. Ribeiro repeats the mistake of Simão's earliest Brazilian commentators, calling the freeborn Cape Verdean a *liberto*.

24 *Diário do Rio de Janeiro*, 19 December 1853.

25 On the peculiarities of race and ethnicity among Cape Verdeans, see Marilyn Halter, *Between Race and Ethnicity: Cape Verdean American Immigrants, 1860–1965* (Urbana: University of Illinois Press, 1993), and Deirdre Meintel, *Race, Culture, and Portuguese Colonialism in Cabo Verde* (Syracuse, N.Y.: Maxwell School of Citizenship and Public Affairs, Syracuse University, 1984).

26 Daryle Williams, "Artists and Models in Nineteenth-Century Brazilian Slave Society" *Art History* 35, no. 4 (Sept. 2012), 702–27.

27 Gonzaga-Duque, *A Arte brasileira* (Campinas: Mercado das Letras, 1995), 103; Guilherme Auler, *O imperador e os artistas* (Petrópolis: Tribuna de Petrópolis, 1955), 26–31.

28 *Diário de Rio de Janeiro* "O Diário" Section, 8 November 1853.

29 Antônio Sena, *História da imagem fotográfica em Portugal – 1839–1997* (Oporto: Porto Editora, 1998), 27; Jill Dias, "Photographic Sources for the History of Portuguese-Speaking Africa, 1870–1914," *History in Africa* 18 (1991), 67–82.

30 Pedro Karp Vasquez, *O Brasil na fotografia oitocentista* (São Paulo: Metalivros, 2003), 13–14.

31 Ibid., 36–38.

32 On blacks in nineteenth-century Brazilian photography, see Boris Kossoy and Maria Luiza Tucci Carneiro, *O Olhar Europeu: O negro na iconografia brasileira do século XIX* (São Paulo: EDUSP, 1994); George Ermakoff, *O negro na fotografia brasileira do século XIX, O* (Rio: Casa Editorial, 2004); Ana Maria Mauad, "Imagem e auto-imagem do Segundo Reinado," in *História da Vida Privada no Brasil*, vol. 2: *Império: a corte e a modernidade*, ed. Luiz Felipe de Alencastro (São Paulo: Companhia das Letras, 1997), 181–232, esp. 201–8; and Robert Levine, "Faces of Brazilian Slavery: The *Carte de Visite* of Christiano Junior," *The Americas* 47, no. 2 (October 1990), 127–59.

33 An original survives at the Instituto Histórico e Geográfico Brasileiro IL 4.25.

34 Joaquim Marçal Ferreira de Andrade, *História da fotorreportagem no Brasil: a fotografia na imprensa do Rio de Janeiro de 1839 a 1900* (Rio de Janeiro: Elsevier, 2004); Orlando da Costa Ferreira, *Imagem e letra: introdução à bibliologia brasileira; a imagem gravada* (São Paulo: EdUSP, 1994); Lygia Segala, "O retrato, a letra e a história: notas a partir da trajetória social e do enredo biográfico de um fotógrafo oitocentista," *Revista Brasileira de Ciências Sociais* 14, no. 41 (1999), 159–68.

35 S[ebastião] A[ugusto] Sisson, *Galeria dos brasileiros illustres: os contemporaneos: retratos dos homens mais illustres do Brasil, na política, sciencias e letras desde a*

guerra da independência até os nossos dias, 2 vols. (Rio de Janeiro: Lithographia de S. A. Sisson, 1861).

36 "Dévouement d'un nègre à Rio de Janeiro," *L'Illustration: Journal Universel* (Paris) 23 (31 December 1853), 448.

37 *Mostra do Redescobrimento*, vol. 6 (São Paulo: Fundação Bienal de São Paulo, 2000), 88.

38 Donato Mello Júnior, "As Exposições Gerais na Academia Imperial das Belas Artes no 2° Reinado," *Revista do Instituto Histórico e Geográfico Brasileiro. Anais do Congresso de História do Segundo Reinado. Comissão de História Artística* 1 (1984), 261–67.

39 On the relationships between sailors and slaves in visual representation see Geoff Quilley's essay in this volume.

40 Arquivo Histórico Nacional do Cabo Verde, Praia. Cx 15 Peça 86 f. 54. Registro Civil de São Vicente, Assentos de Óbitos, Freguesia de Nossa Senhora da Luz (1851–65).

41 Valentim Alexandre, "Nação e Império" in *História da Expansão Portuguesa*, ed. Francisco Bethencourt and Kirti Chaudhuri, 5 vols. (Lisbon: Círculo de Leitores, 1998–2000), 4:90–142.

42 Ibid., 94.

43 Valentim Alexandre, "Situações coloniais: I – A Lenta erosão do antigo regime (1851–1890)," in Bethencourt and Chaudhuri, *História da Expansão Portuguesa*, 4:141–53, esp. 149–51.

INDEX

Page references denoting illustrations appear in *italic*.